LAW, SOCIETY AND COMMUNITY

Law, Society and Community
Socio-Legal Essays in Honour of Roger Cotterrell

Edited by

RICHARD NOBLES AND DAVID SCHIFF
Queen Mary University of London

Routledge
Taylor & Francis Group
LONDON AND NEW YORK

First published 2014 by Ashgate Publishing

Published 2016 by Routledge
2 Park Square, Milton Park, Abingdon, Oxfordshire OX14 4RN
711 Third Avenue, New York, NY 10017, USA

First issued in paperback 2016

Routledge is an imprint of the Taylor & Francis Group, an informa business

British Library Cataloguing in Publication Data
A catalogue record for this book is available from the British Library.

Library of Congress Cataloging-in-Publication Data
Law, society and community : socio-legal essays in honour of Roger Cotterrell / by Richard Nobles and David Schiff.
pages cm
Includes bibliographical references and index.
ISBN 978-1-4724-0982-9 (hardback) -- ISBN)
1. Sociological jurisprudence. I. Cotterrell, Roger, honouree. II. Nobles, Richard, editor of compilation. III. Schiff, David editor of compilation.
K376.L386 2014
340'.115--dc23

2014006172

ISBN 13: 978-1-138-63774-0 (pbk)
ISBN 13: 978-1-4724-0982-9 (hbk)

Contents

List of Figures

Notes on Contributors

Jack Balkin, Knight Professor of Constitutional Law and the First Amendment, Yale University

Reza Banakar, Professor and Director of Research, Faculty of Social Sciences, Lund University

Zenon Bańkowski, Emeritus Professor of Legal Theory, Edinburgh University

Maksymilian Del Mar, Senior Lecturer in Law and Philosophy, Queen Mary University of London

Sionaidh Douglas-Scott, Professor of European and Human Rights Law, University of Oxford

Christoph Eberhard, Legal Anthropologist, Université Paris 1 Panthéon-Sorbonne/Université Saint Louis, Brussels

Marc Hertogh, Professor of Socio-Legal Studies, University of Groningen

Martin Krygier, Gordon Samuels Professor of Law and Social Theory, University of New South Wales

Michael Lobban, Professor of Legal History, London School of Economics and Political Science

Alexandra Lort Phillips, Researcher, University of Westminster

Mikael Rask Madsen, Professor of Law, University of Copenhagen

David Nelken, Professor of Comparative and Transnational Law in Context, Kings College, University of London

Richard Nobles, Professor of Law, Queen Mary University of London

Amanda Perry-Kessaris, Professor of Law, University of Kent

Jiří Přibáň, Professor of Law, Cardiff University

Austin Sarat, William Nelson Cromwell Professor of Jurisprudence and Political Science, Amherst College

David Schiff, Professor of Law, Queen Mary University of London

Paul Schiff Berman, Manatt/Ahn Professor of Law, The George Washington University

Sanne Taekema, Professor of Jurisprudence, Erasmus University Rotterdam

Brian Z. Tamanaha, William Gardiner Hammond Professor of Law, Washington University in St. Louis

Wibren van der Burg, Professor of Legal Philosophy and Jurisprudence, Erasmus University Rotterdam

Mark Van Hoecke, Research Professor of Legal Theory and Comparative Law, University of Ghent

Willem Witteveen, Professor of Legal Philosophy, Tilburg University

Introduction

Richard Nobles and David Schiff

The front cover of the 2nd edition of Roger Cotterrell's *The Sociology of Law: An Introduction* includes nine pictures of some classic writers of sociology, social theory, socio-legal theory, legal history and political theory (Carl von Savigny 1779–1861, Karl Marx 1818–1883, Emile Durkheim 1858–1917, Max Weber 1864–1920, Karl Llewellyn 1893–1962, Talcott Parsons 1902–1979, Michel Foucault 1926–1984, Niklas Luhmann 1927–1998, Jürgen Habermas 1929–). Each of these writers has been adopted as part of the pioneering generation (first and/or second wave) by those writing books, such as Roger's book, on the sociology of law or socio-legal studies. These books not only adopt these classic writers, among others, as the leading theorists, but set the agenda for a new wave of interest in sociology of law and socio-legal studies from the late 1960s. Having contributed to understanding the roots for that new wave of interest, some of the authors of these books have gone on, in their own research and writing, to place themselves amongst the pioneering generation of a second and/or third wave of socio-legal thinkers. Roger Cotterrell is one of them.

Roger's writings have been adopted and are consistently referred to by large numbers of writers who now engage in the range of disciplinary and interdisciplinary subject matter that represents current sociology of law and socio-legal studies, and their many closely related subjects, such as jurisprudence and legal theory. What marks Roger's writings out as one of the new pioneering generation is the consistency of the messages represented within his publications since the 1970s, a consistency that is exemplified by the choice of classic writers' portraits on the cover of *The Sociology of Law: An Introduction*, an eclectic mix but with a concentration on leading theorists, and critical contemporary issues. Although it is obvious from reading Roger's oeuvre that it contains some clear and consistent messages, it is a consistency within his overall eclectic approach that traverses many strands within the compass of sociology of law and socio-legal studies, rather than being dominated by one strand. This is not surprising since, as he is often quoted as saying: 'An important reason for the vitality of the sociolegal community … has surely been its rich, almost anarchic heterogeneity and its consistent openness to many different aims, outlooks, and disciplinary backgrounds' (2002: 632). This is a message which has a definite context and contains a particular critique. The context is the evolution of societies, and our understanding of that evolution (often thought of as 'rapid') in the last 50 years, and the varied and changing challenges that that evolution generates. The critique is of legal studies and, in particular jurisprudence and legal theory, as being too 'conservative', overly dominated by forms of analytic philosophy, and thereby less able to respond to societal evolution and its challenges. But, this is not to say that Roger's eclecticism has reduced his status as making particular contributions to particular theories or topics. For example, Roger has a definite reputation as a leading exponent of Durkheimian sociology, and exploring in depth the nature of community and community networks in relation to law. On the other hand, he consistently responds to other theorists and other developments; his intellectual home is, it would appear, among many socio-legal, jurisprudential, and even legal doctrinal issues, and, in particular, their inter-relationships.

It is in response to Roger's move from texts that engage with the classics,[1] towards his writing about all sorts of significant current theories, issues and debates concerning law in its broadest sense, that this book is addressed. That said, it neither attempts to react to all parts of Roger's oeuvre, nor offer a fair balance between those parts, but rather each chapter discusses a theory, topic, theme, or set of themes that mirror those that can be seen to have engaged and indeed continue to engage Roger's interest.

This book is written to honour Roger at the moment of his formal retirement from his full-time position as Anniversary Professor of Legal Theory at Queen Mary University of London. It has a secondary aim, to write about what he is so interested in, so as to encourage him to continue with his research and writing, partly as constructive criticism of some of the chapters here, which we are confident in itself will be good motivation!

It was not difficult to obtain the agreement of many to write in this volume (indeed we even had requests to participate from others, when they heard of it). However, we were reluctant to go beyond 20 chapters, and we wanted to organize a book that would be written by authors whose work we are aware that Roger specifically admires. Also we wanted to create a book that would be sufficiently diverse, to cover a reasonable range of the subjects that Roger has himself written about, but would include original contributions. At the same time we wanted chapters that would work together as a book. That is what, we believe, we have here. This is a festschrift, but it is a book of original essays that together, we hope, will contribute to the world of ideas and theories of which Roger is known to be a leading exponent.

1. Socio-legal Themes

In Chapter 1, Roger's long-standing fellow traveller, another of the pioneering generation of the second/third wave, David Nelken reconsiders the significant debate that he had with Roger in the 1990s – on how necessary it is to interpret legal ideas sociologically, and on how to do so. He does this following an overall assessment of Roger's writings, contextualized within a biography of Roger as scholar, teacher, colleague and jazz enthusiast. This introduces Roger, not only as a socio-legal scholar with a distinguished academic career, but as the eclectic, kind and deeply committed human being that this festschrift is intended to celebrate. We are very pleased that he makes such an assessment since he is, if anyone, able to put Roger's writings into that broader context (portraying a career in academia as a socio-legal scholar). Many comments in several of the other chapters re-affirm David's assessment of Roger as a teacher, colleague and friend. This first chapter performs this undertaking so well, and so thoroughly, that it relieves us of the need to do so in this introduction.

Moving on from appreciation to critical engagement, David Nelken raises an issue that will re-occur as a major theme within several of the chapters in this book, and which is central to Roger's academic writings. What are the likely results of urging legal theory to take the empirical observations of sociology more seriously? In his earlier work Roger had adopted a more traditional position within the sociology of law, in which law's inability to take account of the knowledge of society generated within sociology is part of its weakness. But later he began exploring the

1 Such as his *The Sociology of Law: An Introduction* (1984/1992), and his editing of various volumes of classic writing or writing about the classics.

possibilities for law to incorporate more knowledge of the social into itself. This is an approach which challenges legal philosophies which stress law's autonomy and independence from the rest of society. But it also raises a question within sociology itself – to what extent is law's limited ability to incorporate sociological knowledge a feature of how law operates within society, which has sociological causes and consequences. This is the basis of David Nelken's debate with Roger in the 1990s, with David arguing that there are sociological reasons why law may see the world as it does, and as such, this is not something which will change by individuals willing it not to be so, or by legal sociology increasing the supply of forms of knowledge which law cannot digest. With this chapter, David rejoins this debate, but in the new context of more recent of Roger's writings in which he attempts to bring sociological insights, arising out of his substantial knowledge of Durkheim, to issues surrounding the role of punishment and regulation in modern society. Roger draws on Durkheim's sociological account of the inter-connections between social structure, solidarity, morality and law, to consider what kinds of law might be appropriate to multicultural societies where law is called upon to reconcile and regulate different communities with different values and systems of belief. David discusses an article in which Roger (2011) considers the appropriate legal response to proposals to ban the wearing of face covering veils by Muslim women. Roger draws on Durkheim to argue that a morality of liberalism and mutual respect is particularly apposite to modern society, as this encourages communication rather than hostility between those who belong to different communities. But Durkheim does not offer a clear guide on this issue, as he also wrote on the need to regulate sexual desire by forms of modesty in every society. In his article Roger is bringing sociological knowledge to bear on a legal issue. A legal issue can be reconstructed as a sociological one. But, and this is David's point, does this mean in turn that a sociological issue can be reconstructed as a legal one, or to put this another way, can the legal issue in cases like *Begum*[2] incorporate sociological knowledge and arguments, and adjudicate upon them? In his conclusion to this chapter, David suggests that Roger may have come closer to his point of view in this latest phase of his work. He describes how Roger distanced himself from another academic's claim that his writings could be used to show the 'correctness' of legal decisions, insisting that in translating legal issues into sociological ones, he was not promoting a form of applied sociology. This kind of broadening – the application of sociology to the understanding of legal doctrine, philosophy and procedures as an exercise *within sociology*, does not give David such cause for concern.

Chapter 2, Michael Lobban's 'Sociology, History and the "Internal" Study of Law', also relieves us of a responsibility as editors: to give some description of the classic sociological theories that Roger has explored in depth, and used in his scholarship. Michael introduces the general theories of Weber, Durkheim and Luhmann, and discusses their implications for law. He does this for a purpose. The springboard for his contribution is Roger's claim, already discussed by Nelken, that legal ideas must be interpreted sociologically. Michael Lobban explores whether sociology offers the only way fully to understand how law and legal ideas operate in society, and whether, in particular, a historical method might contribute as much. This is not a claim that Roger rejects the importance of historical material; Michael notes Roger's insistence that social theory must be 'historically informed ...'. Instead he focuses on two of the central concerns of legal theory – the need to understand what is distinctly legal about law, and how law operates within society – suggesting that historical methods might prove particularly useful in addressing both of these concerns.

Although historians are suspicious of theories of society, treating them as over-general interpretations which prioritize theory over empirical data, Michael notes the overlap between Weber's concept of *Verstehen* and the methodology of historians who stress the need to try to

2 *R (Begum) v Governors of Denbigh High School* [2006] UKHL 15.

comprehend what events meant to the actors at the time. This has proved an important approach within the history of ideas, and he argues that it is as an evolving history of ideas, including ideas of the legal, that law has come to be understood as having a distinct existence. Referring to works that show how historical actors separated customary law from custom, and canon law from theology, he argues that 'it is not enough to distinguish the kinds of community in which law might be located. We need to look further at how particular communities at particular times distinguish the "legal" from other normative or non-normative forms'. The particular communities that he focuses on are specialist interpretative communities – those who are recognized to have special authority to interpret law. And it is the existence of these communities (jurists and judges) who provide the internal attitude to law which gives it its distinct identity. The development of the civilian tradition, from the twelfth century, provides one example of such a community (in that case a community of scholars) that gave law a distinctly separate identity. The artificial reason developed by the intellectual community of common lawyers provides another. But the understandings of these communities (and the understandings of these legal communities by the wider community) represent a multitude of legal languages, which Michael argues need to be studied in their richness and variety, rather than ignored once they have supplied a sufficient overview to support a particular account of social evolution. There is a need to move beyond the models constructed by social theory and legal sociology, to consider the concrete interactions which occur between this specialist body of knowledge and events in wider society.

Before going on to present the historical approach to these questions about law's identity and its operation in society, Michael discusses what he sees as the weaknesses of various approaches within legal and social theory to the identification of what is peculiarly legal, concentrating on Hart, Tamanaha and Luhmann. None of these approaches, Michael argues, adequately recognize that 'the "internal" dimension of law … is less stable and coherent' than such theories tend to assume. And none, thereafter, can adequately illustrate law's impact on society. Considering how sociology of law and history correspond offers a more informed and nuanced understanding that can ameliorate the deficiencies of such approaches, and offer better appreciation of how law as part of society evolves and how it actually impacts on society, namely how law and society interact. Or, as he concludes, 'the historian's method – with its keen focus on the particular context and its scepticism for grand theory – seems in many ways the most useful one'.

Chapter 3 by Zenon Bańkowski and Maksymilian Del Mar entitled 'Images of Borders and the Politics and Legality of Identity' involves an adventurous tour, which employs images to open up our understanding of borders, particularly those territorial borders associated with states or unions of states such as the EU. Images of lines and spaces suggest contrasting possibilities for the meaning of borders within law and politics. Lines represent borders as restraints, places for an inclusion which constitutes identity and an exclusion which defines otherness. Spaces offer us the idea of borders as locations for the exchanges of ideas, opinions, and different kinds of creativity. The chapter stresses the need to think of borders as places for possible enrichment, whereby our identity can be changed through interaction rather than barriers that protect us from external threats. The argument here is not that such threats cannot arise, but rather that we systematically tend to cling to the comfort of what we know, or believe ourselves to be: 'unable and unwilling to see that things could be otherwise.'

The otherwise that might, or probably is, emerging is taken up in the next chapter, written by Sionaidh Douglas-Scott and entitled 'Brave New World? The challenges of transnational law and legal pluralism to contemporary legal theory'. Sionaidh responds to what Roger urges in his important work *The Politics of Jurisprudence*: that participants in legal processes should be 'confronted with wider theoretical perspectives [than conventional legal theory] that can …

broaden our understanding of the nature of law'. The chapter provides a 'survey of the legal field', noting developments which make it increasingly difficult to present law as an autonomous, coherent system. Modern forms of regulation, including 'soft law', not only dissolve the distinction between public and private law, but also that between law and other forms of governance. Municipal jurisdictions involve multiple sources of law that cannot be ordered into the clear hierarchy presupposed by Hart's 'rule of recognition'. And where law operates beyond state borders (as with the EU, international human rights, the contracts of transnational corporations or internet regulation) the multi-dimensionality, complexity and lack of unity of laws becomes increasingly hard to deny or, as is the case with most forms of legal positivism, to ignore. In her discussion of these developments, particularly those arising in connection with the EU, Sionaidh makes a convincing case that the empirical reality of law in modern society is one of legal pluralism, with different legal orders seeking to accommodate each other in response to their factual and normative interdependence.

The tendency to present law as a unified, coherent and non-contradictory system is, she suggests, the internal perspective of a practicing legal professional – a 'mode of construction, an organizational project, rather than a mere representation of laws that actually were organized and clear'. Sionaidh argues that the choice between theories that present law as a unitary system and legal pluralism is a false conundrum, since one is being asked to choose between a theory that fails to present empirical reality, and an empirical reality that is difficult to theorize. One needs to focus on the empirical reality, and identify its various features and interdependencies, even at the risk of failing to identify a separate object of study with clearly defined borders. Multiple legal orders exhibit incommensurability along with interaction and a heterarchical accommodation of different sources and levels of law. This is what needs to be theorized. She offers two further observations as to how this should occur. The first is a suggestive simile – the legal landscape should be likened to the Carina Nebula – a vast complex of dust, stars, gases, forces and energy (though whether one associates this image with chaos, or simply the incomplete explanations available to us through the laws of physics is unclear). The second suggestion is that understanding the complexities of the legal landscape is only a beginning. The key issue is to ask how justice is achievable, given this complexity.

To develop discussion of that key issue, Roger's own work singles out the idea of community. In the next chapter Jiří Přibáň engages with Roger's works on community in order to discuss the nature of constitutional polities. He begins with a discussion of classical sociology's concern with the decline, within modern societies, of traditional local communities, with their close human bonds, mutual affections and common values. Although this is a theme within the works of Durkheim, Maine, Simmel and Spencer, it has a clear expression in the works of Ferdinand Tönnies, with his opposition between Gemeinschaft (community) and Gersellschaft (society). Whilst the values associated with local communities continue within the family, public forms of collective life involve varieties of instrumental rationality. These changes in the nature of collective life lead to corresponding changes to the nature of law: custom and natural law being replaced by legislated positive law. Within modern society, community nevertheless continues to have importance. However, this is no longer the lived experience of a community with affective ties and common values, but the imagined community brought into existence by the decline of religion and the development of political systems into states. This imagined community also forms a nation's 'culture'. The imagined nature of this community is presented most clearly in the paradoxical nature of national constitutions, which identify the national community that has constituent power while simultaneously exercising that power to constitute the organs of government with their self-limitations.

Jiří argues that classical sociology has not provided an adequate explanation for the emergence of this imagined community with its popular culture of shared symbols, political identity and communal bonds. Jiří quotes Roger's statement that 'Law is the regulation and expression of community', but with his acknowledgement of the importance of functional differentiation within modern society this is not a claim that society constitutes a community with common values and a specific morality. Rather, communities arise within society in various forms which include instrumental relationships, affective relationships and relationships drawing on common values. Applying Durkheim to these many communities, law can be expected to arise through conflict resolution, which in deciding who is right, draws upon symbolic values whilst at the same time reaffirming those values and encouraging the conditions of mutual trust which form the essence of communities. Roger contrasts these various communities with the image of a polity as a morally cohesive collectivity linked by its shared members, so often presented in modern philosophy. Jiří extends Roger's arguments. Rather than insist that legal philosophy reflects the multiplicity of communities within society, he wishes to offer a sociological explanation for the symbolic community that arises with a constitutional polity. Drawing on Niklas Luhmann's systems theory, he argues that law and politics, as functionally differentiated social systems, construct their own versions of community 'by turning its systematic operations into the prescriptive language of culture and communal bonds'. This is part of the 'structural coupling' of law and politics. Each system, via its own version of the constitution, also generates its own version of society as a community. In this process culture replaces consensus as a basis for political legitimation. Whilst European nation states share common political features such as liberal democracy, the rule of law and human rights (see Chapter 19 in this book), their political and legal systems construct separate national identities. One particular feature of these processes is the construction of national histories, particularly biographies, which draw on a past particular to a nation's constitution and project forward to that nation's future (see as examples chapters 17 and 18 in this book). This is 'a circular process of integrating a particular nation as cultural community by the state as modern political organisation and recursively shaping the nation's culture by political decision-making and an authoritative definition of nationhood through social and education policies, the state media, state sponsorship of historical science and the humanities, etc'. Thus we can separate community and culture. The former as the many communities present within society, and culture as symbolic and unified, generated separately through the operations of functionally differentiated social systems. Culture, as generated within these systems, forms part of their memories, providing resources through which they can explain themselves to themselves as part of a national totality.

This explanation for a national polity has implications for the development of polities at the transnational level. Roger has identified the possibilities of the kinds of communities that operate within national societies developing at a transnational level, and in turn, self-generating moralities and forms of law appropriate to their need for solidarity. Jiří by contrast doubts the ability of informal networks to generate transnational polities. Roger adopts an anthropological approach, firmly rejecting systems theory's explanation of society as an autopoietic system without specific nature or morality. Jiří however accepts that systems can only constitute polities as part of their operations, selecting memories and constructing identities in order to execute their operations: collectively binding decision making at the local, national and transnational level within the political system; juridical versions of constitutions within the legal system.

Jiří Přibáň's chapter ends where the next chapter can appropriately begin. The leading socio-legal and jurisprudential theorist, Brian Tamanaha, offers a critique of Roger's seminal work *The Politics of Jurisprudence* in the form of the 'Politics' of that work. He is able to distinguish a number of political questions, and a number of different communities who operate, in practice or theoretically, with a focus on law. Brian discusses a theme which runs through many of Roger's writings: the relationship between philosophical and sociological approaches to legal theory. He concentrates on this opposition as it is presented and discussed in Roger's *The Politics of Jurisprudence*.

Brian's is a critical chapter, sympathetic to Roger's desire to promote a more empirical approach to legal theory, but rejecting many of the arguments offered by Roger to justify this endeavour. In *The Politics of Jurisprudence* Roger argues that normative legal theory, by which he means theory that attempts to present law as a unity or system, meets the needs of the legal profession by increasing the legitimacy of legal practices. This occurs at the cost of providing law with an empirically impoverished understanding of its social context, making it a less appropriate form of regulation for the diverse communities which it needs to serve within modern, increasingly transnational society. Brian's critique takes a number of inter-related forms. He questions the shoe-horning of diverse philosophical approaches to legal theory into the category of normative legal theory, preferring Kelsen's two categories of legal science (in which one might place legal positivism) and theories of justice (in which one could place natural law). More fundamentally, he challenges Roger's claim that legal theory has any particular importance for legal practice. The characteristics which Roger attributes to normative legal theory play an important role within the legal academy, where system building and theoretical consistency are valued, but play a relatively insignificant role within legal practice. Local consistency serves the practitioner – whatever is sufficient to provide a solution to the matter at hand. The practitioner has little to gain from normative legal theory, particularly when that theory attempts to provide a general theory of law, i.e. one that is true for all legal systems, which therefore abstracts from the empirical conditions and peculiarities of particular jurisdictions. And even within the academy, there is no consensus that law is a unified system, with counter-views not only presented by post-modern theorists and US Realists, but even by academics writing in the US at the end of the nineteenth century, during the height of the period of what has been retrospectively labelled as one of 'legal formalism'.

Brian marshals a formidable body of evidence in support of his criticisms. He quotes the opinions of numerous legal academics and practitioners, particularly from the US in the nineteenth century, which refutes the relationship between normative legal theory and legal practice claimed by Roger. Rather than providing support to legal practice, normative legal theory is seen by practitioners to be largely an irrelevance: a description of law which bears little or no resemblance to the unsystematic manner in which legal issues are resolved, or the importance of individual judicial attitudes to particular decisions. The support which this form of theory supposedly offers by way of increased legitimacy is challenged and rejected by many legal practitioners, including senior judges. Brian's conclusion is not the direct opposite of Roger's claim. He does not assert that normative legal theory has provided no support to legal practice by way of increased legitimacy, but to be more precise, that one cannot reach such conclusions from identifying the potential for particular forms of theory to present the legal profession in a good light. Rather, one must oneself investigate the empirical reality of the relationships between theories which thrive in the legal academy and legal practice, a situation that is considerably more complex than Roger's approach, which asserts connections based on the possibilities of legitimacy contained within normative theory, would suggest. And if one is seeking to show that normative legal theory may be motivated by a political desire to increase the support for established legal practice, one should also be alert to the manner in which empirical legal theory has been undertaken with the political desire to criticize and reform it.

Having mounted a sustained critique of the account offered by Roger of the relationship between normative and empirical legal theory, Brian ends by considering why Roger maintains a commitment towards their greater integration, asking what 'politics' inform Roger's own contributions to jurisprudence. He finds an answer in Roger's desire to see law informed both by normative and empirical theory, so that it is both non-arbitrary and appropriate to the needs of the communities that it regulates. Although he shares this ambition, he does not feel that it can be achieved by urging either legal practitioners or legal philosophers to take more notice of empirical legal theory. He sees the value of Roger's work in its contribution to sociological jurisprudence which, in contrast to legal sociology, involves the task of 'constituting a theoretical account of law grounded within the concerns and perspectives of jurists seeking an understanding of the social nature of law'.

2. Methodological and Jurisprudential Themes

The book now moves into its second set of chapters. It begins with Chapter 7 by Sanne Taekema and Wibren van der Burg which proposes the sort of cooperative exercise of producing and evaluating knowledge about law that is the hallmark of Roger's tolerant eclecticism. They suggest, relying on the second half of their title: 'How Legal Interactionism May Bridge Unproductive Oppositions.' Responding to Roger's call to interpret legal ideas sociologically, Sanne and Wibren consider the problems of integrating legal philosophy, legal sociology and doctrinal research. They suggest that this involves a process of translation, made more difficult by those who work in these various fields adopting different concepts and definitions. Lawyers and philosophers think of law as coherent doctrine (though, on lawyers, see the previous chapter by Tamanaha), whilst sociologists understand law as a general dimension of social interaction (though, not Luhmannians – see Nobles and Schiff at Chapter 13). Drawing in particular on the work of Postema and Fuller, they offer legal interactionism as a concept that can integrate these three forms of legal research, and make each of them more available to improve legal practice. Legal interactionism is a development of Fuller's division of law into enacted law (of which the primary example would be legislation) and interactional law (the primary example being custom) which 'comes into existence through a gradual process of interaction in which a standard of conduct emerges that is understood as giving rise to legal obligations'. Enacted law is closely associated with legal positivism, consisting of rules laid down by authorities. But the authors go beyond legal positivism, here drawing on the work of Postema, by claiming that the force of a law is not solely a function of its authority, or even authority plus any physical coercion that might be applied in accordance with that law, but also includes its relationship to the obligations that arise through reciprocal interactions. This means that the vertical relations which constitute enacted law gain or lose force according to the manner in which they work with, or against, the obligations that arise between citizens through social interaction. There is a further element to this issue of force, in that the vertical relationship between the ruled and rulers is itself capable of being experienced as a reciprocal relationship, where the rulers too abide by the rules that they create. The key element in all these interactions is 'relatively stable expectations of behaviour'. Enacted law that has this element of reciprocity, or which supports or seeks to give effect to the obligations that arise through social interactions, can also be considered to form part of interactional law (though the authors admit that enacted law may develop in ways that cease to connect it to interactional law, as when a contract at first expresses an underlying reciprocal relationship, and later leads to obligations that run counter to it). Alongside these two sources of law, and in acknowledgement of the fact that some legal instruments constitute relationships that have no prior history, the authors treat mutual consent as a third basis for law, in addition to what is enacted and what emerges from interaction (giving the two examples of contract and treaty). Though here too the force of law arises not from the original consent, or the fact of enactment via contract/treaty, but in the ongoing interaction of the parties and the sense of obligation this generates.

Calling the combination of these three kinds of law 'legal interactionism' allows the authors to present law as a continuum, with enacted law which lacks the force added by interactional law at one extreme (where law is experienced as brute force or ignored) and societies entirely organized on the basis of customary law at the other. Mutual consent seems not itself to be part of this continuum, but to add an extra element of obligatory force to whichever of the other two kinds of law it is combined with. The concept is offered not only as a means to bridge the opposition between sociological, philosophical and doctrinal approaches to the study of law, but to overcome four other oppositions where these different approaches are most in tension: law in the books vs law in action; legal pluralism vs one 'coherent legal order'; law as a static vs law as a dynamic (evolving) order; instrumental vs non-instrumental views of law. The first and second of these are dealt with via the continuum just described. The need for enacted law to gain force through its embeddedness within relationships of mutual consent or ongoing social interaction means that even state law exists only as a form of legal pluralism. From this beginning, it is easy to see all legal orders as only relatively autonomous. The opposition between descriptions of legal systems that are static (doctrinal statements and philosophical attempts to provide an account of law that transcends jurisdictions and historical conditions) and dynamic is less easily reconciled. The idea of continuum is here combined with Wittgenstein's concept of family resemblance. This provides a good argument for abandoning attempts to claim that any features of law are absolutely necessary, but whether it offers an olive branch to those legal philosophers whose raison d'être is seeking to substantiate exactly this, is open to question. Lastly, Sanne and Wibren use legal interactionism to dissolve the means/ends opposition involved in discussions of law's instrumental character. Since social actors are motivated to engage with each other because of the benefits which result, and yet create normative understandings in the process, there is a sense in which all interactional law is both instrumental and not. The same can be said of any enacted laws that support interactional law. Whether this use of pragmatist philosophy really meets the claims of those sociologists who believe that law has a subordinate relationship to other social domains is again open to question. Thus this chapter presents a challenge to both legal philosophers and sociologists, but a challenge that these authors hope might enable them to resolve their 'unproductive oppositions'.

In Chapter 8, Amanda Perry-Kessaris provides an example of the application of Roger's theoretical writings on community to a piece of empirical field work. She describes undertaking an investigation into the relevance of law to foreign companies considering investing in South India. She needed a framework which connected the data that she had collected from economic and legal actors to the social context, and found it in Roger's work on law and community. This allowed her to construct an account of the part played by law in building and supporting the mutual interpersonal trust which was necessary to investment decisions. She goes on to describe how more recently, she has sought to integrate Roger's work on legal communities with Polanyi's thesis on the embeddedness of the economy. Her chapter also provides an opportunity to present something new: the visual communication of legal research. The chapter therefore contains graphical representations of the nature of communal networks, and in so doing gives readers a clear statement of the 'community' part of Roger's oeuvre.

In Chapter 9, Christoph Eberhard seeks to draw the parallels and connections between Roger's work on communities and his own work within anthropology. In doing so he takes some of the description of legal pluralism of Douglas-Scott, in Chapter 4, in other directions. Christoph approaches the world as a pluriverse, an approach that does not rely on identifying universal structures similarly appropriate to all communities, but involves taking a 'pathway' in the discovery of law that involves four stages of cultural or existential disarmament. The first stage is the discovery of alterity. He discusses the usefulness of approaching alterity through concepts of culture, noting Roger's hostility towards monolithic concepts of culture as impeding the comparative study of legal and social relations. Roger has, however, acknowledged the benefits of adopting the concept of legal cultures as a distinct mode of understanding, and one allowing for comparisons. For Christoph, as a legal anthropologist, sensitivity to legal culture is central to alterity – recognizing the plurality of legal experience and accepting that rights, including human rights, states and even notions of the individual do not appear equally in all societies, and that their absence should not lead to the conclusion that those societies have no law. Christoph's own working definition of law is that it 'puts forms, and puts into forms, the reproduction of humanity and the solving of conflicts in the domains a society considers as being vital'.

The second disarmament is of complexity. Rather than looking for the co-existence of diverse but neatly separate legal orders, one has to see plurality in all forms of existence. This makes Roger's idea of community a more fertile basis for investigation than 'legal system'. Christoph reads Roger's ideas of community as an 'invitation to imagine a pluralist and praxis related mileau'. In his own work it led him 'to propose a communitarian paradigm for legal theory inspired by traditional African communitarian legal experiences' where pluralism is the foundation of social life, and in order to maintain harmony all actors are responsible for the negotiation of solutions. Whilst Roger has developed his idea of community as a structural analysis, introducing ideal types as a means to study different aspects and forms of communities, Christoph has utilized the idea of '*jeu des lois*' as developed by Étienne Le Roy, which concentrates on issues such as land law and youth justice, and seeks to identify the rules of the game, as played by the participants. He sees this as a version of 'living law'. This approach does not treat culture as monolithic, but examines it as part of what players bring to the game.

Another theme which Roger has expounded is that interdisciplinarity does not merely add to knowledge, but transforms the terms in which it is sought and conveyed. Christoph sees this as a link to his third disarmament: interculturality. Recognizing the problems of human co-existence and survival in modern society he, quoting Pannkkar, sees the need to transform our approach to pluralism itself. We need to move from universalism and attempts to give a theoretical answer to pluralism and its nature: 'No purely theoretical solution can ever be adequate to the problem of pluralism.' The fourth stage in this process of disarmament is the recognition that we are all humans. This is not a claim that we share a common humanity but that as humans, we have real lives which include both individual and collective experiences.

In Chapter 10, Reza Banakar and Alexandra Lort Phillips present their early research findings into the nationwide UK 2011 riots which began in Tottenham, London, as a case study of the strengths and weaknesses of Roger's ideas of law and community. They begin with a survey of the media reportage in response to the riots which shows a recurring use of the theme of community, both in terms of the riots being an attack on communities, and with suggestions that responsibilities and solutions lie with communities. Next they present Roger's own writings on community, which they read as an extension of ideas of classical social theorists such as Tönnies and Durkheim, which seeks to move away from any totalizing idea of society as community towards communities as networks based on mutual trust. The task for state law according to

Roger, as they represent his analysis by selected extracts from his work, is to offer a form of law that supports these relationships of mutual trust within networks of community, and mediates between different communities within a pluralist society. This support is to be provided, in part, by the devolution to communities of some of the power and responsibility that would otherwise be exercised by state law. The authors draw on their study of the riots to consider the feasibility of this proposal for devolution in light of the experience of community within the inner city areas that suffered the 2011 riots. Their study consists of a series of structured interviews with lawyers, social workers and other professionals, some of whom had first-hand experience of Tottenham or the riots. The interviewees were asked their opinions on the causes of the riots, and then their views on the nature of communities and their own experience of these. Reza and Alexandra conclude that whilst the idea of community continues to play a role in how the majority of people conceptualize their daily lives, they understand this as an ideal to be lived up to, and not a reality of community life. They also interpret the interviews as evidence that the associations and networks existing in London are not integrated through a network likely to produce responsibility, but are at best transitory instrumental communities.

Chapter 11 by Marc Hertogh is also a piece of empirical work, grounded in conceptualization, but rather than that of community and law, a potentially negative form of its expression, namely alienation and legal alienation. In some of his early writings, Roger referred to legal alienation, and the dependence of legal legitimacy on the 'belief of individual actors that law promotes [...] what is most fundamental among the actors' values of justice and order'. Although the idea of legal alienation has not been further developed in Roger's work, Mark demonstrates that it is a promising concept for empirical research on law. Drawing on the work of many theorists, but particularly Seeman, the author seeks to make the concept of legal alienation more precise by breaking it down into different attributes: legal powerlessness (inability to influence legal events); legal meaninglessness (lack of predictability of the outcome of legal procedures); legal cynicism (where the rules of the dominant society are no longer binding in a community or population sub-group); legal value isolation (the alienated assign a low reward value to those legal goals or beliefs that are typically highly valued in society). In his applications of this concept to his study Mark introduces two further sets of categories. In order to address the questions 'Are people aware of the law?' and 'Do people identify with the law?' he uses ideal types: the legalist (aware of law and identifying with its values); loyalists (uninformed but identifying with the law); cynics (aware of law but not identifying with its values); and outsiders (unaware of law and not identifying with its values). His set of categories addresses the nature of protest in response to law. This can take the form of seeking to engage with law to seek change (loyalty); protesting about law from outside the legal system whilst still identifying with its values (voice) and either ignoring the law, or taking illegal action in response (exit). Using these sets of conceptual categories Mark Hertogh analyzes public responses in the US, especially on social media, to the killing of black teenager, Trayvon Martin, by Hispanic neighbourhood watch volunteer, George Zimmerman, and the not guilty verdict that followed.

In Chapter 12 Willem Witteveen offers a fascinating historically informed and, as could be expected from a member of the Dutch Upper Chamber, practically informed, jurisprudential chapter aiming to show how different concepts of law have significant implications for 'the art of legislation'. The concepts he advances are simplified (extracted from Sophocles' tragedy *Antigone*), but serve his purpose. Three main schools of legal thought (legal positivism, natural law and interactive or cultural law) can be seen as attempts to theorize the three sources of justification for legislative provisions: the constitutional authority of the law maker, ideas of justice and the common good and engagement with the normative commitments of those who are subject to the proposed law. The application of these concepts to lawmaking allows for 'the art of legislation' to be 'rhetorically effective' and reflective. What he is able to show is that the story behind the use of different concepts of law to inform lawmaking has been lost, and needs to be re-established. For this he criticizes political theory and modern political ethics, which has become a theoretical science rather than having a focus on the practical art of lawmaking. He demonstrates how classic writers such as Plato, Montesquieu and Bentham each, in their own ways, were insistent on exploring such an art – what the lawmaker needs to delve into in the course of their practical lawmaking. And each represents, as presupposed in their exegeses on lawmaking, different concepts of law. With this discussion he is able to show how such a background (which he believes has been lost) is equally relevant to modern notions such as the rule of law (see Chapter 19 in this book), the EU, delegated lawmaking by bureaucracies, etc. His overall suggestion relates to how different concepts of law are not only relevant to legislative practices, but how their different orientations should always inform those practices.

The final chapter in Part II, 'The Sociology of *The Politics of Jurisprudence*' written by ourselves is the second critical chapter (see also Tamanaha's Chapter 6 'The Politics of *The Politics of Jurisprudence*') on Roger's leading text. We have admired this book and used it in our teaching for some years. Like Brian Tamanaha, we applaud Roger's desire to overcome the tendency of legal philosophy and the sociology of law to remain closed to each other, and each to be insufficiently adapted to the study of legal practice. In our chapter we consider what difference a systems theory approach (namely neo-systems theory as developed by Niklas Luhmann) could make to some of the information contained in that book, and some of its critical engagement with jurisprudence and legal theory. Much of our discussion focuses on the most sociological of the chapters of *The Politics of Jurispurdence*, which deals with common law theory. We ask what role this legal theory has played within day to day legal practice. In answering this question, we draw upon Luhmann's concept of self-description. Systems, through their operations, generate communications that refer to themselves as a totality. These communications, like others of less generality within the system, provide a resource or memory which facilitates the carrying out of operations. One can examine these communications to consider what operations they facilitate that would not otherwise occur. In the case of common law theory we argue that this form of self-description was both generated by, and assisted in the evolution of law in response to changing social conditions at a time when there was relatively little legislation. It allowed adjudication to take a natural law form, in which past judicial decisions are not the law itself, but merely evidence of a form of law that lies within the community. This self-description was not abandoned in response to philosophical criticism, but replaced by a different self-description which emerged from within the legal system when modern legislatures began to create ever more law of a technical, specific and transparently interest-oriented nature. In the rest of our chapter, we seek to show how other topics within jurisprudence could be explored sociologically through the use of systems theory: the paradox of adjudication which identifies the law applicable to a dispute whilst simultaneously changing that law; the nature of the internal/external distinction that operates within the law; and why some kinds of legal theory can have greater capacity to be incorporated within legal practice than others.

3. Globalization, Cultural and Comparative Law Themes

The chapters in the final section of the book deal with a range of subjects, all of which consider law in its evolving international, global, regional, comparative and cultural contexts. Of course, this range is enormously wide, but it reflects subjects all of which Roger has demonstrated his interest in through his writings. It starts at the formal general level of law, 'The Sociology of International Law: An Introduction' by Mikael Rask Madsen. This is, par excellence, a contextual chapter. The subject matter is elusive, or as Mikael says of the rise of 'inter-, supra- and transnational law', that these developments address the 'very idea of society'. The 'politics' of international law is well represented in literature reflecting the relationships of international relations and international law, the 'sociology' of international law is much less well represented. What Mikael is able to offer is a review of the contribution made by sociology to understanding the development and role of International Courts (the number of which is substantially increasing, as is their activity), as those institutions that 'transform international law from its former position as somewhat residual to national law to now becoming "real" law: law in its own right'.

Initially Mikael considers classic sociological theories, those of Weber, Durkheim and Marx and other derivative theories. Weber's interpretative sociology allows the development of International Courts (ICs) to be made intelligible by exploring the motivations of the individuals involved, and their impact on the rationalization of ICs. Durkheim's writings have influenced a functionalist approach to the study of ICs; while Marxist and other critical theories have introduced issues of conflict and power, both symbolic and structural. More recent socio-legal approaches have taken an anti-institutional approach – moving the focus away from courts towards society more generally, and leaving the study of courts and judges to be dominated by political scientists. However, more recent sociological study of ICs (especially Dezalay and Garth, and Hagan) inspired by the sociology of Pierre Bourdieu on elites and professions, explores the role played by ICs within globalization. This approach regards developments of ICs as the outcome of competition between professions and elites in the definition of new areas of legal practice. It stresses the importance of human agents, with their personal and professional trajectories, in explaining the emergence of transnational legal fields. Mikael discusses the application of this approach to International Criminal Courts, and courts within the European law complex. He then briefly considers the relevance to ICs of the sociology of organizations, and the role played by ICs in generating a world culture in action (Lechner and Boli). Despite the differences of these various sociological approaches, they are linked by a commitment to go beyond legal and political studies to approach ICs not only as legal-political phenomena but also as societal ones. Thus Mikael is able to demonstrate the importance of, in the tradition of both Lawrence Friedman and Roger Cotterrell, not leaving the analysis of such developments solely to legal or political theorists. And, where this consideration leads, is to ask whether through the development of the vast plethora of International Courts some form of global society or world culture can be seen to be emerging.

That question takes a different form in the following chapter by Paul Schiff Berman. His chapter is focused on the 'informal' general level of the global, rather than the formal level of international law and international courts, and in particular global legal pluralism that, by definition, opens up the space for what can be considered legal way beyond identifications that are characteristic of nation state, hierarchical, expressions of law. (See the earlier chapters in this volume on other features of legal pluralism, Chapter 4 by Douglas-Scott, and Chapter 9 by Eberhard.) Recognizing that there are significant descriptive, normative and procedural questions involved, Paul focuses his discussion on three substantial issues: in what ways is global legal pluralism global, legal and pluralist?

In arguing for the global nature of legal pluralism, Paul points to the need to recognize the existence of legal orders that cannot be fitted into either state (sovereigntist territorialism) or universalist versions of law. (It is here that he recognizes in particular Roger's contribution to legal pluralism, by his developing concepts of legal community that do not link these to the territoriality associated with state law). Whilst universalism goes beyond traditional international law (law between states) to include universal standards such as human rights that can be asserted against states by non-state actors, it suffers from the levelling effects of seeking to apply single standards throughout the globe. There are descriptive and normative advantages in recognizing the existence of legal orders that incorporate local cultures and differences. These local orders become global through their interaction with universal ones. These interactions occur when members of local orders seek to make strategic use of universal standards, and in the process, transform them. The legal nature of global pluralism raises the problem of where law begins and ends. Paul argues that the advantages of moving beyond a state based understanding of law exceed the drawbacks of losing a clear sense of the boundaries of what is legal. First, he draws attention to the interaction between state legal norms and non-state legal (or quasi-legal) ones. The force of state law is not established by, or limited to, the presence and effects of its powers of enforcement, but lies also in its interaction with other norms which includes its ability to constitute social relations, and to be constituted by them (on this see also Chapter 7 in this book). These interactions are not limited to states and their citizens. International legal norms and institutions influence what state actors regard as legal and binding. As with the relationships that make legal pluralism global, the motivations for these cross-influences are often strategic. He shows, with examples, how transnational jurisdictions and norms come to be accepted by state actors who seek to use them to achieve particular solutions for national legal issues. What we learn from studying these interactions is, he concludes, worth the loss of clear boundaries to what is legal: 'only by going beyond a simplistic law/non-law dichotomy can we see the power of global pluralism coursing below the surface of the seemingly all-powerful state system.' In arguing for the pluralism of global legal pluralism, Paul claims that legal pluralism already exists as an empirical reality in the developments around the globe 'of procedural mechanisms, institutions and discursive practices that attempt to manage the overlapping of legal or quasi-legal communities'. Therefore, the issue he addresses is whether legal pluralism brings a distinct normative perspective to the study of law that is not already accommodated by sovereigntist territorialism, universalism or liberalism. The interactions between the local and the universal which give pluralism its global dimension should, he argues, be viewed positively, as this allows 'more voices, more input from different perspectives and more participation from different communities'. He offers the operation of the doctrine of 'margin of appreciation' by the European Court of Human Rights, and the use of hybrid state/international tribunals in dealing with war crimes, as two examples of pluralism's benefits. In his discussion of liberalism, Paul considers whether pluralism is anything more than the tolerance which a liberal state displays towards other normative orders which operate within its borders. He feels that a legal pluralist approach goes further than the liberalist approach in merely tolerating legal and non-legal norms that rival state law. First, as an empirical matter, pluralism is likely to lead to these other orders being seen worthy of study in themselves, and not simply when they clash with the state legal order, which is when the liberal issue of toleration comes into play. Second, legal pluralism involves a distinct normative approach, which justifies 'procedural mechanisms, institutional designs, and discursive practices aimed at developing habits of mind in decision makers that will encourage those decision makers to use restraint in insisting jurispathically on their own norms to the exclusion of the norms of other communities'.

What Paul's analysis of global legal pluralism anticipates is the possibility of some sort of transference of legal ideas, whether from national, cultural or other community settings to global ones, or vice versa. This is a theme taken up by Mark van Hoecke in the next chapter ('Legal Culture and Legal Transplants'), which delves into questions of the transplantation of legal ideas.

Mark is responding to Roger's criticisms of the use of the concepts of legal transplant (which he has found to be unclear as it confusingly addresses too many complex matters) and legal culture (which he has found to be hopelessly vague and better avoided by comparatists). In his chapter Mark seeks to operationalize these two concepts in the form of the distinction between legal transfers and legal culture: the first referring to attempts to introduce some aspect of one legal system into another, and the second referring to the whole (social, economic, historical and ideological) context of the written law. This opposition provides the basis for a discussion, using a number of examples, of the factors that can impede the reception of a legal transplant.

The first of his examples extends the schema of legal culture beyond the background to written law to include aspects of the law itself. Thus, even where countries develop similar solutions to social problems, they may do so through the extension of different doctrines. This introduces the idea, developed in a discussion of the respective treatments of the European directive on Unfair Terms in Consumer Contracts in Italy and England, of how deeply rooted ways of legal thinking may block the reception of a legal transfer. This tendency is explored further through two Russian examples. First, the thwarted attempt by US lawyers to export the Anglo-American trust into Russian law. Its incorporation threatened to distort too much existing legal doctrine, and was consequently re-interpreted to remove most of its foreign elements. A more focused legal transfer, that introduced new legal provisions limited to specific kinds of investment transactions, was more successful. The second Russian example he uses is of an attempt, instigated by the Russian Higher Commercial Court, to introduce a system of binding precedent on common law lines in order to reduce the work of the appeal courts, and introduce greater consistency into legal interpretations. This was not strictly speaking a legal transfer, but it did represent a conscious attempt to introduce a 'foreign' element. It was resisted by lower courts and legal counsel, being foreign to their tradition, as well as by the Ministry of Justice, who viewed it as an attempt to usurp political power from the legislature. Next Mark looks to China, a country which until recently lacked many of the forms of law associated with business, and therefore did not have an established legal tradition to prevent many legal transfers. However, in this example, he shows how the forms of resistance arose from the wider culture of Chinese society. The particular example he uses is of the failure of Chinese courts to enforce foreign judgments, other than cases of divorce and adoption. Drawing on a Chinese study, he shows that these failures have to be seen in the context of the general hostility in China towards seeking legal redress to solve disputes, and a general opposition to all things 'foreign'. Another example of transfers failing due to the wider social culture comes from sub-Saharan Africa, where an official family law introduced under colonialism and based on monogamy has been almost completely ignored.

In the last section of the chapter Mark offers the beginnings of a theory to explain when legal transfers might be expected to be successful. He distinguishes obstacles arising from internal and external legal cultures. The first refers to the different doctrinal and conceptual frameworks and traditions, which includes the way in which different legal cultures see 'reality' and law in different ways. The second includes the different world views within a society's culture, with Western culture being more individualistic and less communal than others, and very different traditions (often linked to religion) deeply rooted in society, such as through family, ownership, inheritance etc. In more technical matters, unrelated to these traditions, transfers are more likely to be successful. The relationship between transfers and external culture can be made more specific by drawing on Roger's own work on the nature of communities (moving away from a monolithic view of culture, see chapters 8 and 9 in this book). Instrumental communities, such as business, which pursue common purposes across jurisdictional boundaries, can be expected to be more open to harmonization through legal transfers than communities established through traditions. Thus, for example, changes to crime and property law may face stronger resistance than the harmonization of international business law. One also needs to have regard to communities based on belief, and affective communities. Finally, Mark suggests that, whatever the obstacles to successful legal transfers, the opportunities for transfer and influence are growing with increasing globalization, which is likely to lead to increasing harmonization, despite these obstacles.

Mark clearly recognizes that 'legal culture' has had, in ways that Roger has himself demonstrated, an unfortunate tendency as a concept for the analysis of legal patterns, but nevertheless shows how important it is and how much can be lost without it. In doing so he anticipates the two chapters that follow his, from Austin Sarat and Jack Balkin – two leading US academics, whose work Roger has consistently engaged with (and, as with many of us, admired).[3] Both chapters explore a very 'American' compulsion to consider how certain aspects of the constitution of the USA, as an expression of its 'law', also express who 'Americans' are, and what values both 'being American' and 'being legal' represents. Austin Sarat's chapter ('Keeping Civility in its Place: Dissent, Injustice, and the Lessons of History') is a retrospective look at the events in Birmingham, Alabama in 1963, the events that led to the imprisonment of Martin Luther King. These events are clearly etched in the American psyche, ready to be rehearsed anew when contentious laws are being tested, in public, as well as the public fora of legislative bodies and the courts. The tension of different values was tested then, particularly the values of 'civil disobedience' as some sort of 'right', and civility as some sort of restraint on the exercise of rights, as it is in many modern examples. Even at a global level, such tension will operate to construct what Paul Schiff Berman is discussing about evolving standards associated with global legal pluralism. Austin's iconic example also raises issues addressed by Mark van Hoecke and other contributors, of what makes legal systems resistant to particular political and social claims pressed upon them from outside.

Austin locates his chapter within a current US debate on the need for greater civility in political life and the media. Whilst the definition of civility is contested, Austin argues that it is an overrated virtue whose importance is always contingent upon the background conditions (especially injustice) which may lead to incivility. The civil disobedience in Birmingham provides an example of how civility can take a pathological form, in which those who are subjected to extreme injustice are nevertheless expected to act with civility. In the face of a doubtful constitutional and clearly racially motivated injunction prohibiting their demonstration in support of civil rights, in a town that violently enforced racial segregation, the demonstrators continued with their demonstration and were arrested, convicted and jailed for contempt of court. They received calls for civility not only from local church leaders (who argued that their demonstration should not take place as it would cause affront to a hostile white population) but eventually from the US Supreme Court, when the legality of their arrest and imprisonment was considered on appeal. In a judgment which sought to ensure that challenges to court orders take the form of appeals, and not self-help, the US Supreme court found itself siding with those who called for non-confrontation and patience in the face of gross injustice.

Jack Balkin's example of 'originalism' ('Why are Americans Originalist?) is also culturally significant. To argue about originalism's role in interpreting the US constitution is also to ask

3 As with Roger himself, Austin and Jack are eminent socio-legal theorists, consistently engaging moral, political and jurisprudential dimensions of legal regulation and ordering. Consider Roger's recent review of two of Jack's latest books, 2013, his many references to US constitutional questions in his writings, and his chapters in some of Austin's many edited collections (see the full bibliography of Roger's writings at the end of this book).

about what it means to be 'American' and, at the same time, 'legal'. There are some echoes here of Brian Tamanaha's Chapter 6, as originalism may have a much more significant existence within the academy, than it does within legal decisions, where it may be largely ignored except in the context of Federal and Supreme Court decisions when something needs to be decided for which there is little precedent. But Jack raises the question of why originalism is available at all within US constitutional legal argument, politics, the media and the legal academy. He describes the central role played in the USA by the myth of a nation and text brought into being by the revolutionary act of the founding fathers. This myth forms part of the cultural memory through which Americans are able to regard themselves as a dynamic nation, whilst at the same time being a continuation of their past. This myth is not available in other jurisdictions, or even in the context of the separate state constitutions within the US. Jack shows that the use of this myth, in both politics and law, is not a monopoly of the conservative right. It has been used by both liberals and conservatives in order to criticize the status quo, with each side attributing intentions to the founding fathers that are compatible with their own values. However, he argues that consistent resort to extreme forms of originalism are incompatible with the evolution of political institutions and responsibilities that has occurred in the US since independence, and with the legal evolution represented by precedents, forcing both politicians and lawyers to make highly selective use of originalist arguments. Whilst Jack identifies the factors that make this myth specific to US constitutional arguments, there are connections here to the arguments made by Jiří Přibáň in Chapter 5 on the manner in which legal and political systems generate symbolic nations whose constitutional polity is underpinned by symbolic cultural representation. Here Jack describes a mythical history drawing on leading biographies of leading national figures: 'the importance of originalism in American constitutional culture stems from how political and legal actors mobilized these cultural resources to justify and legitimate political and legal transformation in the twentieth and early twenty-first centuries.'

We are close to some of the messages that have been consistently represented in Roger's writings, whether through his discussion of 'community' or his Durkheimian scholarship. How are values embedded in law, and how do such values evolve? While the chapters by Austin Sarat and Jack Balkin are about constitutionality, in some form or other, they also seem to rely on background ideas of rights and, in particular, human rights. In the final chapter of this book, Martin Krygier takes the discourse of rights as a given in the evolution of constitutions in the second half of the twentieth century, and applies himself to what he considers to be the 'minor key' to the 'major key' of human rights, ideas of the 'rule of law' ('The Rule of Law after the Short Twentieth Century: Launching a Global Career'). That 'minor key' is implicit in much of Sarat and Balkin's discussion, as it is in van Hoecke's analysis of transplants, Schiff Berman's global legal pluralism and even Madsen's sociological account of international law. So, in Martin Krygier's chapter, what is implicit or taken for granted in the writings of others, is tentatively discussed. He offers his chapter as an example of Roger's suggestion that the sociology of law should 'allow comparison not of legal doctrine as such, but of legal ideas and practices regarded as inseparable from a broader social context', and that 'ideas and theoretical orientations seem to be adopted and discarded in ways that cannot simply be explained in terms of their intellectual superiority or inferiority'. What Martin draws our attention to is the huge increase in the interest paid to the Rule of Law as an idea since the latter part of the last century, and asks the question: why now?

We can only provide a brief overview here of his answer to this question. He sees his chapter as a development of the work of Samuel Moyn, who in *The Last Utopia. Human Rights in History* offers an account of the genesis and dissemination of human rights since the 1970s. Moyn argues that human rights were seized upon by dissidents who were seeking a moral language in the face of often insuperable obstacles to political action. Rather than seek the ideological opposite of their own countries' regime (capitalist/socialist) these dissidents campaigned for a minimalist and apolitical agenda – universal human rights. For Martin, the Rule of Law gained credence as an idea for similar reasons. Whilst it lacked the morally compelling aura of human rights, and could be seen as technical, it had the same quality of not championing an alternate ideology to existing regimes whilst still providing a basis for dissidence – holding governments up to their own self-proclaimed standards. The fall of communism is, for Martin, the key for understanding the rapid escalation of Rule of Law ideas at the end of the twentieth century. With only one contestant of the Cold War left standing, dissidents who had identified themselves with human rights and the rule of law rather than an ideological vision of society were swept into power and proceeded to give human rights a legal, constitutional form. And on the victor's side, victory over communism generated a temporary self-confidence that the institutions of Western liberal democracies (neo-liberal economies and the rule of law) should be exported around the globe. But as Martin argues, in words that most of the contributors to this book would be happy to echo: 'transplantation of the rule of law is always an intensely social, political, not a merely technical, project'. What is 'true of attempts to generate new law in general, [is] all the more of the rule of law, which involves achieving certain ideals for law, not simply installing an institutional package'. To understand the reality of the rule of law within countries that adopt it, we have to know a lot more about the interaction between this idea and the lives and commitments of those actors who engage with it (see Chapter 7 on legal interactionism). Martin does not see the enthusiasm for the idea of the rule of law around the globe completely dying away any time soon, given the agendas and issues that are currently framed in its terms. Nor would he wish to see the idea disappear, seeing the rule of law as better than the rule of any individual, and moderation in the exercise of power a general good. But he only offers his suggestions modestly, and tentatively. And in response we would like to ask our own question: why modest and why tentative?

Such a question mirrors Martin Krygier's background question, why now, namely why the rule of law has, only in recent times, developed its global attractiveness, its significance for a global understanding of law (a potential modern form of natural law) – about which he is modestly only able to offer some tentative answers (having marked out the significance of needing to ask that question). But the space for asking that question is not only significant for his scholarly chapter, but also for demonstrating, as he shows himself, how his own research and Roger's share much in common.

We repeat. Part of Roger's consistent message throughout his writings is that of critique. 'The critique is of legal studies and, in particular jurisprudence and legal theory, as being too "conservative", overly dominated by forms of analytic philosophy, and thereby less able to respond to societal evolution and its challenges'. Such a critique offers itself as necessarily tentative. The contextualizing involved, and the interdisciplinarity, does not take the form of definite and disciplinary-bounded scholarship. Rather, as Sionaidh Douglas-Scott describes in Chapter 4, it involves 'a variety of perspectives, and acknowledge[s] law's messiness and disorder'. Nothing about Roger's oeuvre would lead anyone to the view that he is anything other than analytically clear, coherent and organized in the way that he presents his research and ideas, but that does not represent how he approaches the task of theorizing about law. Being a theorist of law, and in particular, a social theorist, rather than a legal philosopher[4] (although, of course, so much about these terms depends on agreement about their scope, methods and 'colour') Roger openly asks questions that challenge traditional boundaries, and presents answers that remain modest, tentative and themselves challengeable. Is such an approach methodologically coherent? All the chapters

4 See Roger's very recent discussion of these matters 'Why Jurisprudence Is Not Legal Philosophy' (2014).

in this book, that share to a greater or lesser extent Roger's approach to the sociology of law and socio-legal studies, attest to a definite and, rare, firm and positive answer to this question.

We add one thing. We asked a few contributors to this volume (a few, but definitely not a majority, and certainly not all) to include in their chapters a comment (or a few comments) about Roger's research and writing, his professionalism and personality. We have no hesitation in agreeing with the comments made, as we know that many of our colleagues in Queen Mary, London University, UK universities, and many colleagues from abroad do too.

Bibliography

Cotterrell, R. 2002. 'Subverting Orthodoxy, Making Law Central: A View of Sociolegal Studies'. 29 *Journal of Law and Society*, 632–44.

Cotterrell, R. 2011. 'Justice, Dignity, Torture, Headscarves: Can Durkheim's Sociology Clarify Legal Values?' 20(1) *Social & Legal Studies*, 3–20.

Cotterrell, R. 2013. Reviews of Jack Balkin's *Constitutional Redemption: Political Faith in an Unjust World* and *Living Originalism*. *Public Law*, 411–17.

Cotterrell, R. 2014. 'Why Jurisprudence Is Not Legal Philosophy'. 5/1 *Jurisprudence*, forthcoming.

PART I
Socio-Legal Themes

Chapter 1

Why Must Legal Ideas Be Interpreted Sociologically? Roger Cotterrell and the Vocation of Sociology of Law

David Nelken

It is a delight and a privilege to be asked to write something for this much deserved festschrift for Roger Cotterrell. I have known Roger for more than 30 years and we have remained friends and colleagues for all of this time through the various vicissitudes that life presents. I feel fortunate that our careers have overlapped to a considerable extent, which gave me the opportunity both to learn from him as well as to teach together.[1]

Even if our ideas on most matters are very close[2] we have occasionally also been intellectual sparring partners. During the course of one exchange I sent him a draft of a paper in which I tried to question the force of his claim that law 'must' be interpreted sociologically.[3] He wrote back almost immediately, 'But David, I didn't know we were so far apart. I had to put my coffee down!' However, I see my task here not to tell you stories about this private and modest man but rather to show the importance of his ideas for anyone who wants to think about the possible purposes of studying law sociologically. I shall first briefly summarize his work and achievements. I shall then revisit our earlier exchange and discuss how Roger changed his approach to the goals of sociology of law. I then go on to consider what Roger has had to say more recently about using the writings of Emile Durkheim to illuminate controversial political and legal issues. I conclude by asking whether our positions may now be converging.

1. Roger's Career

After studying for his law degree at University College London, Roger was briefly on the staff of the department of law at the University of Leicester. But, crucially for both his future and the future of sociology of law in the UK, his dissatisfaction with the way law was then taught led him to take a Masters course in sociology and politics at Birkbeck in 1973. There, as he

1 I have especially fond memories of teaching with him, Simon Roberts and Tim Murphy (both from the LSE) on a wonderful Law and Social Theory course of the then federal London LLM in the 1980s. In what was an investment of resources unusual even in those happier times, the four of us rarely attracted more than 10 students a year (though some of these went on to become academics themselves). And I seem to recall that Roger got no teaching credit from his college for his participation in the teaching!

2 We were both influenced by the 'law in context' movement, with its commitment 'to broaden the study of law from within' (Nelken 2009). We each admire the writings of Ehrlich and Durkheim, but are more cautious about the approach of Luhmann and his school.

3 Cotterrell 1998; Nelken 1998. Extracts are reprinted together with extensive commentary in Gallagher (ed.) 2002. Cotterrell's article was a response to Nelken 1996.

readily acknowledges, he gained greatly from the teaching of the late Paul Hirst,[4] Roger spent his entire subsequent career at Queen Mary (University of London) where he rose to be Dean of the School of Law and Anniversary Professor of Legal Theory. He has also been in high demand as a lecturer and examiner in the UK and has lectured in numerous other countries including the USA, Canada, Belgium, Italy, Netherlands, Poland, Sweden, Spain, Switzerland, Finland, Israel, China, Hong Kong, Japan and India. He has also twice taught courses at the Oñati International Institute of Sociology of Law in Spain and is regularly called on to be plenary speaker at its international conferences. Amongst the honours Roger has received for his work he was made a Fellow of the British Academy in 2005 (amongst the highest forms of recognition for academics in the UK and one given to very few law professors), and he was awarded the (UK) SLSA award for his contribution to socio-legal studies in 2013. Roger is thus clearly an exemplary scholar and teacher.

For me and for most of his peers Roger Cotterrell is unquestionably the leading social theorist of law and sociologist of law in the UK, and amongst the very best worldwide. He displays highly sophisticated theoretical skills when offering exegesis and critiques of the literature, but he also has a masterly capacity to appreciate and synthesize the results of empirical work. In a career spanning almost 40 years he has impressed his stamp on the field and been a model for colleagues and students. Roger's major academic contributions (often translated into other languages) are found in the monographs *The Sociology of Law: An Introduction* (two editions, 1984 and 1992), *The Politics of Jurisprudence* (two editions, 1989 and 2003), *Law's Community: Legal Theory in Sociological Perspective* (1995), *Emile Durkheim: Law in a Moral Domain* (1999), *Law, Culture and Society: Legal Ideas in the Perspective of Social Theory* (2006) and *Living Law: Studies in Legal and Social Theory* (2008). In addition, he has authored a number of edited books, book chapters and a stream of path-breaking journal articles (well over 100).

The range of Roger's corpus of work is second to none amongst his socio-legal colleagues. He has written wisely and insightfully about Marx, Durkheim (and his school), Weber, Ehrlich, Gurvitch, Pashukanis, Olivecrona, Radbruch, Luhmann, Neumann, Polanyi, Selznick and Petrazycki, amongst others. He has left an archive of extensive interviews with the late Philip Selznick at Berkeley, and has himself been interviewed, by Hakan Hayden of Lund University, in a set of biographical interviews with leading sociologists of law. And Roger is still at the height of his powers. Roger's work is anchored in particular in a critical and original reappraisal and synthesis of Durkheim (and the Durheimians) and Weber, so as to rethink the relationship between law and community/communities at a time of growing pluralism and globalization. Recent cutting-edge contributions include pieces on law's response to cultural pluralism (to be discussed later, 2011a) as well as cutting edge pieces on the transnationalization of law and the dangers of 'disembedding' the economy from the larger society (2008a, 2012).

But, if Roger's work has been so widely cited in the UK, Europe and beyond, it is because it goes beyond the findings of particular studies and observations about specific authors and offers in addition an overall vision of what sociology of law is for, and what it should be for. Roger has led the way in advocating firmly the virtues of social thinking about law as an essential supplement or corrective to analytical and ordinary language philosophy, whilst also showing how it can maintain a dialogue with related disciplines and subject areas. Few scholars have written as thoughtfully about its links with the discipline of sociology and social science more generally, as well as its relationship with legal philosophy, legal practice and legal education. Roger's sustained and serious engagement, in particular with its epistemological challenges

4 See his obituary for 'Paul Hirst (1946–2003)'. Winter 2003, 41 *Socio-Legal Newsletter*, 6–7.

and value laden justice challenges, has been fundamental for establishing the credibility of the subject. This is seen for example in his acute writings about culture, multiculturalism and community as well as his discussions of the legal profession and the legal academy. Throughout his career he has sought strongly to encourage the growth of sociology of law, e.g. through active involvement with the leading journals – especially so in the cases of the *Journal of Law and Society*, *Law and Society Review* and the *International Journal of Law in Context*. He has helped to make 'sociological perspectives' not only acceptable and welcome, but even seen as necessary for legal scholars. Whilst to his sociological colleagues he has shown how juristic perspectives can sometimes be useful even for sociological purposes. The fact that he is formally qualified in both law (having written on trust, property and administrative law), and sociology has helped in this juristic-sociological balancing act.

But Roger does of course also have a life outside of the academy. Many colleagues (but perhaps not all) will have heard of his fascination for and expertise in jazz,[5] evidenced by the regular contributions he used to make to the Warsaw magazine *Jazz Forum*, and the books about jazz he authored or edited. Some of these are included in the publisher's list of Northway books – in the publishing venture undertaken by his wife Ann with his help. Perhaps less well known is his commitment to his Methodist church, taking part in its management responsibilities and contributing reflections on issues that face those searching for religious ideals against a background of neo-liberal political orthodoxies.[6] Whilst he never attempts to impose his ideas, he nonetheless holds strong convictions about what makes for a fair society and an almost visceral refusal of systems that reinforce social and class hierarchies. To everything he does he brings the same gentle integrity, whether it involves work, the church or his family: his son David is a famous installation artist, his daughter Lin has been a social policy adviser and researcher, and he has four grandchildren.

2. Sociology of Law and the Problem of Allegiances

Though there is a strong common thread in his work, it has also changed significantly in emphasis over time.[7] In a retrospective of his own work (though there would now be ample justification for another one!) Cotterrell explained that when he first 'nailed his flag to the mast of social science' his goal was to discover 'new', more 'objective' and 'realistic' ways of observing and interpreting law. However later on he came to advocate a 'critical, analytical view of the scientific quest itself and a reflexive attitude to the faith in science on which it is founded'. In particular he rejected the boundaries of sociology as a limit to the aspirations of social studies of law. Increasingly concerned 'to go beyond attempts to justify a particular vision of science', his current work has been less motivated by the search for 'scientific means of revealing facets of law often hidden from sight', and more by the desire to formulate a coherent 'moral vision' with the help of which law can and must be made to serve new social purposes (Cotterrell 1995: 15, 16ff).

Work in the first stage, up to and including the first edition of his *The Sociology of Law: An Introduction* textbook, rested on the premise that 'the aim of empirical legal theory (is) that law

5 For a rare glimpse of Roger's 'second life' as a jazz commentator and author, see Cotterrell 2011b.

6 'Voices in the City', in Morna Hooker and Frances Young (eds), *Holiness and Mission: Learning from the Early Church about Mission in the City*. London, SCM Press, 2010, 109–19; 'St. Paul's and the Protesters', *Cross Currents* (West London Mission) Dec. 2011, 8–9; 'After the Olympics', *Cross Currents* (West London Mission) Nov. 2012, 4–6.

7 This section draws freely on Nelken 1998.

is always viewed "from the outside", from the perspective of an observer of legal institutions, doctrines and behaviour, rather than that of a participant' (Cotterrell 1983: 242). In what is still the mainstream rationale of the subject, sociology's strength is here seen as a function of law's weakness; 'sociological analysis of law has as its sole unifying objective the attempt to remedy the assumed inadequacy of lawyer's doctrinal analysis of law'.[8] His early textbook on sociology of law brought together a wide range of its most important sociological empirical findings and showed the achievements and potential of this research field.[9] The book was a success, widely used by law students and social science students in various countries, translated into several languages and published in many foreign editions. But after two editions he lost interest in this enterprise. Subsequently, the focus of his work shifted as he tried to develop socio-legal approaches so as to provide an alternative paradigm within jurisprudence to what he saw as the social myopia of much legal philosophy.

From around 1986 Cotterrell began to focus on the problem that academic sociology might itself be subject to limits. He envisaged sociology and law as different discourses, each with its own conditions of existence, in which 'each constructs its own fields of knowledge and experience' (1986: 11). But he nevertheless found an ingenious argument to show why sociology can still provide a privileged route to understanding law because it is dedicated to a *reflexive* perspective on the development of all disciplines – including itself. Law, by contrast, lacking this interest, is no more than a 'discipline-effect'. Sociology may not have managed to become a successful form of power/knowledge; it is contested both by general common sense and by more specialised disciplines, and for its lack of rigorousness, which makes it, he says, an easy target for 'intellectual sharpshooters'. But rather than any of this constituting an impediment, it is exactly these weaknesses which allow the sociological imagination to play such a positive role in shaping legal discourse. In fact, as he has argued more recently, through this most 'practical' (1998: 178) view of legal ideas, sociological insights can help legal discourses reach interpretative solutions to puzzles that would otherwise be impossible to resolve.

In the debate between us that followed not long after this change of heart I suggested that what was at stake could be better understood if we contrasted two competing ways of looking at the sociology of law. The first approach relates law to its wider historical and social environment and to competing and overlapping disciplines and practices and has little difficulty in showing how legal actors often have little grasp of the factors which shape the 'inputs' and 'outcomes' of their decisions.[10] The second approach presupposes most of these constraints and seeks to improve the quality of decision making in terms that can be used by legal actors. Where the first type of scholarship deliberately transforms legal definitions into sociological categories, the second seeks

8 As Brian Tamanaha notes (1997: 191), legal doctrine is here seen as inadequate in two senses: that there is more to know about law in society than can be found in legal doctrine alone – and second, and more controversially, that legal doctrine mystifies reality so that legal and other actors do not understand their own activities. Tamanaha criticizes Cotterrell arguing that he, and other sociologists of law, soon became 'insiders' because 'the self reflective quality of theoretical practices have a relentless ability to absorb whatever begins as external to the practice when first introduced'. But, as we shall see, Cotterrell is more than willing to embrace this outcome.

9 Susan Silbey (1991), a leading USA sociologist of law, actually accused Roger of being too much the professional sociologist.

10 All the major textbooks, including Roger Cotterrell's own magisterial synthesis of the field, reconceptualize legal phenomena in terms of issues such as social order, social control, regulation, dispute processing, governmentality, desert, distribution, power, symbolism, ideology or rationality, rather than the doctrinal definitions of lawyers or administrative categories.

to translate sociological insights into legal concepts.[11] Importantly, an approach useful for showing the limits of law's sociological understanding of the world is not automatically useful for helping law overcome those limits. This is because it risks creating law in the image of social science (or the particular social science or external discipline being used to interpret law's intentions and criticize its workings).[12]

Roger, however, disagreed. No such dilemma existed. Legal ideas, he argued, *must* be interpreted through employing social insights because this allows 'the deliberate extension in carefully specified directions of the diverse ways in which legal participants themselves think about the social world in legal terms' (Cotterrell 1998: 190) and is a 'necessary means of broadening legal understanding taken as the systematic and empirical understanding of a certain aspect of social life which is recognised as "legal"' (Cotterrell 1998, 191). He was not of course insensitive to the danger that in trying to understand law better than it understands itself sociological interpretation could end up creating law in its own image. To avoid this he suggests we adopt a sociological approach that does not involve any such imposition on law of what he calls an 'alien' or 'colonising methodology' (Cotterrell 1998: 191). His 'transdisciplinary' conception of the sociology of law, he says, is one in which 'the use of the word sociological does not imply adherence to the distinct methods, theories or outlook of the academic discipline called sociology' or that of 'any other specific social science or other discipline' (Cotterrell 1998: 182). Lawyers, and other participants in legal matters, already engage in social theorizing about law. No doubt they could – and should do this better (and more often), but there are no external disciplinary protocols to be followed in deciding exactly when and how they should do this. The social theorist offers his or her insights. But their value is not decided by the contribution they make to the discipline of sociology. Instead of the once proud (if never fully explicated) slogan that 'law is a social science', he now tells us that if sociology of law has any allegiance it is 'to law itself'.

I was not convinced. It would be unwise to assume that law is – by definition – concerned with systematic, empirical, knowledge of the social world. Surely this is exactly what is in question. It is the *variability* in the extent to which legal discourses (or legal systems) express these features that distinguish them from sociology – and it is the study of this variability that forms the subject matter of sociology. Cotterrell at times admits this, even explaining that two of law's essential features can come into conflict because law (but presumably not sociology) is caught in the tension between systematic knowledge and 'the wilderness of single instances'. His argument that legal ideas must be interpreted sociologically thus presupposes but does not demonstrate that law must necessarily be interested in the *maximum* extent of systematic empirical knowledge of the social world. In fact it is the extent to which law does not correspond to this model that he himself relies on in explaining the need for sociology. But even if we conceded for argument's sake that legal discourses are indeed all social, systematic and empirical this would not necessarily guarantee a smooth matching of the discourses of law and sociology. What of the rival claims of other approaches such as those of psychology, history or economics? What about other aspects of law that this characterization of

11 This classification is put forward by John Monahan and Laurens Walker in their leading U.S. University Casebook, *Social Science in Law* (1994: v): 'We here view social science as an analytic tool in the law, familiarity with which will heighten the lawyer's professional effectiveness and sharpen the legal scholar's insights. The principal alternative to the insider perspective on the relation of social science to law is the "law and society" or sociology of law approach which seeks to understand the functioning of law as a social system.' Variations on this distinction are captured in other classifications such as sociology of law versus socio-legal studies, 'law and society' versus sociological jurisprudence, etc.

12 See Nelken 1993, 2009.

law leaves out – for example the idea that it is also a hermeneutical search for correct and coherent textual meaning.

I argued that the best prophylactic against the temptation for sociology to create law in its own image was to search also for insights regarding its differences as much as its similarities to law, to pay *more*, rather than less, attention to their disciplinary practices and allegiances. Cotterrell rightly cites Weber as authority for the possibility of a sociology of legal ideas and doctrine (and not only a sociology of the 'law in action'). But it was Weber himself (and not just Kelsen) who insisted on the sharp difference between the sociological and juristic point of view, a distinction which – significantly for our purposes – Weber based largely on the claim that the juridical view 'takes empirical validity for granted' and is not interested in what 'actually happens in a community'.

As against Cotterrell's recommendation to loosen sociology of law from its disciplinary moorings, I argued that we should seek rather an 'account of law which contextualises the bounded and practical rationality of legal and other actors and the process of legal reproduction without assuming that they could or should have adopted the place, point of view, or practice of the discipline which produces this account' (Nelken 1996b). I went on, 'Even for social scientists, law's lack of awareness, or selective awareness of its context, must be treated as an intrinsic, if changing, feature of its social reproduction, rather than as simply the origin of corrigible errors to be excised by the expert or political activist'. Any call for reflexivity must also be applied to social science itself as well as to law. And this goes beyond Cotterrell's claim that sociology's disciplinary weakness and self-questioning can even be its strength. It requires a serious effort to see why the sociological viewpoint, like any other approach, is also a way of 'not seeing'. In any case, I insisted, it was not so easy to be 'un-disciplined'. By speaking of the 'paradox' of sociology's weakness constituting its strength it is not even that clear whether what Roger still calls 'a sociological perspective on legal theory' (Cotterrell 1998: 181) represents a move away from professional sociology or actually an attempt to make ever-stronger claims on its behalf! In fact when he offers sociological analyses of law he continues to mobilize a working idea of what constitutes social insight that is firmly situated within the boundaries of academic sociology. Many times his argument comes close to the near tautology of claiming that only sociology can satisfactorily explain the way law is constituted by and reconstitutes social ideas. But this does not tell us why our understanding of law *should* privilege social ideas (as against economic, political, psychological, literary or theological insights) unless the term social is taken to embrace every form of knowledge.

This exchange left open a variety of questions concerning the status of sociological arguments around and within legal discourses. When and where – and for who is it a 'must' to interpret law sociologically. Perhaps Teubner is right in arguing that when legal processes try to absorb social science findings they (necessarily) transform them for legal purposes in such a way that they soon lose contact with the sense they had in the discipline from which they were first taken? (Teubner 1989) And what are law's specificities in making, ordering and handling disputes? If 'ever greater broadening' may be valuable for social science, in which legal activities and settings could it be counterproductive? What would this do to the need for legal 'closure' in so many legal contexts?

3. Sociology of Law as a Moral Science

A good way of seeing how Roger responds to these questions is to examine some of his more recent writings where he seeks to show us what sociology of law can offer to the resolution of legal issues. How far do these papers differ, if at all, from his continuing contributions to professional sociology?[13] Does he succeed in producing work that is at the same time both a contribution to sociology and to law? I shall focus in particular on a recent paper (2011a) called 'Justice, Dignity, Torture, Headscarves: Can Durkheim's Sociology Clarify Legal Values?' that discusses the acceptability of torture in defence of national security, and the merits of restricting the wearing of Islamic headscarves (or, more precisely, the face-covering veil). But I shall also make some reference to a related paper (2008b), 'The struggle for Law: Some Dilemmas of Cultural Legality'. In these papers Roger proposes to make social theory relevant to dilemmas facing law as these are manifested in the search for security and worries about what can be asked of minority groups in the search for living together in conditions of mutual respect.

Cotterrell begins his paper on torture and headscarves (2011a) by asking rhetorically: 'Can sociology tell us what is right or wrong? For most social scientists (and surely most citizens) the answer is clearly no. Sociology claims to be science, not moral philosophy. Sociology of law, for example, aims to explain the social character of law, but not whether any particular law or legal regime is just, or morally sound' (3).[14] Yet, he argues, 'it may be that sociology of law's traditional avoidance of the possibilities of a general sociology of legal values has resulted in some missed opportunities' (17). This is true, he says 'in contemporary conditions when law and its practice are often condemned for an instrumental orientation that pays little attention to the moral needs and bases of regulation, or to the necessary moral frameworks of legal relationships' (17–18). For Cotterrell, 'classic sociological theory provides some still useful resources for reconsidering orthodox views about sociology's capacities for informing moral and legal evaluation' (4). In particular, he tells us, 'Durkheim's pioneer work still provides insights that can be related directly to important legal issues of today' (18). Durkheim's 'moral individualism' offers a value system that can help to unite contemporary Western multicultural societies, in which beliefs and values are otherwise very diverse. According to Cotterrell, the idea of moral individualism as the only possible basis for values in modern society is all the more relevant in current globalizing societies. 'More must be assumed, because it cannot be known, about the innumerable "faceless" people an individual must deal with in these systems; and such assumptions need moral-legal guarantees. Developed ideas of human dignity and autonomy become, more and more the basis of these assumptions and guarantees. Hence *universal ideas of human dignity are a function of social and economic complexity*' (10).

What is of particular interest to us here is the way Cotterrell sees Durkheim as moving between description and prescription. He quotes Durkheim's assertion that '"Science can help us in finding the direction in which our conduct ought to go, assisting us to determine the ideal that gropingly we seek", and having observed reality, "we shall distil the ideal from it"'[15] (4). And he explains that the strength of Durkheim's approach lies in the way '(It) detaches morality from seemingly timeless philosophical debates, and grounds analyses of it in empirical study of specific types of

13 For example he has made important recent contributions to comparative sociology of law, the sociology of transnational law and economic sociology of law.

14 Cotterrell tells us that 'only a few leading modern legal sociologists such as P. Selznick have disagreed. Selznick "influenced especially" by John Dewey's teaching on the relations of fact and value, claims that sociology, studying legality as an ideal pursued in practice, can also help to clarify and realize that ideal'. (See also Cotterrell 2004.) But his own approach is less linked to actual practice and closer to what he calls Durkheim's 'normative relativism'.

15 Cotterrell here quotes Emile Durkheim 1984: xxvi. See also the citation from Durkheim, 'the science we are outlining here proposes to attain moral precepts, in their purity and impersonality. It has as its target morality (la morale) itself, ideal morality, floating above human acts, not the deformations to which it is subject when incarnated in current practice', set out in Lukes and Prabhat 2012: 375.

social relations and social organization' (17). Hence 'it can identify moral principles and practices compatible with (or even necessary to) stable social relations in particular kinds of societies'. From this perspective, 'Sociology can provide guidance on moral issues' (5). As with moral individualism itself, '(I)t is not limited to describing what people think in moral terms and what moral choices they actually make. To some extent, it can also provide criteria to evaluate and criticize those choices. Thus, sociology can sometimes advise on what law should prescribe or permit' (5).[16]

It is debatable exactly how this approach gets us from is to ought. Is the argument that the need for social solidarity cannot be questioned without falling into self-contradiction?[17] Arguably, pointing out that given outcomes (solidarity) require particular means (open communication) may only be a technical contingency without moral significance.[18] Be that as it may, Cotterrell insists that Durkheim can show us that certain solutions to policy dilemmas are to be preferred, not because they reflect eternal principles, nor even because they have been agreed to by those involved, but rather because only certain ways of behaving will 'fit' with the underlying needs of living together in given social circumstances.[19] 'Whether, or how far, moral individualism is actually respected in practice, supported in popular opinion or affirmed in government policy is not the issue; it is uniquely appropriate to modern complex societies, *whether recognized or not*' (2011a: 8).[20]

With reference to the two topics addressed in his article, he tells us that Durkheimian ideas 'can be used, for example, not only to show unambiguously why the use of torture is morally indefensible for contemporary complex societies, but also to clarify the context (in terms of various conceptions of national security) in which efforts have been made to *defend* torture' (4). Likewise, '(I)n relation to Islamic dress, an application of Durkheim's ideas on solidarity and the body suggests that prohibiting *certain* forms of this, but not others, contravenes values of human dignity' (4). For Cotterrell, 'Durkheim reveals the complexity of human dignity and autonomy as legal values, and raises important issues about their scope of application'. His approach 'directs attention ... to the *social boundaries* of legal and moral values – their jurisdictional reach and applicability beyond the membership limits of particular societies, or types of society' (17). Cotterrell explains that a Durkheimian analysis of torture will start from the problem of justifying punishment in general: 'the best way to see Durkheimian punishment is as an uneasy *compromise*; a process in which the dignity and autonomy of the offender are,

16 In the forthcoming extended version of his study of Durkheim, *Law in a Moral Domain* now to be published by Edinburgh University Press, originally published by Stanford University Press in 1999, Cotterrell tells us likewise that, according to Durkheim, yardsticks against which law in any society is to be judged are given not juristically or philosophically but by the sociological character of that society.

17 For such an argumentative strategy in the service of quite other purposes see Beyleveld and Brownsword 1986.

18 As Herbert Hart said of Fuller's procedural approach to natural law. See now Cane (ed.) 2010.

19 Philip Selznick offers a somewhat more open-ended view of the relation between social context and ideals. For him, 'Although fidelity to context is essential, and the lure of absolutes should be resisted, we must also recognize that contexts are *transcended*—and also *governed*—by broader standards and ideals. Concepts of growth, freedom, rationality, caring, fairness, and justice are among the criteria by which we *judge* contexts and make proposals for their reconstruction ... Although the context may impose constraints, the latter are not self-justifying. The justifications speak to what may be needed for practical success, but also for the realization of relevant ideals. Fidelity to context is wholly consistent with upholding transcendent values. It does so, however, by learning from the context which values are relevant and how they may be realized. This is the logic of responsive law, which seeks to vindicate legal ideals while adapting to contexts by seizing opportunities and accepting restraints'. Selznick 2002.

20 But, he immediately goes on to add, 'Durkheim sees it as a yardstick against which, increasingly, Western laws and legal systems are widely judged in practice'.

indeed, sacrificed but in a strictly limited, measured way and always with the idea that the damage to these values is, as far as possible, to be repaired' (12). Torture is therefore morally indefensible for contemporary complex societies because it goes beyond any such justification. This can be hidden only 'by thinking of the offender as being *outside* society anyway – not part of the networks of solidarity, an enemy of society who can properly be sacrificed for the good of society' (11).[21]

But what of the potentially serious objection that Durkheim's analysis of punishment in fact treated it as a process closely connected to the reproduction of the boundaries of existing social groups rather than as something requiring universal inclusiveness? To this Cotterrell responds that 'this strategy is ultimately self-defeating for several reasons (13).[22] First, in an increasingly interconnected world the borders of societies are porous and it is not easy to restrict the values of moral individualism to citizens of a particular society, or even a particular type of society. People in complex contemporary societies are increasingly linked through social interaction and mutual awareness with others beyond the borders of those societies. In a globalizing world the moral borders of societies are becoming blurred. The line between insiders and outsiders is less easy to draw, or is drawn in different ways by different people, or is simply rejected by many who may perhaps be unsure about their own insider/outsider status' (13).[23] He goes on: 'Second, even if moral individualism is ultimately given coherence by sociological relativism (an analysis of the distinct characteristics of particular types of society) rather than philosophical universalism (speculations on human nature), it acquires strength the more it can be generalized in popular consciousness into a simple idea of respect for common humanity. The effectiveness of moral individualism, in Durkheim's view, depends on it being an ideal that can be believed in, and since the ideal focuses on human individualism as an abstraction, it is hard to confine that abstraction, *as popularly understood*, within particular, empirically specified social milieux. Third, moral individualism, even if shaped by the experience of complex modern societies, has now become, to some extent, and especially for political reasons, a total value system seen as fitted for export to all societies. While such a view may be sociologically very problematic, the fact that it exists poses obstacles for attempts to treat some people as "less human" than others, whoever and wherever they may be ... Such attempts would create the danger of making the value system appear hypocritical' (13).

The same paper also applies a Durkheimian analysis to the vexed question of the Muslim (face-covering) veil. On the other hand, there are 'the needs of social solidarity. One of those needs is not to prevent the interpersonal communication that can facilitate routine social interaction and encourage social interdependence' (16). 'In so far as forms of dress seem seriously to impede (perhaps, indeed, seem intended to impede) this communication, Durkheimian moral individualism will surely condemn them' (17). Hence, he argues, 'A Durkheimian view thus bypasses much pre-existing debate on the "headscarf issue". On the one hand, it would surely treat the wearing of female Islamic dress as justifiable in so far as it expresses an intention to take part in social interactions normal in an integrated and cohesive society, but to do so while deliberately controlling the impact of sexuality as a factor in those interactions. On the other hand, such an approach presumes that

21 On the other hand, an important if very controversial line of German criminal law theorizing has recently suggested that different procedures are (should be?) used when dealing with those who do not accept the legitimacy of the institutions they are attacking. See Jakobs 2004, discussed in Tondini 2007.

22 The use of the term 'strategy' is not entirely clear here. But Lukes and Prabhat 2012 have also recently tried to apply Durkheim's ideas to the legitimacy of torture. They reach much the same conclusion as Cotterrell about which side of the argument Durkheim would be likely to come down on.

23 But the problem, as posed by Jakobs 2004, is what to do with those who reject inclusiveness – not who are uncertain about being accepted.

individual choices in dress in a modern complex society should ultimately be governed morally by the value system of moral individualism …' (16). Amongst the surprising implications of Cotterrell's analysis is the way it shows the unexpected links between the two issues he discusses.[24] He tells us that 'Legal protection is a more urgent priority, at the same time as legal concepts become harder to apply in practice … Thus, some of the problems surrounding practical protection of women's rights (in domestic violence, rape, etc.) directly parallel those of prisoners' rights, or rights in almost any circumstances in which the individuals concerned are somehow isolated from the ordinary networks of social solidarity that provide the foundation of moral individualism, and so of the law shaped by this value system' (15). Commenting on Durkheim's attitudes towards the sex act (as itself an invasion of the individual) he argues: 'We find in them a moral ambivalence which strikingly parallels the ambivalence underlying his analysis of punishment: both sexual relations and punishment involve a calculated sacrifice of dignity and autonomy, as Durkheim sees it: a sacrifice that amounts to a vaguely defined but essential exception in societies where the values of dignity and autonomy are fundamental' (14).

4. For an Engaged Sociology of Law

What does Roger's advocacy of the continued relevance of Durkheim's ideas and ideals add to his earlier claim that 'legal ideas *must* be interpreted sociologically'? Is he more concerned with helping law to see what it currently fails to see or with using social science to help law do what it has to do as law? Or has he shown this to be a false dichotomy? His formulations on this point are somewhat equivocal. He is certainly willing to recognize that Durkheim's approach to this is partial,[25] can be criticized[26] and is not the only possible one.[27] So there is no 'must' about seeing these issues (just) through Durkheim's eyes.[28] It could also be said that his project here has more to do with developing 'a sociology of morality' than with explaining what law is trying to do, or even what it should be trying to do. As he puts it: 'When sociology reveals the fundamental importance

24 Though bringing these issues together can also be misleading. It is certainly no part of his argument to equate someone who is a citizen of a country but covers her face with a suspected terrorist!

25 In material promoting his forthcoming book on Durkheim, for Edinburgh University Press, Cotterrell warns us that Durkheim's moralistic perspective on law is ultimately not concerned with questions of power except insofar as power is a resource of law. As such it offers only a partial perspective highlighting certain problems and imperatives, while leaving aside others.

26 As he puts it, 'It would be possible to take issue with his understanding of the pre-requisites of social solidarity, of the particular significance which he attaches to moral individualism in relation to this, or indeed with the idea that complex contemporary societies need social solidarity in anything like the terms he describes. It would be appropriate, certainly, to criticize his conception of social solidarity as focused mainly on functional (especially economic) co-ordination and interdependence, and its lack of attention to bases of solidarity that lie in emotional allegiances and commitments, or in customary practices. It would, in any case, be important to consider more fully how diversity of beliefs and values (as well as an over-arching ultimate value system) may contribute to solidarity' (Cotterrell 2011a: 15).

27 Even staying within the realm of sociology, insights from the sociology of the body, gender, minorities, religion, gender and immigration, etc. would certainly be helpful to supplement and possibly even revise conclusions limited to drawing out the implications of Durkheim's ideas about 'moral individualism'. When it comes to the realm of values, these controversies raise questions about patriarchy, liberalism versus communitarianism, minority rights and many other difficult ethical and political issues.

28 Roger says that 'This is not to claim that these values must be seen in Durkheimian terms, but merely that to do so may cast a new, revealing light on their scope and significance' (Cotterrell 2011a: 2).

of certain moral principles in particular social conditions, the question of whether these should be expressed and defended through law will need to be faced' (5).

On the other hand, he argues, just as definitively, that law does need to take on board these sociologically inspired insights. '(W)hat law itself must communicate is a need for adequate respect for the autonomy and dignity of all other individuals. In appropriate circumstances it must firmly enforce this respect. Without such a value system of individualism, stable trans-cultural communication is impossible' (2008b: 382). Likewise, he tells us that 'Where legal communications around culture take the form of battles of rights, it is important that the eventual outcome of these battles – and the aim in processing them legally – should be to produce routine structuring that explicitly recognises cultural differences, while facilitating everyday social interaction that makes possible communication across them' (2008b: 383). Even if it is not obvious that law should always incorporate these moral values sociological argument still has a large part to play in trying to approach these issues. As he puts it, in his paper on torture and headscarves, 'Whether such a sociological assertion of relevant legal values should lead to their direct support through law, and, if so, how,' he says, 'are presumably matters to be clarified further empirically – by examining the conditions and possibilities of social interaction in a particular time and place' (2011a: 17).

As this suggests, the key question remains as to whom Cotterrell's arguments are being addressed. Are they for policy-makers, legal actors, law students or the general (informed) public (or all of the above)? By insisting that sociology of law must seek to go beyond the needs of particular participants 'in the legal process', (1998: 191) his message is also in some ways an anticipation of the recent call for public sociology.[29] But then does an approach based on Durkheim, as he suggests, in fact 'bypass much pre-existing debate'? And would it in any case really be a merit if it failed to take into account the matters that people actually want to talk about? In practice, there is evidence of considerable overlap.[30] Thus there are some, even from the Muslim community, who support the arguments Cotterrell draws out from Durkheim. Yasmin Alibhai-Brown, for example, argues that 'Liberal defenders of the veil have lost their way' and believes the phenomenon of wearing face covering veils to be part of the spread of Saudi Arabian hegemony. She complains that 'The social cost is never considered by upholders of this custom' and that 'the covering declares self-segregation emphatically and it unsettles and provokes people'.[31]

On the other hand, there are other commentators for whom even having a public debate can itself be damaging to the cause of integration (the purported reason for curbing the use of the face covering veil). As one informed insider sees it 'The women who do wear the face veils are a tiny minority within a minority, so the thought that they're any kind of threat to British society as a whole is beyond laughable. But at the same time, [these debates] do, of course, increase the vulnerability of Muslim women as a whole. Time and again, verbal and physical attacks on Muslim women increase when we have these so-called national debates. In emotional and psychological terms, I think it does a huge amount of damage'.[32] And even 'Tehmina Kazi, director of *British Muslims for*

29 See Burawoy 2005. Note in particular his distinctions between professional and critical types of sociology (addressed to academic audiences) and policy and public types of sociology (addressed to non academic audiences). Durkheim's own intervention in the Dreyfus affair is a good example of public sociology.

30 This may of course be because sociological ways of seeing things are already part of common sense.

31 *The Guardian*, Sept. 23, 2013.

32 Salma Yaqoob, formerly a Birmingham city councillor, quoted in *The Guardian*, Sept. 16, 2013: www.theguardian.com/world/…/veil-biggest-issue-uk-niqab-debate.

The same point is made by Maleiha Malik who criticizes the way France and Belgium, 'adopted a criminal ban without any attempt to consult Muslim women, let alone invite them to participate in the creation of laws that would have such an impact on their personal freedom. French and Belgian Muslim women have bitterly *secular Democracy*, is similarly unenthusiastic about having a national debate. "What does need to happen" she says "is an internal debate within Muslim communities, questioning people who push the rhetoric that the veil is obligatory in Islam – or even those who say it's recommended." These conversations are necessary, she says, but when talk turns, at a national level, to a state ban on full-face veils – a measure that passed into French law in 2010 – "it's completely counter-productive." If a woman is, in fact, being oppressed into covering up, then enforcing a stance which makes it difficult or impossible for her to move about in public cuts off her chances of finding any support outside the home'.[33]

Despite insisting that what people think is not the key here, Cotterrell does make some effort to connect his analysis with the reasons people actually give for wearing the face veil. He tells us: '(F)rom a Durkheimian viewpoint, sexuality is a disruptive force, acting on the normal conditions that govern the application of moral individualism. To protect those conditions, "we conceal our body as well as our inner life from prying eyes", partly to make it easier to relate interpersonally on the basis of the neutral individuality that moral individualism celebrates. It is easy to understand in these terms many professed justifications given by women for wearing the Islamic headscarf (hijaˉb) or body-covering gown (jilbaˉb). Although these justifications are very varied, the most relevant here are expressed in such statements as: "The Muslim woman wears al-khimar [head covering] in order to desexualise public social space when she is part of it"; "she does not want her sexuality to enter into interactions with men", and she "is concealing her sexuality but allowing her femininity to be brought out." … Whether or not the wearing of Islamic dress achieves this effect, these justifications for it are clearly consistent with Durkheimian moral individualism' (2011a: 15). What is clear, however, is that, for Cotterrell, the validity of their reasoning needs to be measured by its consistency with Durkheim's analysis, rather than vice-versa[34] even if this priority is hardly likely to be shared by those who base their arguments on their (or some authority's) interpretation of a religious tradition. Arguments from a normative realist are likely to cut little ice with a believer.[35]

But what are legal actors expected to do with Durkheim's arguments (as interpreted by Roger)? He concedes that adjudication in particular cases can be a complex task: 'No doubt the conditions of communication, like other aspects of this value system, will involve compromises in practice … how far any particular practice in fact supports or opposes this value system is an empirical question. In considering it, it will be necessary to take account of both the subjective and objective aspects of dignity and autonomy discussed earlier in this article, and of the varied conditions of social interaction in complex contemporary societies' (2011a: 16). But it nonetheless remains unclear

complained that they experience this as a breach of their democratic rights and an example of double standards by politicians who urge them to be integrated as equal citizens. Rather than serving the goal of integration, the French and Belgian debates left these women feeling alienated, defiant and isolated from mainstream democracy' ('Full-face veils aren't barbaric – but our response can be', *The Guardian*, Sept. 16, 2013).

33 Also quoted in *The Guardian,* Sept. 16, 2013.

34 I have spent the last 30 years trying to persuade law students that Durkheim is an authority because what he says is convincing; he is not persuasive because he is an authority.

35 Paradoxically, however, those in favour of allowing the face veil are sometimes more willing to embrace empirical investigation than those who oppose it. Makhela Malik says we need to have detailed knowledge of the facts on the ground, and are already able to balance the freedom of Muslim women with other important interests such as the education of children, workplace efficiency and fair trial. By contrast, Yasmin Alibhai-Brown makes the (perhaps over-strong) claim that it would be impossible to find out whether the face veil was being worn willingly. See also 'Is France right to "ban the burqa"?', http://www.theguardian.com/commentisfree/2011/apr/02/conversation-yaqoob-alibhai-brown-burqa.

how far judges themselves can and should be expected to get involved in the sociological parsing of these values,[36] or whether, for example, they should just turn to sociologists as expert witnesses.

In this connection it is instructive to consider another paper that Roger wrote at about the same time (based on a speech he gave at Georgetown University). Here Roger is more explicitly concerned with what he calls 'the skill and vision of those who develop, expound and apply law' (2008: 383). He devotes the bulk of his paper to illustrating the social significance of legal communications over the issue of the face-covering veil. But he ends his paper by referring to the case of *Begum*[37] as an example of a House of Lords decision that approved a school policy on school uniforms because the school concerned had made considerable efforts to meet the religious needs of its Muslim students. For Roger, once again, what is central here is the need for legal actors and courts to communicate messages consistent with Durkheim's value of 'moral individualism'. One of the respondents to Cotterrell's Georgetown speech in fact took him to be advocating and approving the judges' level of sociological sophistication in the *Begum* case.[38] Surprisingly, in his reply, however, Roger explained that he had been misunderstood. He insisted strongly on the very different tasks of sociology and legal commentary, saying, 'Professor Mikhail assumes wrongly that I am in the same business as him: that of deciding whether *Shabina Begum* was rightly decided. So he and I are ships passing in the night without making much contact. … I do not "endorse the court's distinction" between the school's approach and that of Shabina Begum and her family; nor do I find "much to admire in the messages communicated by the House of Lords in this case". Professor Mikhail does not seem to recognise that a sociological approach to studying legal ideas might help to explain how messages are being shaped, structured and delivered without necessarily endorsing them' (2008c: 407). He adds: 'The paper's concern was not with the merits of this decision, but with strategies and techniques of communication, and of management of communication, used by the judges and by the litigants. I thought that the case could illustrate some of my arguments, but none of those arguments depends on its outcome. The paper's discussion of the case is not normative (arguing whether the court's resolution of the legal issues was good or bad) but sociological (examining certain strategies and techniques used in communication in and through legal processes)' (2008c: 407). Here we see Roger returning to a familiar sharp divide between the 'normative' and the 'sociological'. On the other hand, having put Professor Mikhail in his place, his next comments again blur the divide somewhat, 'For what it is worth, however, I do think that the court used its management of communications relatively well in some respects. That is only to say that the case produced and relayed communications that, for the moment at least, seem to have been accepted at some level, rather than greeted with outrage, in Britain's diverse population groups (not just those identified as Muslim or non-Muslim). More than that, to the extent that the court's communicative strategies hint at a need to understand complex networks of community as a key to fostering social cohesion, I think they have some merit. But all of that can be a matter for argument. It does not affect what the paper seeks to do, i.e.: (1) to suggest general tasks for law in conditions of multiculturalism; and (2) to argue for reorienting legal thinking to allow adequate recognition of these conditions' (2008c: 407).

But the issue is surely not resolved by Roger admitting that his evaluation of the decision, 'can be a matter of argument'. What we need to know is what kind of argument, and what kind of evidence is suitable. What is involved in what he describes as the task of 'reorienting legal

36 See Tuebner's (1989) warnings.

37 *R (on the application of Begum, by her litigation friend, Rahman) v. Headteacher and Governors of Denbigh High School* [2006] UKHL 15.

38 Mikhail 2008.

thinking to allow adequate recognition of these conditions'? Coming closer to home, what is the message that we want to transmit to law students?[39] As shown by titles such as 'Legal theory in sociological perspective', Roger's life's work has been to broaden legal theory beyond the concern only for philosophical rigour. Although I too wholeheartedly endorse this, I would only add that it is important to teach students how and why sociological insights, too, have their limits. By definition, as Cotterrell himself says, all they do and all they can do are 'allow us to re-describe familiar legal and political ideals from a sociological point of view'.

This process is seen clearly in the careful but sometimes stilted translation of the notion of justice that Roger offers us so as to be able to make it compatible with Durkheimian theorising. 'What is justice?' he asks. 'Justice might be thought of as the oil to lubricate the mechanisms of interdependence in such a society – to ensure the smooth, complex interplay of social and economic roles and functions' (2011a: 7). In addition, 'It will be a value system that not only removes barriers to interaction, but also *actively motivates* all individuals to play their part in society, giving them confidence and status to do so by strongly affirming their human worth. It will foster *communication* across all social divides. It will be *inclusive*: opposing all forms of social marginalization' (2011a: 8). Or again, showing even more clearly the priority of 'the social' in Durkheim's thinking, 'Durkheim's sociology of morals raises the issue of the *justification* of legal values. It addresses the particular character of *justice* as an expression of requirements for stable social interactions and for predictable expectations in social relations. It emphasizes that legal and moral values usually associated (in legal and moral philosophy) with the rights and responsibilities of individuals should be thought of primarily as prerequisites of society's *solidarity* and unity' (2011a: 17).

Roger is right that sociological arguments make a valuable contribution by providing all those interested in creating a better society with new – and often surprising – ways of thinking about law's goals and values. Durkheim's moral science has many advantages over merely formalist or conceptual analyses. But it is only one way of looking at things. His idea of justice for example is some way from the ideal of those for whom justice must be done even if the heavens fall! This underlines the point that it remains an open question how such insights should be (re)formulated in legal discourse and communications. We should be cautious about assuming legal actors can or should be taught to reason in this sort of language (even if, as Roger's studies of Durkheim's disciples show, many of them have tried to do exactly this). If Roger is willing to concede this then I will willingly acknowledge that 'we are not so far apart'. And this way he will not have to choose between reading my comments on his writings and enjoying his coffee![40]

Bibliography

Beyleveld, D. and Brownsword, R. 1986. *Law as a Moral Judgment*. London, Sweet and Maxwell.

Burawoy, M. 2005. 'For Public Sociology'. 70/1 *American Sociological Review*, 4–28.

Cane, P. (ed.) 2010. *The Hart – Fuller Debate in the Twenty First Century*. Oxford, Hart Publishing.

Cotterrell, R. 1983. 'The Sociological Concept of Law'. 10 *British Journal of Law and Society*, 241–55.

39 See Cotterrell 2002.

40 Though it is perhaps only by emigrating to Italy, as I did, that one can fully savour this dilemma to the full.

Cotterrell, R. 1986. 'Law and Sociology: Notes on the Constitution and Confrontations of Disciplines'. 13 *Journal of Law and Society*, 9–34.
Cotterrell, R. 1995. *Law's Community: Legal Theory in Sociological Perspective*. Oxford, Clarendon Press.
Cotterrell, R. 1998. 'Why Must Legal Ideas Be Interpreted Sociologically?' 25 *Journal of Law and Society*, 171–92.
Cotterrell, R. 2002. 'Subverting Orthodoxy, Making Law Central: A view of socio-legal studies'. 29 *Journal of Law and Society*, 632–44.
Cotterrell, R. 2004. 'Selznick Interviewed: Philip Selznick in Conversation with Roger Cotterrell (selected by Jiri Pribán)'. 31 *Journal of Law and Society*, 291–317.
Cotterrell, R. 2008a. 'Transnational Communities and the Concept of Law'. 21 *Ratio Juris*, 1–18.
Cotterrell, R. 2008b. 'The Struggle for Law: Some Dilemmas of Cultural Legality'. 4 *International Journal of Law in Context*, 373–84.
Cotterrell, R. 2008c. 'Culture, Power and the Human Animal: A Reply'. 4 *International Journal of Law in Context*, 407–10.
Cotterrell, R. 2009. 'Spectres of Transnationalism: Changing Terrains of Sociology of Law'. 36 *Journal of Law and Society*, 481–500.
Cotterrell, R. 2011a. 'Justice, Dignity, Torture, Headscarves: Can Durkheim's Sociology Clarify Legal Values?' 20 *Social & Legal Studies*, 3–20.
Cotterrell, R. 2011b. 'Golden Ages: Notes on the Future of Sociology of Law, with Some Comments on its Past, on Poland, and on Jazz'. 12 *Societas/Communitas: Journal of the Institute of Applied Social Sciences*. University of Warsaw, no. 2, 9–23.
Cotterrell, R. 2012. 'What is Transnational Law?' 37 *Law and Social Inquiry* 500–524.
Cotterrell, R. 2013. 'Rethinking "Embeddedness": Law, Economy, Community'. 40 *Journal of Law and Society*, 49–67.
Durkheim, E. 1984. *The Division of Labour in Society*. London, Macmillan, translated W.D. Halls.
Gallagher, M. (ed.) 2002. *Lloyd's Introduction to Jurisprudence*. London, Sweet & Maxwell.
Jakobs, G. 2004. 'Bürgerstrafrecht und Feindstrafrecht'. 5(3) *Höchstrichterliche Rechtsprechung Strafrecht*, 88.
Lukes, S. and Prabhat, D. 2012. 'How Relevant is Durkheim to a Study of Law and Morality?' 12 *Journal of Classical Sociology*, 363–83.
Mikhail, J. 2008. 'Dilemmas of Cultural Legality: A Comment on Roger Cotterrell's "The Struggle for Law" and a Criticism of the House of Lords' Opinions in *Begum*'. 4 *International Journal of Law in Context*, 385–93.
Nelken, D. 1993. 'The Truth About Law's Truth'. In A. Febbrajo and D. Nelken (eds), *European Yearbook of Sociology of Law*. Milan, Giuffrè, 87–163.
Nelken, D. 1996a. 'Can There Be a Sociology of Legal Meaning?' In D. Nelken (ed.), *Law as Communication*. Aldershot, Dartmouth, 107–29.
Nelken, D. 1996b. 'Getting Beyond the Law in Context'. *Socio-legal Newsletter*, 11.
Nelken, D. 1998. 'Blinding Insights? The Limits of a Reflexive Sociology of Law'. 25 *Journal of Law and Society*, 407–26.
Nelken, D. 2009. *Beyond Law in Context*. Aldershot, Ashgate.
Selznick, P. 2002. 'Law In Context, Fidelity to Context'. http://escholarship.org/uc/item/5mp0w9r9
Silbey, S. 1991. 'Loyalty and Betrayal: Cotterrell's Discovery and Reproduction of Legal Ideology'. 16 *Law and Social Inquiry*, 809–83.
Tamanaha, B.Z. 1997. *Realistic Socio-Legal Theory: Pragmatism and Social Theory of Law*. Oxford, Clarendon Press.

Teubner, G. 1989. 'How the Law Thinks'. 23 *Law and Society Review*, 727–58.

Tondini, M. 2007. 'Beyond the Law of the Enemy: Recovering from the Failures of the Global War on Terrorism through Law'. In *Jura Gentium: Rivista di filosofia del diritto internazionale e della politica globale*. http://www.juragentium.org/topics/wlgo/cortona/en/tondini.htm.

Chapter 2

Sociology, History and the 'Internal' Study of Law

Michael Lobban[1]

In his long and distinguished career, Roger Cotterrell has been a consistent champion of the sociological study of law. In his work, he seeks to challenge two approaches, often found in traditional law schools. First, he challenges those legal scholars who see law as 'a set of technical resources for lawyers to harness their clients' interests' (Cotterrell 2008: xiii), reminding them that law is lived by a much larger range of people than the barristers, judges and textbook writers, who are the particular object of study in the law classroom. Second, he challenges those jurists who seek timeless and absolute answers to questions about the nature of law and its relationship to morality and authority, pointing out that law is not a universal abstract entity, but exists only in the practices of people in specific times and places (Cotterrell 2012: 2). For Cotterrell, a proper understanding of law requires both a deeper and broader approach. He has accordingly spoken of his desire 'to develop legal theory as a kind of social theory' (Cotterrell 2008: xiii), which he has defined as 'systematic, historically informed, and empirically oriented theory seeking to explain the nature of "the social"' (Cotterrell 2004: 5).

For Cotterrell, legal ideas *must* be interpreted sociologically: of all the methods offered in the social sciences, the sociological one is, he argues, the most able to provide the necessary insights to understand law. Other disciplines can help, but only in limited ways. While literary or historical approaches may offer 'a richly detailed presentation of particularities of human experience', he argues that they cannot 'provide the means for generalizing from the particular'. Only a 'sociological' approach can 'consistently and permanently [address] the need to reinterpret law *systematically and empirically* as a *social* phenomenon' (Cotterrell 2006: 55). A key part of his approach is to 'reject the familiar dichotomy between internal and external views of law'. In its place, he posits the 'conception of partial, relatively narrow or specialized participant perspectives on (and in) law, confronting and being confronted by, penetrating, illuminating, and being penetrated and illuminated by, broader, more inclusive perspectives on (and in) law as a social phenomenon' (Cotterrell 2006: 59–60).

In what follows, we shall explore whether Cotterrell's method is the only way fully to understand law and legal ideas; and we shall ask, in particular, whether a historical method might not contribute as much to our understanding. It will be suggested that while in some ways Cotterrell's ideas reflect the historian's frame of thought as much as that of the sociologist's (particularly in his emphasis on the importance of empirical work), his desire to erode the distinction between the 'internal' and the 'external' moves him away from one kind of 'historical' approach, which may contribute fruitfully to our understanding. It will be argued that while they are not self-contained, independent 'separate spheres', the 'legal' is a distinct object of study, which should not be collapsed into the 'social'. Indeed, those who study society without paying serious attention to what is distinctly 'legal' within it impoverish their very understanding of that

1 Thanks to Maks Del Mar, Frédérique Lachaud and the editors for their comments.

society. It will be suggested that a historical method can be particularly useful for those seeking to understand both what is distinct about law and its place in society.[2]

1. History and Sociology

Historians and sociologists have generally been thought to be engaged in different, often antagonistic projects (Burke 2005: 2–3). Historians tend to focus on understanding particular societies, tracing and accounting for changes over time, and often stressing the unique and the contingent. From the sociologist's viewpoint, this can look like antiquarian story-telling without rigorous analysis. By contrast, sociologists seek to make scientific generalizations about the structure and development of 'society'. Sociology's remit – understanding and explaining the social world – is a very broad one. It is, in short, the study of everything in the world of human interactions (cf. Cotterrell 2004: 15), with a view to formulating theories about the development or nature of societies. Historians sometimes regard sociology as being overly systematic and prone to excessive generalization on the basis of a limited fact base. Caricatures of the antagonism between the two disciplines are clearly exaggerated, and overlook the fact that there are many schools of sociology and of history, and that members of one discipline often find much to be learned from the other. Nonetheless, there are important differences in methodology and in the use of theory across the disciplines, which merit further exploration.

Unlike history, sociology has long claimed to be a 'science'. The nineteenth-century fathers of the subject wanted it to be scientific in its method. They wanted to create a science of society, akin to the natural sciences, where theoretical propositions about the development of modern society and its structure could be tested empirically, and reformulated if necessary. The idea that sociology was the study of observable facts in the social world which could explain social structures and social systems, and why and how they held together, informed the positivist approach of many of the pioneers of the subject. Detached, social scientific observers would observe the objective data of 'social facts', and record and classify them. By doing this, they would be able to uncover the causes of variations between social phenomena, and subsume them under general laws.[3] For some positivists, only such data as could be scientifically observed and measured counted; but for others, such as Durkheim, social facts included also such matters as collective beliefs and customs, which could be treated as 'things' distinct from the individuals whose conduct was shaped by them (Durkheim 1982: ch. 1). The subject of study was externally observable action, which could reveal causes unknown to the human consciousness, but which nonetheless guided it. In Durkheim's view, in explaining social facts, the investigator was to look at their 'determining causes', which were to 'be sought among antecedent social facts, and not among the states of the individual consciousness' (Durkheim 1982: 134). According to this view, social science could reveal the essential nature of any social phenomenon and even generate predictive laws. As is well known, Durkheim used his methodology to formulate a theory of the development of society, from one based on 'organic' to one based on 'mechanical' solidarity (see Cotterrell 1999).

This positivist method was not the only one, however. Whereas Durkheim's interest was centred on the collectivity, which was distinct from its component parts, Max Weber felt there was

2 In invoking the 'historical' method, I am not suggesting that one should only study the past: as the study of contemporary history shows, one can use the method in studying events and structures into the present.

3 See, e.g., Durkheim's *Suicide: A Study in Sociology* (Durkheim 1952), which aimed to show under what social and economic conditions suicide rates would rise or fall.

no such thing as a collectivity which could act (see Weber 1978: 14). Since all social action was the result of choices which could only be made by individuals, one had to start with the individual. To understand social action, one needed to understand (*verstehen*) its meaning to the actor. In order for social action to be understood, it was not enough simply to describe the act: one had to look for its meaning, by looking from the perspective of the actor. This entailed 'explanatory understanding' (*erklärendes Verstehen*), understanding in terms of motive attached by the actor to his action. Moreover, it required 'a grasp of the complex of meaning in which an actual course of understandable action thus interpreted belongs' (Weber 1978: 9). That is, one needed further to consider the ideas and beliefs of the social group in which the actor was participating.

Weber also developed a notion of ideal types, which were intellectual tools with which to understand the complexity of meaningful social actions. In his view, ideal types were not an accurate reflection of social reality, but entailed the identification and selection of particular features of social action. They provided intellectual models against which to measure reality. In particular, Weber distinguished between four ideal types of rationality: instrumental rationality, value or belief-oriented rationality, affective rationality and traditional rationality. At first glance, ideal types look like theoretical models derived from the process of *Verstehen*, which were to be tested in comparing them with empirical reality – that is to say, tools for understanding social action and social meanings, which were to be modified themselves in light of empirical findings.

However, Weber sought to use them in a different way, to generate causal explanations about social development, in a more 'scientific' manner. A causal explanation of social action could be found if there was a 'correspondence between the theoretical interpretation of motivation and its empirical verification' in a large enough number of cases.[4] One did not test the model by the evidence, but measured the evidence by the model. It was this method which paved the way for his theory of the nature of modern society and how it had emerged. As is well known, for Weber, instrumental rationality was the type which best described the rise of modern capitalist societies. In contrast to older societies which were to be accounted for by other kinds of rationalities, modern Western societies were moving towards the model of rational bureaucracies, where hierarchically organized administrative structures, applying abstract rules in a procedurally formalistic way, directed individuals towards large scale collective goals. According to his view, the modern technical system, so essential for industrial societies, denied spontaneity and trapped people in an 'iron cage'. In effect, Weber was suggesting that the structure of modern society constrained and shaped the individual; he did not use his method of *Verstehen* to explore what modern individuals actually thought they were doing.[5]

In both Durkheim and Weber, the sociological method was used to help create a grand 'scientific' theory of social development, which could explain a large swath of history. Historians have often been sceptical about the power and persuasiveness of such grand theories. They have had a sceptical response to positivist sociology, since they regard the data of history not as a catalogue of objectively true facts, but as interpretations of events. Such interpretations are always open to modification with the addition of new evidence, and can be challenged by rival versions. As an interpretative enterprise, the work of historians cannot generate objectively truthful data.

4 As he put it, causal explanations of social action required both an adequate grasp of the meaning of the action, and 'some kind of proof for the existence of a probability that action in fact normally takes the course which has been held to be meaningful'. He added that '[f]or this there must be some degree of determinable frequency of approximation to an average or pure type' (Weber 1978: 12).

5 The historical interpretation in *The Protestant Ethic* may have begun with an exercise of *erklärendes Verstehen*, getting inside the Calvinist mind; but by the end of the book, their *mentalité* seemed to have become almost reified, a structural device controlling modern man: see Weber 1992: 124.

The higher the generalization, the more vulnerable it is to challenge. Sociological theories resting on broad historical generalizations are hence liable to attract the scepticism of historians. They tend to feel that the desire to find a theory which can explain the whole social order is utopian, and consequently prefer to focus on fragments of it. Historians therefore tend to privilege empirical research over theory, The historian should, the argument goes, always begin with the sources, and read them as best he can, classifying as he goes on, and modifying his classifications as new material is collected. Yet historians are not simple antiquarians: they seek to explain the causes of social change, and not merely to describe it. Such explanations will require some help from theory: the infinite complexity of social life cannot be made sense of unless there is a simplification of the complexity, through models designed to help obtain a better understand of reality. Historians need to develop their own generalizations and abstractions, and often borrow from other areas of social theory. However, these models remain mere tools with which to understand the varieties of social life, which need to be tested and rethought.[6] Thus, from the historian's viewpoint, Max Weber's theory of the development of capitalism in Protestant Europe is merely only one interpretation among many, open to challenge.

When it comes to questions of method, historians have generally eschewed the positivist versions of the social-scientific method.[7] However, many historians have been much more receptive to the kind of interpretive method associated with Weber's notion of *Verstehen*. The interpretivist approach can be seen to be strongly defended, for instance, in R.G. Collingwood's *The Idea of History* (1946). In this book, which attacked the positivist approach, Collingwood argued that the method of history was fundamentally different from that of the natural sciences. The historian could not observe events in nature like a scientist, assigning them to different classes and determining the causal relationship between them. This was because the historian did not study mere 'events', but the actions of agents. He had to take into account not merely the factual event but also the thoughts of the actor which lay behind it, and gave it meaning. He had to consider the 'internal' as well as the 'external' (Collingwood 1961: 213). The only way to do this was to *rethink* the actors' thoughts in one's own mind.[8] For Collingwood, permanent and unchanging laws of human nature could not be found, since for behaviour patterns to remain constant, the social order in which the behaviour occurred had to produce the same situations recurrently. Uniformities might be found within a single social order, but social orders were historical facts subject to change. Collingwood's idealist version did not go unchallenged, but the interpretivist approach, whereby the historian seeks to

6 Thus, medieval historians use the concept of 'feudalism' to help describe and explain the nature of medieval society, even though this concept was never one in the minds of medieval actors, but was the invention of later historians. The very concept is contested and debated: it cannot be used as a simple tool of explanation or description, as is sometimes found in some of the cruder Marxist versions. See especially Brown 1974.

7 Of course, history, like sociology, is a house with many rooms. In some branches of history – notably economic history – statistical and quantitative approaches were used in a manner akin to that of the positivist sociologists, for instance by the 'new economic history' known as 'Cliometrics', which sought to apply economic theory to the study of history in a systematic way. However, there were clear drawbacks to an approach which used an abstract model of how rational economic agents act to study people in different eras and cultures, whose actions did not necessarily share the same motivations as an abstract rational calculator.

8 The historian's task was thus to search for meaning: 'the historian is not interested in the fact that men eat and sleep and make love and thus satisfy their natural appetites; but he is interested in the social customs which they create by their thought as a framework within which these appetites find satisfaction in ways sanctioned by convention and morality'. 'The history of all thought, and therefore all history, is the re-enactment of past thought in the historian's own mind': Collingwood 1961: 215.

understand the motives and intentions of past historical actors has been particularly influential in intellectual history and in the history of legal thought. While many historians continue to claim that they have no overarching 'method', but simply seek to make sense of what they find as they come across it (cf. Baker 2012), a version of the method of *Verstehen* has proved highly influential for over 40 years in the realm of intellectual history (see Skinner 2002).

If we compare these methodologies and approaches with Roger Cotterrell's, it may be suggested that his is in some ways as close to the historian's as the sociologist's. In his article, 'Why must legal ideas be interpreted sociologically?', Cotterrell notes that his proposed method is not tied to any particular discipline – such as the academic discipline of sociology – but can be seen as 'transdisciplinary'. However, he contends that his method is properly termed 'sociological' because it contains three features. The study is 'systematic'; it is empirical; and it studies law 'as a social phenomenon'. A systematic study, he suggests, is to be contrasted with an anecdotal or impressionistic one. It seeks to assess the significance of the particular in a wider perspective, 'to situate the richness of the unique in a broader theoretical context and so provide orientation for its interpretation' (Cotterrell 2006: 55). Only the most narrowly antiquarian among historians would take issue with this. He also stresses the need for study to be empirically grounded – 'based on observation of the diversity and detail of historical experience'. In his view, 'the requirement for empirical foundations of understanding exerts pressure to reject broad speculation which ignores or generalizes beyond what the detail of particular experience and observation can support as plausible' (Cotterrell 2006: 57; cf. Cotterrell 2008: xv). Such a statement is music to the ears of the historian.

Moreover, as his rich discussion and critique of the major social theorists in his book on *The Sociology of Law* shows, Cotterrell is not the follower of any single social theory. The various theories he canvasses are portrayed as having many insights to offer; but they are all shown to omit some important features of the complexities of social life which need to be taken into account. Nor does Cotterrell seek to develop an overarching theory of his own, which can explain how law works or how it has developed. When it comes to methodology, he accepts the interpretivist point that the researcher needs to look for subjective meanings rather than simply measuring observable regularities, and rejects that version of positivism which 'restricts the subject matter of inquiry to a form in which broader understanding is likely to be curtailed by the erection of rigid boundaries between compartments of knowledge' (Cotterrell 1992: 14). But he accepts the 'weak' positivist view that 'scientific method' involves reliance on observed data and a refusal to speculate beyond what observed experience will justify as plausible. So far, this looks much like the attitude of an historian.

The key feature of his method which invites us to describe it properly as 'sociological' is the third one: the notion that we must study law as a *social* phenomenon: 'a field of experience … to be understood as an aspect of social relationships in general, as wholly concerned with the co-existence of individuals in social groups' (Cotterrell 2006: 55). This seems to suggest that we must study law in the context of society *as a whole*. It is the breadth of this ambition and context – and Cotterrell's approach to it – that makes it 'sociological', rather than 'historical'. It invites us to ask whether this is the way we *must* study law. In what follows, it will be suggested that an approach to the study of law and legal ideas as a form of intellectual history, using a method of *Verstehen* which requires us to distinguish (and identify) the 'internal', may offer a more focused understanding of the nature and operation of law.

2. The Study of the Social

The idea that 'law' cannot be studied in isolation from 'society' has informed a great deal of socio-legal research (including legal history) for over 40 years. Such studies have generally been informed by a binary view, that there is a distinct object of study – *law* – which is to be studied in relation to the distinct field of *society*.[9] To borrow Robert Gordon's metaphor, law is seen as a kind of 'box', which contains all the elements which make law 'autonomous'. Outside the box lies 'society', with its social, economic and political features, which may affect or be affected by what is inside the box (Gordon 1975–6). While much traditional legal research (and legal history) has tended to focus on studying what is 'inside' the box (notably the doctrine developed by the superior courts), there has been much work done by those who look outside the box, and concern themselves with 'the interaction between the boxful of legal things and the wider society of which they are a part', in particular by exploring 'the social context of law and its social effects'. Scholars who take this approach – often called the 'external' approach – seek to show the influence of social, political and economic ideas on the legal system, and thereby to undermine law's claims to autonomy and self-sufficiency (cf. Parker 2011). Scholars who take a 'law and society' approach also often take a much wider view of law than traditional 'doctrinal' scholars, taking a more expansive view of what the 'box' of legal materials is.[10] There are wide disagreements over how 'autonomous' law is, with some inclining to the view that whatever is in the box can only be understood as the product of its society (see Friedman 1973: 10–14 and Friedman 2005: 6) and others arguing for a greater degree of intellectual autonomy. Whichever of the multiple theoretical perspectives is taken, there is at least consensus on the focus of study: the conduct and ideas of 'official' governing institutions, primarily in settled western societies.[11] For these scholars, the conceptual distinction of the 'internal' and the 'external' has made much sense.[12]

Roger Cotterrell, by contrast, has challenged the view that one *can* study law from an 'internal' perspective, for there is in his view no distinct line between 'law' and 'society' (see Cotterrell 2006: 60). There is no 'box' of law: rather, it is 'embedded' in society. In recent work, he has explored in greater detail the nature of law's embeddedness in society. A key notion in his recent work has been that there is no such thing as one, undifferentiated 'society'. Instead, 'the social … should be seen as composed of *networks of community*' (Cotterrell 2013: 50). One needs to use the tools of sociology to identify both the 'society' and the 'law' one is studying, and only then will one understand the normative system which is 'embedded' in its social context. While not disclaiming the 'scientific' ambitions of the sociological method, he has in recent years stressed that sociology must study the moral foundations of law, within different types of communities. In developing this view, he makes use of the sociology of both Durkheim and Weber.

Taking his scientific cue from Durkheim, he argues that 'sociology can reveal empirically and theoretically the social structures and conditions in which moral ideas become meaningful for people

9 As Catherine Fisk and Robert Gordon put it, '"Law and" scholarship perpetuates the idea that, even though law is situated in society, law is distinct from society and can, or must, be studied in relation to it': Fisk and Gordon 2011: 520.

10 As Gordon showed, Willard Hurst's idea of the subject of legal study was rather larger than some of his American predecessors: it was not the doctrine of the superior courts (or law professors) which interested him, but covered 'all official activity': Gordon 1975–6: 51.

11 For an expansive and suggestive definition of law, see Gordon 1975–6: 46.

12 At the same time, there has in recent years been increasing critique of the binary of 'internal' and 'external' among legal historians: see in general 'Symposium Issue: "Law As …" Theory and Method in Legal History', (2011) 1(3) *UC Irvine Law Review*.

in particular times and places, and in which moral arguments become urgent' (Cotterrell 2013: 62). Moreover, social science can 'identify the forms of solidarity that are possible in certain types of society' and 'indicate the part that legal and other regulation can play in setting the conditions for solidarity'. Taking his cue from Weber, he has sought to identify four 'ideal types' of community relations which may exist: traditional communities, instrumental communities, communities of belief and affective communities. Following Weber's lead, he stresses that they are not *actual* empirically identifiable communities, since the four types of collective involvement may be combined in an infinite number of ways in real communities, which are 'fluid, flexible, changing, overlapping patterns of social relationships'. However, this differentiation of types of community allows one to think theoretically about the nature of social relations in terms of their general regulatory problems, and allows the theorist to recognise 'the diversity of meanings, understandings and experiences of law produced by the differentiation of the social' (Cotterrell 2003: 258, 261).

The notion that there are different kinds of community with different regulatory needs and expectations is certainly a very useful one. However, two questions may be raised about how this model helps our understanding of *law*. The first relates to Cotterrell's hybrid methodological tools. There may be tensions found in this approach. On the one hand, a Durkheimian commitment to the concept of moral communities held together by social solidarity might entail also a commitment to the notion that the community is a 'social fact', which has a life distinct from the individuals who are in some sense under its control. From this perspective, one might hope to identify particular 'affective', 'instrumental' or 'traditional' communities exerting control over their members, and identify what it is which generates the social solidarity which holds them together.[13] However, this might involve the reification of the concept of community in ways Cotterrell eschews, and raise questions about how far one could be a member of multiple communities. On the other hand, if one takes ideal types to be abstractions from the beliefs and meaningful behaviour of groups of individuals, or tools derived through *Verstehen* with which to understand the infinitely complex world, then it is hard to see why (as Cotterrell argues) the four ideal types encompass *all* kinds of collective involvement, to the exclusion of any other view. There might be a large variety of ways in which people perceive and think about the law.[14]

This is especially so if the focus of one's interest is in legal *ideas*. For instance, Cotterrell argues that gender, race and ethnicity cannot make up legal communities, since these 'categories are too rigid to reflect the complexity of social experiences' (Cotterrell 2003: 258). But if communities of women, or people of different races, have different experiences and understandings of law, and have a sense of being a part of a community of shared experiences, which are articulated and expressed in words and thoughts, why can we not talk of them as constituting communities? One answer might be to say that only the kinds of community outlined by Cotterrell can generate legal regulation – whereas (for instance) there is no extant regulatory community exclusively made up of women.[15] This would be to argue that the notion of a legal community is tied to the

---

13 Cotterrell writes that with this perspective, 'law's relation to morality appears in a new light in this perspective because different types of community have different moral requirements. As law regulates networks of community it has the task of interrelating their moral aspects. Conversely law gets moral authority from its nature as a regulation of networks of community': Cotterrell 2003: 261.

14 As has been seen, Weber uses his 'ideal types' as theoretical constructs against which to measure and test actual behaviour: used as such, however, it might be a tool to explain how *one* form of community came to evolve (and dominate), rather than to explain the existence of multiple communities with multiple understandings.

15 This is, of course, to discount small 'ad hoc' communities, such as clubs. It also rules out larger female communities which are part of broader normative orders, such as religious houses.

idea of communities of *practice*, but this would once more involve a reification of the concept of community. Yet if our aim is to study legal *ideas*, and with the Weberian method of *Verstehen*, we should recognize that women, as well as different ethnic or racial groups, can have distinct legal ideas, which can have a major impact in the wider world. This is to say that we should not let our notion of the ideas we are to study be limited by a predefinition of what counts as a community.

The second question relates to the sense in which these communities are 'legal' communities, and how far identifying them can better help us understand law. We may need to go further and identify what is considered as law *within* these communities. Max Weber himself sought to identify what counted as law at different times and in different societies, showing that different conceptions of law may exist and that 'law' may operate in different ways. However, his version is not unproblematic. Weber sought to define 'law', in contrast to other forms of regulatory order, as the organised and legitimate enforcement of rules. In his view, 'An order will be called [...] law, if it is externally guaranteed by the probability that physical or psychological coercion will be applied by a staff of people in order to bring about compliance or avenge violation' (Weber 1978: 34).[16] The notion of *enforcement* was hence central to his conception of law, though his reference to 'psychological' coercion suggests that the law did not require the physical mechanisms of a state to succeed. Alongside this stood the notion that there are specific people with the legitimate *authority* to state the law. Weber identified three different kinds (or ideal types) of authority, showing variations which can exist in the nature of the legal system: 'traditional', 'legal-rational' and 'charismatic'. Weber also showed that law could operate in different ways, according to the nature of the 'rationality' which characterized the legal system. In this typology,[17] modern civil law systems rested on a 'legal-rational' kind of authority, and were marked by 'formal rationality'. In such systems, the law was a closed and self-sufficient system, which made its decisions without reference to other normative orders. Other legal systems were different in character and operated in different ways: yet insofar as an authoritative figure pronounced a decision which was considered coercively binding, there was a 'legal' order which was the subject of study.

Weber's analysis might help us to seek to identify who makes the rules, but it is not particularly helpful in understanding the working of law as a normative order in non-'legal rational' systems. Rather than giving us an account of how customary normative systems work, he seeks rather to identify the figures whose pronouncements are obeyed. He is not concerned with exploring the content of those pronouncements: they may be 'rational' or 'irrational', they may import norms from outside, or they may not. For Weber, an 'internal' study of the content of law and its implementation seems most suited to modern Western societies, where there is a self-contained system to examine – indeed, it was his desire to explain the very distinct nature of law in modern capitalist societies which encouraged him to identify these typologies. Cotterrell's recent work,

16 By contrast, 'An order will be called *convention* so far as its validity is externally guaranteed by the probability that deviation from it within a given social group will result in a relatively general and practically significant reaction of disapproval'.

17 Weber described four kinds of rationality. They are formal rational (where like cases are treated alike, and where decisions involve the application of general propositions from within the legal system to factual situations); substantive rational (where 'the decision of legal problems is influenced by norms different from those obtained through logical generalization of abstract interpretations of meaning' – that is, by using other norms taken from outside the legal system, such as from ethics or politics); formal irrational ('where one applies in lawmaking or lawfinding means which cannot be controlled by the intellect, for instance when recourse is had to oracles'); and substantive irrational (where 'decision is influenced by concrete factors of the particular case as evaluated upon an ethical, emotional or political basis, rather than by general norms'): Weber 1978: 656–7.

which shifts the focus from the notion of authority to that of community appears to promise a better way to understand how normative orders within different kinds of communities may work, since it promises to show (for instance) how in traditional societies customary norms can generate their own authority. To that extent, it promises to give us a better understanding of normative communities other than modern Western ones than Weber's model does. Yet one may ask whether Cotterrell's model distinguishes the 'legal' aspect from the 'non-legal' sufficiently.

Social theorists have long recognised that 'calling all forms of ordering that are not state law by the term law confounds the analysis' (Merry 1988: 878). In talking of law, we end up simply describing society. Nor should we overlook the fact that many non-state communities clearly identify areas of 'law' which are different from social practice. For instance, from the late eleventh century, the Roman Catholic Church developed an elaborate, technical system of canon law, which came to be administered in church courts by university-trained canonists, who made up a 'legal' community within the church. The 'law' was not simply the reflection of community practices: it entailed professional lawyers, interpreting an authoritatively defined body of rules, in special courts. 'Canon law' was not the same thing as 'theology' (see Brundage 2008). Other religions have similarly specialist bodies of legal learning. Moreover, not all normative social practices are regarded as 'law'. Historians have long pointed out that 'custom' should be distinguished from 'customary law', which (at least in medieval Europe) came to be set down and subjected to interpretation by legal specialists (Kelley 1990: 104–8; Whitman 1991). This 'professionalization' of customary law was in part a movement to subject local communities to greater central control; but it should be noted that the communities so subjected were often ones where the local custom was enforced in a seignorial or manorial court, where complex questions might be referred to 'wise men', who had a particular understanding of the norms in question.[18] Medieval communities often preferred to seek reconciliation between contesting parties rather than to find for one or other party; but when decisions had to be made, suits were decided in 'courts', whose jurisdiction was often underscored by royal authority, by parties using arguments invoking settled norms which were regarded as legal.[19]

This is to suggest that it is not enough to distinguish the kinds of community in which law might be located. We need to look further at how particular communities at particular times distinguish the 'legal' from other normative or non-normative forms. Not every normative practice is usefully regarded as law, and it is helpful to our understanding of societies – and to the development of 'law' and forms of legal argument within them – to be able to distinguish between social norms and legal ones and to see how they interrelated (or did not). There may, of course, be multiple communities within a plural society, in which there may be more than one conception of law and legal authority. This is nothing new, as the clash in 1164 between Thomas Becket and Henry II might illustrate. Where there are such pluralities, we need to examine how the legalities relate to each other, particularly for those who may simultaneously regard themselves as members of more than one community. Plural societies may face new problems of how the state should respond to different expectations among different members of the community. Indeed, such a view can be found in Cotterrell's own view that '[n]ormative legal theory must recognise social diversity by explaining law in terms of the regulatory requirements

18 For instance, in an English case of 1121, in the feudal court of the Bishop of Bath, 'those who were older and *more learned in the law* left the crowd and weighed subtly and wisely all the arguments they had heard and settled the case': Van Caenegem 1990: 193 (emphasis added). The bishop had earlier addressed the court 'as good men and knowledgeable in the law' [jurisperitis].

19 The issue of how far 'legal' or 'social' norms were used in settling medieval cases has been the subject of much recent investigation: see Hyams 2004, Hudson 2000, Wormald 1999.

of different communities' (Cotterrell 2003: 257; cf. Cotterrell 2006: ch. 4). However, a study of the regulatory requirements of different communities may tell us more about what is desired or needed, than about how law works. To understand the latter, we need to take an 'internal' view, and recognize that there may be such a 'box' as 'law.'

3. Identifying Law

This leaves us with the problem of how to identify this 'law' which is our object of study. As shall be seen, to understand what is regarded as law, we need to look from the 'internal' perspective, or the perspective of *Verstehen.* We need to look at how social actors - within the broad social community and the narrower 'legal' community – identify what constitutes the 'legal'. It will be argued that an historical perspective, which focuses on the distinct nature of legal *thought,* and its different operations in different eras and contexts, can open the way for a better understanding of the distinct nature of law and (as shall be seen in the next section) its relation to society. However, before doing so, we need to consider how some philosophers and sociologists have dealt with the question of identifying law, by using the 'internal' perspective.

The pioneering work in this field was that of H.L.A. Hart, whose *Concept of Law* introduced the 'internal/external' distinction to English legal theory. Hart used the distinction as a way to help him identify what was generally understood by 'law'. According to his theory, a legal system is made up of a union of 'primary' and 'secondary' rules. Although some societies could, he admitted, function simply by following 'primary' rules (such as customary rules of conduct), they could not be seen as properly 'legal', since they lacked the mechanisms required to resolve doubts about the meaning of those rules, to make conscious changes in the way the rules operate, or to identify authoritatively whether or when a rule had been broken. A system only became legal when 'secondary' rules existed to remedy these defects, which in effect 'officialized' the system. In particular, there had to be a 'secondary rule of recognition' which was accepted and used to identify the primary rules of obligation. This rule of recognition was the foundation of the legal system, 'providing the criteria by which the validity of other rules of the system is assessed' (Hart 1961: 102). Since, for Hart, the system itself rested on a rule – rather than an Austinian 'habit of obedience' to a sovereign – he felt that it could only be explained in terms of the 'internal' attitude, that is the attitude of the person who 'accepts [rules] and uses them as guides to conduct' (Hart 1961: 86). In Hart's theory, the relevant 'internal' attitude to consider is not that of the ordinary citizen – who might obey the 'law' simply from habit or fear – but officials.[20] Hart's theory has been criticized – particularly by sociologists – for being too essentialist, and for resting too much on his view of what 'ordinary people' meant by law, without looking empirically at what actual people in other contexts thought about law. Such criticisms perhaps fail to give Hart enough credit for developing a model which might have its uses, even for sociologists. Be that as it may, there are flaws in his model, which limit its use as a theory of law. Hart was not interested on exploring 'internally' how 'officials' – or others, including lawyers, jurists or citizens – understood the nature and operation of the law. This was not an exercise of Weberian *Verstehen*:[21] he used the notion of the 'internal' aspect of rules as a philosophical distinction to explain how and why rules are accepted. It said nothing about how the

20 '[W]hat is crucial is that there should be a unified or shared official acceptance of the rule of recognition containing the system's criteria of validity': Hart 1961: 111.

21 Hart had probably not read Weber when he wrote *The Concept of Law*; but he had read Peter Winch's *The Idea of a Social Science and its Relation to Philosophy* (1958). Winch had read Weber, but developed the argument that meaningful social action was invariably tied to the following of rules. Winch's discussion

content of law was understood, or how 'officials' (and others) might think it should be developed. Furthermore, there are doubts over whether Hart's distinction does the job it was intended for, to help identify the boundaries of the legal system. If the ultimate rule which holds together the legal system is the rule of recognition, but the only people ultimately required to accept it are the officials on whose own conduct it confers validity, they are, in effect, validating themselves. In short, Hart's model does not show us either how the legal community understands or identifies its own practices – save to say that they recognise themselves – or how the wider community recognizes the realm of law.

A second approach to the 'internal' view has been developed by Brian Tamanaha. He rejects Hart's essentialism, arguing that there can be no single way to conceptualize law. He also rejects Hart's interpretation of what the 'internal' view entails. For Tamanaha, one can understand any social practice or interpretive community[22] – including law – from an 'internal' point of view without subscribing to it (Raz 1979: 156). This looks much closer to a Weberian notion of *Verstehen*. However, Tamanaha's notion of what law consists of is very broad: 'Law is a "folk concept," that is, law is what people within social groups have come to see and label as "law"' (Tamanaha 2008: 396). It 'is whatever people recognize and treat as law through their social practices'. Consequently, '*any members of a given group can identify what law is, as long as it constitutes a conventional practice*'. For it to count as law, it is enough if '*sufficient people with sufficient conviction*' do so. Such a view 'accepts the possibility that within a given social arena there may be competing groups who claim to constitute law' (Tamanaha 2001: 166–7). Although he is sensitive to the fact that not every kind of normative or regulatory ordering can be described as law, his focus on what people call 'law' means it can encompass everything from 'professional' systems to community practices. While suggestive, Tamanaha's focus on language threatens to blur the line between the 'legal' and the non-legal. We need to do more than report on what others describe as 'law' to understand their concept of the legal. Besides obvious problems of translation – how do we know what correctly translates as 'law' in other cultures, eras or languages? – Tamanaha himself notes that when he looks for languages of 'law', he is referring to something with a particular meaning: 'norms that claim *authority*' (Tamanaha 2001:168–9). This might suggest that we need to look beyond language to wider ideas about authority. In some ways, therefore, Tamanaha's reaction against Hart's essentialism goes too far: although different people may use similar terminology, they may mean different things.

A third approach which explicitly seeks to identify and describe a distinctly legal sphere is the systems theory of Niklas Luhmann. This theory recognizes that there is a distinctly 'legal' language and way of thinking. Luhmann sees law as one of a number of systems of communication found within society (alongside economy, media, medicine and so on). In his theory, each system identifies what belongs to it, and what is external to it (its 'environment'), by 'coding' facts according to a binary format which is unique to the system. In law, coding is done on the binary of legal/illegal. As Luhmann has put it, 'If the question arises whether something is legal or illegal, the communication belongs to the legal system, and if not then not'

evidently influenced Hart's treatment of the internal aspect of rules. Simpson 2011: 106, Lacey 2004: 230 and the useful discussion in Tamanaha 1996.

22 A 'practice' is any socially established co-operative human activity which has its own standards of excellence, which are used to realise the ends of the practice. Participants in the practice understand what those standards of excellence are, and regard them as suitable for judging their own performance. An interpretive community is a group of people 'bound together by socially generated and shared clusters of *meaning* – complexes of ideas, beliefs, knowledge, symbols, and terminology that characterize discrete groups'. See Tamanaha 1996: 176, 180.

(Luhmann 1992: 1428). The code has no meaning in itself. Instead, the legal system develops structures – 'conditional programmes' – for its application. These programmes account for why things are coded either legal or illegal, and provide the normative rules which generate criteria for decisions. They are 'conditional' insofar as they are subject to change. According to the theory, systems are 'operationally closed' but 'cognitively open'. They are operationally closed, and therefore autonomous, since they can only operate through communications which are recognized by the system as belonging to it, and which can be coded by its unique code. However, they are 'cognitively open', insofar as they can alter what is considered as a communication within their own systems in response to perceived changes in their environment. They can therefore change and develop, particularly in response to 'irritations' from other systems.

Systems theory usefully focuses on the question of what is a peculiarly 'legal' way of thinking, and so offers interesting insights in describing how one might conceive of the legal as distinct from the non-legal. Yet questions remain over how far forward the theory takes us. In Luhmann's version, the legal system seems to be tied to an 'official' system, with authority to code legal/illegal, for he gives the courts a central role.[23] The realm of 'legal' communications concerns all those human activities which are (or will be) coded legal/illegal, insofar as they are to be coercively enforced in a court (unlike moral rules). Moreover, it is the *system* which determines its content, rather than any number of individuals expressing their views about the system.[24] This suggests that when people talk about law, they are tapping into the language of a system which they do not control; but where the ultimate decision on legal/illegal will be for the state to make. This seems on the face of it to suggest a high level of determinacy in state law. Yet it is clear that the 'system' is in fact far more indeterminate. The code 'legal/illegal' itself has no meaning: it tells us little more than that a legal question is a legal question.[25] It does not tell us what that 'law' is, or who is to determine that. It is given meaning only by the 'conditional programmes', communications about when and how it has been applied in the past, and when it will be applied in the future. To understand law, we therefore need to look at the level of the 'conditional programmes'. At this level, it is not the language of the 'system' which is the object of study, but the languages of various people discussing what the law is or might be, who may disagree or puzzle over what the law means. Here, we may find a high degree of indeterminacy, where judges and jurists may take the same material and interpret it in very divergent ways.

---

23 Even if the language of law is spoken by others than officials in the courts, it is only insofar as it is directed to the 'legal/illegal' binary, in language which can be understood by the state which determines which side of the binary the action falls, that something is a legal communication. Indeed, Nobles and Schiff suggest that it is not inaccurate to describe premodern societies as lacking autonomous legal systems; and add that it may be unhelpful to use the word 'law' to refer to all normative legal orders: Nobles and Schiff 2012: 290.

24 Nobles and Schiff write, 'Systems theory proceeds on the basis that the process of inclusion within a functional social subsystem is not established through consensus (the number of individuals who express a similar view) but through the operations of that system. The enormous numbers of systematically connected communications that circulate within the legal system of a modern society and create ever more complex meanings do not represent a consensus of individual opinions. And these connected communications severely limit the ability of any individuals to declare for themselves what should be described as "law."' Nobles and Schiff 2012: 274.

25 Luhmann 1992: 1427–8 denies this to be the case: 'To declare something illegal does not mean that it belongs to the environment of the system. We have to differentiate the distinction between self-reference and external reference on the one hand, and legal and illegal on the other.' But he adds 'If the question arises whether something is legal or illegal, the communication belongs to the legal system, and if not then not'.

Each of these theories invites us to think about how to identify the distinct realm of law, by considering 'internal' perspectives which invite us to think about what people *mean* by law. But none of the theories goes quite far enough in identifying what law is and how it works. Theory alone can take us only so far; to get a fuller understanding, we need to look at the ways in which law is used and developed; and it is here that the historical approach can be of particular use. When considering the law, we need to take into account both the 'rules' which people regard as obligatory (and how they are identified), and also the interpretation of those rules by specialist communities, of jurists, judges, lawyers, sages. We need to consider law not only as a mechanism of power – 'law as rule' – but also as a specialist intellectual technique – 'law as interpretation' – which can usefully be studied with the tools of intellectual history. A full understanding of law requires us particularly to take seriously and attempt to understand the world of legal ideas and legal technique. This is not to underestimate the importance of either legislation or custom as sources of law. The power to make law *ratione imperii* – which lay beneath Weber's notion – is clearly central to the idea of law. A rule enacted by a legislator will be part of the world of law before it has been considered by any judge or jurist. Similarly, it would be fatuous to deny the 'legal' status of customary rules, such as (for instance), the English rule that property passed by primogeniture. Many rules of law rest ultimately on customary practices. However, the concept of law also entails the practice of interpreting the law by those recognised as having authority to do so. The authority of judges and jurists to make general pronouncements about the meaning of the law may be said to derive from their expert knowledge: it is *imperio rationis* (Jansen 2010: 1). As soon as we accept that there is such a community of interpreters – which may be much wider than 'officials' – we move to a domain where there is an 'internal' language to be understood. There is a 'box' full of legal ideas and interpretations which is distinct from 'society'. As the interaction between medieval Islamic and Jewish legal thinkers shows (see David 2010), legal ideas and methods can cross cultures and substantive beliefs. Indeed, the idea that the tools of the legal trade – for instance, the techniques of interpreting or analogizing rules of law where they are ambiguous or of distinguishing between kinds of legal concepts – are somehow universal has long had a strong hold on the legal mind.

These specialized communities of knowledge are to be distinguished from the political authority which may ultimately enforce their decisions: the realm of 'reason' is distinct from the realm of 'power'. The most obvious example of this may be the community of jurists who developed medieval Roman law learning after the rediscovery of Justinian's *Digest* in the eleventh century. In the centuries after the recovery of this text, legal scholars at universities throughout Europe puzzled over what different parts of a text composed of many fragments dating from different moments in Roman history meant, working under the assumption that the text must be coherent and correct. In seeking to explain its provisions, they refashioned many doctrines, laying the foundations for more sophisticated and coherent conceptions of legal notions such as contract than had been known before. At one level, this was purely an intellectual exercise: a reconstruction of how best to make sense of the data of the system. At another level, however, it was of immense practical importance, for the learning of the universities soon filtered into the most local of courts, hearing ordinary disputes (Bellomo 1995: 168). Medieval law in all kinds of communities was transformed not by practices within the broad community, nor by the political decisions of rulers, but by an intellectual revolution, based on the rediscovery of a technical law manual lost for half a millennium, which revealed a host of intellectual possibilities that lawyers had not thought of before. Although local courts adapted their practices in response to the new kinds of arguments which were made by those familiar with the vocabulary of Roman law, the realm of ideas which generated the medieval *ius commune* was not tied to any polity or any enforcing authority. The 'Reception' of Roman law was an intellectual event, which cannot be understood by looking either at the practices of communities or the attitude of enforcing authorities alone, but which must be understood by looking at the world of ideas developed by specialists.

The common law itself, which so troubled Weber's model, was also the product of the thought of a particular intellectual community of lawyers. Common lawyers in early modern England may have agreed that the root cause of all legal decisions was what was best for the community – so that the law reflected the community's needs and its values – but they also insisted that this required great specialist knowledge and expertise. The relevant practice was not simply what the community did, but how it had – through its judges – decided disputes throughout its history. For the generation of Coke, the common law was an 'artificial reason'; and the authority of the judges came from the fact that they best knew and understood this system (Lobban 2007: ch. 2). The common law may not have been the kind of system which fitted Weber's view of what a rational, calculable legal system was, since it did not apparently announce clear, systematic rules to guide conduct in society in a predictable way. Yet few common lawyers would have described their system as irrational in Weber's sense. As Matthew Hale saw it, the legal mind involved the application of reason, but within a specialist context. Reason, he said, 'is taken complexedly, when the reasonable facultie is in Conjunction with the reasonable Subject, and habituated to it by Use and Exercise, and it is this kind of reason or reason thus taken that Denominates a Man a Mathematician, a Philosopher a Politician, a Phisician a Lawyer' (Hale 1924: 501). The system of course rested on its ultimate enforcement by political authorities in England: but (as Coke's argument with James I showed), lawyers did not take kindly to the political authorities attempting to tell them what the law meant. While men like Coke accepted the authority of legislation and custom as sources of law, they had the authority to determine what legislation and custom meant, and how it was to be applied.

This is to suggest that there is a body of specialist legal knowledge, which is distinct both from the community at large, and from the political ruler. Wherever we study law, we need to know *something* of this body of knowledge. It is of course true that in many areas, the distinct community of legal specialists may have little to say. As has been shown, the concept of 'law' clearly entails the notion of rules, which may derive from a legislator or custom, which may directly reflect the wants of the community, and which may never require interpretation by a court. Indeed, it might seem that modern legislative states, where there is regular and detailed intervention by political authority, generate much regulatory material, which leaves little room for legal interpretation. Where the 'rule' is clear and there is little debate on its meaning and ambit, it might seem that we have done all the necessary 'internal' work by identifying the pedigree of the rule – that it is a valid regulation issued by authority, and thus is part of the system of rules. Where new legislation seeks to change social behaviour – as with much nineteenth-century legislation enacted to 'tame' the working class – we may be more interested in exploring 'external' questions – such as what it tells us about power relationships in society, or tracing whether the rule was enforced or not, or if it was resisted, avoided or challenged by the communities at which it was aimed. However, we may also find that even the most 'straightforward' rule might require more 'internal' attention, for its meaning may turn out to be ambiguous and contested.[26] Contested meanings open social space, and can reveal that legislation may be a much less potent tool for governments than they hope it

26 Thus, for instance, the wording of the 1853 Betting Act was ambiguous enough to leave doubts over whether it left room for street betting, or gambling at racecourses. The question of what the statute meant came before the courts on numerous occasions, and judges frequently disagreed over its meaning: *Doggett* v. *Catterns* (1864) 17 CB NS 669 (1865) 19 CB NS 765, *Shaw* v. *Morley* (1868) LR 3 Ex 137, *Bows* v. *Fenwick* (1874) LR 9 CP 339, *Eastwood* v. *Miller* (1874) LR 9 QB 440; *Haigh* v. *Town Council of Sheffield* (1874) LR 10 QB 102, *Powell* v. *Kempton Park Racecourse* [1899] AC 143.

would be.[27] Consequently, we cannot understand the social action without understanding also the nature of the contested legal and regulatory understandings.

At the same time, very many rules which are crucial for the working of society are not 'made' by legislators or rooted in custom, but are fashioned by the courts themselves, developing doctrine; many important 'social practices' cannot be understood without an understanding of the legal concepts which constitute them. The social institution of marriage, for instance, is constituted by the 'contract' of marriage. The social understanding, and the social practice, of marriage has been shaped and conditioned by legal meanings and definitions. Historians of marriage have consequently focused much attention on what was considered to be a 'valid' marriage according to canon law at various points in time; and have sought to test how far people in fact complied with its requirements (Probert 2009). What couples did, in making and breaking marriages, were very largely shaped by their conception and use of legal concepts. Economic relations, such as creditor and debtor relations, are similarly constituted by legal relations. One can hardly understand the propertied world of the eighteenth-century English man or woman, without having some idea of the operation of the trust, which was used both to secure provisions for extensive families and to administer large-scale enterprise in this era (Habakkuk 1994). One can no more easily understand the economic position of the twenty-first century citizen without an idea of the legal regime which underscores property, credit and debt. In these 'constitutive' areas, it is important to dig deeper, to try to understand the meanings of 'doctrine'.

The complexities of law cannot be reduced to a single formula. One thing that makes the 'legal' domain distinct is a set of intellectual practices and meanings which are dissimilar from other forms of social practices. But the law is not simply something in the realm of ideas: for the ideas are applied in and to social practice, and are enforced by authority. We therefore need to study not merely the ideas of the 'specialists', how they identify and develop their bodies of ideas, but also the relationship between the 'ideas' and the 'authorities', and the relationship between the community and those it regards as authorities, political and intellectual. One needs both to explore which practices or conventions the community uses to identify those in authority, and to make sense of the practices and understandings of those who have the specialist learning. We may consequently need to look for more than one 'internal view'. We also need to bear in mind that these practices are not constant, but develop, and differ from place to place. Legal orders are clearly not of the same type. Jurists in different traditions have different conceptions and concerns, and different ways of thinking. There are different ways of explaining their authority, both in the language they use themselves, and in the way citizens and subjects explain reasons for allegiance. There are, in other words, a multiplicity of legal languages in different systems, which change and develop. The richness and variety of this development is sometimes overlooked in social theory, either because the detail of the variation and change is not seen as relevant to the theoretical enterprise, or because theorists feel that they can obtain a sufficient overview of the historical change for the purpose of their theories from (often general) secondary sources. Yet there can be no substitute for the detailed, empirical study. To understand how law works, it is not sufficient to generate a descriptive theory from a limited empirical survey: rather the theory should be a tool for understanding the mass of empirical data.

27 Equally, as the nineteenth-century history of the use of the common law to control public order shows, the ambiguous language of law could be a useful tool in the hands of the authorities.

4. Law, Society and Change

Once we accept that there is a distinctly 'legal' box, how do we explain its relationship to the wider society? How autonomous is law? How are we to account for changes in the legal system – do they merely reflect changes in the wider society, or are they wholly 'internal'? The historian's perspective is particularly useful in addressing these questions, since one of the principal tasks of the historian is to seek to trace and explain changes.

To understand the nature of legal change, and its relationship to society, we need to take seriously both the distinct nature of legal reasoning (and the forum in which legal reasoning occurs) and the influences which impact on it. Insofar as law is a system of social governance in practice, and not simply a system of ideas, it cannot be studied solely from 'inside' the box.[28] Nor do many historians seek to study law only from the inside. Rather, as Charles Donahue has put it, most legal historians aim 'to show how law, non-legal ideas, politics and society interact' (Donahue 2009: 332). Indeed, 'doctrinal' legal historians have shown that one cannot understand the nature and development of legal concepts in the past without having some idea of their social contexts. For instance, S.F.C. Milsom's radical reinterpretation of the birth of the common law in the era of Henry II rested on his insights about the nature of feudal society, and about the kinds of disputes which led litigants to call for royal intervention (Milsom 1976). As Milsom has shown, in the later middle ages, the legal system was constantly in a process of change, as lawyers manipulated old forms of procedure to serve new purposes, demanded by litigants in particular social situations. In this vision, legal doctrine – rather than being a static, formalist object of study – was fluid, and constantly recast by lawyers whose main aim was to win cases for clients with real social problems. Equally, it has long been evident that litigants have brought 'test cases' to court, to raise political questions which legislatures may have wanted to avoid.

Can we develop an explanatory model of precisely how this works? An attempt to develop a sociological theory or a model of legal change has been made by Luhmann's systems theory. According to this theory, systems change in response to 'irritations' from outside the system. It is not the case that new information 'enters' the legal system from outside: *society* does not dictate legal change. Rather, change occurs as a result of a process in which the system perceives changes in its environment, and changes itself in response. Since systems produce their own versions of what is external to them – their 'environment' – it is their perception of deviations from what was expected in their environment which matters. 'Irritations' are 'system-internal formulations of the problem', in response to which solutions are formulated by the legal system (Luhmann 2004: 258–9). Luhmann describes the relationship between a 'system' and its 'environment' in terms of 'structural coupling', which can provide an 'influx of disorder' against which the system may modify its operations. Different systems can co-ordinate when one system's communications represents a stable pattern of events which can be perceived by another system, and which 'irritates' communications within that other system. Thus, in his view the structural coupling of the legal and economic systems influenced the evolution of modern concepts of property and contract.

This is an interesting model of change, but still leaves some questions unanswered, which raises doubts about how useful it is in helping us understand the relationship between law and its 'other'. First, it does not explain how or why a 'legal system' comes to perceive 'irritations' from

28 One might think that a legal system with no legislator and no system of courts – such as system of Roman law pieced together by the jurists in medieval universities – might be studied solely 'internally': but even here, the way in which the various generations of jurists studied the texts reflected wider intellectual concerns and changes which cannot be understood without some understanding of context.

other systems at particular times, or why the legal system develops in particular ways. We might want to know more than that its programmes are 'conditional'. Second, it does not explain how or why *different* aspects of the 'environment' are seen to 'irritate' the legal system at different times. When and why does the 'legal' system respond to the 'economic' system, as opposed to the 'moral' system, or indeed, the general societal system as a whole? Thirdly, its systems seem to be too monolithic. After all, ideas within the 'legal' domain – or within the 'economic' or 'moral' domain – may be contested, or unstable and subject to reinterpretation. In some ways, systems theory is *too* 'internal', describing a system that is too autonomous.

In fact, empirical historical research shows that the 'external' influences which affect legal change can be very unsystematic. A catastrophic natural event might change the kinds of cases which come to court, and how the courts respond. Robert Palmer's study of England in the Age of the Black Death suggested that in the wake of this natural event (when the huge population decline had made labour a much dearer commodity), the legal system adapted its writs and forms in order to respond to the desire of litigants to be able to hold people to the performance of their obligations (Palmer 2001, cf. Milsom 1981). This is to suggest that the development of new forms of action – such as *assumpsit* – were to some degree a response to social problems. More incremental economic and social changes may also have an impact on 'internal' doctrine. For instance, it is widely accepted that the initial impulse towards a general tort of 'negligence' in English law came from the escalating number of road accidents consequent to the expansion of stage coach traffic which accompanied the late eighteenth-century transport revolution (Cornish et al.2010: 903–16). The language of the law itself modified and adapted in response to new formulations suggested by litigation. The way that legal doctrines are used might also change in response to the influence of wider social or economic ideas, which impact on the world view of the 'internal' participants. The changing perception of the position of married women in the common law has reflected changes in wider public perceptions, which have been articulated by judges in making clear changes in judicial policy.[29] In numerous other areas, the 'letter' of the law remained constant, but the way it was understood and applied altered, in response to new social needs and new social understandings. An infinite variety of 'external' influences thus constantly 'feeds into' the legal system. Nor do they come 'pre-packaged', as 'irritations' from another coherent system.

A careful study of the 'internal' dimension of law also reveals that it is less stable and coherent than is sometimes assumed. Jurists have often worked under the assumption – found most clearly in the belief of medieval jurists that the Digest of Justinian contained perfect answers to every legal question – that doctrine can be complete, coherent and consistent. Such a view is often said to have been held by the late nineteenth century 'formalists', who (it is said) felt that law was self-sufficient, and independent of politics or social reality, and capable of being turned into a rational order. Some modern doctrinalists also hold to the view that law can be explained in terms of a timeless conceptual apparatus. Once we look at the operations of the legal system over time, it appears much more fluid and less stable. Judges and jurists constantly strive for doctrinal coherence, and try to order their ideas in the most intellectually persuasive way. But there are many obstacles standing in the way of success. First, not only is there a constant flow of new material into the system (as new questions are asked of it), but the way problems can be posed to the system are highly variable. The law does not have a single language, but a choice of languages.

29 See, e.g., *The Queen* v. *Jackson* [1891] 1 QB 671, holding that a man could not detain his wife in his house against her will; and *R.* v. *R.* [1992] 1 AC 599, holding that a man could be convicted of the rape of his wife.

Cases can be framed in various ways, with reference to various doctrines, and judges will have a choice over how to see or characterize the case before them (Waddams 2003). Even within the same area of doctrine – such as 'contract' – there may be a variety of approaches, each of which may be considered appropriate in a different context. Second, the judges themselves – and other legal experts – will disagree over how to interpret the law. Reconstructing the 'internal' is therefore a complicated task: it entails getting inside the mind of actors within the 'system' who may have contending understandings of that 'system'. Different interpretations may prevail at different times, and in response to different social triggers. While a consensus view may prevail, there may continue to be contested interpretations or uncertainties.

In studying the impact of 'society' on law, we must therefore take care to avoid two traps. The first is the assumption that all legal development is the product of a wholly 'internal' debate, as lawyers refine and better understand timeless legal concepts. While it might be argued that this model might describe the refinement and reconstitution of medieval Roman law in the universities,[30] it cannot describe a system of working law which is applied in actual societies. The second is the assumption that legal development straightforwardly reflects wider political or economic or social developments or ideologies, and that law can be seen as a simple instrument to apply these. One example is the widely held assumption that the motor behind changes in nineteenth century contract law was the judges' keenness to promote commercial expansion. Where the first of these views is blind to the importance of social developments, the second is prone to search for the values it wishes to uncover in the 'subconscious' of the judges or 'under the surface', on the assumption that they must be there.

Besides the issue of how to study the impact of 'society' on law, there remains the question of how law impacts on society. In considering this question, two points may be borne in mind. The first is to recall that courts have often been required to act as venues of governance, creating rules for society in situations where the legislature has been silent, but where litigants have asked for problems to be solved. In such situations, courts may have to craft a new policy to deal with pressing social or economic problems. They neither simply apply policies borrowed from the 'outside' nor simply develop 'internal' doctrine: rather they craft a policy for society by developing doctrine. If courts are a forum of governance, they are a distinctive forum: judges cannot make policy in the same way that politicians do, but are constrained by the kind of reasoning they are expected to use, and by the fact that they are dealing with specific questions put to them by individual litigants. Law may be politics by other means, but it has its own processes and own languages, which need to be studied on their own terms. Studying the language and processes of the 'legal' world helps us better understand how and when judges are called upon by society to make rules which other forums of governance have left aside, and at how those rules are crafted. This is in itself to study an important aspect of how society operates.

The second is to note that the deeper question of how the product of 'law' impacts on society is a much more complex one, and one which cannot elicit any simple answers. Since the study of 'society' is the study of 'everything', it is utopian in the extreme to hope for a theory or model which can explain how 'law' impacts on 'society'. What we can do, once we have a rigorous understanding of the 'legal' and how it has been shaped, is to see how its languages are picked up, echoed, avoided, reshaped or ignored, in any number of particular contexts. Rather than asking how 'law' impacts on 'society' in general, we may learn more by looking at particular aspects of law impacting on particular aspects of society. For such an enterprise, the historian's method – with

30 This might be argued of Roman law in the era of the Glossators; though not for the post-glossators, who were interested in addressing actual legal problems using the tools of Roman law.

its keen focus on the particular context and its scepticism for grand theory – seems in many ways the most useful one.

Bibliography

Baker, Sir J. 2012. 'Reflections on "Doing" Legal History'. In A. Musson and C. Stebbings (eds), *Making Legal History: Approaches and Methodologies*. Cambridge, Cambridge University Press, 7–17.

Brundage, J.A. 2008. *The Medieval Origins of the Legal Profession: Canonists, Civilians and Courts*. Chicago, University of Chicago Press.

Burke, P. 2005. *History and Theory.* Cambridge, Polity Press. 2nd edn.

Collingwood, R.G. 1961. *The Idea of History*. Oxford, Clarendon Press.

Cornish, W.R. et al. 2010. *The Oxford History of the Laws of England*, vol. 12. Oxford, Oxford University Press.

Cotterrell, R. 1992. *The Sociology of Law*. London, Butterworths. 2nd edn.

Cotterrell, R. 1999. *Emile Durkheim: Law in a Moral Domain*. Edinburgh, Edinburgh University Press.

Cotterrell, R. 2003. *The Politics of Jurisprudence.* London, LexisNexis. 2nd edn.

Cotterrell, R. 2004. 'Law in Social Theory and Social Theory in the Study of Law'. In A. Sarat (ed.), *The Blackwell Companion to Law and Society*. Oxford, Blackwell, 15–29.

Cotterrell, R. 2006. 'Why Must Legal Ideas Be Interpreted Sociologically?' In *Law, Culture and Society: Legal Ideas in the Mirror of Social Theory*. Aldershot, Ashgate, 45–63.

Cotterrell, R. 2008. *Living Law: Studies in Legal and Social Theory*. Aldershot, Ashgate.

Cotterrell, R. 2012. 'Socio-Legal Studies, Law Schools, and Legal and Social Theory'. Delivered at Wolfson College Oxford, 2012. Available at http://papers.ssrn.com/sol3/papers.cfm?abstract_id=2154404.

Cotterrell, R. 2013. 'Rethinking "Embeddedness": Law, Economy, Community'. 40 *Journal of Law and Society*, 49–67.

Bellomo, M. 1995. *The Common Legal Past of Europe, 1000–1800*, trans. Lydia G. Cochrane. Washington, DC, Catholic University of America Press.

Brown, E.A.R. 1974. 'The Tyranny of a Construct: Feudalism and Historians of Medieval Europe'. 79 *American Historical Review*, 1063–88.

David, J. 2010. 'Legal Comparability and Cultural Identity: the Case of Legal Reasoning'. In 'Jewish and Islamic Traditions'. 14.1 *Electronic Journal of Comparative Law* http://www.ejcl.org.

Donahue Jr., C. 2009. 'Whither Legal History'. In D.W. Hamilton and A.L. Brophy (eds), *Transformations in American History: Essays in Honor of Professor Morton J. Horwitz*. Cambridge, MA, Harvard University Press, 327–43.

Durkheim, E. 1952. *Suicide: A Study in Sociology*, trans J.A. Spaulding and G. Simpson. London, Routledge.

Durkheim, E. 1982. *The Rules of Sociological Method, and Selected Texts on Sociology and its Method,* ed. S. Lukes. Basingstoke, Macmillan.

Fisk, C.L. and Gordon, R.W. 2011. '"Foreword" to Symposium: "Law As": Theory and Method in Legal History'. 1 *UC Irvine Law Review*, 519–41.

Friedman, L.M. 2005. 'Coming of age: law and society enters an exclusive club'. 1 *Annual Review of Law and Social Science*, 1–16.

Friedman, L.M. 1973. *A History of American Law*. New York, Simon and Schuster.
Gordon, Robert. 1975–6. 'W.J. Willard Hurst and the Common Law Tradition in American Legal Historiography'. 10 *Law and Society Review*, 9–55.
Habakkuk, Sir John. 1994. *Marriage, Debt and the Estates System: English Landownership, 1650–1950*. Oxford, Oxford University Press.
Hale, Sir Matthew. 1924. 'Reflections by the Lrd. Cheife Justice Hale on Mr. Hobbes his Dialogue of the Law'. In W.S. Holdsworth, *A History of English Law*, vol. 5. London, Methuen, 500–513.
Hart, H.L.A. 1961. *The Concept of Law.* Oxford, Clarendon Press.
Hudson, John. 2000. Court Cases and Legal Arguments in England, c 1066-c 1166. Vol. 10 (6th ser.) *Transactions of the Royal Historical Society*, 91–115.
Hyams, P. 2004. 'Norms and Legal Argument Before 1150'. In A. Lewis and M. Lobban (eds), *Law and History: Current Legal Issues* vol. 6. Oxford, Oxford University Press, 41–61.
Jansen, N. 2010. *The Making of Legal Authority: Non-legislative Codifications in Historical and Comparative Perspective.* Oxford, Oxford University Press.
Kelley, D.R. 1990. *The Human Measure: Social Thought in the Western Legal Tradition.* Cambridge, MA, Harvard University Press.
Lacey, N. 2004. *A Life of H.L.A. Hart: the Nightmare and the Noble Dream.* Oxford, Oxford University Press.
Lobban, M. 2007. *A History of the Philosophy of Law in the Common Law World, 1600–1900.* Dordrecht, Springer.
Lobban, M. 2012. 'The Politics of English Law in the Nineteenth Century'. In P. Brand and J. Getzler (eds), *Judges and Judging in the History of the Common Law and Civil Law from Antiquity to Modern Times.* Cambridge, Cambridge University Press, 102–37.
Luhmann, N. 1992. 'Operational Closure and Structural Coupling: the Differentiation of the Legal System'. 13 *Cardozo Law Review*, 1419–41.
Luhmann, N. 2004. *Law as a Social System*, trans. Klaus A. Ziegert, ed. F. Kastner, R. Nobles, D. Schiff and R. Ziegert. Introduction by R. Nobles and D. Schiff. Oxford, Oxford University Press.
Merry, S.E. 1988. 'Legal Pluralism'. 22 *Law & Society Review*, 869–96.
Milsom, S.F.C. 1976. *The Legal Framework of English Feudalism.* Cambridge, Cambridge University Press.
Milsom, S.F.C. 1981. *Historical Foundations of the Common Law*. London, Butterworths. 2nd edn.
Nobles, R. and Schiff, D. 2012. 'Using systems theory to study legal pluralism: what could be gained?' 46 *Law & Society Review*, 265–96.
Palmer, R.C. 2001. *English Law in the Age of the Black Death, 1348–1381.* University of North Carolina Press, Chapel Hill.
Parker, K.M. 2011. 'Law "in" and "as" History: the Common Law in the American Polity, 1790–1900'. 1 *UC Irvine Law Review*, 587–94.
Probert, R. 2009. *Marriage Law and Practice in the Long Eighteenth Century: A Reassessment.* Cambridge, Cambridge University Press.
Raz, J. 1979. *The Authority of Law.* Oxford, Clarendon Press.
Simpson, A.W.B. 2011. *Reflections on the Concept of Law.* Oxford, Oxford University Press.
Skinner, Q. 2002. *Visions of Politics, Volume I: Regarding Method.* Cambridge, Cambridge University Press.
Tamanaha, B.Z. 1996. 'The Internal/External Distinction and the Notion of a 'Practice'. In 'Legal Theory and Socio-Legal Studies' 30 *Law & Society Review* 163–204.
Tamahana, B.Z. 2001. *A General Jurisprudence of Law and Society.* Oxford, Oxford University Press.

Tamanaha, B.Z. 2008. 'Understanding Legal Pluralism: Past to Present, Local to Global'. 30 *Sydney Law Review*, 375–411.

Van Caenegem, R.C. (ed.) 1990. *English Lawsuits from William I to Richard.* London, Selden Society, vol. 106.

Waddams, S.M. 2003. *Dimensions of Private Law: Categories and Concepts in Anglo-American Legal Reasoning.* Cambridge, Cambridge University Press.

Weber, M. 1978. *Economy and Society*, ed. Guenther Roth and Claus Wittich. London, University of California Press.

Weber, M. 1992. *The Protestant Ethic and the Spirit of Capitalism*, trans. Talcott Parsons, with an introduction by Anthony Giddens. London, Routledge.

Whitman, J.Q. 1991. 'Why did the Revolutionary Lawyers Confuse Custom and Reason?' 58 *University of Chicago Law Review*, 1321–68.

Wormald, P. 1999. 'Charters, Law and the Settlement of Disputes in Anglo-Saxon England'. In P. Wormald, *Legal Culture in the Medieval West: Law as Text, Image and Experience.* London, Hambledon, 289–311.

Chapter 3

Images of Borders and the Politics and Legality of Identity

Zenon Bańkowski and Maksymilian Del Mar

1. Introduction

Ryszard Kapuściński, the Polish writer known for his literary reportage on revolutions and coups, said the following of borders on the first day of his departure on the Trans-Siberian in 1985 from Peking to Moscow:

> At the approach to every border, tension rises within us; emotions heighten. People are not made to live in borderline situations; they avoid them or try to flee from them as quickly as possible. And yet man encounters them everywhere, sees and feels them everywhere. Let us take the atlas of the world: it is all borders. Borders of oceans and continents. Deserts and forests. Precipitations, monsoons, typhoons, cultivated land and fallow land, permafrost and bog, rocky soil and clay. Let us add the borders of the Quaternary deposits and volcanic flows, of basalt, chalk and trachyte. We can also see the borders of the Patagonian plate and the Canadian plate, the zones of tropical climates and of Arctic ones, the borders of the erosion zones of the Adycha watershed and of Lake Chad. The borders demarcating the habitats of certain mammals. Certain insects. Certain reptiles and amphibians …
>
> And the borders of monarch and republics? Kingdoms remote in time and lost civilisations? Pacts, treaties and alliances? Black tribes and red? Human migrations? The borders to which the Mongols reached. The Khazars. The Huns …
>
> … And our brains? Encoded in them, after all, is an infinite diversity of borders. Between the left and the right hemispheres, between the frontal and the temporal lobes, between the corpus callosum and the cerebellum. And the borders between ventricles, meninx, and convolutions? Between the lumbar region and the spinal cord? (Kapuściński, 1994: 19–20)

There is, as we readily acknowledge, a burgeoning literature of boundary studies, which sees borders all around us. Barbara Morehouse, for example, begins her overview of this realm of scholarship in the following way:

> There seem to be few things in the world today that are as ubiquitous as boundaries and borders. A referee steps in when the soccer ball goes out of bounds. A space shuttle approaches the boundary of the atmosphere. A refugee huddles in a border camp. A two-year old child learns about limits, while a ten year old sibling dreams of exploring the frontiers of space. (Morehouse, 2005: 19)

There are, Morehouse tells us,

> boundary cells in plant roots, borderline personality disorder, boundary conditions in mathematics, boundary layers in the atmosphere and the ocean, and borderlands art and music. (Morehouse, 2005: 19)

This chapter is not, however, the occasion for an interrogation of the concerns of boundary studies. Our aim is not to point to the ubiquity of borders; rather, it is to open up as generous a space as possible for recognizing the many ways in which borders are and can be both imagined and experienced. We then proceed to consider the implications of our examination of the imagination and experience of borders for the legality and politics of identity. We argue that when we look carefully at images of borders, we will recognize that borders can be imagined and experienced as lines or spaces (in a sense, they are both at once, but depending on how we imagine and experience them, these different dimensions of them can appear more pertinent). We argue that it is similarly so with identity (both individual and communal). Persons and communities often imagine and experience the need to demarcate who they see themselves to be and where they consider themselves to belong. They imagine and experience the need to feel safe, at home, surrounded by familiarity. In that sense, persons and communities are always consolidating their identities. But persons and communities are also changing, particularly through interaction and exchange with others. Our further argument is that although persons and communities are both consolidating and changing continuously, it is harder for us to change than to consolidate. In that respect, then, our chapter seeks to emphasize the image of the border as a space, i.e., as a transitional zone where we encounter others and change who we are.

Our tendency to want to consolidate, to escape, to stand above, to believe we have done enough and can now stand in judgement on others, is illustrated best, as is often the case, by a Kafka parable:

> He has two antagonists: the first presses him from behind, from the origin. The second blocks the road ahead. He gives battle to both. To be sure, the first supports him in his fight with the second, for he wants to push him forward, and in the same way the second supports him in his fight with the first, since he drives him back. But it is only theoretically so. For it is not only the two antagonists who are there, but he himself as well, and who really knows his intentions? His dream, though, is that some time in an unguarded moment – and this would require a night darker than any night has ever been yet – he will jump out of the fighting line and be promoted, on account of his experience in fighting, to the position of umpire over his antagonists in their fight with each other. (Quoted in Arendt, 1961: 7)

The dream of an escape can come in other forms too, e.g., as when we make ourselves comfortable in our own home; when we lock ourselves in, hide inside and become unable and unwilling to venture out. Of course, making a home in the first place is often difficult, so that once made, and lived in, it becomes ever harder to change. Consider the following from William James:

> The settler had in every case cut down the more manageable trees, and left their charred stumps standing. The larger trees he had girdled and killed, in order that their foliage should not cast a shade. He had then built a log cabin, plastered its chinks with clay, and had set up a tall zigzag rail fence around the scene of his havoc, to keep the pigs and cattle out. Finally, he had irregularly planted the intervals between the stumps and trees with Indian cord, which grew among the chips; and there he dwelt with his wife and babes—an axe, a gun, a few utensils, and some pigs and chicken feeding in the woods, being the sum total of his possessions. (Quoted in Winter, 2001: ix)

Making a clearing for oneself can be difficult. Beginnings like this are often permeated with violence and hard times, even if not nearly as much for the new occupants as for those (including those of the natural world) whose resistance, if there is any, yields to the incomer. Having got there, having built our home, we will often go about trying to make it as comfortable as we can – and we may loathe to think we might have to do it all again; to venture outside again; risk it all one more time; give up all that we have found; find a new home. Partly because it is often so difficult, so painful, to find one's way, to settle down and carve out one's dominion, does it become so difficult, so painful, to open oneself up to more transformation. Of course, we need a home; we need to feel safe. But the challenge that we wish to emphasize here is how important it is, both for persons and communities, not to not allow themselves to remain locked into the grip of that comfort, unable and unwilling to see that things could be otherwise, and unable and unwilling to face their own limitations.

This challenge also applies to scholars. They too must deal with these issues concerning identity: they too experience the need for reinforcement and the pain of transformation of one's self; the need for closure and the challenge of openness; the need for a home and the experience of otherness. Scholars, too, are perhaps at more risk than before – in these times of increased bureaucratization and professionalization of scholarship – of disciplinary segregation, of finding too sure a footing, too quickly, in the world of academia – and thus losing the ability and willingness to see things in different ways, and recognizing the importance of such diverse ways of seeing.

Roger Cotterrell has always been a scholar who has, in what now seems so clichéd a phrase, 'pushed the boundaries'. He made himself a 'safe home' in the clearing of law and has become a significant interdisciplinary scholar, especially in the application of social scientific insights to the study of law, thus transforming it and his own home. But that is not the only way he touches on our concerns here. Much of his work has been concerned with pluralism, talking about the way pluralism, in respect of different identities and normative systems, is managed and how diverse systems, at points where they touch, influence and interact with each other. And this leads on to looking at what it might be like to live in such zones, to exploring the idea of transnational communities. Living, as he says, in such a world where all these systems cross over us in our daily life, it is necessary to study the boundaries and transitions between them and to see how they intersect with each other and with us. We can do this theoretically by looking at the differences and similarities between belief systems and also practically by considering the boundaries between the forms of our political, social and religious life and the impact that has on polities. What is important, then, are the transition points, the boundaries and the borders.

Our chapter, then, is a meditation on some of the themes that have so concerned Roger and upon which he has offered so much illumination. But it is not just the content but also the method, with ways of seeing, that concerns us here. Thinking by looking at images[1] (here the images of borders) – a process that involves looking at oneself as much as at what one looks at – has proved to be a most fertile method for us.[2] It is a process quite different – at least it has so far seemed to us – to thinking through, or in, or thanks to, linguistic formulations. What we offer below, then, is what emerged as we attempted to walk slowly through images of borders – trying to walk as slowly as possible, to look as much as possible – and what we learnt from that exercise about the legality

1 And *Images of Law* is how one of us started his academic career (see Bankowski and Mungham, 1976). Also, one of us has looked at how the other has 'thought in images' (see Del Mar 2013).

2 Writing and rewriting this essay over a long period of time has led to the burgeoning of other projects, e.g., the AHRC Beyond Text in Legal Education project. See: Bańkowski and Del Mar, 2013, Bańkowski, Del Mar and Maharg, 2013.

and politics of identity. By no means do we claim to have exhausted the images we consider; on the contrary, we feel we have just begun. We know, and hope, that the reader will find much we have not seen. If nothing else, it is the generosity of images that we want to point to; their fertility; their endless lessons – endless, that is, as long as we are willing and able to understand that what we see, at one moment, is but a glimpse, and that we are so dependent upon others and their ways of seeing for learning and growing. And this again touches on Roger the jazz enthusiast.[3] Just as the musician builds his piece by improvising on fixed themes which transforms them and opens the way for future work, we offer, in this spirit and in his honour, this meditation and improvisation on the theme of borders.

The structure of the chapter is as follows: first, in part two, we consider images of borders as lines; second, in part three, we look at images of borders as spaces; third, in part four, we consider the implications of these two ways of looking at borders for the legality and politics of identity; finally, in part five, we offer our conclusions.

2. Borders as Lines

2.1 Against Inherent Properties

There has been a lot written about the legality, ethics and politics of territorial borders: about their benefits and drawbacks. Some say, 'good fences make good neighbours' and much is made, particularly in international law, of the allegedly inherent importance of the stability of international borders and the need for conservatism and circumspection about demands for self-determination (at least in non-colonial contexts). And yet, others call out for a borderless world – a world of global citizens – pointing to the allegedly inherent problems with borders.[4] We acknowledge the arguments on both sides, but wish to distance ourselves here from any argument that is based on the allegedly inherent properties of borders. It is important, then, for us to point out that we do not argue that, for instance, borders-as-lines are inherently bad, whereas borders-as-spaces are inherently good. We recognize there is complexity on both sides, and that much depends on how we imagine and experience borders, on our attitudes to them. Indeed, it is precisely in order to look more carefully – in this part, at borders-as-lines – that we wish to leave behind arguments based on the allegedly inherent properties of borders. Let us proceed slowly, then, looking, collecting echoes of the images of borders-as-lines.

2.2 Walls, Genealogies and Constraints

Perhaps the first associations one is liable to make with the figure of a border are of terrifying walls, separations and cleavages between cultures, communities and civilizations: of the Gatekeeper Operation, for example, on the US–Mexico border, which consisted of the construction of three layers of fifteen-foot-high steel walls – sunk deep into the ground to prevent tunnelling – augmented by

3 Both of the authors are Polish and it gives us great pleasure to recognize Roger's love of Polish jazz and jazz in Poland.

4 The literature here is, once again, immense. For a recent statement from international political theory, see Williams, 2006. For an impressive collection of papers, examining the making and unmaking of borders from Jewish, Christian, Confucian, Islamic, Natural Law, Liberal and International Law traditions, see Buchanan and Moore, 2003.

state-of-the-art sensors and video surveillance, and backed up by a huge contingent of border patrol officers and helicopters (see Davis, 2005).[5]

There are the waters of Australia – recall the story of the Tampa, a Singapore-bound freighter, which was ordered by Australian maritime authorities to rescue boatfuls of Afghans desperate to reach Australia, and then being forced, by a fleet of SAS commandoes, to languish for days at sea, with sickness (especially of children) rife on board, before finally being allowed to port at the distant island of Nauru (Davis, 2005: 97–8). There is also the story of Berlusconi's Italy refusing to allow a German rescue boat to land ashore because it carried 37 shipwrecked Africans – with the additional element that, after finally allowing them to land, but only after substantial pressure from the Vatican, the Italians arrested the German crew for 'abetting illegal immigration' (Davis, 2005: 96).

Some of those physical borders suggest impregnability, but experience has shown that the escalation of border policing only results in escalation of more and more creative methods of transgressing them, as has been the case so clearly on the US–Mexico border – almost inevitably resulting in such an enormous waste of resources, and of course in the loss of so many lives (see Andreas, 2000). Kapuściński comments:

> How many victims, how much blood and suffering, are connected with this business of borders! There is no end to the cemeteries of those who have been killed the world over in the defence of borders. Equally boundless are the cemeteries of the audacious who attempted to expand their borders. It is safe to assume that half of those who have ever walked upon our planet and lost their lives in the field of glory gave up the ghost in battles begun over a question of borders. (Kapuściński, 1994: 20)

The fact that the loss of those lives and the waste of those resources is so rarely reported is testament to the opinion that borders-as-lines function also in a politically-symbolic register: they are paraded in the political theatre of those countries as signs of strength, of the power and toughness of the State – but of course they also exhibit the great fear and anxiety of the State.

Consider, now, other kinds of borders-as-lines: e.g. diasporas (e.g. the Celts, still recognizable over such a long period of time: see Toulier, 2005); or complex heritages and genealogies, such as those found in places such as Bukowina or Trieste. In Bukowina, for example, in the period leading up to the First World War and thus still under the auspices of the Austrian Empire, was a place where Armenians, Germans, Gypsies, Jews, Hungarians, Romanians, Russians, Ruthenians and Slovaks lived side by side on the verge of the collapse of the Austrian imperial state (see Ziegert, 2002). Or Trieste, where its diverse population was the site of so many regimes (themselves identities, borders of some kind): the Habsburgs, the Italian Fascists, the Nazi occupation, the pro-Yugoslav communists, the British American Military Government and then Republican Italy (see Sulga, 2001).

Think of waking up one morning in Palestine or Berlin, unable to reconnect with your family or friends on the other side. Think of the separated family members waking up to the sight of barbed wire in different refugee camps in Australia. Think of Australian Aboriginal children (the victims of the 'Stolen Generation') waking up in foreign homes, with strangers for brothers and sisters. Think of the bridge home to Palestine, as described by the exiled poet Mourid Barghouti in *I Saw Ramallah* (2000) – a bridge seen for the first time after decades of isolation from one's family,

5 The third picture from the top here: www.roaring-girl.com/prod01_a.shtml is not of the Gatekeeper Operation, but it does show a portion of the US–Mexico Border.

one's language spoken in the streets, one's favourite cafes, favourite foods. Still in Palestine, think of the children in refugee camps in Bethlehem, who look out of their school windows (when they are fortunate enough to be at school) and see the wall (covered with Banksy's graffiti) and the dark windows of surveillance towers.

But, as noted above, borders-as-lines are not always bad news. We can think, for example, of lines as constraints, releasing the potential for astounding creativity. That creativity is, or at least can be, enabled by borders-as-lines rather than disabled by them, emerges not only from the constructions of contraptions via which persons have transgressed them, as in the case of the US–Mexico border, or as is visible to any visitor of the Charlie Checkpoint museum in Berlin. It also emerges, for example, in the literary arts. Recall the incredible constructions of the members of *Ouvroir de Littérature Potentielle* (OULIPO, the Association for Potential Literature), founded by Raymond Queneau. One of these constructions, *La Disparition* (1969), by Georges Perec, is a novel written under the constraints of containing no letter 'e' – the most common letter in the French, as in the English, alphabet. The novel has now been translated into several languages, maintaining the constraint, including English,[6] German, Turkish and Spanish, the last of which contained no letter 'a'.[7] Another work to emerge under the influence of OULIPO was *Se una notte d'inverno un viaggiatore* (1979), by Italo Calvino, who addressed a Reader who never manages to go beyond the beginning of a book, and where the meta-story involving the Reader is constructed according to the strict requirements of the semantic squares of A.J. Greimas. Of course, there are many examples of incredible artistic and scholarly achievements produced under constraints that were not self-imposed, such as Erich Auerbach's *Mimesis* (2003; originally published in 1946), which was composed on the basis of the limited sources Auerbach could find in Istanbul, having been forced to leave Germany for Turkey by the Nazis.

2.3 Guidance by Lines

In many of the illustrations above it seems obvious that you have crossed a border – there are large, imposing and sometimes threatening structures. But this is not always the case. Sometimes, we do not *know* or *recognize* that we have crossed a border (imagined as a line), as when we cross the borders of states via a tunnel, emerging from the darkness or artificial lighting into the sudden clamour of another culture. It is only when we encounter signs in another language, and experience a sense of disorientation, do we realize we must have crossed a border.

Borders-as-lines, then, sometimes guide us without us even realizing it: they sweep us up in non-autonomous ways, and channel us thoughtlessly into certain directions. One thinks here of the Parisian arcades, highways for flâneurs, so lovingly described and depicted by Walter Benjamin (2002; undertaken originally between 1927 and 1940), and as soon as one does so, one also sees the enormous maze- or labyrinth-like constructions of modern shopping-centres, bereft of clocks to make you anxious, which sweep you from one corridor of capitalist happiness to another.

In bringing out this feature of borders-as-lines we can draw on the understanding of rules that Judith Shklar (1986) calls legalism. Rules are separated from the outside from the 'dirty business of politics'. They are an autogenerative system which gives stability in the seeming chaos of the 'beyond'. We can see them as institutions, which guide us unseeingly to certain goals, some of

6 It has been translated three times (by John Lee, Ian Monk and Gilbert Adair), though only Adair's (1994) has been published.

7 The translation, dated 1998, is by Marisol Arbués, Mercé Burrel, Marc Parayre, Hermes Salceda and Regina Vega.

which are the system's own. They are like passageways through which you enter into the zone of stability. They are thus the gateway to 'legal institutions' that provide what Neil MacCormick calls 'diachronic practical information', which stabilizes the bits of practical information that we receive and guides us along pre-determined pathways:

> … [at] any given moment, one can then survey the terms of specific existing arrangements interpreted in the light of consequential rules, and, taking account of events and circumstances interpreted in the same light, one can derive the momentary consequential duties, liberties and powers one has in respect of a given arrangement. This indicates how it is possible for practical thought involving law to be, not a chaotic moment-by-moment response to normative requirements or their absence, but at least partly a stable and predictable business in which a measure of secure planning is possible. (MacCormick and Weinberger, 1986: 79)

Once you have entered the institution, it carries you through; the choices are already made by the rules, the border posts of that institution. Certainly, this can be functional and good. Thus, for example, the (legal) fact that someone was married triggers a dependent's pension and one does not have to go into the particularities of the relationship to determine whether there was dependency and desert. The institution pulls you along certain pathways and you do not have to 'think about it'. But 'not thinking about it' also means that in a certain way you do not see the institution and the rules determining your choice, since you do not think of yourself as having a choice – you just do it. You follow the law simply because it is the law.

According to Max Weber (1991), this is how law operates in capitalist economies. The normative turns into the descriptive. For Weber, scientific rationality took away the magic of the world in that it brought the natural world into the sphere of science, thus making it more certain and predictable and more amenable to the emerging capitalist economies. But this was purchased at the price of losing what Weber called the magic of the world:

> That principally there are no mysterious incalculable forces that come into play, but rather that one can, in principle, master all things by calculation. One need no longer have recourse to magical means in order to master or implore the spirits, as did the savage, for whom such mysterious powers existed. Technical means and calculation perform the service. (Weber, 1991: 139)

In the normative world, one can say that the general and abstract rules of formal rationality do the same thing. They take away the magic of the normative world, remove the contingency of individual passion, and make it flat and predictable. In doing so, they again make it amenable to the emerging capitalist economies, e.g., a contract will be honoured because it is a contract, and not because someone thinks it is the right thing to do. In striving so hard to make the normative predictable by ensuring that we 'do not think about it', we start turning the normative into the descriptive so that we act like automata running in a pre-programmed way. In order to be free we become slaves.

2.4 Governance by Lines

Lawrence Lessig draws an analogy between law and the invisible software code, which runs in the background while we work on a computer (Lessig, 1999). It gives people no possibility of non-compliance with internet architecture, while enabling restricted choices within that structure. In this light, law is the invisible programme that limits many choices while facilitating some others.

Thus electronic barrier and automated ticket systems in, for example, subways and libraries, mean that you have to follow the rules and there is no choice. This can and has been generalized in the sphere of situational crime prevention to contexts where the normative is designed out (see Clarke, 1992, and Bańkowski, 2001). You do not ask people not to break the law; you make it impossible for them to break it. In compliance control systems, the computer automatically generates those documents and paper trails that are required by legal regulation (Kerrigan and Law, 2003). They ensure that the organization follows the regulatory provision even if no specific individual within that organization makes a conscious attempt to ensure obedience with the law. People comply without noticing, there being no possibility of non-compliance.

What is happening here is the attempt to make choice more and more a bounded one; to make it more and more constrained by the physical environment, culminating in a situation where there is no choice. The norms themselves become embodied in physical architecture. Think of a police officer directing traffic or controlling a crowd. The police officer embodies a norm; the crowd and traffic flow around them as though they were physical objects. Consider also the regulation of security at airports, which has increasingly become a matter of channelling behaviour through various checkpoints (see Jones, 2008). This makes regulation a sort of symbolic quasi-physical environment cutting down on choice. In this way, the boundaries between the legal/non-legal disappear. We do not see these borders-as-lines because they channel our movement and experience.[8]

3. Towards Borders as Transitional Zones

3.1 Transitions

What we have been talking about so far is the way that the border, imagined or experienced as a line, signals a structure in which one moves from one state to the other – you do not experience the in-between. Recall, for example, the image of the tunnel in section 2.3, where you emerge suddenly into the light in another place. Once you cross you do not see the 'outside' or the border. But borders, even those imagined and experienced initially as lines, can also lead to the flourishing of border-markets, thereby making available goods otherwise not obtainable, and facilitating forms of interactions amongst peoples who may otherwise be loathe to (or at least have no other opportunities to) interact with each other. One striking example is of the exchanges of goods at the Wagah border of India-Pakistan. At the specific times for exchange, the Wagah border comes alive with colours, hands and boxes.[9] Here, porters wear specific colours and hold packets above their heads, thereby facilitating quick exchange, leaving little, if any, room for negotiation.[10] Every now and then, at the same border, there is also border ceremony, facilitating yet another kind of interaction.[11] Although the kinds of interaction here are carefully stage-managed and controlled, there is at least some form of encounter.

Of course, exchange of goods at borders can also quickly become unpleasant. Recall, for example, the incident in 1996, where Bulgarian policemen used rubber batons to control a 300-strong crowd of Macedonians who were breaking through the border, bound for shops on the other side, and fed

8 For an extended discussion of sections 2.3 and 2.4 see Bańkowski and Schafer, 2007.

9 See www.daylife.com/photo/0fP4biOcKogA7.

10 See www.tribuneindia.com/2006/20060216/amritsar.jpg.

11 See www.abc.net.au/reslib/200711/r199773_763793.jpg.

up with the delays in handling their documents – a delay, they asserted, designed to elicit bribes to speed up the process. Perhaps predictably, the Bulgarian authorities replied that Macedonians were doing the same thing to Bulgarians (Donnan and Wilson, 1999).

Whether more or less controlled, more or less pleasant, these borders cease at certain times to function as lines, and become sites of encounter, even of very limited kinds. Sometimes, of course, even this minimal interaction is destroyed, as when Poland's joining NATO and the EU resulted in the tightening of the border of Poland and Ukraine, thus partly destroying the micro-economy built up around that border.

In some images of borders, you can more easily see the border-space, e.g., a long stretch of highway in between two states.[12] When we consider this way of looking, we see not just an immediate crossing over, from one zone to the next, but a motion or movement of longer duration. Architects sometimes create spaces where, in order to cross from one area of the building to the other, we need to experience the process of change, e.g., consider spaces such as the narthex in a church, or the vestibule or doorstep, where people are both looking in[13] and out,[14] and where you can experience the transition from one zone to the next. Let us consider these transitional zones, these in-between spaces, a little more.

3.2 The Space in Between

Gunther Teubner uses the image of *Grenzestellen* (border posts) in the context of the learning process of the legal system, i.e., the complex interplay between the individual trial and the law's evolutionary mechanism (see Teubner, 1993). *Grenzestellen* here can be seen not just as the post marking off one normative space from another, but also as demarcating the space in between. In other words, on the back of this image, one can think of the trial as this in-between space, which is marked off by the posts of the law and the social interactions of ordinary life. It is in this transitional space where claims for changes in the law are articulated. For Teubner, this must be seen as the 'interlocking of two communicative cycles': the trial and the legal system proper. But it must also be seen as interlocking in the normal world of individual disputes. In the trial, individual disputes are resolved and parties in the 'normal' world get satisfaction or not, but, at the same time, questions of legal doctrine are addressed and variations fed into the legal system proper. Thus, a judgement in a trial can be seen as both stabilizing expectations in the outside world and also generating normative renewal in the legal system. It is the '*unum actum*' of systems theory; one act stands for two things.

There is a complex interaction between the two systems. The legal doctrine that is fed into the law through the trial is used to facilitate the solving of further individual disputes that come into the trial, which, at the same time, feed new norms into the legal system. Here then, in 'system speak', the legal system's mechanism of retention (the legal decision) 'bequeaths what has been learnt in the process of interaction'. Stabilization, the final step, involves the play, in law, of all those mechanisms that 'enable insights gained in one trial to … become part of the memory of the law', and thus allow its autopoiesis, as when that memory furnishes new legal expectations to be tested, affirmed or disappointed in future legal episodes. Through this tripartite process, the insight gained in one trial, (a variation possibly), is 'skimmed off as normative surplus', to establish (through retention and stabilization) a principle for future selection in law (Teubner, 1993). For Teubner

12 Consider this image of the German-Poland border: www.berlinka.pcp.pl/kolbaskowo_1996_03.jpg.

13 See www.pinakoteka.zascianek.pl/Bilinska/Images/Bretonka_na_progu.jpg.

14 See jv.gilead.org.il/zydorczak/images/liw_(20).jpg.

and other systems theorists, this and other mechanisms, such as structural coupling and creative misunderstanding, help to explain how even in a theory, where there is supposed to be closure between normative systems, they can interact and be in some sense open to learning from each other (for an extended discussion, see Bańkowski and Christodoulidis, 1998).

3.3 The Borderland

If we go back, now, to real physical borders we can see examples, although regrettably rare, of conceiving of the borderspace as an opportunity for such continual exchange and interactive cross-fertilization. Krzysztof Czyżewski, the Founding Director of the Borderland Foundation,[15] an organization based in the small town of Sejny on the Polish–Lithuanian border that encourages and facilitates cross-border dialogues, writes that 'the existence and development of borderland regions, the number of which will grow in contemporary, multicultural Europe is extremely important in the process of shaping European unification' (Czyżewski, undated: 7). It is within 'these regions', he says, that 'an authentic community, born in the struggle of dissimilarities, is the most likely to appear' (Czyżewski, undated: 8). Czyżewski calls for the 'time of the province' (see Czyżewski, 2003), i.e., for organic work at the grassroots' level and 'in dialogue with neighbours and the natural environment' (Czyżewski, undated: 8). The borderland, as he sees it, is a 'chance to reinvent *agora* – that meeting place that gave rise to democracy itself' (Czyżewski, undated: 8). Indeed, as we have seen with respect to the US–Mexico border, but as has also been the case for the Russia-Kazakhstan and Russia-China borders and others, when the border becomes of interest to national government as a 'reason of State', especially as a result of (easily exacerbated) anxiety about security, a central bureaucracy makes decisions resulting in the effective disappearance of, or at least the imposition of grave burdens on, a local borderland community; no space is left for the local to flourish; no opportunity is provided for the area to develop its own kind of normativity; a 'zone of exclusion' replaces a 'zone of transformation' (for extensive discussion, see Papademetriou and Waller Meyers, 2001). Borderlands do fight back, calling for greater self-governance, despite, typically, a chronic lack of resources, but they are facing an uphill battle. Many of these communities have learnt that when they get attention from the government, it is almost always for reasons that place their very survival in doubt (see, once again, Papademetriou and Waller Meyers, 2001).[16]

4. Transformations of Identity

4.1 The Exchanging Self

Parts 2 and 3 have shown us that we can imagine and experience borders as lines or as spaces. Borders, imagined and experienced as one or other, function either as forms of demarcation and strategies of withdrawal, or as zones for the experience of transition, exchange and interaction. In this part, we extend these ways of imagining and experiencing borders to the politics and legality of identity both personally and socially. As we indicated in the introduction, although we recognize the importance of demarcation and withdrawal, of stability and the safety of the home,

15 Visit www.pogranicze.sejny.pl for more information.

16 We can relate this idea of the 'transistional zone' more spefically to law when discussing Rowan Williams (section 4 below).

we wish also to emphasize the benefits of imagining and experiencing the border as a space, a transitional zone in which, through encounter and exchange with others, we develop and grow. As with borders (see 2.1 above), we also wish to distance ourselves here from relying or proposing inherent properties: we are not arguing that, say, stability is a bad thing, and change is always good (or vice versa). But we do believe that stability is often easier, both for persons and communities, and that, therefore, the importance of change needs to be emphasized.

Our ethical lives are to do with exchange and openness to the other. In exchange, we open ourselves out to others and we receive from them and they receive from us, and in this way we both transform ourselves, and develop and grow. When we are open in this way, we do not hold on to an unchanging identity; rather, it is always in flux, in the process of becoming. This can happen at all levels, from individuals to different levels of community. At the group level, the process of exchange implies being open to the outside – always being ready to go beyond the limit, although that limit is what at the moment defines our existence. Not doing this means a closed and totalizing community. It is, then, at the boundaries that we test and transform our categories in an open encounter.[17] These boundaries might be social, cultural, religious, moral and even spatial. We can certainly use them in order to demarcate and withdraw from one another. But if we experience and imagine them as spaces, thereby transforming them from lines to spaces, we also enable our own transformation, testing our ethical intuitions and sympathies in the contexts of encounter and exchange. So, with the ethics of the limit, transformation comes from the irritation from the outside and it is this that enables us to develop and grow. As we take in the outside, we change in our creative encounter with it. And it is in these border spaces and transitional zones, which we can experience as both physical and normative spaces, where we develop and grow (see Millibank, 1996). It is here that in the exchange we recreate ourselves anew. Again the image of the clearing comes to mind (see part 1 above). But the clearing is to be seen not as some haven carved from and defended against the forest but part of the forest itself – the space that comes from continuous interaction with that forest which becomes part of our 'safe' lives. Another image that comes to mind here is of the new Dominican chapel in Edinburgh. Looking at the sanctuary one cannot distinguish that space from that of the outside. The holy space then becomes part of and undistinguishable from the profane outside – the transcendental is part of the immanent.[18]

4.2 The Space for Democracy

We can expand this by reference to Jeffrey Stout's *Democracy and Tradition* (2004). Stout argues that one can see ethics as a social practice, which is rooted in the contingencies of that practice, but not such as to lose its objectivity. Democratic ethical discourse is social not in giving the democratic community ultimate authority (the We against the I). Rather, its social nature 'needs to be understood in terms of what the individual members of a group do when they keep track of their interlocutors' commitments from their own perspectives' (Stout, 2004: 279). This implies that there is no privileged point of view, that of the community, but an exchange of views and reasons with members, always trying to get at the others' perspectives. It is in that exchange that community exists (an I–Thou model). Although all communities have discursive practices that give authority to some because no community could function in any other way, they are not thereby authoritarian.

17 Though this recalls standard theories of social change which stress 'culture contact and conflict', we are here adumbrating more of an ethical position than a sociological one.

18 Visit https://www.facebook.com/photo.php?fbid=542836762426407&set=a.542836539093096.1073741829.140942489282505&type=1&theater.

For Stout, the only defensible form of democratic community is one where ethical authority is deferred to those who have proved themselves wise in ethical judgement. That authority is not earned by bowing to the will of the majority; rather, it comes through the reflexive giving and receiving of reasons, of exposing ones views in fora where they have to withstand the critical scrutiny of all. Further, the exercise of authority is always defeasible. He gives an idea of what this might mean by the practice of the area where he himself lives and the interactions between races and cultures there. Here, again, there is no idealism, but rather, a realistic account of what it might mean to live in such a community, warts and all.

Rowan Williams's 2008 Foundation Lecture to the Royal Courts of Justice talked about the way in which, among other things, Muslim identity and allegiance had to be factored into the dynamic of the British political and legal system. More specifically, Williams spoke of the way elements of Shariah law would have to be integrated into the system. Though this raised much controversy and outrage, in legal terms his particular solutions were not controversial. However, what interests us is the way his characterization of the Rule of Law might be seen as that transitional space wherein identities are generated and exchanged. He argues that we should not see the rule of a law as the constraint of an absolute universal but rather as the bringing into being of a space:

> accessible to everyone in which it is possible to affirm and defend a commitment to human dignity *as such*, independent of membership in any specific human community or tradition, so that when specific communities or traditions are in danger of claiming finality for their own boundaries of practice and understanding, they are reminded that they have to come to terms with the actuality of human diversity – and that the only way of doing this is to acknowledge the category of 'human dignity as such' – a non-negotiable assumption that each agent (with his or her historical and social affiliations) could be expected to have a voice in the shaping of some common project for the well-being and order of a human group.

The vision here is to try and see society as a form of what Williams calls 'interactive pluralism'. For him, it is a mistake to think of the Rule of Law as some overarching identity of citizenship, which then allows other identities to exist. Rather, it is something which creates the space where irremediably pluralistic societies manage their overlapping identities. In that sense, then, one could see this as the in-between space where identities are created and renewed. This is not a space that manages different identities and cuts them back if they conflict against the lowest common denominator of universalism. Rather, it is a space where, through the medium of a fragile universalism, different identities accommodate each other. In this sense it expresses the conviction that there is something missing if we think of the present form of our identity as self sufficient and expressing all that could be said about our identity free from the determination and views of other forms of identity and life. And participating in that space involves the dangerous and risky process of offering oneself out for negotiation and renewal, and not knowing where one might end up. Our need is, says Williams

> for the construction of "a moral framework which could expand outside the boundaries of particular narratives while, at the same time, respecting the narratives as the cultural contexts in which the language [of common dignity and mutually intelligible commitments to work for certain common moral priorities] is learned and taught".[19]

19 The internal quote from Raymond Plant is from Plant, 2001: 357–8.

Stout's view mirrors Williams' arguments in his lecture and reinforces the points we make in his attempt to leave space for distinctively religious arguments in a liberal democratic polity, as against those theories that would deny such arguments a place in the public arena. This does not mean a rejection of liberal democracy *per se*, and he attempts to provide a plausible alternative in what he calls a 'pragmatic Emersonian democratic tradition'. He describes his project as the attempt to 'tailor the political institutions and moral discourse of modern society to the facts of pluralism'. For Stout, there are at least three commitments for someone engaged in this attempt, someone concerned in the practice of this project: citizens ought to (a) enjoy equal standing in the democratic process; (b) have respect as individuals keeping track of discussion from their own distinctive point of view; and (c) have a stake in expressive freedom through accepting constraints in a reflexive or dialectical manner, seeing them unfold in the process of applying and deciding upon normative concepts. Stout tries to rescue liberalism from those who feel excluded by it. He was writing about America, trying to counter the liberal view that would consign religious discourse and communities away from the public sphere and into the private sphere as do Rawls and Rorty, precisely the form of the Rule of Law which Williams is arguing against. But it also attempts to counter the reaction to it from certain religious theorists (Alasdair MacIntyre and Stanley Hauerwas) who in a way accept the Rawlsian arguments, which see religious discourse as an alien enclave. MacIntyre and Hauerwas, however, see that enclave as dominant, as the master discourse, such that its task is to subvert the liberal public sphere. The political instantiation of that can be moderate and 'liberal' or fundamentalist and terrifying. Stout's arguments allow for a more pluralistic view, where incommensurable arguments can feed on and enrich each other.

4.3 The Ethics of the Limit

On this view of it, we can see boundaries not only as being the agents of exclusion, but also agents of inclusion, i.e., as the means by which we test and renew our moral and other identities. This is important because the most common solution to the divisive and unacceptable pains of a tribalistic and local nationalism, namely that of universalist cosmopolitanism, can itself be divisive and exclusive. For though we might think of cosmopolitanism as a way in which we transcend these divisions and that the way forward is to include everyone in one universal identity, which will be all inclusive – we, all humans, citizens of the world – that assumes that that universal category is necessary and fixed. The problem, then, is that that itself might be exclusive, for it might fix the way we think of ourselves and blind us to what we are doing, making those on the outside invisible to us.

For Judith Butler, the universal is always historically contingent in that it will always be articulated in a certain context. It becomes articulated through challenges to its conventional formulation; the excluded set its contingent limit. Thus the universal becomes an ideal, for it is with that ideal in mind that we can resist the limit (the border where exclusion starts) and include those who are at the moment excluded – thereafter continually repeating the process. Thus, throughout our history, certain groups were not recognized as human and this was a way to deny them rights. We can see this in recent times with respect to Jews, Blacks and homosexuals (Butler, 1996).[20] Consider, for example, the history of the American Constitution, where 'all men' are at first white, slave-owning landowners, but where gradually, as that limit is confronted and resisted, the moral circle is tested and changed and given a new and different life (the election

20 Others, too, such as Peter Singer, have spoken of the expanding moral circle – though this is sometimes cast in an evolutionary discourse that offers a questionable rhetoric of moral progress.

of Barack Obama being an example). What functions as an exclusive universal is precisely that which is often most invisible to us, as when, even today, philosophers and others argue that human beings are distinctively rational (or meta-cognitive, or have sophisticated representational devices, or whatever else it might be) that then sets up an allegedly impregnable wall between humans and animals. According to some philosophers, the task and the difficulty of philosophy lies precisely in revealing, and loosening, such 'hinges' on which our thinking rests (e.g. see the papers in Cavell et al., 2008, responding to a leading paper by Cora Diamond).

Our ethic then is tested and transformed 'at the limit'. But the universalism at that limit or border can be seen as we have detailed above as opaque and impenetrable – there is nothing outside. We reach the limit and all we see at that border when we look beyond is ourselves. Lindahl's (2009) work on the logic of boundaries in the EU can illustrate this. Boundaries there, he says, include by excluding and exclude by including. Thus the internal market that is created within the EU is both a closure – it excludes the outside from that market – and inclusion, because all are seen as part of the global market. But this idea of the market excludes non-market commonality. Europe includes its outsiders by seeing them as market citizens. There is a twofold binary opposition: that of domestic/foreign and own (*Heimweit*) and strange (*Fremdweit*). But those invisible borders also frame one's seeing and make the outside invisible. So the World Social Forum and other forms of polity or commonality are not seen; or, if they are, what is seen is not foreign and strange, but just another market. And so if we do not open up when we get to that limit things also stagnate. We construct a wall to keep the other out and in keeping them out we internally begin to purify ourselves from the other in our midst. So the homogenization of Europe through the market proceeds but there is also something more terrifying. In the name of this 'fortress Europe' that we are trying to create and the European identity that it entails, we also try and purify from within. We see those who are different in culture, religion and values as a danger. We can see this in the growth of European chauvinisms and racism, and the problem of EU citizenship, asylum and migrant labour (those who are already in Europe and those about to come in). Here again growth and progress are seen as more of the same. For convergence, that prospective partners become like the EU can be seen as only opening out to the 'outside' if these partners are already like us – the rigidity of the *acquis communitaire*.

5. Conclusion: Death and the Compass

In conclusion, we come to the final transition point, that between life and death. Why here? If one emphasizes, as we do in this chapter, the process of exchange in and around border zones, where persons and communities reconstruct themselves, moving in new and uncharted directions, then we also open up the figure of death: of the death of our previous selves or ways in which we understand who we are and where we belong. We move from somewhere – our previous demarcation, our current home, and thus also a kind of exclusion – and into a space, a form of inclusion, where we open out ourselves to others and learn from them and are changed by them. In so doing, we leave our old forms of demarcation and strategies for withdrawal behind.

As long as we allow ourselves to dwell in those transitional zones, on the doorstep, our selves will always be 'dying' and recreating. The fear of that ontological insecurity, however, can certainly lead us, sometimes violently, to resist change (or, as we might put it here, the death of our previous self). In trying to conquer this death, we can too easily escape back into the stasis of a fixed identity and law. We then erect barriers around ourselves so that we can resist change and keep ourselves (as we currently understand ourselves) safe; we strive to remain within that which we are comfortable. This also applies to communities and states. For example, part of the fear of immigration is that our national identity will die with the influx of 'alien' cultures; part of the fear of the EU opening out toward Turkey is the fear of Islam swamping our 'Judeo-Christian Heritage'.[21]

It is natural for us to be anxious about such a journey. As we have said throughout, persons and individuals need a clearing, a home. This form of safety and stability is important. But we risk stinting our growth and development if we do not open up to the outside, taking the risk to go forward without knowing our final destination. One way in which we can instigate this journey is precisely by transforming borders-as-lines into borders-as-spaces. We can think of this journey more or less abstractly, or, as scholars, as distant from the practice of scholarship. Nothing could be further from the truth. What we have tried to do in this chapter is mirror, methodologically, what we propose substantively, seeking to turn borders-as-lines (in this case, disciplinary borders) into border-as-spaces, i.e. in this chapter, zones organized via images, which gather up parables, anecdotes, stories, glances, glimpses and stares; repertoires of echoes that offer opportunities for encounter, exchange, interaction, transformation. We finish with a final image and wish Roger a good journey in his retirement.[22]

Bibliography

Andreas, P. 2000. *Border Games: Policing the US-Mexico Divide*. Ithaca, Cornell University Press.

Arendt, H. 1961. *Between Past and Future: Six Exercises in Political Thought*. London, Faber and Faber.

Auerbach, E. 2003; 1946. *Mimesis: The Representation of Reality in Western Literature*. Translated by W.R. Trask. Princeton, Princeton University Press.

---

21 Consider the following statements: 'Europe is a cultural continent, not a geographical one. It is its culture that gives it a common identity. The roots that have formed it, that have permitted the formation of this continent, are those of Christianity. [...] In this sense, throughout history Turkey has always represented another continent, in permanent contrast with Europe. There were the wars against the Byzantine empire, the fall of Constantinople, the Balkan wars, and the threat against Vienna and Austria. That is why I think it would be an error to equate the two continents. It would mean a loss of richness, the disappearance of culture for the sake of economic benefits. Turkey, which is considered a secular country but is founded upon Islam, could instead attempt to bring to life a cultural continent together with some neighboring Arab countries, and thus become the protagonist of a culture that would possess its own identity but would also share the great humanistic values that we should all acknowledge. This idea is not incompatible with close and friendly forms of association and collaboration with Europe, and would permit the development of unified strength in opposition to any form of fundamentalism' (per Joseph Ratzinger in *Le Figaro Magazine*, August 13, 2004); 'Historically and culturally, Turkey has little in common with Europe; for this reason, it would be a great error to incorporate it into the European Union. It would be better for Turkey to become a bridge between Europe and the Arab world, or to form together with that world its own cultural continent. Europe is not a geographical concept, but a cultural one, formed in a sometimes conflictual historical process centered upon the Christian faith, and it is a matter of fact that the Ottoman empire was always in opposition to Europe. Even though Kemal Atatürk constructed a secular Turkey during the 1920's, the country remains the nucleus of the old Ottoman empire; it has an Islamic foundation, and is thus very different from Europe, which is a collection of secular states with Christian foundations, although today these countries seem to deny this without justification. Thus the entry of Turkey into the EU would be anti-historical' (in a speech to pastoral workers, September 18, 2004, in *Il Giornale del Popolo*, Lugano). After his papal visit to Turkey in November 2006 this line appears to have softened.

22 http://nodestone.com/wp-content/uploads/2008/05/leunig_cartoon.jpg.

Bańkowski, Z. 1999. 'The Journey of the European Ideal'. In A. Morton (ed.), *A Europe of Neighbours*, 149–72. Edinburgh, Centre for Theology and Public Issues, University of Edinburgh.
Bańkowski, Z. 2001. *Living Lawfully: Love in Law and Law in Love*. Dordrecht, Kluwer.
Bańkowski, Z. and Christodoulidis, E. 1998. 'The European Union as an Essentially Contested Concept'. 4 *European Law Journal*, 341–54.
Bańkowski, Z. and Del Mar, M. 2013. *The Moral Imagination and the Legal Life: Beyond Text in Legal Education*. Farnham, Ashgate.
Bańkowski, Z., Del Mar, M. and Maharg, P. 2013. *The Arts and the Legal Academy: Beyond Text in Legal Education*. Farnham, Ashgate.
Bańkowski, Z. and Mungham, G. 1976. *Images of Law*. London, Routledge.
Bańkowski, Z. and Schafer, B. 2007. 'Double-click Justice: Legalism in the Computer Age'. 1 *Legisprudence*, 31–49.
Barghouti, M. 2000. *I Saw Ramallah*. New York, Anchor Books.
Benjamin, W. 2002. *The Arcades Project*. Edited by R. Tiedemann. Translated by H. Eiland and K. McLaughlin. New York, Belknap Press.
Buchanan, A. and Moore, M. (eds) 2003. *States, Nations, and Borders: the Ethics of Making Boundaries*. Cambridge, Cambridge University Press.
Butler, J. 1996. 'Universality in Culture'. In M. Nussbaum et al. *For Love of Country: Debating the Limits of Patriotism*. Edited by J. Cohen. New York, Beacon Press.
Calvino, I. 1979. *Se una notte d'inverno un viaggiatore*. Torino, Einaudi. 45–52.
Cavell, S., Diamond, C., McDowell, J., Hacking, I. and Wolf, C. 2008. *Philosophy and Animal Life*. New York, Columbia University Press.
Clarke, R. 1992. *Situational Crime Prevention*. New York, Harrow and Heston.
Czyżewski, K. 2003. 'A Time for the Province', unpublished essay, last accessed on pogranicze.sejny.pl in 2008.
Czyżewski, K. Undated. 'Limes & Agora', unpublished essay, last accessed on pogranicze.sejny.pl in 2008.
Davis, M. 2005. 'The Great Wall of Capital'. In M. Sorkin (ed.), *Against the Wall: Israel's Barrier to Peace*, 88–99. New York, The New Press.
Del Mar, M. (2013). 'Thinking in Images in Legal Theory'. In M. Del Mar and C. Michelon (eds), *The Anxiety of the Jurist: Legality, Exchange and Judgement*, 43–68. Farnham, Ashgate.
Donnan, H. and Wilson, T.M. 1999. *Borders: Frontiers of Identity and Nation State*. Oxford, Berg Publishers.
Jones, R. 2008. 'Checkpoint Security: Gateways, Airports and the Architecture of Security'. In K.F. Aas, H.O. Gundhus, and H.M. Lomel (eds), *Technologies of Insecurity: the Surveillance of Everyday Life*. London, Routledge.
Kapuściński, R. 1994. *Imperium*. London, Granta Books.
Kerrigan, S. and Law, K.H. 2003. *Logic-Based Regulation and Compliance-Assistance. Proceedings of ICAIL, International Conference on Artificial Intelligence and Law* (ICAIL-03). ACM Press.
Lessig, L. 1999. *Code and Other Laws of Cyberspace*. New York, Basic Books.
Lindahl, H. 2009. 'In Between: Immigration, Distributive Justice, and Political Dialogue'. 8 *Contemporary Political Theory*, 415–34.
MacCormick, N. and Weinberger, O. 1986. *An Institutional Theory of Law*. Dordrecht, Reidel.
Milbank, J. 1996. 'Socialism of the Gift, Socialism by Grace'. 77 *New Blackfriars*, 532–54.

Morehouse, B. 2005. 'Theoretical Approaches to Border Spaces and Identities'. In V. Pavlakovich-Kochi, B. Morehouse and D. Wastl-Walter (eds), *Challenged Borderlands: Transcending Political and Cultural Boundaries*, 19–39. Aldershot, Ashgate.
Nussbaum, M. et al. 1996. *For Love of Country: Debating the Limits of Patriotism*. Edited by J. Cohen. New York, Beacon Press.
Papademetriou, D. and Waller Meyers, D. (eds) 2001. *Caught in the Middle: Border Communities in an Era of Globalisation*. Washington, Carnegie Endowment for International Peace.
Perec, G. 1969. *La Disparition*. Paris, Gallimard.
Perec, G. 1994. *A Void*. Translated by G. Adair. London, The Harvill Press.
Perec, G. 1997. *El Secuestro*. Translated by M. Arbués, M. Burrel, M. Parayre, H. Salceda and R. Vega. Barcelona, Anagrama.
Plant, R. 2001. *Politics, Theology and History*. Cambridge, Cambridge University Press.
Shklar, J. 1986. *Legalism*. London, Harvard University Press.
Stout, J. 2004. *Democracy and Tradition*. Princeton, Princeton University Press.
Sulga, G. 2001. *The Problem of Trieste and the Italo-Yugoslav Border: Difference, Identity, and Sovereignty in Twentieth-Century Europe*. Albany, State University of New York Press.
Teubner, G. 1993. *Law as an Autopoietic System*. Oxford, Blackwell.
Toulier, B. 2005. 'Mental Territory – the Celtic Connection'. In G. Dolff-Bonekämper (ed.), *Dividing Lines, Connecting Lines: Europe's Cross-Border Heritage*, 141–7. Council of Europe.
Weber, M. 1991. 'Science as Vocation'. In H. Gerth, and C. Wright Mills (eds), *Max Weber: Essays in Sociology*. London, Routledge.
Williams, J. 2006. *The Ethics of Territorial Borders: Drawing Lines in the Shifting Sand.* New York, Palgrave Macmillan.
Williams, R. 2008. 'Civil and Religious Law in England: a Religious Perspective'. Foundation Lecture delivered at the Royal Courts of Justice, 7 February 2008.
Winter, S. 2001. *A Clearing in a Forest: Law, Life and Mind*. Chicago, Chicago University Press.
Ziegert, K. 2002. 'Introduction to the Transaction Edition'. In E. Ehrlich, *Fundamental Principles of the Sociology of Law*. London, Transaction Publishers.

Chapter 4

Brave New World? The Challenges of Transnational Law and Legal Pluralism to Contemporary Legal Theory

Sionaidh Douglas-Scott

In 2002–03, I co-taught the University of London LLM Law and Social Theory option every week with Roger Cotterrell, Alan Norrie and Amanda Perry-Kessaris.[1] It was an extremely enriching experience. As well as discussing the classics of social theory, we also considered challenges to 'liberal' conceptions of law in the twentieth century from authors such as Karl Schmidt, Hannah Arendt, Jürgen Habermas and those of the Frankfurt School. We looked at the difficult questions posed by EU law and globalization to more traditional theories of law based on state sovereignty. I had already encountered legal pluralism in my own research into EU and human rights law and I had also known Roger's work on jurisprudence for many years, having been captivated by *The Politics of Jurisprudence* at an early stage in my career. But it was only in 2002, in the context of teaching this LLM course, that I started to think in earnest about legal pluralism and its challenges to modern analytical conceptions of law – and for that, I owe a great deal to discussions with Roger, Alan and Amanda, and in particular, to reading many of Roger's deeply insightful and engaging writings about the nature of law.

In *The Politics of Jurisprudence*, Cotterrell (2003: 15) urges, 'Rather than close off law analytically, legal theory should interpret it in ever widening perspectives. As the attempt to understand law as a social phenomenon, legal theory should *require* that the limited views of law held by different kinds of participants in legal processes … be confronted with wider theoretical perspectives that can incorporate and transcend these partial views and thereby broaden understanding of the nature of law'. Yet Cotterrell (2003: 16) continues by reminding us that this is not what legal theory has traditionally done. Instead, legal theory has 'typically asked how it is possible to organize in intellectually satisfying ways diverse doctrinal materials and modes of juristic thought'. Such an endeavour will always be fraught with circularities as well as personal prejudices.

In this chapter, I contemplate other ways of theorizing about law, which do not assert law as autonomous, nor seek to organize it neatly, but instead aim to situate law within a broader social context, allow for a variety of perspectives, and acknowledge law's messiness and disorder. In particular, I consider the challenges of legal pluralism and transnational law to more established ways of legal thinking – a debate in which Roger Cotterrell's work has played an important part.

1 Others were sometimes present – Kenneth Veitch and Tufyal Choudhury, and in subsequent years I also co-taught the same course with Susan Marks, Vanessa Munro and Mary Vogel at KCL.

1. Carving Out the Legal Field: From Legal Autonomy to 'Continuum Network'?

Cotterrell urged legal theory to consider law as a social phenomenon, to situate it, and understand it, within wider perspectives. Yet modern analytical jurisprudence has tended to accentuate an institutional distinctiveness of law from other areas of society, portraying law as a discrete, autonomous discipline, which has an existence in its own right, and may be identified without recourse to moral, value-laden principles.[2]

The critique of legal autonomy asserts that it is problematic to distinguish laws from other normative elements in society – whether one looks to their origin, essence or function in order to do so. It suggests that 'law' is a much broader phenomenon than is often admitted. Such a roomier domain for law has for some time been asserted by pluralists. Earlier pluralists such as Ehrlich (1936) or Malinowski (1926) found law in many places, identifying a coalescence of law with religion, custom, morality, decorum, fashion and etiquette, to the extent that Ehrlich believed jurisprudence to be merely a branch of sociology. Legal anthropologists such as Sally Falk Moore (1972/73) have characterized law as 'semi-autonomous' from, and dynamically interrelated with, other fields. The American legal theorist, Lon Fuller (1965), challenged the positivist tendency to equate law with state authority, instead insisting that law resulted from human interaction, and that activities could be 'more or less' legal, a matter of degree – and he thereby also located law in universities, clubs and associations, proclaiming these to be 'miniature legal systems'. More recently, the theme of pluralism has been embraced by Sousa Santos (2002), for whom much of our social world takes the form of law, including instances that are very informal or unwritten. He describes a cluster of 'interpenetrating legalities', whereby law moves from the old and familiar to the new and innovative, becoming in the process tangled, fluid and difficult to pin down.

A significant dimension of contemporary law is its presence at a transnational level, above and beyond the nation state, whether promulgated by states, international bodies or private parties (Cotterrell 2012). In these contexts too, legal pluralism has become a popular legal theory. Indeed, proponents of legal pluralism are in spirited, expansive mood, making claims such as the following: 'law is everywhere … there has been and still is law without jurisprudence, even law without laws, without legal doctrine, without lawyers' (Fogen 2002: 15, my translation). While such claims may be immoderate, they are evidence of a perception of law's prevalence and ubiquity – an indication that this is something that should be taken into account.

Analytical jurisprudence, with its focus on institutional law from diverse theorists such as Hart, Kelsen or Dworkin, often appears reluctant to capture the hugely varied regulatory practices of contemporary law and governance. Yet law generates organizations that supervise and recognize (in addition to those that promulgate, command and forbid) and that do so in dissimilar and apparently 'non-legal' ways.

Nonet and Selznick (1978) identified a movement from autonomous to 'responsive' law, an evolving concept of law that has become less formal and more purposive and interdisciplinary. In so doing, they reiterated the project of the American legal realists: to make law 'more responsive to social needs' (Frank 1932). Such an approach views law not as a discrete tool external to social life, which can be used to shape society, but instead interprets law as an aspect of social experience. A further example of a search for a legal theory more accommodating to the diversity of legal practices may be found in Gunther Teubner's (1983) advocacy of 'reflexive' law. Teubner argued that reflexive law could be relieved of the burden of direct regulation, instead supporting

2 This last claim is often described as the 'sources' thesis, a feature of theories of law, such as those of Raz, for example, who believe that law must be identified only in terms of its social sources.

and underpinning self-regulation of practices. As examples of such reflexivity he suggested self-regulation of the internet – for example, distribution of domain names by ICANN.[3]

In our survey of the legal field, we may also notice a decline in any sharp distinction between public and private law, together with what Santos (1980: 391) characterized as 'a dislocation of power from formal institutions to informal networks'. As Cotterrell (2002: 632) has suggested, this approach, 'highlights regulation's fluidity, ubiquity and varied consequences, making it possible to describe law as a continuum network or web of regulatory practices or techniques'. Furthermore, an alertness to a broader spectrum of law highlights the complex interrelations between state agencies, 'quasi-government', and the 'private' disciplinary strategies and normative practices that pervade social life – thus avoiding an increasingly implausible public–private dichotomy. For example, EU law makes use of a wide range of alternative regulatory instruments, such as the Open Method of Co-ordination (OMC), benchmarking, peer pressure, networks and standardization in order to circumnavigate the problem of trying to attain a (often impossible) consensus under traditional international intergovernmental law making.[4] Such Governance lacks the 'command and control' measures of traditional law and government. It derives instead from multiple sources of authority – rather than legal hierarchy and the monopoly of force, and it often takes the form of flexible, voluntary measures and fluid, soft law. On account of its multiple and diverse origins, which derive from a plurality of social and cultural sources, it requires a broader investigation from legal, social, cultural and political perspectives if we are to fully evaluate and understand it.

2. 'Expansive' Legal Pluralism

A popular definition of legal pluralism interprets it as an empirically verifiable situation in which two or more legal orders exist in the same juridical space. Presented thus, it appears deceptively straightforward. This still leaves the question of what is to count as a 'legal' order, however. What first appears to be a question of social fact or description may swiftly become normatively charged by evaluations as to *what features* are to be included in the category 'law'.

'Expansive' legal pluralism[5] insists that we be aware of a rich variety of conceptions of law, some incommensurable, suggesting that the dominant Western unitary concept of law is not universal as some of its proponents present it to be, but somewhat more limited and culturally specific, although it has sometimes succeeded in marginalizing other types of law as 'primitive' or defective. Expansive legal pluralism also urges that we acknowledge a continuation, or overlap, between law and other forms of life. Yet this raises some thorny issues. For, if law can span many features of society, when do we dispense with the term 'law' and admit instead to a larger plane of social interaction? Twining (2009) refers to these problems as that of 'definitional stop' – of where to draw the line between the legal and the non-legal.

Ultimately, an overly elastic application of the designation 'legal' might stifle one's ability to talk about law at all. Some writers go so far as to eschew the term law – using instead 'regulation',[6]

---

3 The Internet Corporation for Assigned Names and Numbers (ICANN) is an internationally organized, non-profit corporation that has responsibility for Internet Protocol (IP) address space allocation, protocol identifier assignment, generic (gTLD) and country code (ccTLD) Top-Level Domain name system management.

4 See European Commission, *White Paper on European Governance* (COM(2001) 428 final); and subsequent 'Inter-institutional Agreement on Better Lawmaking' (2003/C 321/01).

5 A term I use in *Law After Modernity*, 2013, Chapter 4.

6 In itself as flexible and problematic a concept as 'law'.

or some other yet more general term to encompass the myriad of practices involved. For example, Rose and Valverde (1998) employ the concept of a 'governable space', which consists of a patchwork of local laws, by-laws and regulation which does not partake of the abstract, universal nature of statute law. 'Governable spaces' are made up of different types of authority – merchants' associations, landlords, shopping complexes and local authorities, which produce codes that embody specific types of desirable or undesirable conduct.

It seems an extreme solution to dispense with the term 'law' altogether. Yet, if everything is complex and variable, how can it be possible to pin down law, or use the term in anything other than a bland and imprecise manner, rendering it useless as a conceptual tool? Does legal pluralism commit one to a wide nominalism, or radical indeterminacy about law? Perhaps all that can be said is – there is this type of law, and those types of law – or should we go even further and cease searching for a precise usage of the term law and instead focus on what is practically treated as law (e.g. Griffiths 2005)? Yet, if 'Law' simply is whatever people identify and treat through their social practices as law, there is a danger of a resigned nominalism taking over, rendering law ephemeral and contingent in nature. This is a disturbing conclusion for some theorists, who assert that there is an 'ideological quality' in legal pluralism's insistence in attaching the label 'law' to different normative orders that may be fundamentally different (Roberts 2005). Will they all concur with their rescue as 'legal'? Does such nominalism as to the meaning of law benefit subaltern or non-official types of law, or does it further empower those who are already powerful enough, such as an elite international business community, enabling it to fashion client-friendly practices into a more official sounding *lex mercatoria* to suit its own needs? Further, if one legal order takes precedence over others, perhaps this is not because it represents some 'focal' or 'core' instance of law but rather a matter of political power – of its ability to impose itself on the rest? This of course says nothing about the desirability of the more peripheral types of law either – indeed, for this reason there is nothing necessarily ethically superior about pluralism – each of the plurality may be good, bad or indifferent.

Notwithstanding these vexed questions, I believe it is necessary to engage with legal pluralism, because it provides a plausible, although ultimately both complicated and demanding, account of the current legal space. Legal pluralism is not itself perfect as a theory. Benda-Beckmann (2002: 40), for example, refers to legal pluralism as a 'useful analytical tool' but not a theory or explanation. While apparently at first offering a better empirical 'fit' of contemporary practises, on closer inspection, it fails to dissolve some of the oldest problems of legal theory, such as that of the nature of law. However, it may be that at least some of these problems present false conundrums. This is because of a tendency to present definitions of the concept 'law' in the misleading guise of a straightforward 'Either/Or' choice between a single, unified concept of law with clear boundaries, or a messy over-inclusive pluralism. A better claim is that these different definitions are dependent on context. From one perspective, that of empirical, descriptive investigation, the contemporary legal space already exists as a messy pluralist world. It could not be transformed into an orderly, united, uncomplicated one if only it were possible to find the right analytical tools to do so – there exists no such Holy Grail, or 'key to the science of jurisprudence'. Seen differently, however, from the internal perspective of a practising legal profession, 'law' may look very different, as a working assumption of coherence, containment and even integrity.

The conclusion is surely not to limit the scope of legal theory to the one 'right' point of view, always inevitably a singular, limited perspective, nor to seek a universal jurisprudence, inevitably so general as to be commonplace, and at its most general what I have characterized elsewhere as a 'banal' positivism, but rather, as Cotterrell insists, to require legal theory to be confronted by ever widening perspectives.

3. From Legal System to Legal Pluralism?

The second of Cotterrell's observations highlighted at the outset of this chapter noted the tendency of modern legal theory to 'organize in intellectually satisfying ways' diverse materials and modes of thought. Yet the attempt to classify and organize is liable to misrepresent law and unify it into something it is not: no doubt a harmony desired by some, but unrealistic and inadequate to characterize the complexity and multiplicity of our contemporary legal world.

Undoubtedly, modern legal theory has often pursued order and tidiness. As Mireille Delmas-Marty (2002: 7) has written, 'An orderly landscape. That is what we want. We ask law for a little order, to protect us from disorder'. Since the times of Hobbes and Grotius in the seventeenth century, 'law has presented itself as the antithesis to fragmentation, leading from the chaos of civil war to unified nation, from inter-state anarchy to an international legal community' (Koskenniemi 2005). Austin wished his work, *The Province of Jurisprudence,* to be 'a region of order and light' by analogy to his impressions of the Roman *Corpus Iuris Civilis*, and believed that, once law was presented as a well-organized subject, it would gain respect within the university environment. Austin's language is striking, and indeed employed by Cotterrell as a heading in Chapter 3 (on Bentham and Austin) of *The Politics of Jurisprudence,* which is entitled 'The Empire of Darkness and the Region of Light'. Austin was not alone in his desire for order – Hart argued that modern law could be distinguished from 'primitive' law by its systematic quality, which, for Hart, takes the form of law as the union of primary and secondary rules, with the Rule of Recognition as the overarching, unifying feature of the system. Hart described this union as the key to the science of jurisprudence – believing that, only when rules form a *system* can we overcome the defects of 'primitive' law, namely its uncertainty, its static nature and its inefficiency. And, to be sure, concern with system is not singular to legal positivism. We also find it in Durkheim and Parsons, Hegel and Marx – concern with 'system' is one of the key features of modernity.

Nevertheless, we may note the historical particularity of legal positivism's orderly impulse. Weber described the modern law era as one of 'disenchantment', and the positivist project to 'demystify' the law may well be seen as a parallel enterprise. Legal positivism, a theory which has tended to pay little attention to history (usually preferring ahistorical techniques of abstract thought) is itself historically situated in seeking to distinguish itself from the perceived 'disorder' of the earlier common law vision. Yet law's historical bearings were acknowledged by Weber (1954), who characterized modern law as 'formal legal rationality', in contrast to the 'charismatic' or 'traditional' authorities of former times. Weber considered that modern law, or at least modern Western law of his time, was *rational* in that it was governed by rules and principles, systematic, intentionally created, logical, clear and self-contained, and, for Weber, formally rational law found its finest examples in the 'legal science'[7] codes of the 19th century German Pandectists.[8] Weber distinguished legal rational authority from law deriving from 'traditional' types of authority, which, for him, lacked the impersonal, formal characteristics of modern law. For Weber, modern

7 The work of the Pandectists is matched by similar developments in the US – e.g. formalists such as Langdell. The purpose of the Restatement projects in the US was to establish a grand consensus, enlightened by legal science, on fundamental principles of common law and to give precision to the use of legal terms, and to make law uniform throughout the US. The scientific impulses of John Austin's work have already been noted.

8 For example, those of Windscheid, a now rather forgotten figure, who infamously suggested that political, moral and economic arguments were irrelevant to the 'lawyer as such', being out of step with argumentative legal reality. Windsheid's major work was *Lehrbuch des Pandektenrechts* (Leipzig: 1862, 1970 reprint).

law had two key features: comprehensiveness – in that no social actions lay beyond its reach, and organizational clarity – such that the principles according to which it was constructed were organizationally clear and self-contained (Kronman 1983).

This desire for organizational clarity is also to be found in Kelsen, as well as in the work of the English positivists. Even in the seventeenth century, Thomas Hobbes (1946: 105) employed lively architectural and organizational metaphors to expound his theory. He suggested that, if a constitution is to be anything other than 'a crasie building, such as hardly lasting out of their own time', then it must be constructed with 'the help of a very able Architect', continuing that, 'The skill of making and maintaining Common-wealths consisteth in certain Rules, as doth Arithmetique and Geometry; not (as Tennis-Play) on Practise onely'. Hobbes' theory was, of course, partly driven by the need for social order and peace in the face of a perceived brutal State of Nature (and also by the brutal actualities of seventeenth century England). However, more than 300 years on from Hobbes, comparable architectural metaphors were employed in the context of the European Union. The EU, which was created by the Maastricht treaty of 1992,[9] was constructed as a structure with 'three pillars'[10] across which it was seen to be desirable for there to be consistency and unity, rather than an unsystematic Europe of 'bits and pieces' (Curtin 1994).[11] The modern legal world has been characterized by an impulse toward 'constitutionalization' – testimony of a desire for a systematic, unified and comprehensive law. Such impulses have their roots in the earlier constitutional codifications of the eighteenth century, particularly those following the French and American revolutions, but continue today in the move toward constitutionalization of EU law and international law, and even appear in the field of legal pluralism – as a device by which pluralism's lack of system and ordering may be reined in (Kumm 2004; Walker 2002).

Indeed, in much legal theory, the terms 'Law' and 'legal system' have been used interchangeably. For Joseph Raz (1980: 2), to comprehend the nature of law is to understand it as a legal *system*. Use of the term 'system' implies a wholeness, a unity of constituent parts or elements that are related in ways that aggregates or collections are not. 'System' suggests a pattern of sorts, or an order of interlocking parts – sense and not randomness. In conceiving law as system, the aim of such an organizational project was, at least for the earlier legal positivists, to provide some sort of certainty and unity of the law. In this way, the law could appear predictable, and people would know where they stood – seen as particularly important to a growing business community, and thus law and capitalism become linked. This unity was presented both as unity of law as a mode of organization and also as a unified understanding of legal experience, and by so doing also provided law with self-validation. It is, however, important to underline that law as system is a mode of construction, an organizational project, rather than a mere representation of laws that actually were organized and clear.[12]

Nor need we restrict our observation of the desire for order and harmony in law to legal positivism. Dworkin's legal theory seeks to find coherence and integrity in law, indeed Dworkin argued that judges are actually required to decide cases in such a way (often by relying on a set

9 As opposed to the EEC, which had been in existence since the treaty of Rome of 1957.

10 The three pillars which made up the EU being the EEC itself (which retained its separate EC treaty) the EU's common foreign and security policy, and thirdly, policies in the area of Justice and Home Affairs. The tripartite pillar structure was abolished by the treaty of Lisbon in 2009, which consolidated all three pillars into a single, unitary structure.

11 Yet the present day EU, with its 'variable geometry' and confusing melée of treaties and law, lacks a well-ordered architectonic structure.

12 Although Austin and Hart do sometimes write as if their work were in fact describing existing practice, i.e. Hart's characterization of *The Concept of Law* as 'an essay in descriptive sociology'.

of principles) that the law is presented as coherent and appears to be the product of a single moral vision. Such a theory places greater demands for order and coherence even than positivism, as it requires not only a coherence in legal theory, but also, at least to a certain extent, in moral theory.

4. Undermining the System

Yet law is not so easily categorized and organized. For example, as Hart so notably pointed out, Austin ignored the variety of laws by restricting laws to the concept of a command, ignoring the ways in which laws function as powers or permissions, and thus the way in which law facilitates – as do areas of contract or testamentary law. Yet, Hart's own system is not watertight. For Hart, as for Weber, law is institutionalized norm enforcement. However, Hart's neat division of laws into primary (duty imposing) and secondary (power conferring) rules distorts a less tidy reality. Are primary rules necessarily duty imposing when much of contract law (which Hart seems to term 'primary') confers *power* on parties to organize, regulate and change their affairs (something which Hart (1994: 96) himself termed private acts of legislation). Similar troubles also bedevil the all-important Rule of Recognition, supposedly the linchpin of Hart's system, which distinguishes 'law' from all other social means of control. Is it, to use Hart's terminology, duty imposing or power conferring? It appears to be duty imposing – requiring officials to recognize things as laws, but, if so, it takes on an unfortunate circularity because officials end up recognizing the rule which recognizes them as officials.

A focus on law as unified and systematic has been understood as requiring a unity of law within the state. Yet is it the case that there should be only one keystone, just one Rule of Recognition or Basic Norm, as stipulated by Hart and Kelsen, for whom the unity of a legal system is essential. For surely laws may derive their essential validity from different sources? English domestic law may derive its validity from a domestic source, but EU law as applied in England may derive its validity from another source – through a decision of the ECJ in Luxemburg, or from the EU treaties or secondary legislation.[13] Judge-made common law and legislation may also have different ultimate sources as argued by Raz (2002: 147).[14] Hart's solution is to dismiss such examples as 'substandard', 'abnormal' or 'deviant' cases (Hart 1994: 123). Yet one could hardly call EU law deviant, given its prevalence and huge importance.

For the earlier positivists (but also later legal thinkers such as Schmitt) divided sovereignty was simply a contradiction in terms and the doctrine of sovereignty was the doctrine of the *unity* of states (*pace* Bentham and the framers of the US federal constitution).[15] A unified legal system was perceived as a key advance of modernity, rectifying the fragmented forms of feudalism and the common law.[16] Dicey (1986/1886), for example, criticized federalism as leading to weak government. He attacked Irish Home Rule, accusing it of undermining the British Constitution,

13 Some interpretations of the nature of EU law would dispute this, deriving the ultimate authority of EU law in its member states from national constitutions, i.e. from the state act which gave effect to EU law in their territory, in the UK this being the European Communities Act 1972.

14 Yet, Raz, while providing a more flexible account, which could accommodate some element of pluralism, still refers to law as a 'system'.

15 See Hart 'Bentham on sovereignty' in Hart 1982, for consideration of Bentham's views on the possibility of divided sovereignty. The US federal constitution of course provides possibly the first example of federalism – a division of sovereignty par excellence.

16 In contrast, Harold Berman (1983) has described the radical legal pluralism of feudalism as 'perhaps the most distinctive feature of the western legal tradition'.

of which he wrote that, '(The) secret source of strength is the omnicompetence, the sovereignty of Parliament'. Where foreign or international law was included at all by twentieth century positivists it was appropriated by their schematic approach (usually at the price of distortion) which squeezed it into a well worn hierarchy. Modern law has also been monist – even though Kelsen (1967) took international law seriously, he stipulated a monist unity of laws, with international law at its apex, tantamount to an account of national law with global dimensions. Where writers were more pluralistic in approach, they tended to be perceived as marginal (sometimes literally – as in the case of Eugen Ehrlich, who writing at the University of Czernitz at the fringes of the old Austro-Hungarian empire, in present day Romania, lamented 'the tragic fate of juristic science' which he complained was devoted 'exclusively to state law' (Ehrlich 1936; Cotterrell 2008). But legal pluralism may no longer be dismissed as 'marginal' and there is now a growing recognition of its highly significant advances – dating back at least as far as those of the framers of the US Constitution who 'split the atom of sovereignty'.[17]

Furthermore, postmodern theory has not shared a desire for order and system, characterizing attempts to systematize law as 'grand narratives' (Douzinas and Warrington 1991). Lyotard (1979) refers to the ideology of the 'system', with its pretensions to totality. He characterizes systematic totality as a silencing of other knowledges, identifying it as a form of 'terror'. Cornell (1992: 94) alludes to Kafka's metaphor of the penal colony, likening the legal subject to the prisoner of modern law and jurisprudence, with its legal propositions etched on its backs, just as was the sentence of Kafka's prisoner in the penal colony. This is in contrast to the conception of Hobbes, who saw social order, and with it organized law, as essential to peace and well-being. The point to note is that propulsion toward order, legal 'system' and the organizational impulse, are capable of becoming oppressive, and not always benign in nature.

In any case, if the notion of 'legal system' is taken as the baseline, then there will be some requirement of orderliness, and structure, which will make it hard to accommodate flailing loose ends, or overlapping or conflicting sources of authority. Even more problematic are the developments in law beyond the state which will now be addressed.

5. Complexity and Multiplicity in Transnational Law

The legal landscape is not orderly and clear. Legal ensembles are untidy and tangled, because law's benchmarks and boundaries are not so easily identifiable. Indeed, Brian Simpson (2011: 139) referred to the 'mind boggling complexity' of UK law, including commonwealth and colonial laws, in 1961, the date of publication of the first edition of Hart's *The Concept of Law*. There exists a profusion of different types of norm – rules, principles, maxims, provisos, ratio decidendi, obiter dicta and their relationship to each other is not always clear, nor hierarchical. Different jurisdictions and areas of law interlock in contemporary law in imprecise and weak or non-hierarchical ways – contrary to Hart's account, whereby rules relate to each other in a clearly hierarchical fashion. The legal world, while it may contain some examples of straightforward, hierarchical 'system', is also a world of crossings, hybrids, inverse hierarchies, fluctuations and fluidity of space. The law is complex in complex and sometimes strange ways.

One immediate way in which the multidimensionality, complexity and lack of unity of laws can be identified is to look at law beyond state boundaries. If we do so, law becomes very hard to systematize. Yet much modern legal theory has tended to focus on municipal law, ignoring the

17 On this, see *US Term Limits v Thornton* (1995) 514 US 779 per Kennedy J at 838.

broader picture. Austin placed the (national) sovereign at the apex of the legal system, denying international law the status of law at all. For Kelsen, state and law are the same thing, expressed in different ways. Hart tended to see international law as a deviant form of law, if indeed, as law at all.[18] With some notable exceptions, such as Neil MacCormick (1999), William Twining (2000 and 2009), Julie Dickson (2012) and Keith Culver and Michael Giudice (2010), analytical jurisprudence has not expressed great interest in developing a theory of law beyond the state. However, within non-state contexts, legal norms and institutions are forming new and intriguing relationships, and the concept of a legal 'system', at least, may be, as Culver and Giudice (2010: 74) suggest, 'outdated and outmoded' and of little conceptual value in explaining what is going on. For example, the EU describes itself as 'a new legal order',[19] seeking to differentiate itself from both state and traditional international law, and to distinguish itself as a legal order of a different kind.

In denying the usefulness of the term 'system', Culver and Giudice propound an 'inter-institutional theory of legality', arguing that laws should be understood not as separate and differentiated legal systems but rather as 'variegated combinations of legal institutions and function oriented, content led peremptory norms and associated normative powers', in which varying relations characterize legality rather than a particular relation to the state. They discern legality as 'shorn from officials, states and geography', to be understood in terms of intra-state, trans-state, supra-state and super-state institutions and norms interacting and engaging in 'mutual relations of varying intensity', appearing in individuals' lives as 'upwellings of normative force' (105, 112, 165).

Hardt and Negri (2000) argue that state-centred systems of power are swiftly unwinding in the face of the forces of world capitalism, and characterize 'Empire' as a system of governing principles without boundaries – an expansive, fluctuating territory – thus presenting a challenge to conventional national sovereignty. In many circumstances, such as the Single Market of the EU, borders have become less significant and legal judgements are frequently enforced across borders. There also exist many situations in which the jurisdiction asserted exceeds national sovereignty – for example, the extraterritorial application of US or EU antitrust, or competition, law. The UN Convention on Torture permits inspection of prisons by those authorized to do so, without any warning, within the territory of any party to the Convention. The internet challenges the geographical model of sovereignty, exceeding territorial jurisdiction in cyberspace, if not real space – making it very hard for states that wish to prohibit certain websites – such as Nazi propaganda in Germany – to do so. The state has therefore become decentred as a source of law and regulation, with other non-state institutions playing a variety of roles generating regulation. For example, the sixteenth century French jurist and political philosopher, Jean Bodin, described the coining of money as one of the 'traditional marks of sovereignty' – and yet this is now done by the EU Central Bank for those countries which are members of the euro, rather than by their national banks.

In other areas, institutions relate to each other in complex, not straightforwardly hierarchical, ways. For example, the Good Friday agreement created a power sharing assembly in Northern Ireland itself, but also a North–South council (i.e. Eire–Northern Ireland) and East–West (Northern Ireland–Westminster) institutions. In a more general context, Judge Gilbert Guillaume, President

18 For example, Hart writes, 'It is indeed arguable, as we shall show, that international law not only lacks secondary rules of change and adjudication … but also a unifying Rule of Recognition … These differences are striking and the question "Is international law really law?" can hardly be put aside' (Hart 1994: 214). He went on to conclude that international law was primitive because it lacked the secondary rules which qualify for a mature, fully developed legal system.

19 This is the famous description of the ECJ in Case 26/62 *Van Gend & Loos* (1963) ECR 1.

of the International Court of Justice, warned that a proliferation of international tribunals (i.e., specialist tribunals on human rights, law of the sea, environmental law and the European Court of Justice, the European Free Trade Association Court, the International Criminal Court, the International Criminal Tribunal for Yugoslavia and International Criminal Tribunal for Rwanda) taking place without any overall plan, might give rise to a serious risk of conflicting judgements, and also spoke of 'the danger of the fragmentation of the law'.[20]

The dissolving boundaries of public and private law have already been mentioned. The distinctions between foreign and domestic policy have also become much less clear within the EU – for example Single Market matters relating to trade fall within both domestic and foreign policy. The International Criminal Court has been described as 'a striking example of the postmodern breakdown of the distinction between domestic and foreign attitudes, whereby moral consciousness applies to international relations as well as domestic affairs' (Cooper 2003: 31). 'Soft' law has also become more important, and increasingly used. It is a term less used by national lawyers but beloved of international and EU lawyers for some time (Mörth 2004). 'Soft' law statements emanating from the European Commission, for example, may have a serious impact on the competition practices of companies, and although not officially legally binding, they may be capable of overriding some 'firm' legal rules. Transnational lawyers negotiate directly with each other, creating binding rules for clients – e.g., netting clauses for insolvency in the context of derivatives trading on global insolvency markets. These informal binding norms acquire such force that national governments are then under pressure to transform them into nationally binding legal norms.

Another example, that of human rights law, illustrates problems of complexity, classification and fluidity of boundaries. In addition to substantive complexity, there is structural complexity. The proliferation of international tribunals noted by Judge Guillaume increases the risk of conflicting judgements.[21] Yet even within a single form of human rights law, there is considerable structural complexity. For example, the recognition or interpretation of a right may depend on a reverse hierarchy. For instance, within the ECHR (European Convention on Human Rights), reference is frequently made to a 'margin of appreciation', namely domestic cultural standards, which may sometimes determine the ruling of the higher court, the European Court of Human Rights.[22] This 'margin of appreciation' may result in a differentiated impact, as illustrated by the coexisting decisions of *B* v *France* and *Rees* v *UK*,[23] which resulted in the different treatment of transsexuals in the UK and France for about 10 years under ECHR law.

A further example of structural complexity in human rights is provided by the EU, which, for the first 40 years of its existence, lacked its own Charter of Rights.[24] In the absence of an EU

20 Per Judge Guillaume, speech to UN General Assembly, 20/10/2000. See also 'Report of the Study Group on Fragmentation and International Law', UN GA OR 55th Session Supp No 10, UN Doc A/CN. 4/L.628, and Koskenniemi and Leino (2002).

21 This fear has been frequently expressed in the context of a possible conflict between the European Court of Human Rights and the European Court of Justice exercising its human rights jurisdiction. So far there has been no real conflict. However, the European Court of Human Rights in its *Loizidou* judgement (*Loizidou* (1995) Series A No 310), gave an interpretation of 'territorial reservations' which was different to that of the ICTY in its *Tadic* judgement (*The Prosecutor* v *Tadic* IT-94–1-A 15/7/99).

22 See e.g. *Handyside* v *UK* (1976) (Series A No. 24) for the European Court's explication of the 'margin of appreciation' doctrine.

23 *Rees* v *UK* (1987) 9 EHRR 56, *B.* v *France* (1993) 16 EHRR 1.

24 The EU *Charter of Fundamental Rights*, proclaimed in December 2000, finally became legally binding with the coming into force of the Treaty of Lisbon in 2009.

Charter, the EU instead imported rights from domestic and international law and then re-applied them to those same national systems in a two-way process of first upward and then downward incorporation. In this way, the state monopoly of broadcasting in Greece was challenged[25] by virtue of a right of freedom of expression derived initially from national law but applied through EU law in a circular looping route, illustrating a relationship of convertible hierarchies. Human rights protection in the EU has taken on a further dimension since 2000, when the EU was given its own dedicated Charter of Fundamental Rights, which was accorded legally binding force by the treaty of Lisbon in 2009. In the *Kadi* case, which concerned the freezing of the applicant's assets on grounds of alleged terrorism, the European Court of Justice referenced the Charter and stressed the primacy and importance of fundamental rights as constitutional principles of the EU treaty, even in the face of obligations under international law. This judgement raised the possibility of a fragmentation of international law, and even ultimately, the insulation of the ECJ from any international human rights standards, because of its choice to look instead to autonomous EU standards.[26]

Therefore, within Europe there now exists a plurality of human rights jurisdictions – domestic, ECHR and EU[27] – as illustrated by the *Bosphorus* case, in which a Turkish airline, whose aircraft had been seized under sanctions against former Yugoslavia, sued in all three of these jurisdictions over a total of 13 years – and lost in all three, illustrating that more choice does not necessarily equate with success for litigants. On a related point, the first European court to refer to the EU Charter of Fundamental Rights was not the EU Court of Justice but the Council of Europe Court of Human Rights[28] – an example of a 'crossing' of legal jurisdictions. However, since the EU Charter became binding in 2009, the ECJ has frequently used it as a basis for its case law, so ECJ case law on fundamental rights is also likely to become a reference point for the ECHR, and provide an example of further crossings. Indeed, the relationship between the EU and the ECHR will be yet further complicated by the planned accession of the EU to the ECHR.

Mireille Delmas-Marty (2002: 8), writing about European law generally, has described it as a situation where, 'incomplete pyramids surrounded by strange loops are mocking the old hierarchies'. European law reveals further interesting interactions and relationships between pluralities of laws and legal systems, indeed it is probably one of the best contemporary examples of legal pluralism, while EU law is one of the most striking examples of rapid legal development and different (sometimes incompatible) legal sources. On the one hand, EU law sees itself as a distinct legal order – it has acquired what MacCormick (1999) named 'self-referentiality'. It has developed its own doctrines and constitutional principles, and, as in the *Kadi* case, stresses the autonomy of EU law. Yet EU law also interlocks and interacts with municipal laws in a post-sovereign Europe, where there are no longer any absolutely sovereign states. In spite of the detailing of some areas as being within the 'exclusive' competence of the EU,[29] it is generally the case that competence is not neatly divided between the EU and its member states, but rather overlapping, symbiotic, incremental and unpredictable in nature. Whether the EU or its member states have competence depends on contingent past events (i.e., on whether the EU has taken some previous action, however small, to 'occupy the field') or on the interpretation or application of vague principles, such as the doctrines of proportionality and subsidiarity. Further, in introducing the concepts of the direct effect and supremacy of EU law, the ECJ has inserted and infused EU law

25 As in Case C-260/89 *ERT* [1991] ECR I-2925.

26 Joined Cases C-402/05P and C-415/05P *Kadi and Al Barakaat* v *Council* [2008] ECR I-6351.

27 And indeed, sometimes, even a fourth, international, dimension may also be at issue.

28 In *Goodwin* v *UK* [2002] 35 EHRR 18.

29 These specifications of EU competence were set out explicitly for the first time by the 2009 Treaty of Lisbon amendments.

into national law, rendering national law anything but hermetically sealed. Yet the EU relies on its member states to enforce and apply EU law and most EU law is litigated in national courts rather than the ECJ – a feature which is problematic for those legal theories (e.g., Raz 1980, 2002) which designate 'norm applying' institutions (i.e., courts) as indicative of distinct legal systems. For if member state courts function as both national and EU courts, then which legal 'system' is at issue when a national court is determining a point of EU law (Dickson 2012)?

Current EU law, therefore, well illustrates that legal systems may not be solid and palpable entities. Further, the European legal space is one of overlapping jurisdictions, segmented authority and multiple loyalties, carrying with it the risk of constitutional crisis and of officials being compelled to choose between their loyalties to different public institutions.

6. Brave New World?

Undeniably, the contemporary legal landscape is challenging. One recent theorist has characterized it as 'a rugged mountainous terrain', (Krisch 2010: 225) and another, describes its primary characteristics as 'imprecision, uncertainty, and instability or … the fuzzy and the soft' (Delmas-Marty 2009: 10).

The perplexities of systematizing and regularizing law have been revelled in as productive paradoxes by autopoiesis theorists (Luhmann 1986). Yet one might ask what is 'productive' about an account that is deceptive, suggesting an orderly landscape when the legal world in fact may be much more chaotic? Contradictions, aporia and a lack of closure are also enjoyed by deconstruction theory. Derrida (1992), who has described law as 'essentially deconstructible', therefore looks not for unity but difference in concepts generally.

Rather than interpreting the legal landscape as a rugged mountainous terrain, or revelling in its contradictions or aporia, or focusing on its perceived originary violence, I have argued (Douglas-Scott 2011, 2013) that it may be more usefully captured by the image of the Carina Nebula.[30]

The Carina Nebula is a vast complex of dust, stars, gas, forces and energy situated 7,500 light years from Earth. Interestingly, this particular image is a mosaic, compiled from 50 frames taken by the advanced camera for surveys on board the Hubble space telescope – interesting, because mosaics are patterns of complexity and intricacy themselves, composed of many interlocking pieces and patterns, and so appear particularly apposite as techniques for portraying contemporary complexity. The image portrays a region many hundreds of light years across, with huge quantities of solar material – stars of all sizes, masses, temperatures and brightnesses forming as well as dying, and gas and dust blown and whirling into all sorts of shapes. There are black holes, dark matter and all manner of imponderable, perplexing shapes. This is a beautiful but disturbing image. With its hugeness, its mysteries and multiplications, its black holes (to which contemporary law has not been immune (Steyn 2004)) it might be compared to the contemporary legal landscape.

In the face of this somewhat nebulous, indeterminate prospect, how to conceptualize law? As a first step legal pluralism (namely, a state of affairs, for any social field, in which behaviour pursuant to more than one legal order occurs) should now be seen as the most relevant and apposite theory of law, most capable of capturing the complexities of contemporary law. Yet, as we have already seen, legal pluralism is not itself uncomplicated. Many pluralists also include the further and distinct claim that not all law-like phenomena have their source in institutionalized law, which leads to

30 This extraordinary image of the Carina Nebula was released (by the Hubble science community) to celebrate its 6,209 days in space.

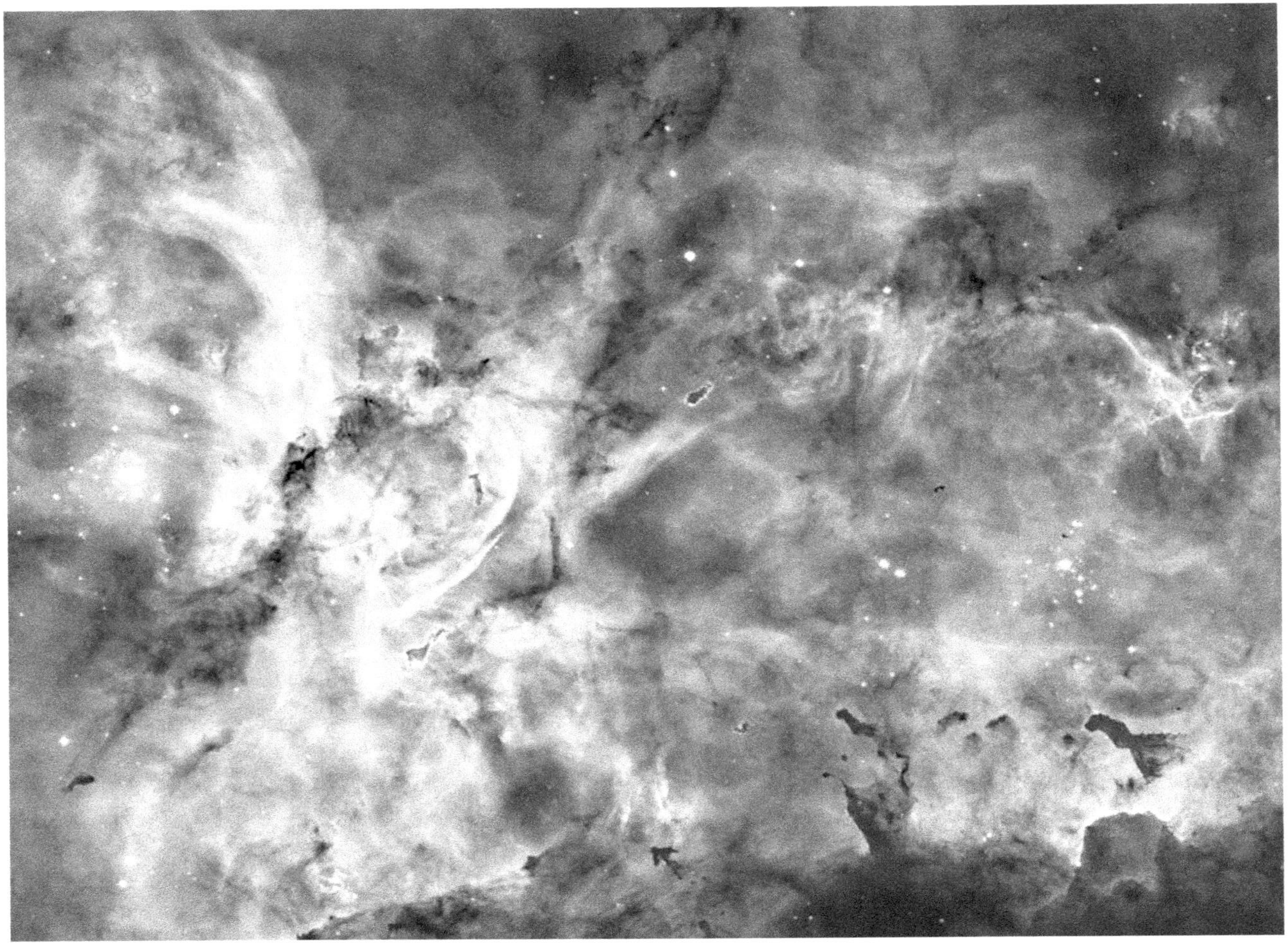

Figure 4.1 The Carina Nebula
Source: Wikimedia commons.

the problems of 'expansive' legal pluralism, already considered in this chapter. Legal pluralism is also usually taken to imply more than just a plurality of laws, but rather a situation in which two or more legal 'systems' coexist in the same societal field, sometimes in a contradictory way, in which each may have equally plausible claims to authority. Thereby, pluralism introduces incommensurability as a feature of legal life to be reckoned with, and, rather than a centralized unity of the legal field, legal relationships as constituted by the heterarchical interactions of different levels and sources of law. Notably, one crucial strand in contemporary pluralism is situated at transnational or global level, where a rich and often competing proliferation of rules and norms are to be found.

Unlike some contemporary theorists, I do not believe that pluralism, plurality, interlegality and the like, present themselves as ethically preferable positions (as opposed to more descriptively accurate) to those monist, or dualist accounts which cleave to notions of a more unified legal space. On the contrary, it is important to be aware that legal pluralism brings with it increased risks of a lack of accountability, or of self-regulating institutions or localized laws being captured by special interests. Yet legal pluralism has not paid a great deal of attention to such questions. The social fact of multiple legal orders says nothing as to their moral worthiness or capacity for justice. By its very definition, pluralism acknowledges the possibility of contradictory laws, of different legal orders imposing competing demands on citizens – a legal space that is not, as Jeremy Waldron (2010) puts it, 'in good shape'. This conclusion opens up a dilemma for those of us who see pluralism as empirically plausible, but who seek some sort of justice or morality within law itself, because it works against pluralism as a normative theory, or as an 'ethical positioning', in the sense that pluralism appears to run the risk of opening up too many opportunities for abuse of power and law, of undermining the rule of law, of glorying in the beauty and wonder of a *Carina Nebula*, without sufficiently acknowledging its black holes.

In particular, many situations arise in which there exists either a weak, or indeed, no functioning, rule of law. This is visible in the growth of informal, flexible, private or non-state 'governance' organizations and networks, which growth undermines accountability and the possibility of justice. Justice becomes further compromised in the global arena where there exists very few, or indeed no trace at all, of formerly familiar mechanisms of state accountability. Too little attention has been paid to this. Complexity, fragmentation, pluralism of laws and globalization can perpetuate injustice. I therefore would argue that justice becomes a *key* issue for law in the era of legal pluralism. Rather than, or at least in addition to, questions of ordering or interpreting pluralism, we should ask how is justice achievable, given this complexity. Recognition of the complexity of the contemporary landscape, and unwillingness to categorize and simplify, is only the starting point for the project of present day legal theory.

Roger Cotterrell's work has been highly significant in alerting us to more nuanced, contextual conceptions of law. As such, it is highly relevant to the contemporary challenges to legal theory posed by transnational law and legal pluralism. Nor has Cotterrell ever been blind to the demands and stresses on our theorizing about justice and authority prompted by these developments. In particular his work on legal community is extremely valuable in this context. Other contributions to this volume consider these issues. One of the purposes of this contribution has been to illustrate how Roger's work is crucial not only to jurisprudence, and social and legal theory, but also to those of us working within fields such as EU, human rights and international law, and how his writings provide an invaluable companion to those of us working in these areas.

Bibliography

Austin, J. 1955 (1832). *The Province of Jurisprudence Determined.* W. Rumble (ed.), Cambridge, Cambridge University Press.

von Benda-Beckmann, F. 2002. 'Who's Afraid of Legal Pluralism?' 47 *Journal of Legal Pluralism*, 38.

Berman, H. 1983. *Law and Revolution: The Formation of the Western Legal Tradition.* Cambridge, MA, Harvard University Press.

Cooper, R. 2003. *The Breaking of Nations.* London, Atlantic Books.

Cornell, D. 1992. *The Philosophy of the Limit.* London, Routledge.

Cotterrell, R. 2002. 'Subverting Orthodoxy, Making Law Central: A View of Social Legal Studies'. 29 *Journal of Law and Society*, 632.

Cotterrell, R. 2003. *The Politics of Jurisprudence: A Critical Introduction to Legal Philosophy.* Oxford, Oxford University Press, 2nd edn.

Cotterrell, R. 2008. *Living Law: Studies in Legal and Social Theory.* Farnham, Ashgate.

Cotterrell, R. 2012. 'What is Transnational Law?' 37 *Law and Social Inquiry*, 500–524.

Culver, K. and Giudice, M. 2010. *Legality's Borders.* Oxford, Oxford University Press.

Curtin, D. 1993. 'The Constitutional Structure of the Union: a Europe of Bits and Pieces?' 30 *Common Market Law Review*, 17–69.

Delmas-Marty, M. 2002. *Towards a Truly Common Law.* Cambridge, Cambridge University Press.

Delmas-Marty, M. 2009. *Ordering Pluralism.* Oxford, Hart Publishing.

Derrida, J. 1992. 'Force of Law'. In D. Cornell, M. Rosenfeld and D.G. Carlson (eds), *Deconstruction and the Possibility of Justice.* London, Routledge. Ch.1.

Dicey, A.V. 1986 (1886). *England's Case Against Home Rule.* London, Public Domain book.

Dickson, J. 2012. 'Towards a Theory of European Union Legal Systems'. In J. Dickson and P. Eleftheriadis (eds), *Philosophical Foundations of European Union Law.* Oxford, Oxford University Press. Ch. 2.

Douglas-Scott, S. 2011. 'Europe's Constitutional Mosaic: Human Rights in the European Legal Space – Utopia, Dystopia, Monotopia or Polytopia?' In N. Walker, J. Shaw and S. Tierney (eds), *Europe's Constitutional Mosaic.* Oxford, Hart Publishing. Ch. 5.

Douglas-Scott, S. 2013. *Law After Modernity.* Oxford, Hart Publishing.

Douzinas, C. and Warrington, R. 1991. *Postmodern Jurisprudence: The Law of the Text in the Text of the Law.* London, Routledge.

Ehrlich, E. 1936. *Fundamental Principles of the Sociology of Law.* Cambridge, MA, Harvard University Press, trans. by W.L. Moll.

Frank, J. 1932. 'Mr Justice Holmes and non-Euclidian Legal Thinking'. 17 *Cornell Law Quarterly*, 568.

Fogen, M.T. 2002. 'Rechtsgeschichte – Geschichte der Evolution eines Sozialen Systems. Ein Vorschlag.' 1 *Rechtsgeschichte – (Legal History) Rg* 14.

Fuller, L. 1965. *The Morality of Law.* New Haven, Yale University Press, revised edition.

Griffiths, J. 2005. 'The Idea of Sociology of Law and its Relation to Law and to Sociology'. 8 *Current Legal Issues*, 49.

Hardt, M. and Negri, A. 2000. *Empire.* Cambridge, MA, Harvard University Press.

Hart, H.L.A. 1982. *Essays on Bentham.* Oxford, Oxford University Press.

Hart, H.L.A. 1994. *The Concept of Law.* Oxford, Clarendon Press, 2nd edition.

Hobbes, T. 1946. *Leviathan.* Oxford, Basil Blackwell, ed. M. Oakeshott.

Kelsen, H. 1967. *Pure Theory of Law.* Berkeley, University of California Press, trans. M. Knight.

Koskenniemi, M. 2005. 'Global Legal Pluralism: Multiple Regimes and Multiple Modes of Thought'. Paper given at Harvard Law School, 5 March 2005.

Koskenniemi, M. and Leino, P. 2002. 'Fragmentation of International Law. Postmodern Anxieities?' 15(3) *Leiden Journal of International Law*, 553.

Krisch, N. 2010. *Beyond Constitutionalism: The Pluralist Structure of Postnational Law*. Oxford, Oxford University Press.

Kronman, A. 1983. *Max Weber*. Stanford, Stanford University Press.

Kumm, M. 2004. 'The Legitimacy of International Law: A Constitutionalist Framework of Analysis'. 15(5) *European Journal of International Law*, 907–31.

Luhmann, N. 1986. 'The Autopoiesis of Social Systems'. In F. Geyer and J. van der Zouwen (eds), *Sociocybernetic Paradoxes*. London, Sage, 172–192.

Lyotard, J.F. 1979. *The Postmodern Condition*. Manchester, Manchester University Press, trans. G. Bennington and B. Massumi.

MacCormick, N. 1999. *Questioning Sovereignty*. Oxford, Oxford University Press.

Malinowski, B. 1926. *Crime and Custom in Savage Society*. London, Routledge and Kegan Paul.

Moore, S.F. 1972/73 'Law and Social Change: The Semi-Autonomous Social Field as an Appropriate Subject for Study'. 7 *Law and Society Review*, 719.

Mörth, U. (ed.) 2004. *Soft Law in Governance and Regulation*. Cheltenham, Edward Elgar.

Nonet, P. and Selznick, P. 1978. *Law and Society in Transition: Towards Responsive Law*. New York, Harper & Row.

Raz, J. 1980. *The Concept of a Legal System*. Oxford, Clarendon Press.

Raz, J. 2002. *Practical Reason and Norms*. Oxford, Oxford University Press, 2nd edition.

Roberts, S. 2005. 'After Government? On Representing Law Without the State'. 68 *Modern Law Review*, 1.

Rose, N. and Valverde, M. 1998. 'Governed by Law'. 7 *Social and Legal Studies*, 541–51.

Sousa Santos, B. 1980. 'Law and Community: The Changing Nature of State Power in Late Capitalism'. 8 *International Journal of the Sociology of Law*, 379.

Sousa Santos, B. 2002. *Towards a New Legal Common Sense*. London, Butterworths, 2nd edition.

Simpson, A.W.B. 2011. *Reflections on the Concept of Law*. Oxford, Oxford University Press.

Steyn, J. 2004. 'Guantanomo Bay: The Legal Black Hole'. 53 *International and Comparative Law Quarterly*, 1.

Teubner, G. 1983. 'Substantive and Reflexive Elements in Modern Law'. 17 *Law & Society Review*, 239.

Twining, W. 2000. *Globalization and Legal Theory*. London, Butterworths.

Twining, W. 2009. *General Jurisprudence: Understanding Law from a Global Perspective*. Cambridge, Cambridge University Press.

Waldron, J. 2010. 'Legal Pluralism and the Contrast between Hart's Jurisprudence and Fuller's'. In P. Cane (ed.), *The Hart-Fuller Debate in the Twenty-First Century*. Oxford, Hart Publishing. Ch. 7.

Walker, N. 2002. 'The Idea of Constitutional Pluralism'. 65 *Modern Law Review*, 317–59.

Weber, M. 1954. 'The Sociology of Law'. In *Max Weber on Economy and Society*, Cambridge, MA, Harvard University Press, trans. M. Rheinstein.

Chapter 5

Polity as Constitutional Law's Community: On the Expressive Function and Symbolism of National and Transnational Constitutions

Jiří Přibáň

Young academics usually meet two or three senior colleagues who influence their research views and ethics in the most fundamental way, and continue to inspire them for the rest of their academic lives. I do not mean ordinary professional encounters with university professors, supervisors and academics supporting the young persons' careers and making them part of academic communities through fellowships and jobs. I have in mind intellectually challenging and revealing encounters with those whose ideas and views remain critically important for everything they do in the future. Thinking of these transforming encounters, my first meeting with Roger Cotterrell was certainly one of them. I met Roger at a conference in Oxford during my first visit to the UK in 1993. I was a young lecturer coming from the Czech Republic for whom everything was new and fresh both at home and abroad. After all, the Czech Republic only came into existence earlier that year as one of many unintended consequences of post-communism – the split of Czechoslovakia. My academic visits to the UK, Germany, Norway and other countries had been a sort of full frontal attack on professors and libraries of partner universities so kindly helping and assisting many academics from post-communist countries throughout the 1990s.

I knew Roger's *Sociology of Law* (1992) and admired its theoretical and philosophical depth without fully realizing how extraordinary the book was within the empirical and policy-oriented context of sociology of law and socio-legal studies in the UK. I was familiar with continental legal and jurisprudential concepts, such as Ehrlich's living law, Savigny's spirit of a people and Weber's legal legitimacy, yet Roger's interpretation of these concepts turned out to be indispensable for comprehending theoretical frameworks, traditions and terminology of social theory and the sociology of the common law. Coming from the Central European university tradition, which often treats professors as semi-deities and their research assistants as slave labour, I immediately admired Roger's manners and friendliness. He looked somewhat more serious, modest and humble than most of his colleagues. When I started asking questions about the social theory of the common law, he kindly responded and took my views and interests seriously by commenting on and asking the most detailed questions about legal, political and social transformations in post-communist Europe. Roger's knowledge of those developments was exceptional as was his ability to generalize and put them in the context of social theory and philosophy of law and I enjoyed every second of our conversation. Nevertheless, while I was fully focused on political and constitutional transformations and believed at the time that these processes were mainly a matter of political decision-making, will-formation and institution-building, Roger, with his typical intellectual clarity and strong focus, offered a different view by raising the question of legal and political cultures as undercurrents profoundly affecting these transformative processes.

In the Central European intellectual tradition, culture is one of the most abused and abusive concepts and the spirit of the 1990s was decidedly universalistic, bringing all the post-communist countries 'back to Europe' with its market economy, democratic statehood, rule of law and human rights. Politics was to generate unity while culture appeared to be suspicious, divisive, destructive and leading to the fragmentation and revival of ethno-nationalism. Czechs and Slovaks managed to resolve differences between their national cultures and political aspirations peacefully by 'the Velvet Divorce' of 1992 following 'the Velvet Revolution' of 1989. However, peoples of former Yugoslavia experienced the series of civil wars and ethnic cleansing in the Balkans in the early 1990s. Roger did not intend to give preferential treatment to either politics, or culture, and certainly did not mean to revitalize Savigny's idiosyncratic concept of *Volksgeist* – the spirit of a people expressed through laws, politics and statehood. His remarks regarding the importance of culture were much more refined and qualified and simply stated that political and legal decisions, actions and concepts involve both recognized and unrecognized traditions, conventions and continuities. Roger did not use culture as a holistic concept determining the form and content of laws of particular communities. It, rather, was another name for legal and political practices to be comprehended and analyzed by the sociology and anthropology of law. It was fascinating to see how this excellent sociologist of law gave me an exemplary private lecture about the persistence of concepts and theories of sociology and theory of law. Without a hint of academic and intellectual conservatism, Roger highlighted the importance of classic sociological and socio-legal thoughts that may clarify our current problems and developments much better than a restless search of new theories and fashionable neologisms. In the last 20 years, I have had many occasions to meet Roger and discuss issues of sociological theory of law, legal culture and transnational law with him. We have collaborated on several projects which would not have succeed without his intellectual rigour, generosity and support.[1] I feel very privileged to know Roger and his friendship is precious to me.

The following chapter, therefore, is a tribute to the academic and friend who manages to use critically the conceptual framework of classic sociology and sociology of law and thus capture fundamental problems of law and politics in world society. Using Roger's concept of law's community, I argue that constitutional polity is internally constructed by constitutional law as its specific community. The concept of polity as the community of the sovereign people is commonly associated with modern nations and the nation state. However, it is not the ultimate foundation of law and politics and the guardian of its values and legitimacy. The semantics of constitutional polity is not limited by the nation state and national imagination and, equally, can lead to the constitution of specific polities of supranational and transnational law.

1. Community Against Society? A Critique of the Classic Sociological Distinction and Cultural Nostalgia

The concept of community and the classic distinction between community and society were intrinsic parts of social, legal and historical theories of the nineteenth century. Nevertheless, the distinction is still popular among some social and legal theorists and continues to be exploited by politicians and ideologues of identity politics even in the contemporary global condition of

1 Roger especially contributed a chapter to the volume *Law's New Boundaries: The Consequences of Legal Autopoiesis* edited by myself and David Nelken in 2001. I also selected Roger's conversations with Philip Selznick for publication in the *Journal of Law and Society* under the title 'Selznick Interviewed: Philip Selznick in Conversation with Roger Cotterrell' in 2004.

world society (Bauman 2000). The concept of community even becomes a conceptual weapon of various anti-globalization movements fighting against injustices and repression and standing for the rights and interests of different communities living in this exploitative global society. It is as if the contrast between the particularity of community and the universality of society with all its political, ideological and propaganda contextualizations had merely entered the global stage in recent times (Castells 2004: 68–70). The community/society distinction was part of a typically modern basket of conceptualizations and distinctions, such as the Marxist distinction between substructure and superstructure, Maine and Spencer's conceptualizations of status and contract, Durkheim's typology of mechanical and organic solidarity, and even the sociology of law's distinction between law in books and law in action or living law. It was a critical response to the process of modernization which contrasted the communal system of close human bonds and mutual affections to the alienating system of modern society and its rational calculations.

Incorporating structural differences between traditional and modern society, the community/society distinction often invited a nostalgic romantic critique of modernity as rationalization destroying the familiarity of social relations (Bond 2013: 169–71). Community was considered a last resort of human sensuality and affections threatened by modern industrial and bureaucratically governed society. It was to guarantee social unity and integration in an evermore functionally differentiated modern society. Using Emile Durkheim's conceptualizations of mechanical and organic solidarity, Ferdinand Tönnies, for instance, associated modern society with mechanistic rationality and contrasted it to the organic community expressing the substance of common life of humankind. No wonder his classic study *Community and Society* starts with the following image of human beings entering the social world:

> All intimate, private, and exclusive living together, so we discover, is understood as life in Gemeinschaft (community). Gesellschaft (society) is public life – it is the world itself. In Gemeinschaft with one's family, one lives from birth on, bound to it in weal and woe. One goes into Gesellschaft as one goes into a strange country. (Tönnies 2002: 33–4)

The image of a human being walking the unknown territory of modern society as a stranger in a strange land is typical of modern culture full of characters such as Robert Musil's 'man without qualities' and Franz Kafka's 'Josef K'. Profoundly inspired by Spencer, Durkheim and Weber's typology and the general *Zeitgeist*, Tönnies thus delivered a variation on the classic theme of the modernization of society but also an exercise in the philosophical search of the meaning of life of human beings in the modern world (Mitzman 1987). Contrasting nature to reason, particularism to universalism, the whole to its parts, collectivity to the self, affectivity to rationality and ascription to achievement, his study of community and society is another exercise in general classifications of modern society which is contrasted to the various forms of traditional life. All these distinctions, therefore, are possible to summarize in the remark that community is *old* and society *new* (Tönnies 2002: 34). Furthermore, specific legal philosophical concepts significantly contributed to the sociological classification of community and society (Tönnies 2002: 171). The specific distinction between rational law valid in the political organization of the modern state and original natural law valid in all social conditions, informs the general distinction between society and community. The complexity and rationality of modern society increases the separation of legislated laws from customary laws and folkways of the people. Similarly, the distinction between religion and public opinion informs the difference between the religious sanctions of moral norms in a community and public sanctions of moral norms arising from collective interests in society. The difference between religious spontaneity and public organization is replicated by the difference between culture and civilization essential for defining one of the most critical differences of political modernity – the difference between the people and the state which is summarized by Tönnies in the following words:

> In the same way as the individual natural will evolves into pure thinking and rational will, which tends to dissolve and subjugate its predecessors, the original collective forms of Gemeinschaft have developed into Gesellschaft and the rational will of the Gesellschaft. In the course of history, folk culture has given rise to the civilisation of the state. (Tönnies 2002: 225)

This sociological explanation of the political evolution of modern statehood provides for the social and legitimation basis of the modern state and the importance of spontaneity of culture in legitimizing the rational state organization and its legal system. However, Tönnies and other social, political and legal theorists of his time also emphasized the state's capacity to create its own culture and establish a morality rising above the state and fostering a new culture founded on the civilizing force of the state (Tönnies 2002: 230). In Tönnies's words, '[L]aw is, in every respect, nothing but common will' (Tönnies 2002: 190), and therefore needs to be treated as both the natural substance of imagined community and the form of its rational will and social ordering. It is both an expression and organization of common life.

Indeed, the classic concept of community involved a warning against social disintegration by emphasizing the need of social unity and integration. Community is 'the whole' contrasted to society dissipating into different 'parts', such as economy, politics, law, etc. The whole of community requires commitment by its members who must obey its rules and, rather than engage in conflicts and pursuits of individual goals and interests, promote commonly shared values. It thus stands in opposition to society as mere coexistence of individuals independent of each other.

Nevertheless, rational will and justification in public opinion involves the capacity to transform political legislation and conventions into a specific culture and order of mores and folkways. The politics of universal civilization symbolized by the modern democratic state and popular sovereignty has the social capacity to construct its particular polity and popular culture – a culture of shared symbols, political identity and communal bonds.

The paradoxical process of general societal structures of modern law and politics constructing its specific culture and folkways, however, is impossible to explain within the classic sociological paradigm of the community/society distinction. It requires different distinctions, conceptualizations and descriptions of the semantics and structures of modern law, politics and culture. Some of these are outlined in the next part of this chapter.

2. Law's Community and Polity

'Law is the regulation and expression of community' (2006a: 28) is Roger Cotterrell's statement replicating Durkheim's moral functionalism which identifies both the law's functions of conflict regulation and symbolic expression of values of modern society (Clarke 1976). Social conflicts are settled by legal procedures of arbitration establishing which party to a conflict is in the right. The same procedures, nevertheless, reaffirm values and thus guarantee the moral integration of modern society. In his influential book *Law's Community* (1995), Cotterrell persuasively delineates culture from the essentialist concept of communal identity. He admits the importance of the functional differentiation of modern society and remarks that it is difficult to imagine that this society could be characterized by a specific morality, common values, nature or essence overarching and overlapping different subsystems. Legal regulation is differentiated itself and these differences can hardly be mitigated by some essentialist morality that could be treated as the legal system's foundation. In Cotterrell's sociological theory of law, there is no space for the conceptualization of the nation as a community of the spirit or folkways unified by the same purpose. It is impossible to contrast the safe world of old community of fully shared values and communally experienced bonds to the alienating world of a new society of individuals calculating and exploiting their interests. Community is not associated with nostalgic longing for things past which are threatened by social evolution. It, rather, is its specific outcome. Communities can be detected in varied forms including instrumental relationships of commerce, affective relationships of friendship and care and relationships drawing on shared beliefs and values. They are constituted by the societal need for solidarity, moral justifications and symbolic collective expressions (Cotterrell 2006a: 28). Furthermore, Cotterrell claims that one of the primary tasks of a sociological theory of law is to debunk naïve concepts of political community, often favoured by philosophies of law, as consensual rather than mired in permanent disputes and controversies (Cotterrell 1995: 309). The image of polity as a morally cohesive collectivity linked by its members' shared values and consensus is specifically produced by state legal systems and state-organized political societies (Cotterrell 1995: 320–21). The legal philosophical view that it is possible to integrate modern society by consensus, constituted by human beings as social actors, is hard to defend vis-à-vis the functional differentiation of modern society and plurality of its communities evolving beyond traditional ethnic and modern national frameworks. Issues of legal philosophy need to be interpreted in their political and social contexts (Cotterrell 2003: 16).

Societies are constituted neither by political constitutions, nor by political citizens and legal subjects as agents shaping their society according to their individual and collective will and intelligent design. However, Cotterrell is well aware that the opposite identification of polity with diversity and plurality of localized communal knowledge contrasted to the state with its social uniformity, so often favoured by various theories of legal pluralism, is equally difficult to defend because it merely represents the other side of the same normative reflection on modern society favoured by philosophies of law and politics. In fact, no community represents a complete form of life, and different networks of social regulations always involve both societal universalism and communal particularism (Cotterrell 1995: 325). Social and legal theorists often surprisingly continue associating community with localized bonds or shared experiences and society with universal values, political statehood and reciprocity, calculation and instrumental reason (Frazer 1999). Against this categorization, Cotterrell states that even communal relationships are reciprocal and involve a great deal of instrumental rationality and that '[T]he essence of community is *mutual interpersonal trust*' (1995: 330). While pleading for the preservation of moral authority of law in contemporary society, Cotterrell critically concludes that

> … [t]he paradox of law lies in its permanent dual appeal to moral and political authority, and in the fact that while political authority is ultimately grounded in moral authority, the former tends to divorce itself from the latter. (1995: 337)

This paradox of law in permanent search of its moral authority while politically self-limiting its legitimation effectively means that law constitutes its community, and such a community remains to be determined as a joint outcome of legal operations and their moral and political reflections.

Extending Cotterrell's argument, it is possible to state that community does not construct its law in the pre-modern fashion relying on foundational collective values, experiences and sets of beliefs. Instead, law constructs its community by turning its systemic operations into the prescriptive language of culture and communal bonds. In this semantics of the system of positive law, the concept of polity can be re-defined as just one of many communities constructed and identified by constitutional law as the structural coupling between law and politics. It signifies the semantic capacity of the modern political and legal systems to reformulate the general image of society as a specific community of constitutional law.

The concept of polity is thus part of political and legal symbolism which has the paradoxical capacity to communicate general images of society as the integrated whole within specific and functionally differentiated systems of positive law and politics (Přibáň 2007: 10–23). When social and legal theorists discuss the expressive function of modern law, they actually refer to this semantic capacity of specific legal and political concepts to communicate social totality and even represent or express it as an ethical goal of 'commonality', 'cosmopolitanism', 'global responsibility', 'universal human rights', 'one world politics', etc.

3. A European History of National Polities and Nation States

In his essay 'Legal Philosophy and Legal Pluralism', Cotterrell quotes Hugh Seton-Watson's comment on Europe as 'a community of cultures' (2006b: 41). Indeed, Hugh Seton-Watson's father was Robert William Seton-Watson, an insightful historian of European nations, the strongest advocate of pre-war Czechoslovakia and a close friend and ally of both its presidents Tomáš Garrigue Masaryk and Edvard Beneš. R.W. Seton-Watson was also the fiercest critic of Prime Minister Chamberlain's policy of appeasement leading to the collapse of Czechoslovak democratic statehood and occupation of Bohemia and Moravia by Nazi Germany in 1939 (Rychlík and Marzik 1996). Hugh Seton-Watson's brief quote and his family history capture the modern tragedy of Europe and its fascination with ethnic diversity and the cultural pluralism of different nations. Europe's plurality of cultures is a reminder that modern politics may draw on the universalistic political ideals of liberty, equality and democracy but materialization of these ideals is culturally embedded and incorporated in particular politics of democratic states. Furthermore, modern history of European nationalism shows that political organization and administration of the nation state managed to constitute democratic republican politics. However, it also facilitated the most extreme forms of cultural ethno-nationalism and violence driven by the ideology of ethnic and racial superiority (Brubaker 1996). The dream of modern nationalism in which the state as a political unit incorporates, determines and symbolizes the nation as a cultural unit is impossible to achieve exactly because of the politically uncontainable plurality of cultures in modern society and its politics organized into statehood (Connor 1994: 118–25). Responding to these historical developments, more recent supra-national projects, such as the process of European economic, legal and political integration, have been normatively driven by a critique of ethnic and cultural nationalism and genuine ambitions to both reconstruct democratic nation states in Europe and construct a postnational European polity. As Ernest Gellner stated, the problem of modern nationalism is the problem of political legitimacy requiring that ethnic boundaries should not cut across political ones and that there is ethnic unity between governors and those who are governed by them (Gellner 1983: 1–3). Political legitimacy, therefore, can proceed only as a circular process of integrating a particular nation as cultural community by the state as modern political organization and recursively shaping the nation's culture by political decision-making and an authoritative definition of nationhood through social and education policies, the state media, state sponsorship of historical science and the humanities, etc.

The nation state takes care of culture because it guarantees its legitimation (Gierke 1990: 160). Culture replaces consensus as a legitimation formula. Instead of the social contract constituting a polity of reasonable individuals, and drawing on the distinction between political society and its natural environment, the concept of culture converts these polities into 'natural' ethnic units established by collective social experiences and not the social contract individually consented to by human beings. Legitimacy becomes a structural problem of social solidarity and collective beliefs which are manifested in individual behaviour and therefore can be measured and scientifically observed. At this historical point, political theory of the Hobbesian tradition gets replaced by general sociology and classic problems of political rationalism and theology become methodological problems of empirical evidence, social statistics, qualitative analysis, etc. In modernity, all societal ways of life have or are culture and therefore may be observed from the comparative perspective (Luhmann 2013: 225). The Romantic paradox of patriotically and nationally differentiated cosmopolitanism of political ideals of the Enlightenment serves as the best example of both the expressive symbolism of modern culture and comparative methodology of social science. The semantics of culture made it possible to keep the image of society as unity which, nevertheless, can be contrasted and compared to other culturally defined communities as specific units of modern society (Cubitt 1998). What can be contrasted and compared remains experienced as different in cultural practices and symbolized in the critical self-reflections of different communities. In this respect, Seton-Watson's quote nicely summarizes political and cultural developments in modern European nation state societies (see, for instance, Seton-Watson 1977). However, it is even more important that it clearly separates the concepts of community and culture – the two most important concepts in Cotterrell's sociological theory of law.

Cotterrell elaborates on the historical and political view that it is possible to have a single community of law and politics even in the social condition of plurality of ethnic and national cultures. The distinction between polity as a single community constructed by modern political constitutions and the plurality of cultural communities is crucial because it opens the possibility to disentangle the notion of polity from nationhood and the nation state. The end of simple identification of polity with a nation and its culture subsequently means that supranational and transnational legal networks and regimes, such as the EU, can constitute their supranational and transnational polities – communities self-constituted by transnational law. Nations may now be defined as specific polities associated with organization of the nation state and its constitution which are historically important, yet hardly unique and ultimate forms of social integration and images of social unity. However, this theoretical move requires a preliminary critique of the holistic concept of the nation and democratic constitutional polity, which is the subject of the next section.

4. The Holistic Concept of the Nation and Democratic Constitutional Polity

The historical emergence and evolution of modern nations and nation states both legitimizing and legitimized by common culture significantly affects the semantics of modern political and legal systems and eventually leads to the reconceptualization of the nation state as the constitutional democratic state. The semantics of the democratic polity represented by its constitution and representing its sovereignty through constitutional settlement draws on the concept of statehood and sovereignty as absolute and exclusive power within the state's territory (Poggi 1994). According to this modern semantics, power is no longer imbedded in a traditional order of social stratification and multiple mediaeval hierarchies but in the politically constructed order of supreme, exclusive and absolute power of a political sovereign. The sovereign state has been described as the 'container' (Taylor 1994: 151–62) of emerging modern society which is delineated by territorial borders, supreme authority and laws.

Political constitution, backed by the sovereign power of the state, traditionally had two important functions – limiting the exercise of sovereign power by means of a system of constitutional checks and balances and symbolically constituting polity as the whole of society. A sovereign act of popular constitution-making is both constitutive of the systems of politics and law as well as expressing the collective identity of the democratic polity governing itself by delegating its sovereign power to its representatives. The expressive mode of collective identity stretches beyond the domain of law and politics and establishes the ethical and cultural self-reflections of the people as a real political force and a symbolically imagined community. According to this view, the order of society is guaranteed by sovereign power and state constitutions are thus the constitutions of political society. However, the constitution of such a statist and territorially defined society does not simply mean the identification of society with its state because modern constitutions and declarations of rights commonly invoke a particular concept of society – polity of civil liberties and self-government as constitutive of the existence of modern society and its statehood.

The modern state thus presupposes a constitutive attribute of the pre-existent polity which pursues its political self-constitution and existence through the state and its sovereign power. Sovereignty may be the absolute and exclusive power of the state but only because it already is the power generated and constituted by a historically new form of polity – the democratic nation as a community of shared destiny of the whole people. This polity is considered a collective entity, both constituting and constituted by its state and therefore both exercising and endangered by its sovereign power. The well known paradox of modern constitutionalism is thus concentrated in the democratic polity constituting its sovereignty to which it is completely and absolutely subjected through the state constitution. Constituent power of this polity draws on the self-reflective concept of collective selfhood and identity (Lindahl 2007b). Law, politics and democratic collective selfhood subsequently redefine the concept of state sovereignty as constitutional sovereignty permanently communicating the constitutive power of the sovereign democratic polity as the constituted power of the sovereign state. The meaning of modern state sovereignty lies in its reformulation as the self-determining command of the democratic polity extending to all citizens in general and dealing with general interests of the polity as democratically self-constituted community.

States are considered sovereign if they integrate and embody the collective will of the polity. This circularity leads to the mutual reinforcement and constitution of both the democratic polity and its constitutional statehood. As Ulrich Preuss states, '[T]he turn from having power to being a power constitutes a polity' (2010: 34). This shift, however, requires adjustment at the level of constitutional law because state constitutions are now required to operate as representative constitutions facilitating a normative framework of the democratic polity and its political will. Constitutional limitation of sovereign power becomes a source of political self-empowerment and juridical self-constitution of the democratic polity. The paradoxical constitution of the sovereign state by the polity as an entity with collective selfhood which, nevertheless, comes into being exclusively through sovereign power of the state has only one solution – the separation of political self-determination from constitutional self-limitation of the polity through the permanent possibility of reformulating the political constitution as legal representation of the democratic polity and the legal constitution as political representation of the democratic state (for a number of conceptualizations of this paradox, see especially Loughlin and Walker 2007).

No wonder political constitutions have become those 'mysterious objects of desire' of modern nations in Europe and elsewhere. They became ultimate representations of 'the people' as political nations and thus have completely changed the concept of the polity by identifying it with political nationhood. The modern constitutional state was thus originally differentiated from the body of social hierarchies, particularisms and loyalties and constituted a new body politic, yet through increasing modernization, as democratization became ever more symbolically representative of the whole society and its sovereign power could be legitimized only by virtue of democratic authority. Constitutionalization became a form of social self-organization of the democratic polity through the state as social organization. The state constitution thus functions both in the Rousseau-like populist sense as self-determination and self-materialization of popular sovereignty and the Locke-like limited government sense as self-limitation of popular will and its transformation to juridical norms and procedures. The biggest invention of modern constitutionalism and constitutional theory of the democratic state, therefore, is its depiction of the polity as both constituent of and constituted by the modern state.

5. Nations and States as Obstacle Epistémologiques?

As Benedict Anderson famously stated, nations are 'imagined communities' politically organized in the nation state (Anderson 1983). They are imagined, first of all, as *limited* because all nations, even the biggest ones, are defined by their boundaries beyond which exist other nations. Furthermore, this us/them distinction is supported by the imagination of nations as politically *sovereign* entities self-governed within the nation state. Apart from this hierarchical political organization, nations finally are imagined as a *community* of a 'deep, horizontal comradeship' and fraternity (Anderson 1983: 7). This imagination opens an entirely new comparison of national cultures evolving in a unique manner, yet synchronically and in parallel to each other. Nations exist because of their unique history and present, yet they proceed along the same trajectory of modernity and their collective identities remain comparable (Anderson 1983: 188). Modern nationalisms and national identities are thus split between past and future. Nations are new polities abolishing the old regimes and proclaiming the new collective future and political settlement, such as the French and American republics. At the same time, this movement and 'new time' recursively constitutes national history and genealogy, so that political rupture coincides with the invention of historical traditions and collective continuities. Political future of modern nations thus has coincided with historical 'national reawakening', and new time of modernity required the imagination of 'old time' of predecessors (Anderson 1983: 194–5).

Regarding culture as a social subsystem, Niklas Luhmann, for instance, states that '[O]nly in modern societies has a sufficiently general concept of culture developed that is suitable for distinguishing social memory from other social functions' (Luhmann 2012: 354). He praises Parsons for having a ground-breaking intuition that social memory should be distinguished from other social functions and that this function consists of 'latent-pattern maintenance'. This latency is the task of the cultural subsystem but it is necessary to ask 'why society invents a concept of culture to describe its memory' (Luhmann 2012: 354). National memory and culture was considered a matter of both remembering national origins and reinventing them through shared collective practices and experiences, such as national memorial days and festivities. Memory is thus always constructed by present uses of the past. Nations are constituted by such present uses of the past and their collective memories are the subject of different uses by the political and legal systems. By definition, national memory is selective. It, rather than the archive imperative indiscriminately collecting evidence of the past events, is modelled on the selective logic of historical narratives and myths. It is not primarily interested in the nation's past but its history – present stories about the past constantly selecting specific events and differentiating between the glorious and inglorious past. The function of memory consists of turning past events into present histories.

Culture consists of parallel processes of remembering and forgetting. According to Luhmann, 'culture is indeed nothing other than the memory of society, hence the filter of forgetting/remembering and the appropriation of the past to determine the variation framework of the future' (Luhmann 2012: 355). National identity as imagined unity, therefore, needs this temporalization of collective existence which had to be brought to life from its historical 'sleep' and can then proceed towards the bright future as a historically unique polity sharing the same destiny. However, this collective memory and shared history is at permanent risk of being forgotten. *Historiographies* of modern nations subsequently need to be supplemented by their *biographies* which treat nations as persons with distinct identity (Anderson 1983: 204). Modern national culture consists of this permanent imagination of the past and present in which national historiographies are as important as present and future biographies of collective identity. The general concept of culture as reflection on self-descriptions of modern society and its national contextualization opens radically new possibilities of social observation and self-identifications (Luhmann 2013: 176). Because culture has different forms in different societies, specific cultures can be compared to other cultures experienced, enjoyed and learned elsewhere. Constant political and social appeals to culture and cultural identity symbolically express the common realm of political society. The concept of nation as the politically and culturally differentiated self-description of society significantly depends on the possibility of comparing historical and regional differences. Cultural comparisons between different habits, practices, systems of beliefs and power struggles have illuminated the concepts of modern nationhood and statehood.

The concepts of culture and collective identity, therefore, should be considered as specific forms of societal differentiation and comparisons conducted within specific social subsystems and the semantics of the democratic polity is one of its examples. It makes it possible to differentiate between democratic and undemocratic political systems, compare different democratic 'cultures' and regimes, analyze their historical evolution, etc. In this respect, the difference between civic and ethnic nationhood, so vital for formulating different political ideals and defining limits and principles of inclusion in and exclusion from the polity (Calhoun 1993), is just another manifestation of the expressive symbolism of the concept of the national polity. Expectations of social unification and political integration were an intrinsic part of the modern concept of nation and the establishment of such unity was facilitated by the modern state organization. Particularisms of ethnically and territorially defined communities coincided with the universalism of the state as modern political organization and the concept of the nation state effectively managed to symbolize both political and societal unity. In the modern state, the people have been transformed from a particular social estate to the general symbol of polity with the sovereign transcending the very realm of politics. National culture became a reservoir of collective memories and practices differentiating 'us' from 'them' in both societal and political terms.

Collective identity and communal bonds are possible to establish and communicate as long as there is parallel reference to those who are different from our polity, its sense of commonality and cultural heritage. In the language of autopoietic systems theory, self-reference of the national polity coincides with other-reference to different polities. Commenting on this historical coexistence of the cultural concept of nation and the political concept of state, Niklas Luhmann states:

> [T]he idea of nation obviously belongs to the set of short-lived semantics that can exercise a fascination for a transitional period without betraying what societal system they refer to. It can therefore be assumed that this idea is now on the wane, a phase in which it does more harm than good and from a sociological point of view constitutes one of those *obstacle épistémologiques* [hypothesized by Gaston Bachelard] that for reason of past plausibilities block urgently needed insights. (2013: 289)

The conceptual difference between universalism and particularism was reconciled by the nation's political theology in theories of sovereignty and modern democratic statehood. However, the concept of the nation as constitutional polity is just one of many semantic forms dealing with the paradox of the constitutional unity of sovereign power symbolically representing the multitude of citizens. If nations are imagined communities brought to their historical existence from sleep and preserved by collective memories, they logically can be imagined as merely historical and biographical communities of limited persistence which, sooner or later, will be forgotten by modern society. Their existence and the political organization of the nation state are subjects of social evolution like any other outcome of social imagination and structural differentiation.

6. From an Ontology of the Collective Self to the Sociology of Transnational Polities

The democratic polity of the people used to be perceived as a mysterious collectivity, turning the social multitude of individuals into the unity of general political will both be exercised through and limited by the constitutional state. This state both organizes popular self-rule and makes it the subject of the exclusive power of its institutions. Popular sovereignty and constitutional sovereignty are identical and explicable only through the metaphor of the people as the self-governed democratic polity organized within the democratic state. Without the democratic polity as the origin of public power, no system of government can meet the standards of the modern constitution (Loughlin 2013). The original function of the democratic polity, therefore, was to guarantee legitimacy of the democratic constitutional system of authority and this system has found its most comprehensive institutional framework in the modern state – a framework impossible to replicate at any international, supranational or transnational societal level. According to this statist view, there are only two solutions for democratic deficits accompanying processes of political and legal globalization, namely limitation of erosion of statehood and coeval enhancement of public accountability and democratization of international, supranational and transnational political and legal institutions (Kuper 2004).

Apart from political coercion, this state enhances the possibility of the polity's democratic self-organization and the capacity of free citizens to interact, deliberate and share common goals and responsibilities. The democratic polity thus needs to be perceived as a self-reflective concept enhancing the capacity of collective self-attribution (Lindahl 2007b: 19) of political decisions and legal norms which turns the social multitude into one self-constituted and self-constituting polity. As Hans Lindahl says, this act of self-constitution, however, may happen only retroactively as an act of self-identification of 'the members of a polity in constituent action by exercising the powers granted to them by a constitution' (2007b: 19). Lindahl's ontology of collective selfhood shows that an act of constituent power – the sovereign people can only retrospectively constitute a legal order because the constitutive act itself cannot be part of that order. The permanent question 'Who are we?' turns the paradox of constituent/constituted power into an ontology of the collective self that 'exists in the modes of *questionability* and, by way of its acts, of *responsiveness*'

(2007b: 21). Lindahl thus argues against Carl Schmitt and his followers that modern democracy is not unmediated political action by the people

> because there can be no such action; it is the form of political organisation that, appealing to the rule of law, postpones acts of attribution by establishing the minimal conditions under which such acts may be viewed, ever provisionally, as acts of the people. (2007b: 24).

This ontology of collective selfhood of the democratic polity clearly shows that the concept of polity cannot operate as a foundational concept of modern society guaranteeing its cultural unity or moral integration (Lindahl 2007a). It rather needs to be interpreted as a retrospective fiction constituted by operations of social memory which merely reconstructs the image of society but cannot justify its unity, centralization or political hierarchization and constitution of ultimate social authority.

Responding to these challenges of the collective self and constituent community of the people, Cotterrell recalls the importance of epistemology and sociological methodology and, while admitting that 'everything is in flux' (Cotterrell 2009: 498) in transnational law and politics, elaborates on the concept of flux and fluidity profoundly different from the philosophical speculations regarding the constituent polity's questionability and responsiveness.

According to Cotterrell, a transnational order of the world replacing the old Westphalian political, juridical and international order, calls for a critical revision of earlier socio-legal and legal pluralist claims that state law is not the exclusive form of law (Cotterrell 1995: 31). Transnational world society certainly challenges the state law form's dominance traditionally associated with modern society, especially since there are limited chances of political and legal convergence in this world. Nevertheless, Cotterrell insists that transnational law, can still keep its moral meaningfulness and integration function in the diverse social networks of world society. Law's social importance and moral ambitions are not diminished by transnational legal pluralism. They rather extend beyond nation state boundaries and technicalities of various transnational legal and political regimes operating without cultural concerns and the notion of the general social good.

Cotterrell's perspective draws on Durkheim's sociological tradition and its critique of law as a mere instrument of balancing of interests (Lukes 1985). Law is not just an abstraction but an effective discipline of wills with its specific moral content without which it would wither away (Cotterrell 1995: 308). The sociology of transnational law, therefore, is not just a sociology of harmonization processes and tendencies in comparative law and must address the problem of multiculturalism including the potential incommensurability of values and beliefs sought by different peoples and communities to be affirmed and recognized by law (Cotterrell 2009: 491–4). Indeed, according to Cotterrell,

> [T]he challenge for legal regulation is to recognise fully (and even-handedly) the different types of communal bonds that unite and differentiate people. Perhaps the distinctiveness of each of these types becomes more obvious insofar as they become *transnationally* focused; not integrated features of a political society but diverse in their range of reference within and beyond nation-state boundaries. The task is to recognise legally the richness of the social, rather than reduce it to regulatory 'packages' that are convenient for purposes of legal harmonisation and for instrumental state-centred views of law. (Cotterrell 2009: 497)

Sociology of law thus avoids international law and relations tendencies of ideal rationalization and harmonization of different interests, by employing non-state and territorially unrestrictive methodology and conceptualizations of social relations, such as Simmel's basic social forms of exchange, conflict and domination or social types of the stranger and the metropolis (Cotterrell 2009: 494). This approach also avoids a stereotypical view of law's exclusive moral function as the guardian of common values and beliefs because it does not equate law simply with these values and beliefs or traditions and collective goals. It rather treats law as an object of collective emotions and affections and a reservoir protecting historical memories, local traditions and customary practices, languages, environments, etc.

7. Transnational Polity Beyond the Moral Groundings

While drawing on the Durkheimian sociological tradition and insisting that the moral groundings of law are still relevant, Cotterrell admits that these groundings are more difficult to detect in law and society beyond the structures and organization of modern nation states. The diversity and contingency of world society and its transnational law and politics make it difficult to 'specify a basis of moral cohesion' (2006a: 27). According to Cotterrell, the question of law's legitimacy and moral authority, nevertheless, persists because the system and networks of transnational law perform the role of socially integrating force.

Analyzing modern law in its expressive function of incorporating the particular characteristics of modern social solidarity and a sense of unity persisting vis-à-vis the increasing complexity, diversity and change of modern society, Cotterrell insists on the continuing importance of law's legitimacy and normative protection of primary values of political modernity and morality – personal autonomy and human dignity. Cotterrell thus principally agrees with Durkheim that modern social integration can only be facilitated by the value system guaranteeing universal respect for the autonomy and dignity of every individual citizen (1999: 103–47). These values must inform current transnational law beyond the sovereign state if it is to be considered legitimate by human beings as both its authors and subjects. Instead of protecting a particular community and giving it a political form, Cotterrell claims that transnational law's bonds are much more general and protect natural and cultural local environments of communities and populations which are not necessarily bounded by political societies and limited by the borders of nation states (2008). Law constitutes various non-state local, national and transnational communities and contributes to the search for both their collective interests and roots (Sousa Santos 2002: 177; Von Daniels 2010).

Polity, therefore, signifies a specific form of the symbolic self-reference of constitutional law which, however, is not limited by the semantics and structures of nation states and national communities. The complexity of modern society rules out the possibility of simple political and legal causality. As Cotterrell notes himself, it, rather, is typical of the absence of a founding principle or a basic norm (2008: 6–7). Contrary to the political and legal intuitions and epistemologies, functionally differentiated modern society evolves through operations of different systems without normative foundations. This functional differentiation rules out the possibility of value integration. No specific system, such as economy, politics, law or religion, can guarantee universal validity of societal norms and rules. The crucial question, however, is whether law's force to constitute specific communities, so carefully analyzed by Cotterrell, still draws too much on the sociological tradition distinguishing between formal and informal rules and associates law's communities with non-political social forces of communal life and its informal spontaneous self-constitution. For instance, despite the long juridical and political tradition of the EU's informal rules of governance, commitology and constitutionalism without a constitution, law's formality remains the ultimate source of political legitimation of both the

EU and its Member States (see, for instance, Griller and Ziller 2008). Turning away from both the normative constructivism of polity-building by constitutional means, so much favoured by philosophies and theories of law and politics, and the moral functionalism of sociological theories of the Durkheimian tradition, of which Roger Cotterrell is one of the most original thinkers, it is then possible to rethink the paradox of constitutional polity as the social multitude represented by the unity of political will beyond the structure of nation states. The general concept of constitutional polity, subsequently, refers to the subsystem of constitutional law and political constitutions evolving at subnational, national, supranational and transitional levels of world society.

Cotterrell and others are right in thinking that society in general and polity in particular can hardly continue to be defined in terms of territory or collective identity. Polity cannot be identified as a collective entity living within territorial boundaries of the nation state or other territorially organized (local, regional, supranational, etc.) political units. Nevertheless, constitutional polity equally may not be treated as a life-world experience reservoir of social systems of law and politics making them legitimate in the sense of preserving social solidarity and expressing the variety of moral grounds and values, or communicative rationality and discourse ethics, etc.

Similarly, prescriptive oppositions between nation state and supranational or international political organizations, such as the EU and the UN, need to be criticized and abandoned. For instance, the EU with its territorial boundaries and system of governance of the European population turns out to be a mere supranational segment of globally functioning world society. It, therefore, hardly can be treated as a political avant-garde acting as a centre of cosmopolitan ethics and political ideals for various peripheries of this world society. In this respect, Niklas Luhmann commented:

> [O]lder societies were organized hierarchically and in function of the distinction between center and periphery. This was in keeping with their world order, which provided for an order of rank *(series rerum)* and a center. Modern society's form of differentiation requires these structural principles to be abandoned, so that this society has a heterarchical world and an acentric world. (2012: 91)

The interplay of political centres and peripheries, typical of modern European empires, has come to its close; the EU cannot appropriate the role of a global political and social centre spreading the message of political multilateralism and ethical universalism of human rights and values binding all humans as members of one *all-inclusive cosmo-polity*. The EU and its recent political and legal history serve as a negative example which actually reveals another important feature of modern society – the impossibility of constituting it by the political and legal process of constitution-making. The EU constitution-making failure is evidence that political constitutions do not constitute society at either national, or supranational, or any other societal levels. The heterarchy of world society coincides with the universalism of functional systems, such as economy, politics, law, science and education, operating in it. Indeed, European society and other supranational territorially segmented organizations, such as the African Union, NATO, ASEAN and national or subnational societies around the world constitute important particularisms in these universally functioning and globally operating and self-constituting systems of law, politics, economy, etc. However, it has to be emphasized that it is the functional systems of world society that select from different particularisms and even traditions while abandoning the operative importance of territorial oppositions or the opposition between traditional communities and modern society. Political constitutions evolving within modern nation states and beyond their organizational limitations, rather, are specific products of societal evolution facilitating the structural coupling between the systems of politics and law. They, therefore, are not a general mirror of the totality of society and social solidarity. Their polities are merely a fragmented reflection of their political and legal evolution. For instance, attempts at constructing the European democratic polity – demos – by the act of constitution-making and adoption of a formal constitutional document for the EU were doomed to fail because of their unrealistic expectation of producing a general European society for particular EU institutions and specific operations of the functionally differentiated systems of EU law and politics.

8. Concluding Remarks: Culture, Memory and Constitutional Polity

Roger Cotterrell's critique of the consensual model of political society and the basic norm/rule of recognition founded system of positive law never leads to the societal neutralization of morality. While acknowledging the complexity of modern society and the impossibility to subject it to either the meta-code of morality, or causality between values and norms, Cotterrell still insists on the expressive symbolic function of law and its moral grounding as a necessary precondition of its legitimacy.

It is correct that society cannot be integrated by a political contract or moral consensus of human beings and fully guaranteed within boundaries of a given space. Its political constitution may be impossible to explain in terms of humanistic values, centralized political power and territorial boundaries. Nevertheless, Cotterrell's description of law and society firmly rejects the self-description of society as, for instance, an autopoietic system without a specific nature and/or morality driven by the need of solidarity, happiness and the harmonization of living conditions (Luhmann 2012: 35). Cotterrell favours an anthropologically grounded view looking for both the function and meaning of law in society. However, he is well aware that this Durkheimian quest is much harder to undertake in the global condition of world society. While using global diversity and complexity of legal structures and networks as persuasive evidence and critique of the modern concept of nation society, its political form and normative self-reflections, Cotterrell can hardly continue describing this society as *societas civilis* of human actors and political institutions integrated by the ethical purpose and vision.

Society is neither polity, nor any other form of civic community constituted and shared by human beings as citizens and political agents. It is a much more complex unity of differences and distinctions, functionally differentiated and specifically organized, yet universally operating social systems and their self-descriptive modes of communication. Different functional systems, such as law, politics, economy, education, science or art, establish their internal and self-referential communication and self-constituted boundaries making distinctions between the system and its environment. Constitutional polity may only be described as the political and legal systems' internal construction of the concept of society. Political identity and the fiction of collective selfhood are constructed out of the remembered past that is meaningful as present and can be linked to future operations of the system. The distinction between past and future constitutes both the present polity and its memory. However, this memory is not collective memory in the sense of individuals sharing the same state of affairs and past. In the case of polity, it is a social memory communicated by the systems of positive law and politics to generate and actualize determinate meaning for the systems' operations.

To conclude, the complex semantics of constitutional polity as society constructed by the political system and juridically communicated through political constitutions is part of the function of memory and culture. However, this culture is a construct of the specific systemic memory and therefore cannot guarantee overall social integration. All 'foundations' and 'constituting' moments of polity merely use memory as an operation selecting between what needs to be remembered and forgotten to facilitate the function of the political system – collectively binding decision-making at local, national, supranational or transnational levels – and its juridical form of constitutions with their specific legal operations.

Bibliography

Anderson, B. 1983. *Imagined Communities: Reflections on the Origin and Spread of Nationalism.* London, Verso.

Bauman, Z. 2000. *Community: Seeking Safety in an Insecure World.* Cambridge, Polity.

Bond, N. 2013. *Understanding Ferdinand Tönnies' "Community and Society": Social Theory and Political Philosophy Between Enlightened Liberal Individualism and Transfigured Community.* Berlin, Lit Verlag.

Brubaker, R. 1996. *Nationalism Reframed: Nationhood and the National Question in the New Europe*. Cambridge, Cambridge University Press.

Calhoun, C. 1993. 'Nationalism and Ethnicity'. 19 *Annual Review of Sociology*, 211–39.

Castells, M. 2004. *The Power of Identity. The Information Age: Economy, Society and Culture, Volume II.* Oxford, Blackwell Publishing. 2nd edn.

Clarke, M. 1976. 'Durkheim's Sociology of Law'. 3(2) *British Journal of Law and Society*, 246–55.

Connor, W. 1994. *Ethnonationalism: The Quest for Understanding*. Princeton, New Jersey, Princeton University Press.

Cotterrell, R. 1992. *The Sociology of Law. An Introduction.* London, Butterworths. 2nd edn.

Cotterrell, R. 1995. *Law's Community: Legal Theory in Sociological Perspective.* Oxford, Clarendon Press.

Cotterrell, R. 1999. *Emile Durkheim: Law in a Moral Domain.* Edinburgh, Edinburgh University Press.

Cotterrell, R. 2003. *The Politics of Jurisprudence: A Critical Introduction to Legal Philosophy*. London, Butterworths. 2nd edn.

Cotterrell. R. 2006a. 'Law and Social Theory'. In *Law, Culture and Society: Legal Ideas in the Mirror of Social Theory.* Aldershot, Ashgate, 15–28.

Cotterrell, R. 2006b. 'Legal Philosophy and Legal Pluralism'. In *Law, Culture and Society: Legal Ideas in the Mirror of Social Theory*. Aldershot, Ashgate, 29–44.

Cotterrell, R. 2008. 'Transnational Communities and the Concept of Law'. 21(1) *Ratio Juris: An International Journal of Jurisprudence and Philosophy of Law*, 1–18.

Cotterrell, R. 2009. 'Spectres of Transnationalism: Changing Terrains of Sociology of Law'. 36(4) *Journal of Law and Society*, 481–500.

Cubitt, G. (ed.) 1998. *Imagining Nations*. Manchester, Manchester University Press.

Frazer, E. 1999. *The Problems of Communitarian Politics: Unity and Conflict.* Oxford, Oxford University Press.

Gellner, E. 1983. *Nations and Nationalisms*. Oxford, Blackwell.

Gierke, O. von. 1990. *Community in Historical Perspective*. Edited by A. Black. Cambridge, Cambridge University Press.

Griller, S. and Ziller, J. (eds) 2008. *The Lisbon Treaty: EU Constitutionalism without a Constitutional Treaty?* Wien, Springer.

Kuper, A. 2004. *Democracy Beyond Borders*. Oxford, Oxford University Press.

Lindahl, H.K. 2007a. 'The Paradox of Constituent Power. The Ambiguous Self-constitution of the European Union'. 20(4) *Ratio Juris: An International Journal of Jurisprudence and Philosophy of Law*, 485–505.
Lindahl, H.K. 2007b. 'Constituent Power and Reflexive Identity: Towards an Ontology of Collective Selfhood.' In M. Loughlin and N. Walker, N. (eds), *The Paradox of Constitutionalism: Constituent Power and Constitutional Form*. Oxford, Oxford University Press. 9–24.
Loughlin, M. and Walker, N. (eds) 2007. *The Paradox of Constitutionalism: Constituent Power and Constitutional Form*. Oxford, Oxford University Press.
Loughlin, M. 2013. 'The Concept of Constituent Power'.12(4) *European Journal of Political Theory*, 1–21.
Luhmann, N. 2012. *Theory of Society, Volume 1*. Stanford, Stanford University Press.
Luhmann, N. 2013. *Theory of Society, Volume 2*. Stanford, Stanford University Press.
Lukes, S. 1985. *Emile Durkheim, His Life and Work: A Historical and Critical Study*. Stanford, Stanford University Press.
Mitzman, A. 1987. *Sociology and Estrangement: Three Sociologists of Imperial Germany*. New Brunswick, Transaction.
Poggi, G. 1994. *The State: Its Nature, Development and Prospects*. Stanford, Stanford University Press.
Press, U.K. 2010. 'Disconnecting Constitutions from Statehood: Is Global Constitutionalism a Viable Concept?' In P. Dobner and M. Loughlin (eds), *The Twilight of Constitutionalism?* Oxford, Oxford University Press. 23–46.
Přibáň, J. 2007. *Legal Symbolism: On Law, Time and European Identity*. Aldershot, Ashgate.
Přibáň, J. and Nelken, D. (eds) 2001. *Law's New Boundaries: The Consequences of Legal Autopoiesis*. Aldershot, Ashgate.
Rychlík, J. and Marzik, T.D. (eds) 1996. *R.W. Seton-Watson and His Relations with the Czechs and Slovaks: Documents, 1906–1951*. Prague, Ústav T.G. Masaryka Publishing.
Selznick, P. 2004. 'Selznick Interviewed: Philip Selznick in Conversation with Roger Cotterrell'. 31(3) *Journal of Law and Society*, 291–317.
Seton-Watson, H. 1977. *Nations and States: An Enquiry into the Origins of Nations and the Politics of Nationalism*. York, Methuen.
Sousa Santos, B. 2002. *Towards a New Legal Common Sense*. London, Butterworths. 2nd edn.
Taylor, P.J. 1994. 'The State as Container: Territoriality in the Modern World-System'. 18 *Progress in Human Geography*, 151–62.
Tönnies, F. 2002. *Community and Society*. Mineola, NY, Dover Publications.
Von Daniels, D. 2010. *The Concept of Law from a Transnational Perspective*. Aldershot, Ashgate.

Chapter 6

The Politics of *The Politics of Jurisprudence*

Brian Z. Tamanaha

Roger Cotterrell's *The Politics of Jurisprudence* is an illuminating book at several levels. On the surface it provides a survey of legal theory past and present. In the course of setting out various theories, Cotterrell critically engages them, astutely pointing out gaps and weaknesses, and indicating how they relate to and measure up against competing theories. That is standard fare for jurisprudence texts. What sets his book apart is that he does not stop with theoretical exegesis: he looks beyond the theories as well, identifying surrounding factors that influenced theorists to take particular positions or focus on particular issues, and factors that help explain how contemporaries responded to these theories. Cotterrell places special emphasis on the need of the legal profession and legal system for legitimation. As he states: 'The claim that there is an important relationship between normative legal theory's concerns with unity or system in law, on the one hand, and legal professionalism and politics, on the other, provides a framework in which to consider, in the following chapters, some influential currents of Anglo-American legal philosophy' (2003: 12). This angle allows Cotterrell to uncover fascinating insights that are not immediately apparent if one examines only the substance of the theories.

His framework prompts a question about the book itself. Cotterrell argues that legal theories – and the legal theorists who construct them – are influenced in subtle ways by their surrounding context of creation. Presumably, this analysis applies to any work in legal theory. Cotterrell's book is not just about jurisprudence – it is a work *in* jurisprudence in so far as he discusses the strengths and weaknesses of various theories as theories of the nature of law.[1] So, what background factors have influenced *this* work of legal theory? And how have these factors affected his presentation of legal theory? I raise these questions not to undermine his analysis, but to shed additional light on his project, a project that I share.

Asking these questions brings to the foreground a context that runs throughout the book, which Cotterrell mentions but does not emphasize. He repeatedly exposes the various ways legal theory has served the needs and interests of the legal profession. 'Thus,' he writes, 'the book suggests that this legal philosophical literature has helped to reinforce views about the nature of law which have seemed important for the legal professions' status and objectives at particular times' (2003: vii). Legal theorists, however, have identified themselves not just with the legal profession but also – and in some cases more so – with an even higher calling (in their minds): developing the philosophy or science of law. This is about the pursuit of fundamental truths about law. Legal theorists are academics with professional scholarly commitments and ambitions that influence their theories of

1 It is possible to engage in a sociological study of jurisprudence that is not itself a work in jurisprudence. An informative example is Richard Nobles and David Schiff, *A Sociology of Jurisprudence*. Although they discuss jurisprudential theories, their focus is on articulating how a systems perspective would construe the same jurisprudential issues being debated, rather than engaging in the jurisprudential debates themselves. Their work is truly sociological. In contrast, Cotterrell relates the debates, offers his assessment of the theories (whether they are convincing jurisprudentially), and offers sociological insights about social influences on the legal theories and their reception.

law in direct and subtle ways. One of the ironies of Cotterrell's argument that certain legal theories can be understood in terms of serving the interests of the legal profession is that lawyers have regularly asserted that theoretical work on law is irrelevant to what they do. Their indifference does not refute Cotterrell's argument, but it evidences a divide that must be taken account of.

Herein I bring out how academic professional commitments have influenced legal theories, and I show how political commitments can conflict with professional commitments among members of the legal profession. Paying attention to these other sources of influence, I suggest, helps provide a richer sense of factors that might influence theory development.

1. Normative Versus Empirical Legal Theory

To understand Cotterrell's argument one must keep in mind a fundamental contrast he draws between 'normative legal theory' and 'empirical legal theory'. Normative legal theory emphasizes the unity, reason, and system in law. Empirical legal theory sees law as a social institution that cannot be isolated and is best understood through application of the social sciences.

> By its nature, normative legal theory tends to exclude systematic consideration of the social context of law. It does so in two ways. First, unlike the empirical legal theory which is a major concern of sociological studies of law, normative legal theory, as it has been defined in this chapter, attempts to explain the nature of law almost exclusively through philosophical analysis and clarification of the values, concepts, principles, rules and modes of reasoning entailed in or presupposed by legal doctrine. Empirical legal theory, by contrast, relies heavily on systematic empirical analysis of legal institutions in their social environment and historical context. These behavioral and contextual inquiries are largely absent from normative legal theory.
>
> ....
>
> Rather than close off law analytically, legal theory should interpret it in ever-widening perspectives .... But normative legal theory has usually been produced from the perspectives of very specific kinds of legal participants – especially lawyers. So it has often served systematically to express (rather than challenge) their outlook, to confirm and refine their views of the nature of law while being influenced by their special practical needs with regard to the ordering and interpretation of legal knowledge. (Cotterrell 2003: 14–15)

Ignorance about surrounding social factors and inattention to empirical information about law, Cotterrell argues (2003: 264–6), renders normative legal theories defective as accounts of law and less useful to the legal profession, legal system and community. 'Ultimately then, the conclusion must be that normative legal theory and empirical legal theory need to become a single enterprise' (2003: 263).

Several odd implications follow from Cotterrell's dichotomy. For one, it classifies as 'normative' theories that the theorists themselves thought were not 'normative', for example John Austin's general jurisprudence, which he presented as 'concerned with law as it necessarily *is*, rather than with law as it *ought* to be' (1869: 33). Austin's theory involved conceptual clarifications aimed at capturing the nature of law. Furthermore, Cotterrell's category groups together theories that stand in opposition: H.L.A. Hart's legal positivist and Ronald Dworkin's anti-positivist theories are both 'normative legal theories' in Cotterrell's scheme.

'Normative' has a special dual meaning here. Normative legal theories, according to Cotterrell, attempt 'to explain the nature of law as a structure of legal ideas or legal doctrine (that is, in terms of the unity, autonomy, rationality, moral justification or systematic character of legal doctrine)' (2003: 182). This appears to invoke 'normative' in two distinct senses: it views law as a system of norms, *and* it involves an effort to portray law as normatively worthy or legitimate. Empirical legal theories, in contrast, view law as a social institution, explain law by reference to external social factors, and draw from social science to provide a fully informed account of law.

Cotterrell identifies his dichotomy with Hans Kelsen's distinction between 'normative jurisprudence' and 'sociological jurisprudence' (2003: 267). But there are major differences. Kelsen meant 'normative' only in the first sense – law as a system of norms. And Kelsen presented a tripartite breakdown: 'The limits of this subject [analytical jurisprudence] and its cognition must be clearly fixed in two directions: the specific science of law, the discipline usually called jurisprudence, must be distinguished from the philosophy of justice, on the one hand, and from sociology, or cognition of social reality, on the other' (1941: 44). Legal positivist approaches and natural law approaches are thus placed in separate categories. Moreover, Kelsen maintained that analytical jurisprudence and sociological jurisprudence cannot be combined. 'The pure theory of law by no means denies the validity of such sociological jurisprudence, but it declines to see in it, as many of its exponents do, the only science of law. Sociological jurisprudence stands side by side with normative jurisprudence, and neither can replace the other because each deals with completely different problems' (1941: 52).[2]

Cotterrell, however, proposes a combination or merger of sorts. 'Normative legal theory,' he urges, 'must ally itself with empirical legal theory to make sense of law's changing circumstances' (2003: 265–6). True to his sociological orientation, he wants legal theories to be more empirically informed and sociologically sophisticated. While I share his desire, Cotterrell fails to appreciate the extent to which the academic commitments of legal theorists stand in the way of his proposal. Legal theorists of various stripes are engaged in different projects, some of which are resolutely anti-empirical. A tripartite division along the lines proposed by Kelsen, I will argue at the close of this chapter, is more likely to succeed in advancing Cotterrell's aims.

2. The Academic Influence on Legal Theory

Legal theorists are *theorists*, not lawyers. They tend to have a theoretical turn of mind attracted to abstraction, generalization, organization, systematization, categorization; they are inclined to logic and structure, to making sense of things, to articulating rational connections, to finding order within apparent chaos, to creating coherence. Academic settings that support the production of legal theory value and reinforce these traits. Notice that several essential qualities Cotterrell identifies with normative legal theory – emphasizing legal unity, rationality, system and order – are also qualities that mark theoretical work in general (at least before the advent of post-modernism). What Cotterrell attributes to serving the interests of the legal profession, therefore, can also be understood as the inclinations and type of work theorists do.

Take John Austin. He died in relative poverty and all but forgotten. Austin failed at the bar after a brief stint, and then he failed as a lecturer of jurisprudence after a few years in a professorship, when his lectures dwindled to a handful of attendees.[3] Austin failed as a lawyer because he lacked

2 Although he identified his theory with analytical jurisprudence, Kelsen uses the term 'normative jurisprudence' to label his 'pure theory of law' because his theory presented law as a system of norms. As Hart observed (1965: 712–13), this choice of labels was a source of confusion.

3 See John Macdonell, Austin, John (1790–1859), *Dictionary of National Biography, 1885–1900*, vol. 2., page 265–8, at http://en.wikisource.org/wiki/Austin,_John_%281790-1859%29_%28DNB00%29.

the aptitude for legal practice, his widow Sarah Austin explained, but he failed as a jurisprudence professor because 'The demand for anything like scientific legal education had to be created' (Austin 1869: 12). When Austin's *The Province of Jurisprudence Determined* was originally published in 1832 it made no apparent impact. Lord Melbourne said at the time, 'it was the dullest book he ever read, and full of truisms elaborately set forth'.[4]

One would not expect such an unfriendly reception for a jurisprudent who Cotterrell contends developed a legal theory that served the interests of the English legal profession. A partial explanation is perhaps that his positivist theory was issued a generation early, before legislation had become a dominant feature of law. But what also helps explain the initial indifference from the bar is Austin's ambition. He aimed to construct a science or philosophy (interchangeable terms then) of positive law that provided an account of the nature of law. Accordingly, his general jurisprudence was explicitly divorced from the English legal system and from any particular legal system. 'My design is to show, *not what is law here or there, but what is law*: As Plato, Aristotle, Cicero and divers others have done, without taking upon them the profession of the study of law' (Austin 1869: 33). Austin believed his analysis would assist jurists working in particular legal systems, but his enterprise was emphatically *scientific* (Austin 1869: 9). 'He was insatiable in the pursuit of knowledge and truth for their own sake,' wrote Sarah Austin (Austin 1869: 19).

His mission to construct a science of law (earning a place within the pantheon of great philosophers) had a significant influence on the tenor and contours of his theory of law. English law and Roman law provided the material he abstracted from when devising his theory of the nature of law, but his account, as Lord Melbourne suggested, is filled with arid distinctions and conceptual clarifications that philosophers might appreciate but practicing lawyers and judges would see little benefit in. This is not limited to Austin. Much legal theory is dispensable in this sense: legal practitioners and judges can carry on just fine with their practices blissfully ignorant of legal theories. For this reason, if legal theory is to flourish, it must find support in *academic* institutions, not legal institutions. Legal practice and legal theory are different enterprises.

3. Rejection of Legal Science by the Bar

The identification of law with science extends back at least to the mid eighteenth century, when Blackstone proclaimed that law is a rational science. Renowned American law reformer David Dudley Field effused in 1859 that there is no science 'greater in magnitude or importance' than 'the science of law' (1859/2000: 740). But this phrase was apprehended in different ways. For some it meant systematic knowledge (Mayes 1833: 349); for others 'science' was a loose synonym for 'philosophy' (Sprague 1876: 648); for many it was an 'honorific' term without real content (Cairnes 1969: 3). Regardless of this ambiguity, the very assertion that law is a science had an impact, requiring that legal knowledge be systematized like other sciences. Nineteenth-century American legal academics were especially enamoured with the idea that law is a science, for that made it a field of learning suitable for the university. Academics were forthright about this. Dean Christopher Columbus Langdell of Harvard asserted, '[i]f law be not a science, a university will best consult its own dignity in declining to teach it' (quoted in White 1978: 220); likewise, the dean of Columbia Law School wrote, 'it is only by regarding law as a science that one can justify its being taught in a university' (Keener 1892: 144, 1894: 710). Thus legal educators had a direct

4 Ibid. 266.

stake in the view that law is a science; jurisprudents in particular would embrace it because it was consistent with their theoretical commitments.

Legal practitioners remained openly sceptical, however. In 1874, the lawyer-editors of the *Albany Law Journal* (1874: 371) marked this gap between theorists and practitioners: 'This view [law is a science] is now taken by all theoretical legists; but it has not come down to the professional level, and for the most part, the jurist and the practitioner do not stop to inquire whether their system is a science …' Henry White, a member of the bar, wrote in the *Yale Law Journal* in 1892 (6): 'If the law were an exact science and furnished a complete system of rules which could be applied without serious difficulty and with certain results in every case, perhaps it would be better not to look beyond the written law in determining controversies. But … most cases of any difficulty present questions of law on which no one can confidently predict the decision. Most important battles in the courts, which do not turn on questions of fact, are fought on the frontier of the law, where the ground is unsettled, and where new rules are being formulated and new precedents made'.

The effort of theoretically inclined legal academics to present law as a science is the source of a major misapprehension of the period. Today, the turn of the twentieth century is widely seen as the 'formalist age' in American law when jurists viewed law as logically ordered and gapless, and believed that judges engaged in mechanical rule application.[5] While a few jurisprudents spoke of law in these terms, many legal academics did not, and practitioners demurred. Austin Abbott (1893: 2), who became a Dean after a long career as a lawyer, expressed scepticism about the assertion that judging involved pure logical deduction (a view he associated with jurisprudence scholars):

> What is the method of reasoning that even common law courts are really pursuing? Is it simply a system of logic, having inflexible lines of a syllogism as its deductions? An examination of the current reports of the decisions will show that while many cases are decided upon that principle a considerable proportion even of common law cases are decided upon principles of utility …. Cases are now frequent in which our courts of last resort are guided in their decision by considering which of several rules will work the best. This is not the jurisprudence of a system of commands; it is the jurisprudence of common welfare wrought out by free reasoning upon the actual facts of life.

A lawyer named Jabez Fox wrote several turn of the century commentaries in the *Harvard Law Review* offering the view from practice. 'If you ask a lawyer whether he really believes that judicial decisions are mathematical deductions', Fox wrote (1900: 42) criticizing the position of a Harvard law professor, 'he will say that the notion is absurd; that when four judges vote one way and three another, it does not mean that the three or the four have made a mistake. It means simply that the different judges have given different weights to divers competing considerations which cannot be balanced on any measured scale'. Fox added that although judges must follow precedents that cannot be distinguished on some rational ground, 'Beyond this the judge has a free hand to decide the case before him according to his view of the general good …. [and] no human being can tell how the social standard of justice will work on that judge's mind before the judgment is rendered' (43). Fox tossed the same sceptical wet blanket on Oliver Wendell Holmes' assertion in *The Path of the Law* that judges saw law as a matter of logic; Fox responded (1897: 6), 'the learned judge finds it necessary to expose a fallacy; namely "the notion that the only force at work in the development of the law is logic"'. 'But is this a common error?', Fox asked. 'I cannot believe … that this particular fallacy has taken a deep hold on the profession'.

5 For a refutation of this characterization of this period, see Tamanaha 2010.

The late nineteenth-century promotion of legal science by legal theorists, when viewed from a certain angle, might be taken to confirm Cotterrell's argument that normative legal theory serves the legal profession by presenting law as an ordered system of principles and doctrines. One must wonder, however, why members of the bar can be heard rejecting these characterizations as unrealistic depictions of law and judging. Their expressions of bemusement at claims of legal science suggests that theoretical portrayals of the systematic nature law by members of the legal academy were perhaps shaped as much by academic norms and interests as the needs of the legal profession.

4. When Politics and Professional Interests Clash

Paying closer attention to what members of the bar say about law and judging exposes the legal profession as not always united and, sometimes, how political commitments clash with professional interests. The turn of the twentieth century was a period of great turmoil in American society that played out in legal arenas. At the time, courts were the target of sharp criticisms for favouring capital at the expense of labour, for aligning with the rich against the poor and for erecting barriers against social welfare legislation. Some members of the bar joined in these criticisms, issuing candid remarks about the social influences on judging.

A remarkably modern-sounding article, 'Politics and the Supreme Court of the United States', was published in 1893 by Walter Coles, a St. Louis lawyer, in the leading *American Law Review*. Coles examined Supreme Court decisions over the prior century, matching the political background of the justices with their decisions. 'Viewing the history of the Supreme Court at large, and stating conclusions somewhat broadly, it may be said that its adjudications on constitutional questions have in their general tendencies conformed, in a greater or lesser degree, to the maxims of the political party whose appointees have, for the time being, dominated the court' (207). He criticized several Supreme Court opinions as 'vague', 'weak, incoherent, and uncandid', (205) best explained not by the stated legal reasoning but by the political views of the judges. '[T]o say that no political prejudices have swayed the court', noted Coles with consummate realism, 'is to maintain that its members have been exempt from the known weaknesses of human nature, and above those influences which operate most powerfully in determining the opinions of other men' (182). Especially when no clear precedent exists, he asserted, a judge's conclusions 'will be largely controlled by the influences, opinions and prejudices to which he happened to have been subjected' (190).

Critical commentary along these lines came not just from lawyers but from prominent *judges*. Walter Clark, Chief Judge of the North Carolina Supreme Court, delivered a series of speeches in the first decade of the new century challenging court decisions that were antagonistic to progressive causes:

> It has never been charged that such judges are corruptly influenced. But the passage of a judge from the bar to the bench does not necessarily destroy his prejudices or his predilections .... [H]aving spent their lives at the bar in advocacy of corporate claims, this will unconsciously, but effectively, be reflected in the decisions they make. Having attempted as lawyers to persuade courts to view debated questions from the standpoint of aggregated wealth, they often end by believing sincerely in the correctness of such views, and not unnaturally put them in force when in turn they themselves ascend the bench. (1906/1950: 570)

The due process and equal protection clauses, Clark said, 'are very elastic and mean whatever the court passing upon the statute thinks most effective for its destruction. This, of course, makes of vital importance the inquiry, "What are the beliefs of the majority of the court on economic questions, and what happens to be their opinion of sound public policy?" A power so great and so irreviewable and therefore so irresponsible, has become the mainstay of the anti-progressive element' (1906/1950: 578).

Another prominent legal progressive, Judge Seymour Thompson (1896: 685), used blunter terms when characterizing the 1895 Supreme Court invalidation of income tax: 'Our judicial annals do not afford an instance of a more unpatriotic subserviency to the demands of the rich and powerful classes'. 'The powerful have been encroaching through the courts', warned John Gibbons (1897: 439), an Illinois circuit judge. 'Security under the law is vouchsafed in unstinted measures to property rights, but niggardly doled out when personal rights seek redress and recognition at the bar of justice. The plea of the powerful is potent, but the plaint of the poor is too often unheard. The mighty forces of wealth compel a hearing where the struggling ranks of work are denied a standing in court.'

What statements like these show is that legal professionals were not united behind the image of law as purely a system of norms, and were willing to raise sharp questions about the legitimacy of law. Legal practitioners and legal academics have long been aware of the openness of law and how judging is sensitive to background social views. Consider these comments by a well-known law professor, Christopher Tiedeman, uttered in 1896 (19–20 emphasis added):

> If the Court is to be considered a body of individuals, standing far above the people, out of reach of their passions and opinions, in an atmosphere of cold reason, deciding every question that is brought before them according to the principles of eternal and never-varying Justice, then and then only may we consider the opinion of the Court as the ultimate source of the law. This, however, is not the real evolution of municipal law. *The bias and peculiar views of the individual judge do certainly exert a considerable influence over the development of the law* .... The opinion of the court, in which the reasons for its judgment is set forth, is a most valuable guide to a knowledge of law on a given proposition, *but we cannot obtain a reliable conception of the effect of the decision by merely reading the opinion. This thorough knowledge is to be acquired only by studying the social and political environment of the parties and the subject matter of the suit, the present temper of public opinion and the scope and character of the popular demands, as they bear upon the particular question at issue.*[6]

Tiedeman advised (1892) that to understand a legal ruling one 'must look beneath the judicial opinion' and take into consideration 'the pressure of public opinion and the influences of private interests' revolving around the case. Tiedeman's account of judging, it should be noted, is consistent with, among others, the historical jurisprudence position that social attitudes make their way into law through the thinking of judges.

Cotterrell's portrayal of normative legal theory – systematic presentations of the unity of legal doctrine that legitimates the law – suppresses the seething criticisms of law and judging that are expressed from *within* the legal profession and legal academia. Cotterrell mentions scepticism and realism as theoretical perspectives on law associated with the legal realists and critical legal studies. That is the standard jurisprudential narrative. But the above statements were uttered over

6 Not surprisingly, given these views, Tiedeman was viewed at the time as something of a sceptic of judging. See Monroe 1924: 745.

a generation before the emergence of legal realism. Every generation has its own political battles played out in law and the losing political side will respond with sceptical criticisms of judging. Legal practitioners are well aware of the realities of law and judging. None of these comments, I should emphasize, detract from Cotterrell's argument that jurisprudential theories are influenced by surrounding political considerations and professional interests. He is right about this and his account places a great deal of weight on the interests of the legal profession in legitimation, which no doubt have played and continue to play a role. My point is only that the picture is considerably more complicated because legal practice and legal theory are two different realms of discourse with divergent orientations, because two professions are involved (legal and academic), and because political-social-moral disputes within society are manifested in various ways within each profession.

Legal theories subtly reflect these influences, sometimes openly but often unannounced. Ronald Dworkin was not just constructing a theory of law to counter legal positivism; he was also providing an account to justify and defend the Warren Court's expansion of rights against conservative attack. In his natural law argument, the 'Basic Goods' John Finnis posits as self-evident have a Catholic feel, perhaps reflecting his personal religious beliefs. To point this out is not to commit the genetic fallacy – identifying what might have shaped a given theory does not detract from its merits. But it is a reminder, one consistent with Cotterrell's own message, that we should be wary of claims that any theory is an objective presentation of the nature of law. Multiple political and professional commitments can sometimes pull a legal theorist in different directions. Roscoe Pound was committed to law and the legal profession. Pound was also committed to the academic profession and to jurisprudence. In addition, he was sympathetic to progressive political causes, he sharply criticized common law judging, he argued that the common law was too individualist in orientation, he advocated legislation to modernize the law, he believed law should be informed by the social sciences, and he advocated an instrumental view of law.[7] Cotterrell flattens much of this (2003: 148–60), painting Pound in the end as a reactionary defender of an organic view of the common law, serving the interests of the legal profession. Perhaps a better way to understand Pound is that his political commitments and professional allegiances resulted in a complex and multifaceted set of views toward law that differed depending upon the issues and the times.

5. The Politics of Empiricism

By placing normative legal theory and empirical legal theory at opposing poles, Cotterrell's dichotomy, in addition to indicating that the former lack empirical grounding, carries the implicit suggestion that empirical approaches are not injected with normative considerations. Social scientific approaches produce verifiably true facts about law: the *is*, not the *ought*. Rather than Austin's legal science or Kelsen's science of law, this is scientific knowledge about law in its social surrounds.

At least in the US, however, the empirical study of law exhibits a marked leftist political bent. A jurisprudence text by Brian Bix (2012: 253) presents this characterization:

7 See Pound 1906, 1908a, 1908b, 1907a, 1907b, 1905.

> The application of sociology to law, known variously as "socio-legal studies", "law and society", and "law in context", has a long history of offering empirically grounded critiques of current laws and legal practices, and suggestions for change. While sociology aims to be descriptive and morally neutral, many of those who identify with this approach have "progressive" or radical views, and so these movements have often been thought of as more "critical" than scientific.

Bix does not contend that sociological approaches to law are incapable of being descriptively and morally neutral – but that, as the field has developed, much of the research is politically oriented. In her Presidential Address to the Law and Society Association, Sally Engle Merry (1995: 13) proudly acknowledged that socio-legal scholars have evinced a 'historical concern for social justice and progressive politics'.[8] A recent overview concurs: 'the field of law and society emerged from a critique of formal law coupled with a commitment to progressive values of scientific methods and pluralist politics.' 'These founding commitments to bridging social science and legal scholarship, progressive social change, a pluralist politics, and a critical perspective on law's internal accounts continue to shape the field's discourse and debates' (Seron, Coutin and White Meeusen 2013: 290).

Law and society studies thus echo the main themes in Cotterrell's challenge to normative legal theory. Marc Galanter in his Presidential Address (1974: 537), for example, drew the same contrast between 'the professionally-based learning that emphasizes law as an autonomous system of general rules' and social science research which 'tries to appreciate the dynamics of social life'. A great deal of empirical work in recent decades has shown how the supposed unity and neutrality of law systematically represses various disadvantaged groups within society. This focus comports with Cotterrell's assertion of 'normative legal theory's need to recognize the diversity of meanings, understandings and experiences of law produced by the differentiation of the social' (2003: 261). Having a leftist political orientation, which might shape what socio-legal researchers choose to study and the angle they take on their subject, does not in itself detract from the empirical soundness of their findings – just as political influences on normative legal theories do not necessarily impugn their integrity. And a great deal of empirical work on law has no evident political orientation. That said, it is important to be cognizant of the potential influence of politics on empirical approaches for the same reasons Cotterrell suggests we should be cognizant of how politics shapes jurisprudence. Awareness of this helps us understand what normative legal theories *and* empirical legal theories are about: why they emphasize what they do, why they tend to take certain positions while ignoring others, and so forth.

6. The State of Contemporary Legal Theory

The final three chapters of the *Politics of Jurisprudence* address various streams of modern legal theory, beginning with the sceptical, instrumental take on law introduced by pragmatism and realism, then covering critical legal studies, critical feminism, critical race theory, postmodernism and deconstruction. None of these schools of thought are normative legal theories in Cotterrell's sense: they do not exclusively focus on legal doctrine to demonstrate unity and system. To the contrary, they are more interested in exposing the failings, partiality and emptiness of law, and its readiness to serve power. He favourably discusses theoretical approaches that emphasize the differentiation of society and that show how law interacts with different groups. Thus, no longer

8 For a critical discussion, see Tamanaha 1997: 20–24, 47–57.

can a single conceptual map be constructed for law, and no longer can law be said to speak for a single community (contra Dworkin and older visions of the common law), at least not without recognition of different perspectives. In his view these are positive developments (254–7). At the end of a book that highlights the shortcomings of normative legal theory, it might come as a surprise to read that Cotterrell hopes to *save* normative legal theory:

> These critiques, valuable as many of them are, do not destroy the worth of normative legal theory as an enterprise. It is still necessary to draw conceptual maps of law, to examine the bases of legal authority, to consider the unity or structure of legal doctrine, to explain the characteristics of legal interpretation and to ask how far law can usefully be analysed independently of morality or ethical debate. (254)

This is puzzling for several reasons. Since the last few decades have been dominated by sceptically oriented legal theories, it is not clear whether any normative legal theories are left standing aside from Dworkin and his followers; perhaps Cotterrell has in mind contemporary legal positivists, though he does not explicitly engage with them.

It is also not clear why normative legal theory *should* be saved. Why is it necessary to 'draw conceptual maps of law' or to 'ask how far law can usefully be analyzed independently of morality?' He explains:

> Certainly, legal practice does not depend on normative legal theory in any direct way. But, as this book has argued, legal theory often develops and rationalizes notions about law that underpin and inform legal practice. Ultimately, a sense of legal professionalism presupposes basic shared ideas among legal practitioners about the nature of law. One of normative legal theory's practical tasks has been to make these ideas explicit and coherent .... It remains important to lawyers that legal doctrine should have some structure and unity, and normative legal theory has plotted and rationalized their efforts to find this. (265)

The first sentence, however, admitting that legal practice does not require normative legal theory, weighs against the sentences that follow. Legal theory work on the nature of law, as I have argued, is an academic endeavour with its own orientation; legal practice and legal systems do not need comprehensive theories of law to function. Nor is it evident that 'legal professionalism presupposes basic shared ideas among legal practitioners about the nature of law'. The 'structure and unity' normative legal theory traditionally provided encompassed the entire legal system. This is not a plausible vision in an age of instrumental legislation and regulation. The only doctrinal structure lawyers require is local structure, sufficient coherence for particular applications, facilitated by methods to reconcile the conflicts among norms and legal regimes that arise. No general legal theory is necessary to accomplish this. Today in the US, lawyers share a content-empty procedural and instrumental view of law along with thin professional norms; the legal system continues to function robustly, although it might suffer in the future.[9]

In the final passages, Cotterrell tells us why he wishes to save normative legal theory:

> But, of course, law is not just a professional preserve. The value of normative legal theory extends beyond the contributions it might make (or has, in the past, made) to legal professionalism. Its intellectual strength and enduring fascination have come from its commitment to make legal

9 See Tamanaha 2006.

> knowledge a system of reason, a structure of thought that does justice as an intellectual creation to the efforts of all legal minds that have sought solutions to practical problems of social regulation through the ages. The main purpose of this book has been to introduce, critically and constructively, some of the most valuable products of that commitment. (266)

He is an idealist in the best sense of the word, upholding two professional commitments I have emphasized throughout this chapter. He believes in law and believes that a well ordered body of legal knowledge is essential to society. And Cotterrell finds deep pleasure in the intellectual aspects of theory construction – in system building and critical analysis. In having these commitments, it turns out, Cotterrell is much like the normative legal theorists he critically discusses in the book: Austin, Pound, Fuller, Kelsen, Hart, Dworkin, Llewellyn and so on. What distinguishes him is his career-long commitment to the sociology of law. Thus his main criticism of these theories is their failure to pay sufficient attention to the complexity of social forces surrounding law and the need to pay attention to empirical studies of law. His normative legal theory versus empirical legal theory framework was structured to deliver this argument. Recall the dual meaning of his 'normative legal theory' label: lack of empirical grounding, and the search for order and system (and need for legitimacy). He objects to the first aspect of normative legal theory but believes in the second.

Now we know the politics behind *The Politics of Jurisprudence*. Cotterrell believes in law and the legal profession. He believes in the value of theory, but thinks theory must be empirically informed. He believes societies are differentiated in various ways and there are different types of communities within social arenas, but in the end the broader community and its legal system must hang together in basic ways or will suffer or be dysfunctional. His wants a suitably reconstructed normative legal theory, not its abandonment.

While there is much in his vision that I find laudable, I take a different view. For the reasons set forth above, I do not believe what Cotterrell calls normative legal theory is necessary, though it may be desirable in the ideal. Legal practice and the operation of the legal system can take care of themselves without an organizing theory of law, and the goal of finding or imposing unity and reason across legal knowledge is a chimera attractive mainly to minds prone to system building.

Nor do I believe that his criticisms will be persuasive to legal theorists who steadfastly reject the relevance of empirical insights. Cotterrell writes: 'In a sense then, normative legal theory has reaped its reward for substantially ignoring the patterned differentiation of the social as a field of meaning and experience. The differentiated social, represented to law by various kinds of radical legal practice, now substantially ignores normative legal theory!' (2003: 235) He reiterates, critics 'warn, rightly in my view, that normative legal theory will become increasingly remote from the changing situation of law unless it looks beyond its familiar ways of conceptualizing legal doctrine to develop a systematic understanding of changes in the social' (2003: 265).

If Cotterrell means to address his warning to contemporary legal positivists, they show little concern about not being read by radical or critical legal theorists, or by anyone else for that matter. Modern analytical jurisprudents are pursuing universal truths about law, seeing no need to incorporate sociological insights, pace Joseph Raz:

> Since a legal theory must be true of all legal systems the identifying features by which it characterizes them must of necessity be very general and abstract. It must disregard those functions which some legal systems fulfill in some societies because of the special social, economic, or cultural conditions of those societies. It must fasten only on those features of legal systems which they must possess regardless of the special circumstances of the societies in which they are in force. This is the difference between legal philosophy and sociology of law.

> The latter is concerned with the contingent and with the particular, the former with the necessary and the universal. Sociology of law provides a wealth of detailed information and analysis of the functions of law in some particular societies. Legal philosophy has to be content with those few features which all legal systems necessarily possess. (2009a: 104–5)

'It is easy to explain in what sense legal philosophy is universal,' Raz asserts. 'Its theses, if true, apply universally, that is they speak of all law, of all legal systems; of those that exist, or that will exist, and even of those that can exist though they never will' (2009b: 91). This aspiration is categorically anti-empirical. Other leading legal positivists have echoed this stance. 'Social sciences cannot tell us what the law is because it studies human society,' Scott Shapiro (2011: 406–7) declares. 'Its deliverances have no relevance for the legal philosopher because it is a truism that nonhumans could have law. Science fiction, for example, is replete with stories involving alien civilizations with some form of legal system .... Social scientific theories are limited in this respect, being able to study only human groups, and hence cannot provide an account about all possible instances of law.'[10]

What explains their rejection of sociological insights goes back to the dual professional orientations of legal theorists. Cotterrell correctly observes that a great deal of legal theory in the past two centuries has been produced by theorists grounded in law. And his main thesis follows from this grounding: 'this book has attempted to relate trends in normative legal theory to the concerns of Anglo-American legal professions' (2003: 264). But in the past few decades, particularly with the influx of legal theorists with advanced degrees in philosophy, the orientation among analytical jurisprudents has perceptibly shifted toward prioritizing philosophical concerns. In this respect contemporary legal philosophers are much like Austin and Kelsen in the pursuit of a science of law. The fact that people in law pay them little heed is unimportant: their conversation is with fellow philosophers. Contemporary analytical jurisprudents of this ilk will not be moved by Cotterrell's critique to incorporate empirical insights into their theory work because there are resolutely abstract, conceptual and analytical (see Tamanaha 2012). As I indicated at the outset, I share Cotterrell's empirically-oriented theory project. I believe there is a better way to advance this project than the path he recommends. Rather than urge other legal theorists to open up to empirical insights – they will do so only if it suits their purposes, not because we urge them to – empirically oriented legal theorists should develop sophisticated social theories of law built on these insights. Natural law theory and legal positivism need not become empirically informed. Legal theory thrives through alternative approaches. A century ago legal theorists recognized a tripartite set of orientations: normative legal theory, analytical legal theory, and social-historical legal theory (see Tamanaha 2013). The first two orientations are well recognized and have made distinct contributions to knowledge about law. The third orientation is the youngest and has yet to be fully acknowledged. Recognition will come as social theories of law are further elaborated. Though it will draw heavily from sociological perspectives on law, this third orientation is not legal sociology per se. Rather, it is distinctively jurisprudential, in the sense of constituting a theoretical account of law grounded within the concerns and perspectives of jurists seeking an understanding of the social nature of law. Through his extensive writings on the sociology of law, jurisprudence, and law's connections with community, Cotterrell has made a major contribution to this effort.

10 Ironically, just as legal philosophers declare the irrelevance of social science, we witness the opposite tendency of scientists denying the relevance of philosophy. See Hughes 2012. On all sides, this has the feel of intellectual border-patrolling and one-upmanship.

Bibliography

Abbott, A. 1983. 'Existing Questions on Legal Education'. 3 *Yale Law Journal* 1.

Albany Law Journal, Editors. 1874. 'Is the Law a Philosophy, a Science, or an Art?' 10 *Albany Law Journal* 371.

Austin, J. 1869. *Lectures on Jurisprudence, or the Philosophy of Positive Law*. 3rd ed. London, John Murray Publishers. Edited and revised by Robert Campbell.

Bix, B. 2012. *Jurisprudence: Theory and Context*. Durham, NC, Carolina Academic Press, 6th ed.

Cairnes, H. 1969. *The Theory of Legal Science*. New York, Augustus Kelly Publishers, originally published 1941.

Clark, W. 1906. 'Some Defects of the Constitution of the United States' (27 April). In *The Papers of Walter Clark*, edited by A.L. Brooks and H.T. Lefler, vol. 2. Chapel Hill, UNC Press 1950, 570.

Coles, W.D. 1893. 'Politics and the Supreme Court of the United States'. 27 *American Law Review*, 182.

Cotterrell, R. 2003. *The Politics of Jurisprudence: A Critical Introduction to Legal Philosophy*. 2nd ed. London, LexisNexis Butterworths.

Field, D.D. 1859. 'Magnitude and Importance of Legal Science'. Reprinted in S.B. Presser and J.S. Zainaldin (eds), *Law and Jurisprudence in American History*, 5th ed. St. Paul, Minnesota, West Pub. 2000.

Fox, J. 1897. 'Law and Morals'. 1 *Boston Law School Magazine*, 1.

Fox, J. 1900. 'Law and Logic'. 14 *Harvard Law Review*, 39.

Galanter, M. 1974. 'Presidential Address: The Legal Malaise: or, Justice Observed'. 19 *Law and Society Review*, 537.

Gibbons, J. 1897. 'Security Under the Law is the Staff and Shield of the Republic'. 5 *American Law*, 436, 439.

Hart, H.L.A. 1965. 'Kelsen Visited'. 10 UCLA Law Review, 709.

Hughes, A.L. 2012. 'The Folly of Scientism'. 37 *The New Atlantis*, 32. http://www.thenewatlantis.com/publications/the-folly-of-scientism.

Keener, W.A. 1892. 'Methods of Legal Education'. 1 *Yale Law Journal*, 143.

Keener, W.A. 1894. 'The Inductive Method in Legal Education'. 28 *American Law Review*, 709.

Kelsen, H. 1941. 'The Pure Theory of Law and Analytical Jurisprudence'. 55 *Harvard Law Review*, 44.

Mayes, D. 1833. 'Whether Law is a Science'. 9 *American Jurist and Law Magazine*, 349.

Merry, S.E. 1995. 'Resistance and the Cultural Power of Law: 1994 Presidential Address'. 29 *Law and Society Review*, 11.

Monroe, A.H. 1924. 'The Supreme Court and the Constitution'. 18 *American Political Science Review*, 737.

Nobles, R. and Schiff, D. 2006. *A Sociology of Jurisprudence*. Oxford, Hart Publishing.

Pound, R. 1905. 'Do We Need a Philosophy of Law?' 5 *Columbia Law Review*, 339.

Pound, R. 1906. 'The Causes of Popular Dissatisfaction with the Administration of Justice'. 14 *American Law*, 445.

Pound, R. 1907a. 'Spurious Interpretation'. 6 *Columbia Law Review*, 379.

Pound, R. 1907b. 'The Need of Sociological Jurisprudence'. 31 *Annual Report ABA*, 990.

Pound, R. 1908. 1908a. 'Common Law and Legislation'. 6 *Harvard Law Review*, 384.

Pound, R. 1908b. 'Mechanical Jurisprudence'. 8 *Columbia Law Review*, 605.

Raz, J. 2009a. *The Authority of Law*. Oxford, Oxford University Press, 2nd ed.

Raz, J. 2009b. *Between Authority and Interpretation*. Oxford, Oxford University Press.

Seron, C., Coutin, S.B. and White Meeusen, P. 2013. 'Is There a Canon of Law and Society?' 9 *Annual Review of Law and Social Science*, 287.
Shapiro, S. 2011. *Legality*. Cambridge, MA, Harvard University Press.
Sprague, A.P. 1876. 'The New Science of Law'. 1 *Law Magazine & Review Quarterly Digest*, 648.
Tamanaha, B.Z. 1997. *Realistic Socio-Legal Theory: Pragmatism and a Social Theory of Law*. Oxford, Clarendon Press.
Tamanaha, B.Z. 2006. *Law as a Means to an End: Threat to the Rule of Law*. New York, Cambridge University Press.
Tamanaha, B.Z. 2010. *Beyond the Formalist-Realist Divide*. Princeton, Princeton University Press.
Tamanaha, B.Z. 2012. 'What is General Jurisprudence? A Critique of Universalistic Claims by Philosophical Concepts of Law'. 2 *Transnational Legal Theory*, 287.
Tamanaha, B.Z. 2013. 'The Third Pillar of Jurisprudence: A Social Theory of Law'. http://papers.ssrn.com/sol3/papers.cfm?abstract_id=2256622.
Thompson, S.D. 1896. 'Government by Lawyers'. 30 *American Law Review*, 672.
Tiedeman, C.G. 1892. 'Dictum and Decision'. 6 *Columbia Law Times*, 35.
Tiedeman, C.G. 1896. 'The Doctrine of Stare Decisis'. 3 *University Law Review*, 11.
White, C.E. 1978. 'The Impact of Legal Science on Tort Law'. 78 *Columbia Law Review*, 213.
White, H.C. 1892. 'Three Views of Practice'. 2 *Yale Law Journal* 1.

PART II
Methodological and Jurisprudential Themes

Chapter 7

Towards a Fruitful Cooperation between Legal Philosophy, Legal Sociology and Doctrinal Research: How Legal Interactionism May Bridge Unproductive Oppositions[1]

Sanne Taekema and Wibren van der Burg

1. Introduction

Roger Cotterrell advocates a broad interdisciplinary approach to law and legal theory. The title of one of his well-known articles is programmatic: 'Why Must Legal Ideas be Interpreted Sociologically?' Similarly, his book *The Politics of Jurisprudence* can be read as an attempt to understand legal theories sociologically – an approach that makes sense of seemingly outdated and unattractive positions in light of the historical conditions of their time. Although Cotterrell's 'strongest intellectual allegiance is to sociology of law, [he] gradually felt dissatisfied with the lack of concern of much legal sociology with any need to engage with legal philosophy' (Cotterrell 2008: 20). His general intellectual programme is nicely expressed in the following statement: 'Legal philosophy and legal sociology are co-workers in a common enterprise of legal explanation' (Cotterrell 2006: 29).

As legal theorists with a background in law and philosophy and a strong interest in legal sociology, we wholeheartedly agree with this advocacy of a broad interdisciplinarity. As co-workers, legal philosophy and legal sociology can fruitfully cooperate with each other in gaining a fuller understanding of law. Theorizing in legal philosophy can be greatly enriched by being empirically informed and tested. Studies in legal sociology may gain depth by being confronted by philosophical normative theories and may gain precision by relying on insights from analytical jurisprudence. Like Cotterrell, we are critical of rigid disciplinarity. Even if it may often be impossible to fully integrate legal sociology, legal philosophy and legal doctrinal research, we should attempt to combine them.

In the cooperative effort of disciplines, we have included legal doctrinal research as a third discipline. We believe that legal doctrinal research is an important partner for legal sociology and legal philosophy, and that the cooperation between these three partners is very fruitful for each of them. The translation of philosophical ideas and empirical insights into practical legal solutions is a good way not only to test the theories by bringing them into practice and to make them practically relevant, it is also enormously enriching for both legal philosophy and legal sociology. The practical

1 This chapter includes materials excerpted by permission of the Publishers from *The Dynamics of Law and Morality. A Pluralist Account of Legal Interactionism* by Wibren van der Burg (Farnham, Ashgate 2014). Copyright © 2013. We would like to thank Briain Jansen and Thomas Riesthuis for their critical comments on an earlier draft.

wisdom and nuances of the legal professions and the mediating role of academic doctrinal research may also provide important starting points for socio-legal and philosophical research.

In this chapter we will mostly focus on the differences between sociological and philosophical approaches to law. For the purposes of this chapter, legal doctrinal research can usually be associated with legal philosophy – both deal primarily with ideas and the meaning, justification and practical implications of those ideas. Only where doctrinal research diverges substantively from legal philosophy, will we pay explicit attention to the differences.

Advocating interdisciplinarity is one thing, actually doing it is another. Interdisciplinary research is not easy, and there are many stumbling blocks to be found. Different disciplines know different methods, different conceptual frameworks, different objects of study, different research goals, different academic cultures. (Taekema and Van Klink 2011: 8–9; Vick 2004: 166–9) Certainly, there are overlaps and fuzzy areas between the disciplines rather than strict separations. Nevertheless, we may usually discern characteristic differences between the mainstream tradition of the various disciplines. Cooperation between disciplines often leads to mutual misunderstandings if we do not explicitly address those differences.

We want to address one important difference that often frustrates successful co-operation between legal sociologists, legal philosophers and doctrinal researchers. That difference is that they rely on different – implicit or explicit – understandings of law, on different concepts and definitions. This makes communication difficult. When lawyers and philosophers implicitly think of law as a coherent doctrine but sociologists rely on an understanding of law as a practice or as a general dimension of social interaction, they have a hard time understanding each other.[2] Of course, there is much variation within these disciplines themselves, as, for example, the debate between legal positivists and natural law theorists testifies. There are, however, important respects in which legal philosophers, sociologists and doctrinal scholars share more with the majority of their own discipline than with sympathetic members of the other two disciplines. It is especially the implicit background character of the differences that hinder a fruitful interaction between the three. The problem we therefore want to address is twofold: how can we make these differences explicit and understand them, and how can we combine the different perspectives on the concept of law without obscuring the insights generated within each perspective? Although we inevitably overgeneralize, we believe that in order to do this it may be helpful to use ideal typical distinctions to formulate the tensions clearly.

2. Four Oppositions

We can discern four basic oppositions regarding the understanding of law. The most basic opposition is that which has become known under the slightly misleading title of law in the books versus law in action.[3] On one side of the spectrum, there are those who conceive of law as the products or enactments of legal institutions such as legislatures and courts, and as the doctrine that can be constructed on the basis of these products. On the other side, there are those who see law as interaction or as a dimension of social interaction, exemplified in customary law or interactional

2 Cf. Cotterrell 2008: 18: 'The sociologists have failed to study law as a world of ideas and as subjective understanding of those ideas in action. The philosophers have failed to study law as a diverse, varied *social and historical experience* ....'

3 This is misleading because it suggests that law itself is an entity that can act rather than the interaction itself. 'Law as interaction' would have been a more adequate phrase. For a critique of Pounds' famous phrase, see Krygier 2012: 141.

law. Most legal philosophers and legal scholars may be found at the pole of enacted law, whereas many sociologists are at the pole of interactional law. As Cotterrell (2006: 45) argues, this is not a strict division of labour, and in our opinion, certainly not a normative distinction that should govern the practice of the various disciplines. Nevertheless, if we look at the work of mainstream legal philosophers and doctrinal scholars, on the one hand, and legal sociologists, on the other, there is a clear difference of focus either on enacted law or on interactional law.

The second opposition is that between monism and pluralism. On the one hand, most legal philosophers and legal scholars still focus on law as one more or less coherent system, usually associated with the state and with a specific territory. Even when philosophers and legal scholars include distinct legal orders such as those of the European Union, and the Council of Europe in their analysis, they usually limit the number of competing legal orders to a few that are all connected with official law-making institutions directly or indirectly associated with the state apparatus. On the other hand, most legal sociologists are pluralists in a broader sense; they accept that there are many different kinds of legal orders, most of which are not associated with official law-making institutions.

The third opposition is that between a focus on the variable and changing characteristics of law and a focus on law as timeless or static. Legal sociology clearly belongs to the first camp, recognizing the importance of variation and processes of change in the study of law (Cotterrell 2008: 18 and 20). However, there is not one opposition here, but two. On the one hand, most philosophers tend to focus on the timeless or universal characteristics of law. For example, classical natural lawyers have tried to find universal normative principles or values underlying law. Many contemporary philosophers would probably agree with Julie Dickson, who argues that the core business of analytical jurisprudence is 'to isolate and explain those features which make law into what it is' (Dickson 2001: 17). She further argues that legal philosophy must analyze the nature of law, that is, 'those essential properties which a given set of phenomena must exhibit in order to be law' (Dickson 2001: 17. See also Shapiro 2011: Chapter 1). On the other hand, most legal scholars construct law as a static phenomenon in a different sense, by providing a construction of the positive law of a certain jurisdiction at a specific moment in time. The aim of legal scholarship is to provide the best picture of law as it currently is.

The fourth opposition is that between instrumentalist and non-instrumentalist views of law. On the one hand, we may regard law as a means to realize policy goals; on the other hand, as a guarantee of interactional norms. Those who focus on enacted law, have a tendency to see enacted law as an instrument in the hands of political institutions; those who focus on customary law or, as many legal professionals do, on law as a distinct and highly autonomous practice upholding values of legality, see institutionalization and codification as a way to guarantee that social norms are actually followed and that distinct legal values are upheld. This is an opposition that is somewhat different from the first three as its division cuts across both legal philosophy and legal sociology rather than between the two disciplines. There is a strong instrumentalist tendency in legal sociology: according to Cotterrell (2008: 21), we may even speak of 'pervasive instrumentalism'. A similar instrumentalism may be found in the works of many modern positivist legal philosophers as well as among law and economics scholars. On the other hand, there are a significant number of researchers, among legal philosophers, legal sociologists, and doctrinal scholars, who are anti-instrumentalist.

Of course, our characterization of these four oppositions provides an ideal typical sketch. Many theorists do not fit in and there are many intermediate positions. Nevertheless, the ideal types may be easily discerned as underlying many positions taken by legal sociologists, legal philosophers and doctrinal legal scholars. Moreover, it is clear that scholars on different poles for each of these four oppositions will encounter difficulties in communicating and co-operating with each other, because they have different things in mind when speaking of law. Therefore, it is important to find ways to transcend these oppositions or at least to understand them as emphasizing different aspects of one common framework in order to transcend the divide between legal philosophy and legal sociology (Cotterrell 2008: 22).

Our claim is that legal interactionism provides such a theoretical approach. Legal interactionism accepts both interactional law and enacted law as law. Therefore, it is very oecumenical in spirit. This broad approach enables us to understand the different poles as part of a full analysis of law, and offers perspectives for integrating the partial insights that a focus on merely one pole can provide.

We will begin by elaborating the first opposition, as it is the most basic (Section 3). Then we will discuss the core tenets of legal interactionism and show that its inclusive approach can transcend this basic opposition (Section 4). In the next three sections, we will show how we may understand each of the remaining oppositions in terms of an interactionist framework, as foci of attention rather than as strict dichotomies (Sections 5 to 7). Finally, we will discuss the theoretical and methodological implications of our analysis for a successful cooperation between legal philosophers, legal sociologists and doctrinal scholars (Section 8).

3. Enacted Law and Interactional Law

What we need, first of all, is a theory that can transcend the unproductive opposition between enacted law and interactional law. These should not be seen as opposites between which we have to choose, but as sources or types of law that are both law in their own right. Here we build on Lon Fuller´s ideas from his book *Anatomy of the Law*, in which he tried to transcend the opposition between natural law and legal positivism and to do justice to the valuable core of truth in both. Fuller makes an important distinction between implicit law and made law (Fuller 1968: 43–84). This analysis, in our view, provides a good starting point for understanding and bridging the difference between sociological and philosophical understandings of law.

Fuller does not explicitly define implicit and made law, but presents them in his discussion of two pure types of law, customary law and legislation, respectively. The two terms are, in our view, unfortunate. In a sense, all law is made law, because law is a human construct – this holds for customary law as much as for statutes. Moreover, the term 'implicit' suggests that once a norm is explicitly formulated – if only in order to explain to the newcomer what the norm is – it no longer counts as implicit law. For these reasons, we prefer two other terms that Fuller uses elsewhere: enacted law versus interactional law.[4] Enacted law is law that comes into existence as the result of an explicit enactment by a legal authority – for example, a legislature, a court, but also an official in an organization, such as the head of a university who makes rules regulating the behaviour of students or staff. Interactional law is law that comes into existence through a gradual process of interaction in which a standard of conduct emerges that is understood as giving rise to legal obligations. Thus, the two names refer to two different sources of law, enactment and interaction.

It may be helpful at this point to explore the characteristics of both ideal types of law in detail. In modern societies, enacted law takes the form of black-letter law, usually consisting of a set of

4 In *The Principles of Social Order* (1981: 232), Fuller uses the terms enacted law and authoritatively declared law as synonyms for made law. Interactional law is used in *The Morality of Law* (Fuller 1969: 221 and 237).

rules. Enacted law is explicitly produced as law by institutions that claim the authority to make law and to pronounce authoritative statements regarding its contents. The most important ones are, of course, legislatures and courts, but these are certainly not the only ones. Many government organizations and officials have delegated regulatory power and can produce regulations that are considered binding upon those who are subject to their powers. Moreover, in every organization of a certain scale, whether it is a governmental organization or a business, there are some officials or institutions that set internal rules for their employees and for those who are dependent on their services.

Gerald Postema explains the concept of enacted law (or, in his terminology, made rules) as follows:

> Made rules are given canonical verbal formulations by a determinate author at a reasonably precise date. The practical force of made rules depends on the authority of their makers or the offices they occupy. Thus, made rules presuppose both authors and relations of authority and subordination. (Postema 1999: 256)

Enacted law emerges out of vertical relationships. It need not be the commanding authority of an absolute dictator, but the relationship is one between lawmaker and subject. Of course, in a democratic legal order, as a voter the legal subject can influence the lawmaker indirectly; moreover, the person or persons constituting the lawmaking institution are also subjected to the rule of law. However, the institution that produces the law, the legislature, stands in a vertical relationship of authority to citizens. This implies that the enacted rule appears as given, as not negotiable, to citizens.

Enacted law therefore depends on authoritative institutions that claim to have law-making and law-enforcing authority. Usually, this type of law can be described in the familiar frameworks of legal positivism, as a union of primary and secondary rules (Hart 1961/1994) or as an institutionalized system claiming authority (Raz 1979). However, for a full understanding of enacted law, we need to go beyond legal positivism, because the reason why enacted law has obligatory force cannot be fully understood from within a legal positivist framework (Postema 1999: 260). In most forms of enacted law, particularly democratic laws, the vertical order is embedded in a more horizontal order. To understand this, we turn to Fuller, who argued that enacted law is embedded in a reciprocal pattern of interactions between citizens, legislators and other officials. Before this relationship can be explained, we need to have a better understanding of what interactional law is.

For a description of interactional law (or implicit rules), we may again turn to Gerald Postema:

> [I]mplicit rules arise from conduct, not conception. Verbal formulations may more or less accurately capture the rules implicit in the conduct, but the formulations are always post hoc and strictly answerable to the conduct. No formulation is authoritative in virtue of its public articulation alone. Although implicit rules arise from the conduct of determinate agents, typically they have no precise date of birth and no determinate authors. They presuppose no relations of authority and subordination; thus, their practical force depends neither on authority nor on enactment, but on the fact that they find "direct expression in the conduct of people toward one another".[5]

The crucial point here is that, in social interaction, we must be able to rely on the predictability of at least most of the actions of other individuals (and of the state). Otherwise we cannot achieve our

5 Postema 1999: 257, quoting in the last sentence Fuller 1981: 232.

own purposes and guide our own behaviour. Therefore, social interaction requires 'relatively stable mutual expectations of behavior' (Postema 1999: 257). These expectations 'emerge over time from a process of mutual accommodation and adjustment of expectations and actions of interacting agents' (Postema 1999: 258).

It is this ongoing practice that is the basis for the obligatory force of interactional law. Interactional law is usually implicit in the interaction, but it can be made explicit by formulating the rules and putting them on paper. For example, the continuing relationship between business partners can be laid down in a contract, and this may acquire a certain legal status in its own right.[6] However, often the contract will not be followed to the letter because the underlying practice requires adaptation and both partners will understand the need for these adaptations. For the partners in the contract, the implicit interactional law is more authoritative than the written contract. As long as this orientation to the underlying practice is considered to be the basis of the obligatory force we can speak of interactional law, even if the norms have also been formulated in contracts, treaties, codes or even statutes.[7]

Contract can therefore both be regarded as enacted law, and as interactional law. However, it is important to note that the contract itself is also a source of law in its own right. Once it has been signed, it constitutes a relatively autonomous legal order, based on mutual consent. The terms of the contract are the primary sources of the obligations following from it; both the underlying interactional law and the enacted law on contracts are, from this perspective, only secondary sources. So there are three perspectives on the meaning of the contract. Each of them can claim to give an explanation for why the contract can create obligations; each of them provides part of the truth.

4. Legal Interactionism

In our view, legal theory must recognize both interactional law and enacted law, as well as other sources such as contract and treaty, based on the possibility of creating obligations by mutual consent. The theory developed here may be called legal interactionism.[8] In an oecumenical spirit, legal interactionism takes seriously interactional law, but tries to do justice to enacted law as well. For legal interactionism, the concept of law refers both to the interaction of legal actors and to the various practices in which legal norms emerge, as well as to the norms themselves, and to the legal doctrine that emerges from these practices. Our account has close affinities with the interactional account of international law recently presented by Jutta Brunnée and Stephen Toope (Brunnée and Toope 2010); however, it differs from their view in developing a more inclusive approach, in line with the later work of Lon Fuller.

6 See Fuller's analysis of the interactional foundations of contract law in Fuller 1981: 244f. Contract also has strong elements of made law; see Fuller 1968: 70–71.

7 However, when, and in so far as the written texts become an independent source of obligatory force we are leaving the domain of interactional law and replacing or supplementing it with enacted law or contract.

8 Fuller's theory has been called interactionist by various authors, e.g., Brunnée and Toope 2010: 24, and Witteveen 1999: 31–2. Witteveen argues that interactionist views on law can also be found with Montesquieu, American pragmatism and the sociology of Georg Simmel. Brunnée and Toope use the term 'interactionalism' for their own position. As our account is closer to Fuller's than to Brunnée and Toope's, on those points where they differ, we prefer the word interactionism. To emphasize that it is a theory about law and not about human interaction in general, we have added the word legal. Legal interactionism is strongly embedded in American pragmatism and symbolic interactionism.

Legal interactionism, in the account advocated here, holds that the obligatory force of enacted law and contract is embedded in an interactional pattern. In a sense, therefore, it regards interactional law as primary because without a general pattern of interaction in which enacted law is accepted as obligatory, enacted law may come close to being merely the exercise of brute force. However, legal interactionism, as we understand it, does not reduce the obligatory force of contract or enacted law to that of interactional law. Both may generate legal norms which have obligatory force once they have been adopted. We do not deny that enacted rules may function directly as guides to behaviour and the basis for law enforcement. Therefore, interactional law is not the sole foundation of enacted law or contract. However, the obligatory force of each of these legal sources is reinforced when there is congruence between the deeper interactional law and the black-letter law of enacted law and contract.

Legal interactionism does claim that enacted law that is not embedded in an interactive practice is not fully law in the sense that a legal order cannot completely depend on enacted law only. There must be some congruence between interactional law and enacted law; otherwise the obligatory force of enacted law is weakened. Enacted law is embedded in a broader interaction and in that sense we could say that interactional law is primary (Fuller 1981/2001: 250). Enacted law without any basis in interactional patterns simply is hardly law, or even no law at all but mere fiction. If someone claims that he is the supreme legislator and everyone should listen to his laws, while no one does, there is simply no law and, instead, the presumed legislator is probably just a lunatic. There must be at least some minimal practice in which individuals act according to what is claimed to be law, underlying the claim to authority. Thus, enacted law not only depends on the formal processes of lawmaking by the relevant authority, but also on underlying interactional expectations. Interaction plays a role in the vertical relationship, because legislature and subjects of the law mutually expect each other to abide by rules. To link it to Fuller again: these expectations are based on the role taken and the internal morality that goes with that position, in the case of enacted law, the principles of the rule of law. However, enacted law is also linked to horizontal interactional patterns, because the rules of enacted law may become part of the reciprocal expectations of citizens among themselves. Ideally, citizens expect each other to conform to enacted law and themselves live up to these expectations. Of course, one of the main insights of legal sociology is that the link between enacted rules and interactional practices is much more complicated (e.g., Moore 1978).

Interactional law and enacted law may give rise to different legal orders that are relatively autonomous in relation to each other; examples are societies in which indigenous groups have strong customary law, which is largely unconnected to the official enacted law of the larger society. Usually, however, they are strongly connected, and their relationship is best regarded as that of two different sources or types of law in the same legal order. They may overlap, they may largely converge, but they may also diverge. Usually, in a relatively stable legal order, there is considerable congruence between interactional law and enacted law. There may, however, be tensions between the two sources of law, as full congruence is rare.

5. Relative Pluralism

The second opposition is that between most legal sociologists usually accepting some form of legal pluralism, and most legal philosophers focusing on one coherent legal order, usually associated with the state. Interestingly, doctrinal legal scholars in Europe increasingly seem to take an intermediate position willing to embrace a narrow form of pluralism, consisting of the competing, and partly interwoven, legal orders of domestic law, EU-law, Council of Europe Law and international law

(Nollkaemper 2011: 10–15; Krisch 2010: 10). The notion of legal pluralism has taken on different meanings, and there have been many attempts to distinguish different forms of pluralism. Here, we distinguish between the narrow pluralism of recognizing a limited set of potentially conflicting official legal orders, on the one hand, and the broad pluralism of recognizing a wide range of conflicting and interacting official and unofficial legal orders, on the other hand.

Legal interactionism embraces a broad form of pluralism, but it tries to address some of the concerns of legal philosophy with authority, unity and coherence. The acceptance of multiple sources of law leads to a broad form of pluralism; each of these sources can be the basis for a multiplicity of legal orders. However, we do not see the broad pluralism of multiple legal orders as necessarily implying conflict and competition between legal orders. In many instances, pluralism is relative and can be accommodated within a larger, open, legal order.

Of course, the most important source of enacted law is that of state legal authorities like legislatures, regulatory bodies and the judiciary and the focus on this type of law as the predominant source of all law is easily understandable. Especially in the Civil Law tradition, this fiction of the legislature as the ultimate source of all law is easily upheld and most civil codes contain provisions declaring customary law and contract only valid under certain conditions, thus claiming that all law ultimately derives its obligatory force from legislation. This may be a legitimate internal perspective of the legal order as held by judges who have to rely on internal, institutional criteria of what is to count as law. (Nevertheless, we should note that, with the rise of the EU, the Council of Europe and international law, this nineteenth-century model of one sovereign legal order claiming ultimate authority in its territorial jurisdiction is rapidly losing its explanatory power.) However, from a broader perspective there is no reason to limit enacted law only to enactments by state legal authorities. For authoritative enactment the association with the state is not necessary. Every institution that has authority over a group of persons can produce enacted law. Church authorities, boards of associations, as well as international organizations such as the FIFA, the IOC or a multinational company can also create law in their own right.[9]

More importantly, once we accept that there may be other sources of law, such as interactional law and contract, legal pluralism seems inescapable. Whenever people interact and their patterns of interaction become denser, interactional law may gradually emerge. This is obvious for ancient customary law as well as for international *lex mercatoria* and public international law, all forms of interactional law that emerged outside the sovereign state legal order. It may even hold true in the global and virtual world of the Internet where possessions in virtual games may be the object of property, or where bitcoins may be accepted as valid money in exchanges. With regard to contract, it is obvious that a contract based on free and mutual consent may give rise to its own legal norms and even to a mini-legal order, whether or not this legal order is also recognized as valid by e.g., state legal orders, and enforced. In this respect the recognition of a contractual legal order established between two parties is not categorically different from the recognition of a foreign state legal order under the rules of private international law.

---

9 As we are still for most practical purposes stuck in the paradigm of national legal orders, lawyers may uphold the fiction that these organizations derive their legal authority from the domestic legal order in which they are formally based, such as Switzerland or the Cayman Islands. Thus doctrinal law can make a closure and provide for effective incorporation of alien legal orders in a state legal order. However, in reality, of course, those organizations were created independently of Swiss or Cayman Islands law and only used the domestic legal orders instrumentally to provide a legal framework for their activities. From a sociological perspective, the legal order created by those organizations is primary, and the domestic legal order is subservient to their purposes.

We may conclude that legal interactionism, in line with Lon Fuller, accepts a wide variety of legal orders (Fuller 1964/69: 125; cf. Berman 2007: 1172). However, this is only one half of the story. Although we claim that legal pluralism is broad and pervasive, it is not necessarily a strong form of pluralism in the sense of separate legal orders competing for normative dominance. In many ways, pluralism is better seen as relative: legal orders are not fully autonomous; they interact in many ways with each other, at times depending on, reinforcing or conflicting with another order. They are embedded in a network of legal orders. Each legal order is relatively autonomous, partly autonomous and partly open to other legal orders. The degrees of autonomy and openness may vary. The legal order of a religious sect will usually be highly autonomous vis-à-vis the state legal order, whereas the internal legal order of state agencies will usually be so strongly embedded in the state legal order that their autonomy is minimal. In fact, the autonomy of the latter may even be so small, and the congruence between the internal norms of the state agency and the official state legal norms so strong, that it is artificial to speak of distinct legal orders. Although theoretically they might be called distinct legal orders (Macdonald 1999), for most practical uses, the norms within the state agency are mere variations within one common state legal order.

In a sense, from a theoretical point of view, it does not matter whether we regard the agency's internal norms as a relatively autonomous, but highly embedded legal order, or as merely a part of the state legal order.[10] There is a continuity from two almost completely separate legal orders to complete identity, somewhere in between it may be helpful no longer to speak of two autonomous legal orders but of one dominant legal order with distinct sub-orders. A confederation of states may slowly evolve into a federative state; there is no clear cut-off point sociologically or philosophically at which it is better to say that there is one legal order rather than a collection of closely intertwined orders, embedded within a confederate order. At this moment, the relation between the EU and member states can best be regarded as a densely knitted network of semi-autonomous legal orders embedded within the EU legal order, but this may gradually change in the future.

Let us take a concrete example of how this might work when the relation between the state legal order and interactional norms is involved. In the past decades, many cyclists in the Netherlands, frustrated by the seemingly purposeless long waits for red traffic lights, have increasingly ignored those lights. It seems that there is an interactional norm emerging that cyclists (and pedestrians) may ignore red traffic lights as long as there is no danger and they do not hinder other traffic, for example when taking a right turn. Prosecution of those traffic lights violations will incidentally occur, but is certainly not a prosecution priority. We may structure this conflict between interactional norms and the state legal order in two ways. Traditional legal sociology would structure it as a conflict between state law and living law as if there were two distinct legal orders. We think this is a theoretical overkill: to conceive of one norm as constituting a distinct legal order unnecessarily complicates the picture. It is better to structure it as a conflict within the state legal order between norms enacted by parliament and competing interactional norms emerging from the actions of citizens. This conflict is not authoritatively solved by the state legal order because of its erratic prosecution policies. In fact, the Dutch state tried to accommodate the interactional practice by introducing a new traffic sign that allows cyclists to ignore traffic lights when taking right turns. However, this traffic sign was placed only at a small minority of traffic lights, and it seems the effect of this attempt for partial accommodation while retaining acceptance of the statutory norm for the rest, has remained futile.

10 From the internal perspective of a state judge or a doctrinal scholar, it may, but we will discuss that later.

The advantage of this notion of relative pluralism is that it enables us to study variation and gradual change, both between and within legal orders, instead of succumbing to rigid theoretical oppositions. It does accommodate broad pluralism, but it allows for the openness of legal orders embedded in a network of legal orders. And it also allows for pluralism within legal orders, to see that there are legal suborders, or competing norms, rather than treating a legal order as one coherent body of norms. By allowing variation of orders and suborders, doctrinal and philosophical concerns with the unity and coherence of legal orders can be recognized, although unity and coherence cannot be realized completely in practice. Thus relative pluralism allows us to accommodate a large variability in legal orders.

6. A Dynamic Understanding of Law

The third opposition is that between a variable and dynamic understanding of law and a timeless and static understanding. Sketching the extremes of the opposition, we can say that legal sociologists have emphasized the dynamic and variable character of law, while legal philosophers have concentrated on uncovering characteristics of law which are true of law in all times and places. As we stated in our introductory comments, doctrinal legal scholars to some extent side with the legal philosophers, but with a different emphasis, not on the universal or essential characteristics of law, but on a legal system as a coherent body of norms. The latter implies that law is described as static, at a certain moment in time. Legal change is not a process, but a series of different descriptions. The gulf between the legal philosophical and the sociological sensibility is not easily bridged, and neither is the divide between the sociological and the doctrinal position, although the first may be more problematic than the latter. In this section we contend that a legal interactionist position can introduce variability and dynamics without giving up the concern for general concepts and accurate descriptions of present law.

Legal interactionism combines pluralism of legal orders (legal pluralism) with a pluralist understanding of the concept of law (conceptual pluralism). Rather than looking for the essential properties of law, we should study the richness of legal phenomena with an open mind to variation as well as change. We should not try to frame all legal phenomena on a Procrustean bed of essential properties. Moreover, even if it were possible to construct some necessary and sufficient legal characteristics – which we doubt – they would likely be such minimal and abstract traits that they would not tell us much that is interesting about law.

We should, therefore, aim for a dynamic and variable understanding of the characteristics of law. Sociological, historical, comparative and philosophical analysis may provide us with insights into both characteristics of law that are fairly general, and characteristics that only some specific legal orders possess. Wittgenstein's idea of a family resemblance is illuminating here. Blond hair may be present in almost all current members of the family, the big nose in only two of them. None of the characteristics is present in all. Both Wittgenstein and the secondary literature discuss the family metaphor in terms of an existing set of family members. However, we can obtain a richer understanding if we realize that families are dynamic phenomena. Families expand and decrease in size. New members are born into the family, other members die. Some members are adopted into the family; in-laws become part of the family too. For example, when we speak about dynasties such as the House of Orange or the Kennedy's, the in-laws like Queen Maxima or Jacqueline Kennedy are as much a part of the family as those who are a biological part of the family – though in a different way. As a result, some family traits may disappear and others emerge.

This dynamic understanding of the family resemblance metaphor is illuminating when applied to the phenomenon of law. Older types of law, such as customary law, may become less important while newer types, such as state bureaucratic law and international law, may emerge. Those types of law that continue to exist, such as constitutional law, may change in important ways, e.g., by becoming intertwined with international human right treaties and European Union treaties and, thus, forcing us to rethink the concept of the constitution of a sovereign state. Perhaps in the future, completely new types of law will emerge that we can hardly imagine today, think of the emerging law of virtual networks. It is important to have a concept of law that is open to such variation and dynamics. A concept that focuses on essential properties is simply not adequate to the task at hand. A more pluralist concept based on the dynamic metaphor of family resemblance is much more productive because it does not, in advance, exclude new types of law.

The concept of law proposed by legal interactionism does not provide a clear definition of what counts as law, but rather a set of characteristics that can be present to a greater or lesser degree. The key to a legal interactionist perspective on the concept of law is the insight that law can exist in degrees and encompasses a wide range of phenomena. A normative order can be more or less law. The idea that a legal order need not be fully law to be at least partly law holds true as much for the legal order of a weak or failing state as for the legal orders constituted by the global climate regime or a professional medical association. Interactionism implies a gradualist conception of law. Therefore, most interactionists eschew a clear demarcation criterion of law, because it would not do justice to the gradual processes underlying the emergence or decline of a legal order. So, what we need is a dynamic conception of law which is sensitive to these degrees of existence. What developing an ideal type of law may help us to reach is a fuller understanding of its variation.

In an interactionist view, law is a normative order. It emerges from intermeshing normative expectations between persons, embedded in a practice of legality. As Selznick has argued, law is a normative practice oriented towards the ideal of legality. We should add that law is not only oriented towards the ideal of legality, but also towards other distinctively legal ideals such as justice, and to ideals that are not distinctively legal, such as democracy (Taekema 2003: 190). In this practice of legality, the normative expectations may gradually thicken (or weaken) and the institutional character of the legal order may also become thicker (or weaker). Secondary rules and law-enforcing institutions may emerge, the implicit rules may be explicitly formulated (if only to make them more easily accessible to all parties and to newcomers), and specific legal institutions may emerge such as adjudication and legislation.

Now, if this is the ideal type of a mature legal order, we can also see how various other elements that are often suggested as distinctive characteristics of law might fit in as contributing to a well-functioning legal order. In a complex society, relying on gradual processes of change may not be very effective. Therefore it may be necessary to have institutions or rules that govern how the contents of the law will be determined, how it will be changed, and how it will be applied. Moreover, for effective discussion about the legal norms, it is helpful if these rules are explicitly formulated. Therefore, in a complex society, law will usually be black-letter law, whether in the form of state law, in the form of contracts or in other forms of private regulation, such as the norms of certification schemes like ISO. Furthermore, it will improve the efficacy of law enormously if there are effective sanctions and institutions that enforce those sanctions. However, it is worth remarking that in the ideal typical description there need not be a connection with the state; effective enforcement can be guaranteed in many ways.

This leads us to the following ideal typical description of law. Law is a normative order, embedded in a practice of legality. There are secondary rules of recognition, change and adjudication. The norms are explicitly formulated, usually as black-letter law, and there is congruence between enacted norms and interactional norms. There is an effective enforcement mechanism and sanctions may be applied.

However, if law can exist in degrees, there are various respects in which it can be less law. Effective sanctions and enforcement mechanisms can be missing, as is often the case in international law. Explicit formulation of the norms may be absent, as is often the case in interactional law. Even a practice of legality may be largely absent, as may be true in state bureaucracies, where internal regulations seem more like general commands, and in dictatorial regimes. Finally, a well-known pathology of legal orders is that there is little congruence between enacted law and interactional norms. In all those situations we may still say that there is law, but that it is lesser law.

Of course, if all those characteristics are missing, there is no law at all. So the question remains: what is minimally necessary in order to characterize a normative order as legal? From the analysis above it will now be clear why we cannot give a general answer to this, let alone suggest a simple cut-off point below which there is no law. Not only would every cut-off point be arbitrary, but it is also true that it is all these characteristics together that justify calling a normative order law, so that various combinations of characteristics in different degrees may be minimally sufficient to call a phenomenon law. Therefore, we cannot construct one universal definition of law, but we may stipulate a definition in light of the purposes for which we need it and the context in which it is to be applied.

This concept of law transcends the opposition between analytical jurisprudence and legal sociology. It incorporates the various characteristics suggested by philosophers as essential for the distinctly legal, but regards them as general rather than as universal traits. They are often present in developed legal orders, in which case they are important for understanding these orders, but they are not universal or essential. It also allows for variation and change, because its conceptual framework allows law to exist in degrees, and it allows elements of the legal order to exist partly and decline or develop.

It can also do justice to the attempts by legal practice and legal doctrinal research to construct law as if it were a static phenomenon. A fully evolved legal order is embedded in a practice of legality, which means that it is oriented towards legal ideals such as legality, justice and legal certainty. Legal certainty can only be provided if law is coherent and does not provide contradictory injunctions. Therefore, it is important for the effective functioning of legal orders that they are modified and reconstructed as much as possible as if they provide a coherent, timeless doctrine, and as if they provide one right answer. Authoritative declarations by judges often provide such a closure, and help the law to work itself pure, the famous dictum Ronald Dworkin derived from the common law (Dworkin 1986: 400). Doctrinal treatises and handbooks similarly provide such a construction as if the law is a coherent static doctrine. So both in practice and in doctrinal research there is a tendency to construct law as timeless or static. Such constructions serve admirable legal and social purposes, but in a legal interactionist perspective they are only temporary and functional sketches of law, which put the variations and changes of law between brackets. As long as the possibilities of change and of unexpected incarnations of law are acknowledged, doctrinal constructions are an important component in making sense of the messy and variable phenomena of law.

7. Pragmatist but not Instrumentalist

The fourth opposition we address is that between instrumentalist and non-instrumentalist views of law. For this opposition, we take our cue from Cotterrell's criticism of law and society scholarship. One of the corollaries of a law and social science perspective has been an instrumental view of law; at the moment, most visible in law and economics research. However, as Cotterrell argues, the instrumental view of law and society scholars has been implied in the projects of legal sociology: supporting or criticizing government policies by means of evaluation research and being engaged in legal reform. Cotterrell criticizes sociology of law for being 'less concerned to *appreciate* the social (and the legal within it), exploring it in its diversity' (Cotterrell 2008: 21). Tamanaha extends this critique of socio-legal studies to legal scholarship broadly: in many different forms, theories of law presuppose that law is an instrument for extra-legal goals (Tamanaha 2009). These may be the policy goals of governments, the utilitarian preference-satisfaction of law and economics, or the political powerplay that is highlighted in critical legal studies.

This broadly held instrumental view of law subordinates the legal order to external ends, and evaluates law in terms of its contribution to such ends. Legal rules are seen as inducements for particular behaviour or as constraints limiting behaviour. The sociological question that needs to be answered from this perspective is whether legal norms are a successful means to achieve this and what causes there might be for law failing to reach such objectives. The underlying premise of such an instrumental view is that any type of end served by law is generated outside of the legal order. Ideally, possible goals are derived from economic modelling or empirically grounded policy research, after which legal rules are designed (and tested) in order to further these goals. Law, in such a view, is a flexible, substantively empty set of norms that can be tailored and tweaked for any purpose.

Such instrumentalism is most easily argued for from an external perspective on law, held by those who observe the legal order from the outside. Things look different from an internal point of view from within the legal practice (compare Taekema 2011). Although it is possible to work within a legal order with the idea that the norms can be used to further external ends, the more common way to link legal norms and ends is to derive purposes from the legal system itself, by reconstructing underlying purposes from the norms or sets of norms themselves. A good example of this line of reasoning is Dworkin's theory of law, in which legal norms and the political morality underlying them are interpreted as an integral whole (1986). Another is Fuller's theory with its idea of an internal morality of law (1969).[11] In such an internal view, law primarily serves its own intrinsic purposes rather than externally formulated goals. Moreover, law is seen as providing the stability and guarantees that make orderly society possible.

Although legal interactionism is closely related to the Fullerian view of law as answering to its own internal purposes, it acknowledges that both aspects of, what we could call, law's purposiveness are important ways of regarding law that are not necessarily at odds. However, to combine the idea of law as an instrument with law as the guarantee of legal purposes and values, the idea of instrumentalism needs to be refined. For this, the pragmatist strand in legal interactionism can serve as a basis. Pragmatism in its classical form highlights scientific inquiry, i.e., systematically examining conditions and consequences; it is focused on problem-solving, i.e., trying to achieve a particular end; and it stresses the flux, change and adaptability of social life. Most importantly, pragmatism's rejection of the dualism of means and ends counters any easy argument about law as primarily instrumental. The basic idea is that ends should be viewed as ends-in-view, that is, as rather particular and tied to the activity at hand. What is an end in one activity might become a means in another. Ends are therefore not fixed, and neither are means. For law, this implies that it depends on the context whether legal norms appear as means

11 As Kristen Rundle shows, Fuller was concerned about the one-directional reasoning of instrumental views of law (Rundle 2012: 194). He also developed an argument against the divorce of means and ends that owed much to John Dewey's ideas (Fuller 1981/2001: 61–78).

or as ends-in-themselves. Another important point, which also follows from the approach of scientific inquiry as a form of problem-solving experience, is that ends are subject to critical scrutiny and evaluation in a similar way as the instruments used. The tendency to take ends as given (e.g., as preferences) is mistaken from a pragmatist point of view because we should also consider what the consequences are of adopting that particular end. (Dewey 1988: 179) The broad instrumentality involved in problem-solving also applies to law: law is not an instrument for independently determined goals, but a tool to serve a variety of purposes.

Pragmatism provides a subtle picture of the way in which legal norms are instrumental: both the rules and the purposes they serve, should be critically evaluated, not in light of some theory, but in the light of their practical use in changing social circumstances. The ends of law are not fixed, nor are they set by legal officials; they arise in the context of a dynamic social environment. The emphasis placed earlier on change and variation is also relevant here. As Selznick points out, in pragmatist theory both ends and means are instrumental, both are valuable in themselves, and the determination of an end depends on a valuation of the means necessary to achieve it (Selznick 1992: 328). Pragmatism therefore sees law as a tool and as an end itself, at the same time.

Importantly, a pragmatist legal interactionism broadens the range of actors involved in using law as an instrument. Legal instrumentalism in its usual forms sees the goals of law as defined by government or legislature, and law as an instrument to be used by government officials. This is not implied by pragmatism: anyone engaged in the solving of a practical problem in need of a legal solution can use legal norms as tools for decision making. It is a democratic idea: all participants in legal practice can make use of it. This form of pragmatist instrumentalism may add something to an interactionist view: an account of how changes in norms get started, namely by a participant of the practice engaging with a problem and challenging the rules (compare Webber 2006: 177).

For legal interactionism, then, law is instrumental to people's own endeavours in a social context. Such a view of legal instrumentality makes law part of everyday life, and by that token, the social interactions and activities that form the core of everyday practices are primary. In one sense, law is even more pervasively instrumental than in the standard, policy-oriented form of instrumentalism, because law is tied to a variety of goals of various actors. Focusing on the underlying interactions of law makes it possible to include instrumentality as a central way in which people may use norms in their lives. However, it also softens the edges of instrumentalism by rejecting the isolation of ends outside of legal discussion and connecting social ends to legal values. Such a view does not do away with the tension between instrumentalist thinking in current politics and scholarship and a value-oriented interactionist view. It will probably not convince hard-core utilitarians or legal economists. However, it makes it possible to see the enterprise of law as embedded in the purposes of everyday life.

8. Conclusions: Implications for Interdisciplinary Research

Taking our cue from Cotterrell, we believe that legal philosophy, legal sociology and doctrinal legal scholarship can and should be co-workers in order to gain a full understanding of law in all its facets. In order to make cooperation meaningful and fruitful, it is essential to have a common concept of law. Such a concept needs to be broad enough to give room to the various concerns of the three disciplines, and we have argued that legal interactionism can offer such a concept. It can do so because it provides an integrative perspective with regard to the four oppositions we have identified, which can explain the importance of the poles of the opposition while also providing a basis for linking them. In these concluding remarks, we want to sketch some implications our view has for interdisciplinary research.

By using a legal interactionist concept of law, three different possibilities for cooperation between the disciplines present themselves. Firstly, the disciplines complement each other: they all contribute in different, but necessary ways to understanding law. Although to some this may sound as a matter of course, it is important to realize that as long as legal sociology and legal doctrine each see a different pole of the law-in-the-books/law-in-action opposition as the right way to view law, this bars any understanding of the other discipline as complementary to one´s own discipline. Softening this opposition is therefore essential for cooperation, even in the form of only providing complementary insights. However, once the oppositions are seen as parts of a larger interactionist picture, contributing disciplines can recognize that the other discipline may be relatively correct. Although the dynamic character of law as studied by legal sociology must be recognized, it is necessary to provide a static account of law at some point to gain an accurate description of a complex legal problem. As long as this account is complemented by historical and sociological research into the origins and development of law, the reduction implied in the static view of doctrinal law is useful.

Another illustration of complementariness is provided by our analysis of the opposition between instrumentalism and non-instrumentalism. We have argued for a rich, pragmatist understanding of instrumentality in which legal norms can be seen both as means and as ends-in-themselves. Theoretically, these two dimensions can be integrated. However, in a pragmatist approach, it depends on the context whether legal norms appear as means, as ends-in-themselves or as both. The same contextualism holds for researchers engaging in research design: they cannot abstract from a particular research setting. Therefore, it depends on the specific purposes and on the specific context – including disciplinary skills – of a research project which of these understandings is emphasized. In many sociological research projects, a feasible research design may require that legal norms are only regarded as means. Such restrictions are often legitimate for specific research purposes and may provide partial but valuable insights. Similarly, philosophers, lacking empirical research skills, will sometimes legitimately abstract from the instrumentalist dimension of law and focus on the internal morality of law in order to design feasible research projects. Consequently, in real life, philosophical, doctrinal and sociological researchers will often have to choose different but complementary research designs. As long as they recognize that each of these projects only provides partial insights that may complement the results from other disciplines, such a restriction may be perfectly acceptable.

Secondly, and slightly more ambitiously, disciplines can learn from each other: they can mutually correct each other´s mistakes. Again, relating the poles of the oppositions helps to achieve this. When legal philosophers are searching for universal characteristics of law, the empirical variations found by legal sociologists may help them to see that the focus on the universal may be traded for a focus on the general, making it possible to acknowledge that some variations may simply be outliers. Providing a general philosophical theory of law that accounts for the majority of legal phenomena may be good enough.

Thirdly, research may attempt to fuse the insights from different disciplines into a synthesis. From the legal interactionist point of view, recognizing the tensions within the four oppositions means that a fusion of disciplines is never completely achievable, but will be partial at best. In practice, this third form of cooperation will be an ideal that is never completely realized. However, as a regulative ideal it is important, because aiming at joint research helps to make the most of the cooperative effort. An illustration where we see possibilities for a partial synthesis can be found in the way legal interactionism bridges the opposition between pluralism and unity through the notion of relative pluralism. It combines the insights of doctrinal scholars studying the intertwinement of national, regional and international legal orders with the broader ideas of legal sociologists about informal, non-state legal orders. However, in emphasizing relativity and partial intertwinement, it also incorporates the concerns of traditional lawyers and legal philosophers about coherence and unity. This enables us to study variation and gradual change, both within and between legal orders. Although we are only at the start of developing it in relation to multi-level legal orders, this integrative concept of relative pluralism offers promising prospects for a real interdisciplinary study of the emergence of such forms of law.

However difficult cooperation between disciplines may be in practice, engaging with each other's work across disciplinary lines is necessary for theory development, for understanding law in context and for engaging with law normatively. Of equal importance, in our view, is what it brings us, and demands of us, as researchers: learning to see things differently, realizing what are the flaws and blind spots of our own perspective, and really trying to incorporate what others do to create something new.

Bibliography

Berman, P.S. 2007. 'Global Legal Pluralism'. 80 *South California Law Review*, 1155–238.

Brunnée, J. and Toope, S.J. 2010. *Legitimacy and Legality in International Law. An Interactional Account*. Cambridge, Cambridge University Press.

Cotterell, R. 2006. *Law, Culture and Society: Legal Ideas in the Mirror of Social Theory*. Aldershot, Ashgate.

Cotterell, R. 2008. *Living Law: Studies in Legal and Social Theory*. Aldershot, Ashgate.

Dewey, J. 1988. 'Reconstruction in Philosophy'. In J.A. Boydston (ed.), *The Middle Works, 1899–1924 Volume 12*. Carbondale and Edwardsville, Southern Illinois University Press (orig: 1920).

Dickson, J. 2001. *Evaluation and Legal Theory*. Oxford, Hart Publishing.

Dworkin, R. 1986. *Law's Empire*. Cambridge, Belknap Press.

Fuller, L.L. 1968. *Anatomy of the Law*. New York, Praeger.

Fuller, L.L. 1964/1969. *The Morality of Law*. New Haven, Yale University Press. 2nd Edition.

Fuller, L.L. 1981/2001. *The Principles of Social Order. Selected Essays of Lon. L. Fuller.* Durham, Duke University Press.

Hart, H.L.A. 1961/1994. *The Concept of Law*. Oxford, Clarendon Press.

Krisch, N. 2010. *Beyond Constitutionalism: The Pluralist Structure of Postnational Law*. Oxford, Oxford University Press.

Krygier, M. 2012. *Philip Selznick: Ideals in the World.* Stanford, Stanford University Press.

Macdonald, R.A. 1999. 'Legislation and Governance'. In W. van der Burg and W.J. Witteveen (eds), *Rediscovering Fuller: Essays on Implicit Law and Institutional Design*. 279–311. Amsterdam, Amsterdam University Press.

Moore, S.F. 1978. *Law as Process: An Anthropological Approach*, Boston, Routledge.

Nollkaemper, A. 2011. *National Courts and the International Rule of Law.* Oxford, Oxford University Press.

Postema, G.J. 1999. 'Implicit Law'. In W. van der Burg and W.J. Witteveen (eds), *Rediscovering Fuller: Essays on Implicit Law and Institutional Design*. 255–75. Amsterdam, Amsterdam University Press.

Raz, J. 1979. *The Authority of Law*. Oxford, Oxford University Press.

Rundle, K.A. 2012. *Forms Liberate: Reclaiming the Jurisprudence of Lon L Fuller.* Oxford, Hart Publishing.
Selznick, P. 1992. *The Moral Commonwealth.* Berkeley, University of California Press.
Shapiro, S.J. 2011. *Legality*. Cambridge/London, Harvard University Press.
Taekema, S. 2003. *The Concept of Ideals in Legal Theory*. The Hague, Kluwer Law International.
Taekema, S. 2011. 'Relative Autonomy. A Characterisation of the Discipline of Law'. In B. van Klink and S. Taekema (eds), *Law and Method: Interdisciplinary Research into Law*. 33–52. Tübingen, Mohr Siebeck.
Taekema, S. and Van Klink, B. 2011. 'On the Border. Limits and Possibilities of Interdisciplinary Research'. In B. van Klink and S. Taekema (eds), *Law and Method Interdisciplinary Research into Law*. 7–32. Tübingen, Mohr Siebeck.
Tamanaha, B. 2009. 'On the Instrumental View of Law in American Legal Culture'. In F.J. Mootz III (ed.), *On Philosophy in American Law.* 27–34. Cambridge, Cambridge University Press.
Vick, D. 2004. 'Interdisciplinarity and the Discipline of Law'. 31(2) *Journal of Law and Society*, 163–93.
Webber, J. 2006. 'Legal Pluralism and Human Agency'. 44 *Osgoode Hall Law Journal*, 167–98.
Witteveen, W.J. 1999. 'Rediscovering Fuller: An Introduction'. In W. van der Burg and W.J. Witteveen (eds), *Rediscovering Fuller: Essays on Implicit Law and Institutional Design*, 21–48. Amsterdam, Amsterdam University Press.

Chapter 8

Discovering the Econo-Socio-Legal Through a Communal Lens

Amanda Perry-Kessaris[1]

> Disciplinary boundaries should be viewed pragmatically; indeed, with healthy suspicion. They should not be prisons of understanding.
>
> Cotterrell 1998: 177

I owe much to Roger Cotterrell – as mentor, collaborator and friend. Almost everything that I have produced in the last decade is set to his communal key. In this chapter I will trace my ever-deepening entanglement in Roger's communal approach to law in the hope of demonstrating why his approach is irresistible to those who, like me, wish to explore connections and incompatibilities between so-called 'economic' and 'non-economic' actions and interactions. And since Roger is an intrepid experimentalist, long committed to the transgression of disciplinary divides, this seems an appropriate occasion on which to attempt my latest something new: the visual communication of legal research.[2]

Since the mid 1990s, Roger has used the concept of 'networks of relations of community' or more recently, 'communal networks' as a unit of analysis with which to map and evaluate the role of law in the world that exists beyond ad hoc and fleeting interactions. His purpose has been 'not to identify "communities" but to study regulatory aspects of types and networks of communal relations' (Cotterrell 2013: Chapter 9 footnote 2).

Figure 8.1 summarizes (my interpretation of) the key concepts and relationships in Roger's communal approach. There are many details and caveats that are not included in this image. Its purpose is to invite the viewer in, reward them with a clear message as to the key elements of the communal approach, persuade them to explore the underlying text-based arguments, offer a point of orientation to which to return if textual times get tough, and perhaps to open new possibilities for dialogue as to the accuracy or otherwise of my interpretation of Roger's work. My understanding of the essence of Roger's communal approach is that law (in particular what one can think of as the 'legal mechanisms' of expression, participation and coordination: Perry-Kessaris 2008) supports trust (of the mutual interpersonal kind), and that trust is a cause and an effect of the relatively stable and sustained interactions that Roger terms 'communal networks'. These networks can, on the basis of shared values and interests around which they cluster, be categorized into the four Weberian ideal types (belief, instrumental, affective, traditional) (Cotterrell 1997: 80–82).

The first prompt for me to reach for Roger's communal framework was my interest in foreign investors and the host state legal system in the Southern Indian city of Bengaluru (Bangalore).

1 Thanks to Tony Pritchard at London College of Communication for heroic quantities of unvarnished, invaluable feedback. This chapter draws heavily on Perry-Kessaris 2008, Perry-Kessaris 2013, and Perry-Kessaris 2011.

2 See econosociolegal.blogspot.co.uk.

Figure 8.1 Key elements of the communal approach to law
Source: © Amanda Perry-Kessaris.

A 2002 application to the Socio-Legal Studies Association for fieldwork funding reveals that I began that project on the following, rather rigid, terms:

> A broad consensus has developed … that states' legal systems are an important factor affecting the location of [Foreign Direct Investment] FDI; that predictable and efficient legal systems are the most effective in attracting FDI; and that efficiency and predictability are best achieved by adopting a Western-style legal system (the "Ideal Paradigm"). The aim of the programme is to test the hypotheses that: (1) The nature of legal systems is a factor in investment location decisions in South Asia; and (2) Foreign investors react negatively to legal systems which are not of the Ideal Paradigm.[3]

I received the funding and completed a series of interviews with Bangalore's foreign investment, government and civil society actors. But as I tried to make sense of what I was hearing I felt smothered by the narrowness of my focus, and the thinness of my analytical frame. I had some law, I had some economics, but I could not breathe for lack of a third, more broadly social, dimension.

Roger ticks some key patriarchal boxes: he is white, male and of a certain age. But he fails miserably on the crucial ones: for he is a modest, thoughtful, open-spirited, egalitarian and an accomplished listener. So, although at this time we were colleagues at Queen Mary and collaborated regularly on reading groups and 'co-teaching' (he was certainly teaching, I was strictly learning), it felt the purest of chance that I should begin to explore the applicability of his 'law and community' approach to my project.

3 'Legal Systems as a Determinant of Foreign Direct Investment in South Asia' SLSA Small Grant application 2003.

Flexible, yet robust, the communal lens allows us simultaneously to visualize a broad range of contemporary actors and their 'fluctuating', 'overlapping', complex and trans-national relations (Cotterrell 2006: 7 and 67). It thereby both requires and enables us to 'seek similarity' (Cotterrell 2002: 49), because it highlights a universal role which law can and ought to fulfil in respect of all social interactions: the support of mutual interpersonal trust. Such trust is the cause and the effect of the interactions and sense of belonging that characterize relations of community, for it 'encourages future interaction and provides the motivation to engage in relatively free, uncalculated relations with each other' (Cotterrell 2006: 73). It is possible to identify three ways in which law supports (or fails to support) trust and, thereby, the productivity that is characteristic of community-like relations. Using 'law' as shorthand for legal rules and processes (such as legislation, adjudication and implementation of law), we can say that law *expresses*, in the form of contracts, institutions and so on, the trust that holds actors together; law draws actors in further by ensuring their *participation* in social life; and law *coordinates* the differences that hold actors – and different networks of community – apart. Just as an integrated analysis of multiple interests and values necessitates and facilitates the appreciation of similarities, so it necessitates and facilitates the identification of differences. We become able to 'appreciate difference' in the values, interests and legal needs that are central to each of these relations (Cotterrell 2002: 49). For this reason, my Bengaluru project was soon entirely transposed to a communal key, as this extract from my 2005 application for a Leverhulme Fellowship reveals:

> Foreign investors, states and civil society regularly interact as part of the globalisation process. However, they share little in the way of objectives, perceptions and expectations. Those who share little in common are unlikely to develop relationships of trust. Trust is important because it facilitates productive interactions. In the absence of trust, productive interactions can be facilitated by legal systems. But legal systems may themselves be ineffective. This project will examine when, why and how investors, the state and civil society use, abuse or avoid the Indian legal system as a mediator of their relationships. ... Drawing on Roger Cotterrell's law-and-community approach, the unit of analysis will be not the investment climate, but the "investment community". Foreign investors, and representatives of government and civil society will be considered as actors within a Karnatakan investment community – an 'instrumental' network of relationships arising as a consequence of foreign investment.[4]

The effect of retro-splicing the tones of communality into my empirical project was, to my eyes at least, dramatic. Roger's framework both enabled and compelled me, a legal researcher possessed with the limited empirical skills and sociological attuning fairly typical of the time, to consider multiple social groups (civil society and government actors as well as foreign investors); and at the same time to consider complexities and (dis)continuities in their relationships with, through and despite law. In the resulting volume, *Global Business, Local Law*, I concluded that:

> Investment climate discourse, like other liberal economic perspectives, tends to applaud law when it operates as an "individual or private resource for channelling power" (Cotterrell, 2002a, p. 643), and to be sceptical of law when it impedes business. Our intrepid investor, armed with the results of the latest [World Bank legal indicators] for orientation, picks his (yes) way gingerly through a tangle of gnarled legislation and dodges the snapping regulators who launch themselves at his

4 'Law and investor-state-civil society relations' Leverhulme Research Fellowship application 2005 (Award LARB7 completed in 2007).

> every limb. Finally, in the half-light, we catch sight of him heroically heaving himself out of a judicial quagmire. Ah, the investor's burden!
> I wish to advocate a move from [this,] the dominant investment climate discourse, according to which law should act as a lure to the touring investor, but is too often an inconvenience; and towards Roger Cotterrell's law-and-community approach, according to which law is not only a resource for individuals to pursue their own interests, but also a communal resource for the support of stable, productive, community-like relations. (Perry-Kessaris 2008)

An ability to appreciate and enunciate difference – in interests and values and, therefore, in legal needs – is especially important whenever there is a risk that the values and interests of certain communal networks might be privileged above others. For example, 'when', as is so often the case today 'the importance of instrumental economic relations is so strongly emphasized politically, and legal analysis seems impelled towards a similar emphasis' (Cotterrell 2002b: 78). So it was to Roger's communal approach that I turned once again in 2011 when trying to think through the legal implications of Karl Polanyi's increasingly remembered 1944 observation that economic action and interaction are always 'embedded' in wider social life.[5] I found that the lens of community allows us to think more specifically about the 'embededdness' of 'the economy' as the fact that any actor is at once engaged, to different degrees (from fleeting to stable), in multiple types (whether focusing on instrumental, traditional, affective and/or belief-based action) of social (including economic) life; and about the 'disembeddedness' of 'the economy' as that fact that the analytical and normative approaches that are central to economic actions and interactions may be confused with, and privileged over, those that are central to non-economic actions and interactions. A communal approach also allows us to specify the role of law within and between all these patterns and types of social life, as a facilitator of both disembedding movements and re-embedding counter-movements, and as itself subject to disembedding. Around this time Diamond Ashiagbor and I began to run a reading group on Economic Sociology of Law – the use of sociological approaches (empirical, normative, analytical) to investigate relationships between 'law' and 'economy' – in which Roger was a central participant.

My (embryonic) thinking on economic sociology of law is largely grounded in communal networks, as well as Roger's wider work on sociological approaches to law. Figure 8.2 is intended to summarize this approach, placing Roger's communal networks in the broader context of other patterns of social interaction, namely, ad hoc and fleeting individual interactions; and levels of social life, namely, regimes and rationalities.

The 'legal' and the 'economic' are both conceptualized 'as social phenomena occurring on all, interconnected, levels of social life' – namely, actions, interactions, regimes and rationalities (Frerichs 2011: 68). Social actions centre on widely divergent values and interests, captured in Figure 8.2 (and, more discretely, Figure 8.1) by reference to the human body: affective (heart), belief (head), traditional (foot) and instrumental (hand). Social interactions occur at different intensities. In Figure 8.2 broken lines indicate individualistic, superficial, impersonal interactions; solid lines indicate communal networks, and the dominant values and interests underlying the interaction are suggested by the section of the body to which the line connects. Laws and other regimes are part-created, used, abused, avoided, and destroyed in the course–of social life. So they appear in Figure 8.2 as part of social interactions: in the colouring of the lines that connect actors

5 See Perry-Kessaris 2011, referring to Polanyi 2001 [1944].

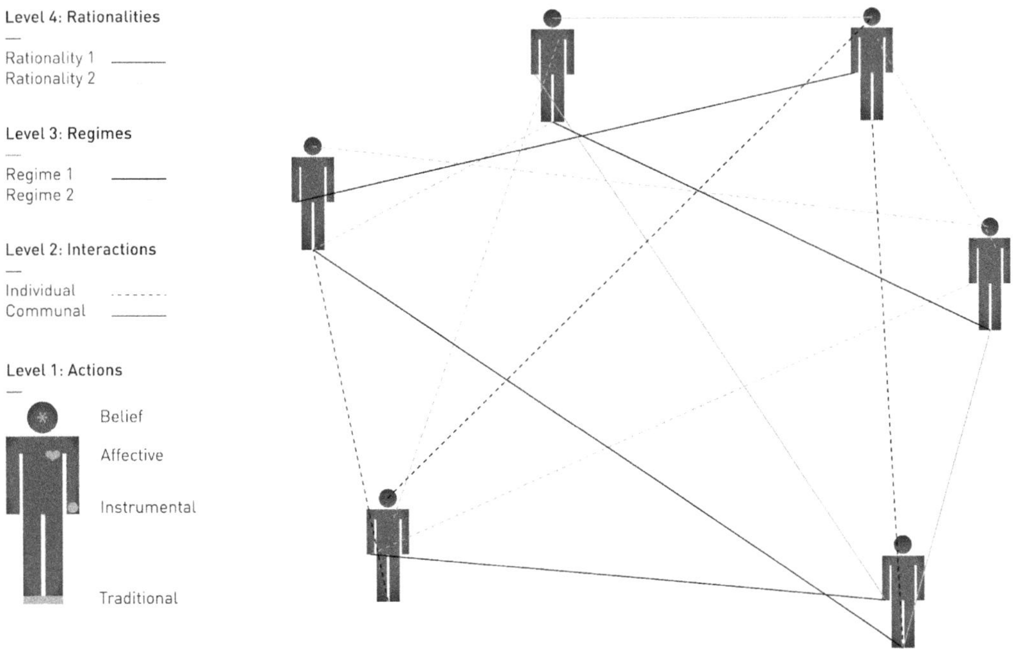

Figure 8.2 Communal networks in context[6]

(black for Regime 1, grey for Regime 2). But the fact that law can trigger, facilitate, hinder or have no effect at all on interactions (individualistic or communal) is not represented in Figure 8.2.[6]

Rationalities or 'shared ways of apprehending the world' influence and are influenced by the creation, use, abuse, avoidance and destruction of laws. So they appear in Figure 8.2 as an overlay on regimes–black for Rationality 1, which is associated with Regime 1; grey for Rationality 2, which is associated with Regime 2.

This communal approach to economic sociology of law seems to me to bear a unique capacity to integrate multiple social levels and perspectives. As any improvising musician will tell you, creativity thrives on well-ordered foundations. Roger's patiently crafted communal framework enables him, and others, to shed light on far flung analytical and empirical quandaries. Long may it, and he, prosper.

Bibliography

Cotterrell, R. 1997. 'A Legal Concept of Community' 12 *Canadian Journal of Law and Society*, 75–91.

Cotterrell, R. 1998. 'Why Must Legal Ideas be Interpreted Sociologically?' 25 *Journal of Law and Society*, 171–92.

6 This figure was designed with and executed by Sara Schrauwen and originally appeared as Figure 1 in Perry-Kessaris 2013.

Cotterrell, R. 2002a. 'Subverting Orthodoxy, Making Law Central: A View of Socio-Legal Studies' 29: 4 *Journal of Law and Society*, 632–44.

Cotterrell, R. 2002b. 'Seeking Similarity, Appreciating Difference: Comparative Law and Communities'. In E. Örücü and A. Harding (eds), *Comparative Law in the Twenty-First Century*. 35–54. The Hague, Kluwer.

Cotterrell, R. 2006. *Law, Culture and Society: Legal Ideas in the Perspective of Social Theory*. Aldershot, Ashgate.

Cotterrell, R. 2013. 'Transnational networks of community and international economic law'. In A. Perry-Kessaris (ed.), *Socio Legal Approaches to International Economic Law: Text, context, subtext*.

Frerichs, S. 2011. 'Re-embedding Neo-Liberal Constitutionalism: A Polanyian Case for the 'Economic Sociology of Law''. In C. Joerges and J. Falke (eds), *Karl Polanyi, Globalisation and the Potential of Law in Transnational Markets*. Ch. 3. Oxford, Hart Publishing.

Perry-Kessaris, A. 2008. *Global Business, Local Law: The Indian Legal System as a Communal Resource in Foreign Investment Relations*. Aldershot, Ashgate.

Perry-Kessaris, A. 2011. 'Reading the Story of Law and Embeddedness Through a Community Lens: A Polanyi-Meets-Cotterrell Economic Sociology of Law?' 62: 4 *Northern Ireland Legal Quarterly* (Special Issue on Socializing Economic Relationships) 401–13.

Perry-Kessaris, A. 2013. '*Anemos*-ity, *apatheia, enthousiasmos*: An economic sociology of law and wind farm development in Cyprus' 40:1 *Journal of Law and Society* (Special Issue on Towards an Economic Sociology of Law), 68–91.

Polanyi, K. 2001. *The Great Transformation: The Political and Economic Origins of Our Time*. Boston, Beacon Press (originally published 1944).

Chapter 9
Culture, Community, Comparison: Approaching Law in the Pluriverse

Christoph Eberhard

> The discoverer perceives relational patterns of functional analogies where nobody saw them before, as the poet perceives the image of a camel in a drifting cloud.
>
> Arthur Koestler 1989: 529

1. Introduction

> All legal theories offer merely partial perspectives. Each theory highlights some matters while ignoring others. A theory is produced from a certain standpoint and reflects a certain range of experience. It may persuade us that matters should be seen from its perspective and that, for the moment, other perspectives should be ignored. Perhaps this is because it develops impressively the image that it presents – sharply, carefully, in illuminating detail. It enables us to make sense of a certain picture of law, to see this picture as informative and interesting, conveying important knowledge, even though we know that it is presented from one viewpoint only, and that the phenomena portrayed would appear differently from another perspective. To evaluate theories should not be to criticize them for giving one picture of experience rather than another. It should be to ask how illuminating is the picture offered. How much does it allow us to see, and how clearly? And how can we go beyond it, locating it in relation to insights provided by other theories? In other words, how can we broaden the perspective the theory offers, not trivialising or dismissing it, but fitting it into a broader picture, albeit one that may never be complete? (Cotterrell 1999: 204)

Contemporary legal theory – and more generally, contemporary social sciences – see a fragmentation in the production of knowledge. This is partly due to the fact of hyperspecialization of knowledge endeavours in current academia. Partly, it is due to the fact that new sources of knowledge make their entry into the academic field. There are many, but no generally accepted grand narratives on law and society to date. At the same time, maybe because of this very lacking of an overarching theory or system that would elicit consensus, one observes an increase in multi-, inter- or trans-disciplinary studies (see Ost and van de Kerchove 1987). These studies, although formally attached to different disciplinary streams (sociology, anthropology, law ...), to a certain degree emancipate themselves from the stronghold of any of the disciplines they draw upon, thus inventing new ways of looking at the legal landscape (see Eberhard 2008). This does not mean that the solid anchoring that diverse disciplines provide becomes irrelevant. Nevertheless, it implies that disciplinary boundaries and affiliations should not obscure the researcher's vision of a new unfolding horizon of meaning. 'Intellectual advance in social studies now often occurs by *ignoring* disciplinary prerogatives, boundaries and distinctions' notes Roger Cotterrell (2006: 6). 'The need is not, however, to weaken the ties of sociolegal studies to academic sociology (...). It is to ensure that those inevitable ties in no way hamper imaginative enquiries across *all* available sources of social insight' (Cotterrell 2006: 6).

Staying rooted while opening up to wider horizons, and thus also realizing through the dialogue with others the pluralism of one's own rootedness, seems to be the current rising horizon, a pluralist and increasingly intercultural and dialogical horizon (Vachon 1997, 1998), which I approach in my work as a pluriverse (Eberhard 2013a). Pluralism, pragmatism, inter-approaches – be they interdisciplinary or intercultural – comparison, dialogue, analysis and imagination, perspective and prospective are part of this rising horizon of thought and action.

Although he does not formulate his quest in these terms, from my point of view, Roger Cotterrell is one of the thinkers who have contributed and continue to contribute to draw out some of the patterns, the motives, the insights from the pluriverse into the socio-legal field.

There is a fine balance to strike between 'general' and 'specific' knowledge, between approaches focusing on 'global' and 'local' knowledge (Cotterrell 2006: 19ff). After having presented and synthesized the pluralistic landscape of legal theory and of the sociology of law in its more theoretical endeavours (Cotterrell 2003, originally published in 1989; 1992), Roger Cotterrell started on a quest of providing a new way of looking at socio-legal realities through the prism of 'community', at least since the mid 1990s (Cotterrell 1996, 1997, 1999, 2006). By doing so, he little by little explored a meaningful way of making 'one camel', 'community', appear out of the existing drifting 'theoretical clouds'.

I met Roger Cotterrell at the beginning of this endeavour. His quest was to contribute to an empirical legal theory (Cotterrell 2003: 3), which is on the one hand addressing the pluralism of our individual and collective existences, and on the other hand does not shy away from the moral dimensions of socio-legal research. This contribution came through his 'Law and Community' horizon that initially drew me to his work and helped me to formalize some of my intuitions and to reveal another 'camel' in the socio-legal cloudscape: the pluriverse. And in his more recent work on culture and comparison (Cotterrell 2006a, 2006b, 2007, 2008), a new set of bridges toward my own work has appeared.

There is a shared outlook in both of our empirical legal theories, but also inevitable differences since mine is not rooted in the sociology but in the anthropology of law,[1] especially in its Francophone version as reflected in the work of the Laboratoire d'anthropologie juridique de Paris (LAJP/University Paris 1 Panthéon-Sorbonne) as chiefly represented in the writings of Michel Alliot (see for example 2003) and Étienne Le Roy (see for example 1999, 2004, 2011), and complemented by a critical legal theory as promoted by François Ost and Michel van de Kerchove (1987). In a nutshell, despite fundamental differences, both our approaches highlight the emergent pluralist condition we are living in and the necessity to relate our legal theories to lived experiences. The main difference in our respective *empiric legal theories*,[2] besides his being rooted more in sociology and mine in anthropology, is that Roger Cotterrell's approach to Law and society appears more structuralist when compared to my more 'dynamic phenomenology' of Law, which is deeply influenced by Étienne Le Roy's dynamic anthropology of law (Le Roy 1999).

In this chapter, I would like to elicit a dialogue, or at least to share some major insights that could serve as starting points for a dialogue between Roger Cotterrell's 'community' and my 'pluriverse' approach, and in a broader sense between rather sociologically and anthropologically informed legal theories, and last but not least between the Anglophone and Francophone worlds of research. In order to do so, I will start – in anthropological fashion – by setting the stage through locating my

1 For a succinct introduction to my approach in English see Eberhard 2001, 2009, 2012a.

2 'For convenience, I term legal philosophy's contributions to legal theory *normative legal theory* and sociology of law's contributions to it *empirical legal theory*' writes Roger Cotterrell (2003: 3), and I am extending his definition here to include anthropology which is sometimes understood as 'comparative sociology'.

own discovery of law. By doing so, I will also pay tribute to how our teachers inspire us and sustain us in our quest for knowledge. This personal account will illustrate the process of (scientific) research through a concrete example that may inspire the younger readers of this volume in their own explorations. Research is not only an objective, intellectual pursuit; it is also an existential path that is enriched and sometimes fundamentally oriented by certain encounters, moulded by circumstances. Leaving a familiar universe for a pluriverse seemed paramount to me in order to understand the pluralist mystery of Law (Eberhard 2013a). I have formalized the pathway from one to the other through what I sometimes call four cultural or existential disarmaments:[3] alterity, complexity, interculturality and humanity. I also refer to the latter as four poles between which legal anthropologists meander in their research and teaching activities. These cultural disarmaments, or poles on the journey of discovery of Law, can be related to Roger Cotterrell's interests in culture, community and comparison. They will constitute the focal points of my exploration.

2. Discovering Law

> Law is assumed to be socially significant, although the nature of this significance, and what kinds of study can best reveal it, are always controversial matters. Law has long been thought worth studying for its intrinsic philosophical or social interest and importance, which relates to but extends beyond its immediate instrumental value or professional relevance. In this sense, law is "a great anthropological document" (Holmes 1899: 444). (Cotterrell 2003: 1–2)

My anthropological interest in Law[4] initially led me to specialize in comparative law (especially between French and German law – Eberhard 1994). It was only in 1995, after a year spent in India, that I became aware of the dire need for intercultural dialogue in the organization of our living together, be it on the global or local scales,[5] and that I explicitly turned to the study of the anthropology of Law. Interestingly enough, remaining in touch with realities of how to act in the world – and thus being highly aware of the social, historical, cultural, political stakes of one's research – actually fuels theoretical investigation and often leads to fundamental research. My quest to move towards an intercultural legal theory that would contribute to ways of rethinking a more dialogical living together on the local and global planes, by linking the anthropology of Law with more general approaches in the field of legal theory, led my path to cross that of Roger Cotterrell at the European Academy of Legal Theory in Brussels.

It was 1996. I had just completed my DEA (*diplôme d'études approfondies* – equivalent to a LLM) in legal anthropology at the LAJP. I had explored the conditions for a more dialogical and intercultural living together in the then emerging new era of a pluripolar globalization through the lens of the *problématique* of human rights in the intercultural dialogue. I subsequently developed this in my doctoral research at the LAJP from 1997 to 2000. My Master's thesis, supervised by Étienne Le Roy (Eberhard 1996), made me aware that in order to rethink human rights – which I

3 For the notion of 'cultural disarmament' see Panikkar 1995a.

4 Whenever I write 'Law' with a capital 'L', I refer to the anthropological 'legal phenomenon', often referred to in French as *juridicité* and of which 'law', 'state law' is but one of many expressions. The distinction will become clearer in the following pages.

5 My interest in comparative law first crystallized during a comparison of German and French Law in my *Magister Legum* (LLM) thesis in 1993–1994 (Eberhard 1994). The next year at the Jawaharlal Nehru University in Delhi where I was introduced not only to international relations but also to anthropology deepened my interest in pluralism and pragmatism that was triggered by this first research.

equated at that time to a kind of *Grundnorm* of the global legal system – it was necessary to rethink Law itself ... and even the underlying modern world vision. But how could one go about this? In order to acquire the necessary tools for the needed work of deconstruction/reconstruction and the rooting necessary to engage in meaningful intercultural dialogue on Law, it seemed necessary to complement my previous studies with a year at the European Academy of Legal Theory in Brussels, which provided an international and interdisciplinary Masters (LLM) in the theory of Law. Three books were required reading for the programme: Hans Kehlsen's *Reine Rechtlehre* (1960), Hart's *Concept of Law* (1994) and Roger Cotterrell's *Politics of Jurisprudence* (2003).

I was seduced by Roger Cotterrell's introduction to legal theory. His concise, simple to read and nonetheless very insightful and contextualized presentation of the different authors and their theories became imprinted on my mind: in his book, theories were not presented as abstract systems but as dynamics of seeking knowledge embedded in broader social and historical contexts, all having their respective merits and limitations. This approach remained one of the horizons for my subsequent studies and then research in legal theory: always try to understand legal theories in an 'anthropological way', from within and in their contexts; then confronting them with different research experiences, just as anthropologists would compare different cultural experiences.

The mid 1990s were also the time when Roger Cotterrell started to develop his 'law and community' approach. He shared it in a seminar at the European Academy of Legal Theory, which I attended. His theory was then in its infancy. He had just published *Law's Community* (1996) in whose final chapter one is invited to 'imagine law's community' (315ff). He shared with me a first draft of his article 'A Legal Concept of Community' that was to be published in 1997 in the *Canadian Journal of Law and Society*. For me this work was very important and the timing prescient.

I was looking for a framework that could welcome anthropological approaches to Law into a legal theory framework. My main aim was to contribute to the move of anthropological insights from the 'edges of law' (Rouland 1993) to its core, to the core of debates in legal theory at large. For me, pluralism, intercultural dialogue, praxis, relationships between the global and the local were not just peripheral anecdotes to the only real and important law: state law. On the contrary, they were essential aspects for rethinking a humane contemporary living together. The 'legal system' could definitely not provide a framework for my endeavour – the promise of a 'communitarian horizon' seemed more appealing (Eberhard 2000).

François Ost and Michel van de Kerchove's work on a dialectical legal theory (1988 and 2002) allowed me to start to present legal anthropology as a dialogical theory of Law – in continuation with their work but also in contrast to it, taking it further for intercultural settings. Their approach to law as game (van de Kerchove and Ost 1992) allowed me to build bridges with Étienne Le Roy's emerging dynamic approach to Law reflected in his model of the *jeu des lois*, the 'game of laws'. At that time, Étienne Le Roy had not yet developed his *jeu des lois* into a general theoretical framework.[6] It had only been presented as a convenient tool to share field data[7] in a comprehensive and clear way without reducing the complexity of the encountered situations.

So here I was, with my own questions of how to rethink our current socio-legal paradigms in order specifically to approach the question of human rights in intercultural dialogue in a meaningful way. The two emerging approaches of the *jeu des lois* and of 'law as community' were clearly useful in doing so, despite – or rather because – they were yet not too developed, giving me more

6 This would only happen a few years later with the publication of his *Le jeu des lois. Une anthropologie 'dynamique' du Droit* (1999).

7 In two settings: land law issues in Africa (Le Roy 1996) and issues of youth socialization in France and in Africa (Le Roy 1995; 1997).

scope to use and adapt them for my own purposes. 'Community' and 'game' became the two pillars for a pluralist paradigm of human rights thought, and more generally for legal theory. I first presented them in the central part, 'Our Human Community: Towards a Plural and Praxis Oriented Human Rights Paradigm', of the Master thesis in legal theory that I wrote under the supervision of Roger Cotterrell (Eberhard 1997: 47ff).

The concept of 'community' provided a 'milieu' in which the phenomenological and dynamic approach to Law developed at the LAJP could make sense in the framework of legal theory (see Eberhard 2000). It must be emphasized that such a vision of 'law's community' is far from being natural to continental European legal theorists who are deeply embedded in highly state-centered visions of law.[8] The Anglo Saxon detour (also including the debates between Communitarians and Liberals) thus allowed me to build bridges and to open up doors in Francophone legal theory which would have remained closed if I had not on the one hand delved into Anglophone research for inspiration, and on the other had not also published in English allowing me to develop insights of community in an environment where this was acceptable (insights to which I could then refer in my French publications).

The Anglophone detour and enrichment allowed me to lay down the foundations on which to develop my actor oriented, pluralist and intercultural approach to Law, which little by little took shape in a *Tao* or *Do* of anthropology of Law, a path of discovery of the legal pluriverse between alterity, complexity, interculturality and humanity (see Eberhard 2010, 2011, 2013a).[9]

3. Culture and the Discovery of Alterity

In his writings, Roger Cotterrell is highly critical of the usefulness of 'culture' as an analytical tool in legal theory as 'the concepts of culture and legal culture are of limited *explanatory* value for sociolegal studies' (Cotterrell 2006a: 8). In his introduction to *Law, Culture and Society*, Roger Cotterrell (2006a: 9) points out that Chapter 5, which introduces the concept of legal culture, is 'one of the few almost entirely negative and critical studies I have written'. Even in the next chapter on 'Law in Culture', where he develops a more positive approach, he argues that in order that it can appropriately be dealt with *juristically*, it is necessary 'to break "culture" down into component parts and see it as expressed in different types of social relations of community' (Cotterrell 2006a: 97). He (2006b: 2) also notes that 'One of the hardest challenges for legal studies today is to decide how to deal with the idea of culture, integrating it into legal thinking but avoiding the kind of reification that treats culture as monolithic, a causal factor in itself, or an explanation of legally relevant behaviour (…)'.

Roger Cotterrell's critical stance towards culture is widely shared in anthropological circles – albeit anthropologists remain to be seen from outside as the specialists in culture. Generally speaking, in current anthropological approaches, 'culture' has evolved into such a fluid, dynamic and changing phenomenon, that it may appear to have lost any analytical usefulness. 'Over the last two decades, anthropology has elaborated a conception of culture as unbounded, contested, and connected to relations of power, as the product of historical influences rather than

8 In a French context 'community' even was – and still largely is – a taboo concept as it is associated with communalism, the ghettoization of particularisms and is basically seen as a fundamental attack to the universalist Republican pact of 'liberté, égalité, fraternité'.

9 The Anglophone reader who does not understand French, may find it beneficial to complement the subsequent developments – which must remain rather succinct due to space constraints – by reading Eberhard 2001, 2002a, 2002b, 2009a, 2012d.

evolutionary change. Cultural practices must be understood in context, so that their meaning and impact change as their context shifts. (…) Cultures consist not only of beliefs and values but also practices, habits, and commonsensical ways of doing things. They include institutional arrangements, political structures, and legal regulations. As institutions such as laws and policing change so do beliefs, values, and practices. Cultures are not homogeneous and 'pure' but produced through hybridization or creolization' (Merry 2006 : 14–15). The deconstruction of essentialized approaches to 'culture' was certainly paramount. At the same time the semantic inflation of the term contributed to discredit the notion itself. Ted C. Lewellen (2002: 49) sums up the current situation in anthropological circles thus: 'The Debate Over "Culture" Goes on (… and on … and on …)' before daring to generalize: 'Nobody likes the concept, but few want to do away with it altogether.'

A few years ago, I was invited to give a lecture on legal anthropology to a class of about 300 students, half coming from a law background and half from an anthropology background. In order to initiate the class, I asked the jurists to explain to the anthropologists what Law was about and vice versa. It was intriguing that culture was not mentioned by any of the anthropology students as distinctive of their disciplinary perspective. When I brought up the point, it did not elicit agreement. The anthropology students perceived culture as something to be deconstructed, rather than a fundamental or even useful tool of their scientific discipline. With the overemphasis on deconstruction, something very valuable and essential seemed to have been lost. A new blind spot was appearing. In my writings, I have pointed out the danger of idealized and essentialized approaches of the 'other', and even the paradox of approaching pluralism and human diversity through the notion of culture (Eberhard 2011: 101–13; 2013a: 103ff). But, what was I witnessing in this classroom? Was not something important getting lost? What is the important reality that 'culture' points to?

Roger Cotterrell provides an insight into this question. He sees a justification for a specific use of the notion of culture such as in the work of Pierre Legrand (see for example Legrand 1996, 2011), especially in comparative endeavours:

> (…) Pierre Legrand's approach contextualizes the traditional comparative law concern for contrasting legal styles of different families of law into a much broader focus on legal cultures as distinctive *mentalities* – 'modes of understanding reality' (…) – informing all aspects of the particular civilization in which law is embedded in a specific time and place. (…) The concept of legal culture in this usage can evoke a sense of rich and complex difference that is important in appreciating, *in a general, preliminary way*, variation between modes of legal understanding or legal styles of analysis and interpretation, even if the elements of difference remain aggregated, diffuse or indistinct and ultimately of unspecified individual significance. (Cotterrell 2006a: 140)

This insight provides a bridge to understanding the legal anthropologists' concern with 'culture' and a framework to understand why I consider it to be an important 'cultural disarmament' in the anthropological discovery of Law.

Legal anthropology shares a lot in common with sociological and comparative approaches to law. Nevertheless, it differentiates itself from them on one major point: it does not take the existence of 'law' for granted. The scope of pluralism runs much deeper in anthropological research than in any other. Developing sensitivity towards different 'modes of understanding reality' is paramount. In the legal field, the legal anthropologist may even be pushed beyond 'legal pluralism' towards a fundamentally pluralist approach to Law (Eberhard 2003, 2005b, 2013a). Why is this so?

Originally, anthropology dealt with societies 'other than the modern ones'. It was a study of 'them' by 'us', as anthropology was originally a Western endeavour to discover the 'other'. Thus, anthropology – and this is a major difference with sociology[10] – dealt with societies that did not share a similar cultural matrix, that did not necessarily have concepts such as 'law', 'rights', 'state', 'individual', etc. An obvious problem arose for legal anthropology: how to compare different societies in regard to certain aspects, such as 'law', without a theory of what one is comparing? Does it make sense to look for law in contexts where there is no reference to law? *Ubi societas, ibi ius*, 'where there is a society, there is law' the jurist would argue. But how to define it? Initially, definitions were based on 'our law' and the 'others' experiences were contrasted to this standard. This comparative attempt – despite being deeply rooted in an evolutionist outlook that put the achievements of Western culture at the summit of evolution and posited them as goals to be sought and little by little attained by all other societies of the world – turned out to be highly ethnocentric and scientifically unsatisfying: it painted a picture of other societies' Law only in terms of what they lacked in comparison to an a priori established standard with no transcultural validity. African Law, for instance, was depicted as non-written, non-systematized, non-distinct from other spheres like morals or religion, non-specialized in terms of institutions and professionals, etc., in direct opposition to our own law (see the comprehensive yet succinct introduction to Freeman and Napier 2008: 1ff).

In the Francophone context, Michel Alliot was influential in questioning this approach. He called for a move towards a non-ethnocentric theory of Law (see Alliot 1983, 1985). His theory did not discard a reference to 'law', in favour for example of 'conflict resolution' which some considered less biased. A change of denomination was not sufficient. It appeared primordial to address the underlying epistemological problems. Michel Alliot proposed defining 'Law' in a phenomenological way, starting from a premise that is beautifully captured in his aphorism: *Dis-moi comment tu penses le monde; je te dirai comment tu penses le Droit* (Alliot 2003: 87), implying that our ways of perceiving the world influence our understanding and organization of it. For Michel Alliot and the researchers of the LAJP, including Étienne Le Roy and myself, 'Law' – which I usually write with a capital 'L' in order to differentiate it from state law – became this phenomenon that puts forms, and puts into forms, the reproduction of humanity and the solving of conflicts in the domains a society considers as being vital. It must be understood that this working definition is especially relevant on the comparative levels of ethnology or anthropology, but may be less relevant in ethnographic descriptions which intend to portray the emic point of view and do not have to bother about the questions of comparison in order to further more general ethnological or anthropological knowledge.[11]

This approach runs parallel to the diatopical and dialogical approach developed by the intercultural philosopher Raimon Panikkar who first presented it in the legal field three decades ago, in a very influential article exploring if human rights were a Western concept (Panikkar 1982).[12] Raimon Panikkar, as Michel Alliot, emphasized that asking if other cultures have the same institutions as we have is meaningless. All cultures do not share the same outlook and questions.

10 Comparative law also, although dealing with law from all over the world, up to now has overwhelmingly only been comparing the modern constructs of law in the diverse national settings of the world (but see Menski 2006).

11 I refer here to ethnography, ethnology and anthropology as the three moments of the anthropological endeavour as outlined by Claude Lévi-Strauss, from the collection of data, through regional comparisons to a general understanding of the human being in society. See Lévi-Strauss 1995: 413, and for more specific elaborations in the field of legal anthropology Eberhard 2013a: 97ff.

12 On the use of this method in the legal field see: Vachon 1990; Le Roy 1990; Eberhard 2011: 183–98.

Hence, it is more fruitful to dig down to similar existential problematics and to try to understand how they are played out in diverse cultural contexts. Without naming it a diatopical and dialogical approach, this is exactly what Michel Alliot did when he proposed his phenomenological working definition of Law and suggested study of how this phenomenon manifested in different contexts. In Michel Alliot's work, what Raimon Panikkar (1982: 29ff) termed a search for homeomorphic equivalents, a search for existential functional analogies from one culture to another, led to a theory of legal archetypes that still constitutes a structuralist foundation for all the subsequent work of the LAJP. I cannot develop this theory here, but I invite readers to familiarize themselves with it in my article *Towards an Intercultural Legal Theory. The Dialogical Challenge* (Eberhard 2001) where I have presented it in connection with the challenges of a diatopical and dialogical approach to Law.

Suffice it to state here that European conceptions of what it is to be human, of what Law is about, are not universal. The recognition of alterity is a challenge to our ethnocentrism. It represents a first cultural disarmament: the realization that our culture, although it wraps itself in a universalistic vision, is but one perspective, among others, to apprehend our existence, and to live. This is not only an ethical wake up call. It also entails an epistemological shift: otherness introduces us to a pluralist world, it invites us to leave the universe of Reason for a pluriverse of being.

Structuralist comparisons, such as Michel Alliot's theory of legal archetypes, constitute an important step to raise awareness of the legal pluriverse by pointing to the existence of very different cosmo-visions informing very different legal visions. When anthropology started to orient its gaze towards modern societies and non-Western anthropology started to emerge, this pluralism, this awareness of alterity, shifted from its geographical location to a special sensitivity for anthropologists. At least until recently, every anthropologist's training involved fieldwork in a cultural context different from their own – usually involving an important cultural shock, an existential shock bearing intellectual consequences, the major one being a raised awareness to 'otherness', to logics, world-visions, representations, social constructions, institutions, informing action even within the same social setting. In this dynamic, Michel Alliot's theory of legal archetypes turned into a stepping stone towards a more dynamic approach which would make law appear in a completely new light. Étienne Le Roy's theory of *multijuridisme* ('multilegalism') and of a tripodic Law (Le Roy 1999: 189ff), which evolved on this basis, hints towards the plural nature of Law itself: Law is not only made up of general and impersonal norms and an imposed order. It also relies on models of conduct and behaviour and a negotiated order, as well as on systems of lasting dispositions to action, or *habitus*, and an accepted order, not to forget the ongoing contestation of established orders, which continuously challenge the status quo and demand to see law as process (Moore 1983). In this view, Western law, state law, appear only as folk systems among many others that crystallize in different ways the underlying anthropological phenomenon of 'Law', or as Étienne Le Roy prefers to call it, *juridicité*.[13]

After this first disarmament, a second one awaits us: the disarmament of complexity. Culture is only one element amongst others to be taken into consideration in order to understand the dynamics of Law. Pluralism not only lies in the coexistence of diverse, but neatly separated and homogeneous different systems. Pluralism lies at the core of all existence. It is a dynamic reality that can only be approached through a processual method, as for example through Étienne Le Roy's *jeu des lois*, 'game of laws' approach. It is obvious that the 'legal system' does not constitute a very adequate intellectual ecosystem for such a pluralist and existential approach. The horizon of community provides a more fertile ground.

13 See Le Roy 2011: 26–7; Le Roy 2004; and the special issue of the *Cahiers d'anthropologie du Droit*, Paris, Karthala, 2006.

4. Community and the Discovery of Complexity

How does one deal with the complexity of legal pluralism in contemporary societies? If the recognition of alterity made us aware of the existence of pluralism, the second disarmament, complexity, urges us not to remain stuck in structuralist simplifications but to approach Law in its dynamic manifestations. Community is a refreshing paradigm to welcome such a praxis oriented and dynamic approach to Law. It emphasizes the participation of all in the legal game, not only a few chosen ones. It echoes current demands for 'participation' that lie at the core of the nowadays fashionable approaches in terms of 'governance' and 'sustainable development' which increasingly question and challenge classical stato-centred approaches to Law (see Eberhard 2005, 2008, 2010, 2012, 2013b).

> The main challenge that faces the legal imagination at the present time is to envisage what "law's community" might be; to draw on the vast accumulated experience of modern legal regulation to imagine and to work towards regulatory structures that are responsive to local moral milieu and that clearly reflect the diversity of social experience of citizens. This is a task of making law morally meaningful as an aspect of everyday existence, rather than an alien intrusion, an inaccessible resource, or a special component only of particular professional or commercial settings. (Cotterrell 1996: 21)

This invitation to imagine a pluralist and praxis related milieu for a more dialogical approach to Law first inspired me to explore Roger Cotterrell's work in relationship to my own endeavour to move towards more dialogical approaches to Law. His work revealed to me ongoing debates in the Anglophone world between liberals and communitarians, which back then did not really have equivalence in Francophone scholarship. Even more importantly, it brought home the point that it may be scientifically legitimate and heuristic to deepen the notion of community in legal studies. This was very welcome news. Indeed, one of the main challenges of my work on human rights and intercultural dialogue consisted in breaking out of the fetters of the universalism versus relativism alternative. Was there no other way to approach things than in terms of the principle of non-contradiction? Were we really facing an either/or situation? Or, was it possible to engage with a more pluralist approach? Was it possible to emphasize the complementarity of differences over the principle of non-contradiction? It appeared to me that the universalism versus relativism dilemma was very much a modern Western construct which reflected a modern legal system *problématique*: how to reduce chaos to order by reducing diversity to unity through the imposition of a universal system of norms (see Bauman 1987). It reflects the archetype of submission that according to Michel Alliot typifies the modern Western legal experience, especially in continental European legal systems. But other archetypes exist. The archetype of differentiation, characterizing many traditional African societies,[14] is based on the recognition of pluralism as the foundation of social life. In order to maintain social harmony, it emphasizes the responsibility of all actors and the negotiation of solutions, rather than the imposing of an external order. It seemed more hospitable to the new dialogical approach to Law I was seeking.

Roger Cotterrell's work on community encouraged me to propose a communitarian paradigm for legal theory inspired by traditional African communitarian legal experiences: community as a horizon allowing an emancipation from the legal system view which, in my eyes, had led continental European jurists to become blind to the realities of their world and thus unable to

14 Alliot 1980, 1983, 1985 – for the communitarian model see more specifically Alliot 1980.

cope with its challenges (see Eberhard 2000).[15] 'An emphasis on community values is thus, in contemporary conditions, an emphasis on the localized as against the centralized, and on diversity as against uniformity. (…) To postulate, with some sociological sensitivity, the utility of a concept of community is necessarily to recognize diversity in social arrangements and radical pluralism in moral life as the essential conditions of existence of those areas of moral agreement that can underpin social solidarity today' Cotterrell (1996a: 322).

Today, as universalism versus relativism debates get replaced by a focus on 'glocal' dynamics, e.g. dynamics articulating diverse global and local fluxes and realities, such an approach becomes increasingly relevant and audible. The current stress on 'reponsibilization' and participation of actors in the elaboration and application of collective action through 'governance' and 'sustainable development', potentially also paves the way for broadened, pluralist perspectives on Law (see Eberhard 2005a, 2008, 2013a). Indeed, 'governance' emancipates legal *problématiques* from the State's shadow and from the legal paradigm in its strict sense. 'Sustainable development', closely related to 'good governance' in the global discourse that can be seen as its 'economic translation', also becomes an increasingly holistic enterprise taking into account social, environmental and even cultural stakes besides the economic ones. In such contexts pluralist and community oriented legal theory appears increasingly pertinent to understanding the possible contributions communities can make to Law, and to step out of purely statist views of Law in order to include what is often referred to as non-state law or alternative practices of law (see Cotterrell 1996a: 296; Eberhard 2010: 147ff).

Roger Cotterrell deepened his approach from a 'system' or 'structural' point of view by starting to operationalize the general notion of community into four ideal types: traditional community (living in the same geographical space or sharing the same language), instrumental community or community of interest, community of belief and affective community (Cotterrell 2006a: 68–70). He subsequently applied this model in his sociologically informed approaches to comparative law (Cotterrell 2006a: 79ff) and recently in order to shed new light on the question of 'embeddedness' in the economic field (Cotterrell 2013).

The researchers of the LAJP chose a different path for approaching Law in a pluralist and dynamic way, without falling into the trap of continuing to be caught in unitary constructions (see Eberhard 2003, 2005b). Instead of reasoning in terms of entities such as 'states', 'societies', 'cultures', 'fields', 'systems', 'clusters' or 'communities' and trying to unveil their pluralist and complex interactions, they chose to study given situations, *problématiques*, such as land law issues, youth justice, the rule of law (*état de droit*), human rights, mediation, etc., in global and local contexts in a processual way. They aimed at revealing the rules of the game, the tripodic Law in action as it emerges through the study of all the relevant actors and dynamics, and their interactions, in given situations. As mentioned in the introduction to this chapter, Étienne Le Roy first modelled this field approach in terms of a 'game of laws' (*jeu des lois*) in the contexts of land law issues in African contexts and questions of youth justice and socialization in Africa and Europe (Le Roy 1995, 1996, 1997), before using it as the general framework for his *dynamic anthropology of Law* (Le Roy 1999).

The *jeu de lois* allows one to study Law in a dynamic and pluralist way and to reveal the complex nature of legal regulation in different situations.[16] It widens the 'legal scope' to embrace

15 The interested Anglophone reader can deepen this endeavour of emancipation from the modern legal system point of view to a more pluralist horizon through the discovery of community in Eberhard 1997: 45–78. In French, the reader can refer to my use of community for a complex approach to human rights in between local and global dynamics in Eberhard 2011: 291–492.

16 Indeed legal pluralism is not a static reality. It is a dynamic interplay, an ever ongoing process. See Moore 1983, Le Roy 1999 and von Benda-Beckmann 2006.

what a law and community approach would call the 'law of communities', which is often referred to in other terms such as 'living law', 'alternative practices of law', etc. The model is presented in the form of a *jeu de l'oie*, a French game similar to the British Snakes and Ladder's game, with ten steps: 1. statuses, 2. resources, 3. conducts, 4. logics, 5. scales, 6. processes, 7. forums, 8. orders, 9. stakes, 10. the rules of the game (Le Roy 1999, p. 35ff).[17] It does not try to establish the embeddedness of Law. Rather, it starts from the very assumption that, from an anthropological perspective, 'Law is not what is in the books. It is what the actors do', as Étienne Le Roy continually reminded his students in his teachings. The state and its institutions are only one set of actors, and state law only one of the manifestations of the underlying plural legal phenomenon, Law or *juridicité*.

The reader may wonder why there is no special entry for culture, although the whole model stems from the aim to move towards a non-ethnocentric approach to legal phenomena. Let us recall that the entry point of the game are the actors and the aim of the *jeu des lois* is to study their interactions. Different aspects of culture thus make their entry into the analysis while examining the different steps which are of course influenced by cultural representations and practices. Thus there is no need for a specific, entry for 'culture' or 'identity' – which is also a safeguard against potential culturalist and essentialist deviations.

In order to analyze Law in any context, the model draws on different disciplinary inputs such as sociology, economics, geography, history, etc., tying them together around the quest of an anthropological understanding of the legal phenomena at work in a given situation. It is thus of an interdisciplinary nature. Being open to culture, it is also an intercultural model, although more on the level of an intercultural legal theory than of an intercultural approach to Law (see Eberhard 2001 for this distinction). Although having taken us already quite a long way from traditional ethnocentric approaches to Law, it must be emphasized that the *jeu des lois* still reflects an anthropocentric 'social sciences' approach. But other world-visions are less anthropocentred and more cosmocentred or theocentred than ours (Panikkar 1993). Another location could change the whole perspective on the legal game giving it more cosmic or divine twists. Thus, I have argued elsewhere (Eberhard 2011: 400–416) that in order to remind us of this positioning, it would be useful to introduce another first square before the current one: the square of our metaphysical positioning (see in this context Panikkar 1999). This leads us beyond intercultural legal theory into the realm of an intercultural approach to Law (see Eberhard 2001) and introduces us to our next disarmament: interculturality.

5. Comparison and the Discovery of Interculturality

> (…) it may be that the only way in which knowledge in the human sciences generally (including the study of law) can escape being limited by the particular configurations of power in the human activities that make possible each of these specific disciplines (…) is by confrontation *between* disciplines, or – to put it in another way – the effective challenging of the mechanisms sustaining the discipline-effect of these fields. Intellectual confrontations of disciplinary knowledge fields may be possible to advance knowledge beyond that encompassed by each of them. It should follow, however that any such effective confrontation will not merely add to knowledge but ultimately *transform the terms in which knowledge is sought and conveyed* by disrupting the taken-for-granted foundations of the disciplines involved. (Cotterrell 1996: 47–8).

17 For a presentation in English see Eberhard 1997: 69–78.

Recognizing *alterity* is like opening up our own window on the world more in order to deal with constructs coming from a different window. *Interculturality* gives credit to the fact that opening up one's window on the world wider in order to see things to which our attention is drawn from the perspective offered by another cultural window is nevertheless not to be equated with looking at the world through that other cultural window. The translation of a different culture's perspective into one's own, necessarily translates the latter. The recognition of indigenous people's rights by the predominant Western world view, for example, transforms their claims into anthropocentred claims on collective rights. It is not really able to deal with the cosmic aspect of these approaches to life and to 'Law'. So, an important question – beyond the opening up of socio-legal sciences to alterity and complexity – another issue needs to be addressed: how to deal with the more radical intercultural pluralism that can never be unified into any system? What happens between windows? A dialogue between Chinese and European partners may happen in English. But once the dialogue is over, how does each of the partners take home what they shared? How do they fit it into their language and world vision and translate it into their Law? We can know various languages. But we cannot speak them all at the same time. Our general perception may be increased by knowing different linguistic, cultural and legal universes. But as soon as we speak and theorize we enter one of them. Our window may be more open than that of people who never looked through another window. But this increased openness does not make the other windows vanish. They continue to coexist.

In the meeting of cultures, comparison – which we have already dealt with above – is not enough. Comparison may be a first step in the discovery of the other. It allows an awakening to alterity. But it immediately raises questions as to what we compare. We discover a fundamental pluralism that challenges our own self-understanding. From comparative, the endeavour little by little becomes 'imparative'. For Raimon Panikkar (1998: 119) this means that beyond comparing, we learn from other existential experiences[18] … and actually get transformed in this dialogical process.

There is no intellectual 'solution' to pluralism. In its profound sense, a pluralist theory is a contradiction in terms. Indeed, the effective confrontation of radically different perspectives, such as those stemming from cultures that do not share the same matrix, does not merely add to knowledge but ultimately *transform the terms in which knowledge is sought and conveyed* by disrupting the taken-for-granted foundations of what knowledge is about, and how it is approached and shared. It obliges us to recognize the importance of *praxis* next to our theories. This is quite a blow to our intellectual academic self-understanding. In a dialogical horizon, as I like to tell my students: 'Questions are not voids to be filled. They are plenitudes to be discovered.' As space is limited, I will simply open up a window to pluralism, by quoting Raimon Panikkar whose intercultural explorations lie at the foundation of my own intercultural theory and approach to Law.

> No purely theoretical solution can ever be adequate to the problem of pluralism; and this almost by definition. A problem which has a theoretical answer is not a pluralistic problem. (…) Pluralism is today a human existential problem which raises acute questions about how we are going to live our lives in the midst of so many options. Pluralism is no longer just the old schoolbook question about the One and the Many; it has become a concrete day-to-day dilemma occasioned by the encounter of mutually incompatible worldviews and philosophies. Today we face pluralism as the very practical question of planetary human coexistence. (…) The problem of pluralism arises only when we feel – we suffer – the incompatibility of differing worldviews and are at the same time

18 See also in this context Vachon 1998, and my attempt to put into practice such an imparative approach in Eberhard 2012a.

> forced by the *praxis* of our factual coexistence to seek survival. The problem becomes acute today because contemporary *praxis* throws us into the arms of one another; we can no longer live cut off from one another in geographical boxes, closeted in neat little compartments and departments, segregated into econonomical capsules, cultural areas, racial ghettoes, and so forth. (…) Puralism is not the mere justification for a plurality of opinions, but the realization that the real is more than the sum of all possible opinions. (…) We may feel disoriented in the face of so many 'orients', so many compasses, medicines and prophets. Yet we should not be resigned and try to withdraw into selfish individualisms, but instead recognize that Man himself and Reality are pluralistic (neither monistic nor dualistic), and thus that the immense variety of what appear to be conflicts (when viewed dialectically) can be transformed (I would even say converted, but this is not an automatic process) into *dialogical tensions* and *creative polarities*. All that is needed is for us to experience, to touch, to reach that very core of reality which makes us so differently unique that we are each incomparable, and so uniquely unique that all our differences appear as so many colourful beams of unfathomable light. (Panikkar 1995b: 55, 56, 57, 86, 87).

6. The Pluriverse and the Discovery of Humanity

The disarmament of *interculturality* leads us to a fourth existential disarmament which is closely related to the discovery of the pluriverse: the recognition that we are humans. Initially, I found this pole important as my intercultural experiences made me aware of how much my discovery of pluralism was rooted in a Western universal outlook on humanity. As a Western jurist and anthropologist, I was intrigued and challenged by pluralism because I believed in a 'universal human nature'…which paradoxically does not exist as such but manifests in a myriad of ways. It is precisely our unity that commands respect for our diversity – this was the starting point and paradox of my whole initial research endeavour on human rights and intercultural dialogue. But this premise is only one amongst many. It is not a universal. Thus, though fundamental in my approach in order to balance all my emphasis on diversity, I hesitated to call it the pole of 'universality'.

Little by little it appeared to me that what was increasingly important in the pluriverse from my perspective was the recognition of our shared humanity. If universality points to abstracts, humanity points to our real lives and encompasses both our individual and collective experiences and beyond. Most importantly, the recognition of our *humanity*, this last existential disarmament on our Tao, Do or Way of legal anthropology (see Eberhard 2011: 11ff; 2013a: 351ff) is closely related to an attitude of humility. We are not Gods. We are not perfect. We are not immortal. We are not beyond suffering. As human beings, we are incomplete, fragile and open beings. This fragility is not a weakness. It is the very condition of our openness to ourselves, others, our environment and beyond. The horizon of humanity hints at the fundamental fragility of the human condition and invites us to a very humble approach to life. A humble approach of critical self-awareness, individual and collective, coupled with a sense of the ensuing responsibilities, is what it points to. Our lives are mysteries, individually and collectively. For me: 'Life is not a void to be filled. It is a plenitude to be discovered.' Let us discover it. Together.

Bibliography[19]

Alliot, M. 1980. 'Modèles sociétaux- 1. Les communautés'. 2 *Bulletin de Liaison du Laboratoire d'Anthropologie Juridique de Paris*, 87–93. Republished in C. Kuyu (ed.), *Le droit et le service public au miroir de l'anthropologie. Textes choisis et édités par Camille Kuyu.* 73–8. Paris, Karthala.

Alliot, M. 1983. 'Anthropologie et juristique. Sur les conditions de l'élaboration d'une science du droit'. 6 *Bulletin de Liaison du Laboratoire d'Anthropologie Juridique de Paris*, 83–117. Republished in C. Kuyu (ed.), *Le droit et le service public au miroir de l'anthropologie. Textes choisis et édités par Camille Kuyu*, 283–305. Paris, Karthala.

Alliot, M. 1985. 'La coutume dans les droits originellement africains'. 7–8 *Bulletin de Liaison du Laboratoire d'Anthropologie Juridique de Paris*, 79–100. Republished in C. Kuyu (ed.), *Le droit et le service public au miroir de l'anthropologie. Textes choisis et édités par Camille Kuyu*, 53–71. Paris, Karthala.

Alliot, M. 2003. *Le droit et le service public au miroir de l'anthropologie. Textes choisis et édités par Camille Kuyu.* Paris, Karthala.

Bauman, Z. 1987. *Legislators and Interpreters – On Modernity, Post-modernity and Intellectuals.* Cambridge, Polity Press.

Cotterrell, R. 1992. *The Sociology of Law: An Introduction.* London, Butterworths. 2nd edition.

Cotterrell, R. 1996. *Law's Community – Legal Theory in Sociological Perspective.* Oxford, Clarendon Press.

Cotterrell, R. 1997. 'A Legal Concept of Community'. 12/2 *Canadian Journal of Law and Society*, 75–91.

Cotterrell, R. 1999. *Emile Durkheim: Law in A Moral Domain.* Edinburgh, Edinburgh University Press.

Cotterrell, R. 2003. *The Politics of Jurisprudence. A Critical Introduction to Legal Philosophy.* London, LexisNexis. 2nd edition.

Cotterrell, R. 2006a. *Law, Culture and Society. Legal Ideas in the Mirror of Social Theory.* Aldershot, Ashgate.

Cotterrell, R. 2006b. 'Culture, Comparison, Community'. 2 *International Journal of Law in Context*, 1–10.

Cotterrell, R. 2007. 'Is it Bad to Be Different? Comparative Law and the Appreciation of Diversity'. In E. Orucu and D. Nelsen (eds), *Comparative Law: A Handbook*, 133–54. Oxford, Hart Publishing.

Cotterrell, R. 2008, 'Comparative Law and Legal Culture'. In M. Reimann and R. Zimmermann (eds), *Oxford Handbook of Comparative Law*, 710–37. Oxford, Oxford University Press.

Cotterrell, R. 2013. 'Rethinking "Embeddedness": Law, Economy, Community.' 40/1 *Journal of Law and Society*, 49–67.

Eberhard, C. 1994. *Die Bedeutung des Abstraktionsprinzips anhand des Vergleichs zwischen dem deutschen und dem französischen Kaufvertragsrecht.* Magister Legum (LL.M.) thesis with Prof. Dr. Dr. Hc. Mult. C.-W. Canaris, Ludwig-Maximilians-Universität München.

Eberhard, C. 1996. *De l'universalisme à l'universalité des droits de l'homme par le dialogue interculturel – Un défi de sortie de modernité*, Mémoire de Diplôme d'études approfondies

19 I would like to apologize to the reader for the very selective bibliography and the overrepresentation of Roger Cotterrell's publications, and my own publications, and those that very directly inspired my scientific path. This is due to the limited space available and the fact that this contribution is foremost an intellectual dialogue between Roger Cotterrell's and my approach to Law.

(DEA) d'Études Africaines Option Anthropologie Juridique et Politique sous la direction de M. Étienne Le Roy, Université Paris I – Panthéon Sorbonne. Available at : http://www.dhdi.free.fr/recherches/droithomme/memoires/ebermemoir1.htm.

Eberhard, C. 1997. *Common Humanities and Human Community – Towards a Dianthropological Praxis of Human Rights.* Master thesis in legal theory with Prof. R.B.M. Cotterrell, European Academy of Legal Theory. Available at: http://www.dhdi.free.fr/recherches/droithomme/memoires/ebermemoir2.pdf.

Eberhard, C. 2000. 'Justice, Droits de l'Homme et globalisation dans le miroir africain: l'image communautaire'. 45 *Revue Interdisciplinaire d'Études Juridiques*, 57–86.

Eberhard, C. 2001. 'Towards an Intercultural Legal Theory – The Dialogical Challenge'. 10/2 *Social & Legal Studies. An International Journal*, 171–201.

Eberhard, C. 2002a. 'Challenges and Prospects for the Anthropology of Law. A Francophone Perspective'. XXXV *Newsletter of the Commission on Folk Law and Legal Pluralism*, 47–68.

Eberhard, C. 2002b. 'Human Rights and Intercultural Dialogue. An Anthropological Perspective'. XXVII *Indian Socio-Legal Journal*, 99–120.

Eberhard, C. 2003. 'Penser le pluralisme juridique de manière pluraliste. Défi pour une théorie interculturelle du Droit'. 2 *Cahiers d'Anthropologie du Droit*, Paris, Karthala, 51–63.

Eberhard, C. (ed.) 2005a. *Droit, gouvernance et développement durable*. Paris, Karthala.

Eberhard, C. 2005b. 'Beyond Legal Pluralism – A Dynamic and Intercultural Approach to Law in India'. XXXI *Indian Socio-Legal Journal*, 131–48.

Eberhard, C. (dir.) 2008. *Traduire nos responsabilités planétaires. Recomposer nos paysages juridiques*. Bruxelles, Bruylant.

Eberhard, C. 2009a. 'Law and Anthropology in a 'Glocal' World. The Challenge of Dialogue'. 12 *Current Legal Issues – Law and Anthropology*, 67–88.

Eberhard, C. 2010. *Le Droit au miroir des cultures. Pour une autre mondialisation.* Paris, LGDJ/Lextenso, Col. Droit et Société Classics, 2ème édition revue et augmentée.

Eberhard, C. 2011. *Droits de l'homme et dialogue interculturel*. 2ème édition revue et augmentée, Paris, Éditions Connaissances et Savoirs.

Eberhard, C. 2012a. *Vers une société éveillée. Une approche bouddhiste d'un vivre-ensemble responsable et solidaire*. Paris, Éditions Connaissances et Savoirs.

Eberhard, C. (ed.). 2012b. *Le courage des alternatives.* Paris, Karthala.

Eberhard, C. 2012c. 'Human Rights and Intercultural Dialogue. European Challenges'. In L. Bekemans (ed.) *A Culturally Oriented and Value Driven European Future*, 97–112. Brussels, Peter Lang.

Eberhard, C. 2013a. *Oser le plurivers. Pour une globalisation interculturelle et responsable.* Paris, Éditions Connaissances et Savoirs.

Eberhard, C. 2013b. 'De l'autre côté … La juridicité'. 70 *Revue Interdisciplinaire d'Études Juridiques. Droit en contexte*, 77–83.

Freeman M. andNapier D. (eds). 2009. *Law and Anthropology*. (Vol. 12 Current Legal Issues). Oxford, Oxford University Press.

Hart, H.L.A. 1994 (1961). *The Concept of Law*. Oxford, Clarendon Press. 2nd edition.

Kelsen, H. 1960 (1934). *Reine Rechtslehre*. Baden bei Wien, Verlag Franz Deuticke Wien.

Koestler, A. 1989 (1959). *The Sleepwalkers. A History of Man's Changing Vision of the Universe.* London, Arkana/Penguin Books.

Legrand, P. 1996. 'How to compare now?' 16 *Legal Studies*, 232–42.

Legrand, P. 2011. *Le droit comparé*. Paris, PUF.

Le Roy, E. 1990. 'Juristique et anthropologie: Un pari sur l'avenir'. 29 *Journal of Legal Pluralism and Unofficial Law*, 5–21.

Le Roy, E. 1995. '"Espace public" et "socialisation" dans les métropoles: quelques préliminaires à une problématique interculturelle'. In S. Tessier (ed.), *L'enfant des rues et son univers – ville, socialisation et marginalité*, 31–45. France, Syros.
Le Roy, E. 1996. 'Prolégomènes à une analyse dynamique de la gestion foncière'. In E. Le Roy, A. Karsentry and A. Bertrand (eds), *La sécurisation foncière en Afrique – Pour une Gestion viable des ressources renouvelables*, 185–211. Paris, Karthala.
Le Roy, E. 1997. 'Sortir d'une représentation injuste de l'enfant des banlieues – Approches anthropologiques des parcours d'insertion et de socialisation des jeunes'. In M. Soulé and B. Golse (eds), *C'est pas juste! L'éthique des enfants devant les actes des adultes – La notion de justice et d'injustice chez l'enfant*, 73–84. Paris, ESF.
Le Roy, E. 1999. *Le jeu des lois. Une anthropologie "dynamique" du Droit*. Paris, LGDJ.
Le Roy, E. 2004. *Les Africains et l'Institution de la Justice*. Paris, Dalloz.
Lévi-Strauss, C. 1995 (1958). *Anthropologie structural*. Paris, Plon.
Lewellen, T.C. 2002. *The Anthropology of Globalization. Cultural Anthopology Enters the 21st Century*. Westport, Conn., Bergin & Garvey.
Menski, W. 2006. *Comparative Law in a Global Context. The Legal Systems of Asia and Africa*. Cambridge, Cambridge University Press. 2nd Edition.
Merry, S.E. 2006. *Human Rights and Gender Violence. Translating International Law into Local Contexts*. Chicago, the University of Chicago Press.
Moore, S.F. 1983. *Law as Process – An Anthropological Approach*. London, Routledge & Kegan Paul.
Ost F. and van de Kerchove, M. 1987. *Jalons pour une théorie critique du droit*. Bruxelles, Publications des Facultés Universitaires, Saint-Louis.
Ost F. and van de Kerchove, M. 2002. *De la pyramide au réseau? Pour une théorie dialectique du droit*. Bruxelles, Facultés Universitaires Saint Louis.
Panikkar, R. 1984. 'Is the Notion of Human Rights a Western Concept?' 82 *Interculture*, 28–47.
Panikkar, R. 1993. *The Cosmotheandric Experience – Emerging Religious Consciousness*. New York, Orbis Books.
Panikkar, R. 1995a. *Cultural Disarmament – The Way to Peace*. Louisville, Kentucky, Westminster John Knox Press.
Panikkar, R. 1995b. *Invisible Harmony. Essays on Contemplation and Responsibility*. Edited by H.J. Carger. Minneapolis, Fortress Press.
Panikkar, R. 1998. 'Religion, Philosophy and Culture'. 135 *Interculture*, 99–120.
Panikkar, R. 1999. 'The Discovery of the Metapolitical'. 136 *Interculture*, 24–60.
Rouland, N. 1993. *Aux confins du droit*. Paris, Odile Jacob.
Vachon, R. 1990. 'L'étude du pluralisme juridique – une approche diatopique et dialogale'. 29 *Journal of Legal Pluralism and Unofficial Law*, 163–73.
Vachon, R. 1997. 'Le mythe émergent du pluralisme et de l'interculturalisme de la réalité'. Conference paper given at the seminar *Pluralisme et Société, Discours alternatifs à la culture dominante*, organized by the Intercultural Institute of Montréal on 15 February 1997, 34pp. Available at: http://www.dhdi.free.fr/recherches/horizonsinterculturels/articles/vachonpluralism.pdf.
Vachon, R. 1998. 'IIM and Its Journal: An Intercultural Alternative and an Alternative Interculturalism'. 135 *Interculture*, 4–74.
van de Kerchove, M. and Ost, F. 1992. *Le droit ou les paradoxes du jeu*. Paris, PUF.
von Benda Beckmann, F. 2006. 'The Dynamics of Change and Continuity in Plural Legal Orders'. 53/54 *Journal of Legal Pluralism and Unofficial Law*, 1–44.

Chapter 10

Law, Community and the 2011 London Riots

Reza Banakar and Alexandra Lort Phillips

1. Introduction

Tottenham riots: A peaceful protest, then suddenly all hell broke loose.

The Guardian headline (7 August 2011)

On 6 August 2011, a group of people marched to the police station in Tottenham demanding answers over the fatal shooting of a local black man, 29-year-old Mark Duggan, by the police. The protest, which had been initially peaceful, spiralled out of control when the police restrained a 16-year-old girl who had allegedly thrown a missile at them. This triggered public disturbances in Tottenham which in turn generated waves of violent unrest that spread first across many parts of London and then to other cities such as Birmingham, Bristol and Manchester.[1] The violence, looting and arson which followed were reminiscent of the Brixton and Toxteth riots of 1981, which were also triggered by confrontations between the police and ethnic minorities. However, the 2011 riots distinguished themselves from the previous disturbances on several points. Social media 'speeded up the exchange of information' (Morrell et al. 2011: 3), allowed the rioters to organize themselves once they were out on the street (Baker 2011) and, according to the tabloid press, to prolong the looting (*The Sun*, 8 August 2011, item 2). Moreover, there was a break in the unfolding of the events, whereby a peaceful political protest was transformed into widespread looting. Admittedly, the previous riots also had been used as a catalyst for looting, but whereas the Brixton and Toxteth riots of 1981 retained their political character throughout the unrest, the 2011 riots quickly lost their political dimension. The apolitical character of the riots remains highly contentious and yet one of the most important aspects of the riots, which might reveal more about how the riots were reported in the media and discussed in the public political sphere, than about how some young people defined and experienced their involvement in the unrests (see Morrell 2011).[2] Perhaps because of their seemingly apolitical character, there were no similar attempts as in previous riots to identify the *social* causes of the 2011 riots in terms of, for example, class differences. Instead, they were presented by politicians and the media generally as random acts of sheer criminality (Cavanagh and Dennis 2012) and

1 Mark Duggan was shot dead by officers working for Operation Trident, which is a Metropolitan Police unit that investigates gun crime among the black community in London. This caused a great deal of anger among many people in Tottenham, who suspected that Duggan, who was black and allegedly involved in criminal activity, had been executed by the police. Trident had apparently mounted this operation without informing the local police. See Lammy 2011.

2 NatCen report on August riots in England (see Morrell et al. 2011) distinguishes between various categories of 'watchers', 'looters' and 'rioters' who were involved in the disturbances. The media reporting makes, however, no such sharp distinction and therefore ignores the fact that not all rioters were involved in looting and that some young people considered their attacks on chain stores as political acts.

eventually blamed on the police service's slow reaction to contain the rioters.[3] Riots in the 1840s in England were about bread and food, the Brixton riots in 1981 were about racial discrimination and racism, and the 2011 riots came to be presented in public political discourse as a meaningless and mindless case of random looting by people who had no legitimate grievance and were only seeking symbols of consumption (Frost and Phillips 2012). Some observers have thus argued that the 2011 riots can only be comprehended fully in the context of a society which is becoming increasingly consumerist in orientation (Moxon 2011).

In a message to the rioters the Prime Minister, David Cameron, promised that they would 'feel the full force of the law', and if they were old enough to commit these crimes they were also old enough to face the punishment (*Daily Mail*, 10 August 2011). Accordingly, magistrates were advised by the courts service to 'disregard normal sentencing guidelines when dealing with those convicted of offences committed in the context of … [the] riots' (*The Guardian*, 15 August 2011). Tough custodial sentences were subsequently handed out for offences such as theft and burglary. *The Guardian* reported that:

> In Manchester a mother of two, Ursula Nevin, was jailed for five months for receiving a pair of shorts given to her after they had been looted from a city centre store. In Brixton, south London, a 23-year-old student was jailed for six months for stealing £3.50 worth of water bottles from a supermarket. (*The Guardian*, 15 August 2011)

In the weeks following the riots, over 3,000 people were arrested and gradually appeared in court (*BBC News*, 4 July 2012) on charges 'ranging from incitement, violent disorder and assault to burglary, theft, handling of stolen goods and criminal damage' (Roberts and Hough 2013: 234). As it transpired, the rioters were a diverse group of people 'drawn from a complex mix of social and racial backgrounds' (*The Guardian*, 10 August 2011). According to the Ministry of Justice (MoJ) and Home Office (quoted in Guardian, 24 October 2011), 'the ethnic background of those in court varied considerably from area to area but overall, 42 per cent were white and 46 per cent black, with only 7 per cent described as Asian' (each of these categories are diverse in themselves). They were, however, predominantly from poorer suburbs (see the *Guardian/LSE* study entitled 'Reading the riots'). Notwithstanding this diversity, frequent references were made to communities in general and to the role of various migrant communities – and among these to the black community in particular – when discussing the breakdown of social order.[4] The rioters were said to be harming their own communities, and 'communities were urged to keep young people off the street' (*BBC News*, 10 August 2011). According to Nick Clegg, the deputy Prime

---

3 Police sources and David Cameron, the British Prime Minister, referred to 'pure criminality' (*The Guardian* 9 August 2011) to describe the riots; the account of one shop owner was given air and press coverage regarding her description of those involved as 'feral rats'. Iain Duncan Smith, the Work and Pensions Secretary, claimed that gangs played a 'significant part' in the riots, and he argued that Britain had to tackle the 'violent gang culture' which had infested the inner cities. (He was, however, proved to be incorrect, as fewer than 10% of those arrested were gang members. See *The Mirror*, 24 August 2011.) The Justice Secretary, Kenneth Clarke, described the rioters as 'a feral underclass' and added that in his opinion the riots could be seen 'in part as an outburst of outrageous behaviour by the criminal classes – individuals and families familiar with the justice system, who haven't been changed by their past punishments' (*The Guardian*, 5 September 2011).

4 Sociologically, community may be regarded as a relational concept expressing the socio-cultural similarities of those who belong to its circle and the differences distinguishing them from other groups and communities (see Cohen 1985: 12). It usually has positive connotations, invoking a sense of belonging, togetherness and harmony (also see Bauman 2001 and Delanty 2010).

Minister, the rioters demonstrated through their actions 'a total and utter lack of responsibility or any kind of loyalty toward the communities in which they live' (*Inside Housing*, 11 August 2011). David Lammy, the Member of Parliament for Tottenham, talked about the 'community' being devastated by the looters: 'A community that was already hurting has now had its heart ripped out' (*The Sun*, 8 August 2011, item 1). Bloggers talked about 'mindless thugs vs. community spirit' (*Hayhurst Consultancy*, 8 August 2011), while headlines such as 'Community spirit keeps the peace in Southall' (*Ealing Gazette*, 10 August) and 'Police and communities have been considering what has fuelled the violence in London' became commonplace (*BBC News*, 8 August 2011). Even in a study of the public's attitude to sentencing responses to riot-related offences,[5] published two years after the unrest, the notion of community continued to loom large, albeit in a more general sense:

> In our view, public opinion is relevant to determining the limits of sentencing practices. If these practices drift too far from the community on whose behalf offenders are censured, there will be a loss of perceived legitimacy, and support for the sentencing process. (Roberts and Hough 2013: 235)

It is unclear to which 'community' the authors are referring, but their survey of attitudes to sentencing is based on a representative sample of the UK population. Their study suggests that there is a single community in the UK whose values and moral standards can and should guide the law (alternatively, one could argue that their study represents an attempt to construct such a community). By contrast, the journalist and broadcaster Cristina Odone stated that:

> [T]he TV reports keep bleating the word "community". London's riots are precisely the opposite: there is no such thing as community. At least, not among the residents of Tottenham. The trouble is, there's no such thing … The broadcasters and the talking heads may try to paint a politically correct portrait of a united community that has come upon hard times (all the fault of the cuts, of course) and is now rent apart by violence; but it's unconvincing. The young hoodies rushing across our screens, plasma screens under their arms, shiny trainers dangling from their hands, have no sense of wronging a community, because they've never felt they belonged to one in the first place. (*Telegraph*, 8 August 2011)

After the riots, instead of setting up a formal inquiry into the causes of the riots, the Government set up the *Riot Communities and Victims Panel* (RCVP) to investigate, among other things, 'how communities can be made more socially and economically resilient in the future to prevent future problems' (Gov.Uk 2012: 4). The RCVP report found the causes of the riots in the breakdown of families, absent fathers, lack of resilience, ill-discipline and the lack of character in the young, but it stopped short of addressing the societal conditions which generated these social problems in the first place (for a discussion see Bridges 2012). They subsequently recommended a number of measures aimed at transforming the lives of 'individuals, families and, in turn, communities'

5 Sentences meted out to those who committed offences during the riots departed from existing sentencing guidelines; they were more severe, thus reflecting the judiciary's view that the riots created an aggravating circumstance 'completely outside the usual context of criminality' (see Sentencing Remarks, *R.* v. *Carter*, [2011] EW Misc 12 (CrownC)). Roberts and Hough's survey of general attitudes to riot-related sentencing shows, however, that 'the courts and the community differ in the quantum of additional punishment deemed appropriate' (Roberts and Hough 2013: 235). The offenders who were sentenced to prison for riot-related offences 'could have been sentenced to a community order, without attracting great public opposition' (ibid.).

(ibid. 117). Politicians who employ the idea of community often know that they are not dealing with functioning associations of people, yet in their rhetoric on law and social order they charge local communities with maintaining their own form of social order. Community is invoked as a distinctive place where solutions to all social problems may be sought and where the state may unburden itself from the responsibility of providing public services. To give an illuminating example, Andrew Ashworth, Professor of English Law at Oxford, recently launched a public debate on sentencing, suggesting abolishing imprisonment for property offences such as theft and fraud. He thought that we should instead 'deal with such offences in the community' (*BBC News*, 14 August 2013). Thus, community is where all social problems may be transported to and where solutions to all our collective challenges may be found – preferably at the level of individual responsibility and without reference to the larger society or societal conditions.

Can the responsibility for bringing social order to people living on the margins of society be passed on to communities whose existence as a functioning association is highly questionable? What type of law (if any) can bring social order to these people? Before addressing these questions we shall consider in the next section how Roger Cotterrell has conceptualized the relationship between law and community. The chapter will then employ ten semi-structured interviews with social workers, police officers, a barrister, a solicitor and other professionals familiar with the Tottenham riots, in order to offer an insider's view into what community means in today's London and how it is linked to law, justice, social order and identity. These pilot-study interviews will not allow us to draw general conclusions about law and community, but they will at least enable us to tease out the empirical complexity of the interplay between the public political discourse on community and social order. This will in turn allow us to reflect critically on the law-and-community approach as developed by Cotterrell.

2. Law's Community

> I believe in the law, I believe that the law in essence is a fantastic thing, but the delivery of it can be very twisted and one-sided. The law … is designed to sit in the middle … very black and white. There should be a real understanding about fairness – this is what the law is all about. As soon as you start taking the fairness out of the law you start losing the community and losing people's respect and their trust.

This quotation, taken from one of our interviews with a gang intervention worker in Tottenham, places law, community, authority, fairness and trust in relation to each other. It draws attention to the tension between state law (with its one-sided authority) and the expectations of fairness at the community level. It thus offers a socio-legal angle from which to view and describe the London riots while reflecting on why law's delivery is 'twisted and one-sided', why its authority does not command local people's respect and trust and why it cannot be applied with fairness. In this section, we throw some light on these questions by briefly discussing Roger Cotterrell's law-and-community approach, which he first formulated in *Law's Community* (1995) and later elaborated in *Law, Culture and Society: Legal Ideas in the Mirror of Social Theory* (2006) and subsequent publications (see, for example, Cotterrell 2008a and 2008b).

Cotterrell's law-and-community approach cuts across numerous discourses in law and social theory, lending itself to multiple interpretations and applications. It may be discussed in relation to law and to capture 'the deep embeddedness of legal ideas, practices and problems in social experience' (Cotterrell 2008a: 18), or in relation to various sociological reflections on the transformation of *Gemeinschaft*, in order to draw attention to the diversity of forms of social experience in contemporary society. It could also be viewed as an idea rooted largely in a common law tradition, which lends itself more easily than its civilian counterparts to the horizontal regulation of social organization and behaviour.[6] Furthermore, it may be employed to explore various socio-legal contexts ranging from ethnic communities existing at the municipal level to transnational corporations operating at the global level. Moreover, we may apply it in the debate on how to develop civil society alternatives to governmental control, or we could employ it as a point of departure for exploring how the forces of globalization are transforming the omnipotent nation state.

Our reading of Cotterrell's law-and-community is, however, in the context of the classical sociology of law, a discourse which has also informed Cotterrell's approach to the relationship between legal and social theory. Cotterrell is treading along the same path as Eugen Ehrlich (2002) and Georges Gurvitch (1947), developing their ideas and replacing their concept of law (Ehrlich's in particular) with 'more precise characterizations of basic types of communal relations' (2007a:24). Ehrlich sought the source of law and the origin of legal authority not in the state – and not as a top-down exercise of political power – but as a horizontal process which starts with the collaborative association of ordinary people. The attempt of a group of people to organize themselves over time is a source of normativity that generates 'living law' (or social order). Ehrlich's 'living law' does not refute the legislative power of the state or the ability of the executive to endow authority upon positive law by bringing the force of the state and the threat of sanctions to bear on non-compliance.[7] As we saw in the case of the London riots, the political and legal systems reacted to the disorders by bringing 'the full force of law' upon those who were arrested, by meting out severe sentences. Nevertheless, as the above quotation suggests, it was an order without fairness (also see Roberts and Hough's study of the sentencing of riot-related offenders, 2013). By contrast, 'living law' emerges as the normative expression of the inner ordering of social associations, thus enjoying a form of legitimate authority which does not require the threat of formal sanctions administered by state officials.[8] Cotterrell develops these ideas in this way:

> ... [L]aw is not limited to the law created by the centralised state agencies (it could be created, for example, by churches or localities), though state law will usually be especially significant. Where social relations have a degree of stability, duration and trust, they can be thought of as relations of community. Law's role is to protect community and to express and to support conditions for it. (2008a: 23)

While Ehrlich and Gurvitch worked with a concept of society that was emblematic of the era of industrialization – when social institutions, structures and relations appeared and were treated as

---

6 According to Ernst Freund (1897: 7) '*communa*' or '*communitas*' were employed in common law prior to the fifteenth century to express 'the collective conception and capacity of an aggregate body, but it appears to have been applied chiefly to municipalities and guilds'.

7 Living law, according to Ehrlich (2002: 493), is 'the law which dominates life itself even through it has not been posited in legal propositions' and it may indeed exist in 'contradiction to [the law] which is enforced in the courts and other tribunals'.

8 More recently, Barden and Murphy (2011) have developed a theory of living law which also emphasises the role of community. According to them, the living law is a moral tradition (or a 'communal moral law') consisting of 'the set of communally accepted norms that express how in certain types of situation, members of community are obliged to act' or 'the set of those ways of acting that, in a particular community are admired and thought appropriate to common types of situations' (ibid: 3). Also see Murphy 2012: 178.

enduring and 'solid' – Cotterrell develops his project in view of the consequences of globalization (2006 and 2012), growing multiculturalism (2008b) and with an awareness of the postmodern critique of knowledge and truth (2007b), which has irrevocably undermined the foundations of classical social theory. As the recent debate within social and legal theory indicates (see Cotterrell 2012 and Zumbansen 2010), the need to identify sources of legal authority, which can exist independently of the state and its institutions, is gaining urgency as globalization transforms the nation state and paves the way for transnational law and legal orders.[9] As Cotterrell explains:

> The long-established "modern" view has been that law is in essence the law of the nation state … But transnational law – harmonising legal practices and legal thought across nation state jurisdictions or irrespective of them – is assuming increased importance, especially in Europe. So also are the problems of autonomous or semi-autonomous regulations of regions, localities, groups and enterprises. (2006: 66)

Cotterrell's concept of community is a social formation below the level of a centralized state, smaller than 'society' and with its own source of normativity. It expands Ferdinand Tönnies' *Gemeinschaft* (1955) from a close-knit and relatively static social construct, based on kin and neighbourhood relations, to a dynamic association or a network of people who do not necessarily constitute tight-knit groups or live in single geographic localities (2013). This notion of community, which Cotterrell conceptualizes using Weber's ideal types of action, 'embraces the diverse, contrasting kinds of moral bonds and legal challenges that arise from many kinds of instrumental, traditional, affective and belief-based social relations' (2006: 161).[10] These communities are held together by a form of *mutual interpersonal trust*, which facilitates 'sustained, stable interaction' between the community members while giving rise to a sense of attachment and belonging among them (2006: 70–71). We are dealing here with a moral force reminiscent of Durkheim's social solidarity, a moral force which varies from community to community, governs the everyday practices of the community members and therefore can be treated as the ultimate source of law. Viewed in this way, Cotterrell's concept of community can explain why the gang intervention worker from Tottenham feels the tension between state law, which exercises its own brand of top-down authority, and his community, with its own sense of normativity, which grows horizontally and perhaps independently of the state. It also provides a methodological approach to socio-legal research, which does not depart from the centralized state (or state law) and is independent of the all-encompassing macro understanding of society we encounter in classical sociological analysis. From this standpoint, society becomes a collection of 'fluctuating, continually reshaped networks of social relations of community, which combine … components of culture' (Cotterrell 2008b: 377). In this particular scheme of things, even the centralized state may be regarded as a form of community network – a political community generating its own form of law, i.e. state law (see Cotterrell 2006: 165).

9 The idea of transnational law is not new and was first coined by Philip Jessup in 1956: 'I shall use, instead of 'international law',' wrote Jessup, 'the term 'transnational law' to include all law which regulates actions or events that transcend national frontiers. Both public and private international law is included, as are other rules which do not wholly fit into such standard categories' (Jessup 1956: 136. Also see Cotterrell 2012).

10 Cotterrell employs Max Weber's ideal types of action to develop the four categories of traditional, instrumental, belief-based and affective communities (see Cotterrell 2006: 69). Since these forms of community are Weberian ideal types, they 'rarely, if ever, exist in pure form in actual social reality. They combine and interact in complex ways as networks of community' (2008a: 23).

Each community has its own form of 'sociability' (to borrow from Gurvitch 1947), interpersonal trust, legal consciousness and subsequently its own specific form of social order, which Cotterrell elevates to a source of law par excellence. Thus, the law which emanates from community – or, alternatively, the form of law which corresponds to community's normativity – reflects the 'social solidarity' of its members (to borrow from Durkheim 1933) and the form of social order which makes the durable association of community members possible. In contrast to the positive law of the centralized state, which makes general laws applicable to diverse groups of people, laws emanating from or corresponding to the inner social ordering of communities are created specifically to regulate life within the community in accordance with the value system of its members. Thus, community law governs horizontally and by definition is therefore legitimate and authoritative, while state law exercises (imposes) its authority and legality in a top-down manner and thus requires legitimizing mechanisms.

What would happen if the moral codes of various communities, their socio-cultural values, forms of legal consciousness and their laws clashed? Such conflicts are not unusual in multicultural settings, where different communities define themselves by reference to divergent value systems and different historical accounts and beliefs. Cotterrell distinguishes between the 'normal plurality of modern society [consisting of] the different value commitments, traditions and allegiances that are combined in networks of community' and a form of pluralism (often associated with multiculturalism) which turns these elements into 'rigid, unbridgeable social divisions' (2008b: 377). Cotterrell means that various communities have to recognize each other's values (even when some aspects of these values might be a matter of on-going public political debate and negotiation) and demonstrate 'universal respect for others as individuals' (ibid: 382–3). The role of state law is to coordinate varying and at times conflicting forms of legal consciousness. State law should therefore be recast into a form of democratic governance designed specifically to aid communication between various communities, foster plural legal forms and cultivate moral commitments at the level of communities: 'What law itself must communicate', Cotterrell adds (2008b: 382), 'is a need for adequate respect for the autonomy and dignity of all other individuals'. This proposed type of state regulation, which breaks with all the fundamental premises of legal positivism, 'can contribute significantly towards restoring moral authority to law in contemporary society' (Cotterrell 1995: 337).

Cotterrell does not assume that all forms of community are good and worthy of support though, and goes on to argue that:

> [T]he social phenomena of community – the existence of social relations based on mutual interpersonal trust – is valuable in itself, because social life in any stable and rewarding sense is impossible without it. To facilitate social relations of community in general is to enrich social life in its various forms. Hence empirical studies of community may help in deciding how the social should be organised and regulated legally. (Cotterrell 2006: 162)

We are therefore dealing with a *normative* theory of community law in this respect. However, it is a normative theory designed in view of the empirical reality of law, i.e. 'what people experience in relation to law and how the experience varies for different parts of a population' (2008: 19). Therefore, it is a theoretical construct crafted intentionally to acknowledge the multiplicity of communities and the plurality of laws in contemporary society and to accommodate the diverse moral codes, worldviews and experiences of groups of people. The question is how can such a pluralistic legal order be realized? In *Law's Community*, Cotterrell argues for 'the devolution of regulatory power from the centralized state to the community as a way for law to retain moral authority and to diminish the current overextension of the regulatory capacity of the state in modern societies' (1995: 336). This approach to law should, on the one hand, allow passing on the responsibility for some forms of regulation (which do not deal with complex national policy matters) to communities, while on the other hand it should strengthen civil society, safeguard the interests of citizenry, promote collective participation in the public political sphere and thus also promote social justice.

In the remaining part of this chapter, we confront Cotterrell's law-and-community ideology with the empirical realities of the late modern age, in order tease to out its points of strength and weakness.

2.1 The Interviewees and Their Conception and Experience of Communities

Ten semi-structured interviews were conducted with lawyers, social workers and other professionals, some of whom had first-hand experience of Tottenham or the riots. The interviews started by asking what triggered the riots on 8 August and why they spread to other parts of London and other cities. These questions were used to create a context for the other parts of the interview, which focused on law and community. The following questions were put to the interviewees as points of departure for discussing their experience of community:

> What sort of an image does the word "community" invoke in your mind?
> Do you know any specific communities?
> Do you think you belong to a community?
> Are there communities which can act in such circumstances (like in the case of the riots) and help to avoid the outbreak of violence and disorder?

The interviews ended by asking about the law, if there had been a loss of respect for law and what the interviewee considered to be the role of law in situations such as the London riots. The average length of the interviews was one hour.

These interviews were conducted as part of a pilot study of the relationship between law and community and do not allow for generalizations. The interviewees were all from London and their sense of community is not necessarily shared by people living in other areas of the UK or even England. This was clearly articulated by one the interviewees, a 25-year-old police woman:

> … I grew up in Somerset, and every single child in my school was white and British. When I moved to London a couple of years ago, suddenly I was faced with massive cultural change, diversity and lots of different groups, and I'm awful for knowing [people's origin]; some people can look at someone and know instantly where they come from. It's bad, and at least I can say I'd never be judgemental, but half the time I'm ignorant. Working in London now, you do get certain areas you seem to have more of a certain ethnic or religious background of people, but I'm probably ignorant of it.

This interviewee underlines two important characteristics of our area of study. Firstly, there is a socio-cultural disparity between a cosmopolitan area such as London (and other large cities, including Birmingham and Manchester, which were also affected by the riots) and small towns and rural areas which constitute the rest of Britain. Secondly, British society is not a homogeneous entity. In such a diverse context we should expect different ideas and experiences of community to flourish.

Our first interviewee, a gang intervention worker from Tottenham, defines community as a collection of people who share some similar experiences and live in the same block. He then goes on to describe community as his 'oasis' – a space with clear social and physical boundaries:

> I class this block as my community, everybody … speaks to each other: "I'm going away on holiday, could you do this for me?" "How's the dog?" "How are you?" What's happening now with our "communities" is that we have been taught to fear our own. You live here, I call it my oasis, but you go 100m that way or 100m that way and you're in war zones, you've got gangs of roaming kids, but they come in here and they sit on the wall; they're cool, they respect everybody – because we demand that. They feel like they're part of it because we get down and say "What's happening, you lot?" "What you been up to?" And we say you're cool and just put your rubbish in the bin. They know they've got someone they can look up to and can have a conversation with who is not going to judge them. That's what I see community is – people helping people in their general area and being able to help people in their area and not to feel fear.

He is also aware of the generational shift which has taken place. When his parents came to England from the Caribbean, they were forced to build their own communities in order to protect themselves against racism directed at them, and 'they became a very close-knit community because no-one else wanted to interact with them'. He adds that life is very different for second- and third-generation immigrants, who feel on the one hand socially excluded, while on the other they are exposed to influences (such as consumerism and popular youth culture) outside the old community in a way that their parents and grandparents never experienced. Expressed differently, the societal conditions which defined the old community of migrants from the Caribbean have changed to such an extent that their children cannot but expose themselves to external forces. Put differently, it is increasingly difficult to sustain an ethnic enclave in today's society because the ideology of individualism constantly undermines a community based on a *collective* sense of ethnic belonging. It also means that what remains of the old community has no authority over its youngsters, and can do very little to either protect them against the outside world or bring order to the way they live their lives. This loss of authority is, however, a characteristic of late modernity and can be described positively in terms of enhanced reflexivity of the individual vis-à-vis social structures (Banakar 2013). While late modernity's enhanced reflexivity generates hyper-individuality – a sense of having rights without corresponding social responsibility – it produces disorder within socially marginalized ethnic populations.

Our second interviewee, a 40-year-old police woman, also mentions the generational problems cutting across migrant communities: 'There are youth issues that the community centres don't know what to do about'. She also paints a less enthusiastic picture of community as a whole. Her views are based on her experience of how people behave once a crime has been committed in their neighbourhood. She asks:

> Is there a community? People mind their own business and think: I don't want to be a witness, I don't want to give a statement, I don't want news outside my door, I don't want to be harassed, I don't want to do anything … they don't have that community feel … Some people haven't got a clue who lives in their street and wouldn't even recognise a burglar if he went next door. You have people who die and no-one knocks on their door for months on end.

Somewhat paradoxically, she nonetheless thinks that there are forms of community at work and these should intervene in cases of crisis such as the London riots. All of these communities are 'ethnic', i.e. non-white and non-British. She says: 'I don't know all the communities, but I can tell you about the Turkish community, black community, the Asian that could intervene'. This echoes the public political discourse in the UK which passes on the responsibility for the riots to 'communities', which once viewed from within are but fragments of ethnic groups with no authority and little sense of collective belonging. This view is largely shared by the next interviewee, a female psychologist living and working for Social Services in Hackney:

> I haven't really … grown up in a community. I grew up out in the countryside. I felt quite alienated from the local community, and I suppose what I see in my work is that people are more and more alienated.

Although some of the families she works with have their own personal networks, they nonetheless do not have what she calls 'a sense of community', a 'kind of spirit of doing something for other people … some sort of common decency, not because you know the person …'. To the question asking if she knows any specific communities in London, she replied:

> I suppose religious communities are quite … like that. I guess the Muslim community. They are quite tight-knit, and ideally they have a sense of their actions attached to a moral framework. I see more of that in my work but I don't particularly see a very big Christian community, although I do know there are ones out there where going to church and stuff like that is seen as a real cohesive force. I suppose there are those sorts of communities.

She also talks about 'an anger that's been building up' in places like Tottenham as a result of 'an underlying sense of injustice' which has in turn undermined respect for law:

> I think there is a massive loss of respect for law, when you see parts of the youth justice system … It is a few years since I worked in the former youth offending team, the disparity in sentencing that you see, the blatant racism … The police are not seen as a force [worthy] of respect.

The fourth interviewee, a youth justice worker, emphasizes the role of media reporting and how the riots were described and defined for most people by the media. Laws appeared to have been suspended and a dream had come true for those who were out looting. As regards community, she thought that it did not exist:

> I don't think communities exist. Although having said that there was some community behaviour going on, in places like Dalston, for example, where the shopkeepers of Turkish descent did stand up as a community to protect their businesses, so therefore you could say that there are communities in London … I think communities aren't fixed, well maybe they are – and do I belong to any? I don't think so, and do I want to belong to any? I don't think so; I don't see a need for that.

We already see a tendency to associate 'community' with the 'other' – the Turks, Blacks and Muslims – while at the same time to regard it as a problematic construction which either does not exist or is precarious, erratic and fragmented. Admittedly this is in the specific context of the London riots, but the community law and order we are seeking is one which can respond to extra-ordinary circumstances. A similar viewpoint is articulated by the fifth interviewee, a 30-year-old social worker, who did not feel that she belonged to any specific community and was uncertain in respect to her commitment to various communities:

> I don't think I belong to just one [community], I feel quite independent within whichever one, I could say my work community, home community, I don't know how much responsibility I feel for people. Work because I have to, home because I have to, not so much because that's what I have chosen. Perhaps a community of friends … where you find that nurture that I think that a community is and I feel more responsibility because I have chosen that rather than being forced into it … It's got to be organic communities, it can't be forced communities. I think a community works because people want to be in it, because it is available, that are solid, that don't let people down. People coming out and clearing up after the riots being a community together is one thing, but I wonder where it is now and what did it actually mean. Maybe there has to be some sort of artificial cohesion to begin with, but there also has to be willingness.

We could force people to build communities but as our sixth interviewee, a 40-year-old criminal barrister, remarked, these forced communities will soon 'fracture' under outside pressure. On a different note, this interviewee describes the impact of the media on the court district in central London, where she was on duty overnight:

> The judges at first were giving bail [to rioters brought before the court] and then when the journalists start coming in and sitting in court, the response of district judges changed … I still think they [the rioters] ought to be treated fairly and in an appropriate fashion, and that worries me that a judge reacts in a different fashion. We are going to find that cases that are now coming into court after a four-month gap onwards are going to be treated a lot more fairly than those that were dealt with on the days.

The seventh interviewee, a 25-year-old police officer, regards community as a big family of people who live and work in the same area. There is, however, 'no sense of togetherness anymore because people don't know who their neighbours are'. She also thinks that the police force is a sort of a community. The problem, according to her, is that it does not reflect the diversity of the people living in London:

> … In London there are lots of different people of all different races and religions and I don't think the police force is reflective of that. It's not that the police only attempt to employ a certain type of person, but unfortunately the majority of the police officers I come into contact with are white and British. We are in England and the majority are white, but it probably would be more helpful if we had a more diverse police force because it would be easier for people to understand. In terms of cultures I feel ignorant, I've not always had a reason to know more, even just little things that I was doing that I wouldn't know were disrespectful, like walking into a home with my shoes on when that is disrespectful. I think it would be easier if the police force reflected the community a bit better.

The eighth interviewee, a 28-year-old supervising officer for the Central London Youth Offending Office, draws attention to the disparity between what he regards to be his understanding of community and what the Government means:

> What [community] is to me and what it is to the Government are very different things. The Government talk about this Big Society, which I think he's been laughed out of now, but his vision of the voluntary sector doing statutory services is a vision of doing things on the cheap and it's this vision of getting away from having to fund services. My understanding and belief in community is

> that if people are part of their community they are less likely to harm it. So my biggest mantra is I get my young people involved in their community as much as possible and they are less likely to mess with it – that's what I believe.

He also does not think that he belongs to any community as such, but he points out that 'in Camden we talk about the Somali community, the Asian community, who typically will live in a similar area or geographical space, and I think they describe themselves as a community as well'. The next interviewee, a 40-year-old criminal solicitor, also suggests that the classification of communities reflects how the Government would like to deal with certain issues:

> When we say in terms of criminology the "black community", the "Asian community", "the young offender community" I see those as parcelled off and isolated, and those definitions of community are parcelled off in ways that the Government is quite happy to keep separate and disenfranchised because that is a method of social control … The communities that kicked off in the riots were the poor and desolate communities; it's a shame you can define a community as poor and desolate ….

Our last interviewee is a Restorative Justice Executive – an ex-career police officer in his 50s. He is keenly aware of what he calls the 'multidimensional make-up of communities':

> This is a mistake a lot of people make; they try to put communities in boxes, and say well that is that community and this is how we are going to police and monitor that community, not recognising that within communities are so many different dimensions. That for me is the real hard bit. In terms of policing directly it's having a response that understands and responds to those significantly different dimensions – it can be gender, race or whatever … I think it is multidimensional; during a week I will engage in a whole host of different communities which I'm a part of. Tonight in London I will be part of a community, professionally I'm part of different communities, my hobby, my home life, all with different values, all with different dimensions.

The interviews suggest that the idea of community as a support network and a source of identity continues to play a role in how the majority of people conceptualize and experience their daily lives. However, almost all of our interviewees are aware of the fact that this is an ideal image rather than the reality of community life. As our last interviewee suggested, what holds these communities (or rather these loose networks of people) together is a 'common purpose', which means that the associations or networks of people we find today in a place such as London are often not integrated through a web of ethical responsibility, and communities are not the 'warm circle' of like-minded and mutually committed people. They are at best *instrumental* communities, to use Cotterrell's typology. In rundown areas such as Tottenham, people live and work in an environment that consists of fragmented and dysfunctional communities and instrumental transitory networks, riddled with racism, social deprivation, youth unemployment and criminality. The police do not – and probably cannot – reflect the diversity of these fractured communities, and their attempts to police them, as demonstrated by the controversies surrounding the police's use of Stop and Search powers,[11] can cause tension and be experienced as discriminatory. The 'elders', first-generation immigrants who created their communities to protect themselves against racism, no longer exercise control over their children and grandchildren. These second- and third-generation migrants, as

11 'Black people are just over six times more likely to be stopped and searched by the police than white people' (Select Committee on Home Affairs Second Report 2007).

one of our interviewees explained, have no alternative but to adapt themselves to the reality in which they find themselves, thus implying that their community is exposed to forces which from the outside undermine its cohesion and lead to its disintegration. These forces, as pointed out above, enhance *reflexivity* vis-à-vis social structures – they insistently remind the individual of existing alternative choices, values, identities and forms of being. However, the Government (and the public political discourse) continues to talk about community cohesion and tries to pass on the responsibility of problems in these deprived areas to the people who live there. Is this because they wish to lay the foundation for a stronger civil society or, as one of our interviewees suggested, to cut back on public expenses and wash their hands of the responsibility for failing communities?

3. Concluding Reflection

A community can generate its own inner social ordering or cohesive normative force – its own living law – as long as it can produce rights and responsibilities and ultimately a durable web of ethical commitment capable of integrating its individual members into a form of collectivity. However, rights and a sense of responsibility are not the characteristics of many transitory networks which increasingly define the constitution of contemporary – late modern – society (see, for example, Bauman 2001 and 2007; Banakar 2010 and 2013). Although Cotterrell recognizes the transitory and instrumental character of many contemporary communities (2013: 54), he nonetheless avoids taking this insight to its final conclusion by acknowledging the need to move beyond a concept of community based on mutual interpersonal trust, durable relational stability and attachment (see 2006: 70–71).[12] Admittedly, we can find old and new communities which foster mutual interpersonal trust in today's society, but the point made here is that these are becoming exceptions to, rather than the rule of, social organization. In late modern society – and the social conditions of large cities such as London are indicative of late modernity – we are moving away from communities based on mutual interpersonal trust to temporary networks of people and interests which neither generate a web of ethical commitment nor require long-term, stable interaction between the members of the network.

In the context of the London riots, for example in Dalston, an area in the borough of Hackney, shop owners and other residents lined up to defend their own shops and property against the looters. In Dudley Road in Birmingham three young Asian men were also reported to have been mobilizing their neighbourhood against the looters when one of them was killed after being hit by a car, allegedly driven by a suspected looter, and the incident was said to have sparked tension between black and Asian communities (*The Guardian* 10 August 2011). The young Asians in Dudley and the residents of Dalston in Hackney appeared to have acted as a community, but their joint move to protect their property was an instrumental ad hoc transitory venture rather than a reaction motivated and necessitated by a sense of ethical responsibility towards each other. As one of the people we interviewed wondered, where are they now? The fact that Asians in Dudley and the residents of Dalston could mobilize themselves and act collectively are, however, important factors that perhaps indicate a 'latent' sense of community – a sense of community which is not realized or does not manifest itself because the everyday conditions under which the residents of

12 In his more recent reflections (see 2013: 55) Cotterrell writes that the idea of community as a distinct social phenomenon needs to be abandoned: 'Community refers to a *quality* of social relationships. It suggests a *degree* of stability and permanence in them – but not necessarily very much' (original emphasis). Yet he hastens to add that '[t]he stability of relations of community comes from *mutual interpersonal trust* between the participants in them' (ibid.).

these areas live are characterized by relational discontinuities and the diversity of values, norms and commitments of individuals. What remains of communities must constantly struggle against the forces which promote individualism and remind community members of alternative forms of life and identity.

Fleeting communities and transitory networks which constitute late modern societies generate neither webs of ethical responsibilities for their members nor enduring relationships capable of providing a basis for creating a living law. The social control which is exercised by the centralized state moves rapidly towards risk management and increased surveillance (for a discussion see Banakar 2013). The harsh sentences handed down to those who had participated in looting during the London riots suggest a central state and a legal system which are more than ever divorced from local communities. The law, which was invoked to meet the riots, did its best to appear in the eye of the public as a forceful deterrent rather than a normative medium for enhancing reciprocity and dialogue. The notion of community survives nevertheless and people continue to act collectively. The protest which started in Tottenham lost its political objective quickly, but even when it had been turned into riots and looting, it continued to signal its 'potential for oppositional collective action' (Scrambler and Scrambler 2012: 4). It is in the collective actions of people seeking justice – a form of justice which transcends their local concerns and recognizes and responds to the rights of the Other – that we should search for a source of law and legality capable of meeting the challenges of late modernity.[13] The common law of the future should be a law which recognizes and acknowledges the plurality of forms of legal consciousness, the diversity of social and moral values and, ultimately, the variety of forms of life, without requiring stable community relations based on mutual interpersonal trust. This law will be more in line with the Kantian notion of cosmopolitanism rather than with the living laws of local communities in Tottenham, Hackney or Croydon (see Benhabib 2008 and Beck 2006). One potential source of cosmopolitan legal order is through late modernity's networks of social movements – through the protesters who occupied the square in front of St. Paul's Cathedral in London in 2011, through the Occupy Wall Street Movement in New York and through similar movements in Spain, Italy, Portugal, Greece, Israel and Brazil.[14]

If for empirical as well as for normative reasons we must continue arguing for a source of law which is rooted in community rather than the centralized state, then our concept of community has to become that of a transnational community designed as the vehicle of cosmopolitanism rather than of local interests. Cosmopolitanism as a form of consciousness and practice, as well as an outlook or an ideal, can easily conflate the empirical and the normative while leading us into the trap of universalism (Inglis 2012). Nonetheless, it is in its ability to link the universal and the particular, thus creating 'a synthesis of modern humanism and postmodern identity politics' (Douglas-Scott 2013: 331), that we may renew our search for a form of law and legality that can meet the challenges of late modernity.

13 An example of such a collective action is found in Occupy Wall Street (OWS). According to Mulqueen and Tataryn (2012) OWS is an open-ended association of people (a type of transitory network or community) created around a set of common experiences, rather than a set of clearly defined political objectives, which characterise traditional social movements. More importantly, it generates its own kind of law as part of its internal processes directed at determining its own constantly shifting boundaries. This law is 'an alternative new law external to the positivist state-centred law', which is unfolded by the process of negotiating 'a set of values that become a community agreement' (ibid: 293).

14 For a discussion on new forms of social movements see Castells 2012.

Bibliography

Baker, S.A. 2001. 'The Mediated Crowd: New Social Media and New Forms of Rioting' 16 (4) 21 *Sociological Research Online.*

Banakar, R. (ed.) 2010. *Rights in Context: Law and Justice in Late Modern Society.* Aldershot, Ashgate.

Banakar, R. 2013. 'Law and Regulation in Late Modern Society'. In R. Banakar and M. Travers, *Law and Social Theory*. Oxford, Hart.

Banakar, R. 2011. 'The Sociology of Law: From Industrialisation to Globalisation'. In *Sociopedia. isa*. Available at SSRN: http://ssrn.com/abstract=1761466.

Barden, G. and Murphy, T. 2011. *Law and Justice in Community*. Oxford, Oxford University Press.

Bauman, Z. 2001. *Community: Seeking Safety in an Insecure World.* Cambridge, Polity Press.

Bauman, Z. 2007. *Liquid Time: Living in the Age of Uncertainty*. Cambridge, Polity Press.

Beck, U. 2006. *Cosmopolitanism Vision.* Cambridge, Polity Press.

Benhabib, S. (ed.) 2008. *Another Cosmopolitanism*. Oxford, Oxford University Press.

Bridges, L. 2012. 'Four Days in August: The UK Riots'. 54/1 *Class & Race* 1–12.

Castells, M. 2012. *Networks of Outrage and Hope: Social Movements in the Internet Age.* Cambridge, Polity.

Cavanagh, A. and Dennis, A. 2012. 'Behind the News: Framing the Riots' 36/3 *Capital & Class* 367–81.

Cohen, A.P. 1985. *The Symbolic Construction of Community*. London, Tavistock.

Cotterrell, R. 1995. *Law's* Community. Oxford, Oxford University Press.

Cotterrell, R. 2006. *Law, Culture and Society: Legal Ideas in the Mirror of Social Theory.* Aldershot, Ashgate.

Cotterrell, R. 2007a. 'Images of Europe in Sociological Traditions' In V. Gessner and D. Nelken (eds), *European Ways of Law*. Oxford, Hart, 21–40.

Cotterrell, R. 2007b. 'Is It So Bad To Be Different? Comparative Law and the Appreciation of Diversity' in E. Örücü and D. Nelken (eds), *Comparative Law: A Handbook.* Oxford, Hart, 133–54.

Cotterrell, R. 2008a. *Living Law*. Aldershot, Ashgate.

Cotterrell, R. 2008b. 'The Struggle for Law: Some Dilemmas of Cultural Legality'. 4/4 *Journal of Law in Context*, 373–84.

Cotterrell, R. 2012. 'What is Transnational Law?' 37/2 *Law & Social Inquiry*, 500–524.

Cotterrell, R. 2013. 'Rethinking "Embeddedness": Law, Economy, Community'. 40/1 *Journal of Law and Society*, 49–67.

Delanty, G. 2010. *Community*. London, Routledge. 2nd edition.

Douglas-Scott, S. 2013. *Law after Modernity.* Oxford, Hart.

Durkheim, E. 1933. *The Division of Labor in Society*. New York, Free Press, originally published 1893.

Ehrlich, E. 2002. *The Fundamental Principles of Sociology of Law*. New Brunswick, Transaction Publishers, originally published 1913.

Freund, E. 2000. *The Nature of Legal Corporations*. Ontario, Batoche Books, originally published 1897.

Frost, D. and Phillips, R. 2012. 'The 2011 Summer Riots: Learning from History- Remembering '81'. 17(3)19 *Sociological Research Online.*

Gurvitch, G. 1947. *Sociology of Law*. London, Routledge & Kegan Paul.

Inglis, D. 2012. 'Cosmopolitans and Cosmopolitanism: Between and Beyond Political Theory and Sociological Analysis. *Journal of Sociology*, Sage.
Jessup, P. 1956, *Transnational Law*. New Haven: Yale University Press.
Lammy, D. 2011. *Out of the Ashes: Britain after the Riots*. London, Guardian Books.
Levi, R. 2009. 'Gated Communities in Law's Gaze: Material Forms and the Production of Social bodies in Legal Adjudication'. 34/3 *Law & Social Inquiry*, 635–69.
Morrell, G. et al. 2011. *The August Riots in England: Understanding the Involvement of Young People*. National Centre for Social Research.
Moxon, D. 2011. 'Consumer Culture and the 2011 "Riots"'. 16(4)19 *Sociological Research Online*.
Mulqueen, T. and Tataryn, A. 2012. 'Don't Occupy this Movement: Thinking Law in Social Movements'. 23/3 *Law and Critique*, 283–98.
Murphy, T. 2012. 'Living Law, Normative Pluralism and Analytic Jurisprudence'. 3(1) *Jurisprudence*, 177–210.
Piper, C. 2011. *The English Riots and Tough Sentencing*. Brunel Law School, at http://bura.brunel.ac.uk/bitstream/2438/5785/2/Fulltext.pdf.
Roberts, J.V. and Hough, M. 2013. 'Sentencing Riots Related Offending'. 53 *British Journal of Criminology*, 234–56.
Scambler, G. and Scambler, A. 2012. 'Underlying the Riots: The Invisible Politics of Class'. 16 (4) 25 *Sociological Research Online*.
Smith, C. 2002. 'The Sequestration of Experience: Rights, Talk and Moral Thinking in "Late Modernity"'. 36/1 *Sociology*, 43–66.
Tönnies, F. 1955. *Community and Association (Gemeinschaft und Gesellschaft)*. London, Routledge and Kegan Paul.
Zumbansen, P. 2010. 'Transnational Legal Pluralism'. 10/2 *Transnational Legal Theory*, 141–89.

Web Sources

Gov.UK. 2012. *After the Riots: The final Report of the Riots Communities and Victims Panel* at http://webarchive.nationalarchives.gov.uk/20121003195935/http://riotspanel.independent.gov.uk/wp-content/uploads/2012/03/Riots-Panel-Final-Report1.pdf.
BBC News, 8 August 2011, 'Communities consider motives behind riots in London' at http://www.bbc.co.uk/news/uk-14452050.
BBC News, 10 August 2011, 'Merseyside sees second night of rioting' at http://www.bbc.co.uk/news/mobile/uk-england-merseyside-14461363.
BBC News, 14 August 2013, 'Do not jail thieves and fraudsters, says Andrew Ashworth' at http://www.bbc.co.uk/news/uk-23686277.
BBC News, 4 July 2012, 'London Riots: Who had been charged' at http://www.bbc.co.uk/news/uk-18681866.
Daily Mail 10 August 2011, 'Fightback! London's looters stay home as 16,000 police flood the streets ready to use plastic bullets' at http://www.dailymail.co.uk/news/article-2023874/UK-riots-2011-16k-police-ready-use-plastic-bullets-lid-Londons-looters.html.
Ealing Gazette, 10 August, http://www.ealinggazette.co.uk/ealing-news/riots/2011/08/10/community-spirit-keeps-the-peace-in-southall-64767-29210921/.
Guardian, 5 September, 'Kenneth Clarke blames English riots on a 'broken penal system" at http://www.guardian.co.uk/uk/2011/sep/05/kenneth-clarke-riots-penal-system.

Guardian, 7 August 2011, 'Tottenham riots: A peaceful protest, then suddenly all hell broke loose' at http://www.theguardian.com/uk/2011/aug/07/tottenham-riots-peaceful-protest.

Guardian, 9 August 2011, 'David Cameron on the riots: "This is criminality pure and simple"' – video at http://www.theguardian.com/politics/video/2011/aug/09/david-cameron-riots-criminality-video.

Guardian, 10 August 2011, 'Who are the rioters? Young men from poor areas … but that's not the full story' at http://www.theguardian.com/uk/2011/aug/09/london-riots-who-took-part.

Guardian 15 August 2011, 'Riots: magistrates advised to 'disregard normal sentencing'' at http://www.theguardian.com/uk/2011/aug/15/riots-magistrates-sentencing.

Guardian, 24 October 2011, 'UK riots analysis reveals gangs did not play pivotal role' at http://www.theguardian.com/uk/2011/oct/24/riots-analysis-gangs-no-pivotal-role

Hayhurst Consultancy, 8 August 2011 'Social Media – enhancing or quashing the London Riots' at http://hayhurstconsultancy.co.uk/social-media/social-media-enhancing-or-quashing-the-london-riots/.

Inside Housing, 11 August 2011, 'ALMO works with police to evict rioters' at http://www.insidehousing.co.uk/tenancies/almo-works-with-police-to-evict-rioters/6517176.article.

LSE/Guardian, 2011, 'Reading the riots: investigating England's summer of disorder' at http://eprints.lse.ac.uk/46297/.

Mail Online, 9 April 2013, 'Now there really is no such thing as society' at http://www.dailymail.co.uk/news/article-2305976/Margaret-Thatcher-quotes-Now-really-thing-society-says-RICHARD-LITTLEJOHN.html.

Mirror, 24 August 2011, 'UK riots: Fewer than one in 10 arrested were gang members' at http://www.mirror.co.uk/news/uk-news/uk-riots-fewer-than-one-in-10-275604.

Select Committee on Home Affairs Second Report (2007) 'Nature and Extent of Young Black People's Overrepresentation' at http://www.publications.parliament.uk/pa/cm200607/cmselect/cmhaff/181/18105.htm.

Sun, 8 August 2011, item 1, 'Tottenham rioters have ripped out our hearts' at http://www.thesun.co.uk/sol/homepage/news/3738875/David-Lammy-MP-Tottenham-rioters-have-ripped-out-our-hearts.html.

Sun (8 August 2011, item 2) 'Rioting thugs use Twitter to boost their numbers in thieving store raid' at www.thesun.co.uk/sol/homepage/news/3738786/Tottenham---riot---thugs---use---twitter.html. Accessed on 14 August 2013.

Telegraph, 8 August 2011, 'London riots: the TV reports keep bleating the word 'community'. The trouble is, there's no such thing' at http://blogs.telegraph.co.uk/news/cristinaodone/100099938/london-riots-the-tv-reports-keep-bleeting-the-word-community-the-trouble-is-theres-no-such-thing/.

Chapter 11
'No Justice, No Peace!' Conceptualizing Legal Alienation in the Aftermath of the Trayvon Martin Case

Marc Hertogh

> We know that justice can never be found in the courts. Next time we will not wait with baited breath for a decision; the distance between those deliberations and what we need in our lives is too vast.
>
> \- block4trayvon

1. Introduction

On 13 July 2013, George Zimmerman, a neighbourhood watch volunteer in Sanford, Florida who shot dead Trayvon Martin, an unarmed black teenager, was acquitted (Luscombe 2013; BBC News 2013). After a three-week trial, the jury agreed that Zimmerman shot Martin in self-defence. This verdict immediately prompted a huge public outcry and ignited a national debate about race and justice in the United States. Outside the courthouse, the acquittal was greeted with angry shouts by protesters who were pumping their fists in the air, waving placards and chanting 'No Justice, No Peace!'(Alvarez and Buckley 2013).The next day, some 2,000 protesters gathered on Times Square in New York City demanding 'Justice for Trayvon' (Sheehan 2013) and there were similar protest marches in other major cities, including San Francisco, Chicago and Washington, DC (Nagourney 2013; Kamens 2013). A week after the verdict, thousands of demonstrators gathered again at rallies in more than 100 cities across the US to protest the acquittal and to commemorate Trayvon Martin (Joseph and Somaiya 2013; Solis et al. 2013). Moreover, polls indicated that while a slim majority of white Americans (51%) approve of the jury's verdict, some 86% of African Americans overwhelmingly and strongly disapprove (Cohen 2013).

This case bears all the signs of what Roger Cotterrell has described as *legal alienation*. The public outcry in the aftermath of the Trayvon Martin verdict illustrates 'a divorce of law from popular needs and the conditions of broad popular acceptance' (Cotterrell 1992: 288). Over the years, and spread over several of his writings, Cotterrell has outlined a social development which he referred to as the 'isolation or alienation of law within the society it is supposed to regulate' (Cotterrell 1992: 288). For example, in a paper critically discussing the work of Max Weber – originally published in the early 1980s (Cotterrell 1983) and republished in the 1990s (Cotterrell 1995) – Cotterrell has argued that 'legal legitimacy depends ultimately on the belief of individual actors that law promotes [...] what is most fundamental among the actor's values of justice and order' (Cotterrell 1983: 87). Yet, he also noted that 'the specific content of legal ideology and the detailed experience of individuals and groups is made increasingly apparent to the broad mass of individuals'. Consequently, 'increasing demands are made on the law from all quarters, and established legal conceptions of justice and order are challenged' (Cotterrell 1983: 87). Several years later, in his much acclaimed book *The Sociology of Law*, he returned to this theme when he described an important trend for the future development of law. In the final chapter of the book, called 'The Prognosis for Law', Cotterrell (1992: 291) observed that 'legal regulation seems to become more alien within citizens' experience, at the same time as it confronts that experience in ever more detailed and intimate ways'. As a result, law becomes 'an alien realm of esoteric knowledge left only to lawyers' (Cotterrell 1992: 46).

'Legal alienation' appears to be a promising concept for empirical research on law in society, but unfortunately Cotterrell does not develop this concept any further in his later work. The approach outlined by Cotterrell only provides us with a general point of departure, but he has offered no further clues to operationalize the concept. Several other authors have used the concept of 'legal alienation' as well. However, most of their work does not discuss the concept at any length either. For example, Gibson and Caldeira (1996) referred to 'legal alienation' as one of the indicators to analyze the legal cultures of Europe. Likewise, Genn (1999: 247), in her study on the legal experiences of ordinary citizens in England and Wales, concluded that '[r]espondents' views of the legal system often conveyed a sense of alienation from the institutions and processes of the law ….'. And Gargarella (2009, 2011) has briefly discussed several examples of 'legal alienation' in his work on the use of criminal law in circumstances of social inequality. These studies suggest that 'legal alienation' may be a promising perspective to analyze the role of law in society, but none of these authors provide us with a detailed frame of analysis for empirical research.

The aim of this chapter, therefore, is to take up Cotterrell's discussion of 'legal alienation' where he left off. Inspired by Cotterrell's early writings, and considering the gap in the present literature, the purpose of this chapter is to explore and to develop the concept of 'legal alienation'. In the next section, I will first examine the general alienation literature and I will discuss those few studies in which the concept of alienation has been applied to the field of law. Here, it will be argued that most previous approaches to 'legal alienation' are either too wide or too narrow to be of much use to socio-legal studies. Therefore, I will try to make the concept more accessible for empirical research. This will be done in three steps. First, the elusive concept of 'legal alienation' will be broken down into several dimensions: 'legal powerlessness', 'legal meaninglessness', 'legal cynicism' and 'legal value isolation'(section 2). The second step I will focus on involves two basic questions in any study of legal alienation: 'Are people aware of the law?' and: 'Do people identify with law?' Based on these questions, I will then introduce four 'normative profiles' to describe people's attitudes towards law: 'legalists', 'loyalists', 'cynics', 'outsiders' (section 3). The third step of the empirical study of legal alienation will focus on different types of social protest: 'loyalty', 'voice' and 'exit' (section 4). Each of these protest tactics provides us with important clues about legal alienation. Finally, to test if these ideas work in empirical research, these three steps will be applied in an exploratory case study of the Trayvon Martin case (section 5). The final section will conclude that, by introducing the concept of 'legal alienation', Cotterrell has indeed made a valuable contribution to the development of socio-legal studies. Although some elements still need further clarification and more rigorous empirical testing, this chapter suggests that 'legal alienation' is a fruitful notion for future research on law in society. Following Cotterrell's ideas of legitimacy, it will be argued that if the American authorities do not produce an adequate response to the public outcry in the Trayvon Martin case, this case may pose a real threat to the legitimacy of the US legal system (section 6).

2. What is Alienation?

The concept of 'alienation' (estrangement or *Entfremdung*) has a long and controversial history. Whereas some argue that it should be considered 'one of the great traditions in sociological thought' (Seeman 1959: 783), others claim that 'we shall always be reduced to confusion when we read about alienation' (Ludz 1976: 3). The concept was particularly popular during the 1960s and 1970s and has produced a small library of literature in many different fields, including sociology, philosophy, social psychology and political science. For example, one bibliography on alienation refers to over 7,000 different titles, including nearly 5,000 articles, more than 1,000 books and some 750 dissertations (Van Reden 1980). It is, of course, impossible to do justice to this voluminous (and slightly intimidating) body of literature within the limited scope of this chapter. Therefore, the following paragraph only offers a brief introduction.

2.1. Alienation in Social Science

According to Ludz (1976: 7) the concept of alienation, as it is used in contemporary social science, can be traced back to two sources: the theory of alienation established by Karl Marx and the theory of anomie developed in twentieth century sociology from Emile Durkheim's work. The development of the concept by Marx, in particular in his Parisian *Economic and Philosophic Manuscripts* of 1843/44 (Marx 1964), has been very influential in most of the early alienation literature. 'Marx pointed out that the estrangement between the worker, his/her tools, and the product of his/her labor led to the removal of work as central moment in human life and thus to the eradication of fundamental self-hood and humanity' (Langman and Kalekin-Fishman 2006: 1). This has produced a vast literature which deals almost exclusively with a Marxian theory of alienation (see, e.g. Ollman 1971; Mészáros 1970). While critics argue that Marx's early writings suffer from an 'alienation syndrome' (Schacht 1976), which comprehends very different relations and therefore severely limits its descriptive content, others claim that 'Marx's analysis of the consequences of the new economic order has a foundational place in social theory' (Langman and Kalekin-Fishman 2006: 1).

Whereas Marx focused on *objective* alienation, most empirical studies in social science look at *subjective* alienation. Here, the focus in no longer on the *circumstances*, but on different *sentiments* of alienation (Seeman 1975: 114). Empirical research on alienation has been concentrated on two main areas: work and politics (see Ludz 1976). In the field of 'work alienation', Pearlin (1962), Zurcher (1965) and many others have studied whether or not people find their work engaging and rewarding. Most studies on 'political alienation' are based on large scale surveys, using several different scales of alienation (see, e.g. Kaase 1988; Dean 1961; Thompson and Horton 1960) or building on material collected in election studies (Levin 1960; Aberbach 1969).

2.2 Different Dimensions of Alienation

Contemporary social science has also been largely influenced by Seeman's (1959) seminal paper 'On the meaning of alienation'. Whereas most of his contemporaries were involved in either fighting or defending different Marxian theories of alienation, Seeman wanted to 'secularize' the alienation concept. 'A concept that is so central in sociological work, and so clearly laden with value implications, demands special clarity', according to Seeman (1959: 783). With his paper he wanted to accomplish two tasks: to present an organized view of the uses that have been made of the concept; and 'to make the traditional interest in alienation more amenable to sharp empirical statement' (Seeman 1959: 783). Seeman identified four alternative meanings of (subjective) alienation.

The first meaning that Seeman refers to is alienation in the sense of 'powerlessness'. In his view, this is the notion of alienation as it originated in the Marxian view of the worker's condition in capitalist society. Seen from the personal viewpoint of the actor, this idea of alienation can be defined as 'the expectancy or probability held by the individual that his own behavior cannot determine the occurrence of the outcomes, or reinforcements, he seeks' (Seeman 1953: 784).

The second major usage of the concept of alienation in the literature can be summarized under the idea of 'meaninglessness'. One may speak of alienation in terms of meaninglessness when 'the individual is unclear as to what he ought to believe – when the individual's minimal standards for clarity in decision-making are not met' (Seeman 1953: 786). Whereas the first meaning of alienation essentially refers to the sensed ability to *control* outcomes, this second meaning refers to the sensed ability to *predict* behavioural outcomes.

The third variant of the alienation theme in the literature refers to a condition of 'normlessness'. This usage of the concept has strong links with Merton's situation of anomie, which occurs when 'the disciplining effect of collective standards has been weakened' (Seeman 1953: 787). Seeman (1953: 788) defines this third variant of alienation as one in which 'there is a high expectancy that socially unapproved behaviors are required to achieve given goals'.

Seeman refers to the fourth and final type of alienation as 'value isolation' (or, in a later version of his paper, as: 'cultural estrangement' (Seeman 1975: 111). The alienated in this sense are 'those who assign low reward value to goals or beliefs that are typically highly valued in the given society' (Seeman 1953: 789). Other studies have described this type of alienation in terms of 'apartness from society' (Nettler 1957). It essentially points to the 'perceived gap between the going values in a society (or subunit thereof) and the individual's own standards' (Seeman 1975: 93).

2.3 The End of Alienation?

Despite its initial popularity, the story of alienation did not become the success-story that many had hoped for. After the heydays of alienation studies in the 1960s and 1970s, scholars have continued to apply the concept in their work, but no longer in the same large numbers as in those early years (see, e.g. Seeman 1983). As one scholar pointed out, after many decades of work there is still no authoritative concept of alienation yet and alienation is thus 'always in danger of becoming an empty formula' (Ludz 1976: 31). As a result of increasing tensions between different theoretical approaches, disappointing results from empirical research, and the fact that alienation soon became 'the all-explaining catchword of the hour' (Lee 1972: 121), many scholars eventually decided to abandon the idea of alienation altogether. One scholar even wrote his own 'obituary for alienation':

> As a term for therapists, for popular spokesmen, and for managerial consultants, "alienation" is admittedly still a "warm body". But as an allegedly scientific conception, it has died of overweening claims and overwork. (Lee 1972: 126)

3. What is Legal Alienation?

Considering the voluminous body of literature, it seems as if there is almost no aspect of contemporary life which has not been discussed in terms of 'alienation'. There are, however, relatively few studies in which the concept of alienation has been (explicitly) linked to issues of law and society. Whereas the general alienation literature could easily fill a small library, there are still only a few studies available on 'legal alienation'.

For example, Gibson and Caldeira (1996) refer to 'legal alienation' as one of the indicators to analyze the legal cultures of Europe. Sampson and Jeglum Bartush (1998) have used a similar approach to study racial differences in the level of 'legal cynicism', dissatisfaction with the police, and the tolerance of various forms of deviance in different Chicago neighbourhoods. Moreover, Rattner and Yagil (2004) have included the concept of 'alienation' in their study among three groups of Israeli citizens about the willingness to take the law into one's own hands. In a more theoretical discussion about the symbolic operations of law, Teubner (2001) focuses on 'law's estrangement from its social and human origins'. In two fairly recent papers, Gargarella (2009, 2011) has briefly discussed the idea of 'legal alienation' to analyze the role of criminal law in situations of social injustice.

These publications have made a considerable contribution to the introduction of the 'alienation' concept in law and society research (and we will use some elements of this work later in this chapter). In most of these studies, however, 'legal alienation' is only mentioned very briefly without any serious attempt to 'operationalize' the concept. Generally speaking, the way in which 'legal alienation' has been employed in previous studies is either too wide or too narrow to be of much use in empirical socio-legal studies. Most theoretical and normative studies use a rather vague (or wide) concept of 'legal alienation' to describe a feeling of generalized discontent (e.g. Teubner 2001; Gargarella 2009, 2011). By contrast, most empirical studies use the concept as one among many different quantitative indicators to measure the level of public support for the law in large-scale surveys (e.g. Gibson and Caldeira 1996; Ratner and Yagil 2004). However, this (narrow) approach is less useful in ethnographic and other qualitative studies. It seems that if we want to develop the concept of 'legal alienation' further, we need to return to the general alienation literature.

3.1 Internal and External Conceptions of Law

As discussed earlier, the present literature includes a great variety of different conceptions of alienation. Yet, several authors have pointed out that there is one feature that all these varied conceptions have in common, namely the feature of 'discrepancy' (Seeman 1975: 93). In the various versions of alienation, the concept refers to some sort of 'separation'– from property, from sanity, or from identity with a group or with society' (Lee 1972: 122). This general insight may also be applied to the field of law. In a much cited, but also heavily criticized (Cotterrell 1997), section of his book Friedman (1975: 223) distinguishes between an internal and an external legal culture.

While 'internal' legal culture refers to the 'legal culture of those members of society who perform specialized legal tasks' such as a judge, a legislator, or a lawyer; 'external' legal culture is the 'legal culture of the general population'. Following this distinction, a preliminary definition of legal alienation may now be formulated in the following terms: legal alienation refers to a perceived gap between an internal and an external conception of law. In the German literature, some authors describe a similar idea using the terms *Rechtsnähe* and *Rechtsferne* (different degrees of 'closeness' to law) (Kölbel 2005).

3.2 Different Dimensions of Legal Alienation

We can now break down this preliminary idea of 'legal alienation' further by applying Seeman's four general types of alienation to the field of law and society. Following his typology, we may now (at least theoretically) distinguish four potential types of 'legal alienation'.

The first type of legal alienation may be characterized as 'legal powerlessness'. In Seeman's terms, this idea of alienation can be defined as the expectancy held by the individual that his own behaviour cannot determine the occurrence of the outcome of legal processes. This is also reflected in Gibson and Caldeira's study (1996: 65/Table 1), when they ask their respondents to react to these two propositions: 'It is rare that law is on my side; usually, I find laws to be restrictive and against my interests.' And: 'My interests are rarely represented in the law; usually law reflects the views of those who want to control me.'

The second potential type of legal alienation is 'legal meaninglessness'. Whereas the previous type of legal alienation refers to the sensed ability to *control* outcomes, this second meaning essentially refers to the sensed ability to *predict* the outcome of legal processes. The most famous illustration of this is the story of the fictional character Jozef K. in Franz Kafka's novel *The Trial*, who gradually becomes completely entangled in a web of unpredictable legal procedures (Kafka 2005). Genn, in her study of the legal experiences of ordinary people in England and Wales, has recorded similar examples of alienation. According to Genn (1999: 247), '[t]here is a lack of sympathy with the jargon of the law [and] the mystifying procedures of the courts …' (Genn 1999: 247). Moreover, '[m]any practices, which are central to preparation for appearance in court and the settlement of proceedings, appear alien and sometimes inappropriate to those who had no relevant experience' (Genn 1999: 224). Or, as one the respondents explained about his day in court: 'It was a bit of mystery to me. I mean it was just like going into sort of a puzzle and coming out' (Genn 1999: 223).

The third type of legal alienation is what Sampson and Jeglum Bartusch refer to as, 'legal cynicism'. This 'anomie about law' refers to 'a state of normlessness in which the rules of the dominant society (and hence the legal system) are no longer binding in a community or for a population subgroup' (Sampson and Jeglum Bartusch 1998: 782). There is, in other words, an expectancy that the law doesn't matter anymore. In their study, this type of alienation is measured by a scale with five items assessing general beliefs about the legitimacy of law and social norms. Respondents reported their level of agreement with statements such as 'Laws were made to be broken' and 'It's okay to do anything you want as long as you don't hurt anyone'. 'The common idea is the sense in which laws or rules are not considered binding in the existential, present lives of respondents' (Sampson and Jeglum Bartusch 1998: 786).

The final potential type of legal alienation is 'legal value isolation'. The alienated in this sense are those who assign low reward value to those legal goals or beliefs that are typically highly valued in a given society. There is, in other words, a perceived gap between the values of the law and one's personal values. Anderson (1999: 9), in his ethnographic study of the inner-city ghetto areas of Philadelphia argues, for example, that 'alienation from broader society's institutions, notably that of criminal justice, is widespread'. This situation has given rise to a kind of 'people's law' or 'street justice'. According to Anderson, 'In some of the most economically depressed and drug- and crime-ridden pockets of the city, the rules of civil law have been severely weakened, and in their stead a "code of the street" often holds sway' (Anderson 1999: 9).

4. Legalists, Loyalists, Cynics and Outsiders[1]

In any empirical study of legal alienation, we need to answer two basic questions. First: 'Are people aware of the law?' How much do they know about the legal system in general, about the official rules and regulations, and – for example – about a particular court case? Second: 'Do people identify with law?' To what extent does the law reflect their own personal values, their own sense of right or wrong, and their own idea of justice? To consider these issues more systematically, we can transfer both questions to a simple two by two matrix (Figure 11.1). The first question, which

1 This section builds on Hertogh 2011.

may be referred to as the 'cognitive' dimension of legal alienation, has been put on the horizontal axis. The second question, which reflects the 'normative' dimension, is placed on the vertical axis. Each field then corresponds with a different 'normative profile'.

Figure 11.1 Four Normative Profiles

		AWARENESS +	AWARENESS −
IDENTIFICATION	+	**I. Legalists** *(informed identification)*	**II. Loyalists** *(uninformed identification)*
	−	**III. Cynics** *(informed alienation)*	**IV. Outsiders** *(uninformed alienation)*

4.1 Legalists

The first normative profile is that of 'legalists'. Here people are well aware of official law. Also, people generally identify with law. This profile reflects the model of the *homo juridicus*, the legal equivalent of the *homo oeconomicus* (Teubner and Hutter 2000), and is often found in publications on legal doctrine.

We know from decades of law and society research, however, that this model is not an accurate description of reality. First, many Knowledge and Opinion (KOL) studies have demonstrated time and again that people are generally not well aware of legal rules (Podgorecki et al. 1973). Second, from the legal consciousness literature we know that not all people equally identify with law. For example in the United States, general attitudes toward law, legal institutions, and legal actors (particularly in relation to the regulation of offensive public speech) vary according to race and gender (Nielsen 2000).

Both the fact that a high level of legal awareness and a high level of legal identification are not self-evident suggests that, besides 'legalists', there are at least three alternative normative profiles.

4.2 Loyalists

The second normative profile is the profile of the 'loyalist'. Here, people generally identify with the law. Contrary to the previous profile, however, people's awareness of the law is limited. They have a general idea of what the law is and they trust that it will be all right. They feel that the legal system should be respected and that it generally serves them well.

Elements of this normative profile are also reported in Genn's study in England and Wales. Generally speaking, this study revealed 'a depth of ignorance about the legal system and a widespread inability to distinguish between criminal and civil courts' (Genn 1999: 247). Nevertheless, a large majority of the respondents in this study also expressed their confidence in the legal system. Of all respondents, 73% (strongly) agreed with the statement that 'courts are an important way for ordinary people to enforce their rights' (Genn 1999: 227) and 53% agreed that they would get a fair hearing if they went to court (Genn 1999: 230).

4.3 Cynics

In the third normative profile, and similar to the first profile, people are generally well aware of the law. The most important difference with the first profile is, however, that the degree in which people identify with law is much lower. They are aware of the law, yet this also makes them critical about law. This profile can be described as that of 'cynics'. They generally do not feel that those norms and values which they themselves consider important are sufficiently reflected in the law.

In recent years, there have been a number of protests in the Netherlands against (alleged) miscarriages of justice (Hertogh 2011). In some of these cases (like the murder trial against the nurse 'Lucia de B.') the protesters included journalists, university professors, novelists and other intellectuals who were generally very well informed about the ins and outs of the criminal justice system and the details of the case. Most of these protesters can be characterized as 'cynics'.

4.4 Outsiders

The fourth, and final, category in Figure 11.1 is 'outsiders'. In this normative profile, people's awareness of the law is limited. People do not identify with the law either. This is the mirror image of the first profile. While 'legalists' regularly turn to law, 'outsiders' have turned their backs to law. This profile is, for instance, reflected in Anderson's (1999) study of life in the inner-city ghetto areas of Philadelphia.

4.5 Sliding Scale

Figure 11.1 may also be read as a sliding scale from 'legal identification' to 'legal alienation'. At one end of the continuum are the 'legalists'. Here there is no sign of legal alienation whatsoever. This profile is followed by 'loyalists'. This normative profile points towards 'uninformed identification' with the law; a first, weak sign of legal alienation. With 'cynics', the level of alienation slowly increases. And at the other end of the continuum are 'outsiders'.

5. Legal Alienation through the Lens of Social Protest

There are considerable differences in how, for instance, 'legalists' and 'outsiders' relate to law. But how do we know if we are dealing with one or other normative profiles? How can, in other words, the concept of legal alienation be employed in empirical research?

5.1 Empirical Approaches to Legal Alienation

A popular way to study alienation is through the use of surveys (see, e.g. Srole 1956). A similar approach has been used to study public feelings or attitudes of legal alienation (e.g. Gibson and Caldeira 1996; Sampson and Bartush 1998; Rattner and Yagil 2004). However, surveys aimed at legal attitudes are limited to record what people *say*, but they do not shed much light on what people *do*. People may, for instance, express a lack of trust in criminal courts, but what does this mean for their everyday behaviour? A second way to study alienation is by focusing on behaviour. For example, in political science non-voting behaviour is an important indicator for political alienation (Levin 1960; Cotterrell 1992: 326). Likewise, many socio-legal studies have focused on legal mobilization. How do people resolve their disputes? How often do they take their disputes to court? And what does this tell us about the way in which people relate to law? (see Genn 1999; Van Velthoven and Ter Voert 2003) These figures may also be interpreted in terms of legal alienation (Hertogh 2011). In this approach, the underlying assumption is that a high level of legal mobilization corresponds with a high level of legal identification, and vice versa. However, this assumption is not always correct. Take, for instance, the national referendum on the European Constitution in the Netherlands in 2005. Nearly two-thirds of the voters (63.3%) participated in this referendum. At first sight, this relatively high level of legal mobilization points towards a low level of alienation. At closer inspection, however, it turns out that most people have taken this opportunity to vote against the ambitions of the European Union and 61.6% rejected the European Constitution (Aarts and Van der Kolk 2006). This clearly indicates that many people do not identify with Europe at all.

Considering the shortcomings of both surveys and legal mobilization figures, we need to look for alternative empirical indicators for legal alienation. One way to do this is by focusing on examples of social protest aimed at the law. In these protests, people's criticism about the law comes to the surface and may be analyzed more directly. Moreover, these examples of social protest not only reflect people's attitudes, but are also translated into observable behaviour.

5.2 Loyalty, Voice, Exit

Studies in political science suggest a strong relationship between (different types of) political protest and (different types of) political alienation (see, e.g. Muller and Opp 1986; Kaase 1988). This may also be true for law, and suggests that the way in which people protest against the law reveals their normative profile. Following Hirshman's (1970) typology, there are three different tactics people may choose to protest against the justice system (see also Toharia 2003). First, when someone disagrees with some element of the justice system, he may choose not to do anything with this or he may try to resolve the matter by mobilizing the law ('loyalty'). This tactic covers a variety of different actions, including writing a petition, filing an official complaint, and bringing the case before a court (of appeal). Second, protest against the justice system may also be expressed by means that are outside, but not against the law ('voice'). This tactic covers, for instance, readers' letters to newspapers, critical blogs on the Internet and protest marches. Finally, the third and most radical way to protest against the law is to look for whatever ways possible to move away from the justice system ('exit'). This may be done by trying to ridicule or to ignore the law, by taking the law into one's own hands (Rattner and Yagil 2004) or by other forms of 'legal disobedience' (Rattner, Yagil and Pedahzur 2001).

5.3 Social Protest as Indicator for Legal Alienation

All three types of social protest tell a different story about legal alienation. According to Jasper (1997: 237), '[t]actics are rarely, if ever, neutral means about which protesters do not care'. In his view, '[j]ust as their ideologies do, their activities express protestors' political identities and moral visions'. Similarly, all three tactics of legal protest (loyalty, voice, exit) suggest a different normative profile of the protesters. 'Legalists' and 'loyalists' are the least critical about the justice system. If, however, they have some form of criticism they will most likely aim to address this within the boundaries of the justice system (loyalty). 'Cynics', on the other hand, are much more critical and they have considerably less confidence in legal procedures and legal authorities. Therefore, it is likely that they will favour different forms of protest outside the justice system (voice). Finally, 'outsiders' who are neither very knowledgeable nor very positive about the justice system will most likely demonstrate their anger and frustration by turning against the law (exit).

6. Legal Alienation in the Trayvon Martin Case

The purpose of this chapter is to explore and to develop the concept of 'legal alienation'. To test if the ideas that were introduced in the previous sections work in an empirical study, let's now return to the Trayvon Martin case already mentioned in the introduction. Data for this exploratory case study was gathered from a variety of public sources such as academic papers; newspaper articles; news websites, blogs and social media (Facebook and Twitter). After a brief summary of the case, I will first look for elements of legal alienation in the public reaction to the jury's verdict. Next, focusing on different types of social protest, I will discuss the normative profile of protesters.

6.1 Case Summary[2]

On a rainy night on 26 February 2012, a 17-year-old black teenager named Trayvon Martin was shot and killed by a 28-year-old Hispanic man named George Zimmerman, a neighbourhood watch volunteer in Sanford, Florida. Minutes earlier, Zimmerman had called 911 to report a 'real suspicious guy' in the neighbourhood who looked as if he was up to no good. Moments later, he got involved in a fight in which he fatally shot Trayvon Martin. Zimmerman told police that he shot Martin in self-defence. Zimmerman was handcuffed and taken to the local police station. But the police eventually released him, citing Florida's 'Stand Your Ground' law, which allows a citizen to use lethal force if he or she feels in imminent danger.

After the shooting, several protests were staged around the United States to demand Zimmerman's arrest. Also, President Obama publicly expressed his sympathy for Martin's family and urged a thorough investigation (Williams 2012). Critics argued that Zimmerman, who the media described as 'a white Hispanic', wrongly suspected Martin of being a criminal because he was black. Six weeks after the shooting, Zimmerman was charged with second-degree murder and his trial began on 24 June 2013. Because of Florida's laws, prosecutors had to persuade jurors beyond a reasonable doubt that Zimmerman did *not* act in self-defence. The case was troubled by the fact that there were no witnesses to the shooting and it remained unclear what exactly happened between the men. On 13 July 2013, a six-woman jury found Zimmerman not guilty of second-degree murder and he was also acquitted of manslaughter. The verdict sparked a fierce debate about racial profiling and was followed by many protest marches. Most protesters also heavily criticized Florida's 'Stand Your Ground' law (and similar self-defence laws in other states), which give people wide latitude to use deadly force if they fear serious bodily harm.

6.2 Legal Powerlessness, Legal Value-Isolation and Legal Cynicism

Immediately after the not-guilty verdict, many public reactions reflected a strong sense of 'legal powerlessness'. In the social media, on news websites and in newspaper articles, people indicated that they no longer felt protected by the US legal system. In particular, many African Americans saw this case as a confirmation that the law treats them differently than White Americans. Or, as one observer put it, the circumstances surrounding Trayvon's death 'were experienced as a fresh cut

2 See, e.g. CNN 2013; Gabbidon and Jordan 2013; Lawson 2013; Lee 2013; Wikipedia 2013.

in an old, but deep, collective wound, for many Blacks' (Lawson 2013: 1). Some public reactions echoed one of the statements from Gibson and Caldeira's study (1996: 65): 'It is rare that the law is on my side; usually I find law to be restrictive and against my interests'. This is also reflected in these examples from Twitter:

Steven Jones @iAMSTEVEJONES
13 juli
This "Not Guilty" verdict is a painful reminder of OUR reality. My heart grieves for #TrayvonMartin No justice. No peace. #ZimmermanTrial

Stoneyy . @StoneyyDOPE_24
13 juli
WHITE people are innocent until proven guilty! Blacks are guilty until proven innocent!! #SadTruth #NoJusticeNoPeace

mommyof2 @kingkee21
15 juli
#106Fortrayon hate that we are always giving the short stick cause we are black no justice no peace.

Nell Scovell @NellSco
14 juli
The best body armor in America is white skin. #NoJustice

Although these reactions were sparked by the Trayvon Martin case, many people emphasized that they demonstrated against the (legal and political) system as a whole. As, for example, Martin Luther King III explained in a newspaper interview, 'People are not as frustrated about the verdict. It's about consistent, systemic kinds of things that don't get reported and happen every day in courtrooms across America' (cited in Joseph and Somaiya 2013). On the day of the verdict, 'Occupy Wall Street' issued a call for a national protest march in over 40 cities (#HoodiesUp). In the flyer for this event, they too indicated that – after the Trayvon Martin verdict – they felt completely abandoned by 'the system':

> No matter what the verdict
> The legal system won't save us
> The clergy won't save us
> The politicians won't save us
> ONLY WE CAN SAVE OURSELVES.[3]

In another example, several protesters in Durham, North Carolina (who had participated in one of the many demonstrations across the US commemorating Trayvon Martin one week after the verdict) wrote in their on-line report that they no longer had faith in the 'so-called' idea of legal neutrality:

3 http://occupywallst.org/archive/Jul-2013/page-2/ [accessed: 1 October 2013].

> We do not have to call into question the legitimacy and power of the Seminole County Courthouse, where Zimmerman got acquitted for cold-blooded murder, nor do we have to call into question the legitimacy of the so-called Durham County Justice Center […]; those halls of corruption and power are designed to divide us and to make it easier for rich folks to get richer and white folks to be white and hide behind the veneer of "color-blind" justice.[4]

Other public reactions in the aftermath of the Trayvon Martin case reflected elements of 'legal value isolation'. For these people, there was a perceived gap between 'justice according to the law' and 'justice according to their own values'. For example, Ralph Reynaud, who was one of the participants in a 'Justice for Trayvon' rally outside the federal courthouse in Washington, DC, told a reporter: 'There was no justice. The letter of the law was executed, but the spirit of it was invalidated' (cited in Solis et al. 2013). This sentiment was also a general feeling in many reactions on Twitter:

Jeff Chu @jeffchu
13 juli
Legally not guilty does not mean morally innocent. #nojustice

Hari Kondabolu @harikondabolu
14 juli
Law & Justice are NOT the same thing in America. #obvious #NoJustice

BA Everywhere @BAeverywhere
14 juli
Obama says respect the Zimmerman verdict-HELL NO! that verdict is legacy of slavery, of lynching #NoJustice

Similarly, one of the protesters – who had participated in several small riots in Oakland on the night of the verdict – wrote on his blog ('block4trayvon') that, in his view, 'the distance' between the law and his personal life had now become 'too vast':

> We know that justice can never be found in the courts and that the prison is not the place for the Zimmerman's of the world. Next time we will not wait with baited breath for a decision, the distance between those deliberations and what we need in our lives is too vast. The police and prison system is theirs not ours.[5]

Other public reactions contained clear elements of 'legal cynicism'. Many reactions on Twitter were quite cynical about the functioning of the US legal system:

4 http://trayvonoc.wordpress.com [accessed: 1 October 2013].

5 http://block4trayvon.wordpress.com/2013/07/19/oaklands-first-night-of-vengeance-for-trayvon/ [accessed: 1 October 2013].

Hari Kondabolu @harikondabolu
14 juli
I wouldn't be surprised if the Prosecution & Defense in the Zimmerman trial went out for drinks after the verdict.#NoJustice

Tyreese Millz @TyreeseMillz
13 juli
What little respect I had for our justice system is now gone.#NoJustice

Other people concluded after the events in the Trayvon Martin case that – for them – the law doesn't matter anymore:

Essence@KittyGanggg__xo
13 juli
Why pledge allegiance to a country that does not value blacks as equals? Why continue being law abiding citizens in a country that states blacks can be discriminated against in all aspects and in case murdered …

Others took this even one step further. After the non-guilty verdict, they felt they now have the 'right' to break the law. For example, on the day of the verdict 'Joe Chimungu' tweeted: 'Take the law into your own hands if they won't serve it equally'. His tweet also included George Zimmerman's home address with the words: 'Let the PURGE BEGIN.' Similarly, a group of activists, who had participated in one of the rallies one week after the verdict, echoed one of the survey statements from Sampson and Jeglum Bartush (1998: 782): 'Laws were made to be broken':

> [W]e never believed the courts could deliver anything resembling justice. Because of this, justice must be conducted in the streets. To that end, we support any and all demonstrations of people power and rage against the system that oppresses and dehumanizes all of us. […] Now is not the time for sorrow, it's the time for rage.[6]

6.3 Cynics, Loyalists and Outsiders

Based on the (limited) public sources that were available for this case-study, the most dominant type of legal protest in the aftermath of the Trayvon Martin case was 'voice' (protest outside, but not against the law). A clear example of this was the extended use of social media like Facebook and Twitter. The story about Martin's shooting led to an 'outrage on social media' (Steel 2012). For example, a 'Justice for Trayvon' Facebook page, which was used to share information about the details surrounding his death, quickly became very popular. Moreover, one month after the shooting, the case was already mentioned more than 500,000 times on Twitter. All these 'tweets' and Facebook 'likes' played a crucial role in turning a local story into a high-profile case which attracted (inter)national attention. After the court case, many people also used the social media to voice their protest. Immediately after the verdict, the hashtags #NotGuilty, #Florida and #nojustice

6 http://trayvonoc.wordpress.com [accessed: 1 October 2013].

were trending on Twitter (Wall Street Journal 2013). According to an analysis by the Pew Research Center of nearly 5 million tweets about the case in the first 26 hours after the verdict, the highest proportion of statements on Twitter (39%) were straight-news updates. But the second highest proportion of tweets (31%) was described as those expressing 'anger at verdict'. In contrast, only 7% expressed 'support for the verdict' (Jurkowitz and Vogt 2013). Finally, celebrities, sports stars and musicians also used Twitter to criticize Zimmerman's acquittal and several rap-artists posted special tributes to Trayvon Martin on Facebook.

A second way in which many people used 'voice' to demonstrate their feelings about the case is by participating in the numerous rallies and protest marches across the United States. For example, right after the shooting there were walkouts by students at over a dozen Florida high schools, calling for Zimmerman's arrest (Emmanuel 2012). Since Martin was killed wearing a hoodie, hoodies were used as a sign of protest, and many cities staged 'Million Hoodie Marches' (CBS News 2012). As indicated before, right after Zimmerman's acquittal, thousands of demonstrators in cities across the US took to the streets to protest the non-guilty verdict (Nagourney 2013). A week after the verdict demonstrators gathered again in several major cities, many of them holding signs that said 'Justice for Trayvon' or 'No Justice, No Peace!' (Joseph and Somaiya 2013).

Others decided to protest by mobilizing the law ('loyalty'), using a petition addressed to the legal authorities. After the shooting, Martin's mother issued a petition on Change.org, calling for Zimmerman's arrest. For this petition, over 2.2 million signatures were collected; the website's largest petition ever.[7] The day after the verdict, the NAACP (National Association for the Advancement of Colored People) also posted a petition, now formally requesting the (federal) Justice Department to open a civil rights case against George Zimmerman. For this petition, 1.5 million signatures were collected within three days.[8]

Finally, although most protests had a peaceful character, there were also some isolated examples in which protesters deliberately acted against the law or decided to take the law into their own hands ('exit'). For example, in an act of civil disobedience, a group of some 50 students who called themselves the 'Dream Defenders' occupied Florida's State Capitol Building to hold a 'sit-in', demanding changes to Florida's self-defence laws (Alvarez 2013). Also, immediately following the verdict there were some reports of riots in several cities, which included vandalizing police cars, breaking windows and burning American flags (Kamens 2013). Taking an even more radical position, after the shooting members of the 'New Black Panther Party' were offering a $10,000 reward for the 'capture' of Zimmerman. According to their leader: 'If the government won't do the job, we'll do it' (Hernandez 2012).

These examples of legal protest give us a first clue about the normative profile of the protesters in the Trayvon Martin case. Considering that the most dominant type of social protest was 'voice' (especially the use of social media and protest marches), most protesters could probably be qualified as 'cynics'. Moreover, both petitions (which may be interpreted as two strong examples of 'loyalty') quickly gained a lot of supporters as well. This suggests that there were a considerable number of 'loyalists' involved in the Trayvon Martin protests as well. Finally, considering the small number of reported riots and other examples of illegal actions ('exit'), the involvement of 'outsiders' in the aftermath of this case was rather limited.

7 http://www.change.org/petitions/prosecute-the-killer-of-our-son-17-year-old-trayvon-martin [accessed: 1 October 2013].

8 http://www.naacp.org/news/entry/naacp-petition-to-doj-reaches-1.5-million-signatures [accessed: 1 October 2013].

6.4 Discussion

The public outcry in the aftermath of the Trayvon Martin case bears all the signs of 'legal alienation'. However, without a more detailed analysis this is just an empty formula. This short case study suggests that the events in the Trayvon Martin case generated three different types of public reactions. While many people felt no longer protected by their own legal system and experienced strong feelings of 'legal powerlessness'; others also experienced a sense of 'legal value isolation' indicating that there was a large distance between the values of the law and their own ideas of justice. Moreover, the events in this case led to strong feelings of 'legal cynicism'; some people no longer felt it necessary to act in accordance with the law.

This case study also illustrates that, although people share general feelings of 'legal alienation', they chose different ways to demonstrate these feelings. While most people participated in protest marches and posted their thoughts about the case on social media ('voice'), there were also many people who supported two legal petitions in response to the events in this case ('loyalty'). By contrast, there were only very few reported riots or other examples of legal disobedience ('exit'). This illustrates that protesters each have different 'normative profiles' and there is no such thing as a single 'standard' protester. Based on their type of protest, our case study suggests that most protesters in the aftermath of the Trayvon Martin case were probably 'cynics' and 'loyalists', with only a limited number of 'outsiders'.

In short, our case study demonstrates that the general label of 'legal alienation' covers a great variety of different attitudes, feelings and ambitions. This is also reflected in the phrase 'No Justice, No Peace!', the central theme of the protests in the aftermath of the Trayvon Martin case (Howard 2013). For some people, this phrase primarily illustrated a sense of anger and frustration; '(There is) no justice (and there is) no peace.' Or, as one commentator explained, 'to me the phrase [...] is a cry of the heart. It is not simply a call to protest, but also a naming of the powers and what those powers have done'. However, for others the same phrase (which was also used during the Rodney King riots in 1992) is a conditional statement and a call for action and riots. In other words, 'If you can't guarantee us justice, we will not let you have peace'.

6.5 Methodological and Empirical Issues

This exploratory case study also raises several important methodological and empirical issues that still need further consideration. From a methodological perspective, it should be stressed that the data for this case study were gathered using public (and mostly online) sources. It is difficult to verify these sources and it remains unclear if these findings can be generalized. Furthermore, the case study illustrates that, although one may differentiate between four dimensions of legal alienation and four normative profiles, this is not necessarily an accurate description of reality. Rather than placing people in one category or the other, in real life it is more likely that people have several (overlapping) feelings of legal alienation and one or more (overlapping) normative profiles.

From an empirical perspective, it is not clear if all people who experience feelings of legal alienation in relation to this case also experience similar feelings when they deal with other fields of the law. Is their criticism about the 'legal system' only limited to criminal law, or does it also cover civil law? Moreover, several commentators have suggested that there was a big 'racial divide' in how the American public reacted to the Trayvon Martin case (e.g. Cohen 2013; Gabbidon and Jordan 2013). Considering these reports, it may also be interesting to find out how the normative profile of the protesters is related to their socio-demographic profile. Are there, for instance, important 'legal alienation' differences between Black and White Americans; between people with high and low educational levels; between people with high and low incomes?

These methodological and empirical issues cannot be resolved within the limited scope of this chapter, but need to be addressed in future with much more elaborate studies of this important case.

7. Conclusion

Recent surveys, for example in the UK and the Netherlands, indicate that there is widespread dissatisfaction with the justice system (e.g. Hertogh 2010, 2011). What is the significance of these surveys and when does this data signal a 'crisis of legal legitimacy'? To analyze these and similar questions, Cotterrell has introduced the concept of 'legal alienation'. In theory, 'law ultimately reflects and depends on the society's shared values' (Cotterrell 1992: 82). However, based on socio-legal research about people's actual knowledge and opinion about law, Cotterrell (1992: 139) has argued that contemporary legal development is characterized by 'a progressive divorce of law from the consciousness of citizens'.

Inspired by these observations, the aim of this chapter was to explore and to develop the concept of 'legal alienation'. This was done in three steps. First, the general concept of legal alienation was broken down into different dimensions. Second, and based on people's level of legal awareness and legal identification, I introduced four different normative profiles. Finally, it was suggested that these normative profiles may be studied more closely by focusing on different types of social protest. Although some elements still need further clarification, this chapter has demonstrated that 'legal alienation' is a fruitful notion for future research on law in society. By introducing the concept of legal alienation, Cotterrell has thus made a valuable contribution to the development of socio-legal studies. Typical for Cotterrell's approach to law and society (1992: 174) is his focus on people's 'subjective conceptions of "order" and "justice" as social and legal values'. When he first wrote about this in the early 1980s, two other approaches with a similar subjective focus – 'legal consciousness studies' and 'procedural justice studies' – were still only in their infancy. However, nearly three decades later, both approaches are now two important and well-established fields of study. An important research agenda for future socio-legal studies is, therefore, to explore how the classic concept of 'legal alienation' may be integrated with the contemporary literature on 'legal consciousness' (see, e.g. Silbey 2005) and 'procedural justice' (see, e.g. Tyler 1990).

The potential dramatic effects of 'legal alienation' were illustrated by the recent events in the Trayvon Martin case. Our exploratory case study suggests that the jury's not-guilty verdict led to strong feelings of 'legal powerlessness'. Moreover, the public outcry in this case illustrated a sense of 'legal value isolation' and 'legal cynicism'. Based on their type of social protest, it was also suggested that most protesters were 'cynics' (using the social media and protest rallies) and 'loyalists' (using legal petitions), with only a limited number of 'outsiders' (who participated in riots).

In the weeks after the non-guilty verdict, the Trayvon Martin case gradually disappeared from the headlines. However, that does not mean that this case will not have a lasting effect on the American legal system. Writing in the 1980s, Cotterrell (1983: 87) already noticed that people were making 'increasing demands on the law' and that 'established legal conceptions of justice' were being 'challenged'. According to Cotterrell (1983: 87), '[t]his in itself poses no threat to legal legitimacy' but 'legal domination begins to become problematic when two conditions are met'. First, when 'the values demanded are seen by those demanding them as ultimately more important than values, considered to be embodied in the legal system …' (Cotterrell 1983: 87) And secondly, when 'the legal system cannot embrace the values demanded' (Cotterrell 1983:88). When we apply this approach to the Trayvon Martin case, there are clear signs that the first condition has already been met. The huge public outcry in this case illustrates that many people consider their own ideas of justice more important than the values of the official system. If the American legal authorities want to prevent the second condition from also being met, they will have to demonstrate that they take the public protest seriously and that they are willing to 'embrace their values' in the legal system. The most obvious way to do this is by repealing or amending the highly controversial 'Stand Your Ground' laws in Florida and elsewhere.

Bibliography

Aarts, K. and Van der Kolk, H. 2006. 'Understanding the Dutch "no": the Euro, the East, and the elite.' 39(2) *PS: Political Science and Politics*, 243–6.

Aberbach, J.D. 1969. 'Alienation and political behavior'. 63(1) *American Political Science Review*, 86–99.

Alvarez, L. 2013. 'Florida sit-in against "stand your ground".' *The New York Times* [Online, 11 August] Available at: http://www.nytimes.com/2013/08/12/us/dream-defenders-arent-walking-out-on-their-florida-protest.html?pagewanted=all&_r=0 [accessed: 1 October 2013].

Alvarez, L. and Buckley, C. 2013. 'Zimmerman is acquitted in Trayvon Martin killing'. *The New York Times* [Online, 13 July] Available at: http://www.nytimes.com/2013/07/14/us/george-zimmerman-verdict-trayvon-martin.html?pagewanted=all&_r=0 [accessed: 1 October 2013].

Anderson, E. 1999. *Code of the Street: Decency, Violence, and the Moral Life of the Inner City.* New York/London, W.W. Norton & Company.

BBC News 2013. *George Zimmerman not guilty of Trayvon Martin murder* [Online, 14 July] Available at: http://www.bbc.co.uk/news/world-us-canada-23304198 [accessed: 1 October 2013].

CBS News. 2012. *"Million Hoodie March" Held in NYC in Memory of Trayvon Martin* [Online, 22 March] Available at: http://www.cbsnews.com/8301-504083_162-57402318-504083/million-hoodie-march-held-in-nyc-in-memory-of-trayvon-martin/ [accessed: 1 October 2013].

CNN 2013. *Trayvon Martin Shooting Fast Facts* [Online, 30 August] Available at: http://edition.cnn.com/2013/06/05/us/trayvon-martin-shooting-fast-facts/index.html [accessed: 1 October 2013].

Cohen, J. 2013. 'Zimmerman verdict: 86 percent of African Americans disapprove'. *The Washington Post* [Online, 22 July] Available at: http://www.washingtonpost.com/blogs/post-politics/wp/2013/07/22/zimmerman-verdict-86-percent-of-african-americans-disapprove/ [accessed: 1 October 2013].

Cotterrell, R. 1983. 'Legality and Political Legitimacy in the Sociology of Max Weber'. In *Legality, Ideology and the State*, edited by D. Sugarman. London, Academic Press. 69–93.

Cotterrell, R. 1992. *The Sociology of Law: An Introduction*. London, Butterworths. 2nd Edition.

Cotterrell, R. 1995. 'Legality and Legitimacy: The Sociology of Max Weber'. In *Law's Community: Legal Theory in Sociological Perspective*. Oxford, Clarendon Press. 134–59.

Cotterrell, R. 1997. 'The Concept of Legal Culture'. In D. Nelken (ed.), *Comparing Legal Cultures*. Aldershot, Dartmouth. 13–31.

Dean, D.G. 1961. 'Alienation: Its Meaning and Measurement'. 26(1) *American Sociological Review*, 753–8.

Emmanuel, L.O. 2012. *List of Schools Staging Walkouts for Trayvon Martin* [Online, 23 March] Available at: http://www.nbcmiami.com/news/local/List-Of-Schools-Staging-Walkouts-For-Trayvon-Martin-143979746.html [accessed: 1 October 2013].

Friedman, L.M. 1975. *The Legal System: A Social Science Perspective*. New York, Russell Sage Foundation.

Gabbidon, S.L. and Jordan, K.L. 2013. 'Public opinion and the killing of Trayvon Martin: A test of the racial gradient thesis'. *Journal of Crime and Justice* (ahead-of-print, 1–16) [Online, 22 May] Available at: http://www.tandfonline.com/doi/abs/10.1080/0735648X.2013.798242#.UjgFiRZ_0So [accessed: 1 October 2013].

Gargarella, R. 2009. 'Tough on Punishment: Criminal Justice, Deliberation, and Legal Alienation'. In S. Besson and J.L. Martí (ed.) *Legal Republicanism: National and International Perspectives*. Oxford, Oxford University Press. 167–84.

Gargarella, R. 2011. 'Penal Coercion in Contexts of Social Injustice'. 5(1) *Criminal Law and Philosophy*, 21–38.

Genn, H. 1999. *Paths to Justice: What People Do and Think About Going to Law*. Oxford/Portland, OR, Hart Publishing.

Gibson, J.L. and Caldeira, G.A. 1996. 'The Legal Cultures of Europe'. 30(1) *Law & Society Review*, 55–85.

Hernandez, A.R. 2012. 'Trayvon Martin: New Black Panthers offer $10,000 bounty for capture of shooter George Zimmerman'. *Orlando Sentinel* [Online, 24 March] Available at: http://articles.orlandosentinel.com/2012-03-24/news/os-trayvon-martin-new-black-panthers-protest-20120324_1_sanford-vigilante-justice-black-men [accessed: 1 October 2013].

Hertogh, M. 2011. 'Loyalists, Cynics and Outsiders. Who Are the Critics of the Justice System in the UK and the Netherlands?' 7(1) *International Journal of Law in Context*, 31–46.

Hertogh, M. 2012. 'The Curious Case of Dutch Legal Culture: A Reassessment of Survey Evidence'. 5(2) *Journal of Comparative Law*, 146–68.

Hirshman, A.O. 1970. *Exit, Voice, and Loyalty: Responses to Decline in Firms, Organizations, and States*. Cambridge, MA, Harvard University Press.

Howard, C. 2013. 'No justice, no peace: What I've felt and what is next in the wake of the Trayvon Martin verdict'. *The Huffington Post* [Online, 14 July] Available at: http://www.huffingtonpost.com/charles-howard/no-justice-no-peace-what-_b_3593307.html [accessed: 1 October 2013].

Jasper, J.M. 1997. *The Art of Moral Protest. Culture, Biography, and Creativity in Social Movements*. Chicago, University of Chicago Press.

Joseph, C. and Somaiya, R. 2013. 'Demonstrations across the country commemorate Trayvon Martin'. *The New York Times* [Online, 20 July] Available at:http://www.nytimes.com/2013/07/21/us/demonstrations-across-the-country-commemorate-trayvon-martin.html?pagewanted=all&_r=0 [accessed: 1 October 2013].

Jurkowitz, M. and Vogt, N. 2013. *On Twitter: Anger greets the Zimmerman verdict* [Online, 17 July] Available at: http://www.pewresearch.org/fact-tank/2013/07/17/on-twitter-anger-greets-the-zimmerman-verdict/ [accessed: 1 October 2013].

Kaase, M. 1988. 'Political Alienation and Protest'. In M. Dogan (ed.), *Comparing Pluralist Democracies: Strains on Legitimacy*'. Boulder, Westview Press. 114–42.

Kafka, F. 2005. *The Trial* (transl. by Richard Stokes). London, Hesperus [1935].

Kamens, L. 2013. 'The system has failed': Hundreds of demonstrators voice their disappointment and anger over not guilty verdict in George Zimmerman trial'. *Daily Mail* [Online, 14 July] Available at: http://www.dailymail.co.uk/news/article-2362829/George-Zimmerman-verdict-Hundreds-voice-disappointment-Trayvon-Martin-case.html [accessed: 1 October 2013]

Kölbel, R. 2005. 'Understellte Rechtsnähe: Zur literarischen Ficktion im (Straf-) Rechtsdiskurs'. 26(2) Zeitschrift für Rechtssoziologie, 249–68.

Langman, L. and Kalekin-Fishman, D. 2006. 'Introduction'. In L. Langman and D. Kalekin-Fishman (eds), *The Evolution of Alienation: Trauma, Promise, and the Millenium*. Lanham, Maryland, Rowman & Littlefield Publishers. 1–22.

Lawson, T.L. 2013. *A Fresh Cut In An Old Wound – A Critical Analysis of the Trayvon Martin Killing: The Public Outcry, the Prosecutors' Discretion, and the Stand Your Ground Law*. Available at: http://papers.ssrn.com/sol3/papers.cfm?abstract_id=2176438.

Lee, A. 1972. 'An Obituary for "Alienation".' 20(1) *Social Problems*, 121–7.

Lee, C. 2013. 'Making Race Salient: Trayvon Martin and Implicit Bias in a Not Yet Post-Racial Society'. 91 *North Carolina Law Review*, 1555–817.

Levin, M.B. 1960. *The Alienated Voter: Politics in Boston*. New York, Holt, Rhinehart and Winston.

Ludz, P.C. 1976. 'Alienation as a Concept in the Social Sciences'. In R.F. Geyer and D.R. Schweitzer (eds), *Theories of Alienation: Critical Perspectives in Philosophy and the Social Sciences*. Leiden, MartinusNijhoff Social Sciences Division. 3–37.

Luscombe, R. 2013. 'George Zimmerman acquitted in Trayvon Martin case'. *The Guardian* [Online, 14 July] Available at: http://www.theguardian.com/world/2013/jul/14/zimmerman-acquitted-killing-trayvon-martin [accessed: 1 October 2013].

Marx, K. 1964. *Early Writings* (translated and edited by T.B. Bottomore). New York, McGraw-Hill Book Company.

Mészáros, I. 1970. *Marx's Theory of Alienation*. London, Merlin.

Muller, E. and Opp, K. 1986. 'Rational Choice and Rebellious Collective Action.' 80(2) *American Political Science Review*, 471–88.

Nagourney, A. 2013. 'Prayer, anger and protests greet verdict in Florida case'. *The New York Times* [Online, 14 July] Available at: http://www.nytimes.com/2013/07/15/us/debate-on-race-and-justice-is-renewed.html?pagewanted=all&_r=0 [accessed: 1 October 2013].

Nettler, G. 1957. 'A Measure of Alienation'. 22(6) *American Sociological Review*, 670–77.

Nielsen, L.B. 2000. 'Situating Legal Consciousness: Experiences and Attitudes of Ordinary Citizens about Law and Street Harassment'. 34(4) *Law & Society Review*, 1055–90.

Ollman, B. 1971. *Alienation: Marx's Conception of Man in Capitalist Society*. Cambridge, Cambridge University Press.

Pearlin, L.I. 1962. 'Alienation from Work: A Study of Nursing Personnel'. 27(1) *American Sociological Review*, 314–26.

Podgorecki, A. et al. 1973. *Knowledge and Opinion about Law*. London, Martin Robertson.

Rattner, A. and Yagil, D. 2004. 'Taking the Law into One's Own Hands on Ideological Grounds'. 32(1) *International Journal of the Sociology of Law*, 85–102.

Rattner, A., Yagil, D. and Pedahzur, A. 2001. 'Not Bound By the Law: Legal Disobedience in Israeli Society'. 19(2) *Behavioral Sciences and the Law*, 265–83.

Sampson, R.J. and Bartusch, D.J. 1998. 'Legal Cynicism and (Subcultural?) Tolerance of Deviance: The Neighborhood Context of Racial Differences'. 32(4) *Law & Society Review*, 777–804.

Schacht, R. 1976. 'Alienation, the 'Is-Ought' Gap and Two Sorts of Discord'. In R. Felix Geyer and D.R. Schweitzer (eds), *Theories of Alienation: Critical Perspectives in Philosophy and the Social Sciences*. Leiden, MartinusNijhoff Social Sciences Division. 133–50.

Seeman, M. 1959. 'On the Meaning of Alienation'. 24(6) *American Sociological Review*, 783–91.

Seeman, M. 1975. 'Alienation Studies'. 1 *Annual Review of Sociology*, 91–123.

Seeman, M. 1983. 'Alienation Motifs in Contemporary Theorizing: The Hidden Continuity of The Classic Themes'. 46(3) *Social Psychology Quarterly*, 171–84.

Sheehan, K. 2013. 'Marchers take over Times Square in protest of Trayvon Martin verdict'. *New York Post* [Online, July 15] Available at: http://nypost.com/2013/07/15/marchers-take-over-times-square-in-protest-of-trayvon-martin-verdict/ [accessed: 1 October 2013].

Silbey, S. 2005. 'After Legal Consciousness'. 1 *Annual Review Law and Social Science*, 323–68.

Solis, S. et al. 2013. '"Justice for Trayvon" rallies in 100 cities across USA'. *USA Today* [Online, 21 July] Available at: http://www.usatoday.com/story/news/nation/2013/07/20/justice-trayvon-martin-vigils-zimmerman/2571025/[assessed: 1 October 2013].

Srole, L. 1956. 'Social Integration and Certain Corollaries: An Exploratory Study'. 21(6) *American Sociological Review*, 709–16.

Steel, E. 2012. 'Trayvon Martin shooting death sparks outrage on social media'. *The Wall Street Journal* [Online, 22 March] Available at: http://blogs.wsj.com/digits/2012/03/22/trayvon-martin-shooting-death-sparks-outrage-on-social-media/ [accessed: 1 October 2013].

Teubner, G. 2001. 'Alienating Justice: On the Surplus Value of the Twelfth Camel'. In D. Nelken and J. Pribán (eds), *Law's New Boundaries: Consequences of Legal Autopoiesis*. Aldershot, Ashgate. 21–44.

Teubner, G. and Hutter, M. 2000. 'Homo Juridicus and Homo Oeconomicus: Communicative Fictions?' In T. Baums et al. (eds), *Corporations, Capital Markets and Business in the Law*. Den Haag: Kluwer. 569–84.

Thompson, W.E. and Horton, J.E. 1960. 'Political Alienation as a Force in Political Action'. 38(3) *Social Forces*, 190–95.

Toharia, J. 2003. 'Evaluating Systems of Justice Through Public Opinion: Why, What, Who, How, and What For?' In E. Jensen and T.C. Heller (eds), *Beyond Common Knowledge: Empirical Approaches to the Rule of Law*. Stanford, Stanford University Press, 21–62.

Tyler, T.R. 1990. *Why People Obey the Law*. New Haven, Yale University Press.

Van Reden, C.W. 1980. *Bibliography Alienation*. 3rd Edition. Amsterdam, SISWO.

Van Velthoven, B.C.J. and Ter Voert, M.J. 2003. *Geschilbeslechtingsdelta 2003: over verloop en afloop van (potentieel) juridische problemen van burgers*. Den Haag, Boom Juridischeuitgevers.

Wall Street Journal 2013. *Reactions to Zimmerman Not Guilty Verdict Flood Social Media* [Online, 13 July] Available at: http://blogs.wsj.com/speakeasy/2013/07/13/reactions-to-zimmerman-not-guilty-verdict-flood-social-media/ [accessed: 1 October 2013].

Williams, M. 2012. 'Obama: Trayvon Martin death a tragedy that must be fully investigated'. *The Guardian* [Online, 23 March] Available at: http://www.theguardian.com/world/2012/mar/23/obama-trayvon-martin-tragedy [accessed: 1 October 2013].

Wikipedia 2013. *Shooting of Trayvon Martin* [Online, 13 September] Available at:http://en.wikipedia.org/wiki/Shooting_of_Trayvon_Martin [accessed: 1 October 2013].

Zurcher Jr., L.A. et al. 1965. 'Value Orientation, Role Conflict, and Alienation From Work: A Cross-Cultural Study'. 30(4) *American Sociological Review*, 539–48.

Chapter 12
Three Concepts of Law and the Lost Art of Legislation

Willem Witteveen

1. The Enduring Problem of the Definition of Law

What is law? There are many answers to this innocent question. In teaching introductory courses to first year students, teachers have to come up with a definition of sorts. But these definitions are never the last word on the issue. Notwithstanding thousands of years of jurisprudential debates, there is still not one generally accepted definition of law. And it is not likely there ever will be, as long as these debates continue. If ever there was one person uniquely qualified to settle the issue once and for all, it was Hermann Kantorowicz (1877–1940). This German scholar of jurisprudence had spent his whole life studying the systems of law developed from ancient times and he was the founder of the *Freirechtschule*, a movement advocating judicial freedom in interpretation and adaptation of the law. In 1938 he embarked on an ambitious project. Kantorowicz would be the editor of the *Oxford History of Legal Science*, a work to be divided into three volumes. The first was to cover ancient and oriental legal science (the Greeks, the Romans, the Byzantines). The second volume would treat medieval legal science (going deeply into Roman, Canon, Jewish, Germanic, French and English law). The third volume on modern legal science would treat the development of general jurisprudence in the United States and Europe. As an introduction, Kantorowicz wrote an essay in 1939 on *The Definition of Law* but his death prevented the further publication of the encyclopedia. The essay appeared as a separate book in 1958 (Kantorowicz 1958).

In order to give a definition that could be meaningful in so many different historical and social contexts, Kantorowicz chose a bare formula. 'Law is a body of rules prescribing external conduct and considered justiciable'. This indeed is a rather elastic formula. A 'body of rules' need not be authored by the state, it can come from all kinds of effective social institutions (including churches). Sociologists and anthropologists of law can begin to identify a body of rules in each social group or other basic unit of analysis. But then the problems begin. Why limit law to guidelines for external conduct only? Does this liberal assumption not needlessly exclude the normative appeal people with legal authority are making on people's mindsets? Does it not seem to deny or belittle the normative convictions, made much of in conservative political philosophies, that turn rules into living law? And the question of how to decide whether a rule is part of the body of rules is delegated to the judges. But judges surely are not a universal category. There may be large varieties of judging, both in the art and in the institution. And how about legislatures, as the decisive agencies promulgating a body of valid rules? Are they not essential to the enterprise of law? How about the complexities of interventions devised by regulatory agencies in interaction with citizens and organizations, extending traditional notions of legislation in a sociological sense to fields of alternative regulation? Can all of that empirical and normative variety be captured in a bare definition? (For a sophisticated sociological concept of law, see Cotterrell 1995: 23–40.) The bare definition turns out to raise a number of further questions. It is no wonder the debate in legal theory on the definition of law continued. In 1961, Herbert Hart would publish his own view under the title *The Concept of Law* and this book spurned a host of other attempts to ascertain the crucial elements that have to be present in social manifestations of the elusive phenomenon we call law.

Before we now conclude that law, like democracy, is an essentially contested concept (Gallie 1956) and that there is at most a family resemblance between various conceptions of law – this is an answer that will not satisfy the aspiring student – it makes sense to investigate the hypothesis that for a very long time in Western culture there have been three elementary conceptual models in circulation. In antagonistic relation to each other they have structured our manifold understandings of law. We can see these models at work in Sophocles' *Antigone*.

2. Three Elementary Concepts of Law

Antigone buries her brother Polynices, who has been killed in his attempt to recover the city of Thebes from the reign of King Creon, a usurper to the throne. For Antigone, burying her brother is a sacred religious duty. She provocatively transgresses Creon's order that Polynices is to be left outside the city walls to rot. Confronting Creon, she declares her understanding of law:

> That order did not come from God. Justice,
> That dwells with the gods below, knows no such law.
> I did not think your edicts strong enough
> To overrule the unwritten unalterable laws
> Of God and heaven, you being only a man.
> They are not of yesterday or to-day, but everlasting,
> Though where they came from, none of us can tell.
> (Sophocles 1974: 138)

In these famous verses, many interpreters have discerned a conception of natural law. The laws that are unwritten and unalterable, 'written in the hearts of men', as Cicero would remark, override all humanly enacted laws. But Creon is not convinced. The law is a King's command. It has to be obeyed because it brings order to the city. The integrity of the state is at issue. To the chorus of citizens, he explains:

> When I see any danger threatening my people,
> Whatever it may be, I shall declare it.
> No man who is his country's enemy
> Shall call himself my friend. Of this I am sure –
> Our country is our life; only when she
> Rides safely, have we any friends at all.
> Such is my policy for our common weal.
> In pursuance of this, I have made my proclamation …
> (Sophocles 1974: 131)

The chorus affirms this view, saying: 'Your will is law'. Creon later repeats his claims as follows:

> To transgress
> Or twist the law to one's own pleasure, presume

To order where one should obey, is sinful,
And I will have none of it.
He whom the State appoints must be obeyed
To the smallest matter, be it right – or wrong.
And he that rules his household, without a doubt,
Will make the wisest king, or, for that matter,
The staunchest subject. He will be the man
You can depend on in the storm of war,
The faithfullest comrade in the day of battle.
There is no more deadly peril than disobedience;
States are devoured by it, homes laid in ruins,
Armies defeated, victory turned to rout.
(Sophocles 1974: 144)

The commands of the sovereign, deciding what the interest of the city requires: that is an early (and unsophisticated) notion of legal positivism, as many commentators have pointed out. The king serves the state and then the citizens ('subjects') must obey the king in an almost Hobbesian notion of survival in a condition of permanent warfare. Antigone's arguments (by Creon called 'woman's law') are totally irrelevant in this respect. Between Antigone and Creon there can henceforth only be a dialogue of the deaf. Now a third understanding of law is brought to bear upon the central issue of the play. Haemon – Creon's son and the betrothed of Antigone – appeals to his father for clemency. Haemon urges his father to listen to the reasonable voice of the citizens of Thebes who sympathize with Antigone and think she committed an honourable action that must be accepted.

Surely, to think your own the only wisdom,
And yours the only word, the only will,
Betrays a shallow spirit, an empty heart.
It is no weakness for the wisest man
To learn when he is wrong, know when to yield. (…)
I think, for what my young opinion's worth
That, good as it is to have infallible wisdom,
Since this is rarely found, the next best thing
Is to be willing to listen to wise advice.
(Sophocles 1974: 145)

Public opinion, the normative convictions of the citizens, must have a voice in the articulation of law and justice. Wisdom and common sense are not confined to those with authority. This interactionist notion, in its simple form, is another approach to the meaning of law, stressing the ongoing deliberations between state officials, elevated to positions of power, and the citizens. Surely, what citizens expect as lawful must be part of their understanding of law, regardless of official pronouncements or even of theories of justice.

Thus three elementary concepts of law are seen to conflict tragically in the course of the play: natural law, positivism and interactionism (which we can also call cultural law). It is possible, of course, that these concepts supplement each other in a much more harmonious form of interrelation. Maybe the legislator in a positivist vein has managed to capture a universal norm that also accords with cultural expectations in his jurisdiction. But the conflict model is much more interesting and illuminating. In situations where the concepts of law are perceived to clash, it becomes possible to alternate between them in a perspectivist mode and thereby to discover relevant arguments regarding the issue. In this way, the three concepts of law may even contribute to the ancient rhetorical art of *invention*, of finding relevant arguments in a controversy.

Interestingly, they will each mobilize different sources of law and do this in their own distinctive ways. Positivism has a clear preference for legislation and international treaties, placing judge made law in second position and denouncing unwritten law which finds favour with both natural law thinkers (as long as it expresses an aspiration toward the just or the good) and interactionists (who see in it a source of legitimate cultural norms). Natural law discourse is fond of referring to the principles of law as dictates of reason transcending positive law, whereas the interactionist authors need empirical sources such as surveys or interviews as evidence of what is or is not a legitimate cultural norm. Neither natural law nor interactionism reject the standard legal sources the positivists recognize but rather deny their exclusivity and both add other sources as relevant to the discourse of law. And Natural law approaches do not have a monopoly on justice as a theme, but positivists seek its importance outside of the domain of law (in a separate sphere of morals or politics) and interactionists depend on a concept of justice in the sense of having norms for fair interaction that may lead to mutual legal understandings. Between the three normative positions an endless dialogue can be heard.

Let us suppose a lawmaking official to be in the position of having to find relevant considerations in defence of a proposed statute drawing a lot of criticism. Let us further assume that the criticisms are directed at the quality of the Bill as a legal act. Often, of course, when the direct impetus for criticism relates to the content of the proposal, the debate will tend towards this secondary question of the legal qualities of the proposal, as this is a theme that supposedly is important for the proponents of the Bill as well as for its critics, and maybe a kind of compromise can be achieved. The lawmaker defending her proposal may now make use of all three models of law, switching between them to find the right mix of arguments. From the standpoint of a positivist lawmaker, the arguments express relations of legitimate authority within the constitutional system of the polity, establishing what role the government and representatives of the people play in the legislative process and claiming that the outcome of the procedure will be binding for all citizens, including critics. Subsequently it can be argued, from the vantage point of natural law, that the proposal is a step towards a just arrangement, not fully there perhaps, but justice and other high norms are aspirational in kind and full justice cannot be reached in one attempt. This argues for respect and patience on the part of the critics; in the long run the legislation may become better still, after this first more tentative articulation. It then helps to be able to turn to the interactionist view that law should be in conformity with cultural expectations, if the lawmaker can show that the proposal does just that, even if the critics do not yet see this. Switching between the three concepts of law, the lawmaker can find a number of arguments providing her with a strategy that may be rhetorically effective, perhaps even overriding a number of content-related criticisms.

3. The Lost Art of Legislation

So we seem to have three elementary concepts of law here which in all their simplicity may yet already serve to provide a lawmaker with a threefold argumentation strategy that can be used to defend a legislative proposal in a public debate. Of course the three concepts can be elaborated into more complex models of law, as has been done for positivism by Austin, Kelsen and Hart; for natural law by a long line of thinkers from Aquinas to Dworkin; and for interactionism by the likes of Montesquieu, Durkheim, Fuller and Llewellyn. But the simple models have two advantages:

they are already a basis for argumentation; and they can be used in many different contexts and situations, across borders of language, religion and culture. Also, these models and the deliberations they engender suggest that it must be possible to develop lawmaking into something like an art of legislation, that is, into a form of reflective knowledge about the practice of making rules for a polity of citizens. Then why has this not happened? The question forces itself upon us. And the surprising answer is that it has indeed happened, but that we have mostly forgotten that an art of legislation has been part and parcel of the legal and political traditions of the Western world.

The story of the lost art of legislation begins in ancient Greece, where Plato devotes his book *Laws (Nomoi)* to a conversation between three men contemplating the foundation of a colony, about the kind of laws that would be right for its future inhabitants. Aristotle reacts with an overview of constitutions, correlating with the organizational principles of different polities. Both philosophers envision the legislator as a wise person possessing a specialized kind of knowledge which has priority over the political knowledge needed in an ongoing public order. In the era of the Roman republic there is then an influential treatise by Cicero, modelled in part on Plato's dialogue, containing fragments of a discourse on the laws. In later times the system of Roman law emerges, with the concomitant invention of an art of codification of legal materials supposedly relevant for many different peoples under the influence of the Roman Empire. This Roman law line of thinking about legislation develops further, but focuses mostly on private law and it is still clearly present in the great codifications of private law of the twentieth century. Meanwhile political theory also brings forth thinkers who devise an art of legislation. Francis Bacon in the common law world of the English renaissance, Montesquieu as monarchical and republican thinker at the start of the Enlightenment, Diderot debating with Catherine the Great the right kinds of laws for the Russian state are some of the most famous examples. The utilitarian philosophy of Jeremy Bentham is presented as 'an introduction to the principles of morals and of legislation'.

In the second half of the nineteenth century a break in the tradition occurs. The science of economics emancipates itself from the art of legislation which was still very much on the mind of Adam Smith. An instrumental approach to law comes forward with the rise of the liberal and later the democratic welfare state. Under an instrumentalist view of legislation laws are mere instruments for political decisions taken prior to and independent from their formulation; the art of making laws becomes a technical activity reserved for legally trained civil servants. Only Lon Fuller draws attention to the lost art of legislation with his ideas about the internal morality of law in his famous story about a king named Rex, failing in eight ways to make law. These imaginary royal failures point at constructive criteria that are important for achieving legislative quality. But then Fuller's interactionist argument was overshadowed by his polemic with Hart which led away from this theme as it centred on the issue of demarcating positivism from natural law (Witteveen 1998; Rundle 2012).

The real story of the lost art of legislation is a lot more complex than this and it cannot be explained here more fully. Let it serve as a background consideration to the work of three authors who did write important treatise about the art of legislation. Each author stands for the sophistication which can be reached in developing a theory of law from one of the three elementary concepts already foundationally present in the drama of Antigone. Plato connects his vision of a just social order to natural law, Montesquieu invents an interactionist framework and Bentham is a forerunner of the legal positivist schools active today. It sounds strange to group them together. Plato, Montesquieu and Bentham are usually studied apart from each other and by different scholarly communities. But this is itself an indication of how the art of legislation has disappeared from view. Apart from the development of legal instrumentalism, already mentioned, a role in this neglect is also played by the prominence of the ethical school in political theory. Rawlsians tend to take up an ideal standpoint outside of the practices and institutions of lawmaking, forgetting that 'the original position is not at all a good model for political deliberation or action' (Geuss 2008: 72). Political ethics post Rawls tends to favour principles over rules and to emphasize the differences between them. Political theory then becomes a theoretical science of principled deliberation rather than a practical art of reflective legislation.

4. Plato's Nomoi

When we say that natural law is all about making a comparison between some idealized state of the polity, in which justice reigns and principles of decent living are upheld, with the ordinary world of mortals which can aspire towards the just city but never realize it entirely, then Plato's political vision espoused mainly in the *Republic* and the *Laws* certainly counts as a model of natural law thinking. At the back of his mind we always find his criticism of the disordered state of democracy in Athens, a democracy that in an unjust political trial killed his hero Socrates. He opposes a vision of a well-ordered hierarchical polity to what he perceives as anarchist tendencies. The possibility of an art of government, which is mostly an art of developing the right kind of laws, is mentioned in passing in his dialogue *Gorgias*. In this dialogue, set against the background of war, Socrates debates with three representatives of the art of rhetoric that is so important for the democratic city. Against young man Polos, Socrates distinguishes good from bad arts. The word used here is *technè,* a term which carries a number of meanings, from technique to profession to art. In his scheme, lawmaking and judging are the good and useful arts, to be distinguished from the bad and dangerous arts of rhetoric and sophistic reasoning.

Do the *Laws* then articulate this true and useful art of legislation? This seems indeed to be the intention of Plato. He situates the dialogue in a meeting of three pilgrims on the road from Knossos to the temple of Zeus. They start discussing the laws of their cities and question what regime is needed to produce the most suitable ones. At that moment Cleinias tells Megillus and the Athenian that he is actually sent on the road by the Cretan citizens to explore the right conditions for founding a new colony and to draw up a legal code, using foreign laws as well when they are useful. He invites the others to discuss the laws of their cities and laws in general. 'Let's construct an imaginary community, pretending that we are its original founders. That will allow us to consider the question before us, and it may be that I'll use this framework for the future state' (Plato/Saunders 1982: 702E). Constructing a city in speech, by reviewing its laws, that is the project. The Athenian in what follows turns out to be the person who does all the talking, he is truly a lawgiver. The dialogue turns into a disguised monologue, very far removed from the dialectical method of Socrates. (And note that unidirectional speech acts will be a troublesome feature of legislative work ever since.)

The art of legislation requires first of all worthy legislators. You can recognize them as being sincere, professional and dedicated to the ideal of a life lived according to stable laws. In a reference that can be taken to be an intimation of the ideal of the rule of law that would be developed much later, the Athenian remarks that a city flourishes 'if law is the master of the government and the government is its slave' (Plato/Saunders 1982: 715D). Plato seems to prefer to place trust in one wise person to be the legislator, but there may also be small legislative councils of the wise. Legislation cannot be entrusted to the mass of the citizens. Good laws always need to have a clear purpose. 'A law is well enacted only if it constantly aims, like an archer, at that unique target [namely virtuous living, WW] which is the only object of legislation to be invariably and uninterruptedly attended by some good result' (Plato/Saunders 1982: 706A). Stability is of the essence for good laws, so that people can understand them, practice them and be educated in them. The Athenian suggests that there may be an experimental period of 10 years during which a law is tried out and its social effects are observed, after which it is made definite and cannot be changed any more (a minority of one magistrate is sufficient as a veto). Education is the main purpose of the laws. This is why the legal text will be preceded by a preamble in ordinary language and this will be a mythical story explaining to the citizen his or her place in life. (Note that the Athenian here advocates the use of deceptive rhetoric, something which had been rejected in the Gorgias. Plato/ Saunders 1982: 723A.)

The general principles of the art of legislation are thus clear. What follows is a bewildering variety of very detailed rules about the most varied subjects that according to the Athenian are all ingredients of the good life for people belonging to various classes. The clarity of purpose seems to get lost in the details. Indeed, we find in this fascinating text something that is highly representative for legal discourse even today: that regulation as a process in institutionalized form tends to acquire its own dynamic, starting out perhaps from limited objectives but unfolding towards a bureaucratic maze of rules and procedures in which the clear sense of purpose, let alone the educational strategy, is lost. This familiar dynamic apparently starts working as soon as a great mind, such as Plato, starts constructing his imaginary community. And that is still what lesser minds as legislators do. On closer scrutiny it appears that the laws according to Plato must fulfill four functions at once. They must have a constitutional function, establishing the polity. They must be effective instruments of governance. They must teach and educate people. And on top of all this, Plato makes clear in his most natural law-like pronouncements that the whole system of laws must mirror the order in the cosmos. Of course it is not easy to connect principled arguments about the right constitution of the polity in classes of people (with the philosophers on top) with exhaustive rules for all aspects of daily life, including for instance rules for the right time of the grape harvest. Many readers have found the *Laws* already unsatisfactory on this count alone. They prefer the stylistic unity of the *Republic*, manifesting the same political vision but avoiding legal excess.

And yet, the confusing mixture of subjects and registers is also challenging. It creates a complexity that makes the *Laws* into what Umberto Eco has called an open work, inviting the reader to develop her own interpretation. The interpretive community of Plato scholars shows that widely different readings are still possible after all these years. Bernardete, for instance, in a very thoughtful commentary, discovers new meaning in the text by taking the secondary meaning of the term 'nomos' as melody in music seriously (Benardete 2000). For the theme of the art of legislation, the interpretation of Pradeau is especially illuminating. He refers to another Platonic dialogue, the *Statesman.* Politics is here compared to the art of weaving. The philosophic ruler masters this art as a way of bringing together the interests of people into a seamless web. Accordingly, the law is not so much an expression of will, not a command but a description of an ideal state of affairs that the governor brings about.

> Plato does not conceive of the law as an order, a proclamation of a governmental decision or an expression of sovereignty. For him, the function of the law is not expressive but supplementary and mimetic: the law should only be paramount in the city if its knowledgeable governor is not up to his task. In such a case – and only in such a case – the law must take over the leadership, rejecting all compromises and making no exceptions. (Pradeau 1997: 95)

The law is thus a substitute for wise leadership, as laws are less dependent on changes of will, shaping order from heterogeneous elements. 'The power of the law is second-best, but it is a second-best that is adequate given the nature of the city' (Pradeau 1997: 97). Laws that reflect the cosmic order will, then, have to be exhaustive; no detail is insignificant, everything having its rightful place. This is why the laws must both be constitutive and instrumental. 'To use Plato's own terms and wordplay more precisely, the law (*nomos*) is the instrument of the intellect (*nous*)'. Turning then to the *Laws*, Pradeau notes a difference. While laws are in the *Statesman* a substitute for the wise decisions of the governor, here the laws constitute the state and have to control the governors themselves. This is expressed in the institution of the Nocturnal Council, a kind of planning board overseeing the development of the polity and intervening when this is not going according to plan. Plato entrusts the science of mathematics to come up with the right kind of proportions for various human activities, prefiguring the economic and utilitarian views of public order. The proportions in the earthly city must match those of the cosmos, the imaginary heavenly city. Because it is never possible fully and definitely to reflect the cosmic order – as a conception of natural law must recognize – governing the city involves a permanent process of transformation, in which the Nocturnal Council plays a central role. 'Through its nocturnal council, the city now becomes the author of its own transformation' (Pradeau 1997: 163).

5. Montesquieu and the Spirit of the Laws

In comparison with Antigone's fierce invocation of natural law and Creon's brutal claim to be the sole positivist ruler, the interactionist appeal of Haemon seems to be but vaguely articulated. There is nothing vague about interactionism, however. In the world re-imagined in Sophocles' tragedies, it was commonplace that even the most autocratic rulers needed to consult the citizens of their city-states. Recent research into the origins of democracy makes clear that not only were there older forms of democracy than that developed in Athens, democratic assemblies were already also a prominent feature of the oriental world in Babylonian times. Keane summarizes this research, saying that throughout the region there were a variety of invented traditions of democratic behaviour, favouring equality, respect for the laws and self-government through assemblies (Keane 2009: 98, 113). Any ruler, claiming to be the commander of the people, would have to come to grips with democratic cultural expectations presuming him to be faithfully consulting the assembly of citizens and listening to their deliberations. Haemon was referring to a social fact of life that Creon vehemently tried to suppress.

The art of legislation has to be adapted to the regime within which it is being practiced. This interactionist insight we owe in a much more theoretically sophisticated sense to Montesquieu. Scholars in constitutional law have usually read his great book *The Spirit of the Laws* of 1748 in a highly selective fashion. They have focused on key passages in Chapter 6 of Book 11, where Montesquieu discusses the English constitution, and where they claim to find the origin of his notion of the separation of powers, with its implication that judges are only to apply the law rather than to develop it interpretively. It is a colossal mistake to overlook all the rest of the work, which consists of 33 books and a total of 624 chapters. It is aptly titled the *spirit* of the laws, because this is indeed its central theme. It is not a handbook of constitutional law, but a treatise on the art of legislation, considering the many variable contexts of its use. A look at the Table of Contents already reveals as much.

The first part of the work (8 Books) is about laws in general, laws in relation to various kinds of governments, the principles of governments, the relationships between laws on education and the principles of each type of government, culminating in the thesis that all legislation needs to be in accordance with these principles. Then the consequences of this approach are discussed for civil and criminal laws, for laws about luxury, and laws about the condition of women, concluding on the ways the principles of governments may be corrupted. The second part (5 Books) deals with the laws in relation to defensive and offensive force, the protection of political liberty in the constitution and for the citizens, with a demonstration of this approach to tax law. The third part (6 Books) concerns a number of variables influencing the laws: climate, the effects of climate on different forms of slavery, the condition of the terrain and finally the relation with the principles forming the general spirit, the mores, and the manners of a nation. The fourth part (4 Books) discusses the relationships of the laws with commerce, the use of money, the number of inhabitants and religious practices. The fifth part (2 Books) considers the laws in their relation to religious law and to the order of things upon which they are to enact. The sixth part (5 Books) treats a remainder of subjects: the origin and revolution of Roman laws on inheritance, the history and the revolution of civil laws in France, maxims on the composition of the laws (and thus an art of legislation in a juridical technical sense), the theory of the Feudal laws among the Franks in relation with the establishment of the monarchy.

These clearly are the contents of an art of legislation with a family resemblance at least to Plato's *Nomoi*. But the supposition that *The Spirit of the Laws* is about an art of legislation can already be confirmed in a wonderful passage in Book 1, Chapter 3, stating the programme at the basis of the whole work:

> Law in general is human reason insofar as it governs all the peoples of the earth; and the political and civil laws of all nations should be only the particular cases to which human reason is applied. Laws should be so appropriate to the people for whom they are made that it is very unlikely that the laws of one nation can suit another. Laws must relate to the nature and the principle of the government that is established or that one wants to establish, whether those laws form it as do political laws, or maintain it, as do civil laws. They should be related to the physical aspect of the country; to the climate, be it freezing, torrid, or temperate; to the properties of the terrain, its location and extent; to the way of life of the peoples, be they plowmen, hunters or herdsmen; they should relate to the degree of liberty that the constitution can sustain, to the religion of the inhabitants, their inclinations, their wealth, their number, their commerce, their mores and their manners; finally, the laws are related to one another, to their origin, to the purpose of the legislator, and to the order of things on which they are established. They must be considered from all these points of view. (Montesquieu/Cohler et al. 1989: 8–9)

Montesquieu designs a typology of political regimes, constitutions and schemes of legislation. In three of them liberty is possible: the republican democracy of Athens and Rome, the representative democracy existing in England and the monarchical system of France. Opposite these regimes there is one regime in which liberty is impossible: despotism (Turkey, Japan, China). In the free regimes the legislative power is in different hands: the people govern themselves in the republic, they are led by their representatives in parliamentary systems (Montesquieu calls them aristocracies), while under a monarchy the laws are made by the King and the nobles. In each free constitutional order there is another basic principle at work, acting as a driving force and actualizing the virtues of the regime. The laws have to be in accordance with this driving force, the spirit of the laws. Virtue is the driving force of democracy, finding expression in the political equality of its citizens. In this system the laws must be simple, equal for all and frugal. Moderation is the spirit of the aristocratic regime; the laws must make sure that the economic and social differences between people – which are of the essence to freedom here – do not become too large. In a monarchy with its many classes of nobles and citizens honor is the basic drive; everybody strives after distinction in relation to others. This requires a lot of often complicated legislation in order to let each class and group live in peace and induce them to respect each other. In comparison with the despotic regimes, the three free regimes have much in common. For under despotic rule fear is the basic motivation of everybody and therefore there cannot be fixed laws that are the basis of order, freedom and security. It is fascinating to see how Montesquieu in his many chapters, using large amounts of historical materials, shows the consequences of this scheme of the order of things and makes clear that a prudent legislator at all times must analyze the social conditions in which rules are made and then has to take care to respect all the factors together forming the spirit of the laws. With Montesquieu the tradition of sociological research – interactionist orientations surely are a key theme here – comes off the ground. (A century later, Durkheim will write his thesis on Montesquieu, in Latin!)

6. Bentham's Code

Positivism in law is not only about assertions of power on behalf of the ruler. Creon is too unsophisticated in his provocative stance as an absolute ruler to be much appreciated by the modern positivists. They are indebted to analytical philosophy in their effort to make clear distinctions between concepts, rules and principles. In their desire to separate the spheres (law is not morals, neither is it politics nor economics) they are also in favour of limited rather than absolute power claims. It is a political project to proclaim a pure law (as Kelsen did), uncontaminated by politics or economics. Jeremy Bentham is one of the founding fathers of legal positivism. But while he is a forerunner of analytical reasoning, he is convinced that there is an overall principle (utility) that is relevant in all spheres of life and in his provocative style of debunking the adherents of natural law, he sounds as bold as Creon.

Bentham's *An Introduction to the Principles of Morals and of Legislation* (1789) begins with a clarion call:

> Nature has placed mankind under the tutelage of two sovereign masters, pain and pleasure. It is for them alone to point out what we ought to do, as well as to determine what we shall do. On the one hand the standard of right and wrong, on the other the chain of causes and effects are fastened to their throne. They govern us in all we do, in all we say, in all we think: every effort we can make to throw off our subjection, will serve but to demonstrate and to confirm it. In words a man may pretend to abjure their empire: but in reality he will remain subject to it all the while. (Bentham 1982: 11)

The author so eagerly attracting the attention of his readers adds right away that he will replace the metaphorical language of this passage by a language of scientific precision, but the choice of images is revealing; this is to be a book about the major forces determining a person's life and these will have to be used in order to make it meaningful. Moreover, the principle of utility works at all levels of society.

> By the principle of utility is meant that principle which approves or disapproves of every action, according to the tendency it appears to have to augment or diminish the happiness of the party whose interest is in question. (…) A measure of government (which is but a particular kind of action, performed by a particular person or persons) may be said to be conformable to or dictated by the principle of utility, when the tendency which it has to augment the happiness of the community is greater than any which it has to diminish it. (Bentham 1982: 12)

In order to make the calculus of pain and happiness as it affects human life, Bentham is convinced a science of legislation must be developed in support of it. This must be a logic of the will. It is for the science of law to produce it.

> Of this logic of the will, the science of law, considered in respect of its form, is the most considerable branch, the most important application. It is to the art of legislation, what the science of anatomy is to the art of medicine. (…) Yet more: a body of proposed law, how complete soever, would be comparatively useless and uninstructive, unless explained and justified, and that in every title, by a continued accompaniment, a perpetual commentary of reasons … There must be therefore, not one system only, but two parallel and connected systems, running on together, the one of legislative provisions, the other of political reasons, each affording to the other correction and support. (Bentham 1982: 8–9)

In this interesting passage we see that Bentham is thinking of an art of legislation which is reflective in nature, where its *nomoi* are not only laws but also rational considerations about laws. Even Plato's scheme of useful and dangerous forms of social knowledge is not absent when we notice that Bentham – who tends to eschew metaphorical language – makes a comparison between the knowledge of human anatomy and the knowledge of human motivations that are amenable to legislative intervention. There are two parallel systems needed, one practical and one reflective, to turn the art or science of legislation into a socially binding normative framework. In his late work on the *Constitutional Code*, Bentham will attempt a synthesis of these two projects, but he was always busy creating the building blocks for this great system. In the *Introduction* there are already elements, such as a doctrine of the four kinds of sanctions that can induce people in the direction of the greatest happiness for the greatest number. In *Place and Time*, Bentham develops a theory about comparative law and addresses the question whether legislation has to be stable over time or requires continuous adaptation. All of these and many more passages are pieces of the great puzzle. Tragically, Bentham will not succeed to put them all together. The *Constitutional Code* remains unfinished. The grand project named *Pannomion* is doomed to remain hauntingly incomplete. But all these writings are an early announcement of something that will indeed come to pass: the notion of the endlessly perfectible society.

We can see from his late *Pannomial Fragments* how Bentham builds his system on the foundation of the greatest-happiness principle. Prefiguring analytical philosophy, he defines his categories in precise, complicating language: what are the axioms, principles and laws in relation to each other and to the utilitarian calculus of motives? Axioms are the foundation, rules articulate the greatest-happiness calculus and principles are by him meant to be short phrases in abridgement of the rules (as what the essential oil is to the plant from which it is distilled, Bentham adds metaphorically). Then how about rights? Bentham takes these to be the obverse of obligations; both are expressions of the utilitarian calculus. He vehemently opposes natural law and the emerging language of human rights. All this talk about human rights, popularized by the French Revolution, adds no meaning to a legal claim and it is a dangerous illusion to believe in them; indeed, human rights are dangerous fictions. And fictions offer no protection against very real tyrannical encroachments of freedom, he argues.

> It may, however, be said, to deny the existence of these rights which you call imaginary, is to give a carte blanche to the most outrageous tyranny. The rights of man anterior to all government, and superior as to their authority to every act of government, these are the rampart, and the only rampart, against the tyrannical enterprises of government. Not at all – the shadow of a rampart is

> not a rampart; – a fiction proves nothing – from that which is false you can only go on to what is false. When the governed have no right, the government has no more. The rights of the governed and the rights of the government spring up together; – the same cause which creates the one creates the other. (Bentham 2011: 256)

Bentham believes that the antidote to tyrannical legislation is to be found in the correct interpretation and systematic application of the political and legal project of bringing about the greatest happiness for the greatest number of persons. When the legislator mistakenly enacts despotic rules, the citizens will resist this attack on their happiness. The citizens themselves profit from striving after all those arrangements that conform to utility. Checks and balances can be created – in another kind of utilitarian calculus of what is conducive to happiness – between the organs of government as an effective form of protection. In all these powerful bodies people will recognize the dictates of utility. It is therefore important to safeguard freedom of speech and make sure that all decision-making occurs in public, under the scrutiny of what Bentham calls the tribunal of public opinion.

With these safeguards in place, Bentham envisages an enduring project of perfecting social arrangements. There are no subjects that cannot in some ingenious way be related to the utilitarian calculus of happiness and pain. This also means there are no other limits to interference with the lives of the citizens. When positivists later deny the idea that there is one encompassing principle regulating all spheres of life, this means that utilitarian legislation can become a mere technical exercise in the hands of those in power. Unlimited instrumentalism is the endpoint of this trajectory.

7. Three Strands in Legislative Thinking

It was seen that the three elementary concepts of law can still readily be mobilized for the purposes of the rhetorical art of invention, as they generate possible lines of argumentation on issues involving legislation. Presumably this is so because they are culturally embedded in the practices and institutions of Western law. The much more refined 'arts' of legislation, developed by Plato, Montesquieu and Bentham, on the other hand, are not often called upon in legislative debates and research. As a general subject of study the art of legislation is a lost art. The canonical texts are read and studied mostly by specialists in the history of political thought who do not consider their relevance for lawmaking today. Yet these classic studies of legislation have deeply influenced current ideas about law. We can detect their influence as three strands in legislative thinking noticeable under the surface of the web of politico-legal discourse.

Take for instance the ongoing debates over the meaning of the rule of law. These debates are structurally characterized by a sense of unease about a governance practice or a political act that seems to be counter to the ideal, followed by an elaboration of the meaning of the ideal as applied to the case at hand. The Platonic heritage of the *Laws* stresses the ideal of public service: officials should consider themselves to be the servants of the laws, working for the public good. Here, the personal qualities of those in power are at issue. Even if they are not members of some tiny philosophical elite, as in Plato's ideal city, they are urged to behave on the basis of whatever practical wisdom they can acquire. The rule of law is then both a government of measures and of men. Montesquieu's concern with the separation of powers and checks and balances is more obviously related to discussions of the organizational framework that effectuates the rule of law and protects the liberties of the citizens. But in this strand of legislative thinking, stressing the priority of laws over execution, the vital issue would be how to keep the integrity of the regime (if it is a free one) intact and how to adapt the constitutional framework to that end. This is a question that is not often debated outside of the university because the regime's integrity of spirit, in the sense Montesquieu interprets it, is not at all clear any more to its inhabitants. What is it that a representational form of democracy requires of the representatives? Many of them simply do not know. Bentham rejects common law making by judges and prefers a codified system of laws; this position is controversial in the Anglo-American world where judges are seen as not only the protectors of civil liberties but also as the motivating force upholding the ideal of the rule of law. But in civil law countries the Benthamite conception of codification is familiar (indeed, Bentham learned much from the French *Code Civile*) and here the critical impulse is in asking whether there is a coherent system present in the codification and whether that system is communicated effectively to the citizens. If not, how can they be expected to calculate their motives in the right way?

There is more to learn from a dialogue with past masters of the art. Plato's highly detailed instrumentalism regarding figs and grapes, which sometimes makes him seem as modern as the European Union, is in fact grounded in a vision of the good life that is deeply principled. Can it be that the only acceptable way of going into detailed instrumentalist regulation schemes is when there is an overall vision of the good life behind it? A lot of bureaucratic lawmaking would fail to survive this test and it would also demand much more effort and inventiveness to articulate visions of the good life relating to our kind of world. When Montesquieu's spirit of the laws is translated into a list of questions that have to be answered before a law may be passed, we would here have a very concrete contribution to legislative practices. In part, this list is available as Fuller's 8 canons of lawmaking, but Montesquieu would go beyond his internal morality of law. From Bentham's *Pannomion* project we can draw both negative and positive lessons. A negative lesson is surely the self-defeating tendency of wanting to create an exhaustive system of well-defined concepts on the basis of one overarching standard of the good; in lawmaking, closed systems are not to be preferred over open ones in which various perspectives compete. But there is a positive lesson as well, because Bentham's demand that all regulation must be based on a calculation of benefits and disadvantages can be a critical yardstick from the point of view of those subjected to regulation: is this really balanced legislation, not only generally, but also at the individual level?

These examples indicate that it may not be necessary and not even desirable to limit the debate over the art of legislation to authors representing one of the three strands. All are relevant, as long as they are used to raise questions in the spirit of rhetorical invention; and it is not unrealistic to expect to find answers for today's problems in ancient texts. We must however, as a matter of methodology, place the texts as much as possible in their historical context while at the same time we must respect the novelty of our own situation. For when any text becomes just another form of ideology, closed off from external criticism, the noble art of legislation cannot engage us in constitutional dialogue.

Bibliography

Bentham, J. 1982. *An Introduction to the Principles of Morals and of Legislation.* London, Methuen. Edited by J.H. Burns and H.L.A. Hart.

Bentham, J. 2012. *Selected Writings*. New Haven, Yale University Press. Edited and with an Introduction by S.G. Engelmann.

Bernardete, S. 2000. *Plato's Laws: the Discovery of Being.* Chicago, University of Chicago Press.

Cotterrell, R. 1995. *Law's Community. Legal Theory in Sociological Perspective.* Oxford, Clarendon Press.

Gallie, W.B. 1956. 'Essentially Contested Concepts'. 56 *Proceedings of the Aristotelian Society*, 167–98.
Geuss, R. 2008. *Philosophy and Real Politics.* Princeton, Princeton University Press.
Kantorowicz, H. 1958. *The Definition of Law.* Oxford, Clarendon Press. Edited by A.H. Campbell and with an Introduction by A.L. Goodhart.
Keane, J. 2009. *The Life and Death of Democracy*. London, Simon and Schuster.
Montesquieu. 1989. *The Spirit of the Laws.* Cambridge: Cambridge University Press. Edited by A. Cohler, B. Miller and H. Stone.
Plato. 1982. *The Laws*. Harmondsworth, Penguin Books. Edited by T.J. Saunders.
Pradeau, J-F. 2005. *Plato and the City. A New Introduction to Plato's Political Thought*. Exeter, University of Exeter Press.
Rundle, K. 2012. *Forms Liberate. Reclaiming the Jurisprudence of Lon Fuller.* Oxford, Hart Publishing.
Sophocles. 1974. *The Theban Plays*. London: Penguin Books. Translated by R.F. Watling.
Witteveen, W.J. 1999. 'Laws of Lawmaking'. In W.J. Witteveen and W. van der Burg (eds), *Rediscovering Fuller. Essays on Implicit Law and Institutional Design*. Amsterdam, Amsterdam University Press, 312–45.

Chapter 13

The Sociology of *The Politics of Jurisprudence*

Richard Nobles and David Schiff

In much of his work, Roger Cotterrell has questioned and lamented the tendency of legal philosophy and sociology of law to remain closed to each other, and of each to be insufficiently adapted to the study of legal practice (e.g. Cotterrell 1975, 1983, 1993, 2002, 2014a). Legal philosophy, with its concerns with what is essential to law, has a tendency to develop concepts that generalize at a level of abstraction which robs it of any obvious relevance to the day to day practices of lawyers, or the information rich empirical studies of the sociology of law (Cotterrell 1989: 2–3). Sociology of law can be criticized in turn for insufficient attention to concepts of law, with a resulting tendency to generate information organized through partial concepts appropriate to the researched sub-field of legal study,[1] which do not build any consensus on the general nature of law as social formation. And there is also a tendency for sociology of law to seek to distance itself from the discourse of lawyers and to focus not on what is said in law by its participants but on the behaviour of those involved in law, and on the causes and effects of particular laws. If, as he has claimed (agreeing here with many leading legal philosophers) law involves the institutionalized generation of doctrine (1983: 243, 251–2), then the study of this doctrine, and the role that it plays within law, should not be excluded from sociological study. He has argued that there needs to be a closer synthesis of the approaches of legal philosophy and the sociology of law, directed to the study of legal practice. This combined approach should generate knowledge of legal practice which is not accessible via each separate discipline and, on a normative note, could improve the work of jurists, those persons who not only study legal systems, but who take some responsibility for their continued existence and enhanced performance (Cotterrell, 2013a, or 2013b). His sense of what might constitute enhancement is associated with ideas of community. The hoped for outcome of this improved understanding is that law will provide a form of regulation that is fit for various kinds of communities (instrumental, affective, traditional and value based) and be better able to reconcile the conflicts between these communities.[2]

In this chapter we focus on one of Roger's best known contributions to jurisprudence: *The Politics of Jurisprudence: A Critical Introduction to Legal Philosophy* (Cotterrell 1989, 2003, hereafter '*PoJ*'). In doing this, we are allowing ourselves, as two of his colleagues at Queen Mary, to continue a discussion which has been ongoing in many forms since we first joined him as colleagues in 2006. Since 2000, we have been exploring the potential of systems theory to increase our understanding of jurisprudence (see especially 2006). Thus we have shared Roger's belief that a sociological approach to jurisprudence could be a profitable addition to a field dominated by

1 Roger observes that sociological concepts of law exhibit more variety and less sophistication than those generated within normative legal theory. He attributes this in part to the fact that, within the latter, these concepts are an end in themselves, whilst within sociological approaches the conceptualization of law is simply a preliminary stage in the organization of empirical study (Cotterrell 1983).

2 'Normative legal theory must recognise social diversity by explaining law in terms of the regulatory requirements of different communities' (Cotterrell 2003: 257).

philosophical approaches. But Roger has expressed considerable reservation as to whether systems theory offers an appropriate way forward, questioning the focus of the theory on law's growth as an abstract system, to the neglect of the 'particular forces and interests that give rise to law's development, inspire its interpretations and guarantee its authority' (Cotterrell 2003: 250).[3] The contrasting approach, offered within *PoJ*, is that 'normative legal theory's abstractions should be seen, in part, as a response to professional and political needs of people (especially lawyers) with specific interests and concerns' (2003: 250).

If *PoJ* were claimed to be a synthesis of philosophical approaches and sociological theory, we could present a straightforward comparison between systems theory and whatever sociological approach Roger has adopted and adapted. But the aims of *PoJ* are more limited. The book offers a critical introduction for undergraduate law students to the theories commonly encountered within a course on jurisprudence.[4] As such, it contains some excellent exposition and discussion of a kind that would be quite at home in a more traditional legal philosophy text. In undertaking this task, *PoJ* expressly eschews dealing with sociologically informed empirical legal theory, in favour of a discussion of the contribution made by legal philosophy (Cotterrell 2003: 3). All of this suggests that it would not be fair or appropriate to use this book to stimulate a debate on how sociological methods and theories might inform our understanding of the issues typically discussed within legal philosophy. But neither is our aim here to criticize *PoJ* for its limitations, namely what it does not attempt to do. Rather, it is to use the material and approaches contained in *PoJ* to consider what a systems theory approach to the issues tackled by legal philosophy offers. We wish to build on those aspects of *PoJ* which offer the beginnings of a synthesis between legal philosophy and the sociology of law. Within *PoJ*, the overall aim or 'organising framework' is that the 'patchwork of philosophical views of the nature of law contained in modern Anglo-American jurisprudence can be understood as a response to social and political change: but a response shaped substantially by perceived problems arising in the professionalisation of legal practice' (Cotterrell 2003: viii). Using some of the material and discussion contained in *PoJ* we wish to utilize systems theory to explore the nature of such links. First we will consider how these links are presented within *PoJ*, concentrating on Roger's first substantive chapter, his exploration of the common law tradition.[5]

1. A Sociology of the Common Law Tradition

This first substantive chapter and approach to understanding the general nature of law discussed in *PoJ* is about the common law tradition; it is in many ways the most sociological chapter in the book and the one that is most closely connected to legal practice. On the other hand, it is also the chapter which is least connected to legal philosophy, or indeed any theory, for the practice of the common law did not deal in theories as such, but in claims. The common law was claimed to be the expression of different things – community, custom, reason, morality, justice and God's will (see Lobban 1991: 59). It was claimed by its practitioners to be unwritten, even when the decisions through which it was formed were recorded in law reports. These claims have some logical interconnection so, for example, the claim that the source of law lies in community, custom,

3 See also Cotterrell 2001.

4 See Cotterrell 1989, Preface.

5 This chapter is called 'The theory of common law', which may be slightly misleading since it explores the failure of common lawyers to develop a theory which could adequately explain the common law. Indeed, Postema (2002) believes that common lawyers never articulated a full-fledged philosophical theory of law, only a 'distinctive approach to understanding the nature of law and legal reasoning' (at 599).

morality or God's will supports the claim that the law is unwritten, as there is no text which both embodies these sources and expresses the content of the common law. The decisions of particular judges are described not as law in themselves, but as attempts to identify the law, which lies in these sources. The manner in which these various claims operate has echoes of classical natural law, since unjust laws (incorrect identifications of justice) are not, therefore, really law – in the sense that they can be discarded in favour of the real or higher law to be found through these sources. At the same time, the decisions of judges can also be described as the best evidence of that law, for these various sources have been cited to, and considered by, those judges on the occasions when they have been asked to provide a new remedy for what is claimed to be a pre-existing wrong.

Whilst these various elements of common law reasoning have a logical connection, it is hard to call them a 'theory', at least by comparison with something like Aquinas' *Summa Theologica* (see the 1959 edition of his writings), which presents a systematic exposition of the sources of law, the relationships between them and the implications of those relationships for everyday legal problems. In place of theory, particularly when it took the form of philosophical speculation, common lawyers tended to stress the practical nature of common law reasoning, terming it 'artificial reason', and claiming that the sense of what it required in any particular dispute could only be acquired through being an experienced legal practitioner.[6]

The discourse of common lawyers prior to the reforms of the nineteenth century poses a challenge to any claim that legal practice needs to be closely connected to legal philosophy. Indeed, one can go further, and point to the resistance of this discourse to the criticisms of legal philosophers, or even empirical evidence. Thomas Hobbes challenged the common lawyers' claim that the common law represented a form of reasoning that could only be known through long practical experience, counter-claiming that the reason within law could be gained by a student within a few months (1681/1971: 56). And when Bentham (1843: 7, 13, 48–9, 63) insisted that the common law was the law of 'Judge & Co.', he was not asserting anything which required systematic empirical enquiry, he was simply pointing out that the only factual bases for the common law were the decisions of judges, whatever claims those judges might make as to their sources of inspiration.[7] How does one account for this state of affairs? Just as one may ask what legal philosophy contributes to legal practice, one may also ask what this a-theoretical collection of claims achieved.

One answer of course is that these claims served the interests of the legal profession. Any claim that legal discourse is something different from other forms of discourse, which requires particular knowledge, gained through experience, supports claims for professionalism. Such claims, if accepted, also legitimate the power that professionals exercise, and the fees that they can charge. And in this the common law tradition, as a non-theory, is not so very different from many of the theories which followed. Legal positivism, with its attempts to present law as a science (Austin 1832/1955; Kelsen 1967), or modern natural law with its various attempts to present law as a restriction on the arbitrariness of power (Fuller 1964; Dworkin 1986) can both be understood as theoretical contributions to the legitimacy claims of the legal profession. But whilst this may say something about the implications of these particular legal philosophies, or even allow us to speculate about the political aims of the respective authors,[8] what does this tell us about the relationship between legal philosophy as an enterprise and legal practice? For whilst

6 The classic statement of this is that of Coke 1628: 97b, discussed by Postema 2002: 593–5.

7 For Bentham, the sources of judicial decisions, or at least judicial desire not to reform the laws and procedures which had resulted from them, were explicable in terms of professional self-interest: to put money into the pockets of the judges, or the lawyers, or the other members of the firm 'Judge & Co'.

8 Inviting a consideration of psychological factors, as one finds in the many books of essays representing a 'progressive critique' of law, such as Kairys 1998.

some philosophical approaches paint the legal profession in a positive light, others decidedly do not. The 'Jurisprudence of Difference', Derrida inspired deconstruction and the sceptical branch of the 'Realist' movement, all challenge the claims of today's legal profession. And in doing this, they are not so very different from Hobbes and Bentham, with their criticisms of the discourse of the common lawyers. Even legal positivism, which can be understood as a theory which supports modern legal practice, has its origins in writings which offered no such supportive role to then existing legal practice.

In *PoJ* the reader is invited to consider a two-way relationship between legal practice and legal philosophy. Firstly, legal philosophy alters as legal practices change. This could be expected to occur in any branch of applied philosophy, for example, one would expect the philosophy of science to be stimulated by changes in scientific practices.[9] If there is any controversy in this claim, it arises from arguments over the parameters of what is legal practice. Practices claimed to be legal by some theories are excluded by others. However, since most modern legal philosophies accept that their theories must be applicable to nation state legal systems and their accompanying practices,[10] *PoJ* is on fairly firm ground in claiming that changes in legal philosophy occur in response to changes which occur to the nature of state legal systems, and it is these kinds of legal systems that are the object of most of the philosophies covered by the book. So, for example, it is plausible to suggest that Hart's stress on power conferring rules (Hart 1961) reflects the changing experience of state law in modern society, with more individuals experiencing more changes to their legal statuses on a regular basis than before, and state power being delegated to more officials through ever more, and ever more complex, legal rules.[11] So it makes some (sociological) sense to claim that when Hart stresses the importance of power conferring rules, he is not really pointing to a feature of law overlooked by prior theories, but to something that has a radically greater importance within modern legal practice than it did in earlier periods.[12]

The second part of the philosophy/practice relationship is more problematic. In *PoJ* the claim that there is an important relationship between normative legal theory and legal practice is broken down into three questions.[13] What practical relevance in professional and political arenas of law does normative legal theory have? How does this relate to particular historical conditions? What assumptions about the nature of societies underlie these theories? One has to take care here that one does not reverse the phrasing of these questions, and return to the previous relationship. The relevance of legal practice to legal theory is demonstrable over and over again, as it provides any

9 A view which adherents of naturalism would extend to philosophy generally: 'Naturalism in philosophy is always *first a methodological* view to the effect that philosophical theorizing should be continuous with empirical inquiry in the sciences' (Leiter 2007: 34).

10 Raz 2009: 105, for example, opines that a theory that did not include clear cases of state law within what it recognized as law would not be an adequate theory.

11 As Maine (1861) famously put it, there has been a change in the basis of modern law from one organized around status, to one organized through contracts, an observation that captures the increased importance of power conferring rules within private ordering, but neglects their equally growing role as a means to distribute state power.

12 Cotterrell (2003: 94) argues that this change in legal practice had already been recognised by Austin and that Hart's desire to identify a role for power conferring rules separately from their relationship to duty imposing ones was motivated by a '*political* concern' to stress law's facilitative functions. The problem for Hart, as an analytical philosopher, was that the change in legal practice which he sought to identify did not readily equate to an analytical distinction, as power conferring rules are always intertwined with duty imposing ones.

13 Cotterrell 2003: 12–13. The particular aspect of normative legal theory which is to be analysed in its relationship to legal practice is legal philosophy's concern with unity and system in law.

such theory with its object. One can subject such theories to a sociologically informed critical analysis, which includes a consideration of the historical conditions which produce both the legal practice that is being theorized, and the resultant legal theories. And one can also examine which assumptions about the nature of societies might inform legal practices, or the particular legal theories which such practices generate. And *PoJ* does all of this, at various points. But whilst all of this would make sociology relevant to legal theory, it does not address the three questions set out above, which focus on the relevance of normative legal theory to legal practice.

If these questions are treated as causal in nature, they are both difficult and easy to answer. It is relatively easy to point to the possibility that a particular theory portrays the legal profession in an attractive light, and then claim this makes that theory relevant in some meaningful way to legal practice. But it is much harder to point to any legal theory and show that, but for the existence of that theory, legal practice would not have developed in a particular way. *PoJ* itself contains a particularly stark example of this difference. Maine's historical school is discussed as an attempt to provide a theoretical basis on which to understand the evolution of law, and therefore something which could compensate for the absence of such a theory within the discourse of common lawyers. His works were widely read by lawyers, and are said to have had 'immense influence' (Cotterrell 2003: 45). But there is no specific evidence that they had any influence on legal practice. The most obvious route for their influence was their inclusion within professional legal education at the end of the nineteenth century, but their lack of relevance to legal practice is perhaps caught by the comments contained in a an early nutshell-type guide to Maine's *Ancient Law,* used by students who had to study this work in order to pass the professional examinations: 'In these books there is a great deal of writing that is absolutely useless to the student for examination purposes, and page after page has to be waded through in search for a criticism or theory …' (Quoted by Cotterrell 2003: 47).

PoJ provides some evidence of legal theory influencing legal practice. One particular example (2003: 194) is Llewellyn's work on the draft commercial code. This code was clearly influenced by Realist views that doctrinal statements could be over general, and thus provide a poor guide (on both a normative and predictive level) to the resolution of disputes. Llewellyn aimed to identify principles that were more specific and appropriate within a narrower range of contexts than had been developed via the common law. And whilst important aspects of his work on the code were not enacted, some of it was. But such specific examples also point to the contingencies of the influence of theory on practice, and the difficulties of claiming that 'but for' a particular legal theory, a particular legal practice would not have occurred.

The relationship between legal theory and legal practice may be open to more sociological analysis if one moves from causal questions to functional ones. What function does legal theory play within legal practice? And in asking this question, can one do more than re-assert the claims that theory which portrays legal practice or the legal profession in an attractive light provides legitimacy? One way to approach this kind of question is to consider the work done by theoretical constructs within day to day legal practice. How, if at all, does the legal system make use of legal theory in its day to day operations?

It is here that we would wish to introduce systems theory, as developed by Niklas Luhmann.[14] For Roger, systems theory is 'not sociological enough' (2003: 250) focusing as it does on law as a system of communication, which he feels ignores the professional, political, organizational and ideological conditions that have made possible law's presentation as an autonomous system. There is no room here to debate this general accusation, except to say that systems theory does, we feel, no such thing. Systems of communication operate at various levels. Society as a whole is

14 Particularly his last monograph devoted solely to law: Luhmann 2004.

a social system (Luhmann 1985) as are its functional sub-systems (see Luhmann 1982: 229–54), such as law or the economy. But so too are interactions (e.g. conversations) and organizations (Luhmann 2005). Thus there is no reason to believe that understanding society in terms of systems excludes professional bodies or other kinds of organizations. What of political or ideological questions and conditions? Tracing how systems exist and change requires one to focus on the operations that their communications execute, and the manner in which those operations change as the system's communications change. But this does not mean that the environment is ignored. For example, if one wished to consider the relationship between the legal and political system, one would track how each evolved in response to the other. To speak meaningfully of a 'relationship' between law and politics requires us to have a sense of their respective self-limitations: what, in each of them, allows them to have stable and on-going (as opposed to fleeting and contingent) reactions to each other.

One can use systems theory to analyze the role played by theory within legal practice. One can ask, along the lines of the first of the questions from *PoJ* set out above, what work such communications might do. What operations do they enable or facilitate that would otherwise have to occur in different ways through different communications? *PoJ* provides the beginnings of this kind of enquiry in the chapter on the common law. This chapter includes a quotation from Coke CJ, taken from *Calvin's Case* (1608):[15]

> … we are but of yesterday … our days upon the earth are but as a shadow in respect of the old ancient days and times past, wherein the laws have been by the wisdom of the most excellent men, in many successions of ages, by long and continual experience … refined, which no one man (being of so short a time) albeit he had in his head the wisdom of all the men in the world … could ever have effected or attained unto. And therefore … no man ought to take upon him to be wiser than the laws. (Cotterrell 2003: 24)

Roger does not criticize this statement as a mystification or ideological presentation of the common law, instead acknowledging it as an honest and direct statement of a set of assumptions that underpin the classical conception of common law judging: law is not made by judges but pre-exists their decisions and is simply declared by them; it is unwritten, and lies in customs and the community at large; it is identified by judges via their powers of reason and experience, or wisdom. He notes that these assumptions amount to a paradox: the law is changed via the endless process of reaching judicial decisions, but at every point in this process the law is claimed to pre-exist and lie outside of the judicial decisions themselves. Even as the law is changed, it is asserted to be unchanging. Roger (2003: 28) presents this paradox as something that was less apparent earlier in the history of the common law, when the decisions of judges were not reported. It also had more empirical truth when the assizes first began in the twelfth century, when judges went out into communities and took evidence of local custom, only combining it into a 'common law' thought through their discussions amongst themselves on their return to Westminster.[16] But according to *PoJ* (2003: 29), the common law tradition 'backed itself into a corner' as empirical conditions offered less and less support to the assumptions of common law judging. And to the extent that judge-made law remains a feature of the legal system, this leaves judges without adequate authority for the decisions which they still have to reach. The remedy which he offers, towards the end of *PoJ*, is for the gap left by the common law approach to

15 7 Co Rep 1, 3.

16 See Baker 2002: Chapter 2 'Origins of the Common Law', Simpson 1986.

adjudication to be filled by a more sociologically informed legal theory, which can assist jurists to find legal solutions that are appropriate to, and thus representative of, the communities that generate legal disputes (2003: 254–66). This offered solution is not only relevant to the role of judges within the unitary and unified communities presupposed to exist within nation states. It would require the law to engage with the multiple communities that exist both within national state boundaries, and across them.[17] In making this suggestion, Roger is, in common with many of the legal theories which he discusses, reacting to the perceived inadequacies of lawyers' own accounts of their own practices.

What could systems theory add to the above analysis? In systems theory the kinds of general statement contained in the quote set out above by Coke, made in the course of a court judgment (rather than in a pamphlet, lecture or diaries) is a legal communication, and of a particular kind. It is an attempt, within the legal system, to describe the totality of the legal system. Where such communications occur within a social subsystem such as law, Luhmann calls them 'self-descriptions'.[18] There is more here than a change of terminology. The theory identifies a relationship between such self-descriptions and other communications within the same system. Within the legal system, communications apply the code legal/illegal to various states of affairs. As part of this process, the legal system generates communications which observe on the application of that code, identifying what it was about state of affairs X that made it legal, in contrast to state of affairs Y, which was coded illegal. These observations, within a system, upon that system's own applications of its code, are second order observations.[19] Such second order observations stabilize, but do not determine, future applications of the code. In the case of law, such observations are more commonly called doctrine – the constant attempt to present law as a non-arbitrary application of the legal code by generating reasons which distinguish what is legal from what is illegal. Doctrine reduces the possibilities of what can be recognized as a meaningful legal communication. In this sense, it stabilizes, but does not determine, what will be found to be illegal, or legal. The communications that constitute a system's secondary observations can be at a high or low level of generality. But those at the highest level, which attempt to describe the system as a unity, to itself, form self-descriptions. And just as law's second order observation stabilizes, but does not determine, what can be coded legal/illegal, self-descriptions have a similar role – stabilizing, but not determining. One might describe these second order observations as facilitating the making of further communications within a system, but this facilitation cannot be separated from their ability to limit what can be communicated. It is only by limiting the possible selection of what might connect next to any communication, which makes complex and technical forms of communication possible.[20]

17 In making these suggestions in the 2nd edition of *PoJ*, Roger is drawing on his own earlier writings on law and communities, most notably Cotterrell 1995, and predisposing himself towards his later writings on 'transnational law' (e.g. Cotterrell 2008, 2009).

18 Luhmann 2004: chapter 11 'The Self-description of the Legal System', and more generally, Luhmann 2013: 167–349.

19 'While first order observation refers to *what* an observer observes, second order observation refers to *how* an observer observes' (Borch 2011: 57). Second order observation can be internal (self-observation) when the communications of a system observe on the system's own application of its own distinctions, or external (hetero-observation) when a system uses its communications to observe upon the communications of another system.

20 '... structure, whatever else it may be, consists in how permissible relations are constrained within the system .... Only by excluding almost all conceivable linkages can there be something like: "Would you

This conceptual scheme focuses our attention, as Roger rightly observes in *PoJ*, on the internal operations of a system, and the possibilities that exist, at any moment, for further communication, including evolution of the system, which alter the possibilities of what can be communicated. He is critical of this: 'the system is portrayed as having a life of its own in some sense. The social context that gives it that apparent life remains only very faintly sketched. The particular forces and interests that give rise to law's development, inspire its interpretation and guarantee its authority remain vague in autopoiesis theory' (250).

Let us examine this criticism, in the context of *PoJ*'s discussion of the common law. What role is played, within law, by self-descriptions in the form set out above by Coke. Our observation is that they facilitate legal judgments within a legal system that faces changing social conditions, where the political system generates (relative to modern conditions) relatively small amounts of legislation. In this, as Roger notes in *PoJ,* the common law attribution of law to the customs of the community duplicated what on the continent was achieved by natural law (2003: 116). Within natural law, any local jurisdiction is, at best, an expression of a higher law. A local law that is unjust is not really a law and, as such, a judge who finds such a law to be unjust, is not legislating, or even changing the law, but simply identifying the law, and correcting an earlier misunderstanding of what the law truly is. In the case of the common law, by describing the law as a standard of right and wrong that lies within the community, common lawyers left law open to change in response to changing conditions. If a dispute revealed a new injustice, the common law would seek to provide a remedy. The sense of injustice which governed this process was not a utopian assessment of the whole social order, for that would open the law to forms of argument that would remove its ability to resolve disputes or support powerful interests. Instead common lawyers looked out on the world using the lenses of the common law (Cotterrell 2003: 32). When identifying a new wrong that needed a new remedy, they would compare the claimed new wrong with whatever wrongs had previously been recognized by the common law. This is not simply a situation of filling in gaps. Wrongs which had not been recognized in past decisions could return to court in a situation where the urgency of the need for remedy had increased, or the distinction between this claim and recognized claims had decreased. In this situation, as the common law communicated to itself that the decisions of judges were simply the best evidence of law, and not the law itself, a judge who accepted a previously rejected claim as a wrong that needed a remedy was not making law, but only correcting an earlier mistaken identification of the law.

This functional analysis of the common law's self-description invites the question, why did this disappear from legal discourse. What changed? The answer given in *PoJ*, with which we would agree, is that the law changed; in particular, due to changes outside of the legal system, particularly in the political system. Parliament began to issue huge amounts of technical and specific legislation, especially in response to the demands of the new middle classes. This was experienced in the courts, and amongst the legal profession, as changes in the forms of legal argument. Prior to this expansion in the amount and nature of legislation, statutes were treated, like judges decisions, as remedies for wrongs, and evidence of the wrongs that they remedied.[21] They were regarded as inferior evidence to court decisions, but with a higher authority in the sense that they had, at least in the immediate aftermath of their passage, to be followed.[22] With the change in the nature

give me a refill?" "You've forgotten to clean the back seat of the car!" or "Tomorrow at three at the movie theater ticket office!"' (Luhmann 1995: 283)

21 The idea that Parliament provided remedies for existing wrongs, led to the recognition of those wrongs, like the decisions of judges, being communicated as declaration of standards that already existed within the community (Stoner 1992: 37–8).

22 An authority from which there was no appeal: McIlwain 1910.

of legislation, the self-observations which generated the common law self-description altered. So much of the law (the application of the code legal/illegal) was law for one reason alone – it was the intention of Parliament. This acceptance of authority was already present alongside the common law tradition, but with the change in the amount and nature of statute, authority, rather than the identification of community values, became the dominant basis for legal decisions. It became implausible to continue to claim that statutes are a remedy for an existing wrong lying within the community, when the overwhelming mass of legislation was seeking to change society. It also became difficult to use the existing law as a framework from which to identify principles or maxims, and in turn use these to identify particular examples of injustice, when so much of the law became detailed, specific, and self-evidently partisan. And when the dominant basis for legal argumentation took the form of an acknowledgement of the need to identify and give effect to the intention of Parliament, the self-description changed. What we would now call positivist self-descriptions replaced the common law tradition in England, whilst on the continent they replaced various forms of natural law self-descriptions.

This history, most of which is found in the *PoJ's* discussion of the common law tradition, would seem to suggest that law does, in very important ways, have a 'life of its own'. The self-description of the common law as the customs of the community, like the functionally equivalent natural law self-descriptions found on the continent, were a feature of law for hundreds of years. As such these self-descriptions cannot be attributed in any direct way to the incalculable number of events that occurred within law's environment during this period. But this does not mean that law was un-influenced by its environment. Rather, the self-description of law formed a significant aspect of law's reaction to, and evolution within, the rest of society. At a time when legislation was, by today's standards, relatively infrequent, the dominant way in which the rest of society sought to influence law's communications was by bringing claims to courts. Law responded to these claims by evolving its doctrines, and in the process, both generated and utilized its self-description as an expression of community values.

2. A Sociological Theory of Jurisprudence

In this section we wish to discuss what systems theory might offer to a discussion of legal theory more generally. The second edition of *PoJ* contains its own introduction to systems theory, which acknowledges that systems theory, with its acceptance that systems contain paradoxes, would echo post-modern theories' focus on the circularity and arbitrariness of the postulates which inform much legal philosophy.[23] Roger claims that 'theorists of autopoeisis' simply answer: 'True, but so what? This is how law is, and works, it does its job' (249). This statement, like the claim that the 'particular forces and interests that give rise to law's development, inspire its interpretation and guarantee its authority remain vague in autopoiesis theory' (250) had more truth at the time that the second edition of *PoJ* was published, than they do today.[24] As a theory of society, systems theory is necessarily abstract. But, like other sociological theories, the issue is not whether the general theory contains lots of information about social phenomena, but whether, in its application, it can

23 Luhmann insisted that his own theoretical writings sought to explain the modern. He did not acknowledge a separate stage of social development which was 'post-modern' (see specifically Luhmann 2000) but only the inadequacy of pre-modern concepts to explain modern conditions (see generally Luhmann 1998).

24 Because, at least as far as English speakers are concerned, some of Luhmann's major works had not been published as translations.

generate concrete observations. Thus, for example, the concept of structural coupling,[25] or co-evolution,[26] which is Luhmann's answer to how closed systems interact with each other in stable and predictable ways, seems no more than a suggestive metaphor. But in our work on reporting of miscarriages of justice we have been able to use this concept to analyze and describe important aspects of the relationship between law and the mass media.[27] And in terms of organizing data, the recent work by Chris Thornhill, *A Sociology of Constitutions*, is a tour de force in its utilization of historical sources, and systems theory, to present the evolution of states and constitutions as a consequence of the increased power which became available to power holders through its expression in, and consequent restrictions by, law. These works,[28] like the above consideration of how the changing nature of statute triggered a change in the legal system's self-description, are not ignoring the forces that give rise to law's development and authority. On the contrary, they are using systems theory to organize complex data and increase our understanding of these forces. And what of the role played by paradox within systems theory?[29] Far from simply accepting that paradox occurs, systems theory directs us towards observation of how and when paradox occurs within systems, and what functions it plays.

Let us begin with the paradox which Roger identifies within the common law: that judges claim to identify a law which exists prior to the decision which establishes it as law. Systems theory has something more to offer here than simple acceptance of this. For a start, what it offers is a clearer idea of where the paradox is situated. This paradox lies within the legal system, in the communications used in adjudication. It does not lie in the beliefs or communications of judges as individuals. Judges are free to acknowledge, to themselves, that their decisions are acts of legislation, structured by their own political beliefs and commitments. They may even, when acting in non-judicial capacities, such as public lectures, admit to making law on this basis. But in their courts judges receive arguments that state what the law is, not what it ought to become, and their judgments follow the same form – they articulate what the law is.[30] In keeping with this

25 Structural coupling occurs when a system 'presupposes certain features of its environment on an ongoing basis and relies on them structurally .... the forms of structural coupling *reduce* and so *facilitate* influences of the [system's] environment on the system'. Luhmann 2004: 382, and generally with regard to the legal system's structural coupling with other systems, see ch. 10. With regard to how this applies to society in general, its operational closure and structural coupling with its environment, see Luhmann 2012: 49–68.

26 On co-evolution with law, see Teubner 1993: ch. 4 'Blind Legal Evolution'.

27 See Nobles and Schiff 2000, 2004. For a succinct statement of the nature of structural coupling between law and the mass media, see Nobles and Schiff 2013b. On the structural coupling between law and politics, and the general nature of structural coupling, see Nobles and Schiff 2013a, chs 6 and 7.

28 For a further selection, see Febbrajo and Harste 2013. There are numerous examples of the application of systems theory on the Continent, and especially in German academic literature where its presence is ever growing and its significance increasing.

29 As an example of the crucial role of paradox within systems theory, see Luhmann 2013: 293–305, and within law(s) more generally, Perez and Teubner 2006.

30 See Nobles and Schiff 2009 and 2013a: 147–63. The paradox is not removed on the rare and exceptional occasions when judges admit, even within the judgments that constitute their decisions, that their decisions represent new law. There are at least two reasons for this. Firstly, because the paradox remains present, but suppressed, on every occasion when no such admission is made and a decision is reached that is not simply an expression of the existing law. As such, no modern legal theorist except Dworkin (and he only during the period when he claimed that the communications of judges alluded to an omnipresent 'right answer') has denied that the paradox occurs within legal adjudication. The only issue that remains between legal theorists is how often this is the case, and on what basis, if any, it can sometimes not apply (i.e. when it is correct for judges to claim that their judgments merely apply existing law rather than create new law). The

form of communication, decisions that mark a break with previous articulations of the law are still applied retrospectively, as if the decision reached in the case had always been the law. And this paradox has, if anything hardened, with the change to more positivistic self-descriptions. When it comes to statutory interpretation, any change of interpretation, no matter how radical, is routinely taken to have always been the law from the moment that the statute was brought into force. This is not because judges cannot see that changing the interpretation of a statute amounts to a change in the standards that will be applied in future, and therefore a change in the law. It is that the very communication that is routinely used to claim authority for the interpretation of law (giving effect to the intention of Parliament) provides no basis for putting temporal limitations on the operation of that interpretation.

The claim that this paradox lies within the legal system as a system of communication, and not in the minds of judges, or within the communications of other systems (such as legal philosophy as a sub-system of education) is related to another distinction that systems theory helps us to draw: the difference between what is external and what is internal to the legal system. We agree with Roger, that it is 'necessary to discard any simple distinction between legal insiders and outsiders, or participants in and observers of law' (2003: 258). Systems theory operates on the basis that there is not simply an inside and an outside to a system of communication. Firstly, a system creates itself through its own communications. But it does this through communications that refer both to itself, *and* its environment.[31] So, for example, when a legal system deals with claims, or evidence, it is recognizing a society that exists outside of itself. It does this with communications that identify the procedures for recognizing claims and evidence as itself – the law, and identifying the events that are being urged and proved as lying outside of the law. So the first sense in which there is an outside and an inside is the boundary that a system constantly creates, for itself, by generating self and hetero-references using its own communications. The second sense in which one can have an inside or outside is when one observes the communications of a system (both the self and the hetero-references) and acknowledges that this is not the manner in which that system and its environment would be described through the communications of another system. To give an example of these two kinds of inside/outside distinctions, consider how the legal system routinely utilizes science as evidence. When this occurs, the legal system does not regard science as part of law just because it has relevance to law. Within the legal system, within discussion of evidence, it will be the norms that establish relevance that are treated as law, whilst the science is external to law. This is the first kind of inside/outside. By contrast to this, a scientist observing on the manner in which the legal system uses science, might well claim that what the law treats as science is not really science at all. This is the second sense of being outside of the legal system.

It is this second version of being inside or outside a system that comes closest to the debate, within much legal philosophy, on whether the existence of law depends on some insider, or participant's perspective. This is usually addressed in terms of the insider's understanding of, and commitment to, the law, with debate on whether the object of this insider attitude is rules, norms, principles, etc. As such, it is typically focused on the legal system's self-reference, tending to ignore hetero-reference. In his call for a more sociologically informed jurisprudence, Roger is alert

second reason, is that even on the rare occasions where judges admit in their judgments to be making law, this is still not presented in terms of a political decision or utilitarianism or efficiency, but on the basis that the decisions reached would be an extension of the present law, or a just solution in light of the context provided by accepted law.

31 '... the system always reproduces a double reference: the distinction between self-reference and other-reference' (Luhmann 2012: 53).

to this hetero-reference: the manner in which law forms its own version of society.[32] This is clearest in his discussion of the common law, where he acknowledges that common lawyers looked out at society 'through the lenses of the common law' (2003: 32) i.e. they formed a view of society in the course of legal operations. As with the paradox of adjudication, systems theory indicates that the internal attitude, or participant's perspective, is not something located in the psyche of individuals, but in the system itself.

The idea of a perspective being located within a system, rather than it being an attribute of the human beings whose voices or bodily movements are interpreted as the utterances by that system, is difficult to grasp. But an example may make clearer what this involves.[33] The communications which are used in law to reach decisions and execute operations typically take a normative form. This normative form will have an implicit meaning that the person who is identified as speaker or writer has a normative commitment towards law. This does not mean that the person in question has any such commitment, in the sense of some psychic identification with law as an appropriate configuration of 'oughts'. It is just that legal operations (claims, legal arguments, legal judgments, etc.) cannot be executed without using communications whose implicit meaning includes this commitment. (This is the experience which makes the political radical on trial refuse to recognize the court or participate in the proceedings. Attempts to affect communications within the legal system constitute an implicit affirmation of commitment to the normativity of the system of which the communication forms a part).[34] Law can be described in a non-committed fashion when one is not seeking to execute legal operations, even by lawyers. And there are some legal operations, such as the giving of advice to clients, which can be presented though communications that are only predictive or instrumental (the so-called 'bad man' approach to law). But this kind of communication will not execute a valid judgment, or make an effective legal argument.

If the perspective of an insider is understood to be the meaning of the communications that construct the legal system – communications whose meanings which identify the relevant human beings as speakers and attribute normative commitments to them – then we can see that the insider perspective is not limited to lawyers. It is a feature of legal communications involving lay people too. Any person who is understood to make a legal claim – 'don't park there, it's a double yellow line' is an insider in the sense that the communications that they are understood to have made contain an implicit endorsement by them of the normativity of the legal system.[35] On the same basis, a judge whose diaries proclaim that they made legal judgments on the grounds of their strongly held personal views, or even bribes, is not an insider. These communications do not execute legal operations (though they may later trigger appeals by being recognized by the legal system as evidence of impropriety). Instead of looking at who is communicating – which

32 In the preface to the first edition of *PoJ*, Roger declares an intention to bring 'to light assumptions contained within [legal philosophy] about the social, political and professional environment of law' (1989: viii, 2003: vi); and in the first chapter entitled 'Legal Philosophy in Context' he argues that 'because "the legal" can never be totally separated from such matters which normative legal theory often treats as external to law, the theory itself often implies interesting ideas about the very social context which it apparently seeks to exclude from its concerns … these ideas … often reveal basic presuppositions on which normative legal theory is based' (2003: 18). Though in our view, the focus here should be on the assumptions which law has about its environment, rather than the assumptions which philosophy makes when seeking to describe law.

33 This example is developed more fully in Nobles and Schiff 2009.

34 While the law remains deaf to communications which challenge or fail to recognize its right to determine what it identifies as the legal issues. See Chistodoulidis 1998: 175–6 discussing the Baader-Meinhof proceedings.

35 See Nobles and Schiff (2013a: 34–46).

kind of human being is involved – we move to focus on the communications themselves – what communications are in play here? This approach not only sharpens our sense of what is involved in internal attitudes, but also points to a wider, less exclusively judge or lawyer centred understanding of what constitutes the legal within society.

At this point we can return to consider how one might tackle the first of Roger's three questions about the relevance of legal philosophy to legal practice: what practical relevance in professional and political arenas of law does normative legal theory have? In *PoJ* the focus is on the possibility that particular theories might serve to present the legal profession in such a way as to increase the political support that it might receive, or the fees which it might charge. But we propose taking this question more literally, and asking what work jurisprudence (in the sense of broad statements about law at its most general) does *within* the legal system. The distinction which we wish to draw is between jurisprudence as self-description, and jurisprudence as legal philosophy. Jurisprudence as legal philosophy, with its concern with what is most general about the legal system, adopts structures similar to the system which it is seeking to describe. It tends towards abstraction, seeking to identify what is general rather than what is particular. In so doing, it replicates the increased generality that is involved in the process of secondary observation, and in turn, self-description. Self-description, in law as in other social systems, does important work in establishing and maintaining a system's identity. But the criteria and restrictions as to what, within philosophy, represents an acceptable description of a system are not the same features that establish what, within a system, is generated as its self-description. The example of common law self-description and its displacement by positivist self-descriptions suggests that a system does not readily alter its self-description in response to external critique. Self-descriptions are generated within a system by the operations which that self-description facilitates, and they are re-affirmed by those same operations. If the operations change, then the self-descriptions that they generate can be expected to alter, as occurred within the legal system with the changing nature and volume of legislation. This is a reflexive relationship, in the sense that what is being created by law's operations (its self-description) is in turn stabilizing (by restricting the possibilities) of what constitutes law's operations. Law is cognitively open, at the level of self-description as at any other level. This means it can adopt communications from its environment. It must therefore be open to legal philosophy as a source of communications that could facilitate its operations. But this also means that it remains closed to communications from the outside that would paralyze its operations.

Applying this systems theory approach, one can see that legal theories which have equal degrees of logical coherence and philosophical respectability may have quite different possibilities for having a second existence (second coding) within the legal system. At what point within the legal system could one introduce a deconstructionist argument, or the more extreme forms of realist arguments?[36] Adjudication cannot be executed by claiming that law is what the judges say it is, or that everything could be different, for such communications provide no basis for the kinds of inter-connected communications that are legal arguments. The same applies to empirical observations on the influence of class, race or gender on legal decisions. Whatever the nature of these causal factors, they cannot operate within law as communications which explain the law to itself, in the course of its own operations. Any judge who is 'honest' enough to admit in the course of their judgment that their decision on a case is the result of their class, gender or race is not offering a communication which fits with those which will have established the legal issues before them. How can such judges articulate their judgments as the product of their class, race,

36 See Nobles and Schiff 2006: chapter 6 'Law's Politics: Criticising Critical Legal Studies'.

gender or self-interest without attributing the same meanings to the precedents cited to them? And how are such judges to decide the issues in question, if the communications that construct their judgments affirm that other judges who come from a different class, or gender, would decide the matter differently? However much these social factors may influence legal decisions, they cannot be internalized within them, without interrupting the ability of law routinely to construct issues, decide cases and execute its other operations. And if they cannot form part of law's self-observations, they cannot in turn form its self-descriptions.

Similar considerations are relevant to the law's construction of itself as a unity. Rather than trying to form a judgement on the extent to which law is, or is not, deserving of this description, or attributing its retention to the self-interest of legal professionals, one can examine the role played by this self-description within the operations of law. Our answer is informed by long historical circumstances, going back to the re-discovery of Roman law in the eleventh century.[37] The assumption that law is a unity and that its parts were systematically inter-related in a manner that can be elucidated through arguments of practical reasoning marked the beginning of the development of legal communications as institutionalized doctrine. As a set of implicit meanings, they are re-affirmed in every attempt by lawyers to contextualize any legal issue within any wider set of legal propositions. The 'truth' (if one can talk of such a thing) that legal communications do not deserve such a self-description will not stop the forms of argumentation which implicitly affirm such self-descriptions, or at least not until forms of inter-connection evolve which dispense with the need for such implicit meanings.

These observations have implications for some of the claims made in *PoJ* about the possibilities for law to become less unified. It is one thing to say that lower courts develop different interpretations of legal provisions from higher courts, or that the police frequently develop interpretations that differ from those of lawyers. But it is quite another to claim that these differences of interpretation can themselves form part of the communications which occur – i.e. that they can become self-conscious communications. And where they cannot, as when a judge or advocate cannot articulate that their own race or gender acts as the basis of their interpretation, then these factors, however much they may influence the actors' attempts to communicate, will not form part of the legal system. The legal system will continue to carry out its operations through communications that fail to recognize these factors. To borrow and develop some of Brian Leiter's writings on legal realism, one can have legal reasons, and non-legal reasons. Some of these non-legal reasons may be capable of forming communications within the system, and offer possibilities for connections to further communications. Examples of these might be the judges' presentations of the justice of the cases before them. But other kinds of non-legal reasons may not be able to form communications within the system at all – or not without undoing the operations which the actors are hoping to induce. Thus judges who attribute their decisions to their own race, class or subjective experiences are likely to be interpreted, within the legal system, as having made errors, due to bias. These kinds of factors may be shown, through other kinds of observation (such as statistical analysis) to make a clear and consistent difference to the reaching of particular classes of decisions. But if they cannot themselves form the subject of communications then they will not simply be non-legal in the sense that the legal system itself identifies them as something, in addition to its formal norms, that can make a difference to a decision. These reasons will be non-legal in a much stronger sense: that they are excluded from the legal system.

In offering systems theory as a sociological approach for investigating the role played by jurisprudence within the legal system we wish to end by saying something about the role of

37 Watson 1991, Stein 1999.

humans, for we suspect that the manner in which this theory de-centres the role of the human actor, is the source of at least some of the resistance which it has generated within the sociology of law (including the resistance presented by Roger in *PoJ*). From the perspective of this theory, human beings are not part of the legal system. This follows from a larger and even more shocking assertion that human beings lie outside of society. For systems theory, society consists of communications, for only these, rather than human thoughts (consciousness) or the internal biological or chemical states of particular human beings, have a social existence. The biology, chemistry or consciousness of human beings can become social as subjects and objectives of (and therefore within) communication. But so can stars and planets, which are accepted to lie outside of society. To quote the title of a recent book by Michael King, *Systems, not People, Make Society Happen*. But this understanding of humans as outside of society, does not lead to an indifference to human beings in our understanding of society. First, systems theory does not exclude most of what is attributed, within sociology, to the human actor. Beliefs, conventions, norms and intentions are observable, but they are only observable, as communication.[38] Second, society and law as part of society, requires the involvement of humans. Unless humans are motivated to seek what operations achieve the necessary communications do not occur.[39] Conversely, where humans are motivated to seek the operations of a system, communication will continue, despite theories that suggest that the communications which affect those operations are groundless, paradoxical, etc. Which, returning to our discussion of *PoJ*, tells us something about the potential of philosophical critique to alter the operations of law, or any other social system.

Bibliography

Aquinas. 1959. *Selected Political Writings*. Oxford, Blackwell. Trans J.G. Dawson, ed. A.P. D'Entreves.

Austin, J. 1955. *The Province of Jurisprudence Determined*. London, Weidenfeld and Nicolson. Reprint of original dated 1832.

Baker, J. 2002. *An Introduction to English Legal History*. Oxford, Oxford University Press. 4th edition.

Bentham, J. 1843. 'Principles of Judicial Procedure'. In J. Bowring (ed.), *The Works of Jeremy Bentham*, Volume 2. Edinburgh, William Tait.

Borch, C. 2011. *Niklas Luhmann*. Oxford, Routledge.

Christodoulidis, E. 1998. *Law and Reflexive Politics*. Dordrecht, Kluwer.

Coke, E. 1628. *First Institute of the Laws of England*. Rep. New York, Garland Publishing Company, 1979.

Coleman, J. and Shapiro, S. (eds) 2002. *The Oxford Handbook of Jurisprudence and Philosophy of Law*. Oxford, Oxford University Press.

Cotterrell, R. 1975. 'Direction and Development in Anglo-American Jurisprudence and Sociology of Law.' 4 *Anglo-American Law Review*, 386–411.

Cotterrell, R. 1983. 'The Sociological Concept of Law.' 10 *Journal of Law and Society*, 241–55.

38 A communication is a unit of meaning within society, and as such, includes not only language but symbols and gestures. A thought is a unit of meaning within consciousness. The possibility of meaning having two existences, within communication and within thought, makes society possible.

39 Whilst the execution of legal operations is something that lawyers are motivated to effect by the material rewards which result, these still would not occur if they failed to motivate their clients – so this is always more than a matter of lawyers' self-interest.

Cotterrell, R. 1989. *The Politics of Jurisprudence: A Critical Introduction to Legal Philosophy*. London, Butterworths.

Cotterrell, R. 1993. 'Sociological Perspectives on Legal Closure.' In A. Norrie (ed.), *Closure and Critique*. Edinburgh, Edinburgh University Press. ch. 10, 175–93.

Cotterrell, R. 1995. *Laws Community: Legal Theory in Sociological Perspective*. Oxford, Oxford University Press.

Cotterrell, R. 1998. 'Why Must Legal Ideas Be Interpreted Sociologically?' 25 *Journal of Law and Society*, 171–92.

Cotterrell, R. 2001. 'The Representation of Law's Autonomy in Autopoiesis Theory.' In J. Priban and D. Nelken (eds), *Law's New Boundaries*. Aldershot, Dartmouth. ch. 4, 80–103.

Cotterrell, R. 2002. 'Subverting Orthodoxy, Making Law Central: A View of Sociolegal Studies.' 29 *Journal of Law and Society*, 632–44.

Cotterrell, R. 2003. *The Politics of Jurisprudence: A Critical Introduction to Legal Philosophy*. 2nd edn. London, Lexis Nexis/Butterworths, and Oxford, Oxford University Press.

Cotterrell, R. 2008. 'Transnational Communities and the Concept of Law'. 21 *Ratio Juris*, 1–18.

Cotterrell, R. 2009. 'Spectres of Transnationalism: Changing Terrains of Sociology of Law'. 36 *Journal of Law and Society*, 481–500.

Cotterrell, R. 2013a. 'The Role of the Jurist: Reflections around Radbruch.' 26(4) *Ratio Juris*, 510–22.

Cotterrell, Roger. 2013b. 'The Jurist's Conscience: Reflections around Radbruch'. In M. Del Mar and C. Michelon (eds), *The Anxiety of the Jurist*. Aldershot, Ashgate. ch. 2, 13–26.

Cotterrell, R. 2014a. 'Why Jurisprudence is not Legal Philosophy'. 5/1 *Jurisprudence*, 1–19.

Cotterrell, R. 2014b. 'Professing Jurisprudence'. In *Law and Michael Freeman*. Oxford, Oxford University Press.

Dworkin, R. 1986. *Laws Empire*. London, Fontana.

Febbrajo, A. and Haste, G. (eds) 2013. *Law and Intersystemic Communication: Understanding 'Structural Coupling'*. Aldershot, Ashgate.

Fuller, L. 1964. *The Morality of Law*. New Haven, Yale University Press.

Hart, H.L.A. 1961/1994. *The Concept of Law*. Oxford, Clarendon Press.

Hobbes, T. 1681. *A Dialogue between a Philosopher and a Student of the Common Laws of England*. Chicago, Chicago University Press, ed. J. Cropsey. 1971.

Kairys, D. (ed.) 1998. *The Politics of Law: A Progressive Critique*. New York, Basic Books, 3rd edition.

Kelsen, H. 1967. *Pure Theory of Law*. Berkeley, University of California Press, trans. M. Knight, 2nd edition.

King, M, 2009. *Systems, Not People, Make Society Happen*. Holcombe, e-publishing.

Lobban, M. 1991. *The Common Law and English Jurisprudence 1760–1860*. Oxford, Clarendon Press.

Leiter, B. 2007. *Naturalizing Jurisprudence: Essays on American Realism and Naturalism in Legal Philosophy*. Oxford, Oxford University Press.

Luhmann, N. 1982. *The Differentiation of Society*. New York, Columbia University Press, trans. S. Holmes and C. Larmore.

Luhmann, N. 1995. *Social Systems*. Stanford, Stanford University Press, trans. J. Bednarz Jr.

Luhmann, N. 1998. *Observations on Modernity*. Stanford, Stanford University Press, trans. W. Whobrey.

Luhmann, N. 2000. 'Answering the Question: What is Modernity? An Interview with Niklas Luhmann'. In Rasch, W. *Niklas Luhmann's Modernity: The Paradoxes of Differentiation.* Stanford, Stanford University Press. 195–221.

Luhmann, N. 2005. 'The Concept of Autopoesis.' In D. Seidl and K.H. Becker (eds), *Niklas Luhmann and Organisational Studies*. Copenhagen, Copenhagen Business School Press, ch. 2, 54–63.

Luhmann, N. 2004. *Law as a Social System*. Oxford, Oxford University Press, trans. K.A. Ziegert, eds F. Kastner, R. Nobles, D. Schiff, K. Ziegert.

Luhmann, N. 2012. *Theory of Society*, Volume I. Stanford, Stanford University Press, trans. R. Barrett.

Luhmann, N. 2013. *Theory of Society,* Volume 2. Stanford, Stanford University Press, trans. R. Barrett.

Maine, Sir Henry. 1861. *Ancient Law*. London, Dent, 1917 edition.

McIlwain, C. 1910. *The High Court of Parliament and its Supremacy: An Historical Essay on the Boundaries between Legislation and Adjudication in England.* New Haven, Yale University Press.

Nobles, R. and Schiff, D. 2000. *Understanding Miscarriages of Justice: Law, the Media, and the Inevitability of Crisis*. Oxford, Oxford University Press.

Nobles, R. and Schiff, D. 2004. 'A Story of Miscarriage: Law in the Media', 31 *Journal of Law and Society*, 221–44.

Nobles, R. and Schiff, D. 2006. *A Sociology of Jurisprudence*. Oxford, Hart.

Nobles, R. and Schiff, D. 2009. 'Why Do Judges Talk the Way They Do?' 5.1 *International Journal of Law in Context*, 25–49.

Nobles, R. and Schiff, D. 2012. 'Using Systems Theory to Study Legal Pluralism: What Could Be Gained?' 46 *Law and Society Review*, 265–96.

Nobles, R. and Schiff, D. 2013a. *Observing Law through Systems Theory*. Oxford, Hart.

Nobles, R. and Schiff, D. 2013b. 'Structural Coupling between the Systems of Law and the Media: The Contrasting Examples of Criminal Conviction and Criminal Appeal'. In A. Febbrajo and G. Harste (eds), *Law and Intersystemic Communication: Understanding 'Structural Coupling'*. Aldershot, Ashgate. ch. 13, 317–25.

Perez, O. and Teubner, G. (eds) 2006. *Paradoxes and Inconsistencies in the Law*. Oxford, Hart.

Postema, G. 2002. 'Philosophy of the Common Law'. In J. Coleman and S. Shapiro (eds), *The Oxford Handbook of Jurisprudence and Philosophy of Law*. Oxford, Oxford University Press. ch. 15, 588–622.

Raz, J. (2009) *The Authority of Law: Essays on Law and Morality*. Oxford, Oxford University Press. 2nd edition.

Seidl, D. and Becker, K.H. (eds) 2005. *Niklas Luhmann and Organisational Studies*. Copenhagen, Copenhagen Business School Press.

Simpson, A.W.B. 1986. 'The Common Law and Legal Theory', In W. Twining (ed.), *Legal Theory and Common Law*. Oxford, Blackwell, 8–25.

Stein, P. 1999. *Roman Law in European History*. Cambridge, Cambridge University Press.

Stoner, J.R. Jnr. 1992. *Common Law and Liberal Theory: Coke, Hobbes and the Origins of American Constitutionalism*. Lawrence, KA, University of Kansas Press.

Teubner, G. 1993. *Law as an Autopoietic System*. Oxford, Oxford University Press, trans. A. Bankowska and R. Adler.

Thornhill, C. 2011. *A Sociology of Constitutions: Constitutions and State Legitimacy in Historical Sociological Perspective*. Cambridge, Cambridge University Press.

Twining, W. 1986. (ed.) *Legal Theory and the Common Law*. Oxford, Blackwell.

Watson, A. 1991. *Roman Law and Comparative Law*. Athens, Georgia, University of Georgia Press.

PART III
Globalization, Cultural and Comparative Law Themes

Chapter 14

The Sociology of International Law: An Introduction

Mikael Rask Madsen[1]

Like many other sociologists of law of my generation, one of my first encounters with the field was through Roger Cotterrell's seminal book *The Sociology of Law: An Introduction* (1984/1992). When you were trained in law and particularly in the approach (still) prevalent at most continental European law faculties as I was, the sociology of law was somewhat of an exotic supplement to an education otherwise firmly founded in the study of black-letter law and legal doctrine. In Copenhagen, at the time of my studies, the sociology of law did not even have its own examination: it was rather pragmatically grouped with the history of law and the philosophy of law regardless of the obviously distinct epistemological premises of each of these disciplines. Nevertheless, since the sociology of law actually existed as part of the curriculum it could still influence a few odd students away from the sombre exegesis of law and legal doctrine and towards the seemingly livelier world of social science. Roger Cotterrell's book was not compulsory reading in Copenhagen, but it featured heavily in the footnotes to the introductory book by Danish sociologist of law Jørgen Dalberg-Larsen. It was however compulsory reading when I enrolled in the MA programme at the International Institute of the Sociology of Law (IISL) in the mid 1990s. This was at the heyday of post-Cold War globalization and an alleged new form of hegemonic Pax Americana – a moment in which theories of McDonaldization, End of History, global network society and the like also featured centrally on the curriculum. Compared to these highly topical (and in some cases sensationalist) theories, Cotterrell's systematic exploration of the sociology of law had a very different appeal: that of sociology of law as a rigorous empirical social science and one that could make law far more intelligible than most so-called legal theories.

The Sociology of Law takes great (and sometimes grand) theories very seriously, just as it takes very seriously the place of empirical sociology in the understanding of law. For students it inevitably comes across as a very serious book and one with a high intellectual ambition, but also a difficult and challenging book for many. Re-reading the book today only confirms these memories of a seminal piece of research and pedagogy. However, if in the meantime you have had the luck to meet the author behind the book, even had a few chats with him at various academic gatherings, it is not easy to maintain the initial image of the author based solely on the seriousness of his writings. Roger Cotterrell is so much more than the author of the perhaps most important introduction to the sociology of law. In addition to being the author of many other and equally interesting books and articles, he is not only a researcher who throughout a long career has always been interested in the cutting-edge of law but also a keen jazz fan. While I personally share his interest in jazz, this chapter is not on the sociology of jazz but on what I believe is the cutting-edge of law. Cotterrell would undoubtedly agree that one of the most important transformations in law in recent years is the rise of inter-, supra- and transnational law as a real force in global society. This

1 The research on which this chapter is based is funded by the Danish National Research Foundation Grant no. DNRF105. Part of it reuses the recently published paper: Madsen 2013.

challenges mainstream notions of law in both legal theory and the sociology of law. It moreover re-opens the foundational question of sociology on the very idea of society.

In this chapter I will focus on the sociology of international law and particularly the sociology of those institutions increasingly put in place to interpret and realize international law: international courts (ICs). ICs are particularly interesting with regard to the study of the globalization of law as they transform international law from its former position as somewhat residual to national law to now becoming 'real' law: law in its own right. This is a recent and still on-going development, and one that is largely under-analyzed, particularly in the sociology of law. The growing importance of international courts can be illustrated by a few facts. While only a handful of ICs existed in the mid 1980s, there are now 25 in operation and indications of further growth. ICs have also become more active during the same period: nearly 90% of the total IC output of legal decisions (24,002 out of 27,060) has been issued over the last two decades. ICs are moreover changing qualitatively: most have compulsory jurisdiction, many allow other agents than states to initiate litigation before them, and several have the authority to review state compliance with international rules.[2] Faithful to Cotterrell's original work, I will focus both on classical sociologies of law and contemporary empirical studies of the globalization of law with the aim of introducing what I term the sociology of *international* law. The goal is not to present any comprehensive outline but rather point to how sociologists of law can further, in my view quite significantly, our understanding of international law and courts in society.

1. Studying International Courts Using Classical Sociology of Law

Sociologists have long studied law and legal institutions in society. This is true for both the classics such as Weber and Durkheim and leading contemporary sociologists, for example Jürgen Habermas (1992), Pierre Bourdieu (1987), Niklas Luhmann (1993) and Bruno Latour (2002). Sociologists, however, study law and courts using a rather distinct starting-point. If law has as its overarching object of inquiry the normative order of legal norms, and political science's key object is politics and associated institutions and actors, sociology is above all concerned with society and its institutions. With regard to studying ICs more specifically, the main difference between sociology and law and political science is the way in which sociologists approach the idea of institutions. While law and political science typically rely on legal delineations of institutions and thus take the circumscription of institutions as a given, sociology for the most part construes institutions in a much broader sense: either as assemblages of practices within larger social fields or more generally as devices for ordering society. Both perspectives will be introduced in the following subsections in which I focus on what classic sociological theories can contribute to our understanding of international law and courts.

1.1 Max Weber and Interpretive Sociology

Max Weber's analysis of the evolution of law in terms of a set of different ideal-typical forms of rationality is probably the most immediately relevant among the classics. It is also the one that comes closest to contemporary mainstream social science studies of ICs. Generally, Weber (1980) provides a set of typologies for describing the rise of modern Western law as an evolution

2 All data from Alter 2014.

from 'formally irrational' and 'substantively irrational' to law becoming 'formally rational' and 'substantively rational'. According to Weber, these rationalities generally correspond to different forms of domination: from charismatic to traditional to legal. Importantly, at no point does Weber claim a complete conversion from one domination or rationality to another. Rather, he maintains that elements of each of these ideal-typical representations of law are present in contemporary society, but to varying degrees. They are indeed ideal-typical representations in the sense that they are abstracted models devised to help identify society in a clearer and more systematic way in order to allow for empirical study and comparison. When used correctly, they provide a conceptual apparatus for the inevitable task of any social science, namely to make a selection and abstraction from the infinite multitude of social reality. With respect to examining ICs, they help turning ICs into tangible empirical objects of research.

As demonstrated in a recent study of the European Court of Human Rights (ECtHR), Weber provides a set of reflexive tools for understanding ICs as evolutionary institutions that develop specific institutional and legal rationalities, which are reflective of institutions' embedded rationality – or situated cognition – in their decision-making processes. (Madsen 2011) This is very different from most law and political science scholarship which generally views ICs in predetermined categories, for example, as transplanted institutions that resemble their national counterparts or other ICs, or on the basis of an abstracted hypothesis of institutional behaviour or institutional design. A Weberian approach rather has its focal point in the historically founded different rationalities of the institution in question, and how these are reflective of both society at large and the very agents of the institution (Madsen 2011a). This unique way of approaching ICs also provides a sociologically-informed alternative for understanding questions related to the legitimacy of ICs; that is, legitimacy in this approach is neither tied to a legalist notion of legitimacy via legality, nor an abstracted political philosophical notion. Max Weber sought instead to explain how legitimacy is contingent on different forms of domination – from traditional to charismatic to legally rational – and thereby embedded in society.

According to Weber, at the end of the day what makes a certain practice of power legitimate is the process through which authority justifies its exercise of power and gains social acceptance. Applied to ICs, it follows that their legitimacy does not stem from them being *representative* of society; it stems from them being *reflective* of society.[3] For example, the US Supreme Court is not demographically or politically representative of American society, but it might very well reflect society and, thereby, justify its practices. In other words, the legitimacy of a given IC cannot simply be statistically deduced from the judges' representativeness of society and politics at large. This also means that even the best and most carefully thought-out procedures of elections of judges, in the most extreme cases seeking to make courts representative as a sort of quasi-democratic political institution, might ultimately fail if the court's practices are not reflective of society. On the other hand, the profiles of a specific set of judges might very well help them gain legitimacy in specific environments, ranging from law to politics and civil society.[4] Using this framework, it has been argued with respect to the genesis of the ECtHR that its institutionalization in a way followed what Weber termed the 'routinization of charisma': the initial institutionalization process was a legitimization process around specific individuals and their practices. Ultimately, the authority of the ECtHR was largely derived from the high status of the bench and the way its judges developed a set of politically fine-tuned legal practices that reflected the social and political conditions under which it operated (Madsen 2011b).

3 The argument is further developed in Madsen 2012: 23.

4 See also Terris, Romano, and Swigart 2007.

From this brief introduction to Weber, the difference between contemporary law and political science explorations of ICs and the particular empirical and conceptual sensitivity of sociology generally speaking becomes clear. While mainstream political scientific examinations of ICs typically test rationalized hypotheses against different sets of data, the goal of a Weberian approach is different: it seeks to make law and courts intelligible as societal institutions.[5] The aim of this so-called 'interpretive sociology' (*Verstehende Soziologie*) is precisely to link habits and motives to action, that is, to make action intelligible by corresponding action to the agents in terms of a specific form of 'methodological individualism'.[6] The prime example of this approach is Weber's famous analysis of the role of the Protestant sprit in the making of capitalism. Here the 'spirit' of the agents – notably internalized norms of duty and correctness – is the backdrop for explaining the rapid growth of a capitalist economy in Germany. But as just shown, the same could be done on a smaller scale with regard to ICs, either by a study of the judges or the normative schemes in society which impel the drive for ICs.

Although Weberian sociology to some might appear as yet another grand attempt at deducing universal socio-logics, it should be stressed that its actual goal is not to devise a universal theory, but to explain society by creating a framework of inquiry that facilitates an exploration of both micro- and macro-levels of society. First of all, Weber is not seeking to get rid of the usual units of middle-range social scientific analysis such as groups, collectives and institutions, but is instead pointing to the basic observation that only individuals can have intentions. Consequently, individuals provide a key unit of analysis, even if the goal is not to understand individuals' motivations as such but societal development as driven by groups of individuals or, for example, institutions. As demonstrated in the above-cited study on the ECtHR, this is directly applicable to analyses of ICs. Yet, different from both the traditional legal realist take on legal actors and many of the subsequent legal realist-inspired studies of judicial behaviour, the focal point of such a Weberian study of ICs is not the individuals as such but societal and institutional developments, which can be made intelligible by exploring the individuals' motivations, and their impact on the rationalization of institutions (cf. Madsen 2011b). Thus, Weber provides above all a historical-sociological approach to law with a focus on the transformation of the institutions of society of which courts are but one. Similarly, ICs are institutions of global society and can be studied as such using Weber.

1.2 From Durkheim to Structural Functionalism and Systems Theory

Emile Durkheim is another of the classical sociologists who made an early contribution to the understanding of law in society. Moreover, as I will argue, Durkheim has had a monumental impact on studies of international law and courts, even if this is rarely acknowledged. According to Durkheim, law is an index of social solidarity – it represents the evolution of social integration. This is explained in Durkheim's famous evolutionary model, outlining the transformation from primitive to modern society and with that, a change in forms of solidarity from mechanical to organic, following a thesis of societal differentiation (Durkheim 1893). Not unlike like Weber, he basically links law and its institutions to the emergence of modern society. Durkheim has, however, less to offer with regard to understanding courts specifically. He views them as mainly 'deliberating on behalf of society in a manner somewhat similar to that of the legislature' (Cotterrell 1999: 172). Rather his main interest is law as a means of stabilizing and integrating society. According to Durkheim, primitive (or traditional) societies are generally kept together by kinship and tribal

5 An exception to this trend is some historical institutionalist scholarship: see e.g. Alter 2001.

6 For an overview of this notion, see Hewa 1988.

justice. In modern societies interdependences between different specialized areas of work secure the integration of society. In this regard, law has an important function as an instrument of integrating these differentiated social spheres. This is precisely what he means by arguing that courts 'deliberate' on behalf of society at large – and with the goal of securing society's coherence against its increased differentiation and specialization.

Durkheim's approach is directly applicable to understanding the role of ICs in contemporary global society. In modern social scientific terms, the question is what function ICs perform with respect to integrating regional or global society, rather than, as is most often the case in the current literature, the more specific and limited functional aims of individual ICs. The heuristic take-away of posing the question in the broader sociological way, which is proposed by Durkheimian sociology, is that it avoids trapping the research in the functional purposes of specific institutions which have tended to dominate debates on ICs. Instead it is concerned with a set of broader questions, which involves states, international courts and organizations as providers of specialized labour of a crucial kind in contemporary society. The overall aim is to understand society at large – both its specialized components and what ensures coherence notwithstanding specialization. Such a macro-level analysis of ICs and global society is yet to be conducted using post-Durkheimian sociology, but the basic social scientific tools are available to those who dare taking up the challenge.[7]

The most direct and pervasive influence of Durkheimian sociology is clearly the focus on functions, as well as what later becomes the notion of systems in structural-functionalism and systems theory, which both draw on the Durkheimian differentiation thesis. In fact, considering the vast body of functionalist literature, particularly in political science and law, the impact of this way of perceiving and constructing the social world can hardly be overstated. To illustrate, two leading scholars, Armin von Bogdandy and Ingo Venzke (2013), simply describe functionalism as the orthodoxy of legal research. Another example is the often-cited thesis of the fragmentation of international law, which equally is based on an (implicit) functionalist reading of public international law (Koskenniemi et al. 2002). In both cases, they build on a very long tradition in international law of perceiving public international law in functionalist terms. Hersch Lauterpacht's *The Function of Law in the International Community* (1933) is an important reference to legal scholarship as well as to the application of the Durkheimian idea of precisely linking international law and international community. In political science, one will come across similar claims to those of legal scholars with respect to understanding ICs and international law in terms of functions and functionalities. Although the bigger societal picture is often missing in the analysis of both lawyers and political scientists, this is nevertheless an important point of convergence between classic sociology and contemporary law and political science explorations of ICs.

Drawing on socio-legal studies of (national) courts and society, Bogdandy and Venzke (2013) offer a very good summary of how functionalism is also helpful for more specifically theorizing the functions of ICs in international society. These are: 1) *settling disputes*; 2) *stabilizing normative expectations*; 3) *making Law*; and 4) *controlling and legitimating public authority*.[8] Although they do not cite Durkheim, these functions clearly echo a Durkheimian way of thinking of courts in society. Similar functionalist claims can be found in a host of sociologies of courts in society in the tradition of structural functionalism and systems theory, starting with Parsons, who argues that a court's main function is to integrate society's different sub-systems by 'mitigat[ing] potential

7 Although not focused on ICs, the most explicit attempt at understanding the international legal ordering of society in functionalist terms is probably found in Teubner 2012. As concerns the European level, see particularly Thornhill 2012. See also Münch 2008.

8 Compare this to the goals defined in Shany 2012: 243–7.

elements of conflicts and to oil the machinery of social intercourse' (Parsons 1962). Building on the combined insights of structural functionalism and notions of differentiation and integration, key students of Parsons have provided even more detailed explorations of particularly the 'integrative functions' of courts in society as in the case of Harry C. Bredemaier (1962) and the specific role of law and courts to 'stabilise normative expectations' as in the case of Niklas Luhmann (1993).

What functionalism basically offers is a general sociological theory of law and courts in society based on a specific rational reading of courts as being functional to a differentiated society. While it is hard to disagree with the overriding claims of these theories, partly because of the level of abstraction at which they operate, it is plain to see that they also tend, to a considerable extent, to reproduce the very claims of formalist legal scholarship and even law itself. This criticism can also be directed at much political science literature using functionalism in a narrow way, establishing a direct causal link between an identified problem and its solution via ICs (e.g. Koremenos, Lipson and Snidal 2001). This critique is also precisely the starting-point for what can be labelled 'critical studies of international law and courts', which as a common thread seek to go beyond the self-descriptions of institutions and agents with the goal of providing what they believe is a more realistic understanding of law and society. In fact, they also seek to study what one well-known sociological functionalist, Robert K. Merton (1949), famously termed the 'dysfunctions of courts' whereby he himself approached critical studies as well as fundamentally challenged functionalism as a viable sociological paradigm.

1.3 Marxism and Critical Approaches

As regards sociology, critical studies can at a general level be said to have their origins in Marxism, traditionally described as the third branch of classic sociology. While it shares with the Durkheimian school an interest in social structures, the underlying assumption of coherence of functionalism is explicitly rejected in the Marxist scholarship, for which the overriding driver of societal evolution is conflict and domination.[9] Classic Marxism has mainly an interest in courts and justice as expressions and tools of social domination as exercised by existing dominant classes. Judges are likewise viewed as agents of a suppressive superstructure mainly put in place to ensure the status quo and, thus, the interests of the ruling elite. Put simply, if functionalism takes its starting-point in a thesis of differentiation, classic Marxism takes it in stratification. There are, however, very important differences between classic (and orthodox) Marxism and its main focus on industrial relations in terms of property owners and labourers, and modern critical studies and their ambition to critique modern society more generally with the goal of liberating the individual from the forms of domination characterizing it.[10]

I will not dwell here on the myriad of schools of critical studies and their differences and convergences, but simply underscore that some important elements of Marxist and critical thinking have made significant impact on contemporary sociological studies of ICs – and often in combination with Weberian readings of institutions and professions. These include, for example, the emphasis on elites as key agents of law, the conceptualization of international law and courts as adversarial social spaces and the focus on the power of law – both as symbolic power, following the Bourdieusian tradition (Bourdieu 1991), and as a structural phenomenon with regard to, for

9 An attempt at devising an explicit Marxist agenda for the study of international law is found in Chimni 1999.

10 The term critical theory is largely contested and covers in practice a whole range of approaches, ranging from the Frankfurter School to many contemporary post-structural sociologies.

example, notions of empire. Whereas functionalist sociology, as argued above, has significantly influenced both legal and political scientific analysis of ICs, starting in the late 1960s, it has overall tended to lose much of its appeal as a sociological paradigm.[11] The actual fate of functionalism is of course debatable, but what is certain is that the combined issues of elites, power, and conflict of the critical camp have come to define much contemporary sociological scholarship on ICs. In the following section, emphasis will therefore be put on this branch of sociology with the goal of accentuating distinct sociological contributions to understanding ICs.

2. The New Sociology of International Courts

I have so far sought to demonstrate how classical sociological theories have provided a series of general studies of law and courts in society with considerable relevance for understanding ICs and society. Of course, sociology has evolved very considerably since Weber, Marx and Durkheim. As concerns the question of courts in society the sociology of law has maintained a general interest particularly in courts[12] – an interest that in recent years has been intensified in the debates on judicialization and the growing role of constitutional courts.[13] However, a considerable part of law and society research was for a long time somewhat anti-institutional and driven by a preference for alternatives to institutional law. As an observable consequence, in the United States, contemporary judicial studies have increasingly been dominated by political scientists and not sociologists. In the following I will outline some recent scholarship which in new ways combines law and society scholarship and contemporary sociology, notably the sociology of Pierre Bourdieu, for explaining ICs and their linkage to global society.

2.1 Some Analytical Preliminaries: Elites, Power, Conflict

The emergence of what now is undoubtedly a growing sociological scholarship on international law and ICs was in part inspired by studies of the globalization and transnationalization of law and legal professionals. Since at least the early 1980s, a number of sociologists of law started investigating what was increasingly termed 'transnational legal phenomena'. Boaventura de Sousa Santos' explorations (e.g. 1995) into the different and interconnected levels of globalization marked a crucial repositioning of sociologists of law in the study of international phenomena, but using distinct sociological tools. Another seminal book in this regard and with greater impact on the new sociological scholarship on international institutions and courts, is the analysis of international commercial arbitration conducted by Yves Dezalay and Bryant Garth in *Dealing in Virtue* (1996).

Using both legal and sociological insights, Dezalay and Garth demonstrated how the battle over the form and the law of international commercial arbitration could be explained as a battle between not only different forms of expertise (European academic law vs. American-style Wall Street law), but also as a clash between different global elites. The work is based on two different research traditions which are brought together via a set of broader conceptual frameworks provided by the sociologist Pierre Bourdieu: first, a sociology of professions with a view to analyzing how professions increasingly compete with one another in the construction of new transnational markets

11 Notable exceptions to this overall trend is the work of Niklas Luhmann and some contemporary organization theory as explained below.

12 For an overview of this literature, see Cotterrell 1992: ch. 7.

13 For a good overview of this literature, see Thornhill 2012: 354–5.

and arenas (Dezalay and Sugarman 1995); secondly, a sociology of elites with the aim of exploring how a set of distinct social groups of (legal) agents hold the power to define new areas of legal practice, with consequences not only for the profession at large, but also for international politics and society (Dezalay 2004). Drawing on Pierre Bourdieu (1987), they frame these battles as social *fields*, that is, as spaces of contestation over defining the law in which different agents occupy positions relative to the portfolio of capitals they can muster and which are 'capitalised' according to the logic of the specific field in question (see also Delazay and Madsen 2012).

Dezalay and Garth's work has also a methodological feature, which has turned out to be of special interest to understanding ICs. Although legal institutions are clearly important to their studies, they are not taking centre stage in the original study on international commercial arbitration and even less so in their subsequent studies of the role of professional battles in the transformation of states in Latin America (Dezalay and Garth 2002) and Asia (Delazay and Garth 2010). What they instead provide is a sociological alternative to the assumption of many studies in both law and political science that institutions in themselves can explain the emergence of new transnational legal fields. Much closer to neo-institutionalist scholarship on organizational fields (e.g. DiMaggio and Powell 1983), yet different, they claim that individual agents, and particularly the agents' personal and professional trajectories into the fields and institutions in question, provide unique data for understanding how institutions come about and transform. Using a methodology, which they term 'collective biographies', a form of prosopography, they map out the social characteristics of the social spaces of institutions in terms of the combined and accumulated trajectories of the main agents.[14] This is also where they deploy Bourdieusian notions of capitals – social, educational, political, legal, etc. – to explore the specific legal elite formations of these socio-legal spaces.

Dezalay and Garth's identification of legal elites as an empirical access point for studying transnational legal fields has had considerable impact on a series of in-depth empirical studies of ICs, ranging from the areas of international criminal law to European law, which emerged at about the same time in the beginning of the 2000s. Basically, Dezalay and Garth provide a subtle way of linking questions of elites, power and conflict for exploring how institutions are built and transformed. Moreover, using these analytical markers enable sociologists of law to repose a number of key questions with regard to ICs, including questions related to the notion of institutions, the legitimacy of ICs and, not the least, their place in contemporary processes of global structuration.

2.2 Studying the Force of International Courts and Law

The International Criminal Tribunal for the Former Yugoslavia (ICTY) was analyzed in the influential book *Justice in the Balkans* by John Hagan (2003). Coming from criminology and law and society studies, Hagan in many ways follows the lead from Dezalay and Garth on the role of legal agency.[15] His goal is, however, more institutional than that found in Dezalay and Garth, yet he uses precisely the described methodology of examining the trajectories of the main agents in order to map the institution in question and its transformation. Hagan more concretely scrutinizes the interplay between investigators, prosecutors and witnesses, as well as specific powerful individuals employed by the tribunal (emblematically Richard Goldstone, Louise Arbour and Carla Del Ponte), in a complex analysis of the making of humanitarian and international criminal law, and how it eventually gains a force of law with a reference to the

14 Compare this to the more institutionalist version of Bourdieusian sociology of organizations presented in Emirbayer and Johnson 2008.

15 Hagan explains the precise usage in ch. 22 of Halliday and Schmidt 2009.

Bourdieusian conception of the legal field (see Hagan and Levi 2005). What is meant by the latter is that to understand the power of law, one has to study the social conditions making that power possible. And that is precisely what John Hagan's study does through its in-depth examination of the various players and emerging institutions producing international justice with legal force in the Balkans.

From Hagan's original study one can trace a more general sociological interest in international criminal law and its new set of associated institutions.[16] Interestingly, this scholarship manages very well to combine insights from earlier law and society studies on the informal sides of law with the analysis of the less institutionalized practices of international law and institutions. An example is the role of mediation and alternative conflict resolution in the area of international criminal law and war crimes (e.g. Ivkovich and Hagan 2008). Similarly, they combine contemporary criminology with new questions derived from the movement towards criminalizing war crimes and its international institutionalization and judicialization. Generally, by defining their object of inquiry in less legal terms than the mainstream law and political science scholarship in the area, they open up for an analysis of the various social spaces in which the possible – and sometimes failed – push for institutionalization and judicialization are played out.[17] A common thread in this literature is the focus on the agency of international law and institutions, yet its actual place is clearly disputed among the scholars in question.

The other branch of sociology of ICs that has found an inspiration in both the work of Bourdieu and that of Dezalay and Garth is a set of projects related to exploring the emergence of a field of European law with a particular focus on the two European inter- and supranational courts: the ECtHR and the Court of Justice of the EU (formerly the ECJ). Using these approaches has enabled these authors to examine the interplay between the agency of European supranational courts and the simultaneous transformation of the social structures in which they evolve.[18] Moreover, this novel approach to the double-structuring of European law by the interplay of agency and structural transformation has allowed them to revise the taken-for-granted story of the emergence of European law and the role played by supra- and international courts in this process.[19] By using a distinct power-perspective on the making of international (European) law and its relative force, they have highlighted how larger societal and geopolitical currents have had an enduring impact on the evolution of European law and institutions, as well as European integration more generally. (Cohen and Madsen 2007; Madsen 2011c) Somewhat similar to many of the studies cited above, these inquiries into the deeper socio-logics of European ICs combine insights from theories of professions and professionals with critical approaches to law and its power in society, which highlights how law is mobilized, in specific cases or as part of broader legal movements.[20] It is exactly because of these combined interests that their analysis tends to find their overriding frameworks in sociological theories in the tradition of, on the one hand, Max Weber and the power and evolution of professions, and, on the other hand, theories of social configurations such as those of Norbert Elias, Michel Foucault and Pierre Bourdieu.

Contemporary sociology-based studies of ICs are not, however, confined to the cited studies, even if they now stand out as perhaps the most distinct sociological contributions to the

---

16 A number of these scholars have contributed to two of the special issues (nos 173 and 174) in 2008 of *Actes de la recherche en sciences sociales*.

17 An example is Serrousi 2012; see also Condé 2012.

18 Most explicitly in Madsen 2011b.

19 See e.g., Vauchez 2010; see also Cohen 2007. On human rights, see Madsen 2010.

20 E.g., Vauchez 2010; see also Ch. 4 on jurist advocacy networks in Alter 2009.

understanding of ICs.[21] Within the broader camps of sociological institutionalism and, to a slightly lesser extent, historical institutionalism, one finds numerous studies, which could be assigned the label sociological. However, as already suggested above, some currents of sociology are by definition more focused on institutions than others and, thus, more inclined to be interested in ICs as such. Functionalism in this respect has a rather large group of followers in both law and political science. In sociology its role has been used in either more organizational analysis of ICs or to depict the global structures of society. The latter is either in a Luhmannian tradition of global society,[22] in terms of world system theory of Immanuel Wallerstein (e.g. 1974) or, in more constructivist terms, as 'global culture' (Lechner and Boli 2005). While organizational studies are focused on deeper institutional logics, neither of the approaches in the second camp is interested in ICs per se, but rather – following broadly speaking the Durkheimian tradition – of how ICs to varying degrees are important institutions in the transformation of the deeper structures of society under contemporary globalization.[23]

It is self-evident that, in the field of sociology of organizations, one comes across studies that more specifically address questions directly relevant to understanding the institutional dynamics and problems of ICs. Yet, while organizational sociologists have offered sophisticated frameworks and theories for such analysis, it has been predominantly lawyers and political scientists who have done the actual empirical work, importing insights from the sociology of organizations for solving puzzles in existing research on ICs. The work of law professor Yuval Shany (2012) on the effectiveness of ICs is illuminating in this regard. With regard to the second camp of research, a particularly interesting branch of sociology is the 'world culture' literature, which in many ways builds on the earlier Stanford school of 'world polity' theory (e.g. Meyer 2010). Frank J. Lechner and John Boli's analysis of the making of the International Criminal Court (ICC) provides in this regard a highly illustrative case of the sociological 'world culture' research paradigm (2005: ch.10). Being precisely interested in the production of world culture by a host of different globalizing practices, they emphasize the ways in which the idea of the ICC and its legal codification triggered the mobilization of more than a hundred states and some 800 NGOs (at 221).[24] This mass mobilization around the ICC they perceive as 'world culture in action' and, thus, as a distinct indicator of the very existence of a global societal layer in certain fields of practice (at 230). Characteristic of this scholarship on the evolving structures of world society, a single court, even one as emblematic as the ICC, is seen as no more than a specific attempt at instituting global culture. It is clearly an important attempt with a long history of fighting war by international law dating back at least a century, but the actual research interest is broader and when it includes ICs they are seen as particular ways, among many others, of instituting and articulating global society.

3. Conclusion

I have in this brief chapter outlined how the sociology of law can make a contribution to the study of the perhaps most striking development of international law in recent years, namely the emergence of

21 These sociological insights have also been widely used by historians interested in European law and integration, e.g. Rasmussen 2008.

22 E.g. Stichweh 2000.

23 A somewhat similar view, although based on a more historical sociological account of globalization is found in Sassen 2006.

24 For a further analysis of the role of NGOs in world culture, see Boli and Thomas 1997.

a significant number of international courts. Considering the rich heritage of both sociology and the sociology of law, it is unsurprising that there are considerable differences to understanding these developments between the various sociological schools I have outlined. They nevertheless have in common the way in which sociological views and imaginations of ICs generally construct different objects of research than what is found in the so far dominant approaches from law and the political sciences. Generally, they do not take the notion of institutions for granted but rather explore where institutions are practiced in a broader societal structure. Secondly, they pose the question of the interplay of agency and social structures in an entirely different way, which helps in approaching ICs not only as a legal-politico phenomenon but also as a societal one. Finally, the often debated question of the legitimacy of ICs is revealed through a very different and ultimately more complex lens than the dominant idea of legitimacy as a legalistic or political philosophical problem.

Developing these different conceptualizations and viewpoints is not about insisting on some kind of sociological exceptionalism. Quite on the contrary, the objective of introducing sociology and the sociology of law to the study of ICs is to find new and perhaps better ways of making ICs tangible empirical objects of study – and ultimately making their development more intelligible as a societal phenomenon. In simple terms, if the dominant nexus for understanding ICs has been law and politics, most of the cited sociological studies are highly evocative of how ICs can be studied using a different nexus consisting of law, politics, *and* society. In many ways this is illustrative of the very core of the sociology of law – both at its genesis and in its modern incarnation. Law and its institutions are, to paraphrase Lawrence Friedman, too important to be left to either lawyers or political scientists. While law is clearly both legal and political, it is at the end of the day also deeply societal. Roger Cotterell has made a very convincing case for viewing law in this manner in his numerous publications. I am merely repeating what he taught us a long time ago and applying it to a relatively new object of study.

Bibliography

Alter, K.A. 2001. *Establishing the Supremacy of European Law: The Making of an International Rule of Law in Europe*. Oxford, Oxford University Press.

Alter, K.A. 2009. *The European Court's Political Power. Selected Essays*. Oxford, Oxford University Press.

Alter, K.A. 2014 (forthcoming). *The New Terrain of International Law: International Courts in International Politics*. Princeton, Princeton University Press.

Bogdandy, A. von and Venzke, I. 2013. 'On the Functions of International Courts: An Appraisal in Light of Their Burgeoning Public Authority'. 26 *Leiden Journal of International Law* 49.

Boli, J. and Thomas, G.M. 1997. 'World Culture in the World Polity: A Century of International Non-Governmental Organization'. 62 *American Sociological Review* 171.

Bredemaier, H.C. 1962. 'Law as an Integrative Mechanism'. In Evan, W.M. (ed.), *Law and Sociology: Exploratory Essays*. New York: Free Press.

Bourdieu, P. 1987. 'The Force of Law: Toward a Sociology of the Juridical Field'. 38 *Hastings Law Journal* 805.

Bourdieu, P. 1991. *Language and Symbolic Power.* Cambridge, Harvard University Press.

Chimni, B.S. 1999. 'Marxism and International Law: A Contemporary Analysis'. 34 *Economic and Political Weekly* 337.

Cohen, A. 2007. 'Constitutionalism Without Constitution: Transnational Elites Between Political Mobilization and Legal Expertise in the Making of a Constitution for Europe (1940s–1960s)'. 32 *Law and Social Inquiry* 109.

Cohen, A. and Madsen, M.R. 2007. 'Cold War Law: Legal Entrepreneurs and the Emergence of a European Legal Field (1945–1965)'. In Gessner, V. and Nelken, D. (eds), *European Ways of Law: Towards a European Sociology of Law.* Oxford, Hart Publishing, ch. 6.

Condé, P-Y. 2012. *Des juges à La Haye. Formation d'une judiciabilité universaliste, des amis de la paix à la lutte contre l'impunité.* Paris, École Normale Supérieure de Cachan.

Cotterrell, R. 1984/1992. *The Sociology of Law: An Introduction.* London, Butterworths.

Cotterrell, R. 1999. *Emile Durkheim: Law in a Moral Domain.* Standford, Stanford University Press.

Dezalay, Y. 2004. Les courtiers de l'international: Héritiers cosmopolites, mercenaires de l'impérialisme et missionnaires de l'universel. 151–2 *Actes de la recherche en sciences sociales* 5.

Dezalay, Y. and Garth, B.G. 1996. *Dealing in Virtue. International Commercial Arbitration and the Construction of a Transnational Legal Order.* Chicago, University of Chicago Press.

Dezalay, Y. and Garth, B.G. 2002. *The Internationalization of Palace Wars: Lawyers, Economists, and the Contest to Transform Latin American States.* Chicago, University of Chicago Press.

Dezalay, Y. and Garth, B.G. 2010. *Asian Legal Revivals: Lawyers in the Shadow of Empire.* Chicago, University of Chicago Press.

Dezalay, Y. and Madsen, M.R. 2012. 'The Force of Law and Lawyers: Pierre Bourdieu and the Reflexive Sociology of Law'. 8 *Annual Review of Law and Social Science* 433.

Dezalay, Y. and Sugarman, D. (eds) 1995. *Professional Competition and Professional Power: Lawyers, Accountants and the Social Construction of Markets.* London, Routledge.

DiMaggio, P.J. and Powell, W.W. 1983. 'The Iron Cage Revisited: Institutional Isomorphism and Collective Rationality in Organizational Fields'. 48 *American Sociological Review* 147.

Durkheim, E. 1893. *De la division du travail social: étude sur l'organisation des sociétés supérieures.* Paris, Alcan.

Emirbayer, M. and Johnson, V. 2008. 'Bourdieu and Organizational Analysis'. 37 *Theory and Society* 1.

Habermas, J. 1992. *Faktizität und Geltung: Beiträge zur Diskurstheorie des Rechts und des demokratischen Rechtsstaats.* Frankfurt am Main, Suhrkamp Verlag.

Hagan, J. 2003. *Justice in the Balkans. Prosecuting War Crimes in the Hague Tribunal.* Chicago, University of Chicago Press.

Hagan, J. and Levi, R. 2005. 'Crimes of War and the Force of Law'. 83 *Social Forces* 1499.

Halliday, S. and Schmidt, P. 2009. *Conducting Law and Society Research: Reflections on methods and Practices.* Cambridge, Cambridge University Press.

Hewa, S. 1988. 'The Genesis of Max Weber's "Verstehende Soziologie"'. 31 *Acta Sociologica* 143.

Ivkovich, S.K. and Hagan, J. 2008. 'La politique de punition et le siège de Sarajevo: Vers une application de la théorie du conflit à la perception d'une (in)justice internationale'. 3 *Actes de la recherche en sciences sociales* 62.

Koremenos, B., Lipson, C. and Snidal, D. 2001. 'The Rational Design of International Institutions'. 55 *International Organization* 761.

Koskenniemi, M. et al. 2002. 'Fragmentation of International Law? Postmodern Anxieties'. 15 *Leiden Journal of International Law* 553.

Latour, B. 2002. *La fabrique du droit: Une ethnographie du Conseil d'État.* Paris, La Découverte.

Lauterpacht, H. 1933. *The Function of Law in the International Community.* Oxford, Oxford University Press.

Lechner, F.J. and Boli, J. 2005. *World Culture. Origins and Consequences.* Oxford, Blackwell.
Luhmann, N. 1993. *Das Recht der Gesellschaft.* Frankfurt am Main, Suhrkamp.
Madsen, M.R. 2010. *La genèse de l'Europe des droits de l'homme: Enjeux juridiques et stratégies d'Etat (France, Grande-Bretagne et pays scandinaves, 1945–1970).* Strasbourg, Presses universitaires de Strasbourg.
Madsen, M.R. 2011a. 'Legal Diplomacy – Law, Politics and the Genesis of Postwar European Human Rights'. In Hoffmann, S.L. (ed.), *Human Rights in the Twentieth Century: A Critical History.* Cambridge, Cambridge University Press.
Madsen, M.R. 2011b. 'The Protracted Institutionalisation of the Strasbourg Court: From Legal Diplomacy to Integrationist Jurisprudence'. In Madsen, M.R. and Christoffersen, J. (eds), *The European Court of Human Rights between Law and Politics.* Oxford, Oxford University Press.
Madsen, M.R. 2011c. 'The Geopolitics of European Law: The ECtHR, the ECJ and the Foundation of the European Legal Field (1950–1980)'. Law and Society Annual Conference, 2011.
Madsen, M.R. 2012. 'Explaining the Power of International Courts in Their Context: From Legitimacy to Legitimization'. RSCAS Policy Paper (Courts, Social Change and Judicial Independence) 7.
Madsen, M.R. 2013. 'Sociological Approaches to International Courts'. In Alter, K. et al. (eds), *Oxford Handbook of International Adjudication.* Oxford, Oxford University Press.
Merton, R.K. 1949. *Social Theory and Social Structure.* New York, Simon & Schuster.
Meyer, J.W. 2010. 'World Society, Institutional Theories, and the Actor'. 36 *Annual Review of Sociology* 1.
Münch, R. 2008. 'Constructing a European Society by Jurisdiction'. 14 *European Law Journal* 519.
Parsons, T. 1962. 'The Law and Social Control'. In Evan, W.M. (ed.), *Law and Sociology: Exploratory Essays.* New York, Free Press.
Rasmussen, M. 2008. 'The Origins of a Legal Revolution: The Early History of the European Court of Justice'. 14:2 *Journal of European Integration History* 77.
Santos, B. de Sousa. 1995. *Toward a New Common Sense: Law, Science and Politics in the Paradigmatic Transition.* London, Routledge.
Sassen, S. 2006. *Territory, Authority, Rights: From Medieval to Global Assemblages.* Princeton, Princeton University Press.
Serrousi, J. 2012. 'The Cause of Universal Jurisdiction: The Rise and Fall of an International Mobilisation'. In Dezalay, Y. and Garth, B.G. (eds), *Lawyers and the Construction of Transnational Justice.* London, Routledge, ch. 3.
Shany,Y. 2012. 'Assessing the Effectiveness of International Courts: A Goal-Based Approach'. 106 *American Journal of Internatioanl Law* 225.
Stichweh, R. 2000. *Die Weltgesellschaft: Soziologische Analysen.* Frankfurt am Main, Suhrkamp.
Terris, D., Romano, C.P.R. and Swigart, L. 2007. *The International Judge: An Introduction to the Men and Women Who Decide the World's Cases.* Oxford, Oxford University Press.
Teubner, G. 2012. *Constitutional Fragments: Societal Constitutionalism and Globalization.* Oxford, Oxford University Press.
Thornhill, C. 2012. 'The Formation of a European Constitution: An Approach from Historical-Political Sociology'. 8 *International Journal of Law in Context* 354.
Vauchez, A. 2010. 'The Transnational Politics of Judicialization. *Van Gend En Loos* and the Making of EU Polity'. 16 *European Law Journal* 1.
Wallerstein, I. 1974. *The Modern World-System I: Capitalist Agriculture and and the Origins of the European World-Economy in the Sixteenth Century.* New York, Academic Press.
Weber, M. 1980. *Wirtschaft und Gesellschaft. Grundriss der verstehenden Soziologie.* Tübingen, Mohr.

Chapter 15

From Legal Pluralism to Global Legal Pluralism

Paul Schiff Berman[1]

1. Introduction

Legal pluralists have long recognized that societies consist of multiple overlapping normative communities. These communities are sometimes state-based but sometimes not, and they are sometimes formal, official and governmental, but again sometimes they are not. Scholars studying interactions among these multiple communities have often used the term 'legal pluralism' to describe the inevitable intermingling of these normative systems.[2] The study of plural normative systems has arisen from a variety of different scholarly traditions. Perhaps the earliest studies of the clashes between state and non-state authority were those penned by lawyers, philosophers and theologians interested in the respective realms of Church and State authority (see, e.g., Figgis 1913). Likewise, historians analyzing the regulatory role of non-state entities such as jockey clubs and stock exchanges noted that these entities often wield more power than formal state law (see, e.g., Maitland 1936). Anthropologists used the idea of legal pluralism to conceptualize the relationship between colonial and indigenous legal systems (see, e.g., Pospisil 1981). And social norms theorists (see, e.g., Ellickson 1991) and scholars in behavioural law and economics (see, e.g., Jolls et al. 1998) have become interested in forms of informal law that often regulate behaviour as much or more than official governmental pronouncements.

In recent years, a new application of pluralist insights has emerged in the international and transnational realm. This new legal pluralism research was born in the decades following the collapse of the bi-polar Cold War order in 1989. During this period, it became clear that a single-minded focus on state-to-state relations or universal overarching norms was inadequate to describe the reality of the emerging global legal system, with its web of jurisdictional assertions by state, international and non-state normative communities. As one commenter puts it:

> The nation-state and the interstate system are the central political forms of the capitalist world system, and they will probably remain so for the foreseeable future. What has happened, however, is that they have become an inherently contested terrain, and this is the central new fact on which the analysis must focus: the state and the interstate system as complex social fields in which state and nonstate, local and global social relations interact, merge and conflict in dynamic and even volatile combinations. (Santos 2002: 94)

---

1 Some of the material in this chapter is derived from Berman 2012 and 2009.

2 The history of 'legal pluralism' is a matter of debate. Some associate the term with legal anthropology (see, e.g., Tamanaha 1993; Merry 1988), while others (see, e.g., Benda-Beckmann 1997) trace the use of the term to lawyers (Hooker 1975). Still others see legal pluralism deriving from Church/State conflicts-of-law analysis (see, e.g., Galanter 1981: 28). For discussions of the history of 'legal pluralism', see Benda-Beckmann 1997; De Sousa Santos 1987; Griffiths 1986; Merry 1988; Tamanaha, 1993; Vanderlinden 1989.

Legal pluralism provided a useful alternative framework because pluralism had always sought to identify hybrid legal spaces, where multiple normative systems occupied the same social field. And though pluralists had often focused on clashes *within* one geographical area, where formal bureaucracies encountered indigenous ethnic, tribal, institutional or religious norms, the pluralist framework proved highly adaptive to analysis of the hybrid legal spaces created by a different set of overlapping jurisdictional assertions (state v. state; state v. international body; state v. non-state entity) in the global arena.[3]

An emphasis on legal pluralism also freed scholars from endless intractable debates about whether international law is truly law given that coercive enforcement power in the international and transnational arena is often indirect or non-existent. Such debates had created stagnation in the international law and international relations literature as both international law triumphalists and nation-state sovereigntists talked past each other with either an overly formalist faith in international law's inherent authority, on the one hand, or an overly formalist rejection of any law beyond the nation-state, on the other.

Global legal pluralism applies the insights of socio-legal scholarship and turns the gaze away from abstract questions of legitimacy and towards empirical questions of efficacy. Thus, pluralists deemphasize the supposed distinctions between a norm, a custom, a law, a moral command, a sociological consensus, a psychological imperative or the like. Instead, a pluralist approach focuses on whether people in actual practice perceive such legal or quasi-legal commands to be binding, whether such commands seep into consciousness over time, and whether the existence of these alternative norms alter the power dynamics or options placed on the table in policy discussions. Finally, global legal pluralism has both a descriptive and normative component. Anthropologists and historians have generally framed the study of legal pluralism in descriptive terms. Accordingly, they have catalogued the inevitable hybridity that arises when two legal or quasi-legal systems occupy the same social space, as well as the resulting strategic interactions that occur among actors in navigating the multiple regimes. As a descriptive enterprise, legal pluralism is relatively uncontroversial. After all, even the most die-hard sovereigntist would likely acknowledge that sub-, supra-, or non-state normative systems do impose real constraints that have real impacts. More controversial is the idea that legal pluralism might be a normatively desirable approach to the design of legal systems.

As a normative project, legal pluralism can be seen to support two different strategies. First, what we might call substantive legal pluralism seeks accommodation of alternative norms, at least in certain delineated spheres. This is more of a multiculturalist project, and for purposes of this chapter I will set it aside. Second, a more proceduralist vision of legal pluralism aims to design procedural mechanisms, institutions and discursive practices that seek to manage pluralism, without making a priori substantive decisions regarding when deference to alternative norms is appropriate and when it is not. This proceduralist version of legal pluralism's normative project argues that the mechanisms, institutions and practices that result may at times be preferable to either sovereigntist territorialism on the one hand, or universal harmonization on the other. Moreover, such a proceduralist version of legal pluralism, unlike the substantive version, need not commit one to a programme of inevitable deference even to illiberal norms. Nevertheless, this proceduralist approach, precisely because it refuses to engage with some of the most contentious

3 In that sense, we might more accurately refer to the 'global legal system' as a 'multiscalar legal system'. For example, Hari Osofsky 2007 has argued that the term 'multiscalar' more accurately captures the variety of normative communities with input at different 'levels' of the legal hierarchy than does the word 'global'.

substantive political battles over when deference is appropriate and when it is impossible, may be distrusted or rejected by those on both sides of the pluralism debate who want more substantive normative certainty.

Among his many other accomplishments as a legal theorist, Roger Cotterrell was one of the first scholars to recognize this pluralism in the sub-national, trans-national and supra-national legal arena (Cotterrell (1995), at 281). And more than simply recognize the phenomena, he made two distinct contributions that have provided a touchstone for subsequent scholars. First, he offered a far more flexible and capacious definition of law – law as institutionalized doctrine – than is typical among legal theorists, but one that is not so capacious that it falls victim to the concern that any normative assertion will be deemed to be law (Cotterrell 1995: at 31–2). Thus, for legal pluralists sceptical of formalist definitions of law, but worried that having no working definition will be problematic, Cotterrell's approach provides a crucial building block. Second, Cotterrell (2006) developed a typology of types of community: instrumental, traditional, belief- or values-based and affective. In a world of legal pluralism, different normative communities vie for authority, and though we are accustomed to defining legal communities solely by reference to territory, there are numerous reasons why such a community definition is unsatisfying (see Berman 2002). In contrast, Cotterrell's typology of community provides flexibility and space for rethinking rigid legal categories. Accordingly, Cotterrell's contributions to the global legal pluralist framework are significant and likely to be influential for many years to come.

In honour of Roger, then, I seek in this chapter to summarize and further refine the move from legal pluralism to global legal pluralism by discussing each component of the inquiry further: in what way is global legal pluralism 'global'; in what way 'legal'; and in what way 'pluralist'? This analysis prompts investigation both of challenges to the global legal pluralist project as well as possible responses to those challenges.

2. Is Global Legal Pluralism Global?

The word 'global' – along with its related word 'globalization' – has been widely used in recent decades to describe the post-Cold War era, but it is fair to say that there is no clear consensus on what we mean when we use the word. For example, if by 'global' we mean only the legal rules governing relations among territorially distinct nation-states, we could use the tried and true word 'international' and speak of international legal pluralism. In contrast, if we mean to invoke a single set of norms or procedures applicable around the globe, what we really mean is a kind of universalism or a unitary set of principles, and we might call it 'universal' legal pluralism (which is likely an oxymoron). The question therefore is whether the word 'global' captures something essential that would otherwise be missed.

I think it does. Indeed, global legal pluralism occupies a crucial cosmopolitan middle ground between what we might call sovereigntist territorialism on the one hand, and universalism on the other. Thus, neither 'international' nor 'universal' fits the bill. It is worth taking a moment to understand why. Recall that the central insight of global legal pluralism is that we live in a world of hybrid legal spaces, where multiple normative regimes may govern (or at least strongly influence) our activities and authority tends to be relative, not absolute. For example, the growth of global communications technologies, the rise of multinational corporate entities with no significant territorial centre of gravity, and the mobility of capital and people across borders mean that many jurisdictions will feel effects of activities around the globe, leading inevitably to multiple assertions of legal authority over the same act, without regard to territorial location.

The problem of multiple states' asserting jurisdiction over the same activity is just the tip of the iceberg, however, because nation-states must also often share legal authority with one or more international and regional courts, tribunals or regulatory entities. Indeed, there are now over a hundred international courts and tribunals, all issuing decisions that have some effect on state legal authority, though those decisions are sometimes deemed binding, sometimes merely persuasive and often fall somewhere between the two. Finally, non-state legal (or quasi-legal) norms add to the hybridity. Given increased migration and global communication, it is not surprising that people feel ties to, and act on the basis of affiliations with, multiple communities in addition to their territorial ones. Such communities may be ethnic, religious or epistemic; transnational, subnational or international; and the norms asserted by such communities frequently challenge territorially based authority.

Sovereigntist territorialism represents a retreat from this messy hybrid world of multiple overlapping normative authority. Instead, the state-centric view of the world rests on the convenient fiction that nation-states exist in autonomous, territorially distinct, spheres and that activities therefore fall under the legal jurisdiction of only one regime at a time. Thus, traditional legal rules have tied jurisdiction to territory: a state could exercise complete authority within its territorial borders and no authority beyond it. In the twentieth century, such rules were loosened, but territorial location has remained the principal touchstone for assigning legal authority. Accordingly, if one could spatially ground a dispute, one could most likely determine the legal rule that would apply. But consider such a system in today's world. Should the US government be able to sidestep the US Constitution when it houses prisoners in 'offshore' detention facilities in Guantánamo Bay or elsewhere around the world? Should spatially distant corporations that create serious local harms be able to escape local legal regulation simply because they are not physically located in the jurisdiction? How can we best understand the complex relationships among international, regional, national, and subnational legal systems? Does it make sense to think that satellite transmissions, online interactions and complex financial transactions have any territorial locus at all? When the US government seeks to shut down the computer of a hacker located in Russia, does the virus transmitted constitute an act of war or a violation of Russia's sovereignty? And in a world where non-state actors such as industry standard-setting bodies, non-governmental organizations, religious institutions, ethnic groups, terrorist networks and others exert significant normative pull, can we build a sufficiently capacious understanding of the very idea of jurisdiction to address the incredible array of overlapping authorities that are our daily reality?

Thus, a simple model that looks only to territorial delineations among official state-based legal systems is now simply untenable (if it was ever useful to begin with). Thankfully, debates about globalization have moved beyond the polarizing question of whether the nation-state is dying or not. But one does not need to believe in the death of the nation-state to recognize both that physical location can no longer be the sole criterion for conceptualizing legal authority and that nation-states must work within a framework of multiple overlapping jurisdictional assertions by state, international and even non-state communities. Each of these types of overlapping jurisdictional assertions creates a potentially hybrid legal space that is not easily eliminated. The influence and application of foreign norms or foreign decision-making bodies may be useful and productive or alien and threatening, but in any event they are inevitable and cannot be willed away by fiat.

Moreover, global legal pluralism recognizes the possibility that at least sometimes this pluralism of normative authority may be *preferable* to a system that imposes a single authority because the reality of legal pluralism empowers individuals to strategically operate among normative and procedural regimes. In a world of multiple overlapping legal and quasi-legal systems, there are always multiple ports of entry. An argument unheard in one forum can gain traction in another. A norm articulated in one place can be persuasive elsewhere. The powerless in one system can access power in another. As Robert Cover (1981) recognized decades ago, there are inherent advantages to a system 'that permits tensions and conflicts of the social order' to be played out in the overlapping jurisdictional structure of the system itself. Of course, powerful repeat players can also strategically use such a plural system to shop for desired norms. Thus, the mere existence of global legal pluralism does not magically level the playing field among parties of disparate power or render such power disparities irrelevant. But there can be little doubt that jurisdictional pluralism opens up discursive space, providing opportunities for agency that may not have existed previously.

As with sovereigntist territorialism, universalism also represents a retreat from the hybrid legal spaces of a pluralist world. Here, instead of responding to normative difference by seeking to impose a single local authority, we see the desire to erase normative difference altogether. Indeed, international legal theory has long yearned for an overarching set of commitments that would establish a more peaceful and harmonious global community. This supposed new world order variously focuses on the religiously-based natural law principles of international human rights or the neoliberal ideology of free trade and its need to harmonize rules that regulate commerce.

One cannot discount the importance of universalism. Certainly since World War II we have seen the creation of a dizzying array of international institutions, multilateral and bilateral treaties, conventions, cross-border regulatory coordination efforts, and the like. In one way or another, all of this activity represents the desire to harmonize conflicting norms. And on many fronts, both in public and private law, norms are in fact converging to a degree, whether through hegemonic imposition or global embrace. Moreover, such harmonization has important benefits because it tends to lower transaction costs and uncertainty as to what norms will be applied to any given activity. Yet, there are reasons to question both the desirability and – more importantly – the feasibility of universalism, at least in some contexts. This is because universalism is based on the premise that people are fundamentally the same despite differences in culture and circumstance. In contrast legal pluralism, founded as it is on anthropological observation (and celebration) of cultural difference, rejects the idea that we should ever expect or necessarily encourage uniformity. From such a perspective, universalism's efforts to dissolve the multi-rootedness of community affiliation into one overarching identity is inherently problematic because it fails to capture the extreme emotional ties people still feel to distinct national or local communities. As Thomas Franck (1996: 374) put it, 'The powerful pull of loyalty exerted by the imagined nation demonstrates that, even in the age of science, a loyalty system based on romantic myths of shared history and kinship has a capacity to endure'. This is what universalism tends to ignore: the very attachments people hold most deeply.

In addition, universalism inevitably erases diversity. Indeed, the whole point of a universalist or harmonization solution is to combat diversity or fragmentation. Yet, although one can appreciate the goal, erasing diversity may involve the silencing of less powerful voices in the global conversation. Thus, the presumed universal may also be the hegemonic. This argument is most often heard by those who resist international human rights norms because they may run roughshod over important local practices, customs or perspectives. For example, in response to the presumed universality of the Universal Declaration of Human Rights, some scholars wonder what such a declaration can mean 'in a universe of competing values and moralities? Is there an objective technique for evaluating systems of morals and cultures? Given the specificity of cultural standards and values, and given the predisposition of human beings to generalize from their situated perspectives and realities, how can we ensure that our presumptions and assertions of universality are not veiled projections onto others of our moral categories?' (Obiora 1997: 277–8). Such arguments have arisen most famously in debates about eradicating the practice of female genital cutting, practiced in many communities on the African continent. On the one hand, many condemn and combat the practice as a violation of women's human rights. At the same time, others suggest that such a position fails to understand the local meaning of the practice. As one scholar argues, 'In the eyes of the Neo-Agrarian cultures of today's Africa, the customary ritual practices of both male and female circumcision are seeable by their practitioners as the supernaturally prescribed, and therefore, indispensable condition of being human' (Wynter 1997: 504–5). Thus, critics contend that the presumed universal tends to become a western or northern imperialist imposition on less powerful communities. In this debate we see replayed the insistence on universal imposition on the one hand and the pristine integrity of the local community on the other. Both positions are retreats from hybridity. In contrast, a global legal pluralist vision focuses on the interactions between these two positions: the ways in which local actors deploy the universalist language of human rights to advance positions strategically, the ways in which so-called local voices interact with seemingly international ones to create change to internationalist regimes and assumptions, and so on. Only through this sort of interactive vision can we avoid reifying either the universal or the local. The word global invokes this multi-rooted process rather than dissolving it into sovereigntist localism or universalism.

3. Is Global Legal Pluralism About Law?

Most critical resistance to legal pluralism has historically revolved around the concern that pluralism's capaciousness as an analytical approach renders it unhelpful because it does not offer a definition of where law begins and ends or how to differentiate law from normative pronouncements that are not law. In this debate, we see that one of the strengths of legal pluralism – decoupling the idea of law from governmental power – becomes a liability. Nevertheless, I think a strong argument can be made that, especially in the context of *global* legal pluralism, the usefulness outweighs the liability. This is because international law debates are often sidetracked by abstract questions regarding whether legal norms asserted by non-nation-state actors are sufficiently law-like to be worthy of attention. Such legal norms might be expressed by nation-states seeking to impose norms extraterritorially, or they might be promulgated by international bodies, or by private non-state entities or multinational corporations. But regardless of the source, much is lost if we try to cabin the study of law on the global scene only to the official pronouncements of nation-states backed by the threat of coercive force. The enforcement power of a norm matters, of course, and power disparities matter as well. But we are unlikely to understand the evolving system of transnational norm creation unless we expand our definition of law.

Legal (or quasi-legal) norms have real impact even in the absence of enforcement power for at least three reasons. First, even if one focuses on state actors pursuing their own interests, those state interests do not exist independently of the social context within which they are formed. Indeed, a policymaker's idea of what is in the state's interest is always and necessarily affected by ideas of appropriate action. And these ideas, in turn, are likely to be shaped – even if unconsciously – by legal norms, including the norms of non-state or international law. Moreover, such government officials, especially in a democracy, are at least somewhat responsive to popular opinion, and such opinion is also likely to be shaped by a variety of forces, again including the moral pull of non-state or international legal norms. As socio-legal scholars have long described, legal norms can effect changes in legal consciousness that in turn alter the categories of our thought, such that they help determine what we are likely to see as a viable policy option in the first place. Accordingly, coercive power is not the only way that law can have an effect, either domestically or internationally. As Martha Finnemore (1996: 15) has noted, '[s]ocially constructed rules, principles, norms of behavior, and shared beliefs may provide states, individuals, and other actors with understandings of what is important or valuable and what are effective and/or legitimate means of obtaining those valued goods'. As a result, law has an impact not merely (or perhaps even primarily) because it keeps us from doing what we want. Rather, law changes what we want in the first place.

In this respect, legal pluralism research can be useful, because it analyzes how the existence of legal or quasi-legal norms changes legal consciousness over time. Legal consciousness scholars have sought to study empirically just how it is that legal categories become reflected in ordinary discourse and thought. Indeed, such scholars have argued that law operates as much by influencing modes of thought as by determining conduct in any specific case (e.g., Bumiller 1988: 30–32; Ewick and Silbey 1998; McCann 1994: 7; Merry 1990; Silbey 1992: 42). Law is a constitutive part of culture, shaping and determining social relations and providing 'a distinctive manner of imagining the real' (Geertz 1983: 173). For example, '[l]ong before we ever think about going to a courtroom, we encounter landlords and tenants, husbands and wives, barkeeps and hotel guests – roles that already embed a variety of juridical notions' (Sarat and Simon 2001: 20). Indeed, we cannot escape the categories and discourses that law supplies. These categories may include ideas of what is public and what is private, who is an employer and who is an employee, what precautions are 'reasonable', who has 'rights', and so on. In short, 'it is just about impossible to describe any set of "basic" social practices without describing the legal relations among the people involved – legal relations that don't simply condition how the people relate to each other but to an important extent define the constitutive terms of the relationship ...' (Gordon 1984: 103). Because legal categories and ideas suffuse social life, scholars have studied both how people think about the law and the ways in which largely inchoate ideas about the law can affect decisions they make. Sally Engle Merry observes legal consciousness in 'the way people conceive of the "natural" and normal way of doing things, their habitual patterns of talk and action, and their commonsense understanding of the world' (Merry 1990: 5). These understandings are often taken for granted. This is because legal consciousness may be so much a part of an individual's worldview that it is present even when 'law' is seemingly absent from an understanding or construction of life events. Thus, '[w]e are not merely the inert recipients of law's external pressures. Rather, we have imbibed law's images and meanings so that they seem our own' (Sarat and Kearns 1993: 29). Law is an often unnoticed, but nonetheless constitutive shaper of experience.

Of course, it is difficult to isolate or prove the precise impact of legal consciousness. Yet, the mere fact that changes in legal consciousness are difficult to quantify and predict does not render them any less important in analyzing state behaviour concerning international or transnational law. Indeed, there are simply too many instances when we do see state actors internalize the norms of international law to dismiss them as flukes or explain them away as mere strategic behaviour. Perhaps the best-known example of a change in international legal consciousness concerns the very idea of crimes against humanity. At the time of the Nuremberg prosecutions, it was not at all clear that the pre-war atrocities committed by the German government against German citizens constituted an international crime punishable outside Germany itself (Orentlicher 1991: 2555). Yet, the statute of the Nuremberg tribunal and the decisions of the tribunal effectively established such a crime. Then, subsequent to Nuremberg, almost every state for the first time voluntarily subjected itself to the Genocide Convention, further enshrining the idea that individuals might have international rights against their own nation-states. Today, this idea is sufficiently well accepted that we commonly see international prosecutions for crimes against humanity committed within state borders, and the International Criminal Court has jurisdiction over such crimes. Significantly, though the US has not ratified the International Criminal Court statute, the basic idea of a crime against humanity under international law is no longer seriously in doubt, signifying an important shift from World War II to the present day.

Just as importantly, it is sometimes not that an international regime is constraining states but that the regime creates the impetus for action in the first place. For example: Prior to the actions of UNESCO, most states, especially less developed countries, had no notion that they needed or wanted a state science bureaucracy. Similarly, European heads of state were not particularly concerned about treatment of the war wounded until Henri Dunant and the International Committee of the Red Cross made it an issue. Global poverty alleviation, while long considered desirable in the abstract, was not considered a pressing responsibility of states, particularly of developed states, until the World Bank under Robert McNamara made it a necessary part of development (Finnemore 1996: 12). Thus, the persuasive power of international norms caused states to develop interests they might not otherwise have had. In these instances, international law is shaping the consciousness of state actors, not operating through coercive restraint. Similarly, as Thomas Berger (1998) argues, in Germany and Japan today, antimilitarism is as crucial to national identity as militarism was in the World War II era. These are changes in the states' conceptions of their own interests, influenced by the international legal regime that Germany in particular has long championed.

Thus, we imbibe legal norms and cognitive categories even when we are not consciously aware of the norm in question. We are persuaded by legal norms even when those norms are not literally enforceable. We act in accordance with law because doing so has become habitual, not because we seek to avoid sanction. We conceive of our interrelations with others in terms of law because our long-term interests require that we do so, even when our short-term interest might seem to counsel otherwise. And the existence of a legal norm alters the constitutive terms of our relationships with others as well as the costs of noncompliance. All of these factors may be overcome in some circumstances. Indeed, people sometimes violate domestic law just as states sometimes violate international law. But in neither case does that mean that the law in question has no significant constraining force. And only by thinking more broadly about changes in legal consciousness and the complicated social, political and psychological factors that enter into the conceptualization of state interests can we begin to understand how international or non-state law operates.

Second, legal or quasi-legal norms have impact on states even absent enforcement power because states are not monolithic entities with a single, definable set of interests. Instead, states are made up of multiple bureaucrats with various spheres of authority, political ideologies, institutional loyalties and interests that range from the goal of re-election, to the need to curry favour with particular interest groups, to the aim of career advancement. And that is not even counting the myriad forces outside of government – NGOs, editorial writers, campaign contributors, political movements and so on – that all exert influence on government actors and all may themselves be influenced by and may consciously deploy the norms of international, transnational, and non-state legal norms in order to press varying agendas. For example, although the celebrated efforts of Spanish Judge Baltasar Garzón to try former Chilean leader Augusto Pinochet were not literally 'successful' because Pinochet was never extradited to Spain, they strengthened the hands of human rights advocates within Chile itself and provided the impetus for a movement that led to a Chilean Supreme Court decision stripping Pinochet of his lifetime immunity. Likewise, Spanish efforts to prosecute members of the Argentine military bolstered reformers within the Argentine government, most notably then-President Nestor Kirschner. In August 2003, Judge Garzón sought extradition from Argentina of dozens of Argentines for human rights abuses committed under the

Argentine military government in the 1970s. In addition, Garzón successfully sought extradition from Mexico of one former Argentine Navy lieutenant who was accused of murdering hundreds of people. In the wake of Garzón's actions, realist observers complained that such transnational prosecutions were illegitimate because Argentina had previously conferred amnesty on those who had been involved in the period of military rule and therefore any prosecution would infringe on Argentina's sovereign 'choice' to grant amnesty (Rivkin and Casey 2003).

But the amnesty decision was not simply a unitary choice made by some unified 'state' of Argentina; it was a politically contested act that remained controversial within the country. And the Spanish extradition request itself gave President Kirschner more leverage in his tug-of-war with the legal establishment over the amnesty laws. Just a month after Garzón's request, both houses of the Argentine Congress voted by large majorities to annul the laws. Meanwhile the Spanish government decided that it would not make the formal extradition request to Argentina that Garzón sought, but it did so based primarily on the fact that Argentina had begun to scrap its amnesty laws and the accused would therefore be subject to domestic human rights prosecution. President Kirshner therefore could use Spain's announcement to increase pressure on the Argentine Supreme Court to officially overturn the amnesty laws. Finally, on 14 June 2005, the Argentine Supreme Court did in fact strike down the amnesty laws, thus clearing the way for domestic human rights prosecutions. Not only was the pressure exerted by Spain instrumental in these efforts, but it is significant that the Argentine Court cited as legal precedent a 2001 decision of the Inter-American Court of Human Rights striking down a similar amnesty provision in Peru as incompatible with the American Convention on Human Rights and hence without legal effect. So, in the end, the 'sovereign' state of Argentina made political and legal choices to repeal the amnesty laws just as it had previously made choices to create them. But in this change of heart we can see the degree to which international legal pronouncements, even if they are without any literal constraining effect, may significantly alter the domestic political terrain.

Likewise, official international institutions, such as the United Nations, can also pressure local bureaucracies by creating international commissions of inquiry concerning alleged atrocities, or by threatening prosecutions in international courts. Such declarations can empower reformers within local bureaucracies, who can then argue for institutional changes as a way of staving off international interference. For example, in the aftermath of the violence in East Timor that followed its vote for independence, there were grave concerns that the Indonesian government would not pursue human rights investigations of the military personnel allegedly responsible for the violence (Dickinson 2003a). Accordingly, an International Commission of Inquiry was established, and UN officials warned that an international court might be necessary. As with Chile and Argentina, such actions strengthened the hand of reformers within Indonesia, such as then-Attorney General Marzuki Darusman. With the spectre of international action hanging over Indonesia, Darusman made several statements arguing that, for nationalist reasons, a hard-hitting Indonesian investigation was necessary in order to forestall an international takeover of the process. Not surprisingly, when this international pressure dissipated after the terrorist attacks of 11 September 2001, so did the momentum to provide real accountability in Indonesia for the atrocities committed. Thus, we can again see that international legal activity (or the lack of it) alters the domestic terrain.

Indeed, even in the United States, the Oklahoma Court of Criminal Appeals stayed an execution in 2004 based in part on a prior decision of the International Court of Justice concerning the Vienna Convention on Diplomatic Relations, despite the fact that the international court had no means of literally enforcing its decision in Oklahoma (Berman 2007). And in the trade context, although ad hoc tribunals convened under Chapter 11 of the North American Free Trade Agreement (NAFTA) have no authority to directly reverse the decisions of national courts or create formally binding precedent, Robert Ahdieh (2004) has argued that, over time, we may see the interactions between the NAFTA panels and national courts take on a dialectical quality that is neither the direct hierarchical review traditionally undertaken by appellate courts, nor simply the dialogue that often occurs under the doctrine of comity. Instead, Ahdieh predicts that international courts are likely to exert an important influence even as the national courts retain formal independence, much as US federal courts exercising habeas corpus jurisdiction may influence state court interpretations of US constitutional norms in criminal cases. In turn, decisions of national courts may also come to influence international tribunals. This dialectical relationship, if it emerges, will exist without an official hierarchical relationship based on coercive power.

There can also be little doubt that local actors, outside of official government bureaucracies or judicial institutions, can at times leverage international and transnational legal norms to press causes within their countries.[4] For example, as late as 1994 women in Hong Kong were unable to inherit land. That year a group of rural indigenous women joined forces with urban women's groups to demand legal change. As detailed by Sally Engle Merry and Rachel Stern (2005: 399), '[t]he indigenous women slowly shifted from seeing their stories as individual kinship violations to broader examples of discrimination'. Ultimately, the women learned to protest these unjust customary laws in the language of international human rights and gender equality. Having done so, they were successful at getting the inheritance rules overturned. While we might regret the fact that these women were forced to 'translate' their grievances into an internationally recognized language in order to be heard, the success of the movement in accessing political power surely attests to the strength and importance of the international law discourse.

Third, it is important to recognize that legal scholars often overestimate the degree to which formal legal pronouncements and institutions actually penetrate social life. As a result, they miss the many sites where the state is non-existent or ignored, or has limited or no power. They also tend to ignore all the coercive systems that get their authority from power centres separate from the state, whether those centres are religious institutions, ethnic or regional clans, or communities of practice. To take an oft-cited example, the international rules governing trade finance are promulgated by a community of bankers with no state involvement at all. Thus, the interaction among plural norms in the global arena cannot simply be viewed as a state pursuing a single set of interests either completely constrained or completely unconstrained by external norms that are either called 'law' or 'not law'. Rather, as part of the multivalent, messy process by which various state constituencies vie to have their preferred policies adopted, alternative legal and quasi-legal norms are a powerful tool, regardless of enforcement power. These norms provide a set of moral, rhetorical and strategic arguments that may empower constituencies that might not otherwise have a voice, or they may be used by already powerful forces to protect their own interests. In any event, only by going beyond a simplistic law/non-law dichotomy can we see the power of global pluralism coursing below the surface of the seemingly all-powerful state system.

---

4 Of course, such local actors do not only 'use' international law as 'given' to them, but also, through their social movements, shape the international legal norms themselves. For an argument that human rights discourse has been fundamentally shaped by Third World resistance to development, see generally Rajagopal 2003.

4. Is Global Legal Pluralism Really Pluralist?

As noted previously, global legal pluralism functions as a middle ground position between sovereigntist territorialism on the one hand, and universalism on the other. As a result, both hard-line sovereigntists and committed international law triumphalists tend to criticize pluralism from their differing perspectives. Sovereigntists think global legal pluralism pays insufficient attention to nation-state prerogatives and is really just universalism in another guise. And universalists tend to view global legal pluralism as giving too much play to parochial local and state-based interests.

So, is global legal pluralism really pluralist, and, if so, what practical benefit does the pluralist approach provide? Given the descriptive reality of global legal pluralism, we should not be at all surprised to find, across a wide variety of doctrinal areas, the development of procedural mechanisms, institutions and discursive practices that attempt to manage the overlapping of legal or quasi-legal communities. Nevertheless, viewing such doctrines through a pluralist lens as a normative matter may offer an important alternative perspective on their efficacy or functionality. Indeed, even if we accept that these mechanisms, institutions and practices are often the product of necessary political compromise between sovereigntist territorialism and universalism, global legal pluralism views these systemic compromises as creating a context for interaction and conversation among multiple constituencies. In consequence, the resulting solution may actually be seen as *better* than if either sovereigntism or universalism had won because it allows for more voices, more input from different perspectives, and more participation from different communities. This pluralist participation may make the resulting decisions more likely to gain support (or at least acquiescence), but the decisions also may be substantively better because more perspectives are included. In any event, it is clear that global legal pluralism offers a distinct perspective that neither sovereigntism nor universalism provides.

Consider two examples to illustrate the point. First, the oft-discussed 'margin of appreciation' doctrine allows the European Court of Human Rights (ECtHR) to pursue a rights agenda while maintaining space for local variation (e.g., Helfer and Slaughter 1997: 316–17). The idea here is to strike a balance between deference to national courts and legislators on the one hand, and maintaining 'European supervision' that 'empower[s the ECtHR] to give the final ruling' on whether a challenged practice is compatible with the Convention, on the other. Thus, the margin of appreciation allows domestic polities some room to manoeuvre in implementing ECtHR decisions in order to accommodate local variation. How big that margin is depends on a number of factors including, for example, the degree of consensus among the member states. Affording this sort of variable margin of appreciation usefully accommodates a limited range of pluralism. It does not permit domestic courts to fully ignore the supranational pronouncement (though domestic courts have sometimes asserted greater independence). Nevertheless, it does allow space for local variation, particularly when the law is in transition or when no consensus exists among member states on a given issue. Moreover, by framing the inquiry as one of local consensus, the margin of appreciation doctrine disciplines the ECtHR and forces it to move incrementally, pushing toward consensus without running too far ahead of it. Finally, the margin of appreciation functions as a signalling mechanism, through which 'the EC[t]HR is able to identify potentially problematic practices for the contracting states before they actually become violations, thereby permitting the states to anticipate that their laws may one day be called into question' (Helfer and Slaughter 1997: 317). And, of course, there is reverse signalling as well, because domestic states, by their societal evolution away from consensus, effectively maintain space for local variation. As Laurence Helfer and Anne-Marie Slaughter (1997: 317) have observed, 'The conjunction of the margin of appreciation doctrine and the consensus inquiry thus permits the EC[t]HR to link its decisions to the pace of change of domestic law, acknowledging the political sovereignty of respondent states while legitimizing its own decisions against them'.

Whereas the margin of appreciation doctrine is a way of working out relationships among different communities, a second example of pluralist procedural doctrines involves hybridizing the decision-making body or process itself. For example, from 1190 until 1870, English law used the so-called 'mixed jury', or 'jury de medietate linguae', with members of two different communities sitting side by side to settle disputes when people from the two communities came into conflict (Constable 1994; Ramirez 1994: 781). Mixed juries were also used in disputes between Jews and Christians, city and country dwellers, and merchants and non-merchants. In the human rights arena, hybrid domestic/international courts continue the tradition of the mixed jury. Such hybrid courts have been employed in transitional justice settings in Kosovo, East Timor, Sierra Leone, and Cambodia. In these courts domestic judges – ideally drawn from the multiple political, racial, or ethnic groups involved in the larger geopolitical conflict – sit alongside international judges, and domestic and international lawyers also work together to prosecute the cases.

Scholars suggest that, at least in theory, hybrid courts hold the promise of addressing some of the problems encountered in post-conflict settings by wholly international courts on the one hand, and wholly domestic courts on the other (Dickinson 2003b). Such problems can be grouped into three categories: legitimacy, capacity building and norm penetration. With regard to legitimacy concerns, the rationale for hybrid courts is largely the same as for mixed juries. If there is broad representation from the various communities involved in the dispute, then the outcome of the trial is more likely to be palatable to a cross-section of the population. Moreover, the presence of judges from the broader international community may contribute to a sense of fairness both for others watching the process from afar and for domestic populations who fear that local judges will rule based on sectarian prejudices. On the other hand, the presence of local judges may protect against rejection of the court as wholly 'foreign', a perception that has, for example, bedevilled the international court for the former Yugoslavia. A hybrid court may therefore be seen as the best available compromise. Turning to capacity building, a hybrid court physically located in the region may be preferable to an international court elsewhere because resources both for physical infrastructure and for training will be more likely to flow into the country. Finally, scholars argue, hybrid courts may help train a cadre of domestic lawyers in international legal standards and give them the tools necessary to develop and adapt those international norms in local settings. Meanwhile, the international actors are more likely to understand better the local nuances that may complicate the application of universal norms. It should be noted that, even if hybrid courts have failed to fully live up to their promise, they may still be preferable to wholly international or wholly domestic courts for many of the reasons set forth above. In any event, a hybrid court will often be the only viable political compromise, reflecting – as with many pluralist solutions – the impracticality of wholly universalist or wholly territorialist responses and the resulting need for some sort of hybrid mechanism. Moreover, as Stephen Krasner (2005: 76) has theorized, the sort of 'shared sovereignty' reflected in the hybrid court structure can be particularly important when domestic institutions are weak because it can 'gird new political structures with more expertise, better-crafted policies, and guarantees against abuses of power'. Following this logic, the Dayton Accords effectively made the Bosnian Constitutional Court a hybrid court, authorizing the President of the European Court of Human Rights to appoint three non-Bosnian judges to the nine-member court. A different kind of hybrid is the Israeli Supreme Court, which has, since its inception, customarily had at least one member who is an expert in Jewish law. Thus, we can see that global legal pluralism does in fact point in a distinctive pluralist direction. As a result, it is a perspective that affords both a way of evaluating existing doctrines and institutions and a way of designing new ones along lines that are distinct from the traditional focus on formal authority, and coercive power.

But is this vision pluralist enough? One might think that there is still too much attention paid to the interaction of formal governmental and juridical actors and institutions. Thus, in the examples above, committed pluralists would decry the relentless reference to official courts, juries, judges, and processes. A truly pluralist account would focus on non-governmental activities as well. After all, part of the point of pluralism is to broaden the lens to include less formal norm-generating activities. Some of this problem, however, simply results from the biases inherent in data collection. In looking for evidence of how a legal or quasi-legal regime operates, it is always easier to gather information about more formal regimes because records are more widely disseminated, official media outlets tend to report on them, and so on. In contrast, less official venues for legal norms tend to require more detailed ethnographies or other forms of empirical, on-the-ground data collection. Nevertheless, most of the normative principles undergirding global legal pluralism would apply to non-state communities as well. These communities can establish decision-making institutions and procedural mechanisms that encourage consideration of alternative communities and their norms, and they can embed permanent forms of structural interaction. Indeed, many scholars have in fact examined such non-state communities, in realms as disparate as the codes governing jewellery merchant enclaves (Bernstein 1992), tuna sellers (Feldman 2006), gypsies (Weyrauch and Bell 1993), the Internet Engineering Task Force (Froomkin 2003: 792–4), and the Gentleman's Agreement of bankers concerning export credits (Levit 2005). In the end, it is clear that global legal pluralism at the very least offers a useful framework to ensure both that we identify these non-state law-making communities and analyze legal procedures and institutions through the lens of pluralist principles.

Finally, one might ask whether this proceduralist pluralist vision is simply liberalism in another guise and not really pluralism at all (Galán and Patterson 2013). After all, liberalism is not unalterably opposed to non-state norms, and even those who focus only on the central legal authority of the liberal state think it important that the state sometimes defer to such norms. Indeed, one of the core notions of liberalism is that government should not take sides in debates about competing visions of the good, and so space is allowed for non-state normative commitments. So long as a non-state normative community does not infringe unduly on the rights of others, liberalism allows those communities a tremendous amount of freedom and scope. For their part most pluralists do not deny the importance of the state, nor even the fact that often the state has greater coercive power at its disposal and therefore is better able to enforce its norms than non-state entities. After all, recognizing non-state lawmaking as important does not in and of itself mean that all sources of law are equally powerful or influential. So, on the surface it appears that legal pluralism and legal liberalism effectively merge into one. The merged statement goes something like this: 'The state is the most powerful lawmaker; it allows scope for non-state norms when it chooses to, and it often does choose to defer because non-state norms have a strong emotional pull and should be accorded deference as long as those norms don't get out of hand.' And if that's all legal pluralism is adding, then the voluminous legal pluralism scholarship does not appear to have altered the basic liberal legal framework very much.

Responding to this objection requires a longer treatment (for a preliminary take on this issue, see Berman 2013), but for these purposes I will simply suggest that legal pluralism is in fact significantly different from the classic liberal vision in at least two important ways, one descriptive and one normative. First, as a descriptive matter (and again it is important to recognize that legal pluralism was historically a descriptive project) legal pluralists are far more likely than traditional liberals even to notice the pluralism of legal and quasi-legal norms that exist apart from the state. A liberal institutionalist will tend to focus on state-based formal entities exclusively and will therefore analyze non-state normative communities only when such communities assert rights before those entities or when those communities propagate norms that seem to present major conflicts with the state. Thus, the low-level day-to-day interaction of normative communities will tend to disappear from view. Moreover, when non-state norms do arise, the question is often framed only in terms of how much the state should defer to or tolerate the non-state community, not as a true conflict of normative systems. Thus, the state-centric view will tend to miss much that legal pluralism uncovers and will bias the analytical framework from the start.

Second, as legal pluralism has developed a more normative bite, it has been used to justify procedural mechanisms, institutional designs and discursive practices aimed at developing habits of mind in decision makers that will encourage those decision makers to use restraint in insisting jurispathically on their own norms to the exclusion of the norms of other communities. Thus, the key normative question from a pluralist perspective is not simply: here are my norms, now how much should I tolerate others? Instead, as discussed above, pluralists will favour hybrid institutional designs and practices that will embed such principles of toleration and accommodation into day-to-day operations. These designs and practices may well be consonant with liberalism, but they result in a very different set of institutional arrangements, inquiries and jurisprudential tropes. For example, consider a governing council of decision makers popularly elected by citizens of a community. Assume that every council member happens to be a member of the same majority ethnic, racial or religious group within that broader community. If the election were conducted fairly and the governing body does not unduly infringe minority rights in its substantive decisions, then under most theories of liberalism of which I am aware there is at least some justification for saying that this is a legitimate arrangement. If one embraces the vision of legal pluralism I pursue, however, one might reach the conclusion that even if this rule solely by members of the dominant group is *legitimate*, it is likely not *preferable*. This is because the procedural pluralist approach adds in a preference for greater dialogue among multiple communities to improve the quality of decision making, to build habits of mind that inculcate tolerance and to make it more likely that the minority will acquiesce in whatever substantive decisions are ultimately reached. Accordingly, following a more pluralist approach, one might decide to set aside certain seats on the governing council for the minority group. Either of these arrangements is likely compatible with liberalism; however, the pluralist perspective adds an additional set of considerations to weigh in the institutional design decision. Of course there are liberal theorists who would similarly seek structural accommodation to minority groups of this sort (see, e.g., Kymlicka 1995). But the point is that a pluralist approach tends to direct our gaze towards the prudential reasons that hybrid mechanisms of this sort might be desirable.

Thus, in the end I believe global legal pluralism offers a fundamentally different analytical framework – both descriptively and normatively – from liberalism. And while it may be that a pluralist perspective can fit comfortably within a liberal philosophical stance (that depends on how far the pluralist impulse is pushed in particular cases), I think a pluralist approach is likely to lead to both a more nuanced descriptive understanding of the world and a more desirable legal and political framework for addressing the hybridity that surrounds us every day.

5. Conclusion

Legal pluralism has long been a useful trope to force scholars away from assuming that all law resides in the sovereign. The move to global legal pluralism allows more detailed analysis of all the ways in which international and transnational legal and quasi-legal pronouncements have potential impact regardless of whether the pronouncements are accompanied by the threat of coercive force. In addition, the normative project of global legal pluralism allows the evaluation of institutions and procedures based on how well they accommodate multiple voices from multiple communities. Thus, global legal pluralism offers a distinctive and useful set of inquiries for understanding the complex multifaceted ways in which law is deployed in the twenty-first century. And Roger Cotterrell, through his decades-long exploration of how social theory contributes to an understanding of law, has ably guided us towards this more nuanced understanding of law in all its plural forms, all around the globe.

Bibliography

Ahdieh, R. 2004. 'Between Dialogue and Decree: International Review of National Courts'. 79 *New York University Law Review*, 2029–163.

Benda-Beckmann, F. 1997. 'Citizens, Strangers, and Indigenous Peoples: Conceptual Politics and Legal Pluralism'. 9 *Law and Anthropology*, 1–42.

Berger, T. 1998. *Cultures of Antimilitarisn: National Security in Germany and Japan*. Baltimore, John Hopkins University Press.

Berman, P. Schiff 2002. 'The Globalization of Jurisdiction'. 151 *University of Pennsylvania Law Review*, 311–529.

Berman, P. Schiff 2007. 'Global Legal Pluralism'. 80.6 *Southern California Law Review*, 1155–238.

Berman, P. Schiff 2009. 'The New Legal Pluralism'. 5 *Annual Review of Law & Social Science*, 225–42.

Berman, P. Schiff 2012. *Global Legal Pluralism: A Jurisprudence of Law Beyond Borders*. Cambridge, Cambridge University Press.

Berman, P. Schiff 2013. 'How Legal Pluralism Is and Is Not Distinct from Liberalism: A response to Alexis Galán and Dennis Patterson'. 11 *International Journal of Constitutional Law*, 801–8.

Bernstein, L. 1992. 'Opting Out of the Legal System: Extralegal Contractual Relations in the Diamond Industry'. 21 *Journal of Legal Studies*, 115–57.

Bumiller, K. 1988. *The Civil Rights Society: the Social Construction of Victims*. Baltimore, John Hopkins University Press.

Constable, M. 1994. *The Law of the Other: the Mixed Jury and Changing Conceptions of Citizenship, Law, and Knowledge*. Chicago, University of Chicago Press.

Cotterrell, R. 1995. *Law's Community: Legal Theory in Sociological Perspective*. Oxford, Oxford University Press.

Cotterrell, R. 2006. *Law, Culture, and Society: Legal Ideas in the Mirror of Social Theory*. Aldershot, Ashgate.

Cover, R. 1981. 'The Uses of Jurisdictional Redundancy: Interest, Ideology, and Innovation'. 22.4 *William & Mary Law Review*, 639–82.

Dickinson, L. 2003a. 'The Dance of Complementarity: Relationships among Domestic, International, and Transnational Accountability Mechanisms in East Timor and Indonesia'. In J. Stromseth (ed.), *Accountability for Atrocities: National and International Responses*. Ardsley, New York, Transnational.

Dickinson, L. 2003b. 'The Promise of Hybrid Courts'. 97 *American Journal of International Law*, 295–310.

Ellickson, R. 1991. *Order Without Law: How Neighbors Settle Disputes*. Cambridge, MA, Harvard University Press.
Ewick, P. and Silbey, S. 1998. *The Common Place of Law: Stories from Everyday Life*. Chicago, University of Chicago Press.
Feldman, E. 2006. 'The Tuna Court: Law and Norms in the World's Premier Fish Market'. 94 California Law Review 313–69.
Figgis, J.N. 1913. *Churches in the Modern State*. London, Longmans, Green and Co.
Finnemore, M. 1996. *National Interests in International Society*. Ithaca, New York, Cornell University Press.
Franck, T. 1996. 'Clan and Superclan: Loyalty, Identity and Community in Law and Practice'. 90 *American Journal of International Law*, 359–83.
Froomkin, A. Michael. 2003. 'Habermas@Discourse.Net: Toward a Critical Theory of Cyberspace'. 116 *Harvard Law Review*, 749–873.
Galán, A. and Patterson, D. 2013. 'The Limits of Normative Legal Pluralism: Review of Paul Schiff Berman, Global Legal Pluralism: A Jurisprudence of Law beyond Borders'. 11 *International Journal of Constitutional Law*, 783–800.
Galanter, M. 1981. 'Justice in Many Rooms: Courts, Private Ordering, and Indigenous Law'. 19.1 *Journal of Legal Pluralism & Unofficial Law*, 1–48.
Geertz, C. 1983. *Local Knowledge: Further Essays in Interpretive Anthropology*. New York, Basic Books.
Gordon, R. 1984. 'Critical Legal Histories'. 36 *Stanford Law Review*, 57–125.
Griffiths, J. 1986. 'What is Legal Pluralism?' 24(1) *Journal of Legal Pluralism & Unofficial Law*, 1–50.
Helfer, L. and Slaughter, A-M. 1997. 'Toward a Theory of Effective Supranational Adjudication'. 107 *Yale Law Journal*, 273–391.
Hooker, M. 1975. *Legal Pluralism: An Introduction to Colonial and Neo-Colonial Laws*. Oxford, Clarendon Press.
Jolls, C., Sunstein, C and Thaler, R. 1998. 'A Behavioral Approach to Law and Economics'. 50/5 *Stanford Law Review*, 1471–550.
Krasner, S. 2005. 'The Case for Shared Sovereignty'. 16/1 *Journal of Democracy*, 69–83.
Kymlicka, W. 1995. *Multicultural Citizenship: A Liberal Theory of Minority Rights*. Oxford, Oxford University Press.
Levit, J.K. 2005. 'A Bottom-Up Approach to International Lawmaking: The Tale of Three Trade Finance Instruments'. 30/1 *Yale International Law Review*, 125–209.
Maitland, F.W. 1936. 'Trust and Corporation'. In *Maitland: Selected Essays*. Edited by H. Hazeltine, G. Lapsley and P. Winfield. Cambridge, Cambridge University Press, 141–222.
McCann, M. 1994. *Rights at Work: Pay Equity Reform and the Politics of Legal Mobilization*. Chicago, University of Chicago Press.
Merry, S.E. 1988. 'Legal Pluralism'. 22 *Law & Society* Review, 869–96.
Merry, S.E. 1990. *Getting Justice and Getting Even: Legal Consciousness among Working-Class Americans*. Chicago, University of Chicago Press.
Merry, S.E. and Stern, R. 2005. 'The Female Inheritance Movement in Hong Kong: Theorizing the Local/Global Interface.' 46/3 *Current Anthropology*, 387–410.
Obiora, L. Amede. 1997. 'Bridges and Barricades: Rethinking Polemics and Intransigence in the Campaign Against Female Circumcision'. 47 *Case Western Reserve Law Review*, 275–378.
Orentlicher, D. 1991. 'Settling Accounts: The Duty to Punish Human Rights Violations of a Prior Regime'. 100 *Yale Law Journal*, 2537–615.

Osofsky, H. 2007. 'Climate Change Litigation as Pluralist Legal Dialogue?' 26 *Stanford Journal of International Law*, 181–238.

Pospisil, L. 1981. 'Modern and Traditional Administration of Justice in New Guinea'. 19 *Journal of Legal Pluralism and Unofficial Law*, 93–116.

Rajagopal, B. 2003. *International Law from Below: Development, Social Movements, and Third World Resistance*. Cambridge, Cambridge University Press.

Ramirez, D. 1994. 'The Mixed Jury and the Ancient Custom of Trial By Jury De Medietate Linguae: A History and a Proposal for Change.' 74/5 *Boston University Law Review*, 777–818.

Rivkin, D. Jr. and Casey, L. 2003. 'Crimes Outside the World's Jurisdiction'. *New York Times*, July 22, at A19.

Santos, B. de Sousa. 1987. 'Law: A Map of Misreading. Towards a Post-Modern Conception of Law'. 14/3 *Journal of Law & Society*, 279–99.

Santos, B. de Sousa. 2002. *Toward a New Legal Common Sense: Law, Globalization, and Emancipation*. London, Butterworths/LexisNexis.

Sarat, A. and Kearns, T.R. 1993. 'Beyond the Great Divide: Forms of Legal Scholarship and Everyday Life'. In A. Sarat and T.R. Kearns (eds), *Law in Everyday Life*, 21.

Sarat, A. and Simon, J. 2001. 'Beyond Legal Realism? Cultural Analysis, Cultural Studies, and the Situation of Legal Scholarship'. 13 *Yale Journal of Law and the Humanities*, 3–32.

Silbey, S. 1992. 'Making a Place for Cultural Analyses of Law'. 17/1 *Law and Social Inquiry*, 39–48.

Tamanaha, B. 1993. 'The Folly of Legal Pluralism'. 20 *Journal of Law & Society*, 192–217.

Vanderlinden, J. 1989. 'Return to Legal Pluralism'. 28 *Journal of Legal Pluralism & Unofficial Law*, 149–57.

Wynter, S. 1997. '"Genital Mutilation" or "Symbolic Birth"? Female Circumcision, Lost Origins, and the Aculturism of Feminist/Western Thought'. 47/2 *Case Western Reserve Law Review*, 501–52.

Chapter 16
Legal Culture and Legal Transplants

Mark Van Hoecke

1. Terminology

'Legal culture' and 'legal transplants' are both controversial concepts. Roger Cotterrell has most notably criticized the usage of the concept of 'legal culture' in comparative law, as it often 'focuses on everything and nothing. It is hopelessly vague and comparatists would do well to avoid it.' (Cotterrell 2003: 149; see also Cotterrell 1997a) 'Legal transplants' is not much more popular with Roger: 'the concept of legal transplant itself is unclear, the matters to be addressed are too complex, the variables are too numerous, or they remain too often insufficiently defined' (Cotterrell 2001: 79). Hence, it was quite tempting to combine both concepts in the title for this chapter, be it at the risk of starting in confusion and ending in confusion.[1]

1.1 Legal Culture

'Legal culture' is a broad concept and indeed needs to be operationalized for empirical research. However, it may well act as an overall concept, which refers to the whole (social, economic, historical, ideological ...) context of the written law. In legal education and in legal scholarship, lawyers tend to analyze the law and to solve legal problems rather isolated from this context. When applying such an approach to comparative law it will often lead to mistaken conclusions. It is the aim of this chapter to illustrate this with the help of some concrete examples, most notably of how 'legal transplants' may work out quite differently in different cultural environments (in the broadest sense). It is not necessary to detect the exact elements of a legal culture that block the actual reception of a legal model, concept, rule or institution in another country. It suffices, within this context, to notice that some elements in the local approach to the law make the reception of a foreign legal element difficult or even impossible.

Identifying the vital building blocks of that legal culture will, of course, be important for solving the problem of the rejection of foreign law in that specific context. In this chapter, the aim is limited to showing the importance of legal culture in blocking or (drastically) re-interpreting the foreign legal element, which is not (fully) accepted by the receiving legal system or society. Also, some suggestions for the operationalization of the concepts of 'legal transplant' and 'legal culture', and their mutual relationship will be added.

1 As it is sometimes said about conferences: 'The Conference started in confusion and ended in confusion, but at a much higher level.'

1.2 Legal Transplants

After the (re)discovery of Alan Watson's 1974 book 'Legal Transplants' by comparatists in the 1990s, the concept 'legal transplant' became commonly used. Michele Graziadei noted in this respect:

> Possibly due to its rapid growth, the terminology of the field is still surrounded by some uncertainty. The term "transplant" is based on a metaphor that was chosen *faute de mieux*, ill-adapted to capturing the gradual diffusion of the law or the continuous nature of the process that sometimes leads to legal change through the appropriation of foreign ideas. (2006: 443)

Several alternative concepts have been proposed, which mostly bear some connotation that fits better with some specific form of 'legal transfer' than with others.

'Transplant' bears the connotation of having been taken from some foreign body or soil to be incorporated in another body (or planted in another soil with a different environment). Typical examples are European concepts and rules which were 'transplanted' in an African or Asian environment, without much adaptation to local traditions and cultures. It is no surprise that such transplants were often rejected by the receiving 'body', although more often in practice than on paper, as we will see later in this chapter.

Legislators in all countries often look for inspiration abroad. During the nineteenth century, the French *Code civil* of 1804 was quite influential, if not largely adopted, in many countries worldwide. After the enactment of the German *Bürgerliches Gesetzbuch* in 1896, it was this civil code that became most influential.[2] When Central and Eastern European countries were looking for new civil law legislation in the 1990s, it was the Dutch *Burgerlijk Wetboek* of 1992 which was widely used as a model. Post-intervention law reform after a period of war and considerable destabilization of a society may require an urgent enactment of, for instance, a new Code on criminal law and criminal procedure. Rules for fair trials and for the protection of human rights are often imposed by the international community on societies with little tradition in these matters. Here, full transplants seem to be the solution. Without sufficient adaptation to local traditions, however, this will not work.[3]

The term 'borrowing' seems appropriate, as it refers explicitly to an active, voluntary transfer by and to the receiving legal system. Also adequate would be the terms 'circulation of legal models,'[4] 'diffusion' (Friedman 2001: 94), 'migration' (Choudhry 2006) or 'travelling', the latter suggesting a more distant, external point of view of the comparative scholar. Whereas 'transplants' suggest a transfer by the 'donor' legal system, 'reception' would rather refer to its (successful) acceptance by the receiver (e.g. the reception of Roman law in medieval Europe and early Modern Times). 'Reception' has also been used in the weaker meaning of accepting to apply foreign law to foreigners in one's home country, such as accepting 'repudiation' under Muslim law as a form

2 For the law of delict/tort law, Gert Brüggemeier showed these mainly French influences in the nineteenth century and the mainly German ones in early twentieth century for Russia, Brazil and China (Brüggemeier 2011: 233 (Russia), 204 (Brazil), 182 (China, where Western influence only started by the end of the nineteenth century, being mainly German)).

3 An example is the introduction of the *Interim Code of Criminal Procedure* in Afghanistan in February 2004, mainly based on the Italian Criminal Procedure Code of 1988. It failed (Jupp 2013).

4 As mentioned by Graziadei 2006 this term has been used, among others, by the International Academy of Comparative Law at its 1992 Congress and by the *Association Henri Capitant*.

of 'divorce' in Europe.[5] The term 'cross-fertilization' (Slaughter 1994: 117) in its turn is only appropriate in cases of mutual influence, such as in the harmonizing process within the European Union. In such cases, the terminology 'legal transplants' may be less adequate.

In this chapter I will mostly use the term 'legal transfer', which may refer to any of the situations above and, hence, be considered, at least to some extent, to be synonymous with the other concepts mentioned, depending on the context.

2. Gradations of Transferability

It is obvious that purely technical, instrumental rules may more easily travel to legal systems belonging to the same legal tradition and with a similar social, economic and historical background, in comparison with legal principles that introduce a value in a quite different cultural context that has always rejected that value. Legal constructions such as 'factoring', 'leasing' or 'franchising' have proved to be rather easily transferable from Anglo-American law (and business practice) to Continental European legal systems and to other parts of the world. Differences however that will, as a rule, complicate legal transfers include the following considerations:

- conceptual legal framework;
- socio-economic context;
- political context;
- internal legal traditions and culture;
- traditions in society related to law;
- mainstream ideology.

2.1. Doctrinal Obstacles

Basil Markesinis (1997: 200, with references) discussed the diverging technical approaches to the problem of a frustrated beneficiary of a badly drawn-up will to sue the lawyer who drafted it negligently. Both this problem and the solution offered are the same in English, German and American law, but the roads these legal systems follow to solve the problem are not transferable to the other systems: contract law in Germany, tort law in England and some hybrid mix of contract and tort in the US. Almost accidentally, the three legal systems are able to reach the same desired solution to this problem with quite diverging conceptual frameworks (terminology and systematics) and rules. As Markesinis argued, English judges who want to allow tort recovery for pure economic loss, as German law does, but English law does not, 'may have to use some kind of contractual thinking if it wishes to preserve the legal result that it currently adopts' (1997: 201). However, this requires imagination and creativity and a willingness to depart from traditional legal thinking, which is not obvious for lawyers. Hence, in such cases the overall doctrinal, conceptual construction of the legal system may considerably hinder a transfer of parts of the legal solution from another country, without there being differences as to the preferred result in the two countries.

5 For example, on 17 February 2005 the *Société de législation comparée* organized a round table on 'La réception en France des répudiations de droit musulman'.

2.2. Judicial Traditions as Obstacles

Paolisa Nebbia (2000) analyzed the way Italian and English judges interpreted the European Directive 93/13 on Unfair Terms in Consumer Contracts in the years following its enactment in both countries. One would expect a high degree of coherence in the way the Directive is applied all over the European Union, for the following two reasons. Firstly, increasing consumer protection has been a trend in most EU countries (15 Member States in the period under consideration) for some decades before the enactment of the Directive: in the UK through the Unfair Contract Terms Act 1977, in Italy for *contratti d'adesione* since the Civil code of 1942. Secondly, European Directives are expected to be interpreted and applied uniformly throughout the Union, even if some divergences are possible as to details and as to the way the rules are incorporated into the domestic legal system. Moreover, EU Member States tend to take over the text of the European Directives literally in their own legislation, without changing a word. Nevertheless, Nebbia's analysis shows how deeply rooted ways of legal thinking may block the 'transfer' of a European Directive into domestic law. In Italy, lawyers were used to the principle of good faith in contract law, but not to the 'consumer' as a legal category. They are inclined to continue reasoning with the narrower category of 'adhesion contracts', which excludes individual consumer contracts. In England, the 'good faith' principle doesn't easily fit with the legal tradition of contract law. English judges will take into account the concrete elements of the case and may reach a similar protection of the consumer with the 'duty of care' on behalf of the professional supplier of goods or services, but both 'general legal principles' and a duty of 'good faith' in contract matters are rather alien to English lawyers' traditions. The former because of the very practical case to case approach in English law, the latter because 'contract' has developed as part of business law.[6] The good businessman is the one who uses opportunities, including the stupidity of the other party. There is no reason, in the Common Law approach, why the businessman should warn the other party or prevent him or her from a disadvantageous deal, except in some specific circumstances where English judges have imposed a duty of information on the professional party to the contract.[7] As a result, tradition is still largely governing the interpretation of the 1993 Directive, narrowing it down, to a large extent, to the domestic law as it was before that European Directive.

2.3. Doctrinal Obstacles Combined with Different Traditions

After the communist era, Russia has been modernizing its law. Contrary to the countries in Central Europe, it could not link up with some previous common (continental) European Roman law tradition or even with any kind of strong legal tradition.[8] For businesses to develop, it was highly desirable to follow international standards and to look for inspiration in those developed countries with a free market tradition. In this process, an attempt was made to introduce the Anglo-American 'trust' into Russian law.

---

6 Hence, marriage cannot be a 'contract' in a way similar to how it is on the Continent, as 'matters of love' do not fit with the business orientation of English contract law.

7 For example, when a wife is invited to stand as a security for a loan by her husband, courts have decided that the bank has to explain the transaction and the risks and recommend the wife to take independent legal advice (House of Lords, *Barclays Bank v. O'Brien*, [1993] *4 All ER*, 417).

8 Before the Russian revolution the country was still largely feudal and agrarian. Attempts to modernize the law in the nineteenth century were partly inspired by French and German legal doctrine. Legal education was limited and largely offered by Germans, at least until the mid nineteenth century.

> It has never been a part of Russian law, *i.e.*, Russian law has developed its own institutions for some of the functions performed by the trust, while other functions of the common law trust simply never existed in Russia. Nevertheless, the discussion of – and even the steps towards – the implementation of the trust concept took place during the recent economic reforms in Russia (1991–2005). (Zhdanov 2006: 179)

Apart from the need for a rapid and radical modernization of Russian law, there was also some pressure by foreign investors, most importantly Americans, 'to secure their investments with legal concepts familiar to them, among them the trust' (Zhdanov 2006: 181). However, this transplant didn't succeed. As Zhdanov noted:

> After several legislative experiments and discussions, lawmakers and the majority of Russian civil law academics rejected the Anglo-American trust. The Russian academics reasonably decided that comprehensive trust transplant would inevitably require substantial revisions in the overall system of Russian civil law, which was hardly desirable. (2006: 182)

This comment points to the problem that, in many cases legal transfers cannot be integrated into a foreign doctrinal and legislative environment, without thorough adaptation to that environment. Here, tradition may strongly oppose such changes, which go beyond what is needed for immediate business purposes. If in the process of transplanting the trust from Anglo-American law, contract law, property law and the law of securities in general are also affected, more traditional legal doctrine in those areas will resist changes that are mainly required for business purposes. As a result, after a failed attempt (Zhdanov 2006: 187) to simply transplant the Anglo-American trust by implementing the concept of fiduciary ownership (1993),[9] a kind of adapted 'Russian trust' was created, but with substantial differences, including that the Russian trust management is a contractual obligation, whereas the Anglo-American trust is a property law concept. This leads Zhdanov to the question whether the Russian trust is still a 'transplant' or rather a (thorough) 'modification' of the Anglo-American trust. (2006: 182) Even if the trust management contract in Russia has proven to fit many of the business purposes for which the Anglo-American trust is applied (Zhdanov 2006: 189), this question should be considered to be rhetorical. Indeed, when the most important characteristic and advantage of the trust, creating rights *in rem* is changed into pure contractual obligations, not much is left of the Anglo-American 'trust'.[10] And this points to another kind of 'transplant', more precisely the import of a word or blank concept, but giving it a quite different content within the 'receiving' legal system. This is not uncommon. Whereas, for instance, the concept of 'federalism' seems to refer to a strong centralization (at the European level) in Common Law countries, it means the opposite on the Continent: decentralizing powers.

The introduction of the 'full (Anglo-American) trust' eventually failed because of the strong opposition of both the Russian Parliament and of legal scholars against the (presidential) Edict, which meant that the concept of fiduciary ownership was never put into practice in Russia. The main reasons for this rejection, apart from the fear that it would have been a tool for fraudulent transfers of state assets, were (a) incompatibility with Russian legal tradition and its doctrinal conceptual framework, and (b) incompatibility with the Russian Constitution and the legislation on property law. It is interesting to note that Edict 2296 had largely been drafted by an American,

9 Edict 2296 on Fiduciary Ownership (the trust) of 24 December 1993 (Zhdanov 2006: 186).

10 Compare this with the essential characteristics of 'trust' as listed by Donovan Waters, of which the first three explicitly require such a right *in rem* (Waters 1995: 347–8).

William E. Butler, who was a member of the team responsible for itspreparation. Hence, it is no surprise that the 'trust' in this Edict met all the requirements listed by Donovan Waters to call it a 'trust' in the Anglo-American sense. Equally, it is no surprise that it was called 'an example of legal ignorance and disrespect to national legal traditions' and that it was largely rejected by Russian legal scholars and politicians (Zhdanov 2006: 186–8, esp. fn 17, with references).

The 'Russian trust' is a kind of legal construction *sui generis*, which has not much in common with the Anglo-American trust. It fits better the Russian tradition, doctrinal framework and legislation, but not completely, as it still needs to be harmonized with other institutions of Russian civil law, with tax law and administrative law. On the other hand, recent developments 'tend to emphasize the property element of the Russian trust in contrast to the contractual approach to the Russian trust as provided for in the RF Civil Code, which raises new theoretical issues regarding the nature and regulation of the Russian trust' (Zhdanov 2006: 193). Indeed, business needs tend to conflict here with doctrinal coherence; modernity tends to conflict with tradition. It opens the possibility that the Russian trust will gradually come closer to the Anglo-American one, not by way of a transplant, but because the law constantly adapts to new needs and to changed views in society. In the context of globalization, this may well lead to an increasing convergence of diverging legal systems, especially in areas such as international business, where the external pressure is high and the internal resistance rather limited, to the extent that it affects only a small part of society. However, to the extent that it affects larger parts of the legal system, the community of lawyers, including advocates, judges and legal scholars, may play an important role in the acceptance or rejection of new legal concepts and rules introduced under the influence of some parts of society.

For instance, Zhdanov notes about more recent legislation that 'The Investment Funds Law[11] treats the management company as a property holder distanced from the investors. As a result, some provisions of the Investment Funds Law contradict the general provisions of the trust management contract established in the Russian Civil Code'. However, 'the Russian courts are likely to accord priority to the Investments Fund Law over the Civil Code', as *lex specialis*. As Zhdanov remarks, what courts accept today may change tomorrow, as long as the appropriate amendments haven't been made to the provisions in the Civil Code (2006: 195–6). Meanwhile it is the community of lawyers which has to accept this more property-oriented trust in Russia, but that may be easier than changing the general provisions in the Civil Code, where a majority of civil law scholars may make the same objections as in 1993.

Clearly, this example of the introduction of the concept of 'trust' in Russia shows to what extent legal tradition and doctrinal obstacles may block attempts to transfer legal concepts and legal institutions from a quite different tradition.

2.4. Political Obstacles

Legal rules and legal institutions are rarely purely a matter of technical, pragmatic regulation. They mostly embody some translation of a value or a balancing of interests. That's why legal transplants may easily conflict with local tradition, but also with conflicting political interests and positions. An example of the latter can be observed in the attempts to introduce binding precedents in Russia, which is more of a civil law country than a common law one.

Binding precedent typically developed in the English Common Law system, because of specific historical circumstances. In the absence of substantial legislation in England in private law

11 Federal Law 156-FZ of 21 November 2001.

matters, at least until the twentieth century, and the historically strong position of courts,[12] the use of precedents was a way to guarantee the unity of the legal system. Genuinely binding precedent, however, was a product of the nineteenth century (Evans 1994). In order to make sure judges follow precedents, they should remain informed of their existence and exact content. This required the availability of published case law, which, in England, had existed since the thirteenth century but only developed in a uniform way in the nineteenth century.

In the history of almost all other jurisdictions, including the US, it has been the Constitution and parliamentary legislation that mainly guaranteed the unity of the legal system. This didn't imply a complete absence of binding precedents, but it kept them marginal. For instance, a second decision of the Belgian Court of Cassation, in the same case and on the same grounds, is binding on the court that will have to take the final decision in that case, but this is the only example of binding precedent under Belgian law. Of course, precedents always had some authority, most notably for lower courts, which generally don't like their decisions to be overruled by a higher court. This persuasive authority has not always been visible through references made to such precedents. On the other hand, when lower courts, on the Continent, think the higher court to have been wrong, the precedent will lose its authority and will easily be discarded. However, as a rule, lower courts will follow the jurisprudence of higher courts and most notably of supreme courts, including the European courts, without always referring explicitly to decisions as precedents. The word 'precedent' will very rarely be used in the decision in this context, as it would suggest a stronger authority than those decisions actually have. This is also true for Russia.[13]

'Transplanting' the system of binding precedent from England to a Continental European legal system would, hence, be not only contrary to the whole civil law tradition, but also problematic in view of the mainstream theory of the State, with its priority for the legislator and the subordinate position for judges. Nevertheless, in Russia, attempts are being made to introduce, at least to some extent, a system of binding precedent. The reasons are political: (a) strengthening the position of the judiciary in relation to parliament and the executive; (b) protecting judges against attempts to influence their decisions; and (c) creating more stability in the legal system (Pomeranz and Gutbrod 2012: 1). A first application of binding precedent was introduced in Russia by the Higher Commercial Court (*Arbitrazh)* in 2008 by a plenum decree of 14 February 2008 aiming at reducing the workload of the court (Pomeranz and Gutbrod 2012: 14–16).[14] This was based on Article 127 of the 1993 Russian Constitution, granting this Court the right 'to provide explanations on issues pertaining to judicial practice'. (Pomeranz and Gutbrod 2012: 9).[15] The 2008 decree of the Higher Commercial Court has been confirmed as constitutional by a decree of the Russian Constitutional Court of 21 January 2010. This decree formally established the right of the Higher Commercial Court (*Arbitrazh)* to issue binding precedents in specific instances (Pomeranz and Gutbrod 2012: 2, with references). Moreover, it offered the Constitutional Court the opportunity

12 As from the early Middle-Ages, the Court of King's Bench was travelling around the country deciding important cases, but also unifying local customary laws and, thus, helping to establish a 'Common Law' for England.

13 See the discussion on this matter and a historical overview in Pomeranz and Gutbrod 2012: 6–9, also 14.

14 'A dramatic increase in the number of cases before the court, many involving similar issues, served as the primary motivation behind this action' (Pomeranz and Gutbrod 2012: 14–15).

15 Pomeranz and Gutbrod (2012: 10) note that 'the custom whereby Russia's high courts issue such instructions stretches back to Imperial Russia. While an internal legislative process existed within the tsarist bureaucracy, Russia lacked an independent legislature (until 1906) that could fulfil the public law-creating functions so essential for a civil-law system'.

to specify the precedential force of its own decisions: 'as soon as the Constitutional Court issues a determination, the legal norms in question "cannot be interpreted in any other way or applied in another sense"' (Pomeranz and Gutbrod 2012: 17, quoting from para. 3.3 of the Constitutional Court decision). The third of the three highest courts in Russia, the Supreme Court, followed with a decision on 14 July 2010 (Pomeranz and Gutbrod 2012: 23).

In its decree of 21 January 2010, the Constitutional Court also called on the Russian Parliament to enact the appropriate legislation so as to give a statutory basis to this doctrine of precedents. The parliament did so on 27 December 2010 – in force as from 28 March 2011 (Pomeranz and Gutbrod 2012: 19). The Higher Commercial Court used its confirmed power to issue binding precedents on 2 March 2010 when overturning a decision that allowed the Russian Bank of Development to unilaterally increase the interest rate charged to its customers. It not only rejected this right because of a violation of Russia's consumer-protection law, but, moreover, stated explicitly that this interpretation was compulsory and has to be applied by commercial courts in analogous cases (Pomeranz and Gutbrod 2012: 20, with the full text in Russian in footnote 90). Pomeranz and Gutbrod noted:

> Nevertheless, as Ivanov and Morshchakova's comments indicate, the Constitutional Courts' recognition of even the limited use of judicial precedent has much broader policy implications, striking at the very heart of the Russian legal system and the power of the judiciary. (2012: 2)

Indeed, binding precedents have largely been alien to the Russian legal tradition. One could argue that binding orders on deciding cases issued from the Tsarist administration until the early twentieth century and, later on, in the Soviet Union from the Communist Party, but these were political interventions, rather than legal precedents. Indeed, in both cases what was operating was external pressure from an organization, which controlled the legislature and the executive powers, rather than pressure from within the judiciary. Although justifiable from a practical point of view, and most notably for attaining a stronger coherence of case law and a reduction of the workload for the highest courts, binding precedents in Russia bear important political consequences and risk to disturb the balance of power between the judiciary and the legislature. Hence, it is no surprise that both the Ministry of Justice and the procuracy have openly contested the Constitutional Court's decree (Pomeranz and Gutbrod 2012: 23). A majority of lower judges appears to be against binding precedents.[16] The bar and existing legal doctrine do not seem to be very enthusiastic either.[17]

One could doubt whether we face here a genuine 'transplant': the word 'precedent' is neither used in the decisions of the highest courts, nor by parliament, no reference was made to the Common Law, the aims of adopting precedents were different in part. Nevertheless, in Russian scholarly legal writing this decree is discussed in terms of of a shift from Civil Law to Common Law, and a binding interpretation imposed on lower courts is actually a 'precedent'. Anyway, a 'foreign element' has been introduced into the Russian legal system, where it meets obstacles, partly because binding precedent doesn't fit with the overall conception of the division of power in Russia, partly because it doesn't fit with tradition, but mainly because of political reasons: too

16 This was the result of a survey between 2003 and 2006 (46.7% against, 28.5% in favour, whilst 24.8% didn't have an opinion). See Svetlana V.Boshno, 'Pretsedent, zakon I doktrina', *4 Gosudarstvo I pravo*, 2007 (as reported by Pomeranz and Gutbrod 2012: 21, fn 95; they also note, at 27, that 'even in the aftermath of the 2008 plenum decree, Russian courts still express scepticism as to whether judicial decisions possess precedential value').

17 As to the bar, see Pomeranz and Gutbrod 2012: 23–4 and, as for legal doctrine, the position taken by Pomeranz and Gutbrod themselves in their article, and part of the literature they refer to.

much power for the judiciary is infringing on the powers of the legislature and the executive. It is this political balance, which may (strongly) limit this development towards binding precedents in Russia or even block them completely.

2.5. Local Culture vs Transplants through Globalization

Globalization has entailed many legal transfers, especially from Anglo-American law, all over the world. This is most notably the case in business law, the law relating to air and sea transport, environmental law, energy law, financial law, and the like. The kind of business or issues to be regulated requires common concepts, a global approach and, hence, uniform rules, at least to some extent. Even if, in this process, new legal principles, rules and concepts are being developed, it will basically entail some legal transfer from the United States or Europe to other parts of the world. Because of the strong economic position of the US over the last century and its presence in all parts of the world, it is mainly American law that has been globalizing in this way. However, the most remarkable globalizing legal transfer is the concept of 'human rights', be it with diverging interpretations in different cultures because some basic assumptions of the Western conception of fundamental rights conflict with basic assumptions of non-Western cultures.

The case I want to discuss here does not belong to one of the areas mentioned, but to procedural law, more precisely the recognition and enforcement of foreign judgments in China. It is based on a recent, not yet published, PhD by Wenliang Zhang.[18] In a globalized world it should be obvious that judgments would be recognized and could be executed in any country, with, of course, the possibility to check the validity of the presented document and its compatibility with basic values in the country where it should be executed. For this purpose, the concept of '*exequatur*' has been introduced: green light given by a local court to execute a foreign judgment. This is also the case in China, but with an obvious reluctance to switch to green.

The Chinese Code of Civil Procedure provides in its Article 282[19] that foreign judgments will be recognized and executed under the following conditions:

- there is a reciprocity with the country of the foreign judgement or an obligation on the basis of an international treaty;
- the foreign decision does not contradict the basic principles of the laws of China;
- it does not violate national sovereignty, security, social and public interest of the People's Republic.

All this looks quite reasonable, but in practice many countries, including India, Japan, Germany, South Korea, UK, US, do not qualify for recognition and execution of their judicial decisions

18 Defended at Ghent University on 28 June 2013: supervisor Professor Johan Erauw.

19 'After a people's court of the PRC reviews, according to the international treaties concluded or acceded to by the PRC or based on the principle of reciprocity, an application or request for recognition and enforcement of a legally effective judgment (*Panjue*) or ruling (*Caiding*) delivered by a foreign court, if [the people's court] considers that such a judgment or ruling neither contradicts the basic principles of the laws of the PRC nor violates the national sovereignty, security, social and public interests of the PRC, the people's court shall make a ruling to recognize its effects. Where the enforcement is necessary, [the people's court] shall issue an order to enforce the foreign judgment according to the relevant provisions of the present law. If a legally effective judgment or ruling delivered by a foreign court contradicts the basic principles of the law of the PRC or the national sovereignty, security, social and public interests of China, the people's court shall refuse to grant recognition and enforcement' (Zhang 2013: 45).

because the first condition is not fulfilled, partly because 'reciprocity' is interpreted narrowly[20] (Zhang 2013: 102–16). On the other hand 'most countries are far from ready to take the initiative to recognize Chinese judgments too' (Zhang 2013: 115). In other words, local and national interests often prevail and block globalization, in this case the recognition and enforcement of foreign judicial decisions. This priority given to the protection of national interests also clearly appears in Article 5 of the Chinese Bankruptcy Act, which adds to the above conditions that the execution of a foreign judgment in cases of bankruptcy should 'not jeopardize the lawful rights and interests of the creditors that are in the territory of the PRC' (Zhang 2013: 65).

The limitations imposed by Article 282 of the Chinese Code of Civil Procedure refer to rather vague concepts, notably 'basic principles', 'sovereignty', 'security', 'social and public interest'. There is no consensus among Chinese scholars on the exact scope of those concepts in this context (Zhang 2013: 143–62) and Chinese courts rarely refer to them (Zhang 2013: 150, 163). On the basis of a survey, Wenliang Zhang concluded that only 8% of the cases involved pecuniary judgments and their recognition: it was always foreigners that applied and were refused in all these cases (Zhang 2013: 305). The other cases involved adoption (2%) or divorce (90%). As for divorce, the possibility of recognition of foreign judgments is more flexible in China. According to Article 12 of the 1991 Regulation on Foreign Divorce Judgments, there are two conditions: (a) the foreign divorce judgments must be 'legally effective', and (b) the original courts must have jurisdiction (Zhang 2013: 193). Possible obstacles to recognition and enforcement include: (a) breach of natural justice, (b) conflicting judgments, and (c) contradiction to basic principles of the Chinese law or sovereignty, security and social and public interest (Zhang 2013: 194). On top of the obstacles for recognition and enforcement of foreign judgments in general, another vague concept is added: 'breach of natural justice.' Nevertheless, all foreign divorce cases in the survey had been recognized by the Chinese court. It may be relevant that the applicants in the divorce cases, and mostly both parties, were generally Chinese. When recognizing foreign divorce judgments, 'hardly any reasoning can be seen. The grant of the recognition almost seems like being unconditional', Wenliang Zhang notes. (Zhang 2013: 309)

This contrasts remarkably with the reluctance in China to recognize foreign judgments in all other matters. The reason for that is the local legal culture: 'Chinese courts just don't like to easily accept foreign things,[21] including foreign judgments' writes Wenliang Zhang, and, although there are many reasons for this, 'parochialism is among the most important ones. The stubborn adherence to the principle of reciprocity can be a good example' (Zhang 2013: 298). This parochial approach with local protectionism is even present when there is a conflict between parties from different Chinese regions (see Clarke 1996: 41).

In addition, transplanted Western rules and concepts are functioning in the different environment of Chinese culture. This culture has traditionally been hostile to the use of law and to court proceedings:

> Chinese citizens' routine fear of law makes the solution of disputes, including international disputes, less effective, and when judgments are delivered, they tend to refute the litigation by refusing to perform the obligations there under. When foreign proceedings involve Chinese citizens, they are far from active to participate in such proceedings. As a result, the recognition and enforcement of the default judgments in China will encounter more resistance and protests. Even in commercial

20 Even between Hong Kong and Mainland China (Zhang 2013: 115–16).

21 One may add here that 'Traditional China regarded herself as the centre of the world and her civilization and culture as superior to all others' (Chen 1992: 20).

> transactions, the Chinese business men are not yet used to taking law as a sword or shield. If international litigation is instituted by their foreign partners, their business relationship is likely to be ended or badly suffered. To resolve disputes through amicable methods appears to be rather important to maintain a business relationship. (Zhang 2013: 299)

Hence, even Chinese judgemnts in private law matters are hardly enforced (Clarke 1996). The possibility of obtaining recognition and enforcement of judicial decision worldwide seems to be one element of globalization, especially for international business. However, notwithstanding apparent legal transfers of Western concepts and rules for this matter, local legal culture, such as the Chinese one, may fully block this possibility in practice, without it being directly visible for outsiders.

In China, there has never been a strong tradition of private law.[22] Since 1979, as China started to rebuild its legal system and to elaborate a modern private law this was not hindered by deeply rooted doctrinal concepts and frameworks, as they simply didn't exist. Hence, a transfer of foreign legal concepts, rules and institutions in China seemed easy, and was easy in the sense that it was fallow land and, for the Chinese, legal rules are more akin to models rather than strong subjective rights and obligations. However, the cultural context puts everything in a different perspective, so that Western transfers do not work, or at least not in the way Western lawyers would expect.

2.6. Transplants through Cultural Colonization

A number of European principles, rules and concepts have been introduced in Africa, mainly in the first half of the twentieth century by colonial powers. These powers belonged to the Common Law tradition (UK) and to the (French private law) Continental tradition (France, Belgium, Portugal). It is remarkable that even half a century after decolonization those imported European rules and concepts largely survived, notwithstanding huge differences in legal traditions, political, social and economic contexts. Paradigmatic differences pertain to:

- the conception of law (tradition, spirits of the ancestors v. rational organization of society);
- the sources of law (customary law, traditional chiefs v. statutory law and courts);
- the underlying dominant ideology (polygamy, traditional gender roles v. monogamy and equality between men and women).

Here, we will briefly discuss some European transplants related to marriage.

All family law legislation in sub-Saharan Africa accepts only monogamous marriages, which are defined as 'the voluntary union for life of one man and one woman, to the exclusion of all others' (Onokah 2003: 69).[23] Once married according to state law, any second wedding is excluded before the first one has been dissolved. Belgian attempts to forbid polygamy by law in the Belgian Congo from 1950[24] have hardly influenced social reality. The weakening of many public authorities

22 Attempts to modernize private law in the first half of twentieth century failed because of revolutions and wars that made it impossible to put this modernization into practice. Between 1959 and 1979 the Ministry of Justice was even abolished as a 'bourgeois' institution (Chen 1992: 20–38). See also Brüggemeier 2011: 182–3.

23 Interestingly enough referring not to some Nigerian text, but to a nineteenth-century decision of the House of Lords.

24 Decree of 4 April 1950 concerning the prohibition of polygamy in the Belgian Congo

because of civil war, military coups, bribery, impunity of crimes committed by officials,[25] etc., together with the inappropriateness of state law in view of local traditions, has led to social life being governed by rules other than those of state law. Professor Camille Kuyu notes that real legal life in Kinshasa is organized completely outside the state and its institutions (Kuyu 2005: 10).

In Gabon, from 1963, dowries have been forbidden.[26] Joseph John Nambo, at that time assistant professor at the University Omar Bongo in Gabon, inquired among his students, asking them whether they would agree to marry without a dowry. Seventy-five per cent of the female students and up to 95 per cent of the male students gave a negative answer. To them a dowry was necessary for the credibility and stability of a marriage.[27] The law of 1963 didn't work in practice and, although formally still valid, has become completely obsolete. In Gabon, the dowry is today more present than ever (Nambo 2001, 89–103, esp. 92–3).

In the case of the import of European law into African countries, the colonizers – but also the generations of politicians, lawyers and academics[28] strongly acculturated following independence – have substantially underestimated the strength of the customary rules of African ancestors, and especially their spiritual and mythical framework (Kuyu Mwissa 2005: 12). In addition, the strong communitarian tradition in Africa could hardly fit with the rather individualistic European approach to law, including to family law.[29]

In the British colonies, legal regulations were better adapted to local traditions. Although monogamous marriage was introduced[30] and promoted, especially by missionaries, colonial legislation left the possibility for native people to marry according to their traditions, including polygamous marriages: 'Nothing … shall deprive any person of the benefit of any existing native law or custom, such law or custom not being repugnant to natural justice, equity and good conscience, … Such laws and customs shall be deemed applicable in causes and matters relating to marriage ….'[31]However, the inevitable interference of courts in the application of customary law in cases of conflict led to the application of 'customary rules' that 'sometimes diverge from the social norms which people customarily regard as binding upon them … Thus, there is divergence between "lawyers' customary law" and "sociologists' customary law", or … between "judicial customary law" and "practised customary law"' (Woodman 1977: 115). Moreover, until now a dual judiciary system, such as that in Nigeria, gives space to apply customary law and Islamic law to official courts up to the level of appeal (Customary Court of Appeal and Shari'a Court of Appeal). But when the case goes to the higher courts (Court of Appeal and Supreme Court), it will be decided by judges who are not intimately acquainted with either customary law or Islamic law, or both. An attempt by British rulers to 'liberate women', by treating them as equal to men and by allowing divorce when requested, led to decisions by the Nigerian 'Native Court' that disturbed

25 See, on this example with regard to Nigeria, Ighorodje and Bamidele 2007.

26 Act 31 May 1963, enacted by President Léon Mba, first president of the Republic of Gabon. For other attempts in Africa to forbid the payment of a bride price in the course of the twentieth century, see Phillips and Morris 1971: 91–4. However, they also give examples of implicit or explicit official recognition of the payment of a bride price in several African countries.

27 Even higher figures (98%) appeared from a Nigerian survey (see Onokah 2003: 97–8).

28 'Dans le monde universitaire, nombre d'enseignants restent encore séduits par la tentation de l'Occident et inaptes à procéder à une décolonisation mentale', Mebenga 2001: 69–87, at 74.

29 It is interesting to note that, after the collapse of the Soviet Union, one of the Baltic States, Latvia, in 1990 reintroduced the dowry (s.111 Latvian Civil Code). However, here it means that the money or property given to the couple by the wife's family remains the property of the wife.

30 For Nigeria: the Marriage Act 1884.

31 s.20 Nigerian Supreme Court Ordinance 1914.

the local customary law considerably. According to the traditional rules, divorce was, in practice, excluded. Nevertheless, divorce was almost automatically awarded by the colonial courts.[32] British colonizers increasingly attempted to control African customary law through courts with English judges.[33] This basically did not change after independence, and has led to a similar situation as in other African countries such as the Congo, namely the increasing segregation between 'official law' and 'real law'.

Today, in large parts of Africa, the 'external' colonizers have been replaced by 'internal' ones: 'There is massive evidence of enormous distances and gaps of communication between modern African states and their peoples' customary, normative orders' (Menski 2006: 470). A Westernized elite of lawyers, businessmen and politicians educated in Europe, has taken over Western values, or at least pretends to have done so, for strategic reasons (being more acceptable internationally and/or strengthening their own power).[34] Most people in those countries, however, bypass the formal courts, for reasons of lack of trust and for practical reasons, and for people living outside towns these courts are often too remote from their village. Hence, they have recourse to traditional patterns of informal dispute settlement (Ebo 1995: 33–4) and the transplanted Western rules are completely ignored.

A similar divergence of the views on family in Asia as compared to Europe explains how identical (imported) rules may be applied in the opposite way in different jurisdictions. Mindy Chen-Wishart shows how, in Singapore, Confucian values have led to a quite different view on the family compared to England. Contract law and commercial law have been fully transferred from England to Singapore, which has been an English colony from its founding in 1819 until its independence in 1965. The same rules are still valid in Singapore today. Nevertheless, the concept of 'undue influence' is interpreted quite differently from the approach of English judges. In England, it is accepted that family members who do not receive independent advice are under undue influence when guaranteeing a loan from their husband or father, etc. In similar cases, Singaporean courts have decided in an opposite way, because of the more hierarchical and less individual conception of the family in the Confucian tradition (Chen-Wishart 2013).

3. Towards a Theory of Legal Culture and Legal Transfer

Which elements constitute a 'legal culture' and which kinds of divergences among legal cultures may prevent legal transfers from being successful?

3.1. Internal Legal Culture

3.1.1. Doctrinal framework

Clearly underestimated in comparative writing is the importance of the different doctrinal conceptual frameworks as obstacles for legal transfers or legal harmonization. Such differences may concern the way reality is structured from a legal point of view (e.g. the liability for a train accident based on tort law or on contract law), but also the way the legal system itself is structured: technical differences, such as cassation for instance, may lead to diverging legal

32 For example, in 1924, in the Ondo region, divorce was granted in 123 cases out of a total 125 petitions (NAI Ondo Division 7/3: Native Court Judgement Book, 1924, cited in Onokah 2003: 44).

33 See on this development in Nigeria: Onokah 2003: 40–50; for Lesotho, see Poulter 1972.

34 See on this last point Menski 2006: 478–82.

cultures, most notably in relation to developing (or not) ways of reasoning for distinguishing facts and norms. This means that different legal cultures see reality in different ways. Hence, the optimistic statement that legal systems may often follow different roads but reach the same result, could be opposed to a more pessimistic hypothesis, arguing that those legal systems with important differences in conceptual framework can never find the same answer to legal questions on points where there are such differences, as the questions cannot be (exactly) the same because of a different legal world view. It is true that some kind of liability will lead to some kind of indemnity in case of accident. However, the legal basis may be different (e.g. tort or contract), the kind of compensation awarded may be different (e.g. for pure economic loss), the kind of liability may be different (e.g. fault based or risk based) and finally, the way the claim is handled may be different (e.g. strict law, with emphasis on rights, or negotiation, with emphasis on reaching a compromise).

Of course, legal transfers may take place at the conceptual level. It is not impossible that Continental legal doctrine may one day accept tort law as the basis for compensation in the case of train accidents, instead of contract law, or that the English system will award damages for pure economic loss, but that would imply a change in those legal cultures, not just a change of rules. Cultures can change, but less easily than rules do. Moreover, in other cases, one change may have consequences for the whole structure of the legal system, which may also block a desirable change on another point.

3.1.2 The paradigm of a legal system

As argued elsewhere (Van Hoecke and Warrington 1998: 513–16), every legal system and legal doctrine has its own fundamental principles and conceptions:

A concept of law (what is law and what other social norms?)
A theory on valid legal sources (who has the power to create law and how?)
A methodology of law (theory of interpretation, style of writing)
A theory of argumentation (acceptability of arguments and argumentation strategies)
A theory of legitimation (internally legal and/or non-legal)
A common basic ideology (shared values and common world view)[35]

The more legal systems share such theories and views, the easier legal transfers may take place. The more they differ on one or more points, the more difficult, and probably becoming impossible beyond a certain degree of difference.

3.1.3 Lawyers' traditions

Some examples discussed above show to what extent a legal or judicial tradition in handling the law, treating a case, interpreting the law, may be kept throughout legislative changes, even *contra legem*. 'We always did it this way' seems sometimes to be a stronger argument for judges than legal change.[36] Lawyers' traditions may not only block new interpretations of old rules, but even an adequate use of new rules according to the aims of the legislator.

---

35 This has to be distinguished from (sometimes hidden) ideological oppositions and debates within the legal culture (see on this, e.g. Kennedy 2012).

36 See most notably Rüdiger Lautmann 1972: 129–32.

3.2. External Legal Culture

3.2.1. World view

A more holistic world view, combining law and metaphysical beliefs, is typical for most non-Western cultures, as opposed to the very rational Western approach, that excludes virtually all religious or other metaphysical elements from law and legal practice. Moreover, Western societies typically have an individualistic approach to law, emphasizing subjective, individual rights, whereas other cultures tend to emphasize the importance of the community, of which the individual is a member. Conceptions of law are strongly influenced by the relevant world view. In the West, law is seen as a system with well-defined rights and obligations, which the individual may use as a weapon or as a shield against other individuals or organizations. Other cultures, however, see law (as far as it can be defined as such) as one of the elements in restoring peace within the community, without offering strong rights and obligations. A lack of distinction between law and religion in most non-Western cultures[37] makes the idea of a legal transplant from the West to these cultures already suspicious. How would it be possible to transplant legal constructions to a mixed system of law and religion (as defined from a Western point of view) or to some 'system' which is not conceived as 'law' by those living in it, and even not as a 'system'?[38]

3.2.2. Traditions

Traditions related to deeply rooted matters in society, such as family, ownership, inheritance, contract, etc., will not only limit the willingness to change among lawyers, but also in parliaments and in society at large. In more or less purely 'technical' matters, such as traffic regulation, for instance, changes, including through legal transfers (e.g. for harmonizing law in the EU) will be much easier. Being used to some technical rule also creates a 'legal tradition', but only in the sense of a habit, of being used to it, without being embedded in a broader cultural framework. As political, social and economic circumstances strongly influence traditions and their cultural framework, even persistent traditions may change one day. The changes in the views on family over the last few decades in Europe, and the legal changes they provoked, are a clear example of this. Harmonization of family law among the States of the US has been facilitated by similar changes in society. Hence, the laws of Texas and Louisiana, based on the civil law tradition, changed under the pressure of the US Supreme Court and of societal changes, so as to align with the laws of other States, which have a common law background (Del Duca and Levasseur 2010).

3.3. Areas of Law

As already noted above and by others,[39] legal transfers are likely to be more successful in international business law than, for instance, in family law. Hence, it may be useful to distinguish areas of law in that respect. For this, Roger Cotterrell's classification of communities (instrumental community, traditional community, community of belief and affective community)

---

37 Werner Menski notes that 'Given the holistic nature of African worldviews, religion (like law) was not seen as a separate concept and many African languages do not have a technical term for "religion"' (Menski 2006: 413). In footnote he adds 'This, again, is a parallel to Hindu law, where *dharma* meant neither "law" nor "religion", although it is often wrongly translated as such'.

38 A rather radical example is offered by the position taken by the Canadian Inuits, refusing their protection as a 'minority', because of denial of the Canadian legal system and its competence and logic as a whole (see Lindahl 2013).

39 See, for example the authors discussed by Cotterrell 2001: 80ff.

proves very useful (Cotterrell 1997b).[40] 'Law is always rooted in communities of various kinds' (Cotterrell 2001: 80). This is partly the entire society (minimum conditions for ordering society, Cotterrell 2001, 85) partly the community of lawyers, partly a specific group of specialized lawyers, such as in tax law; or a group of specialized lawyers in combination with some profession(s), such as with intellectual property rights.

3.3.1. Areas with harmonizing orientation

As a first category, I propose to distinguish areas with harmonizing orientation, such as EU law and international business law. They reflect instrumental communities aiming at a common goal, such as establishing a single common market. Within such areas we may distinguish different modalities:

a. transferring law from one of the countries involved to the others. Within the EU, for instance, German and French law have been by far the most influential. Within international business law, American law has been most powerful;
b. new concepts and principles developed in new areas (internet, environmental law, ...) with partial transfers (nothing is entirely new in all respects);interaction among legal systems, with re-transplants or developing 'new law'.

3.3.2. Areas with focus on identity and tradition

Areas with focus on the given society's own identity and tradition: '...laws concerned only to provide minimal conditions of co-existence in a certain environment, such as basic criminal, tort or property law, are often relatively well defined and settled (like the social environment to which they relate), and their basic ideas or orientation are recognized in popular consciousness' (Cotterrell 2001: 85). Legal transfers are less likely in such areas.

3.3.3. Areas based on belief

Communities of belief may be of different kinds. Traditional world views are typical for all societies. Some of them are strongly embedded in religious beliefs. This used to be the case in all societies in the course of history. It is only in the Western world during the last few centuries that law and religion have been largely disconnected. 'In modern, secular Western societies its main legal reference points may be with human rights or other law seen as expressing a moral individualism in Durkheim's sense; that is the idea of autonomy and dignity of the individual as fundamental values worthy of legal protection' (Cotterrell 2001: 83). Indeed, today 'human rights' have taken the position of a new 'natural law' in Western societies and, to some extent even worldwide. At least the concepts and the principles as worded in international treaties on human rights are globalized, be it with still diverging local interpretations, influence of local values, which are essential within the community of belief concerned.

3.3.4. Areas related to affective communities

The main area, which is directly related to an affective community, is, obviously, family law and its underlying views on the family. Law may not really be appropriate for solving relational problems, but it may offer a way out of relationships that are no longer working. Family law is closely embedded in tradition and, hence, not very open to legal transfers. However in times of change, foreign modernization of (family) law may well be used as a model, including one for legal transfers.

40 And, more applied to the discussion on legal transplants: Cotterrell 2001: 82ff.

3.4. Dynamics of Legal Cultures

This chapter may give the impression of offering a rather pessimistic view on the possibility of legal transfers. However, notwithstanding the obstacles discussed above, one may also be rather optimistic, because of the dynamics of legal cultures. Cultures are not static entities. They change: sometimes very slowly, sometimes dramatically and in a short period, because of important changes in society.

Within the context of globalization, there is increasing communication among cultures, leading to legal transfers, re-transplants and harmonization processes.[41] Again, human rights should be mentioned as an example. First, the idea and the vocabulary of human rights have spread all over the world. Secondly, at a next stage, the conceptions of Western human rights principles are also increasingly influential all over the world. Today, dictators do not argue that there are no political freedoms in their country or that torturing is a perfectly legitimate means to use against political opponents. They will rather assert that those freedoms are guaranteed, except when they jeopardize the general interest of the State (or society). They will deny that torturing is used by the police or the army, even if they know it is actually being used (or indeed want it to be used). In 2012, the 'Arab spring' took on not only the formal Western discourse of human rights, but also its underlying ideas. Even if, in the short term, these democratic movements may not have been successful, it shows a change in those Arab countries in shared culture, influenced by the Western tradition.

Finally, there is also increasing mutual influence between doctrinal frameworks. Lawmakers look around and try to use foreign models. Even if attempts to transfer them into their own legal systems fail, there has been an exchange of ideas around that foreign model and sometimes limited parts of it are used, be it considerably adapted to the needs and (doctrinal) traditions of the 'importing' country. New political constructions, such as regional cooperation, look for models elsewhere. As a result, the European Union has been quite influential on Mercosur in Latin America, on the ASEAN construction in Asia and on OHADA in Africa.

Legal research has become increasingly international too. Whereas before the majority of legal scholars were focusing on domestic law and on publications in their mother tongue, today there is a growing pressure on legal academics to become less parochial, to attend (genuinely) international conferences, to use comparative law in their research, to spend time abroad, to publish in English in internationally recognized journals, and so on. As a result, there is an increasing exchange of information on doctrinal concepts and frameworks among scholars belonging to different legal traditions.

Eventually, this will lead to some degree of harmonization of law.

Bibliography

Brüggemeier, G. 2011. *Modernising Civil Liability Law in Europe, China, Brazil and Russia*. Cambridge, Cambridge University Press.

Chen, A. 1992. *An Introduction to the Legal System of the People's Republic of China*. Singapore/Malaysia/Hong Kong, Butterworths Asia.

Chen-Wishart, M. 2013. 'Legal Transplant and Undue Influence: Lost in Translation or a Working Misunderstanding?' 62 *International and Comparative Law Quarterly*, 1–30.

41 Compare Glenn 2005: 95 and 143.

Choudhry, S. 2006. 'Migration as a new metaphor in comparative constitutional law'. In S. Choudhry, *The Migration of Constitutional Ideas*. Cambridge, Cambridge University Press. 1–21.

Clarke, D.C. 1996. 'Power and Politics in the Chinese Court System: The Enforcement of Civil Judgments'. 10 *Columbia Journal of Asian Law*, 1–92, reprinted in P. Keller (ed.) 2001. *Chinese Law and Legal Theory*. The International Library of Essays in Law & Legal Theory, Second Series. Aldershot, Ashgate. 289–380.

Cotterrell, R. 1997a. 'The Concept of Legal Culture' in D. Nelken (ed.), *Comparing Legal Cultures*. Aldershot, Dartmouth. 13–31.

Cotterrell, R. 1997b. 'A Legal Concept of Community', 12 *Canadian Journal of Law and Society*, 75–91.

Cotterrell, R. 2001. 'Is There a Logic of Legal Transplants?' in D. Nelken, and J. Feest (eds), *Adapting Legal Cultures*. Oñati International Series in Law and Society. Oxford: Hart Publishing. 70–92.

Cotterrell, R. 2003. 'Comparatists and Sociology'. In P. Legrand and R. Munday, *Comparative Legal Studies: Traditions and Transitions*. Cambridge, Cambridge University. Ch. 6.

Del Duca, L. and Levasseur, A. 2010. 'Impact of Legal Culture and Legal Transplants on the Evolution of the US Legal System'. 58 *American Journal of Comparative Law*, supplement, in J. Reitz and S. Symeonides (eds), *US National Reports to the XVIIIth International Congress of Comparative Law*. 1–29.

Chukwuemeka, E. 1995. 'Indigenous Law and Justice: Some Major Concepts and Practices'. In G. Woodman and A. Obilade (eds), *African Law and Legal Theory*. Aldershot, Dartmouth. 33–42.

Evans, J. 1994. 'Change in the Doctrine of Precedent during the Nineteenth Century'. In L. Goldstein (ed.), *Precedent in Law*. Oxford, Clarendon Press. 35–71.

Friedman, L. 2001. 'Some Comments on Cotterrell and Legal Transplants'. In D. Nelken and J. Feest, *Adapting Legal Cultures*. Oxford, Hart. 93–8.

Glenn, H.P. 2005. *On Common Laws*. Oxford, Oxford University Press.

Graziadei, M. 2006. 'Comparative Law as the Study of Transplants and Receptions'. In M. Reimann and R. Zimmermann (eds), *The Oxford Handbook of Comparative Law*. Oxford, Oxford University Press. Ch.13.

Ighorodje, V. and O. Bamidele (eds) 2007. *Reporting Impunity: Giving Voice to the Voiceless*. Lagos, Nigerian Coalition on the International Criminal Court.

Jupp, J. 2013. 'Legal Transplants as Solutions for Post-Intervention Criminal Law Reform: Afghanistan's Interim Criminal Procedure Code 2004'. 61 *American Journal of Comparative Law*, 51–91.

Kennedy, D. 2012. 'Political ideology and comparative law'. In M. Bussani and U. Mattei (eds), *The Cambridge Companion to Comparative Law*. Cambridge, Cambridge University Press. 34–56.

Kuyu Mwissa, C. 2005. *Parenté et famille dans les cultures africaines* (Kinship and family in African cultures). Paris, Editions Karthala.

Lindahl, H. 2013. *Fault Lines of Globalization*. Oxford, Oxford University Press.

Markesinis, B. 1997. *Foreign Law & Comparative Methodology. A Subject and a Thesis*. Oxford, Hart Publishing.

Mebenga, M. 2001. 'Le droit et ses pratiques: expérience camerounaise'. In C. Kuyu Mwissa (ed.), *Repenser les droits africains pour le XXIème siècle*, Bibliothèque de l'Académie Africaine de Théorie du Droit, Yaoundé. Cameroon, Editions Menaibuc.

Menski, W. 2006. *Comparative Law in A Global Context. The Legal Systems of Asia and Africa*. Cambridge, Cambridge University Press. 2nd edition.

Nambo, J.J. 2001. 'Le droit et ses pratiques au Gabon' (Law and its practice in Gabon). In C. Kuyu Mwissa (ed.), *Repenser les droits africains pour le XXIème siècle*, Bibliothèque de l'Académie Africaine de Théorie du Droit, Yaoundé. Cameroon, Editions Menaibuc.
Onokah, M. 2003. *Family Law*. Ibadan, Spectrum Books.
Paolisa, N. 2000. 'Unfair Terms in Consumer Contracts: An Anglo-Italian Comparison'. In M. Van Hoecke and F. Ost (eds), *The Harmonisation of European Private Law*. Oxford, Hart Publishing. 179–88.
Phillips, A. and Morris, H. 1971. *Marriage Laws in Africa*. London, International African Institute.
Pomeranz, W. and Gutbrod, M. 2012. 'The Push for Precedent in Russia's Judicial System'. 37 *Review of Central and East European Law*, 1–30.
Poulter, S. 1972. 'Marriage, Divorce and Legitimacy in Lesotho'. In V. Palmer and S. Poulter (eds), *The Legal System of Lesotho*. Charlottesville, Michie. 66–78.
Rüdiger, L. 1972. *Justiz – die stille Gewalt*. Frankfurt am Main, Athenümverlag.
Slaughter, A-M. 1994. 'A Typology of Transjudicial Communication'. 29 *University of Richmond Law Review*, 99–137.
Van Hoecke, M. and Warrington, M. 1998. 'Legal Cultures, Legal Paradigms and Legal Doctrine: Towards a New Model for Comparative Law'. 47 *International and Comparative Law Quarterly*, 495–536.
Waters, D. 1995. 'The Institution of the Trust in Civil and Common Law'. In *Collected Courses of the Hague Academy of International Law*, vol. 252. Dordrecht, Martinus Nijhoff. 117–453.
Woodman, G. 1977. 'Judicial Development of Customary Law: A Case of Marriage Law in Ghana and Nigeria'. 14 *University of .Ghana Law Journal* 115–36.
Zhang, W. 2013. PhD thesis, defended at Ghent University on 28 June 2013. Supervisor Professor Johan Erauw.
Zhdanov, A.A. 2006. 'Transplanting the Anglo-American Trust in Russian Soil'. 31 *Review of Central and East European Law*, 179–231.

Chapter 17
Keeping Civility in its Place: Dissent, Injustice, and the Lessons of History

Austin Sarat[1]

> It is the right of dissent, not the right or duty to conform, that gives dignity, worth and individuality to man.
>
> Justice William O. Douglas, *America Challenged*

> Just as Socrates felt that it was necessary to create a tension in the mind so that individuals could rise from the bondage of myths and half-truths to the unfettered realm of creative analysis and objective appraisal, we must see the need for nonviolent gadflies to create the kind of tension in society that will help men rise from the dark depths of prejudice and racism to the majestic heights of understanding and brotherhood .... I wish you had commended the Negro sit-inners and demonstrators of Birmingham for their sublime courage, their willingness to suffer and their amazing discipline in the midst of great provocation.
>
> Martin Luther King, *Letter from Birmingham Jail*

1. Introduction

Who can be against civility in an age marked by so much uncivil conduct?[2] Who can be against civility when it is eviscerated daily on cable TV and when we witness the most vile and random destruction of human life in the name of one or another political cause? In what follows I do not want to set myself full bore against civility so much as to remind all of us of civility's limits and its distortions.[3]

Civility is not, in my view, a virtue in and of itself.[4] I agree with Michael Sandel (2005: 54) when he says, 'In politics civility is an overrated virtue'. It is a secondary and contingent virtue whose value ultimately depends on other things. Moreover, all too often we hear the call for civility made with no reference to the background conditions that bring forth breaches of civility. All too

1 This chapter is based on the lecture 'Keeping Civility in its Place: Dissent, Injustice, and the Lessons of History' delivered at 'conference on Civility and American Democracy' at the Center for Civil Discourse at the McCormack Graduate School for Social and Global Policy at UMass Boston and Mass Humanities.

2 On the contemporary crisis of civility see Don Eberly, 'The Reformation of Manners' The Civil Society Project, http://civilsocietyproject.org/_files/ReformationOfMannersEssay.pdf (Eberly 2000); also Marks 1996.

3 In this effort I am following in the footsteps of many others. See, for example, DeMott 1996; Sandel 1996; Rorty 1997; Kennedy 2001.

4 For a contrasting point of view see Calhoun 2000: 275: 'Shouldn't the virtue of civility weigh only lightly in the moral scales? My own view is, no. This is in part because I do not share what seems to be the moral theorists' conviction that morality is first and foremost about 'getting it right' as individuals. The more seriously one takes the social practice of morality ... the heavier civility weighs in the scales.'

often we ignore the limit cases where injustice not lack of civility is the problem that needs to be addressed, and we act as if civility uniformly was aligned with justice and advanced the cause of human dignity. In what follows I call civility to account, or rather hold it to account, in the name of justice.[5]

I hope to make some progress in that endeavour by appealing to history and examining one instance in which civil conduct was not enough to satisfy those who demanded it, in which civility was elevated over justice. Here I take up what might be called a 'pathology' of civility, an instance in which the demand for civility was taken to a frightening extreme. Along the way, I want to offer some modest thoughts on the claims of justice, civility and the problem of political dissent in the United States.

2. Birmingham, Alabama, 1963

Let me take you back 50 years to 1963, nine years after the Supreme Court's *Brown v Board of Education* decision and one year before the enactment of the 1964 Civil Rights Act. Let me take you back to Birmingham, Alabama, which in the early 1960s was one of America's most racially divided cities.[6] City ordinances required that drinking fountains, bathrooms and clothing store dressing rooms had to be segregated by race. Responding to a United States Supreme Court decision that struck down racial segregation in public buses,[7] Birmingham privatized its bus company. Ambulances, police wagons, even elevators were segregated by race, as were theatres, ball parks, jail cells, hospitals, hotels and cemeteries. The public library was open only to whites. Interracial marriage was banned, and it was a crime for African-Americans and whites to play cards, draughts or dice together. Ordered by a federal court to provide equal recreational facilities for blacks and whites, the city closed its 68 parks, 38 playgrounds, six swimming pools and four golf courses. Moreover, all Birmingham public schools were racially segregated by order of the local school board.[8]

Lawyers, police, sheriffs and judges enforced the Jim Crow segregation regime. Notable among those officials was Bull Conner, the Public Safety Commissioner who sent police dogs repeatedly against African-Americans who assembled peaceably and lawfully. Supplementing

5 As Calhoun (2000: 252) explains, 'More so than other virtues, civility has intimate associations with following socially established rules, whether those be rules of etiquette or civil law. For example, the civil debater complies with the written rules of debate; civil neighbors comply with local norms for neighborly behavior; and civil drivers comply with conventional expectations about courteous driving. If civility is a virtue it appears to be more like law-abidingness than justice. Like being a law-abiding citizen, being civil appears to require conforming to whatever the social rules are. Unlike justice, it does not require adopting a socially critical moral point of view'.

6 As Martin Luther King put it in his *Letter from Birmingham Jail*, 'There can be no gainsaying the fact that racial injustice engulfs this community. Birmingham is probably the most thoroughly segregated city in the United States. Its ugly record of brutality is widely known. Negroes have experienced grossly unjust treatment in the courts. There have been more unsolved bombings of Negro homes and churches in Birmingham than in any other city in the nation. These are the hard, brutal facts of the case'. http://abacus.bates.edu/admin/offices/dos/mlk/letter.html. See Garrow 1995; McWhorter 2001; Eskew 1997. See also 'Birmingham Campaign'. http://en.wikipedia.org/wiki/Birmingham_campaign.

7 See *Browder v. Gayle*, 352 US 903 (1956). The description in the next two paragraphs is taken from *Critical Legal Readings of Walker v. Birmingham.* http://cyber.law.harvard.edu/Xchange/Content/Bridge/CriticalTheory/walker.htm.

8 This description is taken from Minow 1998.

this legal apparatus, members of the Ku Klux Klan beat freedom riders who tried to take advantage of court-ordered integration of the city bus terminal. Birmingham gained the nickname 'Bomingham' because so many homes and churches of African–American leaders were bombed (Minow 1998: 80–81).

Responding to the situation in Birmingham, the Southern Christian Leadership Council launched a campaign of non-violent, direct action protests. Led by Martin Luther King, Jr. protesters refused to obey segregationist ordinances in order to 'create a situation so crisis-packed that it will inevitably open the door to negotiation' (King 1963). They initiated a boycott to pressure business leaders to provide employment opportunities to people of all races and end segregation in public facilities, restaurants and stores. When those leaders resisted the boycott, SCLC organizer Wyatt Lee Walker and Birmingham native Fred Shuttlesworth began a series of sit-ins and marches intended to provoke mass arrests. Galvanized by photographs of police using high pressure water hoses and dogs to subdue demonstrators, Birmingham found itself in the national media spotlight.[9]

3. The Dilemmas of Dissent

Protest and dissent of the kind carried out in Birmingham almost 50 years ago has had, and continues to have, a central and important role in America's national story and in our cultural imagination.[10] Whatever the realities on the ground, recognizing a right to speak truth to power, a right to express one's political views through peaceful protest, is advertised as a peculiarly American achievement. 'From the beginning', Henry Steele Commager (1954: 39) notes, 'our own history was rooted in dissent'.[11] Like Commager, Steven Shiffrin (1999: xii) similarly identifies protest and dissent's centrality to America's self-concept. They are, he says, 'crucial institution(s) for challenging unjust hierarchies and for promoting progressive change. [They are] also an important part of our national identity ...'.

Protest and dissent are signs of cultural liveliness and are virtues that Americans most consistently use to explain what makes America distinct and special.[12] Thus the political theorist George Kateb (1992: 89–90) describes what he sees as a uniquely American kind of individualism, what he calls 'democratic individuality', an individualism deeply entangled with protest and dissent. The democratic individual becomes a dissenter as an expression of 'negative individuality', that is 'the disposition to disobey bad conventions and unjust laws, by oneself, and on the basis of a strict moral self-scrutiny, self-examination'. The dissenter takes responsibility for himself and makes the self a project; 'one must become the architect of one's soul'.

This kind of democratic individuality was at the heart of the Birmingham protests. As Martin Luther King wrote in his *Letter from Birmingham Jail*:

> I am in Birmingham because injustice is here. Just as the prophets of the eighth century B.C. left their villages and carried their "thus saith the Lord" far beyond the boundaries of their home towns, and just as the Apostle Paul left his village of Tarsus and carried the gospel of Jesus Christ to the far corners of the Greco-Roman world, so am I compelled to carry the gospel of freedom beyond my

9 See 'Birmingham Campaign, 1963'. http://www.scribd.com/doc/56760488/Birmingham-Alabama-1963.

10 See, for example, Bromwich 2002: 1–21. On the ways in which this proposition is contested see Hunter 1991.

11 See also Fortas 1968: 168, 24.

12 See Kammen 1993. 'America', Shiffrin (1990: 5) contends, 'has had a romance with the first amendment'.

> own home town. Like Paul, I must constantly respond to the Macedonian call for aid. Moreover, I am cognizant of the interrelatedness of all communities and states. I cannot sit idly by in Atlanta and not be concerned about what happens in Birmingham. Injustice anywhere is a threat to justice everywhere. We are caught in an inescapable network of mutuality, tied in a single garment of destiny. Whatever affects one directly, affects all indirectly. Never again can we afford to live with the narrow, provincial "outside agitator" idea. Anyone who lives inside the United States can never be considered an outsider anywhere within its bounds.

In King's description the dissenter is 'everyman' moved to stand up against injustice. In our history we often treat these 'everyman' figures, who were often condemned in their own time, as heroes who bravely confronted power and changed history. We enquire into the psychology of the dissenter, even as we wonder whether we have the courage to stand up for what we believe. In the American story the self of the dissenter is divided. It is desirous of the comfort that patriotism and loyalty provide, but ill at ease if the price of such comfort is silence in the face of the unjust suffering of others. In the American story dissent is both institutionalized and is a cultural practice of engaging the question of injustice. The call of dissent is, in Judith Butler's words (2002), to hear 'beyond what we are able to hear', to attend to an alterity whose presence is overwhelmed by events. Or, as Kenji Yoshino (2010: 221) puts it, 'The dissenter's greatest permission is to imagine a better world, to be the prophet of eternities'.

Protesters, dissenters, like those who took to the streets of Birmingham in 1963, seek to define and occupy an in-between space, resistant to prevailing orthodoxy, but engaged with it nonetheless. Even as she points out its flaws and demands redress, the dissenter affirms her continuing allegiance to the community she criticizes. She is at once within, but outside of, the institutions or the community in which she participates.[13] As King (1963) put it:

> We will reach the goal of freedom in Birmingham, and all over the nation, because the goal of America is freedom. Abused and scorned though we may be, our destiny is tied up with America's destiny. Before the pilgrims landed at Plymouth, we were here. Before the pen of Jefferson etched the majestic words of the Declaration of Independence across the pages of history, we were here. For more than two centuries our forebears labored in this country without wages; they made cotton king; they built the homes of their masters while suffering gross injustice and shameful humiliation-and yet out of a bottomless vitality they continued to thrive and develop. If the inexpressible cruelties of slavery could not stop us, the opposition we now face will surely fail. We will win our freedom because the sacred heritage of our nation and the eternal will of God are embodied in our echoing demands.

In part because of her liminality, the dissenter is often accused of disloyalty and subject to sanction and stigma by state and society. Pulled from the one side by those who say that protest and dissent does not go far enough and from the other by those who demand acquiescence as the sign of loyalty, maintaining the 'in-betweeness' of dissent is very difficult. The dissenter insists, as Henry Louis Gates (1991) puts it, that '[C]ritique can also be a form of commitment, a means of laying a claim. It's the ultimate gesture of citizenship. A way of saying: I'm not just passing through, I *live* here'.

Yet, as Birmingham showed, protest and dissent is always dangerous to those who practice them, no matter how civil that protest and dissent may be. Protest and dissent are vexatious to

13 For a discussion of this tension, see Euchner 1996.

those against whom they are directed. For both the dissenter and her target, dissent stirs up strong emotions and often calls forth strident reactions. Majorities or powerful people seldom appreciate challenge or embrace those who do not profess allegiance to their policies or practices. As King (1963) put it:

> My friends, I must say to you that we have not made a single gain in civil rights without determined legal and nonviolent pressure. Lamentably, it is an historical fact that privileged groups seldom give up their privileges voluntarily. Individuals may see the moral light and voluntarily give up their unjust posture; but, as Reinhold Niebuhr has reminded us, groups tend to be more immoral than individuals.

King's admonition echoes Justice Oliver Wendell Holmes observation that 'Persecution for the expression of opinions seems to me to be perfectly logical. If you have no doubt of your premises or your power and want a certain result with all your heart, you naturally express your wishes in law and sweep away all opposition'.[14] Writing 50 years after Holmes and less than a decade after King, Justice William O. Douglas noted that government's 'eternal temptation ... has been to arrest the speaker rather than to correct the conditions about which he complains'.[15]

While responses to protest and dissent in state and society are contingent and historically specific, the general tendency is toward the containment, if not outright repression, of dissent. Koffler and Gershman (1984: 858) note that in the United States, 'The history of the first amendment has been the history of intolerance of political dissent, a story of dark shadows of fear and orthodoxy illuminated periodically by brilliant rays of enlightenment'.[16] In normal times, the critic, the naysayer, the resister, is not welcomed warmly and comes under intense pressure to evacuate the space of dissent, to take sides, to choose allegiance over authenticity. When the physical security of the community of which the dissenter is a member seems jeopardized these tendencies and temptations intensify.[17]

In the practices of our social and political institutions dissent is accommodated into a defence of rights, in particular the right to freedom of expression. In this accommodation the emphasis is not on the dissenter, but on dissent, and on the value of tolerating dissent for our society. As a result, we may admire the dissenter, but only 'put up with' dissent. Dissent is an annoyance, maybe even an offence. The best that the dissenter can expect is toleration,[18] a toleration which reassures those who express it of their own virtue while, at the same time, allowing them to condemn both those who dissent and the message they seek to communicate. As Shiffrin says,

---

14 See *Abrams v. United States*, 250 US 616, 630 (1919) (Holmes, J., dissenting). See also Schofield 1914: 11. 'Men', Schofield wrote, 'will be fined and imprisoned, under the guise of being punished for their bad motives, or bad intent and ends, simply because the powers that be do not agree with their opinions ....'. As Shiffrin (1999: 92) puts it 'Persons in power also have the all-too-human tendency to believe in good faith that the "right" answers to moral and political issues just happen to be ones that consolidate and enhance their own power'.

15 *Younger v. Harris*, 401 US 37, 65 (1971) (Douglas, J. dissenting).

16 See also Vitello 2000. Susan Ross (2001: 402) argues that 'despite nods to the vital role uninhibited debate plays in democratic self-governance, the Court has not consistently advanced a broad presumption against government action that encourages orthodoxy or discourages open discussion'. See also Chafee 1941.

17 See Sarat 2004.

18 See Heyd 1966, also Mendus 1989. Shiffrin (1999, xiii) argues that given the danger of dissent 'It is not enough to tolerate dissent; dissent needs to be institutionally encouraged'.

> The First Amendment serves to undermine dissent even as it protects it. Of course, the First Amendment protects dissent. It offers a legal claim for dissenters, and it functions as a cultural symbol encouraging dissenters to speak out. Nonetheless, the symbolism of the First Amendment perpetuates a cultural myth. It functions as a form of cultural ideology through which the society secures allegiance. It leads us to believe that America is the land of free speech, but it blinks at the "tyranny of the prevailing opinion and feeling", and "it masks the extent to which free speech is marginalized, discouraged, and repressed. Even as it promotes dissent, it falsifies the willingness of the society to receive it, and it tolerates rules of place and property that make it difficult for people of modest means to address a mass audience." (Shiffren 1999: 27)

The dissenter reserves the right to judge the law and to violate laws deemed to be unjust. As King (1963) put it:

> One may want to ask: "How can you advocate breaking some laws and obeying others?" The answer lies in the fact that there are two types of laws: just and unjust. I would be the first to advocate obeying just laws. One has not only a legal but a moral responsibility to obey just laws. Conversely, one has a moral responsibility to disobey unjust laws. I would agree with St. Augustine that "an unjust law is no law at all" ... An unjust law is a human law that is not rooted in eternal law and natural law. Any law that uplifts human personality is just. Any law that degrades human personality is unjust.

This willingness to violate the law is deeply troubling to those committed to the view that civility is a primary moral virtue. They worry about the righteousness that prompts such disobedience, seeing in it a zealous intolerance of others. As Calhoun (2000: 275) observes, 'I am inclined to weigh civility heavily in the scales because I find something odd ... about the great confidence one must have in one's own judgment .... to be willing to be uncivil to others in the name of a higher moral calling'. Such critics believe that dissent and the pursuit of justice must be tempered by, and sometimes give way, to the demands of civility.

4. Today's 'Crisis' of Civility

Today we are in another of those eras in which political leaders and commentators periodically bemoan a crisis of incivility.[19] Indeed, throughout American history, the discourse of civility has proven quite resilient and concern for a perceived lack of civility has ebbed and flowed in recognizable patterns. Somehow, we continue to find ways to talk about civility and to warn of its demise. Today, 'uncivil' has become synonymous for that horribly dreaded political quality – being wholly and closed-mindedly 'partisan'. President Obama, among others, has been a leading voice highlighting our alleged loss of civility and calling for its restoration. Speaking at Notre Dame's 2009 commencement President Obama called on his listeners to 'temper our passions, and .... be wary of self-righteousness .... to remain open, and curious, and eager to continue the moral and spiritual debate that began for so many of you within the walls of Notre Dame. And, within our vast democracy', Obama continued, 'this doubt should remind us to persuade through reason, through an appeal whenever we can to universal rather than parochial principles, and most of all through an abiding example of good works, charity, kindness, and service that moves hearts

19 See Sherratt (2011), also Powers (2008) and Eisner (2011).

and minds'.[20] Obama returned to this theme in January 2011 at a memorial for the victims of the Arizona shooting of Congresswoman Gabriel Giffords. 'But at a time when our discourse has become so sharply polarized – at a time when we are far too eager to lay the blame for all that ails the world at the feet of those who happen to think differently than we do', Obama observed, 'it's important for us to pause for a moment and make sure that we're talking with each other in a way that heals, not in a way that wounds .... As we discuss these issues, let each of us do so with a good dose of humility. Rather than pointing fingers or assigning blame, let's use this occasion to expand our moral imaginations, to listen to each other more carefully, to sharpen our instincts for empathy and remind ourselves of all the ways that our hopes and dreams are bound together .... And if, as has been discussed in recent days, their death helps usher in more civility in our public discourse, let us remember it is not because a simple lack of civility caused this tragedy – it did not – but rather because only a more civil and honest public discourse can help us face up to the challenges of our nation in a way that would make them proud. We should be civil because we want to live up to the example of public servants like John Roll and Gabby Giffords, who knew first and foremost that we are all Americans, and that we can question each other's ideas without questioning each other's love of country and that our task, working together, is to constantly widen the circle of our concern so that we bequeath the American Dream to future generations'.[21]

In a recent interview with Fox News's Bill O'Reilly, Obama again returned to the issue of civility. 'The media, unfortunately, if I have a nice talk with John McCain, and we're agreeing to do something, nobody is going to report it', the president said. 'But if there's an argument, then that's what gets reported and, as a consequence, I think a lot of politicians think the way I get on the news is if I insult somebody'. Personal attacks are what the media gravitates toward, Obama said, and that fact 'over the long term, is making it harder for the sensible center to get together to solve problems, and I think that is damaging'. Civility and cooperation are necessary, Obama argued, to achieve policy goals like cutting government spending. 'The only way you make those tough decisions is if you're willing to cut the other side a little bit of slack.'[22]

Those who, like President Obama, side with civility variously name and define it. '[C]ivility is concerned with so many different things that it is difficult to specify the range of its applicability' (Schmidt 2000). Yet however it is defined, civility describes how we act. More specifically, it defines how we act or suggests how we *should* act towards one another. According to one dictionary definition, civility refers to refraining from rudeness, while politeness implies some further effort to extend courtesies to others.[23] For some civility is little more than politeness in public discourse.[24] Others, however, claim there is more to civility than manners. In this view,

20 President Barack Obama, 'Commencement Speech, Notre Dame University'. http://www.huffingtonpost.com/2009/05/17/obama-notre-dame-speech-f_n_204387.html.

21 President Barack Obama, 'Arizona Memorial Speech'. http://www.huffingtonpost.com/2011/01/12/obama-arizona-memorial-sp_n_808335.html. For a critique of Obama's emphasis on civility see David Bromwich, 'Obama on Civility and Lincoln on the Rule of Law'. http://www.huffingtonpost.com/david-bromwich/abraham-lincoln-on-violen_b_809546.html.

22 'Barack Obama to Bill O'Reilly: Policy Goals Require Civility'. http://www.politico.com/news/stories/0211/49011.html.

23 *Webster's New World Dictionary*, 3rd College edition.

24 As Kennedy 2001 puts it 'Civility typically connotes courtesy, respectability, self control, regard for others-a willingness to conduct oneself according to socially approved rules even when one would like to do otherwise. Civility, Walzer (1974: 602) notes, makes for 'political peace ... It makes politics less dangerous and less interesting'.

'Civility is an attitude and a mode of action which attempts to strike a balance between conflicting demands and conflicting interests' (Shils 1997: 76). In this view, 'Civility is a disposition that makes political life possible because it allows those with different and conflicting views of the good to live peacefully side-by-side under conditions where a deeper moral agreement about shared purposes or comprehensive systems would be impossible' (Boyd 2006: 865). Thus understood civility is 'primarily a stance toward strangers' (Meyer 2000: 71).[25] It 'requires that we show respect for people we do not know …' (Billante and Saunders 2002: 2).

Still others treat civility as a kind of self restraint. As the psychologist Robert Coles puts it, civility 'means all of us subordinating our feelings to certain shared imperatives'. It is all about collective interest-not 'collective egoism' (Coles 1980: 140).[26] 'Civility', Stephen Carter (1998: 11) notes, 'is the sum of the many sacrifices we are called on to make for the sake of living together'.[27] In Carter's view, 'Respect for rules of conduct has been lost in the deafening and essentially empty rights-talk' of modern American politics. And, he warns, the popular illusion 'that all desires are rights only continues its insidious spread'. Referencing James Q. Wilson, Carter makes the further claim that we, as a culture, suffer from 'an elevation of self-expression over self-control'. He writes particularly of civility's decline in both elementary education and in political life. Even our insults were once expressed in a manner one might call 'civil'. The pointed wit of the nineteenth and early twentieth centuries has fallen to obscenity in the traditional domain of public insult. An unabashed 'witless barbarism' dominates the conversational life and political etiquette of our age. Carter repeatedly mourns a tragic loss of self-restraint: we have developed a 'right to our own offensiveness'. And we take great pride in that 'right' (see Carter 1988). Our society, Carter worries, has lost a necessary degree of 'moral focus'. Instead of emphasizing the protection of valuable speech (whatever that might be), we celebrate the brazenness of the Howard Sterns of American pop culture. The law should not limit the right to free speech, for it is at least backed by profound tradition. Instead, Carter argues, 'We should recognize the terrible damage that free speech can do if people are unwilling to adhere to the *basic precept of civility*'. 'We must sometimes rein in our own impulses', he writes, 'for the sake of those who are making the democratic journey with us'.

---

25 See also Sinopoli 1995. According to Sinopoli, a norm of civility 'defines a *standard of conduct* that citizens can rightfully expect from strangers'.

26 Coles argues, '[civility] has to do with allegiance – a sense that one's behavior ought to be, under a range of circumstances, responsive to and respectful of, certain standards: historically, they have been state-connected; more recently, they have tended increasingly to be social or conventional (in the non-pejorative sense of that last word'. In contrast, Glenn Tinder denies the existence of any collective American interest or 'community' in need of protection. Civility for Tinder, therefore, is something altogether distinct from Carter's manners and etiquette. It is the stance we adopt in response to the discovery of community's impossibility. We place ourselves at a certain distance, 'constituted of doubt and of limits on allegiance', from historical phenomena. Civility defines this distance, our position of conditioned withdrawal from history. For Tinder, civility is derived from man's very nature as communal being in a world where true community is never obtained. In the face of his 'communal impasse', Tinder defines civility as an 'ideal of historical responsibility without historical illusions'. 'Civility', he claims, 'is the stance through which one consciously and responsibly bears the existence of unimaginable multitudes of unpredictable and troublesome fellow humans' (Tinder 1974: 558, 560).

27 Ronald Arnett (2001: 15) describes civility, for example, as a 'pragmatic ethical praxis'. He argues that 'civility is an interpersonal metaphor grounded in the public domain and in a pragmatic commitment to keeping the conversation going in a time of narrative confusion and virtue fragmentation'. Like Carter, Arnett is quick to admit that we live in a cynical age. Civility is therefore an incredibly important value in the negotiation of difference. He speaks of codes of communicative interaction.

Rules of civility, Carter (1998: 11) continues, 'are thus also rules of morality: it is morally proper to treat our fellow citizens with respect, and morally improper not to'. In this vein, civility is equated with 'respect for the dignity and the desire for dignity of other persons' (Shils 1997: 338). Breaches of civility are not simply bad manners; they signal 'disdain' for persons as 'moral beings. Treating someone rudely, brusquely or condescendingly says loudly and clearly that you do not regard her as your equal' (Boyd 2006: 867). Put in the affirmative, civility is 'a precondition of democratic dialogue' (Carter 1998: 25).[28]

Taking up this theme, Anthony Kronman (1996) offers a view of civility as something much more important than mere politeness. When journalists, Kronman observes, bemoan the current crisis of civility, they trivialize civility by equating it with decorum and politeness. In Kronman's view American politicians have always insulted each other's characters and ideas, and citizens have always been fascinated by the prurient details of their representatives' lives. In fact, he argues, we've actually become more civil; for example, politicians' quarrels no longer end in duels. Beyond that, some level of rudeness is necessary, he suggests, because rough candor keeps politicians humble.[29] Yet Kronman believes American society is indeed facing a crisis of civility, not in a loss of politeness, but in a loss of interest in the public good. In his view, the root sense of civility is found in the art of civil government. This art is not innate; it demands experience and training. Civility is the art of creating a government – its laws, customs and institutions-based in concern for the public good. While Kronman concedes that every political and moral judgement is offered from a particular perspective, he insists that the public good is what is held in common. Kronman argues that even if a claim about the public good stems from an individual's perspective, the claim is not about that perspective. The public good is '...what philosophers call its intentional object, the thing the claim purports to be a claim about' (1996: 731). The public good must have value to other people; otherwise, such claims would never be made because they would not sway others. Civility involves an appeal to a public good, and from this appeal, we can, Kronman believes, build institutions and customs.

5. Protest, Dissent, and the Quest for Justice

In the case of the Birmingham, civil rights demonstrators appealed to both the idea of rights and the public good. They tried to make the case that segregation was not just an injury to blacks, but rather was an injury to everyone, a defilement of the Constitution, harmful to America and all Americans, even those who advocated it. As part of their effort to make this case, they planned a protest march to coincide with Good Friday and Easter Sunday, 14 April 1963. King's group applied for a permit for the march in accordance with local law, but their application was denied. Seeking to ensure that there would be no demonstrations on Good Friday or Easter, city officials sought an injunction from a state court to stop it. They argued that the parade ordinance properly prevented marches without permits and that the court should issue an order directly forbidding the planned marches. The court did so barely a day and a half before the march scheduled for Good

28 See also Rehnquist 1973. According to William Rehnquist, civility requires a belief in the necessity for both public and private 'orderliness'; that is, some personal commitment to establishing 'an atmosphere of discussion free of visible and bristling hostility' (4). For Rehnquist, civility is crucially important: 'it is not only form and manner; it is an *underlying attitude*' (5). Civility in this sense constitutes a profound 'commitment to the importance of the process of debate, discussion and even conversation' (6).

29 Trisha Olsen and Karl Shoemaker criticize Anthony Kronman for separating civility from decorum, temperateness of speech and politeness. For Olsen and Shoemaker (1996), civility dwells in the 'art of action'.

Friday. Not surprisingly, the issuing judge, William A. Jenkins, was 'part of the government that implemented racial segregation and ducked orders opposed to it' (Minow 1998: 81). King had encountered a similar order in an earlier civil rights campaign, in Albany, Georgia.[30] 'In Albany, the protesters decided to abide by the court order, to challenge it, and appeal it. In the meantime, though, the momentum of their campaign dissipated. In Birmingham, King decided to violate the order. They made no effort to challenge it before their Good Friday march. They declared their intention to disobey the injunction because it was "raw tyranny under the guise of maintaining law and order".'[31]

On Good Friday, King and 60 others paraded along the sidewalk while a crowd of 1,000 to 1,500 onlookers stood by clapping, hollering and whooping. Some of the crowd followed the marchers and spilled out into the street. The marchers were promptly arrested. On Easter Sunday, 14 April, a crowd of between 1,500 and 2,000 people congregated in the mid afternoon in the vicinity of Seventh Avenue and Eleventh Street North in Birmingham. A group of about 50 civil rights protesters started down the sidewalk two abreast. Some 300 or 400 people from among the onlookers followed in a crowd that occupied the entire width of the street and overflowed onto the sidewalks. Violence occurred. Members of the crowd threw rocks that injured a newspaperman and damaged a police motorcycle. More of the civil rights demonstrators were arrested following the Sunday march. The next day, Monday, attorneys for King and the others appeared in court, and sought to dissolve the restraining order. 'The city moved that the protesters should have to show why they should not be held in contempt. The judge found them guilty of contempt and refused to consider the constitutionality of the restraining order because King and the others had disobeyed it before trying to obtain judicial relief. The judge reasoned that the only issues properly before that court were its jurisdiction to issue the temporary restraining order and whether the defendants had knowingly violated it. He held them in contempt and sentenced each of the violators to a five-day jail sentence and a $50 fine'.[32] They appealed their convictions and eventually sought relief from the United States Supreme Court.

In the midst of the Birmingham protests, eight Alabama clergymen issued a statement condemning the demonstrations in terms reminiscent of several different conceptions of civility.[33] 'We are now confronted by a series of demonstrations by some of our Negro citizens', they said, 'directed and led in part by outsiders. We recognize the natural *impatience* of people who feel that their hopes are slow in being realized. But we are convinced that these demonstrations are unwise and untimely. We agree rather with certain local Negro leadership which has called for honest and open negotiation of racial issues in our area. And we believe this kind of facing of issues can best be accomplished by citizens of our own metropolitan area, white and Negro, meeting with their knowledge and experience of the local situation. All of us need to face that responsibility and find *proper channels* for its accomplishment. Just as we formerly pointed out that "hatred and violence have no sanction in our religious and political traditions," we also point out that *such actions as incite to hatred and violence*, however technically peaceful those actions may be, have not contributed to the resolution of our local problems. We do not believe that these days of new hope

30 For a description of the Albany campaign see Hampton 1990.

31 '*Critical Legal Readings of Walker v. Birmingham*' http://cyber.law.harvard.edu/bridge/CriticalTheory/walker.txt.htm.

32 Ibid.

33 Published statement by Bishop C.C.J. Carpenter, Bishop Joseph A. Durick, Rabbi Hilton L. Grafman, Bishop Paul Hardin, Bishop Holan B. Harmon, the Reverend George M. Murray, the Reverend Edward V. Ramage and the Reverend Earl Stallings (12 April 1963). http://www.priestsforlife.org/articles/kingltroriginal.htm. For a description of the circumstances in which this statement was written, see Bass 2001.

are days when extreme measures are justified in Birmingham. We commend the community as a whole, and the local news media and law enforcement officials in particular, on the *calm manner* in which these demonstrations have been handled. We urge the public to continue to show *restraint* should the demonstrations continue, and the law enforcement officials to remain calm and continue to protect our city from violence' (emphasis added).

Resonant with those who bemoan a crisis of civility in our era, these clergymen treated the civil rights protests as manifestations of 'impatience'. That impatience was contrasted with 'honest and open negotiation' of the kind praised by President Obama in his Fox News interview. Characterizing the demonstrations as inciting 'hatred and violence' was another way of branding them as uncivil. In contrast, the clergymen commended the community and its law enforcement officials for 'the calm manner in which the demonstrations have been handled'. Finally, invoking another dimension of civility the clergymen urged that 'when rights are consistently denied, a cause should be pressed in the courts and in negotiations among local leaders, and not in the streets', and appealed 'to both our white and Negro citizenry to observe the principles of law and order and common sense'.

6. Choosing Civility over Justice

Many of the sentiments in the clergymen's statement were reiterated when the United States Supreme Court heard the appeal of the Birmingham demonstrators. Indeed its *Walker v. Birmingham* decision, 388 US 307 (1967), turned the clergymen's call for civility into a demand for deference even to unjust court orders. The Court, Justice Stewart writing for the majority, cited approvingly the proposition that

> An injunction duly issuing out of a court of general jurisdiction with equity powers upon pleadings properly invoking its action, and served upon persons made parties therein and within the jurisdiction, must be obeyed by them however erroneous the action of the court may be, even if the error be in the assumption of the validity of a seeming but void law going to the merits of the case. It is for the court of first instance to determine the question of the validity of the law, and until its decision is reversed for error by orderly review, either by itself or by a higher court, its orders based on its decision are to be respected, and disobedience of them is contempt of its lawful authority, to be punished. (at 313)

Acknowledging that the Birmingham parade ordinance was of dubious constitutional validity,[34] the Court nonetheless defended the view that civility is the bedrock of civil freedom. 'Civil liberties, as guaranteed by the Constitution, imply the existence of an organized society maintaining public order without which liberty itself would be lost in the excesses of unrestrained abuses.' Here the actions of the Birmingham civil rights demonstrators, who sought an end to segregation and made an effort to insure that blacks would be treated with dignity and recognized as full citizens, were equated with 'unrestrained abuses'. Stewart followed the Alabama Supreme Court's holding that

> As a general rule, an unconstitutional statute is an absolute nullity and may not form the basis of any legal right or legal proceedings, yet until its unconstitutionality has been judicially declared

34 Two years later the Court struck down the Birmingham Parade ordinance as a patent violation of free speech. See *Shuttlesworth v. City of Birmingham*, 394 US 147 (1969).

> in appropriate proceedings, no person charged with its observance under an order or decree may disregard or violate the order or the decree with immunity from a charge of contempt of court; and he may not raise the question of its unconstitutionality in collateral proceedings on appeal from a judgment of conviction for contempt of the order or decree.

He ended his opinion by echoing the clergyman's description of the Birmingham protesters as 'impatient', and portrayed their impatience, however 'righteous' its source, as a threat to civilization itself. 'This Court', Stewart said, 'cannot hold that the petitioners were constitutionally free to ignore all the procedures of the law and carry their battle to the streets. One may sympathize with the petitioners' impatient commitment to their cause. But respect for judicial process is a small price to pay for the civilizing hand of law, which alone can give abiding meaning to constitutional freedom' (at 321).[35] In Stewart's view the only way for the civil rights protesters to demonstrate their 'respect', their commitment to civility, would have been to defer to an unconstitutional injunction, issued by an ardent, segregationist judge. Here Stewart's opinion replays the response that Rosa Parks received when she asked the policeman who came to arrest her for refusing to move to the back of a segregated bus 'Why do you treat us so badly? I don't know' she recalled the officer responding, 'but the law is the law, and you're under arrest'.[36] Stewart imaginatively inverted the positions of the protestors who demonstrated in the hope of advancing constitutional values and the segregationists who distorted the very meaning of the Constitution. The former are uncivil, disrespectful and dangerous; the latter are owed respect and deference.[37]

Stewart's call for civility, the call to respect the 'judicial process', has the effect of discouraging ordinary citizens from seeing themselves as active interpreters of the law and of suppressing conflict over basic principles of justice while diverting it from the streets to the courtroom. The apparently moderate call for civility and respect became, in this case, a 'tool of the regime of oppression' (*Critical Legal Readings of Walker v Birmingham*: 4). Thus as Minow (1998: 89) notes, 'King and others had to lose their liberty despite an unjust order, an unjust local process, and an unjust state legal system'.

7. Conclusion

Reading Stewart's opinion calls to mind Herbert Marcuse's (1965) critique of what he called 'Repressive Tolerance'. Writing in the mid 1960s, Marcuse argued that tolerance was not itself a

35 For a careful analysis of this kind of argument see Peller 1987. Peller argues that dominant groups justify their privileged status by associating the 'other' with base, animal urges – a pattern extending from Nazi caricatures of Jews, to white racist caricatures of Blacks, to the middle-class vision of the poor, to male visions of femininity, to factory owners' visions of workers, to skyscraper office images of the people on subways. In each class relation, the dominant group projects the other as emotional and primitive, ruled by irrational passion. In this interpretation, the language of the distinction between reason and passion seems to be simply the language by which the powerful and dominant justify their own power on the basis that they are more civilized and human – and as such, the very categories of reason and passion, far from giving us a vantage point from which to distinguish politics from truth, seem to be merely one form of the rhetoric of social power (93).

36 Quoted in White 1996: 816.

37 As Minow (1998: 88) notes, 'Surely the Supreme Court justices knew that no defense of purely procedural values could prevent the watching world from reading their opinion as exonerating those who administered racial apartheid in Birmingham'.

primary political virtue and we should not extend tolerance to 'policies conditions, and modes of behavior which should not be tolerated because they are impeding, if not destroying, the chances of creating an existence without fear and misery' (1). Marcuse opposed tolerance of that which is 'radically evil' (like racial segregation) even if that came at a cost to 'the cohesion of the whole' (1). In his view, only when tolerance was practiced by 'the rulers as well as by the ruled, by the lords as well as by the peasants, by the sheriffs as well as by their victims' should it be 'tolerated' (2). Marcuse warned that the call for tolerance masked, or ignored, background conditions that gave it a particular political tilt. He warned that society should not be indiscriminate in its embrace of tolerance 'where the pacification of existence, where freedom and happiness themselves are at stake: here, certain things cannot be said, certain ideas cannot be expressed, certain policies cannot be proposed, certain behavior cannot be permitted without making tolerance an instrument for the continuation of servitude' (5).[38]

This is, I think, one of the most important of the lessons taught in Birmingham 50 years ago. This is, I fear, what Stewart's opinion in *Walker* became, namely 'an instrument for the continuation of servitude'. It represented an extreme extension of the call for civility, an elevation of civility over justice, or perhaps an undue deferral of the call for justice. Today it is a useful reminder both of the burden that dissent carries even when its cause is the cause of the Constitution itself and of the need to keep civility in its place.

Civility is, as I said at the beginning of this chapter, not a primary virtue. It is not an end in itself. In so far as it aids the cause of justice, civility has a powerful claim on democratic citizens; in so far as it impedes the attainment of justice civility can, and should, be breached. What Marcuse (1965: 10) said about tolerance applies with equal force to civility, 'When tolerance mainly serves the protection and preservation of a repressive society, when it serves to neutralize opposition and to render men immune against other and better forms of life, then tolerance has been perverted'. Many embrace civility out of a humble recognition that no one is in 'possession of truth and capable of defining what is right and wrong, good and bad', just and unjust (Marcuse 1965: 5).[39] While there is much to praise in such epistemological and ethical modesty, it should not disable us from recognizing that, as Randall Kennedy once put it, 'if you are in an argument with a thug, there are things much more important than civility'.[40]

Fifty years ago the 'incivility' displayed by the Birmingham civil rights demonstrators toward the thugs who oppressed them helped to enlarge the USA's collective vision and to build a more inclusive and more just community. That is the standard against which their actions should be judged. That is the standard by which anyone's conduct should be judged. If the protest and dissent of the Birmingham civil rights demonstrators indeed was 'impatient' and 'righteous' rather than civil, it was in its time, and is in our time, nonetheless worth praising and emulating.

Bibliography

Arnett, R. 2001. 'Dialogic Civility as Pragmatic Ethical Praxis: An Interpersonal Metaphor for the Public Domain'. 11 *Communication Theory*, 15.

38 As Dumm (1999: 102) puts it, 'To identify a decline of civility in public discourse with the breakdown of civil society is itself to engage in a political strategy that excludes and marginalizes subordinate groups .... '.

39 As Emily Gill (2001) notes, part of civic virtue is recognizing that any belief is contestable and that to achieve a public good we must respect each belief enough to argue it.

40 Quoted in DeMott 1996: 13.

Bass, J. 2001. *Blessed Are the Peacemakers: Martin Luther King, Jr., Eight White Religious Leaders, and the 'Letter from Birmingham Jail'*. Baton Rouge, Louisiana, Louisiana State University Press.

Billante, N. and Saunders, P. 2002. 'Six Questions About Civility'. Volume 82 of CIS Occasional Papers Series. St Leonards, NSW Australia, Centre for Independent Studies.

Boyd, R. 2006. 'The Value of Civility'. 43 *Urban Studies*, 865.

Bromwich, D. 2002. 'Lincoln and Whitman as Representative Americans'. 90 *The Yale Review*, 1–21.

Butler, J. 2002. 'Explanation and Exoneration, or What We Can Hear'. 5 *Theory and Event* http://muse.jhu.edu/journals/theory_and_event/v005/5.4butler.html.

Calhoun, C. 2000. 'The Virtue of Civility'. 29 *Philosophy and Public Affairs*, 251.

Carter, S. 1998. *Civility: Manners, Morals, and the Etiquette of Democracy*. New York, Basic Books.

Carter, S. 1988. 'Just Be Nice'. *Yale Alumni Magazine*. May.

Carter, S. 1998. *Civility: Manners, Morals, and the Etiquette of Democracy*. New York, Basic Books.

Chafee, Z. 1941. *Free Speech in the United States*. Union, New Jersey, Lawbook Exchange. 2nd edition.

Coles, R. 1980. 'Civility and Psychology'. 109 *Daedalus*, 136.

Commager, H.S. 1954. *Freedom, Loyalty, Dissent*. New York: Oxford University Press, 1954.

Critical Legal Readings of Walker v. Birmingham http://cyber.law.harvard.edu/bridge/CriticalTheory/walker.txt.htm

DeMott, B. 1996. 'Seduced by Civility: Political Manners and the Crisis of Democratic Values'. 9 December, *The Nation*, 11.

Dumm, T.L. 1999. *A Politics of the Ordinary*. New York, New York University Press, 1999.

Eberly, D.E. 1998. *America's Promise: Civil Society and the Renewal of American Culture*. Lanham, Maryland, Rowman & Littlefield.

Eberly, D.E. 2000. (ed.) *The Essential Civil Society Reader: The Classic Essays*. Lanham, Maryland, Rowman & Littlefield.

Eisner, D. 2011. 'The Civility Crisis is Real, Not Imagined'. 13 April. http://articles.philly.com/2011-04-13/news/29413925_1_incivility-civil-war-discourse.

Eskew, G. 1997. *But for Birmingham: The Local and National Movements in the Civil Rights Struggle*. Chapel Hill, North Carolina, University of North Carolina Press.

Euchner, C. 1996. *Extraordinary Politics: How Protest and Dissent Are Changing American Democracy*. Boulder, CO, Westview Press.

Fortas, A. 1968. *Concerning Dissent and Civil Disobedience*. New York, New American Library.

Garrow, D. 1995. *Birmingham, Alabama, 1956–1963: The Black Struggle for Civil Rights*. New York, Carlson Publishing.

Gates, H.L. Jr. 1991. 'Patriotism'. *The Nation*. July 15/22, 91.

Gill, E. 2001. 'Neutrality, Autonomy, and the Liberal State'. 11 *The Responsive Community*, 15.

Hampton, H. 1990. *Voices of Freedom: An Oral History of the Civil Rights Movement from the 1950s through the 1980s*. New York, Bantam Books.

Heyd, H. (ed.) 1996. *Toleration: An Elusive Virtue*. Princeton, Princeton University Press.

Hunter, J.D. 1991. *Culture Wars: The Struggle to Define America*. New York, Basic Books.

Kammen, M. 1993. 'The Problem of American Exceptionalism: A Reconsideration'. 45 *American Quarterly*, 1.

Kateb, G. 1992. *The Inner Ocean: Individualism and Democratic Culture*. Ithaca, Cornell University Press.

Kennedy, R. 2001. 'State of the Debate: the Case Against Civility'. 19 December, *The American Prospect*. http://prospect.org/article/state-debate-case-against-civility.
King, M.L. 1963. 'Letter from Birmingham Jail, April 16, 1963'. http://abacus.bates.edu/admin/offices/dos/mlk/letter.html.
Koffler, J. and Gershman, B. 1984. 'The New Seditious Libel'. 69 *Cornell Law Review*, 858.
Kronman, A. 1996. 'Civility'. 26 *Cumberland Law Review*, 727.
Marcuse, H. 1965. 'Repressive Tolerance'. http://ada.evergreen.edu/~arunc/texts/frankfurt/marcuse/tolerance.pdf.
Marks, J. 1996. 'The American Uncivil Wars'. 22 April, *U.S. News and World Report*, 67–8.
McWhorter, D. 2001. *Carry Me Home: Birmingham, Alabama, the Climactic Battle of the Civil Rights Revolution*. New York, Simon and Schuster.
Mendus, S. 1989. *Toleration and the Limits of Liberalism*. Atlantic Highlands, New Jersey, Humanities Press International.
Meyer, M. 2000. 'Liberal Civility and the Civility of Etiquette: Public Ideals and Personal Lives'. 26 *Social Theory and Practice*, 71.
Minow, M. 1998. 'Politics and Procedure'. In D. Kairys (ed.), *The Politics of Law: A Progressive Critique*. New York, Basic Books. 3rd edition. Ch.3.
Olsen, T. and Shoemaker, K.B. 1996. 'Civility and Remembrance'. 26 *Cumberland Law Review*, 887.
Peller, G. 1987. 'Reason and the Mob: the Politics of Representation'. 2 *Tikkun*, 28.
Powers, K. Kristen 2008. 'A Crisis of Civility'. 5 December. http://www.nypost.com/p/news/opinion/opedcolumnists/item_0x1JWLgsTVsNbCXCmzSUJO.
Rehnquist, W.H. 1973. 'Civility and Freedom of Speech'. 49 *Indiana Law Journal*, 1.
Rorty, A.O. 1997. 'From Decency to Civility by Way of Economics: 'First Let's Eat and Then Talk of Right and Wrong''. 64 *Social Research*, 114.
Ross, R. 2002. 'An Apologia to Radical Dissent and a Supreme Court Test to Protect It'. 7 *Communication Law & Policy*, 401.
Sandel, M. 1996. 'There's A Big Difference Between Making Nice and Doing Good. December 26, *The New York Times*, A4.
Sandel, M. 2005. *Public Philosophy: Essays on Morality in Politics*. Cambridge, MA, Harvard University Press.
Sarat, A. (ed.) 2004. *Dissent in Dangerous Times*. Ann Arbor, MI, University of Michigan Press.
Schmidt, J. 2000. 'Is Civility a Virtue?'. In L. Rouner (ed.), *Civility*. South Bend, Ind., University of Notre Dame Press, 22.
Schofield, H. 1914. 'Freedom of the Press in the United States'. In *Essays on Constitutional Law & Equity*, 11.
Sherratt, T. 2011. 'A Crisis of Civility and Representation'. August 19. http://www.capitalcommentary.org/christian-democracy/crisis-civility-and-representation
Shiffrin, S. 1990. *The First Amendment, Democracy, and Romance*. Cambridge, MA, Harvard University Press.
Shiffrin, S. 1999. *Dissent, Injustice and the Meanings of America*. Princeton, Princeton University Press.
Shils, E. 1997. *The Virtue of Civility: Selected Essays on Liberalism, Tradition, and Civil Society*. S.E. Grosby (ed.). New York, Liberty Fund.
Sinopoli, R. 1995. 'Thick-Skinned Liberalism: Redefining Civility'. 89 *The American Political Science Review*, 612–20.

Tinder, G. 1974. 'Transcending Tragedy: The Idea of Civility'. 68 *The American Political Science Review*, 548.

Vitello, M. 2000. 'The Nuremberg Files: Testing the Outer Limits of the First Amendment'. 61 *Ohio State Law Journal*, 1175.

Walzer, M. 1974. 'Civility and Civic Virtue in Contemporary America'. 41 *Social Research*, 593.

White, L. 1996. "'Why Do You Treat Us So Badly?' On Loss, Remembrance, and Responsibility'. 26 *Cumberland Law Review*, 809.

Yoshino, K. 2010. 'Of Stranger Spaces' in A. Sarat, L. Douglas, M.M. Umphrey (eds), *Law and the Stranger*. Stanford, Stanford University Press.

Chapter 18
Why Are Americans Originalist?

Jack Balkin

During an oral argument before the United States Supreme Court in 2010, Justice Samuel Alito poked fun at his usual ideological ally, Justice Antonin Scalia. The issue before the Court was whether violent video games were protected by the First Amendment, which guarantees freedom of speech. 'I think what Justice Scalia wants to know', Alito deadpanned, 'is what James Madison thought about video games. Did he enjoy them?' Scalia, who did not seem to find this at all funny, growled in response, 'No, I want to know what James Madison thought about violence. Was there any indication that anybody thought, when the First Amendment was adopted, that there – there was an exception to it for – for speech regarding violence? Anybody?' (Oral Argument Transcript 2010).

This exchange symbolizes one of the most distinctive features of American constitutional culture: its fascination with (and debates over) originalism in constitutional interpretation. The term 'originalism' refers to a family of theories and rhetorical approaches. They have in common the idea that the US Constitution should be interpreted according to the meanings, purposes, intentions or understandings of those who framed or adopted the Constitution, or who lived at the time of its framing and adoption. (For convenience, I will sometimes use the phrase 'founders, framers, or adopters'.)

One must offer all of these alternative formulations because, among American legal academics at least, the theory of 'originalism' has split into multiple competing versions (Colby and Smith 2009). Among the general public, however, the idea of originalism is captured by the deceptively simple notion that judges should interpret the Constitution according to 'what the framers wanted'. In popular discourse, this advice is primarily directed at judges, who, it is feared, are tempted repeatedly to stray from the framers' vision and substitute their personal political predilections for the country's basic law.

Originalism is mostly unknown outside of the United States. It has made a few inroads in Australia, Malayasia and Singapore, but it is hardly a dominant tendency there (Tew 2014 forthcoming; Weis 2013; Goldsworthy 1997). The most widespread approach to constitutional interpretation in contemporary constitutional courts is proportionality review, which is decidedly not an inquiry into original meanings (Matthews and Stone Sweet 2011). Similarly, Kim Scheppele explains that although purposive interpretation is common in 'advanced constitutional systems', constitutional courts do not generally inquire into original meanings or original intentions. (Scheppele 2013: 24). 'In Europe', Michel Rosenfeld tells us, 'recourse to originalism is virtually nonexistent' and 'even implicit references to originalism in substance are quite rare' (Rosenfeld 2004: 656n83). And Canada, the country perhaps most similar to the United States culturally, nevertheless has a very different *constitutional* culture (Greene 2009). 'Originalism', Peter Hogg assures us, 'has never enjoyed any significant support in Canada' (Hogg 2011: 83). In fact, there have been some recent stirrings of originalist theory among Canadian academics (Miller 2011). Nevertheless, Canada's constitutional culture is perhaps most famous for developing the doctrine of the constitution as a 'living tree' (*Edwards v. Attorney-General for Canada*, [1930]).

Most Americans know comparatively little about what the framers and adopters actually wanted or sought to achieve in the creating the Constitution. Even seemingly non-controversial statements phrased at the most abstract level, such as 'the founders believed in limited government' may turn out to be seriously misleading (Raphael 2013; Edling 2008; Amar 2005). On some issues there was no consensus among the adopters, and in still other cases – due to significant changes in technology and society – the adopters could not have had any intent at all. This was the premise of Alito's little joke at Scalia's expense. Finally, some of the most important features of American constitutionalism were put in place after the Civil War during Reconstruction, but the Reconstruction framers and adopters are almost unknown to most Americans and are rarely invoked.

Nevertheless, the idea of fidelity to the founders and a desire to follow their example and their wisdom – even when wholly imagined – is a powerful trope in American constitutional argument, although not in most other constitutional democracies. The purpose of this chapter is to explain why that might be.

1. Original Meanings Versus Original Expected Applications

At the outset it is worth distinguishing two different conceptions of originalism, one of which is hardly controversial, even outside the United States.

In an ancient constitution like America's the semantic (i.e., dictionary definition) meanings of words may change over time. Imagine, for example, a constitution written in Chaucerian English – many of the words would have acquired new or different meanings over the years, not to mention different spellings. In the case of the United States Constitution, largely written in the eighteenth and nineteenth centuries, most words and phrases have the same semantic meanings as they did at the time of adoption. But there are a few exceptions or possible ambiguities. Article IV, section 4 of the Constitution, for example, speaks of the federal government's duty to respond to 'domestic violence' in the states, which refers to riots or insurrections, not interspousal battery; the same clause requires the United States to guarantee the states a 'Republican form of government', meaning a representative government, not a government controlled by the Republican Party (founded many years after these words were written). Article I, section 8 speaks of 'magazines', which are places for storing ammunition, not glossy publications, and the Second Amendment speaks of the right to keep and bear 'arms', which refers to weapons, not limbs or appendages.

In addition, some terms in the Constitution, like 'letters of marque and reprisal' in Article I, section 8, are legal terms of art. To apply the text today it is important to know what these terms of art meant at the time of adoption. Many of these terms were taken from the common law, and therefore it is possible that they would be subject to common law evolution. Even so, it is helpful to know what the terms originally referred to.

Finally, some features of the text require an understanding of background context: for example, the fact that when the constitutional text refers to 'the Senate' it is talking about the US Senate and not the Roman Senate; the fact that when the Constitution mentions dates and months it refers to the Gregorian Calendar and not the Jewish lunar calendar; the fact that all numbers mentioned in the text should be understood as calculated in base ten rather than in base 12, and so on. These features of the text, although not expressly stated, require us sympathetically to understand what the text's authors meant and to avoid twisting their words out of context (Balkin 2013a).

Consider these three ideas together: that interpreters should pay attention to linguistic change in order to avoid unintended puns and plays on words; that interpreters should recognize the existence of legal terms of art and that interpreters should read the text consistent with basic assumptions about background context. We might call each of them requirements of fidelity to 'original meaning' or 'original communicative content' in a thin sense (Balkin 2013a; Solum 2013).

That lawyers and judges should try, as far as possible, to decide cases consistent with this thin version of original meaning is not particularly controversial in the United States – most adherents of a 'living constitution' that evolves with changing times would probably agree to it. One expects it would not be controversial in many other countries as well.

I consider myself to be an originalist precisely because I think that contemporary interpreters in the United States should follow original meaning in this thin sense. I also believe, however, that where the text is vague or uses open ended standards or principles, like 'freedom of speech' or 'equal protection of the laws', later generations must engage in constitutional construction; they must build out the constitution by creating doctrines that, in their view, best realize the Constitution's words in their own time. My version of originalism, which I call framework originalism or living originalism, views the constitutional text as a framework for making politics possible, leaving to each generation the duty of building out and implementing the Constitution's text and principles in their own time (Balkin 2011b). This version of originalism is fully consistent with the idea of a 'living Constitution'.

What makes originalism controversial in the United States – and largely unheard of outside it – is a far stronger claim than framework originalism. It is the claim that judges must interpret and apply the Constitution in the same way that people living at the time of adoption would have. Conversely, to the extent that judges decide cases or create doctrines inconsistent with how the adopters would have understood and applied the Constitution, their interpretations are illegitimate. This version of originalism presumes a very different conception of 'original meaning' than the thin version of original meaning I just described; and it is this version of originalism that mystifies many lawyers and judges outside the United States – and within it as well. It offers what appears to be an exclusive approach to interpretation – if judges do not follow the way that the adopters would have understood and applied the text, they act illegitimately and lawlessly (Bork 1987).

This approach has many theoretical problems, which have produced a substantial academic literature. I will not repeat that debate here. But I will note that the practical problem with such a view is that it cannot account for a very large proportion of current legal practices – the modern administrative and regulatory state; federal protections for workers, consumers and the environment; many aspects of the modern social safety net including Social Security and Medicare; the modern conception of the presidency and the National Security State; and large swaths of constitutional civil rights and civil liberties. Under this model of interpretation, most of the federal programmes and protections that Americans rely on today are beyond the Constitution. It is a theory of American constitutional interpretation that renders most of modern American governance unconstitutional.

2. Cafeteria Originalism

As a result, American lawyers and judges, even self-described originalist ones, do not consistently adopt this approach to interpretation. Instead, American lawyers and judges invoke the framers and adopters selectively, often describing their views and principles at varying levels of generality so that they cohere with most of current practice. In other words, understood as a rhetorical practice of lawyers and judges, originalism is a far more flexible and pragmatic phenomenon than originalism understood as an exclusive theory of legitimate constitutional interpretation. Thus, to understand why Americans engage in originalist rhetoric, we must understand originalism as a set of cultural practices of justification in politics and in law as well as an academic theory of correct legal interpretation.

In this chapter, I shall explain that American originalism is America's distinctive way of invoking cultural memory and arguing about the nation's political and legal traditions. Precisely because originalist arguments appeal to the nation's political traditions and cultural memory, they will normally not be persuasive unless the audience can accept the values of the founders, framers or adopters as their own values, or can recharacterize them so that they can plausibly accept them as their own (Balkin, 2013b; Post 1990). When the adopters' values and expectations seem too alien or irrelevant to contemporary audiences, lawyers and judges simply refrain from making originalist arguments. (Sometimes this is justified on the grounds that substantial reliance on longstanding non-originalist precedents forecloses an originalist inquiry.)

Thus, American lawyers and judges do not feel obligated to consult or follow the views of the founders, framers or adopters in every case. And when lawyers and judges do invoke the founders, framers or adopters, they do not treat their views as binding when there are more pressing considerations. Thus, in practice, American originalism is not really an exclusive theory of interpretation, no matter what particular academic theories might suggest or American politicians might claim.

We might make an analogy to American religious practice. American Catholics are sometimes called 'cafeteria Catholics' because they pick and choose which parts of the Church's teachings to accept and under what conditions. Many American Catholics, for example, disregard the Church's admonitions against contraception and divorce. In the same way, although American culture is saturated with references to the founding and the wisdom of the framers, Americans are essentially 'cafeteria originalists'. They pick and choose when to follow the views of the founders, framers, or adopters and often artfully re-characterize these principles to support contemporary political and legal arguments.

Obviously, this flexibility is helpful for accommodating existing political and legal practices. But it is equally important for another reason. Strange as it may seem, one of the most important uses of originalist rhetoric in the United States is not to *preserve* existing traditions but to *transform* them. Americans regularly invoke the memory of the founders and their principles to justify political and constitutional reform. That is why they use the framers to criticize contemporary politicians and especially contemporary judges. Americans employ originalism as a political practice for critiquing the status quo (whether in a liberal or conservative direction) and arguing for change, sometimes quite radical. In order to do this, however, one must be able to invoke the founders, framers and adopters on only some subjects but not others; and to read their insights generously, abstractly and creatively so that they appear directly relevant to political and social contexts that few of them could have imagined.

What is interesting about American constitutional culture, then, is not that it is thoroughly and uncompromisingly originalist. It is not. Americans are as pragmatic about their originalism as they are about almost everything else. What is interesting is that American constitutional culture takes originalist arguments seriously in a way that most other counties with constitutional courts rarely do. And this is what requires explanation.

3. Cultural Memory and Constitutional Modernity

Why is originalism so prominent in American constitutional culture? The answer is complex, and shows the powerful influence of American society and culture on American jurisprudence. American originalism has been produced by a combination of historical and cultural factors. These include:

1. America's revolutionary tradition;
2. the long dominance of a protestant religious tradition with its emphasis on close reading of scriptural texts and redemptive calls for a return to origins;
3. the emergence of the American state, nation and people (at least in the popular imagination) roughly contemporaneously with the creation of the American Constitution;
4. the fact that the Constitution is strongly identified with American nationhood and peoplehood;
5. a long tradition of reverence for the Constitution and the Declaration of Independence as foundational scriptures in the American civic religion; and
6. Americans' special veneration of the founding generation and particular figures within that generation (like George Washington and James Madison) as culture heroes. (The idea of 'culture heroes', an idea taken from the study of mythology, is discussed *infra*.)

Finally, the importance of originalism in American constitutional culture stems from how political and legal actors mobilized these cultural resources to justify and legitimate political and legal transformation in the twentieth and early twenty-first centuries.

Throughout American history lawyers and judges have made claims about the purpose and intentions of the Constitution's framers. They made these arguments in conjunction with a wide range of other legal arguments about text, structure, purpose, precedent and consequences. Yet American originalism – as a *self-conscious* and *general* theory of legal interpretation – is a relatively recent invention. It arose from the way that first liberal and then later conservative political movements from the middle of the twentieth century onwards have explained and justified their constitutional projects of reform.

During the twentieth and early twenty-first centuries the United States has experienced multiple upheavals and changes in the constitutional order. These include the New Deal and the rise of the administrative and regulatory state, the creation of the National Security State, the Great Society and the creation of the American welfare state, the civil rights revolution, the sexual revolution, the second wave of American feminism, the gay rights movement and a series of conservative counter-mobilizations that often reacted to these changes.

Indeed, one might call the twentieth century an age of 'constitutional modernity', in which actors became increasingly self-conscious about how much constitutional practices had changed from traditional understandings (Levinson and Balkin 1991). With modernity usually come modernist crises of belief, and one of the standard cultural effects of modernity is a schizophrenic attitude toward the past. On the one hand, the past is increasingly left behind, sometimes proudly or deliberately; on the other there is a repeated longing to regain the past and its authority, even in an imagined form. Thus, the experience of modernity is *both* about transcending the practical and cultural constraints of the past *and* the anxiety that this freedom creates.

It is no accident that many fundamentalist movements emerge from modernist challenges to belief and practice; they respond to periods of change when, in Marx's and Engel's famous words, 'everything solid melts into air' (Marx and Engels 1972). But in constitutional modernity, the invocation of the past – and the great deeds, principles and commitments of the past – is useful not only as a means of *forestalling* change, but also as a way of *justifying* change and *consolidating* change. In America, originalism is like the spoonful of traditionalist sugar that helps the modernist medicine go down.

In a period of continuous constitutional struggle and change, both liberals and conservatives have sought to invoke the past as a justification for moving constitutional understandings in their favoured direction. Hence the founders, framers and adopters have increasingly been mobilized on both sides of these debates, first by political liberals in the middle of the twentieth century, and then by political conservatives beginning in the 1970s.

What is remarkable about liberal constitutional rhetoric in the middle of the twentieth century is that it featured *both* arguments for progressive adaptation to changing times *and* circumstances and appeals to the wisdom of the framers. During the constitutional crisis over the New Deal, for example, President Franklin D. Roosevelt argued that a conservative Supreme Court had strayed from the founders' design of a flexible, pragmatic Constitution that gave the federal government power to solve national problems. He compared the Constitution to the Bible, and explained that, '[l]ike the Bible, it ought to be read again and again'. He extolled the framers' wisdom in providing for a flexible document that provided 'all the powers needed to meet each and every problem which then had a national character and which could not be met by merely local action'. Roosevelt denounced the conservative Justices of the Supreme Court for disregarding the framers' meaning. The Justices were 'reading into the Constitution words and implications which are not there, and which were never intended to be there'. He called for the restoration and the redemption of the true Constitution created by the framers: 'We must take action to save the Constitution from the Court and the Court from itself. We must find a way to take an appeal from the Supreme Court to the Constitution itself' (Roosevelt 1937a).

Roosevelt's speeches are eye-opening today precisely because he is widely regarded as a prominent liberal symbol of living constitutionalism, which is generally assumed to be the very opposite of originalist thought. Yet Roosevelt's argument was a characteristically liberal use of the founding. He claimed that the constitutional text was *designed* to be forward-looking and sufficiently adaptable to deal with new national problems then unforeseen. The Constitution was a wise and flexible document written by wise and pragmatic men. It was, in Roosevelt's words, a 'layman's document, not a lawyer's contract' and 'a charter of general principles'. The framers, Roosevelt explained, 'used broad and general language capable of meeting evolution and change when they referred to commerce between the States, the taxing power and the general welfare' (Roosevelt 1937b). The founders were political experimentalists, just like the New Dealers.

It is therefore fitting that Roosevelt's first appointment to the Supreme Court was Hugo Black, an Alabama Senator who became the most famous liberal advocate of original intention and one of the Supreme Court's greatest civil libertarians. Black was truly an originalist *avant la lettre*, for the term itself would not be coined until 1980. From the 1940s to the 1960s, Justice Black, and later, various Justices on the liberal Warren Court repeatedly invoked the framers to legitimate elements of the New Deal/Civil Rights regime, to secure equality in voting rights, to reform police practices, to require separation of church and state, to protect civil liberties, and, above all, to justify overturning many existing legal doctrines.

In his famous critique of how American lawyers use (and misuse) history, *Clio and the Court: An Illicit Love Affair*, Alfred Kelly (1965: 122) accused Black and other liberal justices of 'law office history' – that is, using history selectively to justify politically desirable results. Moreover, he pointed out that throughout American history appeals to the framers have often been used as a 'precedent-breaking device'; by breaking with existing doctrine and returning to the original meaning of the Constitution, a court can claim that it is actually preserving constitutional continuity

(Kelly 1965: 125–6). ‘In search of some adequate guiding principle upon which to support their libertarian interventionism in the social order’, Kelly argued, ‘the reformist activists on the Court initiated a new era of historically oriented adjudication’ (Kelly 1965: 131). The Warren Court turned to history to justify its increasingly muscular exercise of judicial review. Thus, it is no accident that, as Frank Cross has shown, the liberal Warren Court cited *The Federalist* ‘more than any previous Court [in] American history’ (Cross 2013: 136–43, Cross 2012). In short, to justify constitutional transformation mid century American liberals employed *both* a rhetoric of change and evolving social values *and* a rhetoric of return to founding-era verities.

The work of the Warren Court and the early Burger Court, in turn, served as targets for powerful conservative counter-mobilizations that dominated American political culture through the end of the twentieth century and into the early twenty-first century. Far more than mid century liberals, conservative social and political movements adopted originalism and fidelity to the founders’ Constitution as key tropes in their attack on legal liberalism and key rhetorical justifications for political revolution. Conservatives like Reagan Attorney General Edwin Meese and Judge Robert H. Bork denounced the ‘living constitutionalism’ of legal liberalism and promoted originalism as the sole legitimate method of constitutional interpretation. Moreover, conservatives sought to identify originalism and fidelity to the founders with conservative political and legal ideals (Post and Siegel 2006). So effective were these attacks that most Americans today have forgotten that legal liberals both before and during the Warren Court had themselves often invoked adoption history to justify many of their most celebrated innovations (Balkin 2013b).

Originalism in American constitutional law, therefore, is a product both of the distinctive construction of American cultural memory and the way that political and legal actors in the twentieth century have built on that cultural memory to struggle over American politics and American constitutional law. Although Americans pride themselves on being cultural innovators and repeatedly breaking with past traditions, there are deep strains of traditionalism in American thought and life. Founder and Constitution worship is Americans’ characteristic way of articulating American traditions and arguing about how to adapt those traditions to contemporary problems. Originalism allows Americans to argue about American ethos and political tradition in the present by reference to honoured founders and framers. Although it may offer itself as a jurisprudential theory about correct legal interpretation, originalism’s roots are political and cultural.

4. American Originalism and the Revolutionary Tradition

American political and legal discourse is shaped by American cultural memory. In American memory, the revolutionary founders of the American nation, and the framers of the American Constitution are conflated as ‘The Founding Fathers’, the ‘Founders’ or the ‘Framers’. Americans share an origin story about how they came to be Americans. According to this story, the American state (the United States of America), the American nation (America), the American people (‘We the People of the United States’) and the American Constitution (whose preamble begins with that famous phrase) were born virtually at the same time. America was created through an act of political revolution. Equally important this revolutionary act was a *self-creation*, in which Americans acted as the midwife to their own birth. Through political revolution, the American people brought themselves into being as Americans and created a state and a Constitution under which they still live.

The American political mythology is one of self-birth (autochthony); yet Americans, as a settler nation, were clearly *not* the indigenous inhabitants of the land that came to be called America. They may claim to have made themselves, but they did not spring from American soil. In fact, the very presence of indigenous peoples and a forcibly imported slave population may have led Americans reactively to over-emphasize how much they created themselves and their nation out of a wilderness (Rana 2010).

The story of American origins ties the creation of American national and political identity closely to the creation of the American Constitution. The fate of America is linked to the fate of its Constitution, and vice-versa. The members of the Revolutionary generation, and the framers and adopters of the American constitution (who are not always the same people) become the veritable symbols of American identity, American statesmanship and American values. Particular individuals in the story – George Washington, Benjamin Franklin, Alexander Hamilton, Thomas Jefferson, James Madison and John Adams – stand metonymically for the entire generation that produced the nation and the Constitution and are especially venerated. These men – we might call them the 'Big Six' Founders – are the most prominent culture heroes in American mythology. Perhaps ironically, Jefferson and Adams did not even attend the Philadelphia Convention – they were engaged in overseas diplomacy – and Hamilton was absent for long stretches of time.

The creation story that connects the creation of the Constitution to the creation of the American state, nation and people is a fiction, omitting the presence of Native Americans and slaves, who were not originally counted as part of We the American People. It also conveniently collapses time frames. From 1776 to 1781 the American government (such as it was) was the Continental Congress. From 1781 to 1789 the country was governed by the Articles of Confederation, which proved unworkable; the failure of the Articles led to the Philadelphia Convention.

Americans' cultural memory tends to collapse these events. Most Americans have never even heard of the Articles of Confederation; those who have do not regard the Articles as America's first Constitution. Instead people tend to think of the Articles as a sort of transitional document or trial run which led to the real Constitution, the Constitution of 1787.

The irony is that the Articles were anything but a transitional document. They were styled as 'Articles of Confederation and perpetual Union' and were unamendable without agreement of all the states. Article XIII provided that 'the Union shall be perpetual; nor shall any alteration at any time hereafter be made in any of them; unless such alteration be agreed to in a Congress of the United States, and be afterwards confirmed by the legislatures of every State'.

The Philadelphia Convention, convened under the pretence of suggesting amendments to the Articles, was in fact a 'runaway' convention, which eventually jettisoned the Articles completely and proposed a new Constitution that would become effective on ratification by conventions in nine states rather than the 13 required by the Articles. It was, therefore, a revolutionary act of its own, breaking from the previous revolutionary government.

American cultural memory, therefore, is the memory not only of a revolution, but of political autochthony or self-birth in which key documents – the Declaration and the Constitution – emerge with the formation of We the People and are bound up with its identity and political self-conception. These documents are more than merely the birth certificate of a nation and a people; in the American imagination they become akin to Scripture in an American civic religion based on this powerful myth of origin.

In his study of comparative originalism, David Fontana has suggested that originalist rhetoric is most likely to appear in countries in which a constitution is strongly identified with the creation of the nation itself. '[T]he most relevant' feature that explains whether a country's constitutional culture will embrace originalism 'is whether … its constitution created the nation that lives under the constitution, or … merely reorganized the institutions of the country'. Countries with 'revolutionary' constitutions, Fontana explains, are more likely to have originalist cultures than countries with 'reorganizational' ones (Fontana 2010: 190).

This helps explain important differences between the United States and Canada. Despite Canada's many cultural affinities to the United States, Canadian cultural memory is quite different. Canada does not have a revolutionary tradition, and Canadian nationhood and the Canadian Constitution emerged in phases, beginning with the 1867 British North America Act, which was passed by the British Parliament, and not by 'We the Canadian People'.

Moreover, although many countries have revolutionary traditions, very few have a revolution that – in the nation's cultural memory, at least – simultaneously creates the people, nation, state and constitution. France's revolution was close in time to America's, but the French people existed long before the events of 1789. The French do not consider their current 1958 constitution as the very essence of what it means to be French. Nor could they, given the many changes in French government since the Revolution. France has had five Republics, and multiple constitutions; Americans claim to have had only one Republic and one Constitution, despite the previous failure of the Articles of Confederation, the constitutional breakdown of the American Civil War, and the twentieth-century transformations of the New Deal and the National Security State. No matter how much America changes, Americans continue to insist that they have had only one Republic, one Constitution, and, as the Pledge of Allegiance explains, 'One nation, under God, indivisible, with liberty and justice for all'.

As noted previously, the characteristic American response to – and justification for – constitutional change during the twentieth century has been to call for a return to origins and fundamental principles, using the heroes of the founding as sources of quotable wisdom. In fact, this cultural gesture predates the American Revolution – it emerges out of the radical protestantism of American puritanism. As Sacvan Bercovitch famously explained, the characteristic American complaint is the jeremiad – the fervent denunciation of corruption and decline in American institutions, coupled with a stirring call for return and renewal. 'In virtually every area of life', Bercovitch argued, 'the jeremiad became the official ritual form of continuing revolution' in the United States (Bercovitch 1978: 141). In politics, the cultural memory of the Revolution and the Founding has allowed Americans to engage in a series of constitutional jeremiads, making originalism a potent vehicle for justifying continuing revolution in American constitutional law.

5. The Constitution and Culture Heroes

America's reverence towards its founders is just as important as its revolutionary tradition in explaining the American tendency toward originalism. In his study of the secularism provisions of the Turkish Constitution, Ozan Varol has suggested that 'originalism blossoms when a political leader associated with the creation or revision of the nation's constitution develops a cult of personality within the nation' (Varol 2011: 1246). This would explain another difference between the United States and France. Not only does the French nation predate the French Constitution(s), but the French Revolution is the central object of civic devotion, rather than particular revolutionaries like Danton or Robespierre, who are admittedly complicated figures.

America's origin myth, which fuses the American Constitution together with the creation of the American state and American national identity, treats its founders quite differently. Americans think of the same group of people as responsible for creating the American state, the American nation and the American Constitution, and they are given enormous reverence. I call this phenomenon the 'ethical trifecta'. The ethos of American constitutionalism, statehood and national identity are all projected onto a single group of people. Hence Americans imbue the generation that produced the American revolution and the generation that produced the American Constitution (which are often run together as one generation) with enormous symbolic importance and ethical significance. They are the Founders, the Framers, or the Founding Fathers, almost always described reverently in capital letters.

Although the founding generation is revered collectively, not all members have the same ethical status or receive the same degree of attention. Members of the founding generation thought to have key roles in the creation of the American nation, like the Big Six mentioned earlier – Washington, Jefferson, Franklin, Madison, Adams and Hamilton – take on a mythic status. Recently the National Archives created an online resource, the Founders Online, which includes the complete papers of these six figures (The Founders Online 2013).

In American mythology, these six figures, and the founding generation considered collectively, are treated as *culture heroes*. In the study of mythology, a culture hero is a figure of legend that stands for a people's values, characteristics and aspirations. Culture heroes are often credited with important innovations or achievements. King Arthur stands for British unity and chivalry; the legendary Chinese emperor Fuxi is said to have invented the arts of writing, trapping and fishing. As these examples demonstrate, culture heroes are often people of high rank or status (including kings or demigods), but they can also be pioneers or explorers (like Daniel Boone or Davey Crockett), artists (like Homer or Hesiod to the Greeks) or people who symbolize extraordinary achievements (like Alexander the Great or Aeneas) or virtues (like Cincinnatus). Culture heroes need not be perfect in all respects – indeed, their failures and defects may themselves be topics of legend – but they are often held up within the culture as sources of wisdom and examples for emulation.

6. Originalism and Nationalism

Defenders of originalism sometimes argue that originalism is required by the democracy, the rule of law or constitutional fidelity. If that were so, we would expect to see originalism adopted around the world, which it is not. Perhaps equally importantly, we would expect to see originalism as the dominant practice in the interpretation of the 50 American state constitutions. Yet if we examine interpretive practices involving state constitutions we find that originalism has relatively little influence.

One cannot explain this fact on the ground that state judges are foreigners who do not understand true American democracy and its philosophy of limited government. From a cultural standpoint, state constitutions are every bit as 'American' as the federal Constitution, and the judges who sit on the state courts themselves are just as imbued with American legal culture as their federal counterparts. They go to the same law schools and they learn the same interpretive techniques.

Unlike the federal constitution, which was originally drafted in 1787, the 50 state constitutions have a wide variety of ages, and most states have had multiple constitutions. Some state constitutions are products of the late twentieth century, while the constitution of the State of Massachusetts is even older than the federal Constitution, having been written in 1780 by John Adams. Moreover, unlike the federal Constitution, most of these state constitutions, regardless of their age, are constantly being amended, sometimes by the legislature, and sometimes by the public through propositions, initiatives, and referenda (Levinson 2012b).

State courts, like federal courts, may sometimes make originalist arguments, but for the most part their practices are not originalist at all. Nor do politicians or social movements routinely invoke the founders of individual states as justification for their positions. If anything, state courts are especially likely to engage in forms of 'living constitutionalism', interpreting their constitutions according to evolving contemporary mores (Usman 2010). That is because state courts are often the initial venues for promoting legal theories that are later introduced in the federal courts – involving such diverse issues as race relations, sex equality, property rights, gun rights and positive rights of education and housing. The litigation campaign to secure equality of marriage rights for gays and lesbians is only the most recent example. This is not surprising, given how constitutional development operates in the United States. Political mobilizations (and counter-mobilizations) often turn to local venues – city councils, state legislatures and state courts – to win converts for their novel constitutional claims. As they succeed in state and local jurisdictions, they attempt to extend their influence nationally, through litigation in the federal courts and through pushing for new legislation and new administrative regulations. Originalist argument is not always useful in this process, and, sometimes it is almost entirely beside the point.

The example of state constitutional development provides further evidence that originalism in the United States is a cultural phenomenon rather than one required by democracy or the rule of law. More precisely, originalism is a product of the construction of American *national* identity and a feature of *national* constitutional culture. Americans often make originalist arguments about the federal Constitution – but far less frequently about their state constitutions – because originalism as a political practice draws on cultural memories about America as a nation. This is especially so when the issue is federalism. Disputes about state prerogatives and limits on federal power are debates about the nature of the national Constitution and about the nature of the American nation; hence it is not surprising that originalist rhetoric frequently appears in such debates.

7. Originalism and the Judicial Role

Most legal arguments in American courts are doctrinal. They reason from the authority of previous precedents, not from the authority of the framers or founders. This is especially the case in federal trial and intermediate appellate courts, because these courts must apply the law of higher courts (Levinson 1996). This means that courts will tend to rely most on originalist arguments when there are relatively few precedents on point – the most recent example being the debate over the meaning of the Second Amendment to the Bill of Rights, which guarantees the right to keep and bear arms (Barnett 2013). Where judicial precedents are plentiful, originalist arguments rarely dominate judicial analysis; they are mostly added as spice or seasoning. A Supreme Court opinion may throw in a quote from *The Federalist*, or a letter or speech from a famous framer, but it will likely decide the case on other grounds.

Although originalism offers itself as a theory of how judges should decide cases, originalism appears most prominently in legal and political rhetoric *outside* of courts. Crucial to understanding the phenomenon is recognizing its variants in different sites of political and legal culture. In particular, one must distinguish the practice of originalist argument in the courts (which we might call 'judicial originalism') from originalist theorizing and argument in the legal academy ('academic originalism') and the frequent rhetorical use of originalist tropes in American popular culture ('popular originalism'). Academic originalism and popular originalism often direct their advice to courts, but for the most part, American courts do not take their advice.

An important feature of originalist rhetoric in the United States – which stems from the cultural memory of the Founding – is its deep connection to movements for political reform and revolution in American politics. Americans have often used constitutional language and debates about the Constitution in order to press for social reforms that in other countries would be approached as questions of legislation and public policy (Goldsworthy 2012).

American politicians regularly refer to the values of the Founders and Framers; so too do social and political movements like the first wave of American feminism in the nineteenth century and the Tea Party in the twenty-first century. (The Tea Party – the latest incarnation of radical conservatism – takes its name from the Boston Tea Party in December 1773 and seeks to identify the movement with a key symbol of American patriotism.) Politicians, movement faithful and media pundits quote the framers and founders frequently, and with an almost religious zeal. A few conservative Christians, in fact, have argued that the Constitution, like the Bible itself, is divinely inspired. Popular (or populist) originalism is primarily an appeal to national ethos and to an imagined tradition. Often it does not seriously engage with the historical record, which may be quite complicated and equivocal, and in some cases not particularly flattering. Popular originalism is a way of attacking the status quo and pressing for reform; it is a mood rather than an enforceable dogma, much less a coherent theory of judicial practice.

As noted previously, contemporary conservative originalism is the result of conservative political mobilizations that began in the late 1960s and early 1970s and came to fruition with the election of Ronald Reagan in 1980. Movement conservatives adopted originalism as a way of explaining what they believed was wrong with legal liberalism, and, in particular, the decisions of the Warren and early Burger Courts in the 1960s and 1970s. These decisions had revolutionized criminal procedure; created guarantees of sexual autonomy, the right to abortion and women's equality; mandated racial integration of public schools; and increased judicial oversight of prisons, schools and hospitals. Originalist appeals helped conservatives explain how liberal federal judges had strayed both from the correct interpretation of the nation's charter and from their proper role as unelected judges. Thus, modern conservative originalism has been a call for reform through the rhetoric of return and restoration. It was also, at least in its early years, a call for judicial restraint and for respect for democracy. Conservatives argued against liberal ideas of a 'living constitution', which, they claimed, gave insufficient deference to democracy and failed to restrain judges from imposing their personal political views on the law.

Nevertheless, as conservatives won elections, they began to control the federal courts; in particular, they gained a conservative majority on the United States Supreme Court. In this changed political context, arguments for judicial abstention increasingly made less sense. Conservatives wanted courts to strike down liberal legislation, rein in federal power and protect the kinds of rights that conservatives favoured – the rights of property owners against environmental regulation, the rights of corporations and wealthy donors against campaign finance regulation, the rights of gun owners against gun control, the rights of states against guaranteed federal health care and federal protections of voting rights, the rights of whites against affirmative action programmes, the rights of conservative Christians to promote religion in the public square and in public expenditures, and so on. Promoting these kinds of rights required a muscular judiciary unafraid to exercise the power of judicial review in order to protect important constitutional values.

In this new world of conservative judicial hegemony, originalism could no longer serve primarily as a justification for judicial restraint. It had to be re-conceptualized in order to legitimate conservative judicial activism (Whittington 2004). The difficulty was that the term 'judicial activism' had been rendered politically radioactive by continuous assaults by conservatives against liberal decisions and liberal jurists. Therefore new euphemisms like 'judicial engagement' or 'judicial fidelity to text, history and structure' better explained the role appropriate for conservative judges (Neily 2013; Tushnet 2012). In this way, conservative originalism gradually shed its associations with judicial restraint and respect for majoritarian politics. Once conservatives solidified control over the federal courts, they once again become defenders of robust judicial review to protect important constitutional values, just as they had been before the New Deal.

8. Academic Originalism

A quite different form of originalist practice from popular originalism is *academic* originalism. Today conservative academics in American law schools, conservative think tanks like the Heritage Foundation and lawyers affiliated with conservative policy networks like the Federalist Society regularly discuss and develop originalist arguments. These academics and organizations are affiliated with the conservative political movements that blossomed in the last decades of the twentieth century. As noted above, conservative political movements essentially adopted originalism as their official theory of constitutional interpretation, and conservative legal intellectuals have seen it as their job to theorize and articulate these commitments.

Conservative academics, think tanks and policy networks like the Federalist Society tend to be far more interested in originalist dogmatics than most American judges. Nevertheless, their work has surely influenced American judges, and especially Republican-appointed conservative judges. That is because Republican presidents have appointed many judges who are connected to these intellectual networks; and many law students who end up clerking for these federal judges are also connected to these intellectual networks.

A small number of conservative judges (and two Supreme Court Justices – Clarence Thomas and Antonin Scalia) have declared themselves as originalists, although most federal judges have not. Nevertheless, conservative policy networks like the Federalist Society have helped originalist ideas become part of the common coin of conversation among conservative legal intellectuals. The conservative blogosphere, often connected to these intellectual networks, also helps spread discussion of originalist legal theories. Originalism has provided a common reference point and a common language for conservative legal thinkers and for conservative constitutionalism (Hollis-Brusky 2014).

American legal academics have debated the merits of originalist theories of constitutional interpretation since at least the 1970s and 1980s. In fact, the term 'originalist' was coined by a liberal legal academic, Paul Brest, in a famous critique of early versions of academic originalism (Brest 1980). Legal academics of all persuasions regularly shower the law reviews with learned articles about originalist theory and the original meaning of this or that clause of the Constitution. Even so, their arguments have only a limited direct influence on judges, except in the small number of cases of first impression where there are no developed judicial doctrines. That is why originalist scholarship mattered most to the Justices in two recent decisions about the Second Amendment – *District of Columbia Heller* and *McDonald v. City of Chicago*. Legal academics also often provide judges with originalist research in amicus briefs; although courts may cite this research, originalist arguments by themselves rarely determine the outcome.

Although the American Supreme Court currently has two originalist Justices, they tend, like most other judges, to invoke originalist arguments opportunistically. Justice Antonin Scalia has described himself as a 'faint-hearted' originalist who has no interest in overturning the vast expansion of federal power that came with the New Deal (Scalia 1989: 864). Justice Clarence Thomas has shown himself more interested in bringing modern doctrine closer to original meanings, often leading him to argue for overturning wide swaths of settled doctrine in the interest of constitutional fidelity. In this respect, however, Justice Thomas is an outlier on the Supreme Court and among the federal courts generally. His often radical positions have made him among the most interesting Justices to American legal academics. Nevertheless, even Justice Thomas ignores originalist arguments in areas such as affirmative action in which originalist inquiries are likely inconsistent with his considered legal judgements. Not surprisingly, American legal academics on both the left and the right never seem to tire of pointing out how often the Court's two self-proclaimed originalists deviate from originalism in practice (Lund 2009; Post and Siegel 2006, Barnett 2006).

Within the American legal academy, originalism has been a staple of legal scholarship. But, like all belief systems that lack a central enforcing authority, it has split into a vast array of conflicting and inconsistent versions. There are multiple schools and flavours of originalism. They include original intention, original understanding and original public meaning originalism, strong originalism, weak originalism, abstract originalism, moderate originalism, originalism as translation, the New Originalism, the New New Originalism, living originalism, and the list goes on. Academic originalism offered itself as a theory for correct judging, and, in some versions, as the one true and legitimate way to interpret the Constitution. It therefore became as much legal theology as legal science, and like other theologies, it is likely to split and fracture into multiple versions as different members of the faithful express their disagreements with each other. Moreover, the dialectical nature of the American legal academy virtually ensured that there would be no easy consensus on the merits of originalism, or on which form of originalism was the correct one.

As academics have sharpened their critiques and defences of originalism, academic originalism has become increasingly distinct from popular originalism. Academic originalists have engaged in elaborate debates about the justifications for appealing to the past, the differences between original intention, original understanding, and original meaning, what kinds of sources should be treated as authoritative and why.

Much of this debate is irrelevant to the way that politicians and political movements invoke the framers or the founding. Popular originalism is deeply connected to the protestant tradition in American constitutional culture (Levinson 2012a; Balkin 2011a). The Constitution belongs to We the People – it is written in a comparatively brief text that anyone can read and that each citizen has the right to understand and interpret for themselves. This protestant tradition is populist and anti-elitist; it has generated many popular studies and histories of the Constitution aimed at general audiences, some of which are quite well-informed and brilliant, while others are decidedly less so.

Academic originalism is also strongly textualist, but it often leads to complicated historical investigations and elaborate philosophical arguments. Thus, although academic originalism begins with a text that anyone can read, it soon leads to esoteric argument in which most citizens do not participate and specialized forms of knowledge that most citizens do not share.

What academic and popular versions have in common is a desire to invoke the authority of the past and to criticize and discipline judges. Nevertheless, academic originalism is to popular originalism what the most esoteric debates in Christian theology are to the everyday beliefs and practices of the faithful. The two are surely connected, but no one would mistake the former for the latter.

The majority of American legal academics are liberal, not conservative, and most of them are not advocates of originalism. They do not believe that judges should be bound by the original intentions, understandings, or meanings of the founders, framers or adopters. Nevertheless, they have been major contributors to the proliferation of academic writing about originalism and adoption history.

Since the 1980s there has been a 'turn to history' in American legal scholarship, especially constitutional scholarship, much of it produced by liberal legal academics (Kalman 1996; Kalman 1997). This turn to history has many overlapping causes. Some scholars turned to history in response to the emergence of rational actor and law and economics models in legal scholarship beginning in the 1970s. History was a way of preserving the study of law as a humanistic enterprise; moreover the turn to history also occurred in other disciplines, and as American law schools became increasingly interdisciplinary, ideas migrated between departments. For other scholars the turn to history was partly a response to attempts in politics and law to claim the Founders and Framers for conservative ends. Liberal scholars sought to show that liberal and progressive values equally characterize American traditions. An example is the 'republican revival' of the 1980s. Liberal constitutional academics drew on the writings of Gordon Wood, J.G.A. Pocock, and other historians to argue that the founders were civic republicans and that their political philosophy, properly understood and translated into contemporary concerns, actually supported the liberal egalitarianism of the late twentieth century (Kalman 1996, 1997).

Some American legal academics have set out to do better historical work than earlier originalists, who were usually not professional historians and often had only a basic knowledge of the relevant historical materials. There continues to be a healthy debate about 'law office history': who is engaged in it, the role that professional historians should play in arbitrating legal disputes, and how and when lawyers' uses of history may appropriately differ from those of professional historians (Flaherty 1997; Tushnet 1996; Flaherty 1995; Sunstein 1995). Finally, many liberal legal scholars turned to history not to gain authority from the past; but to understand how different the past was from today's world and how past struggles have led to our present circumstances. As a result of the turn to history, liberal legal academics have offered a wide range of scholarly analyses of the original purposes, meanings and designs of various parts of the US Constitution. In this way, historical inquiry has become a standard feature of academic research agendas even for legal scholars who do not consider themselves originalists.

9. Conclusion

In many countries legal academics may have close relationships to sitting jurists and many jurists are taken from the ranks of academics. Legal academics from these cultures are therefore likely to be misled about the practical importance of originalism when they read American legal scholarship and listen to the speeches of American politicians. American legal scholars and American politicians care far more about originalism than most federal and state judges do, and they take debates about originalism far more seriously. American judges may employ research into adoption history, especially if it appears in amicus briefs prepared by academics, but they tend to use it as an additional justification for legal positions they already hold. Citing to *The Federalist*, Madison's notes of the Philadelphia Convention, or other adoption-era materials offers lawyers and judges a way of bestowing additional legitimacy on their legal conclusions, especially if they seek to alter or overturn existing precedents. As Alfred Kelly pointed out in his study of Warren Court originalism, originalist appeals often appear in legal opinions when judges are trying to change the law; the use of originalist sources helps them justify jettisoning existing traditions and practices in the name of older ones (Kelly 1965).

Every political culture must deal with change, but different countries articulate and struggle over their traditions in different ways. In some countries, political tradition can be associated with a common culture, a shared religious or ethnic identity, or the shared memory of wars, struggles, victories and defeats. In the United States, however, national identity is bound up with the memory of the American Revolution and the enactment of the American Constitution. American political identity is strongly shaped by what Sanford Levinson has called America's constitutional faith (Levinson 2012a).

Americans like to imagine themselves as forward-looking pioneers – itself a quasi-originalist image. They celebrate American dynamism. Yet at the same time Americans need to believe that something remains constant about themselves in the face of constant change. Constitutional originalism offers Americans a language to express their longing for continuity as well as pride in their past achievements. Originalism, which on its surface appears to defy the very idea of a continuously changing Constitution, is actually a key device through which Americans articulate and justify political change to themselves and to each other. It is the language of revolutionaries as well as defenders of the old order, of constitutional reformers as well as constitutional conservatives. It offers a familiar language through which Americans can disagree with each other and remember who they are in the midst of constant political transformation.

Bibliography

Amar, A.R. 2005. *America's Constitution: A Biography.* New York, Random House.

Balkin, J.M. 2011a. *Constitutional Redemption: Political Faith in an Unjust World.* Cambridge, MA, Harvard University Press.

Balkin, J.M. 2011b. *Living Originalism.* Cambridge, MA, Belknap Press of Harvard University.

Balkin, J.M. 2013a. 'Must We Be Faithful to Original Meaning?' 7(1) *Jerusalem Review of Legal Studies*, 57–86.

Balkin, J.M. 2013b. 'The New Originalism and the Uses of History'. 82 *Fordham Law Review*, 641–719.

Barnett, R. 2006. 'Scalia's Infidelity: A Critique of "Faint-Hearted" Originalism'. 75 *University of Cincinnati Law Review*, 7–24.

Barnett, R. 2013. 'The Gravitational Force of Originalism'. 82 *Fordham Law Review*, 411–32.

Bercovitch, S. 1978. *American Jeremiad.* Madison, University of Wisconsin Press.

Bork, R.H. 1987. 'Original Intent: The Only Legitimate Basis for Constitutional Decision Making'. 26(3) *Judges Journal*, 13–17.

Brest, P. 1980. 'The Misconceived Quest for the Original Understanding'. 60 *Boston University Law Review*, 204–38.

Colby, T.B. and Smith, P.J. 2009. 'Living Originalism'. 59(2) *Duke Law Journal*, 239–307.

Cross, F.B. 2012. 'Originalism – The Forgotten Years'. 28 *Constitutional Commentary*, 37–51.

Cross, F.B. 2013. *The Failed Promise of Originalism.* Stanford, Stanford University Press.

Edling, M.M. 2008. *A Revolution in Favor of Government: Origins of the U.S. Constitution and the Making of the American State.* New York, Oxford University Press.

Edwards v. Attorney-General for Canada, [1930] A.C. 124 (P.C.) (The Persons Case).

Flaherty, M.S. 1995. 'History 'Lite' in Modern American Constitutionalism'. 95 *Columbia. Law Review*, 523–90.

Flaherty, M.S. 1997. 'The Practice of Faith'. 65 *Fordham Law Review*, 1565–80.

Fontana, D. 2010. 'Comparative Originalism, See Also'. 88 *Texas Law Review*, 189–99.

The Founders Online, http://founders.archives.gov/.

Goldsworthy, J. 1997. 'Originalism in Constitutional Interpretation'. 25 *Federal Law Review*, 1–50.

Goldsworthy, J. 2012. 'Constitutional Cultures, Democracy, Implications, and Underlying Principles'. *University of Illinois Law Review*, 683–710.

Greene, J. 2009. 'On the Origins of Originalism'. 88 *Texas Law Review*, 1–89.

Hogg, P.W. 2006. 'Canada: From Privy Council to Supreme Court'. In J. Goldsworthy (ed.), *Interpreting Constitutions: A Comparative Study*, 55–105. Oxford, Oxford University Press.

Hollis-Brusky, A.L. 2014 forthcoming. *Ideas With Consequences: The Federalist Society and the Conservative Counterrevolution*. New York, Oxford University Press.

Kalman, L. 1996. *The Strange Career of Legal Liberalism*. New Haven, Yale University Press.

Kalman, L. 1997. 'Border Patrol: Reflections on the Turn to History in Legal Scholarship'. 66 *Fordham L Review*, 87–124.

Kelly, A.H. 1965. 'Clio and the Court: An Illicit Love Affair'. *Supreme Court Review*, 119–58.

Levinson, S. 1996. 'The Limited Relevance of Originalism in the Actual Performance of Legal Roles'. 19 *Harvard Journal of Law and Public Policy*, 495–508.

Levinson, S. 2012a. *Constitutional Faith* (rev. ed.). Princeton, Princeton University Press.

Levinson, S. 2012b. *Framed: America's Fifty-One Constitutions and the Crisis of Governance*. New York, Oxford University Press.

Levinson, S. and Balkin, J.M. 1991. 'Law, Music, and Other Performing Arts'. 139 *University of Pennsylvania Law Review*, 1597–658.

Lund, N. 2009. 'The Second Amendment, *Heller*, and Originalist Jurisprudence'. 56 *UCLA Law Review*, 1343–76.

Marx, K. and Engels, F. 1978. Manifesto of the Communist Party, in *The Marx-Engels Reader*, edited by R.C. Tucker. New York, W.W. Norton. 2nd Edition, 469–500.

Mathews, J. and Stone Sweet, A. 2011. 'All Things in Proportion? American Rights Review and the Problem of Balancing'. 60 *Emory Law Journal*, 797–875.

Miller, B.W. 2011. 'Origin Myth: The Persons Case, the Living Tree, and the New Originalism'. In G. Huscroft and B.W. Miller (eds), *The Challenge of Originalism: Essays in Constitutional Theory*. Cambridge, Cambridge University Press, 120–47.

Oral argument transcript, *Schwarzenegger v. Entertainment Merchants Association*, No. 08-1448, November 2, 2010. http://www.supremecourt.gov/oral_arguments/argument_transcripts/08-1448.pdf.

Neily, C.M. III. 2013. *Terms of Engagement: How Our Courts Should Enforce the Constitution's Promise of Limited Government*. New York, Encounter Books.

Post, R.C. 1990. 'Theories of Constitutional Interpretation'. 30 *Representations*, 13–41.

Post, R. and Siegel, R. 2006. 'Originalism as Political Practice: The Right's Living Constitution'. 75 *Fordham Law Review*, 545–74.

Rana, A. 2010. *The Two Faces of American Freedom*. Cambridge, MA, Harvard University Press.

Raphael, R. 2013. *Constitutional Myths: What We Get Wrong and How to Get it Right*. New York, The New Press.

Roosevelt, F.D. 1937a. 'Fireside Chat Discussing the Plan for Reorganization of the Federal Judiciary, March 9, 1937'. In *The American Presidency Project*, J. Woolley and G. Peters (eds) online at www.presidency.ucsb.edu/ws/index.php?pid=15381.

Roosevelt, F.D. 1937b. 'Address on Constitution Day, Washington, D.C., September 17th, 1937'. In *The American Presidency Project*, edited by J. Woolley and G. Peters (eds), online at www.presidency.ucsb.edu/ws/index.php? pid=15459 ; 'The Constitution of the United States Was a Layman's Document, Not a Lawyer's Contract (Sept. 17, 1937),' in 6 *The Public Papers and Addresses of Franklin D. Roosevelt*, Rosenman, S.I. (ed.). New York, Macmillan 1941. 359, 367.

Rosenfeld, M. 2004. 'Constitutional Adjudication in Europe and the United States: Paradoxes and Contrasts'. 2 *International Journal of Constitutional Law*, 633–68.
Scalia, A. 1989. 'Originalism: The Lesser Evil'. 57 *University of Cincinnati Law Review*, 849–65.
Scheppele, K.L. 2013. 'Jack Balkin is an American'. 25 *Yale Journal of Law and the Humanities*, 23–42.
Solum, L. 2013. 'Originalism and Constitutional Construction'. 82 *Fordham Law Review*, 453–537.
Sunstein, C. 1995. 'The Idea of a Usable Past'. 95 *Columbia Law Review*, 601–8.
Tew, Y. 2014 forthcoming. 'Originalism at Home and Abroad'. 53 *Columbia Journal of Translational Law*.
Tushnet, M. 2012. 'From Judicial Restraint To Judicial Engagement: A Short Intellectual History'. 19 *George Mason Law Review*, 1043–51.
Tushnet, M. 1996. 'Interdisciplinary Legal Scholarship: The Case of History-in-Law'. 71 *Chicago-Kent Law Review*, 909–35.
Usman, J.O. 2010. 'Good Enough for Government Work: The Interpretation of Positive Constitutional Rights in State Constitutions'. 73 *Albany Law Review*, 1459–534.
Varol, O.O. 2011. 'The Origins and Limits of Originalism: A Comparative Study'. 44 *Vanderbilt Journal of Transnational Law*, 1239–97.
Weis, L. 2013. 'What Comparativism Tells Us About Originalism'. 11 *International Journal of Constitutional Law*, 842–69.
Whittington, K.E. 'The New Originalism'. 2 *Georgetown Journal of Law and Public Policy*, 599–613.

Chapter 19

The Rule of Law After the Short Twentieth Century: Launching a Global Career[1]

Martin Krygier

Though we operate at very great distances from each other and have met only a few times, my own intellectual sympathies, interests and concerns have overlapped closely with those of Roger Cotterrell, in areas both general and particular, for many years. Generally we are both drawn to what Philip Selznick has called an ecumenical view of social science, one that happily, with no sense of disciplinary guilt, encompasses philosophical, moral and legal concerns. More particularly, we share an interest in the thought of Selznick himself,[2] and with him a view of sociology of law that is not just ecumenical but relentlessly (though not exclusively) contextual.

We both believe, as Roger (2006: 81) has put it, that 'what is required for [sociology of law] is a conceptual framework allowing comparison not of legal doctrine as such, but of legal ideas and practices regarded as inseparable from a broader social context'. One such legal idea which has intrigued us both (and intrigued Selznick) is the rule of law. That idea also, as Roger wrote (2007: 101) of Franz Neumann's writings on it, must be considered – not reduced to, but considered – contextually, within 'the changing social and political contexts in which the Rule of Law ideal, variously interpreted in different nations but with a certain common core of meaning, was invoked'. Such consideration is likely to find, as Roger demonstrated (1989) of several of the canonical works of jurisprudence, that 'changing intellectual fashions [are] related to the changing social context of legal development' (15); 'ideas and theoretical orientations seem to be adopted and discarded in ways which cannot simply be explained in terms of intellectual superiority or inferiority' (18). And so, 'if we are to try to understand how legal philosophy has developed and how its debates and disputes have been formed and conducted, the answers cannot be found entirely in the logic of philosophical argument. They are, in part at least, located in the wider context of ideas and activities in which theories are developed and evaluated … content is to be understood not as timeless but as a response to conditions and problems existing at particular historical moments in Western legal development' (15).

This is not, to repeat, an argument for sociological reductionism. It is clear to Roger, and it is my belief as well, that ideas need to be understood 'on [their] own terms *and* in context'

1 Earlier versions of this chapter were presented to panels at the Law and Society Conference, Boston, 2013, the Institute for Global Law and Policy Conference, Harvard University, 2013 and the International Association for Philosophy of Law and Social Philosophy Conference, Bela Horizonte, 2013. I am grateful to the participants in those panels, and also to Deval Desai, Samuel Moyn and Kenneth Winston, for their comments. It draws upon research supported under Australian Research Council's *Discovery Projects* funding scheme (project number DP110101029).

2 See Cotterrell 2004; Krygier 2012. For the full text of the Cotterrell/Selznick conversations, and for videos of my and others' interviews with Selznick and other materials on him, see the Philip Selznick Memorial Page, Center for the Study of Law and Society, UC Berkeley, at http://www.law.berkeley.edu/selznick.htm.

(1989: 19). If they are important ideas, they need to be subjected to immanent appreciation and critique, not merely explained away by their circumstances of origin. But one learns something, sometimes lots, from exploring those circumstances. My aim in this chapter is to seek to demonstrate the truth of these propositions in a specific and recent context: that in which 'the rule of law' has become a global logo.

1. Introduction

Fashion is a curious thing. Items lying around in attics for long periods suddenly get brought out and everyone wants to be seen wearing them. It's hard to say why, though *they* haven't changed, peoples' attitudes to them have; so much so that a new industry often starts, producing cheap and insubstantial replicas of old classics. In my home town, Sydney, harbour views were always prestigious, but those of the ocean were not. So houses near the waves were cheap. Now you can't buy one for love nor money. The architecture is less attractive than the view, since there are still a lot of standard-issue houses there and now new follies, but no one seems to mind. Those with enough money to afford one can tear it up and start again. The result seems to please the new owners, but it's not always a pretty sight.

What is true of clothes and views is also true of concepts. Some are very old, dusty and suffering from ages of neglect, even distaste. And suddenly we find ourselves talking of little else. The rule of law is one such. It's scarcely a new term and an even older concept, sometimes lauded, sometimes decried. Today however, among the 'posts' that litter the planet – post-communist, post-conflict, post-authoritarian, post-Washington; now post-post – it figures as a non-negotiable item in virtually every public agency's recipe for reform. Those with long memories might think something has been lost in translation, but the industry doesn't falter on that account.

In the last 20 to 30 years, rule-of-law-as-panacea has become extraordinarily popular. Rule of law is today an international hurrah term, on the lips of every political leader, development agency and world body, offered as a support for economic growth, democracy, human rights, and much else. 'RoL' promotion is booming. Lots of people and organizations are contracted to work on it, lots of money is spent on it, lots of academics study it. It wasn't always so. And even though the term is everywhere it's hard to say that we see more rule of law in the world. All sorts of thugs and murderers are not now, just as they were not then, constrained by law, whatever they say. And notwithstanding heaps of rule of law promotion, that doesn't seem likely to change. But my story in this chapter is about concepts and ideology, not practice, though ideology is of course a form of practice, and it affects other forms of practice as well.

Recall Lenin for a moment. He was after all leader of a post-authoritarian transition (to totalitarianism, as it happens, but the point remains). The rule of law was not high on his agenda and he was not embarrassed about it. He said, and it was true, that his government was 'based directly upon force and unrestricted by any laws. The revolutionary dictatorship of the proletariat is rule won and maintained by the use of violence by the proletariat against the bourgeoisie, rule that is unrestricted by any laws'. And it was not hard for such views to find support. In the old days, if British patriots were to laud the rule of law, they could easily find themselves drowned in choruses deriding bourgeois ideology, at least in academic circles. When one such, E.P. Thompson, who had distinctively managed to combine Marxism with his patriotism wrote, as recently as the mid 1970s, that the rule of law is a 'cultural achievement of universal significance' (1977: 265), he was not thanked by his erstwhile comrades. And critical legal studies, a movement of the 1970s and 1980s, spent much of its time denouncing the allegedly false-consciousness-inducing ideology of the rule of law.

Things are different now. If any evidence is needed, I offer just one piece which speaks volumes: out of a litany of encomia to the rule of law collected by Brian Tamanaha, perhaps Robert Mugabe's is the most poignant. He explains that '[o]nly a government that subjects itself to the rule of law has any moral right to demand of its citizens obedience to the rule of law'.[3] If hypocrisy is the tribute vice pays to virtue, this is tribute indeed. Since I think that the rule of law, understood in a particular but historically far from exotic way, is a good thing (Krygier 2011a: 64–104), precious even, I should be happy about its newfound popularity. But it does lead to a question about the contingent nature of the enterprise in which so many of us are engaged: why now? The answer can't simply be that the rule of law is valuable or important, as so many now say. For it is not obvious that it is any more important today than when Lenin was happy to abuse it without apology. What's changed? Perhaps we've just become smarter, but it is hard to say why that would be. What made us so? And again: why now?

A third possibility is that we've had such success in global rule of law promotion, and that in turn has been so beneficial in so many ways to so many countries, that we're merely facing obvious, undeniable, facts. But, in light of the evidence, that is not altogether plausible either; indeed some might say it's more risible than plausible.

Another suggestion might be that some experts, among them institutional economists of neoliberal persuasion, hit upon the idea that the rule of law was important, convinced international agencies, and the rest followed. That has to be part of the truth, because we can point to examples. Economists have without doubt appropriated and boosted the vogue for the term world-wide over the past 20–30 years. But experts have ideas all the time. Most of them share the fate Marx misguidedly anticipated for his and Engels' first manuscript together, *The German Ideology*: subject to nothing but 'the gnawing criticism of the mice'. Why were ideas about the rule of law taken up – by men not mice, and not only economists – with such enthusiasm, and all over the globe? Why indeed did economists' ideas about law, which could be and have been expressed in terms other than 'the rule of law', come to be so? What made the concept so widely available, so ready-to-hand at that time and not another?

My own hunches are, first, that it is no surprise that the rule of law began its global career so late in the last century. There was no room for it earlier, because of ideological features which shaped and distinguished that century and specifically its core, the 'short twentieth century' that Eric Hobsbawm (1994) identified as beginning in 1914 and ending in 1991 (central Europeans would argue plausibly for 1989, and indeed that date is more relevant to the concerns of this chapter). Secondly, the rule of law began its global rhetorical apprenticeship, with 'human rights' and for many of the same reasons, as disillusion set in with the short century's ideologically driven 'grand narratives', though before anyone realized one of them was about to disappear. Third, the career of the rule of law began its ever-upward trajectory, after and because of the ignominious and complete debacle of one of the short century's two protagonists. This, fourthly, was grist to the mills of neoliberal economists and other enthusiasts, whose ideas about the significance of law came to be expressed in terms of the rule of law, added to its global charms, boosted its ratings sky-high, and changed the terms and the tone in which it was discussed. Whether, finally, this career will survive the complicating transformations that have occurred since, are matters of conjecture, in which I will indulge tentatively and briefly.

3 Quoted in Tamanaha 2004: 2.

At the moment I have more confidence that such questions are worth asking than that I have answers worth giving. They should be asked, even so, because when a concept becomes fashionable enough to set agendas, it tends to drive out alternatives. We think within those agendas, rather than about them. Even if we find ourselves in a conceptual hole, it is hard to ask whether we might stop digging, or dig somewhere else, or for something else, or in some other way. We exhaust our energies trying to dig ever better, rather than ask why we got into the hole in the first place. Such questions are not always easy to answer, however, since the rise and fall of concepts is often over-determined, while evidence that would allow us confidently to assign causes is typically underwhelming. It is rare that any one thing explains the career of a concept, and unless one is attached to some sort of vulgar materialism or idealism it's not always even clear what might count as an explanation. So my claims are modest: I try here only to suggest a few plausible linkages – neither necessary nor sufficient conditions, perhaps only 'elective affinities' – between what I postulate as effective and what we see as effects.

1.1 The Short Twentieth Century

Shortly after the French Revolution, the French philosopher Joseph de Maistre observed that 'for a long time we did not fully understand the revolution of which we were witnesses; for a long time we took it to be an event. We were mistaken; it was an epoch'. The same could be said of the Russian Revolution. At the very least, it spawned an epoch that lasted until 1989, though its triumphal moments were long behind it by then. The end of European communism, and with it even the dream of world communism, in turn, was itself not just an event but, as many thinkers have observed, the end of that epoch.

There was a lot that was special about that century, short though it may have been. One was that the 'conceptual geography' (Judt 1990: 25) of the globe became framed as a battle between states seen as the creatures, incarnations and bearers of particular, programmatic ideas with global claims. This is rare. The United States, after their revolutionary inception developed ideas with which they later became identified, and revolutionary France for its brief life was associated with novel ideas that certainly infected subsequent history. However, no other great state had ever before been destroyed and reconstructed with the manifest intent of realizing the secular intellectual, and revolutionary project of one thinker. The Soviet Union began as just such a state.

Certainly the Soviet Union's European neighbours and opponents in 1917 were nothing like that: no one invented them, and while there were texts and ideologies, most came well after, at any rate during, the events and few were canonical. In many ways there are parallels with a later invention, Nazism, also the thought of one man, also an unprecedented and defining part of the epoch, also a response to many of its dislocations, especially the War, also revolutionary and totalitarian in its ambitions, also attractive to many intellectuals in the 1930s, and also responsible for almost unimaginable levels and kinds of 'violence, hubris, ruthlessness and human sacrifices' (Tismaneanu 2012: i). Communism and Fascism were both ideological regimes and, as François Furet (1999) has stressed, we don't have many of those. Arguably, and he does so argue, these two were the first. Whether the concepts that defined the geopolitical rivalries of the century would have been ideological had Communism and Nazism not been there is anyone's guess. For while contention seems inescapable from human affairs, *ideological* contention is not the norm.

There were of course immense differences, intellectual and moral, between Marx and Hitler, between their roles in the movements that followed them, and between the mythologies and narratives that inspired their followers – world emancipation in one, world domination in the other. The movements they inspired both excelled in human catastrophe though. The epoch could have ended in a competition between them both, and indeed could have been won by either. Had that been the case, I doubt we would be talking about the rule of law today. As it happened, however, Nazi Germany was defeated, and only one of these novel ideocratic creations remained. Its influence, as actor, model and counter-model, was profound. The post-War world was framed by the bipolar contest – over ideas as much as territories – between the liberal-capitalist 'West', its allies, subalterns, vassals and dependents on the one hand, and the Communist – first Soviet, then Soviet and Chinese – powers with their attendants, acolytes, emulators and victims, on the other. The rest of the world was an arena of competition – between countries of course but more distinctively between frames and views of life, including political, economic and social life, that were in intense competition and diametrically opposed. As Hobsbawm (1994: 4) has noted:

> The world that went to pieces at the end of the 1980s was the world shaped by the Russian Revolution of 1917. We have all been marked by it, for instance, inasmuch as we got used to thinking of the modern industrial economy in terms of binary opposites, "capitalism" and "socialism" as alternatives mutually excluding one another, the one being identified with economies organized on the model of the USSR, the other with all the rest.

That's one – Marxist – way of putting it, with economics as the core. Another – political – way is to contrast ideological one party dictatorship versus pluralist liberal democracy. Either way the geopolitical map of the short century turns out the same, and radically different from what it was and what it has become. Much of the century was dominated, then, by a stark and at times dramatic ideological, political, economic and often military contest between exemplars of antithetical and contending social/economic/political regimes for life. Their conflicts were holistically conceived as between incompatible *systems* of social, political and economic organization and operation; not – as traditionally – as occurring from time to time between entities of more or less the same sort, even if differently adorned and even if hostile.

Law had no part in the glorifying myths and narratives of communism. It was at best viewed as a piece of (transitional) social technology of subordinate significance in the life of a society, treated always instrumentally, often with suspicion or contempt; often simply ignored. The rule of law in particular was no part of what Hobsbawm describes as 'the special house-style [communism] imposed on its successors'. On the other side, by contrast, law and the rule of law were vaunted, sometimes considered national treasures, but there were hefty barriers to export, not open to globalizing ambitions, since 'we' only owned a part of things and no one thought that was going to change in a hurry. On occasion, and especially in the US backyard or where it sought influence,[4] tentative experiments in law and development [L&D] occurred, but given the competitive struggling and ideological posturing that dominated the world, the rule of law could never be part of any international *lingua franca*. L&D was not even a hint of what was to come. As David Trubek (2006: 78) has noted:

> The L&D movement had a brief and intense life. Of course, by today's standards it was never a major enterprise. It was focused on a few countries in Latin America and Africa. Projects were small and short lived, and finances were limited. … by the middle of the 1970s there was disillusion in the academy, foundation interest declined, and the official aid agencies showed no interest in moving into legal reform. So, for the moment, the L&D movement seemed to have run out of steam.

4 See Trubek and Santos 2006.

Somehow L&D came, after some 20 years, to be replaced by RoL. And that was something else. As Trubek again (2006: 81) observes:

> Today, the enterprise of law reform in developing and transition countries is big business, far eclipsing even the wildest dreams of the L&D pioneers. Aid agencies like the World Bank, which once focused primarily on building roads and dams and getting macroeconomic variables right, now proclaim the importance of the "rule of law" (ROL) and spend billions to reform the legal systems of countries as different as Albania and Argentina, Bangladesh and Bolivia.

1.2 Apolitical Politics

Why did this begin to change, as I believe it did, in what were, but were not yet recognized to be the waning years of the short century? There is an economic story, which Trubek and his colleagues tell well, that focuses on the development of institutional and neoliberal economists' ideas of that period, their political incarnations in Margaret Thatcher and Ronald Reagan in the late 1970s, and their later influence on world mega-development institutions, such as the World Bank and the IMF in the 1990s.[5] The back story, though without reference to law, is part of an intriguing new book on 1979 as the harbinger of things to come (Christian 2013). That is clearly a key part of the story of the take-up of the rule of law, and later perhaps a dominant part, but I want to stress another strand, that started elsewhere, had to do with politics more than economics, so far as I can tell began earlier (anyway not later), and has received less attention.

Here I develop some intriguing claims of Samuel Moyn (2010), in his remarkable *The Last Utopia. Human Rights in History*. Moyn's work is part intellectual history, part political lament. Both are relevant to the career of the rule of law, though in different ways. I begin with the history, and will later return to the lament. Moyn has nothing to say about the rule of law but his argument, about the genesis and dissemination of 'human rights' in the 1970s has profound implications for the career of the former concept. The core of his argument is that most of the current purported genealogies of human rights, which have them emerging from old precedents, such as the American or French Revolutions, or more recent world-historical calamities, such as the Holocaust, are false. The international omnipresence of 'human rights' is a recent thing, and its sources other than those we usually identify. He argues that while the concept of human rights was certainly around for a while, and had precedents and bursts of documentary crystallization after World War II, it really only gained its current international state-questioning character, ubiquity, salience and rhetorical space-filling dominance over other moral languages, from the 1970s. It was, Moyn argues, a recent story spawned at a particular moment, largely by the writings of Russian and east European dissidents, Latin American revolutionaries and others, who were seeking a moral language for an ideologically exhausted, and politically blocked, time.

Moyn's discussion of why human rights were found so appealing to dissidents in the 1970s seems extremely plausible to me, and to the extent that it is so, extendable to the later embrace of the rule of law as well, perhaps even more so. My borrowings from Moyn do not depend on one of his central and most controversial claims – the lack of real precedent for the international vogue for human rights before the 1970s. Whatever the case with that concept, the rule of law was not new coin, and it is no part of my argument that the concept was 'invented' in the very recent past.[6] However, notwithstanding the old lineage of the concept, it simply wasn't there as the universal

5 See Kennedy 2004; Trubek and Santos 2006; Haggard, MacIntyre and Tiede 2008.

6 See my 'Rule of Law (and Rechtsstaat)', forthcoming.

panacea it has since become, before the 1990s. It had local roles and traditional partisans, but not the cosmopolitan reach it has come to enjoy.

Moyn's basic claim about 'human rights as a powerful transnational ideal and movement' (2010: 7) is that:

> they emerged in the 1970s seemingly from nowhere. … Yet within one decade human rights would begin to be invoked across the developed world and by many more ordinary people than ever before. Instead of implying colonial liberation and the creation of emancipated nations, human rights most often now meant individual protection against the state … Westerners left the dream of revolution behind – both for themselves and for the Third World they had once ruled – and adopted other tactics, envisioning an international law of human rights as the steward of utopian norms, and as the mechanism of their fulfilment … The moral world had changed. (3–4)

Why such a turn? For even if there are more precedents for the internationalization of human rights than Moyn allows, it seems incontestable that the 1970s saw a dramatic quickening and spread of recourse to them.[7] Moyn attributes this to the exhaustion of, a turning away from, the grand ideological alternatives that had framed political choices for much of the century. Communism had discredited itself internally, for a huge number of reasons, and internationally at least after its brutal crushing of the Hungarian revolution in 1956 and the Czech in 1968. These showed that politics were unavailable in any real, 'normal' sense in Communist states, at the same time as they destroyed utopian political transformative projects as an ideal. However, neither anti-communist dissidents in Russia and Eastern Europe nor dissenters in Latin America, also politically blocked, were enthusiasts for replacing one of the two grand projects on offer with the other, or indeed with *an* other. They were not, at this stage, enthusiasts for capitalism either (though later this came to change for many of them), and many of them had had enough of the *scale and ambition* of either alternative. Moreover, throughout the West, the 1960s – the war in Vietnam, the rise of the New Left, the West-wide student movement, the Rolling Stones – had shaken ideological confidence there also. It was common for critics to concede 'moral equivalence' to the two camps, to cast a plague on both their houses.

> This fed the appeal of rights: The best general explanation for the origins of this social movement and common discourse around rights remains the collapse of other, prior utopias, both state-based and internationalist. … In this atmosphere, an internationalism revolving around individual rights surged, and it did so because it was defined as a pure alternative in an age of ideological betrayal and political collapse. (Moyn 2010: 8)

East European dissidents preached 'apolitical politics', the 'power of the powerless', civil society. They abhorred conventional politics in general, and in any event there was no place for them in Communist states. And, having felt the consequences, they abhorred utopian politics in particular. Better to secure some minimal basic moral rights that apply to everyone, than to pursue contentious fantasies of social, economic and political regeneration that had been seen only to generate catastrophe. Distrusting political utopias and politics more generally, they sought a morally untainted alternative. Human rights seemed, Moyn suggests, to fit the bill.

In such a context, Moyn (2010) argues, human rights had many attractions. First, they seemed more modest, 'involving smaller and more manageable moral acts' (147) than the utopias they

7 See also Moyn 2012.

replaced: 'Human rights emerged as a minimalist, hardy utopia that could survive in a harsh climate … the winter of discontent that swept the West [in the early 1970s] also resulted in the mistrust of more maximal plans for transformation – especially revolutions but also programmatic endeavours of any kind' (121). Second, they could combine modest aspiration with universal appeal; human rights were everyone's rights, no one should be denied them, and no one could claim exemption from their demands. Third, they were grounded in the purity of moral self-evidence, not the dirt of (in any event unavailable) political manoeuvring; 'The disavowal of earlier utopias took place in part out of the aspiration to achieve through a moral critique of politics the sense of a pure cause that had once been sought in politics itself' (171–2). Finally, they offered an ecumenical language; 'It also mattered that the language proved to be highly coalitional and ecumenical in providing a lingua franca for diverse voices' (144). As Andrei Sakharov, whom Moyn quotes, summed it up in 1978:

> The ideology of human rights … serve[s] as a foothold for those who do not wish to be aligned with theoretical intricacies and dogmas, and who have tired of the abundance of ideologies, none of which have brought mankind simple human happiness. (174)[8]

Moyn's is a rich book and human rights a larger and more captivating ideal than the rule of law. The ambitions are greater, the sweep, the beyond-the-state grounding and reach, all go beyond the rule of law. So one cannot simply say, 'quite so, and so too – with a slight delay – for the rule of law'. He is, after all, not interested in the connections between human rights and the rule of law, but with international law, and that is a different if overlapping story. However, as a subaltern attendant to Moyn's story, the launch of the global career of the rule of law – concept not achievement – is illuminated by his argument. It might indeed turn out to be the next chapter in his story. For so much that Moyn says about the appeal of human rights in a time of ideological exhaustion applies to the revving up stage of the next universalistic cab off the rank, the junior relative (and increasingly-presumed vehicle) of human rights, the rule of law. Even more than human rights, the rule of law can seem to be a minimalist goal, applicable everywhere and to everyone, independent of political ideology or system. It is certainly not the stuff of popular utopian fantasy. All it has seemed to involve is the demand that regimes respect legal undertakings they have already and explicitly given. It also incarnates the displacement of politics by judicial assessment that Moyn sees as the crucial shift from earlier talk of rights to contemporary human rights talk. Indeed it seems utterly prosaic, much more so than human rights, and perhaps for that very reason more appealing to those to whom it has come to appeal.

It is true that the rule of law has little of the morally compelling aura of human rights; its appeal is instrumental not fundamental. That indeed might be why it is talked about more by technocrats, diplomats, and professional promoters than by ordinary folk, but that might even seem an advantage to some among its constituencies, particularly official ones. Though Moyn does not say this, one could even more easily say of the rule of law what he says (2010: 213) of human rights: 'human rights could break through … because the ideological climate was ripe for claims to make a difference not through political vision but by transcending politics.' Indeed, though this takes us into a later part of our story, after the short twentieth century had ended and the global career of the rule of law was well under way, Rajagopal has argued that one reason the UN took up the rule of law was that:

8 Sakharov 1979.

> The rule of law came to be seen, in many ways, as a convenient substitute for human rights. Unlike human rights, the rule of law does not promise the achievement of any substantive social, political, or cultural goal. It is much more empty of content and capable of being interpreted in many diverse, sometimes contradictory, ways. The human rights discourse is a discourse of social transformation, and even emancipation, whereas the rule of law discourse does not have that ambition and may be seen as inherently conservative.[9]

Moreover, not only did the rule of law share many of the sources of attractiveness of human rights, if in a minor key, it also became a vehicle for them. One key if subsidiary theme in Moyn's account is the extent to which this human rights discourse became legalized. It was not just an international movement but a movement of international law. Also novel was the extent to which law more generally was entrusted with the delivery of human rights, Moyn notes (2010: 134) the extent to which, already in the late 1960s early Soviet dissidents chose to pursue a 'legalist' approach, insisting on the terms of the law, which in reality mattered to no one, in order to highlight 'the failure of the regime to abide by its own enacted rules'. In the 1970s, Vaclav Havel also insisted on a strategy of 'legalism', and dissidents took inspiration and also tactical support, from a landmark event, the Helsinki Accords of 1975. These traded recognition by the West of post-War boundaries that the Soviet Union had secured by force, for recognition of human rights by the East, recognition that Henry Kissinger memorably said, could be written 'in Swahili for all I care'. However, what to many anti-communists seemed a poor deal, since boundaries were tangible and human rights commitments not so, proved to be the opposite of expectations: the boundaries evaporated in 1991 and the commitments provided a focus for increasingly embarrassing Soviet and East European dissent.

The point has been nicely captured in a recent memoir by a later visitor to Eastern Europe, Marci Shore (2013: 26–7), seeking to recapture the distinctive ethos of the Czech dissident movement, Charter 77:

> In Prague that summer of 1993 I was trying to understand Charter 77 – what it was and what it was not. It was not anti-Marxist. It appealed for neither the restoration of capitialism nor the introduction of multiple political parties. It proposed no alternative political system. It called on the government only to take seriously its own laws. Everyone told me this; it was a kind of refrain. I was interested in democratic politics, but in Czechoslovakia the dissidents had been interested in "antipolitics." The Helsinki Accords had inspired a language that was not only post-Marxist but also postpolitical. Inside politics, the dissidents had believed, it was impossible to have clean hands. Political opposition would always imply something shared with the regime it opposed. The language of Helsinki was a language of human rights, transcendent of communist – or capitalist – ideology.

Dissidents developed a legal strategy of insisting that laws, which had never counted for much in their experience or parts of the world, be taken seriously and solemnly, *as if* the regimes that were harassing them could be assumed to heed the rule of law, in order that they might be forced to do so. Conventional political participation being unattractive and unavailable, law offered a kind of authority and impersonal appeal, immediately at the level of rhetoric, and perhaps in an unforeseeable future in fact. It was a powerful strategy by that time, deeply uncomfortable for floundering, de-legitimized regimes. Some of those regimes, Poland's for example, desperately

9 Rajagopal 2008: 13–59.

launched a strategy of legitimation through law – new courts, Ombudsman, Constitutional Tribunal, Tribunal of State[10] – in their last decade, since all other forms of legitimacy had disappeared. Mikhail Gorbachev, too, a lawyer like Lenin but with somewhat different views about law, sought in the flickering moments of his rule to construct a 'state based on the rule of law' (Foster-Simons 1989), but it was too late. And when to everyone's surprise, European communism collapsed like dominos in and after 1989, one of the central demands of the unprepared victors of those unprepared revolutions was the rule of law. Trubek (2006) is illuminating here. He identifies as the first of two strands for 'the rediscovery of law in the development community' what he calls '"the project of democracy," [that] came out of the human rights movement of the 1970s and 1980s.' Of that strand he writes:

> For our story, the most important move was the recognition that purely international approaches to human rights protection were insufficient without strong counterparts in domestic law. Events such as the Helsinki process drew attention to the lack of protection for human rights in domestic institutions. The human rights movement began to look at domestic institutions, championing the creation of constitutional guarantees, judicial review, greater judicial independence and "access to justice." This path naturally led to ideas about the construction of "the rule of law." It was understood that the project would require substantial effort both to dismantle older systems that had buttressed authoritarian rule and to create the new culture and institutions needed to protect democratic freedoms. (84)

1.3 Back to the Future

In 1992, the rule of law for the first time became an item on the agenda of the United Nations General Assembly. In 2012 it was for the first time the exclusive subject of a 'High level meeting' of the Assembly, which declared, in its 'Declaration on the Rule of Law at the National and International Levels', that human rights, the rule of law and democracy are interlinked and mutually reinforcing and that they belong to the universal and indivisible core values and principles of the United Nations', (even though it had only explicitly begun to notice the place of the rule of law in this pantheon 20 years before). Again, Jeremy Farrall notes a 'transformation of the rule of law from curiosity to familiar friend in the term's increasing appearance in the Council's resolutions. During the Cold War, rule of law featured in Security Council resolutions a mere handful of times. By contrast, in the nine years from the beginning of 1998 until the end of 2006, the phrase "rule of law" appeared in no fewer than sixty-nine Council resolutions' (Farrall 2007: 22). The reasons are not far to seek. Many people have noted, Agnès Hurwitz (2005: 4) among them, that 'It is only after the end of the cold war that the rule of law became the big tent for social, economic, and political change generally – the perceived answer to competing pressures for democratization, globalization, privatization, urbanization, and decentralization'. Why so?

My conjecture is that the ground was ploughed and the seeds sown by the factors that Moyn has argued mobilized the language of human rights. The subsequent collapse of communism fertilized the soil, but also opened the field up to others to sow, graft and harvest. Out of all this came a curious hybrid, born of political disillusion but nurtured in a time of apparent geopolitical triumph and evangelical confidence ('the end of history'), some of it political (democracy and the rule of law), some of it economic (the triumph of the market), some of it – later – fearful (the

10 See Czarnota 1994: esp. 190–95.

war on terror). The result was a product available for many different consumers, with varying tastes and uses, some of them discordant with others; but not every discordance within the 'big tent' was immediately, or later, noted. This led to continuity, rapid advance, but also significant transformations in the career of the concept. On the one hand, the existing distrust of untested utopian experiments was augmented when communism collapsed so dramatically, without even having been pushed. Had nothing else been involved than that collapse, it might have led to an incremental increase in attention to law. However, when one contestant collapsed, the other was left standing. This radically altered the balance between the two protagonists of the short century: now, it seemed clear, one had won, in practice, in real time. No more was heard of moral equivalence or indeed any equivalence at all. One side was out the window; the other came confidently through the door. The task, many came to believe, was now to move rapidly into the future by emulating what were taken to be the lessons of the Western past. The result of this reconfiguration was a windfall for the career of the rule of law, but also an amplification of the ambitions of its partisans. It emerged out of politics and in modesty, but was promoted in economics and, for a time, in glory. These are not always easy traits to combine, and so it has proved.

2. 'No adjectives'

On the one hand, then, the trajectory begins with the insistent *modesty* of initial demands for what was to follow communist collapse, modesty, in keeping with Moyn's thesis. The spectacular collapse of European communism in 1989 puzzled many observers. For it spawned a phenomenon virtually without precedent: a cascade of revolutions that while having truly world-historical practical and ideological implications, put the rule of law central among their programmatic themes and demands. Apart from the American Revolution, no other world-historical revolution can be similarly characterized. Clearly something significant – indeed unprecedented – was going on. However, the rhetoric of these world-historical transformations was restrained in the extreme. First of all: 'No Experiments!'[11] That has never been the call of any other revolution. No new ideas seemed to emerge, and this not for lack of thought but deliberately. And many observers agreed. Timothy Garton Ash (1990a: 20), for example, couldn't decide whether to call them 'refolutions' or 'revolutions' since the collapse of one country after another and the end of a political, economic and social system is clearly something more than ordinary reform, but it lacked many of the dramatic trappings of revolutions, among them new ideas. And, Romania apart, there was very little blood. Debates followed about whether it had generated any new ideas at all.

This combination of centrality, novelty and modesty was all played out in relation to law and the rule of law. On the one hand, law was unusually central to the rhetoric of the dissidents-turned-statesmen. As Sajó and Arato (1991: 101) have observed:

> From many points of view the post-Communist systems, at least in the first two years of their existence, are strongly legalistic. ... the East European transitions did not only aim at constitutionalism and the rule of law, but also the process of change itself which, in all countries with the exception of Romania and Soviet Union, took a constitutional form. This paradoxically involved taking the existing communist constitutions seriously for the first time (an odd proposal

11 Originally used by Konrad Adenauer of German reconstruction after defeat in World War II.

> of the dissidents!) and using their own mechanisms to produce constitutions with an entirely new spirit.

This centrality of law is unusual of revolutions, particularly in this part of the world. But also unusual for revolutionaries was that the rule of law they sought should be 'without adjectives': not bourgeois, socialist, or whatever, just law. Rule of law and constitution-building was largely considered a work of emulation, not invention. As Garton Ash (1990b: 21) noted at the time:

> ... in politics they are all saying: There is no "socialist democracy," there is only democracy. And by democracy they mean multi-party, parliamentary democracy as practised in contemporary Western, Northern, and Southern Europe. They are all saying: There is no "socialist legality," there is only legality. And by that they mean the rule of law, guaranteed by the constitutionally anchored independence of the judiciary.

It has turned out to be a more complicated undertaking than that,[12] but that is certainly how many viewed it at the time.

3. The End of History

One reason it all seemed so cut-and-dried is that, while post-communist dissidents shared with their former selves and predecessors distrust for political utopia, they were no longer even-handed about it. In a moment, it was all over, and one side had won: decisively and without striking a blow. European communism simply dropped away, in a manner unpredicted and widely unlamented; a fascinating and singular achievement itself: its rise was without precedent, and so was its fall. With it, and not coincidentally, the role of intellectuals in framing alternative social imaginaries has all but vanished, especially in former communist countries and at least for now. That, as Judt observes, 'is in large measure because Lenin and his heirs poisoned the well' (2008: 124).

So now it wasn't even handed ideological exhaustion: communism was out and rule of law was in; part of, for a time, a confident triumphal package for export. There was a negative and a positive aspect to this. For many opponents of communism, the characteristic absence of the rule of law under communist regimes, the patent 'instrumentalization' of law by rulers or its irrelevance to their exercise of power, were seen as central to the ways in which communist despots ruled. That was a negative lesson: a good regime doesn't behave that way. And for the surprised participants in and inheritors of that *annus mirabilis,* who eschewed experiments, and boasted that their revolution was 'self-limiting' (Poland) 'negotiated', 'velvet' (Czechoslovakia), indeed 'legal' (Hungary), and that they would establish the rule of law, a 'law-governed state', or other canonical rephrasings quickly included in new constitutions, there were positive lessons apparently readily available. They were to be found either in the pre-communist past or in the present of all those 'normal' countries, as the West used to be described, where constitutions were thought to set the rules for the exercise of power, and citizens could petition courts if they thought their governors had broken the rules; where politicians were supposed to be constrained by law; and more generally and fundamentally, where law *counted* in social life, and where people thought it could, should

12 Cf. Krygier and Czarnota 1999; Czarnota, Krygier and Sadurski 2005.

and would so count.[13] And so law and the rule of law came to have unusual significance in the non-Utopian Utopias of post-communist reformers. Given these circumstances, it is probably no accident that law and ideas of the rule of law were more central to the aftermath of the revolutions against communism than elsewhere.

Thus what was involved in 1989 was not just a continuation of the 'modesty' born of failed experiments, that had already been learnt in the 1970s, but a novel linking of it with a renewed belief in the resilience, for some the unique appropriateness, of Western liberal capitalist arrangements. All the more because the absence of the rule of law had pervaded all domains of what Ernest Gellner called the 'Caesaro-Papist-Mammonist' regimes of the Soviet bloc. Thus it could be, and was, boosted as a cure for pathologies in all three domains. Not everyone spoke of the end of history, but no one had much clue about alternatives. So the ideological context had radically changed. There was, it clearly appeared, a winner – the liberal capitalist West – and a clear loser – Soviet communism – and it was not obvious for a time that there was anything else. The rule of law was touted as a Western achievement, and it became a Western export industry. Good time to have come up with the Washington Consensus, described by Peerenboom and Bugaric (2013: 2) as 'a universal, one-size-fits-all approach to development based on imitation of "international best practices" – i.e. the historically contingent and surprisingly diverse institutions, rules and practices of primarily high-income countries in North America and Western Europe'.

4. Economists Turn to Law

I mentioned earlier that Trubek had identified two strands to the rise of the rule of law in the 1990s. One was the 'project of democracy'. The other, which came from elsewhere, had different goals, and no humility at all, which he calls 'the project of markets and the discovery of institutions':

> This approach stressed export-led growth, free markets, privatization, and foreign investment as the keys to growth. To pursue these goals, it was necessary to create all the institutions of a market economy in former command economies and remove restrictions on markets in *dirigiste* economies such as those in many Latin American countries. (2006: 84)

With roots in the institutional economics of the 1960s and the Hayekian transformations of the 1980s, the new economic approach laid great stress on law, property rights and security of contract guaranteed by law, and more general economic predictability, also said to flow from law. The tone was very different from that of the disillusioned 'apolitical' politicians of the 1970s. These people had a doctrine to sell.

I won't explore this economic turn here, partly from lack of competence and partly because it has been well done elsewhere (Trubek and Santos 2006). I just stress that its priorities and tone were very different – not necessarily inconsistent, but different – from those of the political and ideological sceptics who in the 1980s and 1990s had turned to law. Securing property rights is not the same as taming despotism. You might want both, but typically those interested in one had less to say about the other. Nevertheless, as often happens in matters of rhetorical fashion, they fastened onto the same slogan, and together pushed it along. Trubek (2006: 85) is again useful:

13 On late communist and immediately post communist ideas of the rule of law and 'normal countries,' see Krygier 1990: 636–7.

> Once the economic development agencies realized that the neoliberal turn involved positive intervention to create the institutional conditions for markets, development agencies were committed to investing in legal reform. They found their concerns overlapped with those of the proponents of human rights and democracy. For both, the rule of law was a common goal.
> While the project of democracy and the project of markets seem very different, they both identified "the rule of law" as an essential step toward their objectives.

5. The Global '89

This was a combination pregnant with significance in relation to law. On the one hand, the revolutions of that year galvanized unusually explicit and strong hopes for the transformative significance of the rule of law, while, on the other, the attention was deliberately more imitative than path-breaking in self-conception and ambition. The assumption was that the future would be nothing fancy, but would be modelled on legal arrangements that have already been tried and that had *worked*, usually somewhere else. Rather than indulge in novel legal experiments, still less attempt to do away with law, or for that matter do something new with it, the task was one of reverse engineering a successful achievement, and then constructing and reconstructing the sources of its success. Moreover, given the dichotomous terms in which the short twentieth century was understood, the collapse of one of its protagonists was taken by many observers to mean not merely the signal victory of the other, but that the sources of its superiority would be found in institutions and practices that were the reverse image of those that had failed: in place of maximal state intervention, minimal state intervention; in place of no property rights, untouchably secure ones, and so on. This was a great boost to the neoliberal 'take' on Western achievements, for some time squeezing out other interpretations of a more mixed, complex and variable sort, of possible relations between states, laws and civil societies. For some time, and to some people, the notion that there were indispensable 'virtuous circles' (Krygier 1997), rather than stark oppositions between states and civil societies, for example, or property-securing rule of law on one hand, and regulatory interventions, on the other, could only seem to be squeamish temporizing.

You might think that if one were to take these limited ambitions seriously, there would be little of more than local interest to be expected from the transformations that occurred in Central and Eastern Europe; all emulation, no invention, no demonstration. And yet these concept-importers became concept exemplars and even exporters before very long. What began as regional fixes quickly became experimental sites and provocations for international recipes, because it seemed to have been established that, as core elements of the model system, they should be core elements of every other system. So though the so-called post-communist 'region' was where much of this emulatory practice started, this new vogue for the rule of law did not stop there. The apparent victory – economic, political, ideological – in Central and Eastern Europe and the former Soviet Union of one of the two contenders in the contests of the previous century had reverberations in both the real and conceptual geography of the world.

Within relatively few years, demands for the rule of law echoed throughout the world, particularly among people and agencies concerned with so-called 'transitional' societies. This rather hopeful label ultimately came to include many different sorts of societies, at different stages of development, with different orders of problems, and only three unifying features: there was hitherto little rule of law within them, the 'transitional' moment seemed to be one in which this might be changed, and rule of law promoters were thought to know the ways to change it. Thus was born the international rule of law promotion industry.[14] As Venelin Ganev (2009: 263) has observed, '[t]hroughout the 1990s Eastern Europe was arguably the region most intensely studied and discussed by the community of scholars interested in the spread of the Rule of Law around the world'. And, as Veronica Taylor (2009: 46–7) has noted,

> Legal reform as a component of multilateral or bilateral development assistance is not new. However, the fall of the Berlin Wall signalled an emphatic "turn to law" in multilateral and bilateral flows of finance, development aid and technical assistance, to developing and transition economies. Beginning in Central and Eastern Europe but expanding rapidly to other regions, this "new" wave of legal reform was funded at dramatically higher levels than in previous decades. As a result, over the last two decades, the creation, diffusion and enforcement of law and legal institutions has become both a set of free-standing goals and a tool-kit for achieving other policy aims, such as resolving armed conflict, entrenching electoral democracy, restructuring public administration, igniting economic growth, strengthening market mechanisms or improving public health and education.

The collapse of European communism, then, not alone but crucially thus altered the conceptual space, rendering it available for the rule of law and created conditions for its epidemic spread. It also made rule of law seem attractive in ways it never had. It led first to a *quickening* of interest, because there were suddenly plenty of new states or newly liberated states that lacked the rule of law, on *any* definition; for which these were not academic questions, but urgent; and there was at the same time space, lack of ideological competition and hindrance, and a sense that this was a global turning point. Secondly, a new sense of *salience*: it came to be said worldwide that these are central issues, not just good things or local achievements, since the main proponent of a contrary view had just disappeared. Third, *spread*. There was no obstacle to the spread of the good news, and no obvious alternative. The time to propagate our models of the rule of law, markets, and democracy had apparently arrived throughout the world.

5.1 Moyn's Lament

I mentioned that Moyn did not simply argue a historical case. His book has a powerful polemical thrust as well. He claims that having been taken up as a non-political, anti-utopian, moral minimum, human rights have come to fill the space they sought to empty. Increasingly, he argues, the language of human rights has become a maximalist language, which squeezes out other ways of imagining problems, ways of conceiving what they are, what they might be, and how they might be dealt with, other than in terms of the language of rights; 'their substitution of plausible morality for failed politics may have come at a price' (2010: 175):

> After all, they [human rights] have done far more to transform the terrain of idealism than they have the world itself. … Though they were born as an alternative to grand political missions – or even as a moral criticism of politics – human rights … were forced, slowly but surely, to assume the very maximalism they triumphed by avoiding. (2010: 9)

14 As to which, see Magen 2009.

Though as always in a minor key, similar things might be observed about the rule of law. In the hands of its international promoters, rule of law at least does sometimes grow rhetorically into maximal versions.

There was always something falsely, perhaps disingenuously, technicized and depoliticized about the rule of law story, as Moyn suggests of human rights. It was manifest in what Thomas Carothers (2006: 21) has called a 'breathtakingly mechanistic approach' based on the notion that 'a country achieves the rule of law by reshaping its key institutions to match those of countries that are considered to have the rule of law'. This legalistic stuff didn't look like transformative projects; just fixing obvious wrongs, even just technical problems, on the basis of solutions obvious to those experienced with the rule of law in its secure homes. The story was a condescending one, but in the first years after 1989, there was a certain plausibility to it. What else was there? Wasn't the West a success? Wasn't it true that the rule of law was associated with that success? Wasn't it true also that there were experts in law who knew how to identify, pack and transport its ingredients? And wouldn't everyone benefit? Thus, and not too slowly, it came to be that, as Charles T. Call (2007: 4) observes:

> Among a plethora of development and security agencies, a new "rule of law consensus" has emerged. This consensus consists of two elements: (1) the belief that the rule of law is essential to virtually every Western liberal foreign policy goal – human rights, democracy, economic and political stability, international security from terrorist and other transnational threats, and transnational free trade and investment; and (2) the belief that international interventions, be they through money, people, or ideas, must include a rule-of-law component.

And yet transplantation of the rule of law is always an intensely social, political, not a merely technical, project. Whatever forms and methods are chosen inevitably embody social and political aims, have social and political conditions of success and failure, (see Krygier 2011a) the effort sometimes causes social and political harm, (see Massoud 2013) and it always produces winners and losers (see Kennedy 2004). Indeed, though it is commonly viewed as a kind of technology transfer, I doubt that a great deal of the rule of law is well understood in terms of technological metaphors at all, since it so involves culture, social practices, traditions and ways of life. But even if it makes sense to think of it in such terms, the rule of law is what Stephen Holmes has called an 'interaction technology', not a production technology. That means we have to know a lot about the inter-actors and the ways they interact in particular societies, and, for a host of reasons, rule of law promoters know much less about them than they do about what they bring to them (see Krygier 2011b). That is true of attempts to generate new law in general, and all the more of the rule of law, which involves achieving certain ideals for law, not simply installing an institutional package. This should have been obvious, if not in the first moments of enthusiasm then pretty early on (Krygier 2001). In moments where there seemed to be only one game in town, however, it was easy to forget this and imagine 'there is no alternative'. Fortunately or unfortunately, that is not a stable state. Francis Fukuyama notwithstanding, it soon became clear that there are alternatives, for better and for worse, and other games to play.

5.2 Towards No One's World[15]

The rule of law came, then, to be internationally modish at one particular moment – when it *seemed* that the major ideological competition that framed our lives was over, and there was a winner. It was associated with that victory, part of the triumphal machinery, many came to think a key part. Unfortunately for the confidence of those manning the programme, history did not end in 1989, even if the short century did. If there is any significance to the ideological stories I have been sketching, the international career of the rule of law must be affected by this. For it is all a lot more complicated now, and everyone knows. The afterglow of the short century was even shorter. September 11, 2001 and what followed, including the lengthy, costly, painful and inconclusive wars in Iraq and Afghanistan, challenged both the confidence of the West and also the cheerful logic that had propelled the transplantation of the rule of law. Perhaps the rule of law is not the obvious good that the West has claimed. Perhaps it is not part of an economic/technical package of the sort that rule of law promoters have suggested. Perhaps there are other ways to it, uncountenanced by Westerners and compatible with antithetical beliefs and practices. Perhaps we need to reconfigure our understanding of the rule of law to encompass (as it has come to do) goals and means quite other from those envisaged in the early days, now that security sector reform has come to vie with, often to swamp, the secure restraint on arbitrary power. Perhaps we truly don't know what we're doing. Perhaps it is all too hard.

The global financial crisis challenged the notion of a success-package too, this time from another angle; the economic package now seems altogether less seamless and sturdy than once it did. The success of China in economically rivalling the West, and the rise of (some of) 'the rest' form third and fourth challenges to what now seems to have been the premature triumphalism of 1989. A lot looks very different now. Whatever settles from all these shocks, challenges and disappointments will also be different from what seemed likely in 1989. If these are signs that we might be moving from the end of history to 'no one's world', my conjecture is that one should expect this to be reflected in the future career prospects of the rule of law.

None of this means that its career is over. Once a rhetorical balloon is launched it doesn't come down quickly. It is too full of air, some of it extremely hot. It frames agendas, concepts, the very ways we think and speak. And too many people have a stake in keeping it aloft. They also have a stake in continuing to do things the way they have done them; so old models and mistakes are unlikely to disappear overnight, and old language often masks new priorities, as when post-September 11 rule of law came to have a much higher dose of SSR (security sector reform), a mutation not always matched by change in language coined in an older, more confident time, even where some of the new imperatives are inconsistent – often systematically inconsistent – with the old, at home (see Holmes 2009) and abroad (see Taylor 2010).

And, not to forget, in pre-hubristic, traditional, politically-oriented understandings, the world needs the rule of law, the effective constraint on arbitrary power,[16] as much or more than it ever did. Properly understood, as a value or cluster of values that have to do with taming and moderating the exercise of power, the rule of law is an extremely precious thing. It is a good in itself[17] as well as

15 See Kupchan 2012.

16 See Montesquieu 1748; Thompson 1977; Shklar 1998; Reid 2004; Krygier 2011a.

17 See Amartya Sen 2000: 9–10. 'We cannot very well say that the development process has gone beautifully even though people are being arbitrarily hanged, criminals go free while law-abiding citizens end up in jail, and so on. … Legal development is constitutively involved in the development process … even if legal development were not to contribute one iota to economic development … even then legal and judicial reform would be a critical part of the development process.'

for other good things, however implausible the suggestion that it can be a panacea for all the many problems for which it has been prescribed, or that there is one way to achieve it *anywhere,* still less that we have a recipe that can be followed worldwide. In its rise, something fundamentally healthy has undergone a kind of rhetorically and bureaucratically self-regenerating metastasis. If that could be slowed, the differences between health, pathology and placebo clarified, and the role of law and other social institutions and practices in contributing to the values we seek from the rule of law explored, we would perhaps do better than we have.

Having risen so high, the rule of law balloon won't deflate or disappear soon. However it might without loss be injected with some more humility, and its eager promiscuity moderated a little more successfully than in the recent past. If so, that might be one salutary consequence of the setbacks of the present age. And if that happens, it won't simply be due to what we could only learn after our most recent shocks and disappointments. These are lessons we should have learnt from those who have thought about the rule of law for a very long time. After all, Aristotle knew some of them and Montesquieu others. The rule of law *is* better than the rule of any individual, and moderation in the exercise of power a general good. These are large and general values, perhaps indeed universal, but they are complicated achievements. Of course, it's never too late. If the 'next generation reform' (Kleinfeld 2012) of rule of law promotion, and the amendments to the Washington Consensus forced on promoters by failures of earlier generations (only a couple of years before), and perhaps by reflection, are examples of hard-won humility about how complex and variable are the ways of attaining the values of the rule of law, they will be valuable lessons – even better than 'international best practice' – to have learned.

Bibliography

Call, C.T. 2007. 'Introduction'. In C.T. Call (ed.), *Constructing Justice and Security after War.* Washington, DC, United States Institute of Peace Press.

Carothers, T. 2006. 'The Problem of Knowledge'. In *Promoting the Rule of Law Abroad.* Washington, DC, Carnegie Endowment for International Peace.

Christian, C. 2013. *Strange Rebels.1979 and the Birth of the 21st Century.* New York, Basic Books.

Cotterrell, R. 1989. *The Politics of Jurisprudence: A Critical Introduction to Legal Philosophy.* London, Butterworths.

Cotterrell, R. 2004. 'Selznick Interviewed: Philip Selznick in Conversation with Roger Cotterrell'. 31 *Journal of Law and Society*, 291–317.

Cotterrell, R. 2006. 'The Concept of Legal Culture'. In *Law, Culture and Society. Legal Ideas in the Mirror of Social Theory.* Aldershot, Ashgate, 81–96.

Cotterrell, R. 2007. 'The Rule of Law in Transition: Revisiting Franz Neumann's Sociology of Legality'. In *Living Law.* Aldershot, Ashgate, Ch. 8.

Czarnota, A. 1994. 'Marxism, Ideology, and Law'. In M. Krygier (ed.), *Marxism and Communism: Posthumous Reflections on Politics, Society, and Law.* Amsterdam, Rodopi. Ch. 9.

Czarnota, A., Krygier, M. and Sadurski, W. (eds) 2005. *Rethinking the Rule of Law after Communism: Constitutionalism, Dealing with the Past, and the Rule of Law.* Budapest, Central European University Press.

Farrall, J.M. 2007. *United Nations Sanctions and the Rule of Law.* New York, Cambridge University Press.

Foster-Simons, F. 1989. 'Towards a More Perfect Union? The "Restructuring" of Soviet Legislation'. 25 *Stanford Journal of International Law*, 331–73.

Furet, F. 1999. *The Passing of an Illusion, The Idea of Communism in the Twentieth Century*. Chicago, University of Chicago Press.
Ganev, V.I. 2009. 'The Rule of Law as an Institutionalized Wager: Constitutions, Courts and Transformative Social Dynamics in Eastern Europe'. 1/2 *Hague Journal of the Rule of Law*, 263–83.
Garton Ash, T. 1990a. *We the People*. Cambridge, Granta Books.
Garton Ash, T. 1990b. 'Eastern Europe: The Year of Truth'. *New York Review of Books*, February 15, 21.
Haggard, S., MacIntyre, A. and Tiede, L. 2008. 'The Rule of Law and Economic Development'. 11 *Annual Review of Political Science*, 205–34.
Hobsbawm, E. 1994. *The Age of Extremes. The Short Twentieth Century 1914–1991*. London, Michael Joseph.
Holmes, S. 2009. 'In Case of Emergency: Misunderstanding Tradeoffs in the War on Terror'. 97 *California Law Review*, 301–56.
Hurwitz, A. 2005. 'Towards Enhanced Legitimacy of Rule of Law Programs in Multidimensional Peace Operations'. In A. Hurwitz and K. Studdard (ed.), *Rule of Law Programs in Peace Operations*. New York, Peace Academy.
Judt, T. 1990. 'The Rediscovery of Central Europe'. 119/1 *Daedalus* 23–54.
Judt, T. 2008. *Reappraisals. Reflections on the Forgotten Twentieth Century*. New York, Penguin.
Kennedy, D. 2004. *The Dark Side of Virtue*. New Jersey, Princeton University Press.
Kleinfeld, R. 2012. *Advancing the Rule of Law Abroad. Next Generation Reform*. Carnegie Endowment for International Peace.
Krygier, M. 1990. 'Marxism and the Rule of Law. Reflections after the Collapse of Communism'. 15 *Law and Social Inquiry*, 633–63.
Krygier, M. 1997. 'Virtuous Circles. Antipodean Reflections on Power, Institutions, and Civil Society'. 11/1 *East European Politics and Societies*, 36–88.
Krygier, M. 2001. 'Transitional Questions about the Rule of Law: Why, What, and How?' 28/1 *East Central Europe-L'Europe du Centre Est. Eine wissenschaftliche Zeitschrift*, 1–34.
Krygier, M. 2011a. 'Four Puzzles about the Rule of Law: Why, What, Where? And Who Cares?' In J.E. Fleming (ed.), *Getting to the Rule of Law*, Nomos no. New York, New York University Press, 64–104.
Krygier, M. 2011b. 'Approaching the Rule of Law'. In W. Mason (ed.), *The Rule of Law in Afghanistan. Missing in Inaction*. Cambridge, Cambridge University Press, 15–34.
Krygier, M. 2012. *Philip Selznick. Ideals in the World*. Stanford, Stanford University Press.
Krygier, M. 2014/15 (forthcoming). 'Rule of Law (and Rechtsstaat)'. *Encyclopedia of the Social and Behavioral Sciences*, 2nd edition. Amsterdam, Elsevier.
Krygier, M. and Czarnota, A. (eds) 1999. *The Rule of Law after Communism*. Aldershot, Dartmouth.
Kupchan, C. 2012. *No One's World: The West, the Rising Rest, and the Coming Global Turn*. Oxford, Oxford University Press.
Magen, A. 2009. 'The Rule of Law and its Promotion Abroad: Three Problems of Scope'. 45/1 *Stanford Journal of International Law*, 51–116.
Massoud, M.F. 2013. *Law's Fragile State: Colonial, Authoritarian, and Humanitarian Legacies in Sudan*. Cambridge, Cambridge University Press.
Montesquieu, 1748. *The Spirit of the Laws*. Cambridge, Cambridge University Press (Cambridge Texts in the History of Political Thought, 1989 edition).
Moyn, S. 2010. *The Last Utopia. Human Rights in History*. Cambridge, MA, Belknap Press.

Moyn, S. 2012. 'Substance, Scale, and Salience: The Recent Historiography of Human Rights'. 8 *Annual Review of Law and Social Science*, 123–40.

Peerenboom, R. and Bugaric, B. 2013. 'The Emerging Post Washington, Post Beijing Consensus: Prospects and Pitfalls'. Paper presented at Law and Society Conference, Boston, June 2013.

Rajagopal, B. 2008. 'Invoking the Rule of Law in Post-Conflict Peacebuilding: A Critical Examination'. 49/3 *William and Mary Law Review*, 1347–76.

Reid, J.P. 2004. *The Rule of Law,* DeKalb, Illinois, Northern Illinois University Press.

Sajó, A. and Arato, A. 1991. 'Editors' introduction'. 13/2 *Law and Policy*, special issue on 'Eastern Europe and the 'Western' Policy Dialogue', 101.

Sakharov, A. 1979. 'The Human Rights Movement in the USSR and Eastern Europe: Its Goals, Significance, and Difficulties'. *Trialogue*, January 1979.

Sen, A. 2000. 'What is the Role of Legal and Judicial Reform in the Development Process?' Washington, DC, World Bank Legal Conference, June 5. http://siteresources.worldbank.org/INTLAWJUSTINST/Resources/legalandjudicial.pdf.

Shklar, J. 1998. 'The Liberalism of Fear' and 'Political Theory and the Rule of Law'. In S. Hoffman (ed.), *Judith Shklar: Political Thought and Political Thinkers*. Chicago, University of Chicago Press. 3–20, 21–37.

Shore, M. 2013. *The Taste of Ashes. The Afterlife of Totalitarianism in Eastern Europe*. New York, Crown Publishers.

Tamanaha, B.Z. 2004. *On the Rule of Law: History, Politics, Theory*. Cambridge, Cambridge University Press.

Taylor, V.L. 2009. 'Frequently Asked Questions About Rule of Law Assistance (And Why Better Answers Matter)'. 1/1 *Hague Journal on the Rule of Law*, 46–52.

Taylor, V. 2010. 'Displacing 'Development': The new agenda for rule of law assistance'. 104 *Northwestern University Law Review*, 260–61.

Thompson, E.P. 1977. *Whigs and Hunters: The Origin of the Black Act*. Harmondsworth, Penguin.

Tismaneanu, V. 2012. *The Devil in History.* Berkeley, University of Calfifornia Press.

Trubek, D. 2006. 'The 'Rule of Law' in Development Assistance: Past, Present, and Future'. In D. Trubek and A. Santos (eds), *The New Law and Economic Development. A Critical Appraisal*. Cambridge, Cambridge University Press.

Trubek, D.M. and Santos, A. (eds) 2006. *The New Law and Economic Development. A Critical Apppraisal*. Cambridge, Cambridge University Press.

Appendix
Roger Cotterrell: Academic Writings

1. Authored Books

The Sociology of Law: An Introduction. London: Butterworths, 1984. Partial Chinese trans. Beijing: Huaxia Press, 1989. Spanish trans. as *Introducción a la Sociología del Derecho.* Barcelona: Editorial Ariel, 1991. Korean trans. Soeul, South Korea, 1992.

The Politics of Jurisprudence: A Critical Introduction to Legal Philosophy. London: Butterworths, 1989. Revised US edn. Philadelphia: University of Pennsylvania Press, 1992.

The Sociology of Law: An Introduction. 2nd edn., revised, updated and expanded. London: Butterworths, 1992; republished by Oxford University Press, 2004. Lithuanian trans. as *Teises sociologija: jvadas*. Kaunas: Dangerta, 1997. Chinese trans. Beijing: China University of Political Science and Law Press, 2014.

Law's Community: Legal Theory in Sociological Perspective. Oxford: Clarendon Press, 1995.

Emile Durkheim: Law in a Moral Domain. Stanford, CA: Stanford University Press/Edinburgh: Edinburgh University Press, 1999.

The Politics of Jurisprudence: A Critical Introduction to Legal Philosophy. 2nd edn., revised, updated and expanded. London: LexisNexis Butterworths, 2003; republished by Oxford University Press, 2004. Chinese trans. Beijing: Peking University Publishing House, 2013.

Law, Culture and Society: Legal Ideas in the Mirror of Social Theory. Aldershot: Ashgate, 2006.

Living Law: Studies in Legal and Social Theory. Aldershot: Ashgate, 2008.

2. Edited Books

Law, Democracy and Social Justice (with B. Bercusson). Oxford: Blackwell, 1988. Also published as (1988) 15 *Journal of Law and Society*, no. 1 (special issue).

Law and Society. Aldershot: Dartmouth, 1994/New York: New York University Press, 1994.

Process and Substance: Lectures on Comparative Law. London: Butterworths, 1995 (Butterworth Lectures 1994).

Sociological Perspectives on Law. vol. 1 (*Classical Traditions*); vol 2. (*Contemporary Debates*). Aldershot: Ashgate, 2001.

Law in Social Theory. Aldershot: Ashgate, 2006.

Emile Durkheim: Justice, Morality and Politics. Farnham: Ashgate, 2010.

3. Essays and Articles

'The Teaching of Jurisprudence in British Universities' (with J.C. Woodliffe) (1974) 13 *Journal of the Society of Public Teachers of Law*, 73–89.

'Direction and Development in Anglo-American Jurisprudence and the Sociology of Law' (1975) *Anglo-American Law Review* 386–411. Revised abbreviated reprint as 'Jurisprudence and

Sociology of Law' in W.M. Evan (ed.), *Sociology of Law: A Social-Structural Perspective*. New York: Free Press, and London: Collier-Macmillan, 1980, pp. 21–9.

'Durkheim on Legal Development and Social Solidarity' (1977) 4 *British Journal of Law and Society* 241–52. Reprinted in Cotterrell, *Sociological Perspectives on Law*, vol. 1, pp. 291–302.

'Legal Theory, Legal Practice and Social Science' (1979) 129 *New Law Journal* 532–3.

'Commodity Form and Legal Form: Pashukanis' Outline of a Materialist Theory of Law' (1979) 6 *Ideology and Consciousness* 111–19. Trans. (C.N. Kashiura Júnior) as 'Forma mercantil e forma jurídica: Pachukanis e o esboço de uma teoria materialista do direito' in M.B. Naves (ed.), *O discreto charme do direito burguês: ensaios sobre Pachukanis*. Campinas, Brazil: Universidade Estadual de Campinas, Instituto de Filosofia e Ciências Humanas, 2009, pp.103–16.

'Interdisciplinarity: The Expansion of Knowledge and the Design of Research' (1979) 11 *Higher Education Review* 47–56.

'Professional Autonomy and the Construction of Professional Knowledge: Sociology and the Professional Practice of Law and Medicine' in P. Abrams and P. Lewthwaite (eds), *Development and Diversity: British Sociology 1950–1980*, vol. 1. London: British Sociological Association, 1981, pp. 280–96.

'The Impact of Sex Discrimination Legislation' (1981) *Public Law* 469–76.

'The Development of Capitalism and the Formalisation of Contract Law' in R. Fryer, A. Hunt, D. McBarnet and B. Moorhouse (eds), *Law, State and Society*. London: Croom Helm, 1981, pp. 54–69. Reprinted in Cotterrell, *Living Law*, pp. 167–82.

'Conceptualising Law: Problems and Prospects of Contemporary Legal Theory' (1981) 10 *Economy and Society* 348–66. Reprinted in adapted form in Cotterrell, *Law's Community*, pp. 113–33.

'Legality and Political Legitimacy in the Sociology of Max Weber' in D. Sugarman (ed.), *Legality, Ideology and the State*. London and New York: Academic Press, 1983, pp. 69–93. Reprinted in adapted form in Cotterrell, *Law's Community*, pp. 134–59.

'The Sociological Concept of Law' (1983) 10 *Journal of Law and Society* 241–55. Reprinted and extracted in Lord Lloyd of Hampstead and M.D.A. Freeman, *Introduction to Jurisprudence* (various edns). London: Stevens and Son. Reprinted in K. Rokumoto (ed.), *Sociological Theories of Law*. Aldershot: Dartmouth/New York: New York University Press, 1994, pp. 3–17; and in adapted form in Cotterrell, *Law's Community*, pp. 23–40. Trans. (M.I. Bergoglio) as 'El Concepto Sociologico de Derecho' (2010) *Revista de la Facultad de Derecho de la Universidad Nacional de Córdoba* [Argentina], n.s.II, 1(1) 51–62.

'English Conceptions of the Role of Theory in Legal Analysis' (1983) 46 *Modern Law Review* 681–99.

'Sociology of Law in the United Kingdom' in W.E. Butler and V.N. Kudriavtsev (eds), *Comparative Law and Legal System: Historical and Socio-Legal Perspectives*. Dobbs Ferry, NY: Oceana, 1985, pp. 11–22.

'The Law of Property and Legal Theory' in W.L. Twining (ed.), *Legal Theory and Common Law*. Oxford: Blackwell, 1986, pp. 81–98. Reprinted in Cotterrell, *Living Law*, pp. 183–200.

'Law and Sociology: Notes on the Constitution and Confrontations of Disciplines' (1986) 13 *Journal of Law and Society* 9–34. Reprinted in adapted form in P.A. Thomas (ed.), *Legal Frontiers*. Aldershot: Dartmouth Press, 1997, pp. 10–40; and in Cotterrell, *Law's Community*, pp. 41–72.

'Critique and Law: The Problematic Legacy of the Frankfurt School' (1986) 3 *Tidskrift för Rättsociologi* No. 2. pp. 99–112. Reprinted in adapted form in Cotterrell, *Law's Community*, pp. 204–17.

'The Recovery of Judgment Debts in the County Court: Some Preliminary Results' (with B. Davies, R. Goode, H. Gravelle and J. Phipps) in I. Ramsay (ed.), *Debtors and Creditors: A Socio-Legal Perspective*. Abingdon: Professional Books, 1986, pp. 68–100.

'Power, Property and the Law of Trusts: A Partial Agenda for Critical Legal Scholarship' (1987) 14 *Journal of Law and Society* 77–90. Reprinted in P. Fitzpatrick and A. Hunt (eds), *Critical Legal Studies*. Oxford: Blackwell, 1987, pp. 77–90; and in part in G. Moffat and M. Chesterman, *Trusts Law: Text and Materials*. London: Weidenfeld and Nicolson (various edns).

'Liberalism's Empire: Reflections on Ronald Dworkin's Legal Philosophy' (1987) *American Bar Foundation Research Journal* 509–24.

'The Rule of Law in Corporate Society: Neumann, Kirchheimer and the Lessons of Weimar' (1988) 51 *Modern Law Review* 126–40. Reprinted in adapted form in Cotterrell, *Law's Community*, pp. 160–77.

'Feasible Regulation for Democracy and Social Justice' (1988) 15 *Journal of Law and Society* 5–24. Reprinted in adapted form in Cotterrell, *Law's Community*, pp. 249–73.

'What is Legal Theory for? (Comment on Lermack)' (1989) 12 *Legal Studies Forum* 419–24.

'Law's Images of Community and Imperium' in A. Sarat and S. Silbey (eds), *Studies in Law, Politics and Society* vol. 10. Greenwich, CT: JAI Press, 1990, pp. 3–27. Reprinted in adapted form in Cotterrell, *Law's Community*, pp. 221–48.

'Sociology of Law in Britain: Its Development and Present Prospects' in V. Ferrari (ed.), *Developing Sociology of Law: A World-Wide Documentary Enquiry*. Milano: Giuffrè, 1990, pp. 779–803. Reprinted in adapted form in Cotterrell, *Law's Community*, pp. 73–90.

'Realism, Pragmatism and the Appellate Judge' (1991) 54 *Modern Law Review* 594–605.

'The Durkheimian Tradition in the Sociology of Law' (1991) 25 *Law and Society Review* 923–45. Reprinted in adapted form in Cotterrell, *Law's Community*, pp. 178–203.

'Some Sociological Aspects of the Controversy Around the Legal Validity of Private Purpose Trusts' in S. Goldstein (ed.), *Equity and Contemporary Legal Problems*. Jerusalem: Hebrew University, 1992, pp. 302–34. Reprinted in Cotterrell, *Living Law*, pp. 201–33.

'Viewing Legal Discourses Sociologically' in G. Skapska, J. Czapska, K. Daniel, J. Gorski, K. Palecki (eds) *Prawo w Zmieniajacym sie Spoleczenstwie* [Law in a Changing Society]. Festschrift for Maria Borucka-Arctowa. Krakow: Uniwersitytet Jagiellonski, 1992, pp. 55–70.

'Law's Community: Legal Theory and the Image of Legality' (1992) 19 *Journal of Law and Society* 405–22. Reprinted in adapted form in Cotterrell, *Law's Community*, pp. 274–95.

'Jurisprudence of Reason and Jurisprudence of Fiat' in Peter Birks (ed.), *Examining the Law Syllabus: Beyond the Core*. Oxford: Oxford University Press, 1993, pp. 89–92.

'Filosofia del Derecho y Sociología del Derecho en Gran Bretana', trans. A.E. Ves Losada. (1993) *Revista de Sociología del Derecho* [Argentina], no. 8, April, 6–10.

'Sociological Perspectives on Legal Closure' in A. Norrie (ed.), *Closure or Critique: New Directions in Legal Theory*. Edinburgh: Edinburgh University Press, 1993, pp. 175–93. Reprinted in adapted form in Cotterrell, *Law's Community*, pp. 91–110.

'Trusting in Law: Legal and Moral Concepts of Trust' in M.D.A. Freeman and B.A. Hepple (eds), *Current Legal Problems 1993* (vol. 46). Oxford: Oxford University Press, 1993, pp. 75–95. Reprinted in Cotterrell, *Living Law*, pp. 235–55.

'Sociologie', trans. W.M. de L. Capeller, in A.-J. Arnaud et al. (eds), *Dictionnaire encyclopédique de théorie et de sociologie du droit*. Paris: Librairie Générale de Droit et de Jurisprudence, 1993, pp. 564–5.

'Introduction: The Law and Society Tradition' in Cotterrell (ed.), *Law and Society*. Aldershot: Dartmouth/New York: New York University Press, 1994, pp. xi–xxii.

'Judicial Review and Legal Theory' in G. Richardson and H. Genn (eds), *Administrative Law and Government Action: The Courts and Alternative Mechanisms of Review.* Oxford: Clarendon Press, 1994, pp. 13–34.

'The Symbolism of Constitutions: Some Anglo-American Comparisons' in I. Loveland (ed.), *A Special Relationship: American Influences on Public Law in the UK.* Oxford: Clarendon Press, 1995, pp. 25–46. Extended version published as 'Some Aspects of the Communication of Constitutional Authority' in D. Nelken (ed.), *Law as Communication.* Aldershot: Dartmouth, 1996, pp. 129–51. Reprinted in Cotterrell, *Living Law*, pp. 257–79.

'Sociological Interpretations of Legal Development' (1995) 2 *European Journal of Law and Economics* 347–59.

'The Rule of Law in Transition: Revisiting Franz Neumann's Sociology of Legality' (1996) 5 *Social & Legal Studies* 451–70. Reprinted in Cotterrell, *Living Law*, pp. 101–20; and in Cotterrell, *Law in Social Theory*, pp. 485–504.

'The Concept of Legal Culture' in D. Nelken (ed.), *Comparing Legal Cultures*, Aldershot: Dartmouth, 1997, pp. 13–31. Reprinted in adapted form in Cotterrell, *Law, Culture and Society*, pp. 81–96.

'Pluralismo y Communidad en Sociología de Derecho', trans. A.E. Ves Losada (1997) *Revista de Sociología del Derecho* [Argentina], no. 13, November, 6–9.

'A Legal Concept of Community' (1997) 12 *Canadian Journal of Law and Society* 75–91. Reprinted in Cotterrell, *Sociological Perspectives on Law*, vol. 2, pp. 45–61; and in adapted form in Cotterrell, *Law, Culture and Society*, pp. 65–78. Trans. (A.E. Ves Losada) as 'Un concepto juridica de Comunidad' in (1998) *Revista de Sociología de Derecho* [Argentina], no. 15, November, 8–16.

'Why Must Legal Ideas be Interpreted Sociologically?' (1998) 25 *Journal of Law and Society* 171–92. Reprinted in M. Del Mar and M. Giudice (eds), *Legal Theory and the Social Sciences.* Farnham: Ashgate, 2010, pp. 89–110; and in Cotterrell, *Sociological Perspectives on Law*, vol. 2, pp. 151–72. Reprinted in part in M.D.A. Freeman, *Lloyd's Introduction to Jurisprudence*, 7th and 8th edns, London: Sweet & Maxwell; and in adapted form in Cotterrell, *Law, Culture and Society*, pp. 45–63.

'Social Theory and Law' in E. Craig, gen. ed., *Routledge Encyclopedia of Philosophy*, London: Routledge, 1998, vol. 8, pp. 872–9.

'Law and Community: A New Relationship?' in M.D.A. Freeman (ed.), *Legal Theory at the End of the Millenium: Current Legal Problems 1998* (vol. 51). Oxford: Oxford University Press, 1998, pp. 367–91. Reprinted in Cotterrell, *Sociological Perspectives on Law*, vol. 2, pp. 357–81; and in adapted form in Cotterrell, *Law, Culture and Society*, pp. 29–44.

'Common Law Approaches to the Relationship between Law and Morality' in *Societas Ethica Jahresbericht 1998: Ethik und Gesetzgebung.* Zurich: Institut für Sozialethik de Universität Zurich, 1999, pp. 23–38. Reprinted in (2000) 3 *Ethical Theory and Moral Practice* 9–26; and in Cotterrell, *Living Law*, pp. 313–30.

'Transparency, Mass Media, Ideology and Community' (1999) 3 *Cultural Values* 414–26. Reprinted in A. Alexander and J. Hanson (eds), *Taking Sides: Clashing Views on Controversial Issues in Mass Media and Society*, 7th edn. New York: McGraw-Hill, 2000.

'Gurvitch, Georges' in C. Gray (ed.), *The Philosophy of Law: An Encyclopedia.* New York: Garland Publishing, 1999, vol. 1, pp. 337–9.

'Criminology' in C. Gray (ed.), *The Philosophy of Law: An Encyclopedia.* New York: Garland Publishing, 1999, vol. 1, pp. 169–71.

'Pandora's Box: Jurisprudence in Legal Education' (2000) 7 *International Journal of the Legal Profession* 179–87. Reprinted in M. Del Mar, W. Twining and M. Giudice (eds), *Legal Theory and the Legal Academy*. Farnham: Ashgate, 2010, pp. 75–83; and in Cotterrell, *Living Law*, pp. 45–53.

'The Representation of Law's Autonomy in Autopoiesis Theory' in J. Pribán and D. Nelken (eds), *Law's New Boundaries: The Consequences of Legal Autopoiesis*. Aldershot: Ashgate, 2001, 80–103. Reprinted in Cotterrell, *Living Law*, pp. 121–44.

'Introduction: Classic Traditions in the Sociological Study of Law' in Cotterrell, ed., *Sociological Perspectives on Law* vol. 1. Aldershot: Ashgate, 2001, xi–xxii.

'Introduction: Contemporary Debates in the Sociological Study of Law' in Cotterrell, ed., *Sociological Perspectives on Law*, vol. 2. Aldershot: Ashgate, 2001, xi–xxii.

'Is There a Logic of Legal Transplants?' in D. Nelken and J. Feest (eds), *Adapting Legal Cultures*. Oxford: Hart Publishing, 2001, 71–92. Reprinted in adapted form in Cotterrell, *Law, Culture and Society*, pp. 109–26.

'Law as Constitutive' in N.J. Smelser and P.B. Baltes (eds), *International Encyclopedia of the Social and Behavioral Sciences*. Amsterdam: Elsevier, 2001, pp. 8497–500.

'Seeking Similarity, Appreciating Difference: Comparative Law and Communities' in E. Örücü and A. Harding (eds), *Comparative Law in the Twenty-First Century*. The Hague: Kluwer, 2002, pp. 35–54. Reprinted in adapted form in Cotterrell, *Law, Culture and Society*, pp. 145–59.

'Subverting Orthodoxy, Making Law Central: A View of Sociolegal Studies' (2002) 29 *Journal of Law and Society* 632–44. Reprinted in Cotterrell, *Living Law*, pp. 3–15.

'Law in Culture' (2003) 7 *Associations: Journal for Social and Legal Theory*, no. 1, pp. 213–25. Revised and expanded version published in (2004) 17 *Ratio Juris* 1–14. Reprinted in adapted form in Cotterrell, *Law, Culture and Society*, pp. 97–108.

'Comparatists and Sociology' in P. Legrand and R. Munday (eds), *Comparative Legal Studies: Traditions and Transitions*. Cambridge: Cambridge University Press, 2003, pp. 131–53. Reprinted in adapted form in Cotterrell, *Law, Culture and Society*, pp. 127–43.

'Law in Social Theory, and Social Theory in the Study of Law' in A. Sarat (ed.) *Blackwell Companion to Law and Society*. Malden, MA, and Oxford: Blackwell, 2004, pp. 15–29. Reprinted in adapted form in Cotterrell, *Law, Culture and Society*, pp. 15–28; and in M.D.A. Freeman, *Lloyd's Introduction to Jurisprudence*, 8th edn, London: Sweet & Maxwell, 2008, pp. 957–68.

'Emmanuel Lévy and Legal Studies: A View from Abroad' (2004) 56/57 *Droit et Société* 131–41. Reprinted in Cotterrell, *Living Law*, pp. 73–84; and in Cotterrell, *Law in Social Theory*, pp. 161–71.

'Selznick Interviewed: Philip Selznick in Conversation with Roger Cotterrell' (selected by J. Pribán) (2004) 31 *Journal of Law and Society* 291–317.

'Ideals and Values in Law: A Comment on *The Importance of Ideals*' (2004) 33 *Nederlands Tijdschrift voor Rechtsfilosofie & Rechtstheorie* 288–98. Reprinted in Cotterrell, *Living Law*, pp. 351–61.

'Constructing the Juristic Durkheim? Paul Huvelin's Adaptation of Durkheimian Sociology' (2004) 10 (n.s.) *Durkheimian Studies* 56–69. Reprinted in Cotterrell, *Law in Social Theory*, pp. 147–60. Revised version as 'Durkheim's Loyal Jurist? The Sociolegal Theory of Paul Huvelin' (2005) 18 *Ratio Juris* 504–18. Reprinted in Cotterrell, *Living Law*, pp. 85–99.

'Legal Effects and Moral Meanings: A Comment on Recent Debates on Approaches to Legislation' in N. Zeegers, W. Witteveen and B. v. Klink (eds), *Social and Symbolic Effects of Legislation Under the Rule of Law*. Lewiston NY: Edwin Mellon, 2005, pp. 339–58. Reprinted in Cotterrell, *Living Law*, pp. 331–50.

'From 'Living Law' to the 'Death of the Social': Sociology in Legal Theory' in M.D.A. Freeman, ed., *Law and Sociology* (*Current Legal Issues* vol. 8). Oxford: Oxford University Press, 2006, pp. 16–31. Reprinted in Cotterrell, *Living Law*, pp. 29–44.

'Introduction' to Cotterrell, ed., *Law in Social Theory*. Aldershot: Ashgate, 2006, pp. xi–xxi.

'Living Law Revisited: Communitarianism and Sociology of Law' in P. van Seters (ed.), *Communitarianism in Law and Society*. Lanham, MD: Rowman and Littlefield, 2006, pp. 33–48. Reprinted in Cotterrell, *Living Law*, pp. 57–72.

'Lawyers and the Building of Communities' (2006) 18 *Student Bar Review* (NLSIU Bangalore), no.1, 25–30. Reprinted in Cotterrell, *Living Law*, pp. 373–8.

'Culture, Comparison, Community' (2006) 2 *International Journal of Law in Context* 1–10. Reprinted in Cotterrell, *Living Law*, pp. 363–72. Revised version as 'Culture, Comparison, Community: Social Studies of Law Today' in M. John and S. Kakarala (eds), *Enculturing Law: New Agendas in Legal Pedagogy*. New Delhi: Tulika Books, 2007, pp. 22–34.

'Comparative Law and Legal Culture' in R. Zimmermann and M. Reimann (eds), *Oxford Handbook of Comparative Law*. Oxford: Oxford University Press, 2006, pp. 709–37. Reprinted in Cotterrell, *Living Law*, pp. 281–309.

'Community as a Legal Concept? Some Uses of a Law-and-Community Approach in Legal Theory' (2006) 2 *No Foundations* electronic journal [Helsinki] (November) 15–26. Reprinted in (2007) 2 *Revista Jurídica* (Facultad de Derecho Universidad Nacional de Mar del Plata, Argentina) 101–12; and in Cotterrell, *Living Law*, pp. 17–28.

'Durkheim, Emile (1858–1917)', 'Durkheim School' and 'Olivecrona, Karl (1897–1980)' in D.S. Clark (ed.), *Sage Encyclopedia of Law and Society: American and Global Perspectives*. Los Angeles: Sage Publications, 2007, pp. 442–3 and 443–5 (vol. 1), and 1082–3 (vol. 2).

'Sociology of Law' in D.S. Clark (ed.), *Sage Encyclopedia of Law and Society: American and Global Perspectives*. Los Angeles: Sage Publications, 2007, pp. 1413–20 (vol. 3).

'Is It So Bad To Be Different? Comparative Law and the Appreciation of Diversity' in E. Örücü and D. Nelken (eds), *Comparative Law: A Handbook*. Oxford: Hart, 2007, pp. 133–54.

'Images of Europe in Sociolegal Traditions' in D. Nelken and V. Gessner (eds), *European Ways of Law.* Oxford: Hart, 2007, pp. 21–39. Reprinted in Cotterrell, *Living Law*, pp. 145–63.

'Comment penser le multiculturalisme en droit?' (with A.-J. Arnaud) (2007) 23 *L'Observateur des Nations Unies: Revue de l'Association Française pour les Nations Unies* (Section Aix-en-Provence) no. 2 (Automne-Hiver Dossier spécial: *Multiculturalisme et droit international*) 7–26.

'Transnational Communities and the Concept of Law' (2008) 21 *Ratio Juris* 1–18. Reprinted in M. Giudice, W. Waluchow and M. Del Mar (eds), *The Methodology of Legal Theory*. Farnham: Ashgate, 2010, pp. 403–20.

'Sociological Jurisprudence' in P. Cane and J. Conaghan (eds), *New Oxford Companion to Law.* Oxford: Oxford University Press, 2008, pp. 1099–101.

'Is Law Just 'a Means to an End''? (2008) 4 *Socio-Legal Review* (NLSIU, Bangalore) 1–8.

'Ehrlich at the Edge of Empire: Centres and Peripheries in Legal Studies' in M. Hertogh (ed.), *Living Law: Reconsidering Eugen Ehrlich*. Oxford: Hart, 2008, pp. 75–94. Russian trans. (M. Antonov) in *Russian Yearbook of Legal Theory,* No. 1, 2008. St Petersburg: University Publishing Consortium, 2009, pp. 546–64. Reprinted as appendix to Russian trans. of E. Ehrlich, *Fundamental Principles of the Sociology of Law*. St Petersburg: University Publishing Consortium, 2011, pp. 673–99.

'Law and Culture – Inside and Beyond the Nation State' (2008) 31 *Retfærd: Nordisk Juridisk Tidsskrift*, 4 (123), 23–36.

'The Struggle for Law: Some Dilemmas of Cultural Legality' (2009) 4 *International Journal of Law in Context* 373–84.
'Culture, Power and the Human Animal: A Reply' (2009) 4 *International Journal of Law in Context* 407–10.
'Spectres of Transnationalism: Changing Terrains of Sociology of Law' (2009) 36 *Journal of Law and Society* 481–500. Reprinted as 'The Growth of Legal Transnationalism' in A. Febbrajo and G. Harste (eds), *Law and Intersystemic Communication: Understanding 'Structural Coupling'*. Farnham: Ashgate, 2013, pp. 31–50.
'Introduction: Durkheim on Justice, Morals and Politics' in Cotterrell (ed.), *Emile Durkheim: Justice, Morality and Politics*, Farnham: Ashgate, 2010, pp. xi–xxiv.
'Conscientious Objection to Assigned Work Tasks: A Comment on Relations of Law and Culture' (2010) 31 *Comparative Labor Law & Policy Journal* 511–22.
'Justice, Dignity, Torture, Headscarves: Can Durkheim's Sociology Clarify Legal Values?' (2011) 20 *Social & Legal Studies* 3–20.
'Golden Ages: Notes on the Future of Sociology of Law, with Some Comments on its Past, on Poland, and on Jazz' (2011) 12 *Societas/Communitas*: *Journal of the University of Warsaw Institute of Applied Social Sciences*, no. 2, 9–23.
'What is Transnational Law?' (2012) 37 *Law and Social Inquiry* 500–524.
'Comparative Sociology of Law' in D.S. Clark (ed.), *Comparative Law and Society*. New York: Edward Elgar, 2012, pp. 39–60.
'Responsibility, Solidarity and State Regulation in Classical Continental Social Theory' in M. Lobban and J. Moses (eds), *The Impact of Ideas on Legal Development*. Cambridge: Cambridge University Press, 2012, pp. 34–56. Revised version as 'Classical Social Theory and Ideas of Responsibility and the State in France and Germany' in (2013) 15 *Comparative Law Review* [Poland] 21–44.
'Socio-Legal Studies, Law Schools, and Legal and Social Theory'. Paper delivered at Wolfson College Oxford, June 2012. Queen Mary School of Law Legal Studies Research Paper No. 126/2012. SSRN electronic publication.
'Transnational Networks of Community and International Economic Law' in A. Perry-Kessaris (ed.), *Socio-legal Approaches to International Economic Law: Text, Context, Subtext*. London: Routledge, 2013, pp. 133–49.
'Rethinking "Embeddedness": Law, Economy, Community' (2013) 40 *Journal of Law and Society* 49–67. Also published in D. Ashiagbor, P. Kotiswaran and A. Perry-Kessaris (eds), *Towards an Economic Sociology of Law*. Oxford: Wiley-Blackwell, 2013, pp. 49–67.
'The Jurist's Conscience: Reflections around Radbruch' in M. Del Mar and C. Michelon (eds), *The Anxiety of the Jurist: Legality, Exchange and Judgement*. Farnham: Ashgate, 2013, pp. 13–26. Also published as 'The Role of the Jurist: Reflections around Radbruch' (2013) 26 *Ratio Juris* 510–22. Revised version as 'Jurists and Philosophers: Radbruch and Dworkin' [in Russian], trans. M. Antonov [2014] *Jurisprudence* [St Petersburg State University Faculty of Law], no. 1.
'Northern Lights: From Swedish Realism to Sociology of Law' (2013) 40 *Journal of Law and Society* 510–22.
'Petrazycki and Contemporary Socio-Legal Studies' [in Russian], trans. M. Antonov [2013] *Jurisprudence* [St Petersburg State University Faculty of Law], no. 5.
'Why Jurisprudence is Not Legal Philosophy' (2014) 5 *Jurisprudence*, forthcoming.

'A Concept of Law for Global Legal Pluralism?' in S. Donlan and L. Heckendorn (eds), *Concepts of Law: Comparative, Jurisprudential, and Social Science Perspectives*. Farnham: Ashgate, forthcoming.

'Law as Constitutive' (revised and expanded entry) *International Encyclopedia of the Social and Behavioral Sciences* (2nd edn). Elsevier, forthcoming.

'The Concept of Crime and Transnational Networks of Community', in P. Alldridge, L. Cheliotis and V. Mitsilegas (eds), *Globalisation, Criminal Law and Criminal Justice: Theoretical, Comparative and Transnational Perspectives*. Oxford: Hart, forthcoming.

'The Politics of Jurisprudence Revisited: A Swedish Realist in Historical Context' *Ratio Juris*, forthcoming.

'Professing Jurisprudence' in A. Diduck et al. (eds), festschrift for Michael Freeman. Brill, forthcoming.

4. Book Reviews

Law as Fact (K. Olivecrona) 2nd edn. (1971) 34 *Modern Law Review* 589–90.

Pashukanis: Selected Essays in Marxism and Law (P. Beirne and R. Sharlet) (1980) 7 *British Journal of Law and Society* 317–21.

Research in Law and Sociology (S. Spitzer) (1981) 44 *Modern Law Review* 607–9.

Law and Social Inquiry: Case Studies of Research (R. Luckham) (1982) 45 *Modern Law Review* 602–4.

Earl Warren: A Public Life (G.E. White) (1983) *Public Law* 508–10.

Marxism and Law (H. Collins) (1983) 11 *International Journal of the Sociology of Law* 317–20.

No Access to Law: Alternatives to the American Judicial System (L. Nader) (1983) 46 *Modern Law Review* 252–4.

Max Weber's Insights and Errors (S. Andreski) and *The Limits of Rationality: An Essay on the Social and Moral Thought of Max Weber* (R. Brubaker) (1985) 33 *Sociological Review* 370–4.

Lord Denning: The Judge and the Law (J.L. Jowell and J.P.W.B. McAuslan) (1985) 63 *Public Administration* 374–6.

The Role of Courts in American Society (J.K. Lieberman) (1985) *Public Law* 344–6.

Women in Law: Explorations in Law, Family and Sexuality (J. Brophy and C. Smart) (1986) 20 *Sociology* 105–6.

Legal Systems and Social Systems (A. Podgorecki and C. Whelan) (1986) *Public Law* 495–6.

The Legal Mind: Essays for Tony Honoré (N. MacCormick and P. Birks) (1987) *Public Law* 307–8.

Verdict According to Conscience: Perspectives on the English Criminal Trial Jury 1200–1800 (T.A. Green) (1987) *Criminal Law Review* 288.

Theories of Evidence (W. Twining) (1988) 21 *Law and Society Review* 853–6.

The Jurisprudence of Orthodoxy: Queen's University Essays on H.L.A. Hart (P. Leith and P. Ingram) (1989) *Public Law* 367–8.

Judges, Legislators and Professors (R.C. van Caenegem) (1989) *Public Law* 662–3.

Languages of Law (P. Goodrich) (1991) 11 *Legal Studies* 223–7.

The Barrister's World (J. Morison and P. Leith) and *Justice Outside the City* (M. Blacksell, K. Economides and C. Watkins) (1992) *Public Law* 182–4.

Patterns of American Jurisprudence (N. Duxbury) (1996) 23 *Journal of Law and Society* 597–600.

Max Weber: The Lawyer as Social Thinker (S.P. Turner and R.A. Factor) (1997) 6 *Social & Legal Studies* 153–4.

Social Cohesion and Legal Coercion: A Critique of Weber, Durkheim and Marx (L.S. Sheleff) (1998) 27 *Contemporary Sociology*, no. 2, 198–9.

Roscoe Pound and Karl Llewellyn: Searching for an American Jurisprudence (N.E.H. Hull) (1999) 26 *Journal of Law and Society* 256–9.

Christian Perspectives on Law Reform (P.R. Beaumont, ed.) and *Beyond Fear: Vision, Hope and Generosity* (Z. Bankowski et al.) (1999) 3 Edinburgh Law Review 414–16.

Introduction à l'analyse sociologique des systèmes juridiques (A-J. Arnaud and M.J. Fariñas Dulce) (2000) 44/45 *Droit et Société* 319–22, trans. R. Vanneuville; abbreviated English version in (2001) 10 *Social & Legal Studies* 273–5.

Feminist Perspectives on Equity and Trusts (S. Scott-Hunt and H. Lim) (2001) 64 *Modern Law Review* 951–2.

Merging Law and Sociology: Beyond the Dichotomies in Socio-Legal Research (R. Banakar) (2004) 31 *Journal of Law and Society* 266–71.

Law, Modernity, Postmodernity: Legal Change in the Contracting State (B. Edgeworth) (2005) 14 *Social & Legal Studies* 139–41.

Law as a Means to an End: Threat to the Rule of Law (B.Z. Tamanaha) (2008) 42 *Law & Society Review* 441–3.

Ubiquitous Law: Legal Theory and the Space for Legal Pluralism (E. Melissaris) (2009) 19 *Law and Politics Book Review*, no. 10, 27 October, 774–9.

Globalisation and the Western Legal Tradition: Recurring Patterns of Law and Authority (D.B. Goldman) (2009) *Public Law* 415–17.

The Making of Law: An Ethnography of the Conseil d'État (B. Latour) (2011) 11 *Journal of Classical Sociology* 506–10.

Law and Justice in Community (G. Barden and T. Murphy) (2012) 8 *International Journal of Law in Context* 531–5.

Constitutional Redemption: Political Faith in an Unjust World (J.M. Balkin) and *Living Originalism* (J.M. Balkin) (2013) *Public Law* 443–9.

5. Other Writing

'The Requirement of 'Benefit' Under the Variation of Trusts Act' (1971) 34 *Modern Law Review* 96–9 (case note).

'Gifts to Charitable Institutions: A Note on Recent Developments' (1972) 36 *Conveyancer and Property Lawyer* 198–204.

'Extradition and 'Offences of a Political Character'' (1973) 89 *Law Quarterly Review* 476–9 (case note).

'The Lessons of Impeachment' (1974) 124 *New Law Journal* 784–94.

'Charity Law Reform and the Charity Commission' (1975) 125 *New Law Journal Annual Charities Review* 40–50.

'Charity and Politics' (1975) 38 *Modern Law Review* 471–4 (case note).

'Legal Control of Election Campaign Expenditure' (1976) 39 *Modern Law Review* 730–33 (case note).

'A Legal Re-Definition of Charity' (1976) 126 *New Law Journal Annual Charities Review* 30–40.

'The Goodman Report and the Future of Charity Law' (1977) 127 *New Law Journal Annual Charities Review* 3–14.

'Prosecuting Incitement to Racial Hatred' (1982) *Public Law* 378–81.

'Introduction: Law, Democracy and Social Justice' (with B. Bercusson) (1988) 15 *Journal of Law and Society* 1–4.
'Prefacio del Autor a la Edición Española' in Cotterrell, *Introducción a la Sociología del Derecho*. Barcelona: Ariel, 1991, pp. 13–14.
'Context and Critique in Law Teaching (With Reference to Property and Trusts)' in P.B.H. Birks (ed.), *Examining the Law Syllabus: The Core*. Oxford: Oxford University Press, 1992, pp. 28–32.
'Foreword' to Berry Fong-Chung Tsu, *The Common Law in Chinese Context*. Armonk, NY: M.E. Sharpe/Hong Kong: Hong Kong University Press, 1992, pp. vii–ix.
'Lord Lloyd of Hampstead' (obituary) *The Guardian* 13 January 1993. Longer version in (1993) *SPTL Reporter: Newsletter of the Society of Public Teachers of Law*, no. 6, Spring, p. 20.
'Per Una Deontologia Della Ricerca Sociologico-Giuridica', trans. V. Pocar (1994) 20 *Sociologia del Diritto*, no. 3, 169–71.
'A Pluralist Perspective in Socio-Legal Studies' (1996) *Socio-Legal Newsletter*, no. 18, Spring, pp. 4–5.
'Establishing Sociology of Law in Sweden' (1997) *Socio-Legal Newsletter*, no. 23, p.4.
'Optimal Legal Structures of Community' (1998) 8 *Framtider* [Sweden] 5–7.
'Professor Francis Roger Crane (1910–2001)' (obituary) *SPTL Reporter*, no. 22, Spring 2001, p. 4. Extract in *The Times* 29 January 2001.
'Global Law in a Moral Domain' (2002) *Socio-Legal Newsletter*, no. 37, Summer, p. 6.
'Paul Hirst (1946–2003)' (obituary) (2003) *Socio-Legal Newsletter*, no. 41, Winter, pp. 6–7.
'Foreword' to P. Shah, *Legal Pluralism in Conflict: Coping with Cultural Diversity in Law*. London: Glasshouse Press, 2005, pp. ix–xi.
'Per Stjernquist 1912–2005' (obituary) (2006) *Socio-Legal Newsletter*, no. 48, Spring, p. 9.

Publications in addition to those in this listing include some occasional pieces, shorter book reviews and many journalistic and other writings on music.

Index

Note: Entries in *italics* refer to figures and entries in **bold** refer to tables.

www.ingramcontent.com/pod-product-compliance
Ingram Content Group UK Ltd.
Pitfield, Milton Keynes, MK11 3LW, UK
UKHW050753180926
475701UK00007B/1017
* 9 7 8 1 1 3 8 6 3 7 7 4 0 *